Lillian and Edwar[illegible]

The Piozzi Letters

Mrs. Thrale and her daughter Hester Maria (Queeney), ca. 1781. Painted by Sir Joshua Reynolds. *(Gift of Lord Beaverbrook, Beaverbrook Art Gallery, Fredericton, N.B., Canada.)*

The Piozzi Letters

Correspondence of Hester Lynch Piozzi, 1784–1821 (formerly Mrs. Thrale)

Volume 1
1784–1791

EDITED BY
Edward A. Bloom
AND
Lillian D. Bloom

NEWARK: University of Delaware Press
LONDON AND TORONTO: Associated University Presses

Associated University Presses
440 Forsgate Drive
Cranbury, NJ 08512

Associated University Presses
25 Sicilian Avenue
London WC1A 2QH, England

Associated University Presses
P.O. Box 488, Port Credit
Mississauga, Ontario
Canada L5G 4M2

The paper used in this publication meets the requirements of the American National Standard for Permanence of Paper for Printed Library Materials Z39.48-1984.

Library of Congress Cataloging-in-Publication Data

Piozzi, Hester Lynch, 1741–1821.
The Piozzi letters.

Includes bibliographical references and index.
1. Piozzi, Hester Lynch, 1741–1821—Correspondence.
2. Authors, English—18th century—Correspondence.
3. London (England)—Intellectual life—18th century.
I. Bloom, Edward Alan, 1914– . II. Bloom, Lillian D.
III. Title.
PR3619.P5Z48 1988 828′.609 [B] 87-40231
ISBN 0-87413-115-4 (v. 1 : alk. paper)

Printed in the United States of America

We dedicate these volumes
to
Mary Hyde Viscountess Eccles
and
Dr. Frank Taylor
who "protected [her] Remains—
The poor Remains of the Piozzi:
her *never-forfeited honour*—and
secondly at immeasurable distance,
***her* literary fame."**
28 [June] 1819.

Contents

Illustrations

Acknowledgments

Many people encouraged us to undertake an edition of the "notorious" widow's correspondence, that of Hester Lynch Piozzi from 1784 to 1821. They offered not only moral encouragement but access to the Piozzi letters that were in their care. We are especially grateful to Herbert Cahoon of the Pierpont Morgan Library; Roy L. Davids, director of printed books and manuscripts at Sotheby's, London; Mary Hyde Viscountess Eccles; the late James Gilvarry; Glenise Matheson, keeper of manuscripts at the John Rylands University Library of Manchester; Stephen R. Parks, curator of the Osborn Collection, Yale University Library; Paula F. Peyraud of Chappaqua, New York; Charles Maurice Petty-Fitzmaurice, the earl of Shelburne, Bowood House near Calne, Wiltshire; Lady Stewart of Lexbourne Ltd., London; Lola Szladits, curator of the Berg Collection, New York Public Library; Frank Taylor, the John Rylands University Library of Manchester; and Virginia Clifford, New York City.

As always, we are grateful to Maynard Mack, as well as to Hugh R. Trevor-Roper, Lord Dacre of Glanton, for everything one scholar can give to another.

Archivists throughout the United Kingdom have helped us to identify the names of people long dead and obscure but meaningful to Mrs. Piozzi. We are particularly indebted to Patricia Allderidge, archivist, Bethlehem Royal Hospital, Beckenham, Kent; Robert Bryant and his successor Colin Johnson, the Guildhall, Bath; B. C. Cooper of Drummond's Bank (Charing Cross branch), the Royal Bank of Scotland; Marian Halford of the Salop Record Office; Nia Henson, assistant keeper of the department of manuscripts and records, the National Library of Wales, Aberystwyth; Jane Langton, registrar of the Royal Archives, Windsor Castle; M. Joyce, Bath Reference Library; Mary E. Williams, Bristol Record Office; and A. G. Vesey of the Clwyd Record Office.

Often perplexed by allusions made faint by distance, time, and alterations of taste, we called upon individuals who graciously provided answers and gave willingly of their expertise. So many people have helped that we may inadvertently have omitted the names of some. To these we offer both gratitude and apologies.

Among our supporters and fellow scholars at Rhode Island College, we thank the Faculty Research Fund Committee for financial support; Taki Votoras, who unraveled the strands of complicated Italian research; the late Nelson Guertin, who spent arduous hours in deciphering Fanny Burney's stumbling "French Exercise Book" that spelled out the Burney-Mrs. Thrale association; Dean John

Salesses; the late President David Sweet, who not only tolerated scholarship but actively supported it; the secretaries, Natalie DiRissio and Arlene Robertson.

At Brown University we are indebted (and the indebtedness runs both long and deep) to Nelson W. Francis of the Linguistics Department; Alan S. Trueblood, Franco Fido, Walter Schnerr, and Albert Salvan, all of the Modern Languages Division; Caroline and Paul Flesher; David E. Pingree of the History of Mathematics Department; Andrew J. Sabol of the English Department; Michael Putnam of the Classics Department; Barbara and Leonard Lesko of the Egyptology Department; Dwayne Davies of the Rockefeller Library.

Among those with whom we worked at Oxford University, we are enriched by the dedication and friendship of Bruce Mitchell and Richard Fargher, both of Saint Edmund Hall; David Fleeman of Pembroke College; Alan S. Bell of Rhodes House; and Sheila Gordon-Rae of the Bodleian Library.

Several scholars at the Huntington Library, San Marino, California, tossed aside—to use Mrs. Piozzi's language—many of the hedgehogs that cluttered our path. Clearing the way to knowledge and understanding were Elizabeth S. and Daniel Donno, the late William Ringler, Jr., Hallett D. Smith, Sr., James Thorpe, Robert C. Wark, and Daniel H. Woodward.

Although it is ungracious to name so few among people to whom we owe so much, we gratefully recognize Ruth Battestin of Charlottesville, Virginia; Alain Bony, Université de Lyon; the late Frank Brady, Graduate Center, City University of New York; A. R. Braunmuller, University of California at Los Angeles; the late Bertrand H. Bronson, University of California at Berkeley; B. Cooper, Trinity College, Hartford, Connecticut; James C. Corson, Melrose, Roxburghshire; Margaret Doody, Princeton University; the Right Honorable Michael Foot, M.P.; Philip H. Highfill, Jr., George Washington University; Susumu Kawanishi, the University of Tokyo; Slava Klima, McGill University; Joan E. Klingel, University of Colorado; Gwin J. Kolb, the University of Chicago; Herman Liebert, Yale University; Mary Lightbown, University College, London; Professor David Quinn, University of Liverpool; Valerie B. Pearman Smith, Porthmadog, Gwynedd; Helen Ramage, Menai Bridge, Anglesey, Gwynedd; Raymond Refaussé, Representative Church Body, Dublin; F. P. Richardson, the Law Society Library, London; John Riely, Boston University; Ronald Rompkey, University of Newfoundland; Anthony W. Shipps, Indiana University Library; John Tearle, Berkhamsted, Hertfordshire; Lars Troide, McGill University; Bruce W. Wardropper, Duke University; Christopher White, the Paul Mellon Centre for Studies in British Art, London; Sarah Wimbush and Kae Kim Yung, both of the National Portrait Gallery, London.

Ours is a special indebtedness to Inge Chafee, who dominated the word processor, guarded us against inconsistencies, and in general improved the manuscript wherever she could. Similarly, we are grateful to Ruth Oppenheim, of the Brown English Department, whose administrative acumen and enlightened concern eased the burden of numerous practical obligations.

To all whom we have named and to others whose names may have momentarily eluded us, we record our profound thanks for scholarly generosity and care.

In the more than twelve years since we began letting Hester Lynch Piozzi tell her own story as she felt and understood it—a literally expensive tale—we have enjoyed the support of the Guggenheim Foundation, the American Council of Learned Societies, Brown University, and the Huntington Library. The preparation of these volumes was also made possible by two grants from the Division of Research Programs of the National Endowment for the Humanities, an independent federal agency. Its help made the edition a realistic possibility so that even long periods of plodding research were converted into times of quiet joy. The grants that we have received have permitted Mrs. Piozzi to speak in her own voice and, more importantly, in her own spirit.

We admire her, especially her unstated determination to stand up to death, which she deemed an "unnatural" but "conquering" force. Nevertheless, as annotators we have tried for a certain objectivity, a detachment that provides a background for much that H: L: P. had read or quoted, for her commentary on the political world and the times, for her friendships and enmities. If the letters set forth the Piozzi world, then the annotations, which elucidate rather than interpret, amplify the record. In short, through text and notes, we want the "notorious" widow to appear as a woman, whether dull or vibrant, joyous or melancholy, pretentious or very much bound to the productive earth as a member of the landed gentry.

Of course, the work on the letters could not have been finished—or even begun—without the pioneering efforts of the late James L. Clifford and the late Katharine C. Balderston.

Introduction

1

Within the last half century interest in Hester Lynch Piozzi has been sparked by Professor Clifford's biography and Professor Balderston's edition of the diary *Thraliana,* both published by the Clarendon Press in 1941 and 1942 respectively. Most of her letters to Samuel Johnson—written when she was the wife of Henry Thrale and then his widow—were edited by R. W. Chapman in 1952. Mary Hyde, now Viscountess Eccles, concentrated first upon the Thrale-Boswell association in *The Impossible Friendship* (Harvard University Press, 1972) and some five years later upon the family itself in *The Thrales of Streatham Park,* an analysis and reproduction of the manuscript called "The Children's Book or Rather Family Book."[1]

The ground-breaking work of our predecessors has fixed the starting point for this edition of Hester Lynch Piozzi's correspondence. Specifically, we are committed to editing the letters written by H: L: P.—as she often signed and thought of herself—between 23 July 1784, when in London she married for the second time, and until close to 2 May 1821, when she died in Clifton. In actual fact, these letters are introduced by others written shortly before her remarriage. This prefatory material anticipates the return of Gabriel Piozzi from Italy. It bursts with nervous exuberance, or anxiety, or a feisty disdain of those who challenged what she justified as her right to happiness. Among these letters are those to Samuel Johnson in which the tone seesawed between peacemaking and defiance. Among them too are the resolute yet troubled pieces to her eldest daughter, Queeney, and those to Fanny Burney which started in confidence and broke off with the moral exile of the "aimable traitresse." These twenty-three letters usher in a virtually new life that continued for the next thirty-seven years.

Mrs. Piozzi of course emerged from Mrs. Thrale just as the young bride of 1763 had emerged from Hester Lynch Salusbury. But her life changed as the circumstances altered. Energized in 1784 by her newly realized power to make decisions, she accepted the fact that she was free of Thrale's sexual demands and his overt promiscuity, that she was released from the obligation of childbearing and the need to watch children die. No longer was she compelled to preside over the houses in Streatham and at Grosvenor Square where in her own mind she was dwarfed by the personalities of Johnson, Reynolds, the elder Burney, and others. No wonder that she published almost exclusively as Mrs. Piozzi. Not even a honeymoon dampened her enthusiasm to become a professional writer with its attendant fame. Between 1785 *(Florence Miscellany)* and 1803 she contributed to or published six books *(Retrospection,* 1801, the last) and a few pamphlets. Even when deserted by the booksellers, she did not allow her commitment to falter. She wrote on, and if success in her lifetime became evanescent, there was always the future.

At the moment the epistolary Mrs. Piozzi interests us, and she penned about two thousand letters. Their precise number cannot be determined since they, whether isolated or in blocks, disappear or surface sporadically. The edition will make available more than half of them, most of which have never before been published.

If Mrs. Piozzi took offense too hastily, she never suffered from excessive humility. Even in the process of admitting mistakes, she did not denigrate herself. At the same time that she "scribbled" her letters, she assessed their worth as literary and historical documents that cried out—she assumed—for preservation and publication.

She was frustrated in this desire. The relatively few letters of H: L: P. that have been printed hitherto are fragmented and bowdlerized or edited haphazardly. We have only to examine those to Samuel Lysons, which appeared in *Bentley's Miscellany* in 1850, or the ninety-four to the Reverend Edward Mangin—bits and pieces entitled *Piozziana* (1833). The letters to Mrs. Pennington—important because they are woman-to-woman—were edited by Oswald G. Knapp in 1914. Some of the most candid, more than forty which we have seen, were ignored, the remainder purified by ellipses.

Even as she carried on epistolary exchanges, Mrs. Piozzi suggested that certain recipients safeguard her correspondence, as she would theirs. In short, she created a "coterie" of writers who communicated gladly and deferred to one another's wishes. So her "poor dear old Friend Mr. Chappelow" did as he was told. Just after he died in 1820, his executor George Jenyns wrote to inform Mrs. Piozzi that he had found "amongst" the priest's papers "a packet of letters carefully tied up with directions to be forwarded to you."[2] She soon retrieved this correspondence, some 154 letters written between 1786 and 1818.

Others—friends, neighbors, stewards, lawyers, business acquaintances, even her daughters—were as dutiful as Chappelow. From several large or special blocks of letters we have therefore drawn those which enable H: L: P. to tell her own story—biographical and intellectual. We want the genuine text of her letters to generate a history of her life and times. For them to function in this twofold capacity, we rely of course on specific collections, without allowing any one to dominate: her letters to Samuel Lysons (1784–ca. 1814) in the Hyde Collection, the Houghton Library of Harvard, and the Huntington Library; to Sophia Byron (1787–89) in the John Rylands Library; to the Reverend John Roberts (1804–21) in the library of the Victoria and Albert Museum; to her daughters (1780–1821), especially Queeney, in Bowood House; to Penelope Sophia Pennington (1788–1804, 1819–21) in the Princeton University Library; to the Reverend Thomas Sedgwick Whalley (1789–1816) in the Berg Collection; to the Williams family of Bodelwyddan (1796–1821) in the Rylands Library; to John Salusbury Piozzi Salusbury and his wife (1804–21, 1813–21) in the Rylands; to the Reverend

Edward Mangin (1816–21) in the Princeton University Library; to Sir James Fellowes and his family (1815–21) in the Osborn Collection at Yale and in various libraries—the Beinecke, the Pennsylvania Historical Society, and the Pierpont Morgan (to name but a few); to Fanny Burney, later Mme d'Arblay (ca. 1778–1820) in the Berg and Osborn Collections. But smaller groups of letters also add to the autobiography: for instance, those to her youngest daughter Cecilia (1795–1821) in the Rylands; and to Robert Ray (1797–99) in the Princeton University Library.

With all these recipients Mrs. Piozzi maintained a flexibly intimate or personal connection. In other cases she was the employer and the recipient an employee to whom she transmitted orders and inquiries and bewailed the state of her finances. In these business letters she seems less studied, indeed more genuinely casual, than in the correspondence with her friends. Never writing down to her stewards, for example, she admitted her sense of dependence upon them (albeit expressed somewhat peremptorily) and therefore her gratitude. A large number of business letters—some 142 to her steward Alexander Leak and his wife, a smaller number to the architect Clement Mead[3]—lays bare Mrs. Piozzi's reactions when she was fretted by the need for money, bewildered or infuriated by Streatham Park's tenants and her daughters' attitude toward the remodeling of the great house. In addition, there remain the occasional letters: to theater people like Eliza Farren, Sarah and William Siddons, William Augustus Conway; to the antiquary Daniel Lysons; to Arthur Murphy, always her friend and for a short time her lawyer; to tough-minded publishers, like Thomas Cadell, James Robson, and John Stockdale; to the philanthropic Duncan brothers; to Bishops Thomas Percy and Robert Gray; to the medievalist Joseph Cooper Walker and the joking schoolmaster Reynold Davies of "Streatham University"; to Cambridge students like Clement Francis and John Williams; to her Welsh neighbors, Thomas Pennant, the Ladies of Llangollen, John "Philosopher" Lloyd, and many others.

As we said earlier, we do not intend total inclusiveness. Within the process of selection, however, we have represented everyone to whom Mrs. Piozzi wrote. Not all her letters were available to us. For example, the Pennants of Nantlys, near Saint Asaph, lately owned nine of her letters to the steward Jacob Weston (1794–99). We were allowed to see but not to print them. (Fortunately, some of them have made their way into different repositories, like the Paula Peyraud Collection, and we could, therefore, provide some insight into the nature of the exchange.)

On the other hand, there is no longer any trace of twenty letters to Sophia Pugh (of 22 Gay Street, Bath), formerly in the Bath Reference Library. Missing too are some ninety-seven letters written by Mrs. Piozzi to Dr. William Makepeace Thackeray (1795–1816) of Chester. They were once the property of Albert Ashforth, Jr., of New York City, who died in 1958. We can find no record of their sale; and none of the surviving Ashforth family—generous in their time and desire to help—know the present location of these letters or whether in fact they still exist. Similarly, Mrs. Piozzi's correspondence with the Reverend Robert Gray, in time bishop of Bristol, has disappeared, its disposition unknown since late in the nineteenth century. In this instance, because we had no alternative, we used the obviously truncated versions of the letters reproduced by Haywood.

On one occasion a large body of Piozzi letters vanished, only to be rediscovered. As recently as October 1975, Sotheby's sold to a protoplasmic Mr. Barber 551 letters, bound in eleven volumes, the correspondence of Mrs. Piozzi with the Williams family, neighbors in North Wales.[4] This collection, covering the years 1796 to 1821, has not been published previously. It constitutes the lengthiest known series of her letters and ranges in subject from Sarah Siddons to Napoleon, from whist-table gossip and fashions to international news and politics. When the correspondence fled with Mr. Barber, we resorted to one hundred of these letters that had long ago been deposited in the library of the Victoria and Albert. Of them twenty-five were originals; the remainder were copies that had been viciously doctored: names and dates changed, significant statements omitted, and sometimes two letters cut and spliced as one. Compulsively, we chased after Mr. Barber. We hunted for eight years, following any lead that seemed minimally credible. Finally, with the help of the Right Honorable Michael Foot, M.P., we found in 1983 their owner, who soon sold the lot to the John Rylands Library where they are now housed.

2

We have chosen to exclude certain letters because not all that Mrs. Piozzi wrote inform the autobiography or contribute to a cumulative study of social and cultural history. That twofold intention would not have been served by orders to shopkeepers, cards of thanks, tea or dinner invitations, notes of formal acceptance or regrets. What we have in mind is an ort of letterwriting, such as the following: "Mrs. Piozzi returns Compliments, and is by no means well enough today to answer for herself next Wednesday; hopes Mr. and Mrs. Layard are well. No 8 / Gay Street. October 23d—1819—*Bath.*"[5] We do not know the outcome of this invitation, but she probably did visit the Layards, probably did play a rubber of whist with them for modest stakes. The note itself, however, adds nothing to her life narrative or to a commentary on the times.

Actually, the lady played an epistolary game, one that tested her sensitivity to individuals and proved her ability to write for a diverse audience. On 26 September 1808 she confessed her game to her nephew John Salusbury, then a fifteen-year-old school boy. "I am just Thinking," she confided, "how unlike my Letters to *you* are to those I write to my young friend Marianne Francis; who works at the Greek Verbs in *mi* till I am forced to *beg* She will make Truce with Study, and go see a Play or something to divert Thought; and not fancy Scholarship the sole Clue to Felicity, although Ignorance is the certain Road to Ruin."[6]

In writing to these two young people Mrs. Piozzi altered the contents of her letters. But more often than not, her correspondence to different recipients varied less in subject matter than in tone. Given the quantity of the correspondence, she had to repeat information, describe a particular piece of news to three or four people to whom she wrote on a single day or even within a single week. In short, the facts stayed the same, but the language and verve were adjusted to the personality and interests of the recipients. Such alteration becomes an act of intellectual prestidigitation, fascinating to watch. For this reason, we do print now and then letters that tend to repeat the contents of others, but never with deadening sameness of language. Mrs. Piozzi, except in her sermonizing letters to young John Salusbury, was rarely a bore.[7] Why impose upon her the sin of dullness that she deemed unpardonable? Emulating her sense of an audience, we have passed by letters that deal with trivia or merely restate information already provided.

While we do not edit all the letters of Hester Lynch Piozzi, we have sought another kind of totality. Whenever we print one of her letters, we include the other side of the correspondence, in whole or relevant part, if it is extant. As important as are her letters to others, so very often are the replies. Rylands makes available a large number of these: at least 1,371 from correspondents as diverse as Arthur Murphy, Michael Lort, Sir Lucas Pepys, Sophia Byron, Samuel and Daniel Lysons, Sarah and William Siddons, the Ladies of Llangollen, the erudite Clement Francis and his sister Marianne, called with some understatement the "prodige" by her grandfather, Dr. Charles Burney.[8]

3

Convinced of her talent, Mrs. Piozzi believed that much of what she had written and put aside was publishable. Her own publishing life ended in 1803 with an anonymous penny broadside called *Old England to Her Daughters. Address to the Females of Great Britain.* During the last few years of her life when her vanity was threatened and the wrinkles smarted, she searched for a literary executor and chose Sir James Fellowes. She even outlined his responsibility: he was "to cull what poems and anecdotes he might think fit from Thraliana and her miscellaneous papers."[9] A bit more than a year after their introduction, she wrote him into her last will, dated 29 March 1816, and left him a token two hundred pounds so that he could fulfill his editorial function.

She wanted Sir James to "be careful of [her] Literary Fame," to salvage the creative recognition that had eluded her through most of her life. In July 1820, she remarked in her diary: "At my Death the Battle about my Merits and no Merits will be renewed over my Memory. Friends wishing to save it—Foes contending for the Pleasure of throwing it to the Dogs like the Body of Patroclus in Homer."[10] Her savage imagery suggests that she accepted the ferocity of debate as long as she was remembered; what she feared was oblivion. So she could write as early as March 1799 to her eldest daughter: ". . . 'tis a melancholy Thing . . . to outlive Lovers and Haters, and Friends and Foes; and find one's self surrounded by those with whom one has no Ideas in common,—no Care for Applause nor no Strife of Competition."[11] Hers was a curious mind willing to explore ideas on the run; it was a generous yet combative intelligence that enjoyed rivalry and found in acclaim its natural habitat.

Long before she appointed her literary executor, she anticipated publication of certain blocks of letters. She prompted her friends to save them, as we have already seen, and to promise their return. She saw her power as a letter writer not dissipating with time but rather becoming more finely honed. She thus boasted to John Salusbury, " 'Tis the Fashion to say my Letters of the Years 1817,

18, 19—are better than those of 1768 or 70 &c. &c. &c." She wrote in what she called "a large loose hand" and usually dated precisely, confirming her eagerness to make an editor's effort as congenial as possible.[12]

Mrs. Piozzi always conceived of her letters as part of a literary genre, but not until her later years did she think of mining this rich vein. Even before she consciously considered them as marketable products, their potential could not have been repressed too deeply. For this reason—and perhaps for others—her letters sometimes appear more guarded than we would have expected from a woman who never denied her passion or her biases or suspicions. For instance—and this is an extreme illustration of her tight-lipped restraint—she and Penelope Sophia Pennington were friends for a long time and over large distances that separated them. Yet in 1804 the friendship ended abruptly. Why? we asked. And since both sides of the correspondence exist, we should have discovered a decisive answer, but we have not. Why? asked Mrs. Pennington, who sent letter after letter from late 1804 until 1809. She too was left to wonder, at least until 1819 when they renewed their friendship.

Control is written into some of Mrs. Piozzi's letters. For the most part, however, she held back little of her private world, deliberately highlighting its dramatic episodes. What she emphasized was her adoration of Gabriel Piozzi and her almost silent grief at his death on 26 March 1809. What she underscored also were her quarrels and truces with her four daughters; her pleasure and chagrin at the critical reception of her published work; the tremulous start of her second widowhood and her adjustment to Bath society whose rumormongering entertained her; her exile and poverty-ridden boredom first in Weston-super-Mare and then in Penzance; finally her pavane-paced return to Clifton and death.

But what emerges from all these letters? Hester Lynch Piozzi was so dynamic a personality, so much a creature of both reason and mood that she sometimes appears to whirl as a paradox. She struck out for independence and a realization of self; yet she needed the reassurance of people about her. She applauded successful women, whether Elizabeth Carter or Helen Maria Williams or Hannah More, all different from one another; above anyone else she exalted Sarah Siddons. She believed that a woman who triumphed in a man's world deserved adulation. But a woman who faltered deceived not only herself but every other woman who pushed against the bonds that encircled her. So, when the young and talented Anna Lee committed suicide in 1805, Mrs. Piozzi was without pity. The suicide, she wrote, was a "disgraceful Exploit! my opinion is that careful as She used to be of her Toilette She misplaced her Garters terribly that fatal Morning,—and left the Sisterhood a bitter Legacy of Shame and Sorrow. Our Critical Reviewers will *enlarge* the *Sisterhood,* and make all us demiscavantes look foolish on her Account I suppose:——stringing us up in a Row like Penelope's Maids at the End of Homer's Odyssey. I am very angry to be sure."[13] She directed her anger against a person who, she believed, gave credence to the cliché of feminine weakness and, conversely, annulled examples of feminine courage.

Or to pursue her paradoxes still further: wishing to be learned, she nevertheless saw erudition as alien to a woman whose role by class definition was social and domestic. In a journal written for her nephew and adopted son, she commented: "I would not advise you to breed your Girls to Literature. My Happiness was almost all made by it, but it is not the natural Soil, whence Females are likely to find or form some Felicity."[14] While she enjoyed the act of composition, she had to confess that "Life is scarce long enough to talk, & to write, and to live to rejoyce in what one has written." She tried for literary approbation even as she conceded that applause was the sound that went nowhere. Still she relished the fact "that grave Mr. Lucas brings his son to her that he might see *the first Woman in England*."[15]

The paradoxes continue. She fulfilled her duties as daughter and wife with a show of acquiescence. At the same time she sought to dominate family and friends; her tongue, her money—when she had it—her determination, all became instruments of manipulation. Yet she felt that her capacity for love was not matched by others. Not even Piozzi could provide "the soft Passion" she needed from him. She wanted to be a published author, whether of scholarly volumes or flag-raising pamphlets. Yet she seldom triumphed in the marketplace. Certainly we can sense frustration and repressed rage under her avowed commitment to husband and children.[16] We can sense too her anger at being mauled by critics who found her guilty of sins that ranged from deception and betrayal to feminine perversity. We can, indeed, intuit her painful consciousness of failed effort and of not belonging. Almost a year and a half before she died, in a letter to Mangin dated 4 September 1819, she confessed she was in fact "houseless."

> Life is a Magic Lanthorn certainly, and I think more so to Women, than to men: who often are placed very early in a Profession which they follow up regularly, and slide on; Labetur et Labetur almost unconsciously:—but We Females (myself for Example,) I passed the first 20 Years in my Father and Uncle's Houses, connected with their Friends, Dwelling-Places and Acquaintance; and fancying *myself at home* among them;—No such Thing.
>
> Marriage introduced me to A *new* Set of Figures, *quite* new; nor did I ever see but distantly and accidentally, any of the old Groupe or their Residencies from that Day to this. . . . another Marriage drove that Set of Figures quite away, and I began the World anew——with new Faces around me, and in new Scenes too. . . . I did however fancy when Piozzi built me a beautiful House on the Estate and in the Country my Parents quitted in my early Childhood—that I was got *home* again . . . *quite* a Mistake was *that*. . . .

Her wanderings were not yet over; she never found the niche that she believed hers until she was buried in a vault under Tremeirchion Church in the Vale of Clwyd.

Hester Lynch Piozzi evades comfortable understanding because she encompasses so many contradictions and because—like many others—she hid a part of her private self. Yet a few facts stand clear. Her soul could suffer but could not be stifled, and it continued steady beneath the mutability of her external life. Whether innocent or provocative, she endured those who bartered away her confidences or sneered at her. Her daughters distrusted her and she them, with each side threatening and taking legal action against the other. Yet she played out the role of "mère de famille" even when she abandoned them in 1784 and when—years later—she was barred from the weddings of Sophia and Queeney, from Cecilia's lying-in. She cajoled and badgered her adopted son Sir John Salusbury Piozzi Salusbury into becoming the moral English gentleman when he could be neither moral nor gentle. He mangled her love and trust, siphoned off her money until almost none was left.

While her epithet "Enemies" may be too strong to describe certain of her associations, she was abused, sometimes offensively so. But she also had many friends, prominent, or humble, who gave her affection, loyalty, compassion, and the ego-fulfilling admiration that sustained her. She nonetheless had gray days when she was ready to renounce love and friendship as well as study and the learning groped for but never fully attained. What, she asked, are any of them good for except to erode health and good will? The gray days, however, slipped away, and back she went to the values that gave her definition as a person—love and friendship, study and learning. What can be said of Hester Lynch Piozzi is that she exhibits a strong personality and that her letters mirror this fact. We may respect her for courageous independence and a capacity to survive, or we may disdain her for self-indulgence and vain pretensions. Whatever we feel about her, her very boldness and vibrancy preclude indifference.

The distinction of her correspondence stems ironically from her ability to speak, to give an individual all her attention, and so to dominate the talk. Most people who knew her enjoyed her conversation and clever repartee. As Dr. James Currie described the voluble Mrs. Piozzi on 1 September 1789: "She expects to talk and to be listened to, & her conversation flows in a perpetual stream. We travelled over France and Italy together, and discussed the manners and characters of the people. . . . She has observed them with a penetrating tho' with a female eye, & her remarks are therefore the more amusing. We talked of love, cicisbeoism, marriage, intimacies, & various points of that kind; on which she was very explicit . . . tho a lady, she is quite a philosopher."[17]

Mrs. Piozzi would have recognized the masculine patronage, while lapping up the doctor's delight in her natural fluency. She was an animated conversationalist, dramatically alert to her audience. Her letters become an extended dialogue with hers the controlling voice among others less dominant. Their style emulates the power to speak, and she took care to speak well. Her correspondence, then, strives for informality; it is often colloquial and even slangy but the matters pursued usually have substantive weight. Indeed, a few of her letters, seeking profundity, fall into a trap of strained learning. Thus, in the give-and-take with Joseph Cooper Walker, Mrs. Piozzi wanted her scholarship either to match or to outshine his. She, consequently, flew from one bit of erudition to another with the speed of a frenetic hummingbird.

4

Despite a rare flight into fancy, slips into the coyness of vanity, some errors, Mrs. Piozzi considered her letters as assertions of self, a public record of her life and times stated with easy grace. We are then faced with the inevitable question. How reliable, in literal fact, are they? The answer comes quickly. When she writes of immediate events, she reports accurately. Yet her accounts are shaped by her heritage and values, whether new or old. She writes as a member of the landed gentry, as a monarchist and a Tory; her beliefs are grounded in the image of England as both spirit and fighting machine. Fortunately, she never conceals her point of view, and so she allows us to achieve a balance that perspective fortifies. We find in her correspondence a running commentary on the politics of George III and the Regency, with Pitt and Perceval as near-epic figures. Also dominant in her news reportage is a mass of emotional responses: antipathy to the French Revolution whose contagious anarchy had, she felt, spread across the Channel; surprise at the Napoleonic onslaught; pride in her aggressive management of an expanding landed estate during hard times and incipient rebellion; loathing of corn factors and merchants who for gain forced up the price of bread while the poor went hungry; moral disgust with British behavior in India. She makes clear in her letters the excitement of travel on the Continent and in Great Britain; the polite huffing and puffing of salon behavior, whether at Streatham Park or Brynbella, in Bath or London.

When in her correspondence she indulges in recollection, often set forth as dramatic episode or as anecdote and parable, she is probably honest enough in the broad outlines of these earlier experiences. But the people who acted out their roles in them did not always speak as she recalled the conversation. It is usually witty dialogue, quite sparkling, but as often as not it is her aphorism or mot seasoned with the flavor of the original speaker. For example, in a letter to Mrs. Pennington dated 10 January 1798, she described an adventure early in her new marriage. "When I was going over the Alps with Mr. Piozzi the sight of a dreadful Precipice made me afraid and I said I would walk—it was very late in a fine Summer Evening——*Sit still,* cried my Master. I cannot sit still, replied I. *Stop, stop,* You disturb the Drivers you will make them overturn us—pray sit still. No I would *not* sit still, I would *walk:* Well walk away then said Mr. Piozzi if you *will* walk; There are a Troop of Wolves ranging the Mountains now—I was told so at the last Inn: They will find their Prey out in an Instant. Oh! You can't imagine after that how still and quiet I sate in the Carriage."

When she records the opinions of people like Johnson, Burke, Garrick, Reynolds, Hogarth, and others, she perpetuates the substance of their remarks, given the blurring effects of time, or she may exaggerate their essence to enhance her stature. To illustrate: certainly, she knew Hogarth, who frequented her uncle's house where she was a happy visitor, and certainly he might have proposed that she be the model for *The Lady's Last Stake,* if only to attract the attention of a precocious child. But did she sit for the genre painting? In short, the milieu supports a possibility; the fact itself remains in doubt despite her frequent insistence that she posed for the harried woman in the Hogarth portrait.[18]

She wanted to be part of a creative tradition. If her correspondence alone supported that desire, so be it. Indeed, those letters, which she meant to be preserved in print, place her in the epistolary heritage of the eighteenth century represented by Lady Mary Wortley Montagu, Elizabeth Carter, Anna Seward, Lord Chesterfield, and Horace Walpole (to single out those whom she would have named). She was sensitive to letter writing as an art, to the techniques of her contemporaries and near-predecessors. Like them, she emphasized intellectual quality, saying something about whatever mattered—a significant event, a great man, a new book, the high fashion of prophecy or flesh-colored clinging fabrics. Quite deliberately, she used the material of her letters to link herself with those correspondents whose judgment she respected. Many in number, disparate in professions and financial worth, they nevertheless were familiar acquaintances who shared similar responses to art and music, to history and politics, to a set of social institutions. Not that she was a prig, feeling comfortable largely in an epistolary world of men. On the contrary. Like many of the women letter writers of her time, she worked the familiar themes of courtship, marriage, and children but probably with less intensity than they; each of those subjects cost her pain. How could she unquestioningly revere them in a manner suitable to a woman or even dwell upon them?

Above all, Mrs. Piozzi liked to formulate personas who appeared to write spontaneously about various subjects but exercised the restraint that would guard her private self. Like Samuel Johnson, she assumed that, in most instances, "a friendly letter is a calm and deliberate performance in the cool of leisure, in the stillness of solitude. . . ." She would have agreed further that one of the "pleasure[s] of corresponding with a friend" is a waiver of "doubt and distrust" and the assurance that "everything is said as it is thought."[19]

5

Sir James Fellowes never brought out the edition of Mrs. Piozzi's letters—or of her poems and anecdotes—that she hoped he would. She did not err in her choice of literary executor. She just mistook the nature of her heir. A consummate fox hunter and squire, Sir John Salusbury Piozzi Salusbury suspected anyone and anything literary. At the same time that he promised to cooperate with Sir James, he concealed his aunt's papers at Brynbella. Obviously resentful of the image he projected in the letters, he prevented their posthumous publication even when they were owned by others. His threat of legal action against the Williams family, who wished to print their Piozzi letters, offers presumptive evidence of his anxiety. In any event, he held the correspondence and journals hostage and sold, as if for retribution or ransom, a large part of her library, paintings, prints, silver, and other valuables, first in 1823 and then again in 1831 and 1836. Not until 1901 and for several years during the first decade of the twentieth century were significant numbers of her holograph materials sold by Sir John's grandson, Major E. P. Salusbury. Since then, the sale of her letters and diaries has been steady with a falling off, understandably, during the depressed thirties and two world wars.[20]

From these diaries and letters emerges the portrait of an intricate woman whose energy and curiosity seemed immune to fatigue. Almost everything piqued her interest, no matter how practical or how recondite. She was attracted to people, to "coteries" with whom she could hold forth and to whom, less frequently, she could listen. Her correspondence, particularly, and her journals record the events, the stories, the "chatteries" that fascinated her. These documents—and so she thought of them—offer a lasting, often allusive delineation of her world, both intimate and social. "This is her chief claim to remembrance; this her value to the social historian of to-day."[21]

Notes

1. *The Letters of Samuel Johnson with Mrs. Thrale's Genuine Letters to Him*, ed. R. W. Chapman, 3 vols. (Oxford: Clarendon Press, 1952). Prior to the work of Professors Clifford and Balderston, the following also stimulated awareness of Mrs. Piozzi: *Johnson and Queeney* (London: Cassell; New York: Random House, 1932), *The Queeney Letters* (London: Cassell; New York: Farrar & Rinehart, 1934), both edited by the marquis of Lansdowne; and *The French Journals of Mrs. Thrale and Dr. Johnson*, ed. Moses Tyson and Henry Guppy (Manchester: Manchester University Press, 1932).

2. The John Rylands University Library of Manchester, England, 559.1. The letter is dated 19 September 1820.

3. The letters to Alexander Leak and Clement Mead are in the Donald and Mary Hyde Collection.

4. For the sale of the Williams letters, see Sotheby's *Catalogue of Valuable Autograph Letters, Literary Manuscripts, and Historical Documents*, 29 October 1975, p. 94, lot 206. The same correspondence had been advertised five years earlier by Dawson of Pall Mall in *Catalogue 209* (June 1970), pp. 37–41, lot 21.

The Williams-Piozzi correspondence was again sold, ca. 1984, to the John Rylands University Library.

5. Piozzi, "Miscellaneous Papers," Firestone Library at Princeton University.

6. The John Rylands University Library, 585.12. The letter is dated 26 September 1808 and is addressed to John P: Salusbury Esq. / at the Rev. T. Shephard's / Enborne Cottage near / Newbury / Berks.

7. 473 letters, in six volumes from 1807 to 1821. See the John Rylands University Library, 585–90.

8. Frances Burney d'Arblay to her husband, dated 10 December 1812, in the Henry W. and Albert A. Berg Collection, New York Public Library.

9. James L. Clifford, *Hester Lynch Piozzi (Mrs. Thrale)*, 2d ed. (Oxford: Clarendon Press, 1968, 1987), p. 458.

10. The John Rylands University Library, 616.

11. The Bowood Collection of Thrale-Piozzi letters, Bowood House, Calne, Wilts. The letter is dated 19 March 1799.

12. The John Rylands University Library, 590.433. The letter is dated 12 May 1819, Bath. For the description of her penmanship, see *Thraliana: The Diary of Mrs. Hester Lynch Thrale (later Mrs. Piozzi)*, ed. Katharine C. Balderston, 2d ed., 2 vols. (Oxford: Clarendon Press, 1951), 1:158.

13. The John Rylands University Library, 561.132. The letter is dated 14 November 1805.

14. "Minced Meat for Pyes," Houghton Library, Harvard University.

15. *Thraliana* 1:257; see her letter to Sir James Fellowes, dated [19 October 1815].

16. Patricia M. Spacks, *The Female Imagination* (New York: Knopf, 1975), p. 200.

17. As Katherine Plymley later reacted to HLP: "She is 74 but has an expression of youthful vivacity and animation of her countenance very uncommon at that age. She appears much younger, expecially when lighted up by conversation. . . . I was struck by the nonchalance with which she spoke upon subjects that I should have supposed she would have avoided to mention," for example, the intimacy between Sophia Streatfield (or Streatfeild) and Henry Thrale.

For the Plymley diary, see MS 567 / Book 92, County Record Office, Salop. Cf. Mangin, pp. 18–20. For Currie to Francis Trench, see J. L. Clifford, "Mrs. Piozzi's Letters," *Essays on the Eighteenth Century Presented to David Nichol Smith* (Oxford: Clarendon Press, 1945), p. 157 and n. 1.

18. See Mrs. Piozzi to Queeney, 22 March 1810, n. 12. For the ways in which she manipulated Johnson's portrait, see Clifford, *Hester Lynch Piozzi*, pp. 255–72, 314–21. See also his *From Puzzles to Portraits* (Chapel Hill: The University of North Carolina Press, 1970), pp. 77–79.

19. Johnson, *Lives of the English Poets*, 3 vols., ed. G. B. Hill (Oxford: Clarendon Press, 1905), 3:207; Chapman, *Letters of Samuel Johnson* (to Mrs. Thrale, 27 October 1777), 2:228. See also Bruce Redford, *The Converse of the Pen* (Chicago: University of Chicago Press, 1986), pp. 214–15; Howard Anderson, Philip B. Daghlian, and Irvin Ehrenpreis, *The Familiar Letter in the Eighteenth Century* (Lawrence: University of Kansas Press, 1966), pp. 269–82.

20. For a partial listing of the significant sales of Piozzi letters, see Edward and Lillian Bloom, and Joan E. Klingel, "Portrait of a Georgian Lady: The Letters of Hester Lynch (Thrale) Piozzi, 1784–1821," *Bulletin of the John Rylands University Library of Manchester* 60 (1978): 315.

21. Clifford, *Hester Lynch Piozzi*, p. 460.

Short Titles for Major Manuscript Repositories

Barrett	The Barrett Collection of Burney Papers, British Library, London, 43 vols., Egerton [Eg.] 3690–3708
Berg	The Henry W. and Albert A. Berg Collection, New York Public Library, New York City
Bodleian	Bodleian Library, Oxford University
Bowood Collection	The Bowood Collection of Thrale-Piozzi letters in the possession of the marquis of Lansdowne, Bowood House, near Calne, Wilts.
Brit. Mus. Add. MSS	British Museum [now British Library] Additional Manuscripts
C.R.O.	County Record Office[s], England, Wales, and Ireland
Harvard University Library	Houghton Library at Harvard University
Historical Society of Pennsylvania	Historical Society of Pennsylvania, Philadelphia
Huntington Library	Huntington Library, San Marino, California
Hyde Collection	The Donald and Mary Hyde Collection at Four Oaks Farm, Somerville, New Jersey; and at the Houghton Library, Harvard University
N.L.W.	National Library of Wales, Aberystwyth

N.P.G.	The National Portrait Gallery, Trafalgar Square, London
Peyraud Collection	The Paula F. Peyraud Collection of Piozzi letters and marginalia, Chappaqua, New York
Pforzheimer	The Carl H. Pforzheimer Library, New York City
Pierpont Morgan Library	Pierpont Morgan Library, New York City
Princeton University Library	Firestone Library at Princeton University
P.R.O.	Public Record Office, Chancery Lane, London
Ry.	The John Rylands University Library of Manchester, England
Victoria and Albert	Victoria and Albert Museum Library, London
Yale University Library	James Marshall and Marie-Louise Osborn Collection; and the Beinecke Collection at Yale University

Locations of miscellaneous collections of Piozzi manuscripts not listed above are identified at the foot of each relevant letter under *"Text."*

Short Titles for Hester Lynch Piozzi's Manuscripts and Books

Anecdotes	*Anecdotes of the Late Samuel Johnson, LL.D., During the Last Twenty Years of His Life.* London: Printed for T. Cadell, 1786.
British Synonymy	*British Synonymy; or, An Attempt at Regulating the Choice of Words in Familiar Conversation.* 2 vols. London: Printed for G. G. and J. Robinson, 1794.
"Children's Book"	For "The Children's Book or rather Family Book" from 17 September 1766 to the end of 1778 (Hyde Collection), see Hyde, Mary. *The Thrales of Streatham Park.* Cambridge and London: Harvard University Press, 1977.
"Commonplace Book"	"The New Commonplace Book." Random entries made by HLP after the completion of *Thraliana,* the first entry written at Brynbella in 1809 and the last in 1820 at Penzance (Hyde Collection).
Florence Miscellany	*Florence Miscellany.* Florence: Printed for G. Cam, Printer to His Royal Highness. With Permission, 1785. Hester Lynch Piozzi contributed the preface and nine poems.
French Journals	*The French Journals of Mrs. Thrale and Doctor Johnson.* Edited by Moses Tyson and Henry Guppy. Manchester: Manchester University Press, 1932. Hester Lynch Thrale's *French Journal* (1775) includes pp. 69–166; Hester Lynch Piozzi's *French Journey* (1784), pp. 191–

	213; Samuel Johnson's *French Journal* (1775), pp. 169–88.
"Harvard Piozziana"	"Poems and Little Characters, Anecdotes &c. Introductory to the Poems." 5 MS vols., 1810–14, for John Salusbury Piozzi Salusbury. Harvard University Library, MS Eng. 1280.
"Italian and German Journals"	"Italian and German Journals, from 5 September 1784 to March 1787," 2 MS notebooks (Ry. 618).
"Journey Book"	"Journey through the North of England and Part of Scotland, Wales, &c." 1789 (Ry. 623).
Letters	*Letters to and from the late Samuel Johnson, LL.D.* 2 vols. London: Printed for A. Strahan and T. Cadell, 1788.
"Lyford Redivivus"	"Lyford Redivivus or A Grandame's Garrulity." [Signed by] "An Old Woman" [1809–15] (Hyde Collection).
Merritt	*Piozzi Marginalia.* Edited by Percival Merritt. Cambridge: Harvard University Press, 1925.
"Minced Meat for Pyes"	"Minced Meat for Pyes" (1796–1820)," a collection of extracts, jottings, quotations, verses, &c. "Harvard University Library, MS Eng. 231F.
Observations	*Observations and Reflections made in the course of a Journey through France, Italy, and Germany.* 2 vols. London: Printed for A. Strahan and T. Cadell, 1789.
Old England	*Old England to her Daughters. Address to the Females of Great Britain.* [Signed by] "Poor Old England," penny broadside. London: Printed by J. Brettell for R. Faulder, ca. June 1803.
Retrospection	*Retrospection: or A Review of the Most Striking and Important Events, Characters, Situations, and their Consequences, which the last Eighteen Hundred Years have Presented to the View of Mankind.* 2 vols. London: Printed for John Stockdale, 1801.

Thraliana	*Thraliana: The Diary of Mrs. Hester Lynch Thrale (later Mrs. Piozzi), 1776–1809.* Edited by Katharine C. Balderston. 2d ed. 2 vols. Oxford: Clarendon Press, 1951. The original MS, 6 vols., is at the Huntington Library, San Marino, California.
Three Warnings	*The Three Warnings.* Kidderminster: Printed by John Gower, 1792. This work appeared originally in Anna Williams, *Miscellanies in Prose and Verse* (1766).
Three Warnings to John Bull	*Three Warnings to John Bull before He Dies. By an Old Acquaintance of the Public.* London: R. Faulder, 1798.
"Verses 1"	"Collection of Hester Lynch Piozzi's MSS Poetry." 140 leaves, of which 60, i.e., 120 pages, contain HLP's original poetry (Hyde Collection).
"Verses 2"	"Collection of Hester Lynch Piozzi's MSS Poetry." 34 pages of Hester Lynch Piozzi's verse plus 19 blank pages (Hyde Collection).
Welsh Tour	*Mrs. Thrale's Unpublished Journal of her Tour in Wales with Dr. Johnson, July–September, 1774.* In A. M. Broadley's *Doctor Johnson and Mrs. Thrale*, pp. 155–219. London and New York: John Lane, 1910.

Short Titles for Secondary Sources

We have used standard encyclopedias, school and university rosters, biographical dictionaries, law lists, peerages, armorials, baronetages, knightages, medical and clerical rosters, town and city directories, almanacs, and so forth. Along with these we have consulted annual army and navy lists; *Boyle's Court Guide; Royal Kalendar;* the Reverend William Betham, *The Baronetage of England,* 5 vols. (1801–5); the numerous editions of Burke's *Peerage and Baronetage* as well as Burke's *Landed Gentry;* Burke's *Royal Families of the World,* 2 vols. (1977); Burke's *Irish Family Records* (1976); George Edward Cokayne, *The Complete Peerage,* revised by Vicary Gibbs, et al., 13 vols. (1910–59); *The Complete Baronetage,* 6 vols. (1900–1909); W. A. Shaw, *The Knights of England,* 2 vols. (1906); Howard M. Colvin, *A Biographical Dictionary of British Architects, 1660–1840* (1954; 1978); Joseph Haydn and Horace Ockerby, *The Book of Dignities,* 3d ed. (1894); Gerrit P. Judd IV, *Members of Parliament, 1734–1832* (1955); Sir Lewis Namier and John Brooke, *The House of Commons, 1754–1790,* 3 vols. (1964).

These works will be cited only when specifically appropriate.

AR	*The Annual Register, or a View of the History, Politics, and Literature. 1758–*
Baronetage	Cokayne, George Edward, ed. *Complete Baronetage.* 6 vols. Exeter: W. Pollard, 1900–1909.
Bayle	*The Dictionary Historical and Critical of Mr. Peter Bayle.* 2d ed. 5 vols. London: Printed for J. J. and P. Knapton [etc.], 1734–38.
Boaden	Boaden, James. *Memoirs of Mrs. Siddons, Interspersed with Anecdotes of Authors and Actors.* 2 vols. London: Henry Colburn, 1827.
Boswell's Johnson	*Boswell's Life of Johnson.* Edited by George Birkbeck Hill and L. F. Powell. 6 vols. Oxford: Clarendon Press, 1934–64.
Broadley	Broadley, A. M. *Doctor Johnson and Mrs. Thrale.* London and New York: John Lane, 1910.

Brooke	Brooke, John. *King George III*. New York: McGraw-Hill, 1972.
Campbell	Campbell, Thomas. *Life of Mrs. Siddons*. 2 vols. London: Effingham Wilson, 1834.
Chandler	Chandler, David G. *The Campaigns of Napoleon*. London: Weidenfeld and Nicolson, 1966.
Chapman	Chapman, R. W., ed. *The Letters of Samuel Johnson, with Mrs. Thrale's Genuine Letters to Him*. 3 vols. Oxford: Clarendon Press, 1952.
Clifford	Clifford, James L. *Hester Lynch Piozzi (Mrs. Thrale)*. 2d ed. Reprinted with corrections and additions. Oxford: Clarendon Press, 1968, 1987.
Corr. George IV	*The Correspondence of George, Prince of Wales, 1770–1812*. Edited by A. Aspinall. 8 vols. New York: Oxford University Press, 1963–71.
Décembre-Alonnier	[Joseph] Décembre–[Edmond] Alonnier. *Dictionnaire de la Révolution française, 1789–1799*. 2 vols. Paris [1866–68].
Diary and Letters	*Diary and Letters of Madame d'Arblay*. Edited by Charlotte Barrett. 7 vols. [1842–46.] London: H. Colburn, 1854.
Dodsley	*A Collection of Poems in Six Volumes by Several Hands*. [Edited by Robert Dodsley.] London: Printed by J. Hughs, for J. Dodsley, in Pall-Mall, 1765.
Early Journals	*The Early Journals and Letters of Fanny Burney*, vol. 1 (1768–73). Edited by Lars E. Troide. Oxford and Montreal: Oxford University Press; McGill-Queens University Press, 1987–
English Poets	Johnson, Samuel. *Lives of the English Poets*. Edited by George Birkbeck Hill. 3 vols. Oxford: Clarendon Press, 1905.
Farington	*The Diary of Joseph Farington*. Vols. 1–6 edited by Kenneth Garlick and Angus D. Macintyre. Vols. 7–16 edited by Kathryn Cave. New Haven and London: Published for the Paul Mellon Centre for Studies in British Art, Yale University Press, 1978–84.

Genest	Genest, John. *Some Account of the English Stage, from the Restoration in 1660 to 1830.* 10 vols. Bath: Printed by H. E. Carrington and sold by Thomas Rodd, Great Newport Street, London, 1832.
GM	*The Gentleman's Magazine.* Edited by Sylvanus Urban. London, 1731–1907.
Hawkins	Hawkins, Sir John. *The Life of Samuel Johnson, LL.D.* 2d ed. Revised and corrected. London: J. Buckland [etc.], 1787.
Hayward	Hayward, A., ed. *Autobiography, Letters and Literary Remains of Mrs. Piozzi (Thrale).* 2d ed. 2 vols. London: Longman, Green, Longman, Roberts, 1861.
Hazen	Hazen, Charles Downer. *The French Revolution.* 2 vols. New York: Henry Holt, 1932.
Hemlow	Hemlow, Joyce. *The History of Fanny Burney.* Oxford: Clarendon Press, 1958.
Highfill	Highfill, Philip H., Jr., Kalman A. Burnim, and Edward A. Langhans. *A Biographical Dictionary of Actors, Actresses, Musicians, Dancers, Managers & other State Personnel in London, 1660–1800.* Carbondale and Edwardsville: Southern Illinois University Press, 1973–
Hodson	Hodson, V. C. P. *List of the Officers of the Bengal Army 1758–1834.* 4 pts. London: Constable; Phillimore, 1927–47.
Howell	*Epistolae Ho-Elianae, The Familiar Letters of James Howell.* Edited by Joseph Jacobs. 2 vols. [1645–55.] London: David Nutt, 1892.
Hyde	Hyde, Mary. *The Thrales of Streatham Park.* Cambridge and London: Harvard University Press, 1977.
Idler	*The Idler and the Adventurer.* Edited by W. J. Bate, John M. Bullitt, and L. F. Powell. Vol. 2 of *The Yale Edition of the Works of Samuel Johnson.* New Haven and London, 1963.
Jerningham	*The Jerningham Letters (1780–1843).* Edited by Egerton Castle. 2 vols. London: Richard Bentley and Son, 1896.

Jesse — Jesse, J. Heneage. *Memoirs of the Life and Reign of King George the Third.* 2d ed. 3 vols. London: Tinsley Brothers, 1867.

Johns. Misc. — *Johnsonian Miscellanies.* Edited by George Birkbeck Hill. 2 vols. Oxford: Clarendon Press, 1897.

Johns. Shakespeare — *Johnson on Shakespeare.* Edited by Arthur Sherbo. Vols. 7–8 of *The Yale Edition of the Works of Samuel Johnson.* New Haven and London, 1968.

Journals and Letters — *The Journals and Letters of Fanny Burney (Madame d'Arblay).* Edited by Joyce Hemlow et al. 12 vols. Oxford: Clarendon Press, 1972–84. Especially vol. 7, edited by Edward A. Bloom and Lillian D. Bloom (1978); vol. 8, edited by Peter Hughes et al. (1980): vols. 9–10, edited by Warren Derry (1982).

Knapp — Knapp, Oswald G., ed. *The Intimate Letters of Hester Piozzi and Penelope Pennington 1788–1821.* London, Toronto, and New York: John Lane; Bell and Cockburn, 1914.

Lefebvre — Lefebvre, Georges. *The French Revolution.* Vol. 1, *From its Origins to 1793,* translated by Elizabeth Moss Evanson. Vol. 2, *From 1793 to 1799,* translated by John Hall Stewart and James Friguglietti. London: Routledge and Kegan Paul; New York: Columbia University Press, 1962–64.

Lloyd — Lloyd, J[acob] Y. *The History of the Princes, the Lords Marcher, and the Ancient Nobility of Powys Fadog, and the Ancient Lords of Arwystli, Cedewen, and Meirionydd.* 6 vols. London: T. Richards [Whiting], 1881–87.

London Stage — *The London Stage 1660–1800.* Edited by William Van Lennep, Emmett L. Avery, Arthur H. Scouten, et al. 5 vols. in 11 and index. Carbondale: Southern Illinois University Press, 1960–79.

McCarthy — McCarthy, William. *Hester Thrale Piozzi: Portrait of a Literary Woman.* Chapel Hill: University of North Carolina Press, 1985.

Mangin — [Mangin, Edward.] *Piozziana; or, Recollections of the Late Mrs. Piozzi, with Remarks.* London: Edward Moxon, 1833.

Manvell — Manvell, Roger. *Sarah Siddons: Portrait of an Actress.* London: Heinemann, 1970.

Marshall — Marshall, John. *Royal Naval Biography.* . . . 4 vols. London: Longman, Hurst, Rees, Orme, and Browne, 1823–35.

Nichols — Nichols, John. *Illustrations of the Literary History of the Eighteenth Century.* 8 vols. [7 and 8 by John Bowyers Nichols.] London: Nichols, Son, and Bentley, 1817–58.

Oxford Proverbs — *The Oxford Dictionary of English Proverbs.* 3d ed. Revised by F. P. Wilson. [1970.] Oxford: Clarendon Press, 1982.

Parliamentary History — *The Parliamentary History of England from the earliest Period to the Year 1803, from which last-mentioned Epoch it is continued downwards in the work entitled "Hansard's Parliamentary Debates."* 36 vols. London: Printed by T. C. Hansard [etc.], 1806–20.

Pastor — Pastor, Baron Ludwig Friedrich August von. *The History of the Popes, from the Close of the Middle Ages.* 40 vols. London: J. Hodges [etc.], 1891–1953.

Peerage — Cokayne, George Edward. *The Complete Peerage of England, Scotland, Ireland, Great Britain and the United Kingdom.* 2d ed., rev. and enl. Edited by Vicary Gibbs et al. 13 vols. London: St. Catherine Press, 1910–59.

Poems — *Poems.* Edited by E. L. McAdam, Jr., with George Milne. Vol. 6 of *The Yale Edition of the Works of Samuel Johnson.* New Haven and London, 1964.

Prayers — *Diaries, Prayers, and Annals.* Edited by E. L. McAdam, Jr., with Donald and Mary Hyde. Vol. 1 of *The Yale Edition of the Works of Samuel Johnson.* New Haven and London, 1958.

Queeney Letters — *The Queeney Letters.* Edited by the marquis of Lansdowne. London: Cassell; New York: Farrar & Rinehart, 1934.

Rambler — *The Rambler.* Edited by W. J. Bate and Albrecht B. Strauss. Vols. 3–5 of *The Yale Edition of the Works of Samuel Johnson.* New Haven and London, 1969.

Redford — Redford, Bruce. *The Converse of the Pen.* Chicago and London: University of Chicago Press, 1986.

Repertorium — Winter, Otto Friedrich. *Repertorium der diplomatischen Vertreter aller Länder seit dem Westfälischen Frieden (1648),* vol. 3, 1764–1815. Graz-Köln: Verlag Hermann Böhlaus, 1965.

Rothenberg — Rothenberg, Gunter E. *Napoleon's Great Adversaries: The Archduke Charles and the Austrian Army, 1792–1814.* Bloomington: Indiana University Press, 1982.

Sale Catalogue — 1. *Streatham Park, Surrey. A Catalogue of the . . . Household Furniture . . . a Collection of Valuable Paintings . . . also the Extensive and Well-Selected Library . . . the genuine Property of Mrs. Piozzi . . . will be sold by Auction, by Mr. Squibb, on the Premises, on Wednesday the 8th of May, 1816, and Four following Days (Sunday excepted).*
2. *Collectanea Johnsoniana. Catalogue of the Library, Pictures, Prints, Coins, Plate, China, and other Valuable Curiosities, the Property of Mrs. Hester Lynch Piozzi, Deceased, to be sold by Auction, at the Emporium Rooms, Exchange Street, Manchester, by Mr. Broster, on Wednesday, [September 1823] the 17th instant, and [six] following days, Saturday and Sunday excepted. Chester.*

Seward, *Anecdotes* — Seward, William. *Anecdotes of Some Distinguished Persons, Chiefly of the Present and Two Preceding Centuries.* 4 vols. and supplement. 2d ed. London: T. Cadell, Jr., and W. Davies, 1795–96.

Seward Letters — *Letters of Anna Seward: Written between the Years 1784 and 1807.* 6 vols. Edinburgh: Archibald Constable and Co.; London: Longman, Hurst, Rees, Orme, and Brown, William Miller, and John Murray, 1811.

Shakespeare — *The Riverside Shakespeare.* Boston: Houghton Mifflin, 1974.

Siddons Letters — Burnim, Kalman A. "The Letters of Sarah and William Siddons to Hester Lynch Piozzi in the John Rylands Library." *Bulletin of the John Rylands Library* 52 (1969–70): 46–95.

Spectator — *The Spectator.* 8 vols. London: Printed by H. Hughs for Payne, Rivington [etc.], 1789. This is Hester Lynch

Piozzi's copy, bought in 1794, with her marginalia (Peyraud Collection).

Stanhope — Stanhope, Earl. *Life of the Right Honourable William Pitt.* 4 vols. 3d ed. [1867] New York: AMS Press, 1970.

Tilley — Tilley, Morris Palmer. *A Dictionary of the Proverbs in England in the Sixteenth and Seventeenth Centuries.* Ann Arbor: University of Michigan Press, 1950.

Walpole Correspondence — *The Yale Edition of Horace Walpole's Correspondence.* Edited by W. S. Lewis et al. 48 vols. in 49. New Haven, 1937–83.

Warton — Warton, Thomas. *The History of English Poetry, from the Close of the Eleventh to the Commencement of the Eighteenth Century.* 4 vols. London: J. Dodsley [etc.], 1774–81.

Watson — Watson, J. Steven. *The Reign of George III, 1760–1815.* Oxford: Clarendon Press, 1960.

Welsh Journey — Johnson, Samuel. *A Journey into North Wales, in the Year 1774.* In *Boswell's Johnson* 5:427–61.

Wheatley — Wheatley, Henry B. *London Past and Present.* 3 vols. London: John Murray; New York: Scribner and Welford, 1891.

Wickham — Wickham, The Reverend Hill, ed. *Journals and Correspondence of Thomas [Sedgwick] Whalley, D.D.* 2 vols. London: Richard Bentley, 1863.

Names and Abbreviations of Major Figures in the Piozzi Correspondence

AL	Alexander Leak (1776–1816)
CB	Charles Burney (1726–1814)
CMT CMM	Cecilia Margaretta Thrale (1777–1857); in 1795 Mrs. Mostyn
DL	The Reverend Daniel Lysons (1762–1834)
EM	The Reverend Edward Mangin (1772–1852)
FB FBA	Frances "Fanny" Burney (1752–1840); in 1793 Mme d'Arblay
HLS HLT HLP	Hester Lynch Salusbury (1741–1821); in 1763 Mrs. Thrale; in 1784 Mrs. Piozzi
HMP HMS	Harriet Maria Pemberton (1794–1831); in 1814 Mrs. Salusbury; in 1817 Lady Salusbury
HT	Henry Thrale (1728 or 1729–81)
JB	James Boswell (1740–95)
JF	James Fellowes (1771–1857); in 1809 Sir James, knight
JSPS	John Salusbury Piozzi Salusbury (1793–1858); in 1817 Sir John, knight
JW	John Williams (1794–1859); in 1830 Sir John, second baronet
LC	The Reverend Leonard Chappelow (1744–1820)
Ly W	Margaret Williams (1768–1835) of Bodelwyddan; in 1798 Lady Williams
MF	Marianne Francis (1790–1832)
MW	Margaret Williams (1759–1823) of Bath
PSW PSP	Penelope Sophia Weston (1752–1827); in 1792 Mrs. Pennington
Q	Hester Maria "Queeney" Thrale (1764–1857); in 1808 Lady Keith
RD	The Reverend Reynold Davies (1752–1820)
RG	The Reverend Robert Gray (1762–1834)
SAT	Susanna Arabella Thrale (1770–1858)
SJ	Samuel Johnson (1709–84)
SL	Samuel Lysons (1763–1819)
SS	Sarah Siddons (1755–1831)

ST } SH }	Sophia Thrale (1771–1824); in 1807 Mrs. Hoare
TSW	The Reverend Thomas Sedgwick Whalley (1746–1828)
WAC	William Augustus Conway (1789–1828)

Genealogical Abbreviations

cr.	created
fl.	flourished
M.I.	monumental inscription

Editorial Principles

Manuscript Sources

All letters are arranged chronologically. Mrs. Piozzi's correspondence creates few textual problems since she prided herself on her penmanship and wrote with a strong hand. We have transcribed literally, changing only what we believe would detract from clarity. We have retained original spellings, capitalization, and punctuation. Certain accidentals—the omission of a period or a closing parenthesis—are silently emended. Superior letters are lowered. Her intermittent use of an elision to form a past tense—a usage that she came to see as outmoded—is normalized: e.g., "defer'd" becomes "deferred." Most abbreviations—except in a few instances or in addresses and postmarks—are expanded.

Mrs. Piozzi's paragraphing can puzzle. Occasionally she follows normal practice by dropping a line and then indenting. At other times to indicate a new paragraph she merely extends a space on the same line. Sense usually dictates where a visibly uncertain paragraph begins. Dashes, similarly, are hard to decipher since her lines for that mark can be of any length or even appear as a seemingly extended ellipsis. Dashes, consequently, are transcribed as "—" or, when elongated to suggest emotional response, as "——."

The writer's address is shown at the upper right of the letter along with the date. The complimentary close and signature for each letter are presented in run-on fashion with slash marks to indicate line breaks or divisions. At the foot of each letter are provided, where available, repository, address of recipient, and postmark. Franked letters are marked as such.

Pertinent complementary correspondence usually appears in notes in order to explain obscurities, clarify cryptic remarks, or solve problems. In a few instances, however, when Mrs. Piozzi answers a letter—say, of Sarah Siddons, Leonard Chappelow, Joseph Cooper Walker, or Daniel Lysons—point-for-point, we incorporate in the body of the text the letter that initiated or continued the correspondence.

Generally, square brackets "[ ]" signal such defects in the holographs as blots, tears, seals, oversights. In addition, when a date of composition is conjectural, it is enclosed in square brackets and annotated. Angle brackets "< >" indicate places where a printed date, as in a postmark, a word, or a phrase is blurred. When warranted by the context, emendations are made within the appropriate square or angle brackets.

Printed Sources

Texts are reprinted literally although erroneous datings and obvious misprints are corrected with explanations when necessary, and certain typographical eccentricities, such as the arbitrary and inconsistent use of small capitals in words and phrases, are not reproduced.

We have consistently used the names of Welsh counties as HLP would have known them. Since 1974, however, following reorganization under the Local Government Act (1972), the new county of Clwyd, e.g., was created from Flintshire, most of Denbighshire, and the Edeyrnion district of Merioneth. Similarly, the new county of Gwynedd was formed out of Anglesey, Carnarvonshire (or Caernarfonshire), the rest of Merioneth, and the Conwy valley in Denbighshire.

Inventory of Letters from Hester Lynch (Thrale) Piozzi to the Following Recipients

In 1784:

14 to Hester Maria "Queeney" Thrale
11 to Fanny Burney
3 to Samuel Johnson
3 to Samuel Lysons
1 to Charles Burney

In 1785:

10 to Samuel Lysons
5 to Hester Maria "Queeney" Thrale
4 to Thomas Cadell
1 to Lord Cowper

In 1786:

9 to Samuel Lysons
4 to Thomas Cadell
3 to the Reverend Leonard Chappelow
3 to Hester Maria "Queeney" Thrale
2 to William Parsons
1 to Lord Cowper

In 1787:

10 to Samuel Lysons
3 to the Reverend Leonard Chappelow
3 to Hester Maria "Queeney" Thrale
2 to Sophia Byron
2 to Sir Robert Murray Keith
1 to William Parsons

In 1788:

14 to Sophia Byron
6 to Samuel Lysons

5 to Thomas Cadell
3 to Ann Greatheed
2 to the Reverend Leonard Chappelow
1 to George Colman, the elder
1 to Elizabeth Lambart

In 1789:
7 to Sophia Byron
6 to Penelope Sophia Weston
4 to Samuel Lysons
2 to the Reverend Leonard Chappelow
1 to Henry Barry
1 to Hugh Griffith
1 to Charlotte Lewis
1 to the Reverend Thomas Sedgwick Whalley

In 1790:
3 to Penelope Sophia Weston
2 to the Reverend Thomas Sedgwick Whalley
2 to Samuel Lysons
1 to the Reverend Leonard Chappelow
1 to Charlotte Lewis
1 to Jonathan Sterns

In 1791:
12 to Penelope Sophia Weston
2 to Hugh Griffith
2 to Charlotte Lewis
1 to John Cator
1 to the Reverend Leonard Chappelow
1 to John Field
1 to William Wilshire

In 1792:
13 to Penelope Sophia (Weston) Pennington
4 to Hugh Griffith
3 to the Reverend Leonard Chappelow
3 to Henry Drummond
2 to Samuel Lysons
1 to John Cator
1 to James Drummond
1 to [French Laurence]
1 to Charlotte Lewis
1 to Thomas Pennant
1 to Bishop Thomas Percy

In 1793:

16 to Penelope Sophia Pennington
5 to the Reverend Leonard Chappelow
4 to Hester Maria "Queeney" Thrale
3 to the Miss Thrales
1 to Charles Este

In 1794:

9 to Penelope Sophia Pennington
7 to Hester Maria "Queeney" Thrale
4 to the Reverend Leonard Chappelow
2 to the Reverend Daniel Lysons
1 to Elizabeth Farren
1 to Samuel Lysons
1 to Thomas Pennant
1 to Sarah Siddons

In 1795:

11 to the Reverend Leonard Chappelow
9 to Penelope Sophia Pennington
4 to the Reverend Daniel Lysons
4 to Hester Maria "Queeney" Thrale
1 to Daniel Leo
1 to Samuel Lysons
1 to John Meredith Mostyn
1 to Thomas Pennant
1 to Robert Ray

In 1796:

15 to the Reverend Leonard Chappelow
13 to Hester Maria "Queeney" Thrale
5 to the Reverend Daniel Lysons
4 to Penelope Sophia Pennington
1 to Elizabeth Burney
1 to Thomas Cadell and William Davies
1 to John Cator
1 to Sophia Thrale
1 to the Williams family

In 1797:

14 to the Reverend Leonard Chappelow
3 to Robert Ray
3 to the ladies of the Williams family
2 to Arthur Murphy
2 to Penelope Sophia Pennington

1 to Anne Poole
1 to the Miss Thrales
1 to Joseph Ward

In 1798:

11 to the Reverend Leonard Chappelow
9 to Penelope Sophia Pennington
4 to Robert Ray
3 to Anne Poole
3 to Jacob Weston
1 to Thomas Bellamy
1 to Richard and Maria Cecilia Louisa Cosway
1 to the Reverend Robert Gray
1 to the Reverend Daniel Lysons
1 to the proprietors of *The Monthly Mirror*
1 to Thomas Pennant
1 to Hester Maria "Queeney" Thrale
1 to Lady Williams
1 to Margaret Williams
1 to the ladies of the Williams family

In 1799:

18 to the Reverend Leonard Chappelow
9 to Penelope Sophia Pennington
3 to Joseph Cooper Walker
2 to the Reverend Reynold Davies
2 to the Reverend Robert Gray
2 to Hester Maria "Queeney" Thrale
1 to John Gillon
1 to Elizabeth Gray
1 to John Griffith
1 to John Lloyd
1 to Margaret Owen
1 to Robert Ray
1 to James Robson
1 to Lady Williams

In 1800:

20 to the Reverend Leonard Chappelow
10 to Penelope Sophia Pennington
4 to Lady Williams
3 to the Reverend Reynold Davies
2 to Lady Eleanor Butler
2 to John Lloyd
2 to Hester Maria "Queeney" Thrale
1 to [John Gillon]
1 to the Reverend Robert Gray

1 to the Ladies of Llangollen
1 to the Reverend Thomas Sedgwick Whalley
1 to the ladies of the Williams family

In 1801:

13 to Penelope Sophia Pennington
7 to the Reverend Leonard Chappelow
5 to Hester Maria "Queeney" Thrale
4 to the Reverend Robert Gray
2 to the Ladies of Llangollen
2 to the Reverend Thomas Sedgwick Whalley
2 to Lady Williams
1 to Lady Eleanor Butler
1 to the Reverend Reynold Davies
1 to John Lloyd
1 to Lady Salusbury

In 1802:

10 to Penelope Sophia Pennington
6 to Lady Williams
3 to the Reverend Robert Gray
2 to the Reverend Leonard Chappelow
1 to John Ewen
1 to the Reverend Daniel Lysons
1 to John Lloyd
1 to the ladies of the Williams family

In 1803:

11 to the Reverend Leonard Chappelow
7 to Penelope Sophia Pennington
4 to the Reverend Reynold Davies
2 to James Robson
2 to Hester Maria "Queeney" Thrale
1 to Elizabeth De Blaquiere
1 to John Lloyd
1 to Eleanor Williams

In 1804:

9 to Lady Williams
4 to Penelope Sophia Pennington
2 to the Reverend Leonard Chappelow
2 to the Reverend Robert Gray
1 to the Ladies of Llangollen
1 to the Reverend John Roberts
1 to John Salusbury Piozzi Salusbury
1 to Hester Maria "Queeney" Thrale
1 to Lady Williams and Eleanor Williams

In 1805:

3 to Hester Maria "Queeney" Thrale
2 to the Reverend Leonard Chappelow
2 to the Reverend Robert Gray
2 to the Reverend Thomas Sedgwick Whalley
2 to Lady Williams
1 to Isabella Hamilton
1 to Robert Myddelton
1 to Margaret Owen
1 to Lady Williams and Eleanor Williams

In 1806:

4 to Hester Maria "Queeney" Thrale
2 to the Reverend Leonard Chappelow
2 to Lady Williams
2 to Margaret Williams
1 to the Reverend Robert Gray
1 to the Reverend John Roberts

In 1807:

7 to Margaret Williams
3 to Hester Maria "Queeney" Thrale
2 to the Reverend Leonard Chappelow
2 to the Reverend John Roberts
2 to John Salusbury Piozzi Salusbury
2 to Lady Williams
1 to Charles Burney
1 to the Reverend Charles Burney
1 to the Reverend Robert Gray
1 to Robert Ray
1 to John Stockdale
1 to Susanna Arabella Thrale
1 to the Miss Thrales

In 1808:

11 to John Salusbury Piozzi Salusbury
3 to the Reverend Leonard Chappelow
3 to the Reverend Thomas Sedgwick Whalley
2 to the Reverend Robert Gray
2 to Margaret Williams
1 to John Gillon
1 to Samuel Lysons
1 to Caleb Hillier Parry
1 to William Siddons
1 to William Makepeace Thackeray
1 to Eleanor Williams

1 to Lady Williams
1 to William Wilshire

In 1809:

16 to John Salusbury Piozzi Salusbury
7 to Lady Williams
4 to Lady Keith
3 to the Reverend Leonard Chappelow
2 to Margaret Williams
1 to John Lloyd
1 to Samuel Lysons
1 to the Williams family

In 1810:

17 to John Salusbury Piozzi Salusbury
4 to Lady Williams
3 to Lady Keith
2 to Clement Francis
1 to [Jesse Foot]
1 to the Reverend Thomas Sedgwick Whalley

In 1811:

12 to John Salusbury Piozzi Salusbury
3 to the Reverend Thomas Sedgwick Whalley
2 to Margaret Williams
1 to the Reverend Leonard Chappelow
1 to the Reverend Robert Gray
1 to Lady Keith
1 to Alexander Leak
1 to John Oldfield
1 to John Perkins
1 to John Perkins, Jr.
1 to Lady Williams
1 to Lady Williams and Margaret Williams

In 1812:

10 to John Salusbury Piozzi Salusbury
6 to Clement Mead
4 to Alexander Leak
3 to Lady Keith
2 to the Reverend Thomas Sedgwick Whalley
1 to Thomas Cadell and William Davies
1 to the Reverend Leonard Chappelow
1 to Amelia Perkins
1 to Lady Williams

In 1813:

10 to John Salusbury Piozzi Salusbury
8 to Clement Mead
7 to Alexander Leak
5 to the Reverend Thomas Sedgwick Whalley
3 to Lady Williams
2 to Lady Keith
2 to Harriet Maria Pemberton
2 to John Williams
1 to James Disney Cathrow
1 to the Reverend Reynold Davies
1 to Marianne Francis
1 to Lord Liverpool
1 to Samuel Lysons
1 to the Reverend John Roberts

In 1814:

8 to Alexander Leak
8 to Harriet Maria Pemberton
8 to John Salusbury Piozzi Salusbury
7 to John Williams
3 to Anna Maria Pemberton
2 to the Reverend Leonard Chappelow
2 to Clement Francis
2 to Ann Leak
2 to Samuel Lysons
2 to the Reverend Thomas Sedgwick Whalley
2 to Lady Williams
1 to Charlotte Barrett
1 to the Reverend Robert Gray
1 to Lady Keith
1 to Clement Mead
1 to Frances Whalley
1 to Thomas Windle

In 1815:

12 to Sir James Fellowes
10 to John Salusbury Piozzi Salusbury
8 to Lady Williams
5 to Alexander Leak
5 to Ann Leak
3 to the Reverend Thomas Sedgwick Whalley
2 to Alexander and Ann Leak
2 to the Reverend John Roberts
2 to John Williams
1 to the Reverend Leonard Chappelow

1 to Robert Dalgleish
1 to Ann Fellowes
1 to [Count Lieven]
1 to Cecilia Margaretta Mostyn
1 to Edward William Smythe Owen
1 to Anna Maria Pemberton and Harriet Maria Salusbury
1 to Anna Maria Pemberton and John Salusbury Piozzi Salusbury
1 to Harriet Maria Salusbury
1 to Doctor William Makepeace Thackeray

In 1816:

16 to Sir James Fellowes
13 to Alexander Leak
9 to John Salusbury Piozzi Salusbury
5 to Lady Williams
4 to Ann Leak
2 to the Reverend Robert Gray
2 to Anna Maria Pemberton
2 to the Reverend John Roberts
1 to Richard Duppa
1 to Ann Fellowes
1 to Mary Fellowes
1 to Clement Francis
1 to Mary Mangin
1 to the Reverend Thomas Sedgwick Whalley
1 to John Williams
1 to Thomas Windle

In 1817:

16 to Sir James Fellowes
8 to the Reverend Edward Mangin
6 to Harriet Maria Salusbury
6 to John Salusbury Piozzi Salusbury (after 21 March, Sir John)
3 to the Reverend Leonard Chappelow
3 to Mary Mangin
3 to Lady Williams
2 to the Reverend Robert Gray
1 to the Reverend Reynolds Davies
1 to the Reverend Edward and Mary Mangin
1 to John Salusbury Piozzi and Harriet Maria Salusbury
1 to John Williams
1 to Margaret Williams

In 1818:

12 to Sir James Fellowes
7 to Sir John Salusbury Piozzi Salusbury

6 to the Reverend Edward Mangin
3 to Frances d'Arblay
3 to Mary Mangin
3 to John Williams
2 to the Reverend Leonard Chappelow
2 to Marianne Francis
2 to Harriet Maria Salusbury
2 to Harriet Maria and John Salusbury Piozzi Salusbury
1 to Lady Keith
1 to Lord and Lady Keith
1 to John Upham
1 to Lady Williams
1 to Margaret Williams
1 to Harriet Willoughby

In 1819:
15 to Sir James Fellowes
10 to William Augustus Conway
8 to Penelope Sophia Pennington
7 to Sir John Salusbury Piozzi Salusbury
3 to the Reverend Edward Mangin
3 to John Williams
2 to Harriet Maria Salusbury
1 to Ann Fellowes
1 to Sir James Fellowes and Sir John Salusbury Piozzi Salusbury
1 to William Dorset Fellowes
1 to Marianne Francis
1 to the Reverend Edward and Mary Mangin
1 to the Reverend John Roberts
1 to George Watson Taylor
1 to Margaret Williams
1 to John Wilson

In 1820:
19 to Penelope Sophia Pennington
7 to William Augustus Conway
6 to Sir James Fellowes
5 to Harriet Maria Salusbury
5 to Sir John Salusbury Piozzi Salusbury
3 to William Dorset Fellowes
3 to the Reverend Daniel Lysons
2 to Marianne Francis
1 to Frances d'Arblay
1 to Alfred Bunn
1 to Sir James Fellowes and Sir John Salusbury Piozzi Salusbury
1 to Clement Francis

1 to the Reverend Robert Gray
1 to Bishop John Luxmoore
1 to John Williams
1 to Harriet Willoughby

In 1821:

6 to Penelope Sophia Pennington
3 to Harriet Maria Salusbury
2 to Frances d'Arblay
2 to William Augustus Conway
2 to Sir James Fellowes
2 to John Williams
1 to John Shute Duncan
1 to the Reverend John Roberts
1 to John Thomas Smith
1 to Margaret Williams
1 to Harriet Willoughby

The letters *to* Hester Lynch (Thrale) Piozzi included in these volumes will be cited under appropriate headings in the index.

The Piozzi Letters

Letters, 1784–1791

TO FANNY BURNEY[1]

Thursday
20: May 1784.

When I came home I found a letter from Mrs. Parker,[2] setting forth that Mrs. or Miss Delane[3] was not to be found, and leaving me free to make another Choice—and now where shall I chuse Dearest Burney? For the Times come on apace, or shall I accompany my Misses to Brighton myself, settle them there, and return back hither to receive my Husband.[4]—I shall not speak to them about it till I have your Answer, for I know not that this Scheme will succeed; as it may not peradventure so loudly notifie to the World that Dislike of my Conduct which their quitting my house on Piozzi's Approach would more particularly testifie!—Tell me your Mind as quick as possible, and give me a Hint where to look for a *Lady* if this Notion don't answer——it would save me a World of Expence—that it would—and the Journey to Sussex would be of Service to my Health: I am all the better for the sweet Visit I paid my Burney in London, and Dr. Dobson[5] says so himself. Miss Thrale says the Lady will not be wanted for a Month, as *She* will go to some of these famous Matrons who take *grown Ladies* under their care. [Ten and one-half lines have been obliterated.] Shall I escorte them to Brighthelmstone, leave them there with their old Friends and their old Nurse[6] and return?—or shall I let them leave *me?* God knows they are the fittest Women in the World to act for themselves. Queeney's whole Diversion was saving *my Money* in my Absence, with an Activity that warm Friendship seldom inspires: Dear Tit! and she brought me the Bills, and told me with such Triumph that they were only 4£.3*s*.

My Love's Letter was a tender one, he had got three of mine that pleased him, and he *thinks* I *do* love him *now.* What hopes and Fears had the Signor Abate, as Pacchierotti[7] calls him, after the evening spent at Le Texier's.[8] And what says my charming Friend to the World about her zealous Visitor from Bath, about the Meat Breakfasts she made in her Company so kindly?—and with a tender Sweetness unknown to any but herself.

It was a pretty Meeting after all was it not? And I had a very good Journey home, with a Dissenting Teacher and his humble Obadiah in the Stage:[9] what one liked least was the Companies of the two Stage Coaches joining at the Dinner, but there was no harm in it; I sate at the head of the Table and Carved for the Men, who absolutely would treat Johnson[10] and I for Love of her Beauty and my Wit, I trow.

The Misses were at the Play[11]—since I begun this Letter I have repented on't, and *will not have you* give me any advice about the Trip to Sussex: My dearest and most delicate-minded Friend shall not be pained by her own Virtue as far as I can defend her; You *never have* given me any Advice in this Matter, except to let it alone!—and you *never shall:* I will get through it how I can, if dishonour should come near the transaction, how should I deserve a Man whose Soul is Susceptible of the nicest Sensibility, and whose Rest is broken by Scruples of Refinement. I have resolved in Consequence of this Reflection, and told Queeney, before her Sisters, ten Minutes ago, my Purpose of accompanying 'em—at the same time saying that I might have the Appearance of Collusion to the Town most certainly, and if She thought public disclaiming of my behavior the best way to keep peace with that World she preferred to me——I would still look for a Lady. I told her also, and I told her truly, that tho' I resolved to prefer Piozzi to the good will of all Mankind, I never should blame her for giving me the second place to so respectable an Aggregate; that it was fit She should *esteem* the World, and very fit I should *despise* it; that it was natural for me to wish She would shake hands with him on his Arrival; but that if She would not do so, for fear People should blame her; I thought the way to shew those People her Disapprobation, was to leave me on his Approach:[12] if however she had a mind to part good Friends, and let all see that she did so, I would go with her to Brighthelmston, and leaving her in her own House, as I left her the other Day in *mine* here, return back to Bath and wait for my Husband, leaving my Maid (whom you like so) to hold him fast if he should come before I can get hither again. Now make me no Answer at all to all this Rhodomontade, but tell how much you love me, and that shall content your H: L: T.

Text: Berg Collection.

1. HLT had just returned from London where she had gone to consult with attorneys; to discuss marriage plans with GP's friend Borghi (HLT to Q, [27 June], n. 2); to find a governess for her three eldest daughters; to solicit the support of FB, her still-trusted protégée and confidante.

HLT took lodgings on Mortimer Street, Cavendish Square, about 11 May, writing to FB: "[Y]ou will come to Breakfast in the morning [i.e., the 12th] as early as *ever you can,* and you will keep your kind and tender Promise of objecting no more to what now is absolutely and irreversibly determined. To this determination alone I owe my Life and Senses, which will endure no more Struggles, and they must have no more" (Berg). The two women saw much of each other, but the futility of their meetings is implicit in FB's diary entry on 17 May: "I parted most reluctantly with my dear Mrs. Thrale, whom, when or how, I shall see again, Heaven only knows! but in sorrow we parted—on *my* side in real affliction" (*Diary and Letters* 2:263).

2. Mary Parker, née Whitwell, later Griffin (1729–99), wife of the Reverend William Parker (1714–1802), rector of Saint James's, Westminster, and a chaplain in ordinary to George II and George III. On the death in 1797 of her brother John Griffin Whitwell, cr. Baron Braybrooke (1788), she acquired a share of his large fortune. The Parkers had been longtime friends of HLT since the days of Dr. Parker's intimacy with her father, John Salusbury.

3. "The Miss Delane whom I had settled with to come from Ireland, and take charge of my Misses; could not be found forth coming when we wanted her, and Mrs Parker wrote me a Letter to lament her Death" (*Thraliana* 1:595).

4. HLT was to accompany her daughters and their governess as far as Salisbury and then hurry back to Bath. Her intense desire for marriage is evident in letters to FB. As of

19 April, e.g.: "Don't grieve seriously my loveliest Friend: I *must* either quit you for Heaven or for Italy—and which is nearest? I told you Ages ago that Death or Piozzi should be my Lot——I told it you not in passion, but in deliberation; and I told you what *I knew to be true*" (Berg).

Again, in May to FB: "The man I mean to marry is wise, virtuous and honourable—let those who chuse on other Principles be ashamed, and never Oh never shall I have Cause to be ashamed unless of sending out an honest Man to suffer Torture from Compliance with Prejudice and Pride.—Forgive me my dearest but it is of a *Husband,* not a Lover I am speaking—he has my Promise, and will return to claim it" (Berg).

See also FB to Q, 24 May, in *Queeney Letters,* pp. 96–97.

5. Matthew Dobson (ca. 1732–84), M.D., University of Edinburgh (1756), author of *De natura hominis* (Glasgow, 1753); *Experiments and Observations on the Urine in a Diabetes* (London: T. Cadell, 1776); *A Medical Commentary on Fixed Air* (Chester, 1779). He had been the Thrale family physician in Bath.

6. Identified only as Tibson, she had joined the Thrale family by 1773 and become attached to the Thrale sisters, especially Q. When HLT married GP, Tibson went to live with Q, at least until 1799.

HLT resented the nurse's gossip about GP and her influence on the three eldest Thrale children.

7. Gasparo Pacchiarotti, or Pacchierotti (1740–1821), was an Italian soprano castrato, who sang for several seasons at King's Theatre, London. (He made his last London visit in 1791.)

He was said to be the greatest of the late eighteenth-century castratos. A consummate musician, he had a genius for rendering sentimental airs. For his association with CB and GP, see CB to HLP [21 January 1807], n. 5.

8. Anthony Le Tessier (d. ca. 1814) was a French actor-manager associated with London operatic productions from at least 1778 onward. After March 1787, he was to figure often in the Piozzis' soirées, and in the 1790–91 season was to be acting manager of King's Theatre. See *Thraliana* 1:268; *Diary and Letters* 2:227.

9. A Quaker and his companion. Obadiah was once a colloquialism for a Quaker.

10. Mary Johnson, HLT's femme de chambre who accompanied the Piozzis on their Continental honeymoon.

11. They would have seen at the Bath Theatre Royal on Tuesday, 18 May, a benefit performance of the comedy *The Suspicious Husband* (1747), by Dr. Benjamin Hoadly (1706–57). The benefit was for a member of the Bath company, Charlotte Wright (1761–ca. 1834). The performance was sponsored by Lady Charlotte Murray (1731–1805), Baroness Strange, *suo jure,* wife of John, 3d duke of Atholl. See the *Bath Chronicle,* 13 May 1784.

12. HLT had sought Q's approval by urging her and her sisters to come to Italy. Q rebuffed her, arguing that the guardians would not consent and that the girls wished to settle in Brighton before GP's arrival in Bath.

TO FANNY BURNEY

2: of June [1784] a day I shall always dote on.[1]

My dearest Fanny—

I only write six Words lest you should think me sick, dead, or distracted——

I have been to London, and got me a Lady:[2] I would not see nor say a Word to you from reasons of Delicacy; and I've now no Time to tell Adventures.

I hope Miss Cambridge is better,[3] and her amiable Family less distressed./ Adieu.

I'll write whole Volumes when I've Time: but I'm illish from Harry[4] just now.

Text: Berg Collection.

1. GP was to leave Italy on 2 June although HLT did not expect to see him until about 2 July. See HLT to FB and to Q, both letters on [27 June]. Word of his actual departure from Italy did not reach HLT until 24 June, and they met a week later in Bath, on 1 July. See *Thraliana* 1:599–600, and HLT to FB, 1 July.

2. The lady was Jane Nicolson (1755–1831), possibly daughter of the dean of Exeter. She accompanied the sisters to Brighton as chaperone and companion, a role she was to undertake later for Charlotte Charpentier (or Carpenter), future wife of Sir Walter Scott. Known to both Borghi and GP, Miss Nicolson won HLT's regard as an elegant and mature "woman of fashion." She remained in Brighton until 16 August, when Cator and Crutchley dismissed her, apparently because she was partial to the Piozzis. She joined them in London the next day and was with them until their departure for the Continent in September. See *Thraliana* 1:596 and n.1; Hyde, pp. 240, 242; *Queeney Letters,* pp. 157, 163, 166, 178, 183.

3. Charlotte (1746–1823) was the only surviving daughter of Richard Owen Cambridge and his wife Mary. About this time she began to suffer intermittently from a form of mental or nervous instability but was spared its continuous effects until about 1812. For the Cambridge family, see HLT to FB, 30 June 1784.

4. That is, from worry or emotional pressure.

TO FANNY BURNEY

Thursday
[24] June 1784[1]

I am delighted my sweetest Soul to receive your pretty dear Scrap: I had forgotten my own promise, and was thinking only of suspicion lest your Love should be diminished towards your H: L: T. The dismal Stories I heard in London when Lady-hunting, were such that as kept me in a perpetual Transition from Laughing to crying and back again. Chance threw in my way at last however, a very *elegant Woman of Fashion:* whose pleasing Carriage and correct Manners *must* meet everyone's Approbation more than halfway.

Tall, fair, and beautiful as a Woman of 35 years old and battered by sorrow *can* be beautiful; with Hair like your eldest Sister's,[2] and Teeth like the Duchess of Devonshire's.[3] Something like *Harriett* Streatfield,[4] but *much* more quiet and delicate: something like Lady Shelley[5]—Ay *very* like Lady Shelley in Movement and Disposition of her Person: the Voice like Miss Cooper who lives here at Bath,[6] and the Mind and Conversation very like hers as can be. Haven't I been amazing lucky? She is too partial to *me* tho'——I want her to please the Misses, and adoring me is not the way. [Two lines have been obliterated.] She behaves with a Dignity and politeness that surprize me.

Piozzi set out the 2d. of June, but will not be here I fancy till the 2d. of July, he is far from well I am sure, and so am I.

The Ladies will leave me this Day sennight. And Now my charming friend *tell me something* the *only* thing that can interest, and delight me out of my own Conjuring Circle: tell me *how* you have conquered, and *whom*. Dear irresistible, *perfect* Burney! you I believe could conquer even yourself; but when other People pretend to such Powers I despise them—tell me *who* adores, admires, and esteems, who loves and venerates my sweetest friend, as does her H: L: T.?

I am ashamed to think that I could suspect you of alienated Kindness:[7] you are all Virtue——and tho' so much has evaporated in Tenderness, it has never lost in Quantity: like Musk when it has perfumed a Whole House for a Whole Year—and lent some of its Sweets too to occasional passers by——yet suffers at last no diminution either in Weight or Fragrance.

Fare you well! and write quickly.

Poor Miss Cambridge!!

Text: Berg Collection.

1. The letter was originally dated 27 June 1784. By then, however, HLT was already separated from her daughters. Probably the "Ladies" decided to leave Bath more quickly than their mother had anticipated upon news of GP's arrival in England. The Thursday on which this letter was written was the 24th.
2. Esther Burney, née Burney (1749–1832), had married on 20 September 1770 her cousin Charles Rousseau Burney (1747–1819), harpsichordist and music teacher.
3. Georgiana (1757–1806), duchess of Devonshire, wife of William Cavendish (1748–1811), fifth duke (1764), and eldest daughter of John (1734–83), first earl Spencer (1765). Although HLT was proud of being accepted by the beautiful duchess, a social leader of her day, she ridiculed her literary pretensions (*Thraliana* 1:536; Clifford, p. 172; Hyde, p. 212).
4. Harriet Streatfeild, or Streatfield (d. 1824), was the younger daughter of Henry Streatfeild (1706–62) of Chiddingstone, Kent, and Anne, née Sidney (1732–1812), natural daughter of Jocelyne, earl of Leicester. Harriet had two brothers, Henry (1757–1829) and Richard Thomas (1759–1813), and a sister Sophia (1754–1835), the close friend of HT. Harriet was living with her mother and Sophia at Tunbridge Wells.
5. Elizabeth Shelley, née Woodcock (d. 1808), second wife of Sir John (d. 1783), fifth baronet (1771), of Maresfield Park in Sussex, one-time keeper of the Tower of London records, privy councillor and treasurer of the king's household. Sir John had been a friend of HT, and the eldest Shelley daughters had been Q's playmates. Lady Shelley and HLT had organized a benefit for GP in 1780 (*Thraliana* 1:452; Hyde, pp. 169–70, 178, 192, 210).
6. Margaret Cooper (d. 1806), a Bath acquaintance, married in 1785 Jean André Deluc, or de Luc (1727–1817), geologist and mineralogist, one of the readers to Queen Charlotte.
7. The suspicion became reality for HLP. See her letters to FB, 6 and 13 August.

TO HESTER MARIA THRALE

[Bath] Sunday Noon
[27 June 1784][1]

This Moment brings me a charming Letter from Borghi,[2] but why do I say *one* charming Letter; here are four from Piozzi and him together—I'll enclose one of

Henry Thrale, the Streatham portrait, 1777. Painted by Sir Joshua Reynolds. *(Reproduced by permission of Viscountess Eccles, the Hyde Collection, Four Oaks Farm, Somerville, New Jersey.)*

'em. Oh! here's new ones—Good God! he's come sure enough! he must be come by now, & enraged at my being from home no doubt—I felt he was coming; I said I would not stay till Monday for all Wilton House,[3] and its Contents. I was right. Well! Johnson has cleaned the house up pretty well, & is set down *to bind the Petticoats* while this Monkey is getting the Licence from Drs Commons he says.[4] Oh Lord! how nervous I am! but the Comfort is, so is he; and I may cry 'Griah, Griah, Griah,' to him like Meunie;[5] for I find him very ill in earnest poor Soul.

A Letter from Greenland[6] too all about the *Money Stuff;* why I shall have need of Cold Bathing. I have been at Mrs Greenway's[7] just now, & breakfast in my Dressing Room, whence I dispatch an *Express* to Borghi's House to say I am safe & alone in my own.

Pray for me my dearest Tit, I am really half out of my Mind—Now shall I lose all the pleasure of *Hope* in *Possession.* Well! Hope is a sweet soft Passion; mild & nourishing like Milk, but like Milk too, when *long kept* it turns sour on the Stomack, and is the hardest of all things to *bring up again.* Elegant Metaphors indeed! but this is a very exact one; and I wonder it never came in anybody's head. 'Ay,' says you,—'into Seward's.'[8]

Now are all my dear Girls seeing the Cathedral at Salisbury; while I am writing and praying by Fits, but crying all the while; and ready to burst into a Laugh too, was anyone near me to encourage the Motion. how is poor Sophy?[9] Mrs. Lambart has been here & Johnson raves about her Ugliness, which she says surpasses all she ever saw in Woman—poor Lambart![10] but Mr Burgess & She are going to be married however, he has 1000£, pr Ann: Estate & She 100£ for her Life, so he weds her for Love as ugly as she is, that's *plain.*[11]

I'll send my Letter to the Guardians[12] tomorrow, God knows I think not of them; nor care one Straw about the Talkers & Advisers, and Spitters and praters any more than if I was alone in the World, just now. I think of you & of Sophy, of Piozzi and Susan, I think of each and all, and over again, and still the same Thoughts, till I am at best half crazy; and often fancy I hear Sophy's Voice cry 'Johnson! Johnson!' in her slow Tone: so dear, so sweet, to her adoring Mother. Oh if I lose my Sophy's Love or yours, not this World—no, not t'other would content me.

Farewell!

There is a shift & an apron of Susan's, besides other Things that will all be taken care of: I will execute everything *a puntino* you may be sure, & think each Commission a new Mark of that Friendship, which to preserve will be my constant Care.

Tell Miss Nicholson her Box went directly; only think how Lady-like She behaved among us, offering Johnson money which She refused, & then sending her Scissors from Salisbury by the Husband; that is really a sweet young Woman—or I think so:—I have never said a truer Word than that I had not Leisure to love her as She deserves.

God bless you charming Tit, and get yourself some Money—or I'll send you all mine; the Idea of your wanting Cash haunts me with Horrors, but sure it is impossible—I half long tho' to enclose 10£: but that I fear you would be angry. Farewell—I long for a Letter.

I shall go to Church in the Afternoon—I know I shall cry all prayer-Time—but that will do me good. Oh Lord strengthen me Body and Soul, to do thy Will I pray.—

Text: Queeney Letters, pp. 138–40.

1. HLT misdated—4 July 1784—by one week. On 4 July GP had been in Bath since the 1st.

2. Aloisio Borghi (fl. 1750–90), an Italian violinist who emigrated to England and became a "Musical Professor" at John Street near Oxford Street (HLT to FB, 19 April [Berg]). He entertained HLT and GP in London, recommended that Augustine Greenland be their attorney, and with his wife Angelica witnessed the marriage performed at the ambassador's chapel on 23 July. See HLT to Q, 12 July, n. 1; *Thraliana* 1:593, 597; 2:611 n. 1.

3. Wilton, the Wiltshire estate (designed by Inigo Jones) of the Pembroke family, was celebrated for its gardens, woods, and art collections. On 26 June HLT had traveled with her daughters through Wilton and Fonthill (William Beckford's "abbey," also in Wiltshire) to Salisbury. From the last place she returned to Bath for her meeting with GP while the girls and Miss Nicolson proceeded to Brighton. For her impressions of Wilton and Fonthill, see *Thraliana* 1:598.

4. HLT lightly alludes to the housecleaning activities of Mary Johnson in anticipation of GP's arrival. "Monkey" is a term of endearment for GP.

5. The wailing sound of a cat named Meunie. A possible variation on "guash, guash, guash," the cry of a cat in an old nursery rhyme.

6. Augustine, or Augustus Greenland (d. 1803), solicitor at Newman Street, near Oxford Street, and Manchester Street in the parish of Saint Marylebone; eventually a commissioner in bankrupts (1793) and a deputy teller of the exchequer. Acting as GP's attorney (1784–92), he "found out that I [HLT] needed not have fretted so about Money Matters:—for there lay four Years Interest of 13000£ never called for by me, who knew not of its Existence" ("Harvard Piozziana" 2:21). See also Ry. 601.14–19.

7. Mrs. Greenway (fl. 1740–1800) was the proprietor or supervisor of the "cold bath" house. She took her surname from Thomas Greenway, a mason with a yard in Widcombe, who had erected the building on Claverton Street in 1707. HLT had gone there for therapy on other occasions. In March 1780, e.g., when HT was being treated after an apoplectic fit, the doctors prescribed cold bathing for her "shatter'd Nerves."

See "Harvard Piozziana" 1:110; *Thraliana* 1:432–36, 439–40; *Robbins's Bath Guide* (1780).

8. William Seward (1747–99), man of letters, anecdotist, and confirmed albeit truly ailing hypochondriac, was a member of the Thrale-Johnson circle as early as 1777. See *Thraliana* 1:28 and passim.

9. For several months ST had been in frail health following a severe illness (November 1783). See *Thraliana* 1:580.

10. Elizabeth Lambart (1730–1821), sister of Sir Philip Jennings Clerke (see HLT to FB, 30 June, n. 6) and widow of Hamilton Lambart (d. 1771), lieutenant general in the army and colonel of the sixty-seventh regiment, M.P. for Kilbeggan (1753–60), third son of Charles Lambart (d. 1753) of Painstown.

11. Possibly John Burgess (1727–post 1785) of North Molton, Devon. An unfulfilled rumor: no marriage occurred between him and Elizabeth Lambart or between her and anyone else.

12. The four guardians listed in HT's will (P.R.O., Probate 11/1077/216–17, signed 17 March and proved 30 March 1781) were Jeremiah Crutchley, Jr. (1745–1805), of 14 Clarges Street, London, and Sunninghill Park, Berks.; John Cator (1728–1806), timber merchant, of Bank Side, Southwark, and Beckenham, Kent; M.P. for Wallingford (1772–80), later for Ipswich (April–June 1784) and Stockbridge (1790–93); SJ; and Henry Smith (1756–89), of New House Farm near Saint Albans, a cousin once removed of HT.

TO FANNY BURNEY

[27 June 1784][1]

[A portion cut away.] . . . high time for me to write to you while I yet sign myself *your* H: L: T. Miss Thrale good-naturedly wished for my Company on their Journey as far as Salisbury—so I set out with them and Miss Nicholson Fryday, and paid their Road Expences, (no small ones let me tell you;) till I had shewed them Wilton, and Stonehenge, and Salisbury, and Fonthill, and then parted last Night pretty late, and drove hither as [fast as] I could drive——but not too soon; for the dear long-expected Exile is come home, or coming, on this very day, seventeen Months since we were parted in and by a Tempest, which has wrecked the peace of both; and now we must try to get into the Harbour with our *Jury Masts*.[2]

The parting yesterday was tender on all sides, and that dear Miss Nicholson's doting on *me* so, is quite astonishing—for I have had no Leisure to love her as I verily think she deserves [a portion mutilated].

You are at dear delicious Norbury Park by now; a Place which will be famous in future Times, as it is delightful in these.[3] The Residence of Genius, the Centre of Beneficence,[4] and the Birthplace of a Youth whose Excellence seems to set Praise at a Distance and make Words superfluous—beyond any Artist of any Age or Nation.

Mr. George James[5] once known among the painters shewed me the other day a Collection of Drawings done by this astonishing young Man[6]—but we were soon past trying to commend——and I turned all my Thoughts upon the Lady, who is loved by Mr. Locke, admired by Miss Burney, and Mother to that Boy!!!!!——

I was out of Breath when I left off, those Drawings overpower me; weak Nerves have strong Sensations——but James is a Giant in Person——and his Tears of delight choked his Utterance, who knows nothing of the Family but that such performances came out on't—What must I feel who have [bottom line of the page mutilated].

Text: Berg Collection. *Address:* Miss Burney / at The Seat of Locke Esq. / near Dorking / Surrey. *Postmark:* BATH 29 JU [1784].

1. Although the letter was not posted until 29 June, HLT probably wrote it on the 27th, the day after her return from Salisbury to Bath. In a letter to Q, dated 26 [June 1784], she promised to write again (and presumably wrote to FB as well) on the day following (*Queeney Letters*, p. 137).

2. Emergency improvisations. For HLP's interest in the etymology of this phrase, see her letter to JSPS, 26 April 1809.

3. Norbury Park was the country residence of mutual friends, William (1732–1810) and Frederica Augusta Locke, née Schaub (1750–1832), near Mickleham and Dorking in Surrey. See Vittoria Caetani, *The Lockes of Norbury* (London: Hutchinson [1929], passim; *Journals and Letters*, vols. 3, 4, 7, passim; HLT to Q, 29 [June].

The estate consisted of 527 acres of parks, meadows, woods, and farmland, in the midst of which was an elaborately refurbished manor house. Locke "conceived an original and ingenious design of uniting the grand amphitheatre of nature, viewed from the windows of his saloon. . . . The magnificent scenery with which he has embellished the walls, is artfully managed to appear as a continuation of the view." Here "the lakes and mountains in Cumberland and Westmoreland" were made to merge with the tamer Surrey landscape. In other sections of the house, the scenes shifted so as to represent all the changes of nature, from the gloomy and sublime to the classical, complemented by sculpture and even by a carpet that "resembles a new-mown lawn." See John Timbs, *A Picturesque Promenade Round Dorking in Surrey* (London: J. Warren, 1822), pp. 4–9.

See also HLP to TSW, 28 March 1811.

4. Locke was a philanthropist as well as an art collector. He and his wife, for example, were to provide substantial help for the French émigrés living in a nearby colony called Juniper Hall.

HLT thought the Locke children talented, especially the eldest son. The Lockes had at this time four sons: William (1767–1847), Charles (1769–1804), George (1771–1864), and Frederick Augustus (1785–1805). There were also two daughters: Mary Augusta (1775–1845) and Amelia (1776–1848).

5. After receiving an inheritance from his grandfather, George James (ca. 1750–95), a minor portrait painter, studied in Rome. Upon his return to London, he resided in Meard's Court, Dean Street, Soho. He exhibited as a member of the Incorporated Society of Artists until 1768. In 1770 he was elected an associate of the Royal Academy of Arts, exhibiting there until 1790. On 14 February 1774, he had married the affluent Frances Boissier (d. 10 February 1816) at Saint George's Church, Bloomsbury. They had three children: George, Jr., Frances, and Gertrude. Curtailing his professional activities, James moved his family to Bath in 1780, residing primarily at Brunswick Place and then in Kelston near the city. For his final years, see HLP to PSP, 26 June [1795]; and for his work, Algernon Graves, *The Royal Academy of Arts: A Complete Dictionary of Contributors and their Work from its Foundation in 1796 to 1904*, 8 vols. (London: H. Graves, 1905–6), 4:234; Samuel Redgrave, *A Dictionary of Artists of the English School* (London: Longmans, Green, 1874), p. 228.

6. William Locke the younger. For further testimony of HLT's enthusiasm, see *Thraliana* 1:595.

TO HESTER MARIA THRALE

[Bath] Monday night
[28 June 1784][1]

Well! my dearest, I have been this morning to Coward's[2] & paid your Bill & mine, & have seen the sweetest strip'd Taffeties: I will have one as sure as Day, for demi-Saison. Mother Greenway has heard I am going to be married, and prayed with true Presbyterian Tenderness & Devotion that Piozzi might be put in his Coffin before we met—and this with a serious earnestness.—I asked her the Reason: 'Reason!' says She—'why he has *no Money* has à!' I came home laughing more than shocked, but it was very horrid of a Fellow Creature who never had offended or even seen her—was not it?

Foolish Jemmy says to me this morning—'Your Daughters will come back in half a Year, and then I'll have the second!' 'What do you think half a year means Jemmy?' 'Six Months my Lady;—12 months make a year, I know that, tho' I am a Fool.'

M[rs] Lambart persecutes me oddly, I wonder what She wants;[3] I have not seen her yet; Hudson was not at home, I tried for admittance but in vain;[4] The Weather gets warmer & dryer but I am still very bad—Good Heaven what a Night I past—A little more Sorrow & Suspense would yet do my Business effectually, & I am morally and physically assured on't.

D[r] Johnson is very low spirited & writes me word that old *Macbeane* is dead,[5] who was the last Screan between him and Death.[6] I am sorry he is so miserable. Sophy will be pleased to think that her favourite Johnson is in the way to be a Marshall Man, & to Stand at S[t] James's swaggering with a little Stick while She goes in & out to Court &c.[7]

I am going to dine with James & his wife, but expect to be called home to tea by my dear Italians: our last Letters said *parto domani, volo a voi,* from Paris; & they were dated 23: he flew from Lyons in two days to the Capital; that is in 48 Hours—for he never lay down he says—and so got tired and ill &c.

I have not written the Letters to the Guardians yet, because M[rs] Greenway's Prayers may still prevail, but I think they will not.

No Messenger returned & 'tis 8 at Night—very dreadful indeed—something *must* have happen'd to the Boy at least. / Ever yours / H: L: T.

Text: Queeney Letters, pp. 141–42. *Address: To Miss Thrale, at her House, / West Street, Brighthelmstone, Sussex.*

1. This letter, misdated 5 July, was probably written one week earlier. On 28 June HLT had one from SJ with news of Macbean's recent death (n. 5 below). HLT wrote on the present occasion before sending the circular letter to SJ on 30 June.
2. In a Bath directory for 1783, Thomas Coward (fl. 1763–1809) is listed as a linen draper at 17 Bond Street, where he also ran a lodging house. In other directories (1800–1809), he is also identified as haberdasher, lace-man, and hosier.
3. Elizabeth Lambart, suspecting the imminence of the HLT-GP marriage, nagged in vain for details of the secret.
4. A Bath embroiderer or seamstress, who taught needle work to SAT and other children, she suffered from delusive persecution. HLT had attempted, with little success, to elicit SJ's sympathy, although he conceded: "To know at least one mind so disordered is not without its use; it shows the danger of admitting passively the first irruption of irregular imaginations" (8 July 1783, *Letters* 2:292; cf. 260, 263, 266).
5. On 26 June, SJ wrote to HLT: "A message came to me yesterday to tell me that [Alexander] Macbean, after three days of illness, is dead of suppression of urine. He was one of those who, as Swift says, *stood as a screen between me and death.* He has I hope made a good exchange. He was very pious; he was very innocent; he did no ill; and of doing good a continual tenour of distress allowed him few opportunities: he was very highly esteemed in the [Charterhouse].

"Write to me, if you can, some words of comfort. My dear girls seem all to forget me" (*Letters* 2:373–74).

The often poverty-stricken Macbean was one of the six amanuenses on the *Dictionary.*

6. *On the Death of Dr. Swift:*

> The Fools, my Juniors by a Year,
> Are tortur'd with Suspence and fear;
> Who wisely thought my Age a Screen,
> When Death approach'd, to stand between.

(lines 219–22)

7. HLT facetiously dignifies John Johnson, Mary's husband, with Court status. A "marshal-man"—once under orders of the knight marshal—belonged to the royal household. His function was to clear the way before the king in processions.

TO HESTER MARIA THRALE

[Bath] 12 at Noon
Tuesday [June] 29 [1784]

No letter from Salisbury yet. I think the Time terribly long since I heard ought of my sweet Girls: and yesterday's continual Anguish about the Creature who alone could have divided my Heart with them, was truly cruel. He's safe in London at last though, but very ill; and if I did not know that Borghi would take Care of him, I would go and enter on my office of Attendant—He is *safe* however, and but 100 Miles off, so I ought to be grateful and hope I am so. The Express came just now, & saved the *Ippe*[1]—which was just weighing out; for I had a horrible Night you may be sure—The Fellow remained on the road but *ten* hours, Borghi kept him at his House till he could send me *felice Nuova—He* Johnson cried to see my Distress, & said it was like what I suffered for dear Miss Sophy. 'Ah Johnson!' says I—'if those two Beings should *not love me* after all!' 'They would,' says the Fellow, 'be fit neither to live, nor die.' Johnson will get a Place sure enough.

I have seen Mrs. Lambart & her Son, a fine Youth enough, & a professed Admirer of Susan Thrale;[2] whose Name he has written on every Window between here & Brussels;—did not I say She would have a Lover speedily? he is much grieved She has left Bath, and I am as much rejoyced—for he is a forward, pushing Fellow, and ten to one it might have been better Earnest than there was any need of. *Mrs L.* continues her Kindness, & tires me with Instances of her Brother's too constant Attachment:[3] I fancy she thinks I have broken off with Piozzi.

The Jameses saw me so ill yesterday, that I told them all whether they would hear it or not. He behaved like a Man of the World about it, & She behaved *nohow.*[4] Does Miss Nicholson know it yet? I'll tell her. You left your fine Purple Irish Stuff here my love, I begin to wonder what you carried . . . but all shall be taken care of . . . have you left me any Share of your Heart?—I will defend *that* Trust with what remains of my Life.

The Muffs and Books are all safe as can be. Fanny Burney is safe embosomed in Music, Painting and Poetry at Norbury Park; Mrs. Ord[5] is expected at Weston to watch her Mother's Pockets:[6] I am now miserable only for Letters, & this Cross Post will plague my Heart out, everybody says that one might with more certainty expect Letters from Paris than Portsmouth. Well my Parisian Correspondence is over, and my Correspondent will be here tomorrow, and lodge at Old Harford's on the South Parade:[7] He laments his ill Health & his *ill Looks* cruelly—but you say we shall both recover—I saw a Fortune-telling Fan at a Shop just now, and tried my Luck for Fun;[8] these were the words presented to me

He will be jealous, queer, and flat,
But a fond Husband with all that.

I went away laughing at the oddity.

Adieu my sweet Love, and pray do write to me: my Heart is eating itself up, for want of Food . . . Oh send me Letters *per Carità*.—how sorry I am that I *must* hate that Scoundrel Dobson! for there is no Friend like a Physician, & no Physician like him.[9]

Text: Queeney Letters, pp. 143–44. *Address: Miss Thrale, at her House, / West Street, Brighthelmstone, Sussex.*

1. Possibly ipecacuanha, a South American plant used medically as an emetic, nauseant, diaphoretic, and expectorant. HLT dosed herself with it as an antidote to nervous tension.

2. Elizabeth Lambart's only surviving child, Edward Hamilton Lambart (d. 1803) married in 1789 his cousin Frances, daughter of the wealthy John Dodd. See HLP to Elizabeth Lambart, 19 February 1788, n. 9, and *Thraliana* 2:748–49; also *GM* 59, pt. 1 (1789): 371, and 73, pt. 2 (1803): 791.

3. Sir Philip's attraction to HLT was abetted by his sister. Usually finding him agreeable company, HLT in the years just before her marriage to GP nevertheless thought his attempted courtship offensive (*Thraliana* 1:538).

4. The wife of George James, Frances was the daughter of a wealthy merchant, John Boissier (d. 7 May 1770), of Austin Friars, London (buried in Putney, Surrey). With her three brothers—James William, John Lewis, and Peter—she shared a substantial inheritance. See P.R.O., Prob. 11/957/1770, and *GM* 40 (1770): 239.

5. Anna, or Ann Ord, née Dillingham (ca. 1726–1808), one of HLT's Bluestocking friends. The mother of nine children (but survived only by Rev. James, ca. 1759–1843), she was the widow of William (d. 1768) of New Castle, Fenham, and Whitfield Hall; high sheriff of Northumberland. Initially she had scorned the Piozzi marriage. But by 1789 she, along with other censorious acquaintances, "now sneak about, & look ashamed of themselves" (*Thraliana* 2:745).

6. Her mother Susanna Dillingham, née Noble, was not to die until 1789 at Bath. Mrs. Ord had little reason to worry about her mother's financial loyalty since the latter left her, as an only child, the bulk of her sizable estate, with bequests to certain of the Ord offspring: William (1752–89), who had succeeded to his father's landed estate; Robert (d. 1788); John, "master in chancery"; Jemima (d. 1806), married in 1772 to Thomas Charles Bigge (d. 1794); and Charlotte (1753–95). See the will of Susanna Dillingham, witnessed 8 April 1784, and proved 14 July 1789 (P.R.O., Prob. 11/1181/357). For Charlotte's death, see HLP to DL, 22 February 1795; *GM* 65, pt. 1 (1795): 257.

7. William Harford lived at 14 South Parade (ca. 1766–97). The "Bath Abbey Register," C.R.O., Somerset, lists his burial as of 27 June 1797.

8. However they are termed, gypsy, fortune-telling, and necromantic fans were popular in the latter part of the eighteenth century. The "Oracle," typical of the fortune fan, has in the center a wheel of fortune with two winged children on the clouds, one of whom holds a scroll inscribed "Oracle." On the sides of the fan are the names of ten gods and goddesses, in ten columns, the names listed variously in each. On the lower part of the fan appear the "Explication" of the oracle and "examples," together with the questions, such as "Whether one is to get Riches; Whether one will be successful in Love; What sort of a Husband shall I have"; and so forth. See G. Woolescroft Rhead, *History of the Fan* (London: Kegan Paul, Trench, and Trübner, 1910), pp. 254–56.

9. For the "Enmity" of HLT (and HLP) toward Dr. Dobson, see, e.g., her letter to Q, 25 July (*Queeney Letters*, pp. 170–71). The antagonism extended to his wife Susannah. "I care not (but in Xtian Charity) if She & her Husband were tyed together, & thrown into the Sea" (*Thraliana* 1:588, dated 13 January 1784).

TO SAMUEL JOHNSON

Bath
30: June, 1784.

My dear Sir,

The enclosed is a circular Letter which I have sent to all the Guardians, but our Friendship demands somewhat more;[1] it requires that I should beg your pardon for concealing from you a Connection which you must have heard of by many People, but I suppose never believed. Indeed, my dear Sir, it was concealed only to spare us both needless pain; I could not have borne to reject that Counsel it would have killed me to take; and I only tell it you now, because all is *irrevocably settled*, and out of your power to prevent. Give me leave however to say that the dread of your disapprobation has given me many an anxious moment, and tho' perhaps the most independent Woman in the World—I feel as if I was acting without a parent's Consent—till you write kindly to your faithful Servant.

I shewed James this letter and he cried.[2]

Sent this day to Dr. Johnson enclosed in what is written on t'other side the paper.

[The Enclosure]

Sir,

As one of the Executors to Mr Thrale's Will, and Guardian to his daughters, I think it my duty to acquaint you that the three eldest left Bath last Fryday for their own house at Brighthelmstone,[3] in company with an aimiable Friend Miss Nicholson, who has some time resided with us here, and in whose Society they may I think find some advantages and certainly no Disgrace: I waited on them myself as far as Salisbury, Wilton, &c. and offered my Service to attend them to the Seaside; but they preferred this Lady's Company to mine, having heard that Mr. Piozzi was coming back from Italy, and judging from our past Friendship and continued Correspondence, that his return would be succeeded by our Marriage.

I have the honour to be Sir, Your most humble Servant / H: L: T.

Text: Chapman 3:172–73. *Address:* Doctor Sam: Johnson. In the *Letters* (2:374–75) HLP publishes a slightly altered version of the first paragraph, omits the following two brief sentences and the entire "Enclosure."

1. On 18 September 1777 HLT recalled: "It was on the second Thursday of the Month of January 1765 [10 January] that I first saw Mr Johnson in a Room." Arthur Murphy, a mutual friend of SJ and the Thrales, effected the introduction at Streatham. The accord was immediate, and SJ's intimacy with the Thrale family continued after the death of HT (4 April 1781) until HLT's letter of marital intention. On 2 July SJ denounced her "ignominious" marriage (not in *Letters*). (The wedding did not in fact take place until 23 and 25 July in Catholic and Protestant ceremonies respectively.) He repented in a letter of 8 July, but there no longer seemed to be room for reconciliation, even though she made two subsequent efforts. Rarely, as on 3 November 1784, did she make a passing allusion to his "*rough* Letter" of 2 July. After her initial hurt began to fade, she was able to put their

friendship into perspective and to idealize it for the rest of her life. See *Thraliana* 1:158–59, 568, 593 n. 3; 2:615 n. 2, 617, and passim; SJ to HLT, 8 July; HLT to SJ, 15 July.

2. That is, George James.

3. On 28 August 1755, HT's father Ralph Thrale (1698–1758) had bought a "copyhold" property on West Street in Brighton. The house passed from father to son, and eventually to CMT. The explanation for this line of inheritance came from the Reverend John Delap (1725–1812), writing to HLP on 6 February 1791 (Ry. 547.7): "The late Mr. Thrale died seized of a copyhold estate on the manor of Brighthelmston, and having surrendered it to the use of his will, the same on his death descended to his youngest Daughter, by the custom of the manor." See also "Brighton Land Tax Assessments," C.R.O., East Sussex.

TO FANNY BURNEY

Bath
Wednesday 30: June 1784.

I *did* detain them till the last Moment my ever dearest, my ever-kindest Friend; That strange Creature flew from Lyons to Paris in two days, and is now ill in London from Fatigue and Agitation: Our kind Friend Borghi detains him to recover a little, and sends me pacifying Letters by Express, but he will be here himself tomorrow, I have got him Lodgings at our old Habitation on the South Parade, and shall put him under Dr. Dobson's Care immediately: The Waters will be very beneficial too I'm sure.—

My Heart and the State of it is wholly undescribable, but it rejoyces in the Tranquillity of yours: I hope the dear Cambridges will recover,[1] and enjoy once more their Family and Friends: they know how to chuse Friends, and will I doubt not, long retain them. You are in the very Place, and with the very People I would wish:[2]—if an Angel was to tell me I should never see Seward more, my health would mend with the Intelligence.[3] The Jameses are all my Solace; 'tis vexatious that I can't have any Comfort out of *The Red Cow's* Mate[4]——that would indeed be *milking the Bull* as the phrase is; yet a Physician is so sweet a sort of Friend. Apropòs I shall write to Sir Lucas[5] this Day, or rather tomorrow when I have seen my Husband.

Mrs. Ord is coming hither directly, so we may canvass her at our Leisure: Sir Philip's Sister Mrs. Lambart is returned too, and tires me with Accounts of her Brother's rooted Attachment, and tender Regard:[6] She always *did* teize me with her Hopes on that Side: en attendant they would I see have no Objection to poor Susan Thrale's Fortune for her once gawkee—now flashy Son:[7]—but I hope She's born to better Luck, and am glad She left Bath before he came;—he is gay, bold, and saucy, and looks all alive in his new Red Coatt.

Here is the Copy of the Letter written to the Guardians

Sir— Bath 30 June 1784

As one of the Executors to Mr. Thrale's Will, and Guardian to his Daughters, I think it my Duty to acquaint you that the three eldest left Bath on Fryday last for their own house at Brighthelmstone, in Company with an amiable Friend, Miss Nicholson;—who has some Time resided with us here, and in whose Society they may I think find many Advantages, and certainly

> nothing like Disgrace. I waited on them myself as far as Salisbury, Wilton, Stonehenge &c. and would have attended them to the Seaside, but they preferred this Lady's Company to mine; having heard that Mr. Piozzi is coming back from abroad—and judging by our past Friendship, and continued Correspondence, that his Return will probably be succeeded by our Marriage. / I have the honour to be Sir / Your most humble Servant / H:L:T.

Well Dearest Burney! wish me happy, and to make me So—continue your Kindness——shall I tell you a comical Thing? I went into a Shop two Minutes ago where they were selling Fortune-telling Fans——let me try *my* Luck said I in Sport—They rattled the Thing about and produced these Lines

> He will be jealous, queer, and flat
> But a fond Husband for all that.

Not far from the Truth I do verily believe—so Adieu, and may God send you as honest and amiable a Partner,[8] with the only Thing I shall not possess——General Approbation![9] Farewell! my Fingers are shaking, my Heart——I do not know what my Heart is doing besides loving and reverencing *you* with all the Sense it has left.

Thinking the mere circular Letter too dry for dear Dr. Johnson, I sent it him inclosed in this for a Softener and Sedative.

> My dear Sir — Bath 30 June
> The enclosed is a circular Letter which I send to all the Guardians; but our Friendship demands something more: it requires me to beg your pardon for concealing from you a Connection you must have heard of from many, but I suppose never believed. Indeed, my dear Sir, it was concealed only to spare us both needless pain: I could not have borne to reject that Counsel it would have killed me to take, and I only tell it you now, because all is irrevocably settled, and out of your power to prevent. Give me leave however to say that the dread of your disapprobation has given me many an anxious Moment, and though the most independent Woman in the World perhaps, I feel as if I was acting without a Parent's Consent till you write kindly to your Faithful Servant.

Text: Berg Collection, no. 1784, folder 3. *Address:* Miss Burney.

1. Residing at Twickenham Meadows, Middlesex, Richard Owen Cambridge (1717–1802), dramatist and poet, was married to Mary, née Trenchard (ca. 1716–1806). They had three adult children in 1784: Charlotte; Charles Owen (1754–1847); George Owen (1756–1841), archdeacon of Middlesex and prebendary of Ely, once thought to be FB's suitor.
2. FB was visiting the Lockes at Norbury Park.
3. As early as October 1783, while yearning for GP, HLT agreed "To trust [William Seward] with the Secret of my Love . . . He will assist us I am sure, & smooth the Difficulties in our Passage to each other." Apparently he played a double game, assuaging her anxieties, yet revealing to both Q and FB many confidences. FB remarked to Q (November 1783): "And poor Mrs. T. thinks him her first friend, & says his behaviour has been angelic!—How every way she is deluded, & how all ways by herself." But by now HLT was bitterly aware of Seward's duplicity. See *Thraliana* 1:574, 576 n. 3, 579–80; *Queeney Letters*, pp. 70, 76; HLP to SL, 7 December 1784.

4. The "Red Cow" was Matthew Dobson's wife Susannah, née Dawson (d. 1795), who in 1775 translated from the French a life of Petrarch. HLT thought her mad (*Thraliana* 1:588 n. 2). For the derivation of the epithet, see the satiric Spanish lines, in HLT to Q, 1 July. For FB's opinion of her, see *Diary and Letters* 1:296.

5. Sir Lucas Pepys (1742–1830), cr. baronet (1784), physician-extraordinary (1777) and physician-ordinary (1792) to King George III, whom he treated for recurrent mental disorder. Sir Lucas, a friend of HT and HLT, attended them (and later GP) during various illnesses.

6. Sir Philip Jennings Clerke (1722–88), of Duddleston Hall, Salop, and Lyndhurst, Hants., M.P. for Totnes (1768–88). He was created baronet October 1774 upon succeeding to the estates of his uncle, Sir Talbot Clerke, sixth baronet. He also assumed the surname Clerke.

The first son of Philip Jennings by his second wife Dorothy, née Clerke, he was educated at Westminster and Oriel College, Oxford. HT had been partial to him as a political and social crony; but HLT thought him intellectually shallow. She became antagonistic when, after HT's death, he flirted with her. Nevertheless she regretted his death; see her letter to Elizabeth Lambart, 19 February 1788, and *Thraliana* 2:705–6 (cf. 1:349–51, 444 and n. 4, 445 and n. 1).

7. Edward Hamilton Lambart. Mrs. Lambart's hopes were futile. See HLP to Elizabeth Lambart, 19 February 1788, nn. 2, 9.

8. HLT's wish for FB's marital happiness was long-standing. As early as 1781 she had contemplated a Burney connection with Jeremiah Crutchley (*Thraliana* 1:496–97). But FB was attracted (in vain) to the taciturn George Owen Cambridge. See *Thraliana* 1:562–63; *Diary and Letters* 2:188–89; Hemlow, pp. 187–93.

9. HLT anticipated the hostility her marriage would provoke. Not only did she offend her three eldest daughters, but she lost friends as well: FB, Elizabeth Montagu, Elizabeth Handcock Vesey, Sarah Scott, née Robinson (Mrs. Montagu's sister), Leonard Smelt, Hester Chapone, Mr. and Mrs. William Weller Pepys, among others. Her marriage to GP did not escape the newspapers and periodicals. The *Morning Herald*, for example, flatly announced on 18 August that she "in consequence of her marriage with Piozzi, has the children taken away from her. This the guardians insisted on." (See also the issues for 6, 10, 12, 14, 27 August; 7, 14 September.) As late as 1788, Baretti in his "Strictures" for the *European Magazine* continued to attack both HLP and her second marriage as a betrayal of all values that an English gentlewoman should cherish. See also HLP to SL, 27 July 1785, n. 3.

TO FANNY BURNEY

written in the Night at Bath
1: of July 1784.

I cannot sleep—how should I! my Piozzi is come home;[1] he lives, he loves me, he sleeps tonight at Harford's on the North Parade, in the Bed *you* slept in there.[2] I have seen him, I have rejoyced over him: I have cried, and prayed, and thanked God—and cried again for Joy, a whole Day, and almost a whole Night. Let me now write to my Burney; She will forgive and soothe my Frenzy, think, my dear Creature! Seventeen Months of Absence, and no Alteration but what Kindness for me has caused: *Can* I love him too well? has he not cost me my life almost? have I not purchased him with my very Vitals? Oh! we will part no more tho',—per non separarti piu as he says.

Tell Mrs. Philips my Happiness—She will not laugh *much* at me, She has been in Love herself, and I hope will continue so to her Life's end.[3]

Piozzi says Mr. Locke has written to him[4]—how sweet that was of Mr. Locke! but Norbury Park is the Place for Agrémens—and it now contains my Burney. This Letter goes to Town, they will send it forward from thence: my Nerves are cruelly agitated, who can wonder? but Dr. Dobson says we shall both recover, as our Disorder is of the same Kind exactly. I hope we *shall* recover——To live and love so true &c.

The separated Ladies write constantly, but the eldest writes *very coldly,*[5] and though I sent 'em a fond open-hearted Letter, expressing my Agitation of Mind on Piozzis expected Arrival,[6] they none of them name his Name, nor take the smallest Notice, just as if such a Creature had never existed!—*You know* how to do so to be sure, and yet shew affectionate Regard all the Time; but it amazes me to see *their* Proficiency in such a Power.

God bless you sweet Soul, and love me in any way you *will,* and in every [way that] you *can:* for in *all* ways of true Friendship and unalterable Esteem will I be *ever yours.*

I have written to the Misses just as they do to me—taking their *Ton* exactly—cold and kind—They shall begin first I assure you in all that relates to him whom I have chosen to be my Husband with the most constant and deliberate Esteem.

Text: Berg Collection, no. 1784, folder 3. *Address:* Miss Burney.

1. On 2 July HLP wrote: "The happiest Day of my whole Life I think—Yes, *quite* the happiest; my Piozzi came home Yesterday & dined with me: but my Spirits were too much agitated, my Heart too much dilated, I was too painfully happy *then,* my sensations are more quiet to day, and my Felicity less tumultuous" (*Thraliana* 1:599–600).
2. She meant South Parade. See her letter to Q, 29 [June], n. 7.
3. On 10 January 1782 FB's youngest sister, Susanna Elizabeth Burney (1755–1800), married Molesworth Phillips (1755–1832), an officer in the Royal Marines. He is remembered for killing James Cook's assassin in the Sandwich Islands, 14 February 1779.
4. HLT assumed from the missing letter a promise of the social acceptance she wished for GP.
5. Of her three eldest daughters, the suppressed resentment of Q was unremitting. As late as 6 December 1816 Q—now Lady Keith—wrote to FBA: "I would advise your never referring in any way to any of us. She could not bear to come so near to old Times which She knows *you* must so well remember. To others she can say what she pleases, and no doubt as she has invariably done, will ever continue to justify herself, in every Particular, at our expence: but that, she well knows, would not do with you" (Barrett, Eg. 3699B, fols. 22–24b); *Journals and Letters* 7:119 n. 4.
6. The letter written on 27 June but misdated 4 July.

TO HESTER MARIA THRALE

[Bath] Thursday,
July 1, 1784

A sweet & delightful Letter is at last brought me from Salisbury dated June 26: and here is the 1st of July, and a Day as hot as can be wished. That cursed Cur I suppose threw *Joh*[1] into her Disposition to have a Fit: but what Blockheads were we all to set out without due provision of Asafoetida! 20 Drops of the Tincture would however always be efficacious, perhaps more so than the white Draught.

Dr Dobson has called, but Mr James was with me, and Johnson would not let him in: 'tis a Grief to me that I cannot help hating and despising him; for he is naturally pleasant & comfortable—Yet what, (as I said to Mr James) can one hope for from the *Mate of the Red Cow?* 'tis at best but *milking the Bull* you know.

El Marido de la Vaca
Qué puede ser sino Toro?[2]

Give Miss Nicholson the enclosed my Love, She deserves pretty words I find, & She shall have them—I really do fancy she is a good natured Girl, and loves you.

My poor Heart is in a State wholly undescribable; *saltando, balzando,* &c. Let me have your dear Friendship continued to me; there is nobody's on Earth which I esteem more highly, exclusive of the Tenderness we have some right to from each other. I expect my Sposo[3] tonight, & have prepared his Apartment at Hartford's;[4] 'tis very airy there, tho' excessive hot—Miss Hudson is never at home somehow.

I can read thank God to amuse myself, and Coxe's Book[5] is come out in a happy Hour; you will work at it night and day—the Subject—and I think the Style—is much to your natural Taste. We shall ruin each other in Postage, for to be without Letters from you distracts me, Sr Lucas Pepys being at Brighthelmston is a rational cause of your desire to be there—poor old Woodward is dying,[6] the old Countess of Harrington gone too,[7] and the once beautiful Duchess of Argylle[8]

With all that Plenty—all that Pomp e'er gave;
Await alike th' inevitable Hour,
The Paths of Splendour point but to the Grave.[9]

Young Lysons[10] has been kindly received by old Charles,[11] & what is stranger—the Boy has found Time to thank me for my Civilities to him—an attention I did not expect—but he wrote in the warmth of his heart from the Somerset Coffee house[12] as soon as he got out of Bolt Court.[13] Vanbrughs,[14] Goulds,[15] Lambart all come to the Door—like the Waiters round your *blue* Feathers—*to see what is:* as you used to say when a Baby. the Bennetts[16] & Browns[17] have sent for me to a Card party naming next Saturday, but I wrote 'em word a sick Friend had engaged me, who was coming to Bath for health. True enough God knows! I want you to like my Letter to Dr Johnson,[18] which is equally firm & tender, and will I hope defend me from his undesired Company.

Sophy will show you what I have done for *her* Favourite Johnson; That poor Fellow lives in a spin as badly as myself, and will end at last like Prince Prettyman in the Rehearsal,[19] I fear, by being nobody's Son at all.

God bless you my charmer, keep your Health steady if possible; there is no being happy, there is no being *good* without Health. While I write, I feel the Truth of all I say—for the Dustman rings his Bell on one side my Ears, the People hammer up Shelves on the other Side—till I am ready to run wild with nervous irritation, and half renounce my own Existence. Oh pray for your poor H: L: T.

Text: Queeney Letters, pp. 145–47. *Address: Miss Thrale, at her House, / West Street, Brighthelmstone, Sussex.*

1. A nickname for Mary Johnson, HLT's maid.
2. In Howell 2:498, see the anecdote about "*de Vaca,* husband to *Jusepe de Vaca,* the famous Comedian who came upon the Stage with a cloke lin'd with black plush, and a great Chain about his neck; whereupon the Duke of *Medina* broke into these lines:

Con tant felpa en la Capa
Y tanta cadena de oro,
El marido de la Vaca
Que puede ser sino toro."

3. He was accompanied by his friends Baretti and Mecci, for whom see HLP to SL, 27 July 1785, nn. 2 and 3.
4. William Harford.
5. William Coxe, *Travels into Poland, Russia, Sweden, and Denmark,* 3 vols. (London: T. Cadell, 1784).
6. Francis Woodward (d. 1785), M.D. He had begun his practice in Bristol but moved to Bath, where his patients, including the Thrales, were generally people of fashion (*Thraliana* 1:155; Chapman, passim).
7. The wife of William Stanhope (1719–79), second earl of Harrington (1756), and the eldest daughter of Charles Fitzroy (1683–1757), second duke of Grafton. Lady Caroline (b. 1722) had died on 28 June.
8. John Campbell (1723–1806), fifth duke of Argyll (1770), had married on 3 March 1759 Elizabeth, née Gunning (1733–90), widow of the sixth duke of Hamilton. Acknowledged as one of the most beautiful ladies of the Court, she was created Baroness Hamilton of Hambledon, Leics., 20 May 1776.
9. HLT's alteration of Thomas Gray's *Elegy written in a Country Churchyard* (lines 34–36).
10. Samuel Lysons—lawyer, antiquary, talented illustrator and artist—became one of HLP's principal correspondents during the early years of the Piozzi marriage. On 13 January 1784 she recorded her first favorable impressions of him (*Thraliana* 1:586).

He was the son of the Reverend Samuel Lysons (1730–1804), rector of Rodmarton, and Mary, née Peach (d. 1791). His elder brother Daniel was a priest and topographer, and his uncle Daniel (1727–93) a well-known physician. Called to the bar in 1798, SL practiced law until 1803, when he became keeper of the records in the Tower of London, a post that he held until his death.

In 1786 he had become F.S.A. (subsequently a vice-president and honorary director); in 1797 F.R.S. (later vice-president and treasurer). Between 1785 and 1796 he exhibited occasionally at the Royal Academy, specializing in views of old buildings. Among other artistic activities he contributed etchings to his brother's *Environs of London* (1792–96) and assisted him with *Magna Britannia* (1806–22). He became a favorite of the royal family, to whom Sir Joseph Banks had introduced him in 1796.

11. CB, the musicologist.
12. In the eighteenth and nineteenth centuries, the Somerset Coffee House was in the Strand, near the present entrance to King's College.
13. SJ on 26 June informed HLT: "This morning I saw Mr. Lysons [at Bolt Court]. He is an agreeable young man, and likely enough to do all that he designs. I received him as one sent by you has a right to be received, and I hope he will tell you that he was satisfied; but the initiatory conversation of two strangers is seldom pleasing or instructive to any great degree, and ours was such as other occasions of the same kind produce" (*Letters* 2:373–74).

14. Prisca, née Holt ? (ca. 1727–1804) was the wife of Edward Vanbrugh (ca. 1722–1802) of 6 Brock Street, Bath. They came from the parish of St. Stephen Walbrook in the City of London.

15. Probably Nathaniel Gould (ca. 1731–86), colonel of the Third Regiment of Guards (M.I. All Saints, Weston) and his daughter Frances (ca. 1752–1832), who in 1791 was to marry Lieutenant General Charles Horneck (ca. 1751–1804) and in 1812 TSW.

16. William Bathurst Pye Benet, or Bennet (1764–1806) and his wife Elizabeth (d. 1826), initially of Salthrop House, Wilts., were now residents of Gay Street, Bath. "He was descended from the ancient Family of the Pyes of Farringdon House in the County of Berks." (M.I. Bath Abbey). See *Bath Journal,* 3 May 1806; *GM* 76, pt. 1 (1806): 484. HLP (*Thraliana* 2:1071) hints that he was a suicide.

17. Frances Browne (fl. 1760–94), daughter of Lyde Browne (d. 1787), of Wimbledon: a virtuoso, antiquary, and a director of the Bank of England. She had eloped in 1779 with Thomas Gunter Browne (1756–1834), an officer in the Thirty-seventh Regiment. He retired as a half-pay captain in 1783. See *Thraliana* 1:407, and *Whitehall Evening Post*, 16 September 1779. For Lyde Browne, see *GM* 57, pt. 2 (1787): 840.

18. Cf. the tonal differences between her letters to SJ and the guardians (both on 30 June). In the first she is firm but hopeful of reconciliation. In the second, she is terse and uncompromising (*Queeney Letters*, pp. 148–49).

19. A character in Villiers's *The Rehearsal* (1672). While an infant he is stolen by a fisherman who rears him as a son (3.2). Later on, the fisherman is seized on suspicion of murder and Pretty-man laments:

> What Oracle this darkness can evince?
> Sometimes a Fisher's Son, sometimes a Prince.
> It is a secret, great as is the world,
> In which, I, like the soul, am toss'd and hurl'd.
> The blackest Ink of Fate, sure, was my Lot.
> And, when she writ my name, she made a blot.

The play never comes to terms with Pretty-man's paternity.

SAMUEL JOHNSON TO HESTER LYNCH PIOZZI

2:July 1784.

Madam

If I interpret your letter right, you are ignominiously married, if it is yet undone, let us once talk together.[1] If you have abandoned your children[2] and your religion, God forgive your wickedness; if you have forfeited your Fame, and your country, may your folly do no further mischief.

If the last act is yet to do, I, who have loved you, esteemed you, reverenced you, and served you, I who long thought you the first of human kind, entreat that before your fate is irrevocable, I may once more see you. I was, I once was, / Madam, most truly yours. / Sam: Johnson[3]

I will come down if you permit it.

Text: Chapman 3: 173–74 (not in *Letters*). *Address:* to Mrs. Thrale at Bath. *Postmark:* 2 JY. See also Hayward 1:239.

1. FB had early in 1783 convinced herself and Q that SJ knew only the incidentals of the affair, and that with GP departed, he believed it to be ended. But on 24 May FB wrote to Q: "Since I began & writ thus far, I have seen Dr Johnson—& find he knows the whole affair!" (*Queeney Letters*, p. 97 and n. 2). He therefore could not have been startled by HLT's circular letter (30 June). But as late as 2 July he still hoped there was time to dissuade her. See also *Thraliana* 1:599–600 n. 2.

2. SJ thought precisely that, responding on 1 July to a lost letter from Q:

"I read your letter with anguish and astonishment, such as I never felt before. I had fondly flattered myself that time had produced better thoughts. I can only give you this consolation that, in my opinion, you have hitherto done rightly. You have not left your Mother, but your Mother has left you" (Chapman 3:173).

3. John Nichols reproduced a questionable variation of this letter in *GM* 54, pt. 2 (1784): 893:

"If you are already ignominiously married, you are lost beyond redemption—if you are not, permit me one hour's conversation, to convince you that such a marriage must not take place. If after a whole hour's reasoning you should not be convinced, you will still be at liberty to act as you think proper. I have been extremely ill, and am still ill; but, if you grant me the audience I ask, I will instantly take a post-chaise, and attend you at Bath.—Pray do not refuse this favour to a man, who hath so many years loved and honoured you!"

SJ, according to Hawkins (p. 568), discredited the *GM* version as "an *adumbration* of" the one that appears in the present edition of HLP's letters. It is purportedly "spurious, as to the language . . . but in respect of the sentiments, he avowed it."

TO HESTER MARIA THRALE

Bath
Sat: 3; July [1784]

I should not have *grudged Postage* for any Letter that told me you were well, and loved the Heart which so esteems your Virtue, and admires your Talents: but the longest Letters are the best. I have had a very charming one from Mrs Strickland.[1] She will soon quit her emancipated Son, and *his* House at Sizergh;[2] when She and her Husband think of retiring to Italy, to end their Days in a warm Climate, and enjoy all the Comforts that mutual Kindness, and Freedom from Care can bestow: her Daughter is going to be married,[3] I wish the Mother had a larger Income[4]—but

Dans un lieu du bruit retiré,
Où pour peu qu'on soit modéré,
On peut trouver que tout abonde![5]

The stuttering Man that Sophy tells me of, must lend you the Book which Coxe has written about the Northern Nations; his Account of the Jews in Poland entertain'd me vastly—I worked thro' that huge Quarto (in my way of working) between 4 o'clock o' Monday Noon, and four o'Clock o' Wensday Noon.[6] Mrs Carey of the Pump weeps very prettily, and yet the cruel Corporation will not let her continue; so we are to have all new People now. Sophy's Account of John is ridiculous enough; I fancy he finds Brightelmstone a shabby Place compared to

Bath, which for emptiness may however vye with anything but Antwerp where I have heard that the grass grows in the Streets.

I enclose a letter to Sophy[7] and am ever both hers and Yours in all possible Affection. Adieu.

I write to Susan tomorrow.

Text: Queeney Letters, p. 154. *Address: Miss Thrale, at her house, / West Street, Brighthelmstone, Sussex.*

1. Cecilia "Stricky" Strickland, née Towneley (1741–1814), of Sizergh Park, Westmorland. A childhood friend of HLS, she later attended her at the birth of CMT (who was named after her) (*Thraliana* 2:975 n. 2).

She had married twice: first, in 1762 to Charles Strickland (1734–70) of Sizergh Park, and second, in 1779 to her late husband's cousin Gerard (Jarrard) Strickland (1741–95). See Henry Hornyold, *Genealogical Memoirs of the Family of Strickland of Sizergh* (Kendal: Titus Wilson and Son, Printers, Highgate, 1928), esp. pp. 185–87.

2. The elder son of Charles and Cecilia Strickland was Thomas (d. 1813) of Sizergh. As early as 1784 he knew that he would inherit the estates of his childless uncle Edward Towneley-Standish (1740–1807). In return he was to assume the arms and surname of Standish, i.e., Thomas Strickland-Standish.

3. Mary Cecilia Strickland (1766–1817), the only daughter of Cecilia and Charles, had been placed in Saint Mary's Convent, Micklegate Bar, Yorks., in 1772, and then in the convent of the Poor Clares at Rouen. After a year or two she completed her education at the Canonesses of the Holy Sepulchre in Liège, returning to England about 1783. At Kendal, on 27 February 1786, she married Edward Stephenson, the banker, of Queen's Square, London; Scaleby Castle, Cumberland; and Farley Hill, Berks.

Edward (1759–1833) was the son of Rowland Stephenson (ca. 1728–1807), who was M.P. for Carlisle (1787–90) and nephew of Edward Stephenson (1691–1768), onetime governor of Bengal (1728). The last had owned Scaleby Castle and the house in Queen Square. Without issue, he left a fortune "supposed to be upwards of £500,000" to his nephew.

4. Cecilia Strickland's parents were William Towneley (d. 1742) and Cecilia, née Standish (d. 1778), who was the sole heiress of her parents, Ralph Standish (d. 1755) and Lady Philippa (d. 1732), daughter of Henry Howard, sixth duke of Norfolk.

Cecilia Strickland had two brothers: Charles (d. 1805) and Edward (d. 1807). Her parents' wealth had to be divided three ways, with the greatest shares going to her brothers. Moreover, the bulk of her first husband's estates went to their sons: Thomas and William.

5. Probably HLT's own verse. See "Harvard Piozziana" 2:2, in which she indicates that her "power of writing Verses in Other Languages has always been a subject of Wonder—even to my Enemies."

6. HLT refers to bk. 1, chap. 7 (5th ed. [1802], 1:118–19).

There Coxe describes the Polish Jews as an economically influential (virtually elite) society who enjoyed privileges of commerce and trade unprecedented anywhere except in England and Holland.

7. The enclosure to Sophia is missing.

TO SAMUEL JOHNSON

4: July 1784.

Sir—

I have this Morning received from You so rough a Letter, in reply to one which was both tenderly and respectfully written, that I am forced to desire the conclusion of a Correspondence which I can bear to continue no longer. The Birth of my second Husband is not meaner than that of my first,[1] his sentiments are not meaner, his Profession is not meaner,—and his Superiority in what he professes—acknowledged by all Mankind.—It is want of Fortune then that is *ignominious,* the Character of the Man I have chosen has no other Claim to such an Epithet. The Religion to which he has been always a zealous Adherent, will I hope teach him to forgive Insults he has not deserved—mine will I hope enable me to bear them at once with Dignity and Patience. To hear that I have forfeited my Fame is indeed the greatest Insult I ever yet received, my Fame is as unsullied as Snow, or I should think it unworthy of him who must henceforward protect it.

I write by the Coach the more speedily and effectually to prevent your coming hither.

Perhaps by my Fame (and I hope it is so;) you mean only that Celebrity which is a Consideration of a much lower kind: I care for that only as it may give pleasure to my Husband and his Friends.

Farewell Dear Sir, and accept my best wishes: You have always commanded my Esteem, and long enjoyed the Fruits of a Friendship never infringed by one harsh Expression on my Part, during twenty Years of familiar Talk. Never did I oppose your Will, or controal your Wish: nor can your unmerited Severity itself lessen my Regard—but till you have changed your Opinion of Mr. Piozzi—let us converse no more.[2] God bless you!

Text: Chapman 3:175 (not in *Letters*). *Address:* Dr. Johnson.

1. If HLT had granted SJ an interview, he might well have pointed out the chief charges against GP: that he was a foreigner, a musician and therefore of questionable professional and class standing; that he was a Roman Catholic. HLT would have undoubtedly rebutted these accusations with the fact that HT, despite his wealth and university education, was still a brewer and therefore middle-class—a fact that distressed her father and herself as members of the landed gentry.

2. HLT's equally "rough" letter evoked a conciliatory one from SJ (8 July) and his resigned note of 6 July to Q: "You will soon [17 September 1785] be mistress of yourself. Do your best; and be not discouraged. Serve God, read, and pray. You have in your hand all that the world considers as materials of happiness. You have riches, youth, and Health, all which I shall delight to see you enjoy. But believe a man whose experience has been long, and who can have no wish to deceive you, and who now tells you that the highest honour, and most constant pleasure this life can afford, must be obtained by passing it with attention fixed upon Eternity. The longest life soon passes away . . ." (Chapman 3:176).

For HLT's further correspondence with SJ, see n. 4 of SJ to HLT, 8 July.

TO HESTER MARIA THRALE

Bath,
Sunday, 4 July [1784]

You are very kind my Dearest in caring for my Safety: All is well; he is come, and I have need of his support: Mr. Johnson has written me a letter even rougher than one could have thought for. The Delays about [our] Marriage too are numerous and incredible: but I have had *one happy Day!* It was the 2nd. of July, I never had so happy a Day in all my Life—Thursday was Tumult, & Terror, & Hope & Anxiety—but Fryday was all Tranquillity & Peace & Comfort—and now comes the Storm.

Sperai vicino il lido,
Credei calmato il Vento;
Ma trasportar mi sento
Fra le Tempeste ancor.[1]

I must enclose Johnson's Letter and my Reply; will he come after that Letter reaches him?—perhaps so: When come the others? I am less murdered than Piozzi is: for his Health is still more shaken than mine, & his Temper less ruffled by Sorrow—he cried bitterly however over his poor little *Sposa,* who they tell me must now live 26 Days more in hot water before she has a right to say She is wedded to the Man of her Heart, Meanwhile how are we to live? Together? and lose my Reputation so dear, so necessary to both?—Asunder? and be separately baited by Bulldogs, Curs, and Puppies? We should neither of us see the 26th Day. I always did hate that rascally Marriage Act, and now I have Cause to curse it—for we are told it obliges people to reside 26 Days in a Parish before they are married, & that the expence of bringing Lawyers &c, hither will be such, that we must go to Town & be Parishioners 26 days—

Che Seccatura mai! We have however written to Greenland to know. I shall think the Answer as tedious as if it came from *Greenland* in good earnest. Lord bless me! What will they do to us meantime?

My spirits are very low, I'll write again soon: beg Susan's Pardon for me—on second Thoughts I *cannot* copy the Letter. Tis *too bad,* & has hurt us both sadly—Adieu—Mr Johnson has stabbed my Peace more than I thought him capable of doing—but I am ashamed to think any Ill usage not coming from you should affect me—and you are sweetly kind. It was generous & lovely of you to give the Chintz to Miss Nicholson. Farewell & love each other *half* as well as I love you all.

Text: Queeney Letters, pp. 155–56. *Address: Miss Thrale, at her House, / West Street, Brighthelmstone, Sussex.*

1. The poet and dramatist, Pietro Antonio Domenico Bonaventura Trapassi Metastasio (1698–1782), *Demofoonte* (1733), 1.4.238–41. See CB, *Memoirs of the Life and Writings of the Abate Metastasio. In which are incorporated, translations of his princpal letters,* 3 vols. (London: Printed for G. G. and J. Robinson, 1796).

SAMUEL JOHNSON TO HESTER LYNCH THRALE

London 8: July 1784.

What you have done, however I may lament it, I have no pretence to resent, as it has not been injurious to me.[1] I therefore breathe out one sigh more of tenderness perhaps useless, but at least sincere.

I wish that God may grant you every blessing, that you may be happy in this world for its short continuance, and eternally happy in a better state. and whatever I can contribute to your happiness, I am very ready to repay for that kindness which soothed twenty years of a life radically wretched.

Do not think slightly of the advice which I now presume to offer. Prevail upon Mr. Piozzi to settle in England. You may live here with more dignity than in Italy, and with more security. Your rank will be higher, and your fortune more under your own eye. I desire not to detail all my reasons; but every argument of prudence and interest is for England, and only some phantoms of imagination seduce you to Italy.

I am afraid, however, that my counsel is vain, yet I have eased my heart by giving it.

When Queen Mary took the resolution of sheltering herself in England,[2] the Archbishop of St. Andrew's attempting to dissuade her, attended on her journey and when they came to the irremeable stream[3] that separated the two kingdoms, walked by her side into the water, in the middle of which he seized her bridle, and with earnestness proportioned to her danger and his own affection, pressed her to return. The Queen went forward.——If the parallel reaches thus far; may it go no further. The tears stand in my eyes.

I am going into Derbyshire,[4] and hope to be followed by your good wishes, for I am with great affection / Your most humble servant, / Sam: Johnson.

Any letters that come for me hither, will be sent me.

Text: Chapman 3:177–78 (not in *Letters*). *Address:* To Mrs. Thrale at Bath. *Postmark:* 8 JY.

1. The prophetic implication is that the intended marriage will be socially injurious to HLT. "Poor Thrale!" SJ wrote to Sir John Hawkins from Ashbourne (Chapman 3:183), "I thought that either her virtue or her vice would have restrained her from such a marriage. She is now become a subject for her enemies to exult over, and for her friends, if she has any left, to forget or pity."
2. The anecdote may have been derived from Adam Blackwood, *Adami Blacvodaei Opera* (1644), p. 589. See Chapman (citing G. B. Hill) 3:178 n. 2.
3. From "irremeabilis unda," *Aeneid* 6.425.
4. Suffering from dropsy and asthma, SJ wrote to William Adams on 11 July: "I am going into Staffordshire and Derbyshire in quest of some relief" (Chapman 3:180). Finding little, he returned to London on 16 November (*Boswell's Johnson* 4:377).

According to HLT, writing to Q and FB, both on 12 July, she sent SJ a mild letter (now missing) expressing her "adoration," her "best respects and those of my dear Futur." On 15 July (below), she sent him another conciliatory letter.

TO HESTER MARIA THRALE

No. 30 Berners Street [London]
12: July [1784]

I write from London only to say I am there, for the Purpose of attending and urging on our dilatory Lawyers, We must be married here too it seems at the

Ambassador's Chapel,[1] & then return to St. James's Bath, my Parish Church—We swore to the Residence before we broke it, & obtained the Licence which Piozzi keeps safe, & his Friends joke him for kissing it—and tell him he will wear it out.[2]

Borghi gave me a Dinner yesterday all Italiano—but would suffer no Friend to come in but ourselves & his beautiful Wife! he is a Man of very elegant Manners indeed, & I have seen few like him: he hired us our Lodging—for me in one Street, for Piozzi in another: he appointed Greenland to meet us—& turned his Wife out that Com^y^ might not break in upon Business the 1st Night of our Arrival.[3] Viva Mr Borghi, I never saw his Fellow.

I wrote Mr Johnson a sharp answer to his first Letter—not sharp neither but exculpatory; and he has recanted so sweetly, & prays so prettily for my Felicity and Piozzi's that I adore him and have sent him my best Respects and those of my dear *Futur,* whose Reception among all the People I wish to call Friends, is far more precious to me than my own,—those who love me *in earnest* will love *him,* and dear Dr Johnson is the 1st to promise me, not the 1st tho'—for so should I wrong my dearest Dr Pepys who gives us all his Heart.

This Moment brings me yours forwarded from Bath.[4] Hateful Crutchley! and *that's* his love, to tyrannize the Woman of his Heart, & that's his Virtue, to sow Discord among Friends & Family Affection.[5]

Fye on such specimens of Virtue. / Ever & ever Yours / H: L: T.

I am not well but better—I am not married but I shall be. I write in the Dark.

Text: Queeney Letters, pp. 159–60. *Address: Miss Thrale, at her House / West Street, Brighthelmstone, Sussex.*

1. The priest at Bell Tree House, the Roman Catholic chapel in Bath, had created difficulties about performing the marriage ceremony. GP and HLT therefore went to London on 11 July and were permitted to calculate their legal residence from 27 June, the Sunday of GP's arrival there. On 14 July another vexing complication arose. "The Ambassador's Chapel Folks won't marry us," she told Q, "till the Ceremony has been performed Protestant-wise, & that must be done at Bath—and there, the Man of the Bell-Tree house won't marry us—so we must come back to London" (*Queeney Letters,* p. 164).

She was still irritated as she recalled the circumstances in the "Harvard Piozziana" (2:22): "We had been married according to the Romish Church on one of our Excursions to London by Mr. Smith—Padre Smith as they called him: Chaplain to the Spanish Ambassador——because such is the Pride of that Religion, they acknowledge none but themselves for Xtians, and consider marriage with a Protestant as not in any wise binding:——but as you would think of a *Hottentot Wedding*—A Matter to be set aside *as a Jest."*

Finally the marriage was celebrated in the French ambassador's chapel and not—as she faultily recollected—the Spanish. "Padre Smith" was in fact chaplain to comte Jean-Balthazar d'Adhémar de Montfalcon (1731–91), French ambassador to Great Britain from 1783 to 1787 (*Repertorium,* p. 118). Comte d'Adhémar as well as Richard Smith signed the marriage certificate (Ry. Ch. 1242): "Anno Domini 1784, die vero 23 July, nullo impedimento detecto, ritè in Matrimonio conjuncti fuère, Gabriel Piozzi, et Hester Lynch Thrale, presentibus notis testibus, Aloisio Borghi, Francesco Mecci, et Angelica Borghi."

For Padre Smith, see HLP to Q, 25 July, n. 1.

2. In addition to the license from Doctors Common applied for in absentia as early as 24 June, GP on 8 July signed a bond before the bishop of Bath, attesting that there existed no legal bar to the marriage.

3. The major business concerned the marriage settlement, witnessed by Greenland and the banker Richard Cox. It is dated 19 July 1784 and described: "Settlement of the Interest of £51,805.1.8—3% Consolidated Annuities and of £13,400 Life Annuities during the Life of Mrs. Thrale" (Ry. Ch. 1239).

4. Most of Q's letters to her mother are missing.

5. For the causes and intensity of HLT's detestation see, e.g., *Thraliana* 1:552; 561 n. 4; 596 n. 1, and passim. Among other flaws, Jeremiah Crutchley was—she thought—HT's illegitimate son.

She was to characterize him in 1788 as "a Man of delicate Honour, with Manners so very coarse and so very cold, that he scrupled not to shew his ill Opinion of People to their Faces . . ." (*Thraliana* 2: 707).

TO FANNY BURNEY

Berners Street
12: July 1784.

I received your Letter *here* my Love, it was transmitted me from Bath: I cannot get married yet, here are so many delays and Difficulties, for I *will* settle my Affairs first; and have no one to assist me in so doing, but *new* Friends—the old ones are so angry: in good Time! being angry is so easy a way to shew Kindness. Dr. Johnson wrote me a most ferocious Letter in answer to that you saw the Copy of, but when he read my Reply to it, he softened at once; has sent Prayers and Wishes for mine and my Piozzi's happiness—and behaved with all the Tenderness you can imagine. Lord Dudley[1] has given me Letters to Dr. Harris,[2] to smooth our road through the Ecclesiastical Courts; The Bishop of Durham has interested himself warmly in our Cause—his Lady hearing Piozzi sing,[3] cried out *She wondered no longer* and good old Lord Conyngham[4] promised for *his* Lady that She should be the first to wait on us after our Marriage.—so the Last shall be first, and the first last as the Scripture says.[5]

In the mean Time our charming Sir Lucas Pepys has offered me every Service, every Civility in his Power—so perhaps We may yet be *fashionable* and then the People so justly called People of *Fashion* will be all on our Side; and I shall know what their Tenderness amounts to.

Dr. Johnson is going to Derbys—and in very good humour with me I am sure: This Moment I write again to him with Piozzi's Compliments &c.

I went to Portland Chapel yesterday, and heard Mr. George Cambridge read prayers and preach;[6] he did both very well, and saved me by Attention from fainting away with the Heat.

Bath and London are indeed so hot this Weather that I may defie Naples itself:[7] it will take us a week to stay in Town I dare say, before the Writings are compleated;[8] we are then to be married *here* in the Romish Chapel, and return to my Parish Church at Bath to be married there *again* as the Law directs.

Mean Time I am ill enough and so is my Caro Sposo: but we must get well when we can, and how we can; we shall at least be sick or well *together* and to us that is no small Consideration. / Ever yours my dear / sweet Friend Ever Yours / Adieu!

Text: Berg Collection, no. 1784, folder 3. *Address:* Miss Burney / at Norbury Park, The Seat of / Locke Esq. / near Dorking / Surrey. *Postmark:* 12 JY.

1. John Ward (22 February 1724/25–1788), second viscount Dudley and Ward, seventh baron Ward (1774); skilled in the law, he had been M.P. for Marlborough (1754–61), for Worcestershire (1761–74). See *GM* 58, pt. 2 (1788): 937.
2. George Harris (1722–96), trained in ecclesiastical law at Oriel College, Oxford, earned the degrees of B.C.L. (1745) and D.C.L. (1750). He was admitted in the latter year to the College of Advocates and subsequently became chancellor of the dioceses of Durham, Hereford, and Llandaff (where his father John [1680–1738] had been bishop).
3. John Egerton (1721–87) after studying at Eton was admitted to Oriel College (1740) and ordained deacon and priest (1745). He took the degrees of B.C.L. (1746) and D.C.L. (ca. 1756), was appointed King's Chaplain (1749), consecrated as bishop of Bangor (1756), and translated to the see of Durham (1771). He first married (21 November 1748) Lady Anne Sophia (d. 1780), daughter of Henry de Grey, duke of Kent. His second wife (31 March 1782) was Mary, née Boughton.
4. Francis Pierpont Burton, later Conyngham (d. 1787), second baron Conyngham (1781) of Mount Charles [Ireland], had married on 19 March 1750 Elizabeth (1731–1814), eldest daughter of Nathaniel Clements, and sister of Robert (1732–1804), first earl of Leitrim.
5. Matt. 19:30. See also Matt. 20:16, Mark 10:31, Luke 13:30.
6. In Great Portland Street, Saint Marylebone, a chapel designed by S. Leadbetter, was built in 1765–66 at a cost of five thousand pounds; it was not consecrated until 1831. Cambridge preached there as archdeacon of Middlesex.
7. The exceptional, "insupportable" heat and thunderstorms are reported in the *Bath Chronicle,* 15 July.
8. The banns and marriage contract.

TO HESTER MARIA THRALE

Written in Bed at 7 o'clock in the Morning,
No. 30 Berners Street, Tuesday
14 July [1784]

Never was there such hot weather sure, it half kills by Relaxation us *nervous patients;* How can poor Sophy support it? I almost fainted away at Portland Chapel o' Sunday, where nothing kept me alive but the desire of watching how Mr George Cambridge pray'd preached &c.—You would scarcely believe how much more *genteely* than *well* he did both; talked of the weight of a 'high' Charge instead of a 'heavy' one, & such sort of Newspaper Language it was. My agreeable Friend Mr Borghi & his pretty Wife wait on us most politely indeed; he hears the Settlements read, & explains all the Law Terms to Piozzi, (which he else could never comprehend)—with a Facility & affection that would charm you.—They dine with me today, I shall give them Venson; Good God! how these Foreigners do eat and talk, it is distraction to hear their Rapidity, to me however they are very pleasing, and if I had wanted a fresh assortment of Adoration, this Plan was just the Thing! I have seen Bartolozzi now;[1] for tho' he lived in the House, Borghi would not suffer him to appear till yesterday—for fear he said, lest I should be frighted & suffocated with Italians. Shall I tell our odd dishes of

Meat? a Soup like thick Water gruel stuff'd with the pipe Macaroni boyld very soft, & scraped Parmezan Cheese carried round on a Salver, for each to put a Spoonful into his Plate—this is the middle dish: at Top Pulpettis, oh how odious a Mess! like Veal Olives to look at, but so impregnated with Cabbage, Cheese & Garlick that sure it has no Fellow. Bologna Sausages on this Side, & stewd Pease on the other; but the Pease are not like Pease somehow, I do not know what they are like. Their Conversation is interesting and animated, their Singing heavenly, & they *all* sing: but the *manging* as we call it, worse than I could conceive. You know how little that touches *me* however.

I am enraged with Crutchley; what a mean Creature 'tis! and I hear *such* Things of Cator:[2] Poor, pretty, dear Tit! you will perhaps pay on all Sides both of Comfort & Fortune for the high Situation you will at least be commended for maintaining: I laid down *my* Magnificence most willingly, and like my new associates very much; bred among Artists,[3] I delight in their Talk & take an interest in their Disputes: the Reverence they have for my Talents, and those of my Husband make me happy in my new associates. Lord Conyngham at Bath said that my Piozzi and I left no one else a chance except Mr James; for that *his* Art alone was unknown to our joint Skill, or beyond our Joint powers—A very pretty Speech, I *liked* it, as the Nawdowessies say.[4] So Reputation is safe enough; He shews his Licence, and Greenland swears he shall *only* shew it, till all Matters are so settled as to prevent every future entanglement: he bathes in the Cold Bath & so do I; and we drown ourselves in Lemonade but both are far from well: I have all my Nerves so distressed that 'tis incredible,—and from Smelling quicker than others—I have now no power of distinction by my Nose; if a Window rattles or a Coach passes in the Street it kills me—there is not however so desert a place as London at this Time, & glad at heart am I. Johnson will take care of all your Things, we shall go back to Bath to marry after performing the Ceremony here according to the Romish Institution, but we will not stay any longer there than just to rejoice in one another's Company a little, and to take leave of our friends who have been civil to us; this is indeed a Whalleian letter,[5] but one longs to be talking of one's self to those one has talked to so long. You shall see the whole of my Correspondence with old Charles some day,[6] I *thought* (as the stuttering lawyer in Steele's Play says) he could not stand my Argument about Gr, Gr, Gr, Grim Gribber.[7]

Do not be too tame, my dearest, sweetest Friend—there has come no Good of it to *me* you may perceive.

Tender-hearted touch a Nettle
And it stings you for your pains;
Squeeze it like a Man of Mettle
And it soft as silk remains.[8]

Love to the Dears and kind words to Miss Nicholson from y^r^ affect^e^ & faithful / H: L: T.

Johnson laughs herself blind at Piozzi's English. He told her yesterday he was her 'Quarter Master.'

Text: Queeney Letters, pp. 161–63. *Address: Miss Thrale, at her House, / West Street, Brighthelmstone, Sussex.*

1. Francesco Bartolozzi (1727–1815). In 1764 he emigrated from Italy to England, there becoming engraver to the king. Some four years later he was one of the original members of the Royal Academy.

2. Several years earlier HLT had expressed the bases of her lasting distaste for Cator as a coarse and vulgar "purse-proud Tradesman," although she questioned neither his intelligence nor his financial acumen (*Thraliana* 1:220, and passim). SJ, on the other hand, admired his fellow guardian as one with "a rough, manly, independent understanding, [who] does not spoil it by complaisance; he never speaks merely to please, and seldom is mistaken in things which he has any right to know" (21 January 1784, *Letters* 2:347–48).

3. According to HLP's autobiographical account (17 June 1798) for the *Monthly Mirror:* William Hogarth taught her to recognize good art. She knew the famous actors James Quin and David Garrick. She learned the art of conversation from Arthur Murphy, SJ, Edmund Burke, and CB. Throughout her life, she was comfortable among theater people—SS, Elizabeth Farren, WAC—even John Philip Kemble, whose morality she deplored.

4. A nursery coinage for "Now-do-Essie [Hester]." Cf. *Queeney Letters*, p. 162 n. 3.

5. That is, a long and egocentric one. For a biographical account of TSW, see HLP to SL, 17 September 1784, n. 11.

6. The letters from CB are now scattered. Some thirteen to HLT and two poems—between 1777 and 1781—are at the John Rylands Library (Ry. 545.1–16). Three more letters—dated 11 January 1778, 19 November 1778, 16 October 1779—are deposited in the Beinecke and Osborn collections of the Yale University Library. In addition he had sent her a complimentary poem of seven quatrains when she "made him a Present of a Gold Pen" (7 October 1777). ("Harvard Piozziana" 1:74–75; "MSS Verses 2," pp. 41–43, Hyde Collection.) See *Thraliana* 1:216–17.

If CB admired HLT, she professed equal regard for him, as in this excerpt from a draft letter (Yale University Library, 14 June 1782), to an unknown recipient, in support of CB's aspiration for court preferment: ". . . If a consummate Knowledge of the Theory of his Art, if Perfection in the practice of it; if the Knowledge of a Scholar, the elegance of a Gentleman, and the Conduct of an amiable inoffensive Man, can be urged as Claims—my dear Doctor Burney will not fail of Success—. . . ." See also Roger Lonsdale, *Dr. Charles Burney: A Literary Biography* (Oxford: Clarendon Press, 1965), p. 295 n. 4.

7. Target (*The Conscious Lovers*, 1722) speaks: "He could not bear my argument, I pincht him to the quick, about that Gr-gr-ber." An argument had been staged between two bogus lawyers, and Target drove his adversary from the room by repeated attempts to pronounce "Grimgribber" (3.1.408–9).

8. Aaron Hill (1685–1750), "Verses written on Windows in several Parts of the Kingdom, in a Journey to Scotland," *Works* (1753–54)), 4:120:

> Tender-handed stroke a nettle,
>   And it stings you for your pains,
> *Grasp* it like a man of mettle,
>   And it soft as silk remains.

TO HESTER MARIA THRALE[a]

[London July 15, 1784]

Poor, little, lovely, dear Tit! why thou wilt be plagued indeed;[1] and spited, and mortified, and all for what?—whom, and how can you have offended?

Miss Nicholson's Sister[2] laments the Guardians' objecting to Miss Jane's continuing with you, & says it breaks all their Hearts, because her Sister is attached to Miss Thrale so.[3]

Berry is a *Goose* Berry as well as a *Black* one;[4] but you have learned of your Mother to be merry & *sad* I see. She never found out the Way herself to be merry & *wise* poor Soul! The Rascal wrote me three Letters, just such as I intended sending poor Susan out of Fun, only more impudent. Reject all Offers of Kindness from Mrs Byron,[5] as you value your Reputation; Cator's Coldness is cruel, & undeserved—unprovoked too, I do not comprehend it. Teizers to marry you will spring up like *Dorbeetles,* and you may rely upon it Harry Cotton[6] is no *otherwise* offensive to you I believe than as a Sollicitor for what you do not mean to bestow—in any, in every Situation, it would be Misery to me to keep that puppy Company. A propos Piozzi met Seward in the Street, who would have embraced him as if for Joy—but the Honour was rejected with sudden, and I doubt not *apparent* Aversion by a Man who does not know the nature or meaning of Duplicity. Seward asked for me it seems, but Piozzi *troncò il Discorso,* and ran hither to charge me not to let him in if he call'd,—for *such* Reasons as will make me shut him out I'll warrant you, for all Mrs. Montague says I so love *Bloody Noses*.[7]

Poor Mrs Montagu! Miss Gregory has married without her Consent, & professing to prefer Competence and the Company of an honest Man to *Tonism,* & *Blueism,* has oddly enough, as I think, got the World on her side.[8]

—sed Victa Catoni—[9]

Fanny Burney seems to be against her, I am sorry.[10] If I had Time to learn a new manner of working, I have got a nice Master. Mr Borghi, with the finest Talents for Music, with general powers of Conversation, with Knowledge of Life, Manners and Literature; with a Memory that I think scarce knows its own Limits; that can repeat long Passages from every Author—among the rest *Walton's complete Angler*—(What a Book for a Foreigner!) with a Wife who is all Beauty & elegance—dies for Amusement: and makes Straw Boxes, and will teach me *how.* The Straw is all prepared and dyed in Shades, and has the sweetest effect; he learned the Trick of a Capucin Friar at Loretto, when he was *ennuié à la Mort* in his own charming Country, & tells me if I *cared a Straw* for him, I would be willing to learn—There's a fine Fellow for you, quibbling in a foreign Language as if it was his own—and one never heard there was such a Creature existing!

Well! now I feel in health, for this last Fit is gone off again—I do sincerely believe there is not so happy a Woman as I am, out of Heaven. Dear, precious, charming Queeney, accept my truest, my tenderest Thanks: All that this Earth can give—for which I have any Taste at least, do I now enjoy; your Company alone excepted and that I will not despair of. Some Franks tho' would be good additions to my Felicity.

I will not teize you with saying how very comfortably I live; but you *should* know that your sweet saving Kindness was not flung away upon your grateful & / faithful & Obliged / H: L: T.

Oh! one very comical Thing I will add to make you grin: I called on Miss Hudson before we left Bath, & told her I was going to be married, and that she should drink Tea with me some Evening, & hear Piozzi sing. 'Yes, dear M[rs] Thrale' says she, 'so I would; but the People here say he is very handsome, & a great Musician—& so it might produce *dissention* you know, if you should be *jealous* of me, for *indeed* I would give you no Cause.'

Text: Queeney Letters, pp. 166–68. *Address: Miss Thrale, at her House, / West Street, Brighthelmstone, Sussex.*[11]

1. According to HLT Crutchley was in love with Q (*Thraliana* 1:541), and so he plagued her with unwanted (perhaps incestuous) advances. Moreover, Q, along with ST and SAT, were to be denied their chaperone and hence the immediate use of their West Street house in Brighton.

2. Jane Nicolson had two sisters: Catherine (1749–1814), who had married a London banker, Stephen Barber (1749–1823); and Sarah Ann (1750–1838), housekeeper to the family of Charles François Dumergue (1740–1814), surgeon to George III, dentist to the Prince of Wales and duke of Sussex.

3. Cator and Crutchley came to Brighton, planning to dismiss Miss Nicolson by 15 August. Thereafter the Cators brought Q to live with them either at Beckenham Place in Kent or at the Adelphi in London. SAT and ST were sent to Mrs. Murray's school in Kensington, with CMT remaining at Streatham at a school run by Mrs. Ray and Miss Fry.

4. James Barry (1741–1806), Irish-born painter and fellow of the Royal Academy. Among his many works was a portrait of SJ that pleased the sitter. Barry was a member of the Essex Head Club and, if HLT can be believed, her unwanted suitor.

5. Sophia, née Trevannion (d. 1790), wife of Admiral John "Foul Weather Jack" Byron (1723–86). This was a remarkable statement; HLT thought of herself as Mrs. Byron's loyal friend.

6. Henry (Harry) Calveley Cotton (1755–1837), youngest son of Sir Lynch Salusbury Cotton. According to FB, Harry was "sweet-tempered and good, and soft-hearted; and alas! . . . also soft-headed" (*Thraliana* 1:518 n. 1).

7. Elizabeth Montagu, née Robinson (1720–1800), had predicted that HLT would suffer for her marriage to GP. HLP remembered with cause (in 1789) that before her second marriage the Bluestocking "turned her Back upon me & set her Adherents to do the same" (*Thraliana* 2:745). In a letter to Q, dated 10 August, FB reported: "I have heard that Mrs. Montagu & Miss More have written long letters about this cruel business, which are read about the Town" (*Queeney Letters*, p. 102).

8. Dorothea (ca. 1755–1830) was the daughter of the Reverend John Gregory (1724–73), whose most popular work was *A Father's Legacy to his Daughters* (1774).

Dorothea was a protégée of Mrs. Montagu, who had once called her "my spiritual Daughter" (in a letter to HLT, 15 January [1781], Ry. 551.5). Without Mrs. Montagu's concurrence, Dorothea had married (14 June) the Reverend Archibald Alison (1757–1839).

9. From Lucan [M. Annaei Lucani], *De Bello Civili* 1.128.

10. FB's displeasure was probably prompted by Mrs. Montagu's adverse criticism of her fiction. As HLT had written to SJ (19 October [1778]), "Mrs. Montagu cannot bear Evelina . . . her Silver-Smiths are Pewterers She says, and her Captains Boatswains" (Ry. 540.83).

Moreover, FB thought Mrs. Montagu cold, "a character rather to respect than love, for she has not that *don d'aimer* by which alone love can be made fond or faithful; . . ." (*Diary and Letters* 2:7).

11. The dating of this letter and the one that follows it is dependent on HLT's description of "two Whalleian Letters [sent] in one Day." See HLT to Q [23 July 1784].

TO HESTER MARIA THRALE[b]

[London] Thursday,
July 15 [1784]

Well! now for our Dinner & Concert of yesterday: both were really very charming, & Miss Greenlands sang in good earnest, and finely:[1] The lady of the House is a wellbred pleasing Woman; mad after Belles Lettres, modern Languages, Accomplishments &c., doting on the Italian Artists, and apparently fearless lest her fair Daughters instead of turning these Arms on the proper Prey of rich Traders, or illustrious Levee Hunters, should unwittingly enter themselves into the Society of the people she wishes to polish them up for another Purpose. A gallant Entertainment they gave us indeed, such as our *own* House in its high days need not have scorned;[2] & the Desks were set about 8 o'clock, when Giardini's Quartettes were very sweetly performed;[3] and Mr Borghi played a Solo divinely on his Violin, tho' he had been forced to run from Table too, poor Fellow, with a Fish-Bone in his Throat, which we never could get at last either up or down, but Piozzi & the Girls sung all the singing, & when the Violoncello Player broke his Bow, my Solemnity quitted me, & I felt all upon the Giggle. *The Gift of Phoebus* thought I—*my faithless Bow!* &c. as Pandarus complains in the Iliad.[4] The Man's Face express'd no less Affliction & Dismay, & I wished heartily for you to help laugh. Well! about 11 o'clock I came home in a Chair, & my Futur to see me safe, & to teize my heart out because the Ambassador's Chapel Folks won't Marry us, till the Ceremony has been performed Protestant-wise, & that must be done at Bath—and there, the Man of the Bell-Tree house won't marry us—so we must come back to London before my *personal* Reign is over, tho' Piozzi is entitled to *legal* Possession, that he is, the moment we come out of St. James's Church Bath,[5]—but a little Coquetry Miss Queeney, says I,—a little Coquetry in an *Eve*ning—like pompous Langley and his *Society.*[6] So I am not sorry, not I; the World can't part us when Morgan[7] has married us, so then I play the fool upon sure Ground at least—and if by delay one *can* make valuable, that which no one could make a woman of your age think *really* so—why all's fair an't it?

When I am sick I am more willing to be happy, but the nervous Fit is off, and my Spirit of Procrastination returns, much to the Misery of my Companion, whose native Country gave him a warmer Temperamento than fell to the Lot of a snow-nursed Welchwoman. All this however is *but* Nonsense, for till the Writings are executed—(and they are now before Council [*sic*], for the sake of seeing that all goes right, & that no future Plagues may arise in consequence of present Neglect) we *cannot* be married; and Piozzi was more contented with stipulations in *my* favour, and *so* solicitous for my Pin money to exceed that of the Marchesa Litta,[8] who is the first woman in Milan; that all *present* Delays are his own Fault; and if I don't reward him with *future* ones—then am I not my lovely Hester's most Affectionate & faithful/ H: L: T.

Text: Queeney Letters, pp. 164–65. *Address: To Miss Thrale, at her House, / West Street, Brighthelmstone, Sussex.*

1. The only daughter mentioned in Greenland's will (P.R.O., Prob. 11/1396/628) was Emma. If another daughter existed, she like her mother died prior to the execution of the will in 1803.

2. An allusion to the lavish fetes at Streatham.

3. Felice (de) Giardini (1716–96), Italian violinist and composer who made frequent concert appearances in England.

4. The bow and arrows given to Pandarus by Apollo.

> This unavailing Bow
> Serves not to slaughter, but provoke the Foe. . . .
> If e'er with Life I quit the *Trojan* Plain,
> If e'er I see my Spouse and Sire again,
> This Bow, unfaithful to my glorious Aims,
> Broke by my Hand, shall feed the blazing Flames.
> (*Iliad* [Pope's trans.] 5.262–71)

5. "The Church dedicated to St. James, is both low and small; the tower (which was built in 1726) is pretty lofty, and has a musical peal of eight bells" (*The Bath and Bristol Guide,* 4th ed. [ca. 1765], p. 13). Reconstructed in 1768 and 1769, the church "is a very neat freestone building with fronts in the gothic taste" (*The Bath Directory* [1792], p. 8).

6. William Langley (ca. 1722–95), headmaster of Ashbourne School and rector of Fenny Bentley. Langley, an acquaintance of SJ and the Thrales, was constantly at odds with the junior masters of the school, which he mismanaged badly (*Boswell's Johnson* 1:xv; 3:494–95).

7. Nathaniel Morgan (ca. 1740–1811), rector successively of Glooston, Leics.; Corby (1778–81) and Deene (1781–1811), Northants.; Charlcombe, Somerset; prebendary of Wells Cathedral (1779–1811). From 1778 to 1811 he was headmaster of the Bath Grammar School.

8. Marchesa Barbara Litta (1757–1834), daughter of Prince Alberico Barbiano di Belgioioso d'Este, was married to Antonio Litta (1748–1820), visconti Arese, elevated by Napoleon I to all ducal honors.

TO SAMUEL JOHNSON

15: July 1784.

Not only my good Wishes but my most fervent Prayers for your Health and Consolation shall for ever attend and follow my dear Mr. Johnson; Your last Letter is sweetly kind, and I thank you for it most sincerely. Have no Fears for me however; no *real* Fears. My Piozzi will need few Perswasions to settle in a Country where he has succeeded so well; but he longs to shew me to his Italian Friends, and he wishes to restore my Health by treating me with a Journey to many Places I have long wished to see:[1] his disinterested Conduct towards me in pecuniary Matters, His Delicacy in giving me up all past Promises when we were separated last Year by great Violence in Argylle Street,[2] are Pledges of his Affection and Honour: He is a religious Man, a sober Man, and a Thinking Man—he will not injure me, I am sure he will not, let nobody injure him in your good Opinion, which he is most solicitous to obtain and preserve, and the harsh Letter you wrote me at first grieved him to the very heart. Accept his Esteem my dear Sir, do; and his Promise to treat with long continued Respect and Tenderness the Friend whom you once honoured with your Regard and who will never cease to be / My dear Sir Your truly Affectionate and faithful Servant / <Signature erased>.[3]

The Lawyers delay of finishing our Settlements, & the necessity of twenty six days Residence, has kept us from being married till now. I hope your Health is mending.

Text: Chapman 3:184 (not in *Letters*). *Address:* Doctor Sam: Johnson / Bolt Court / Fleet Street / London. *Postmark:*[4] BATH 16 JY 1784.

1. An early reference to the Piozzis' Continental tour that was to begin 5 September and end with their return to London on 10 March 1787.
2. HLT's allusion to the crises with her daughters, FB, and Crutchley, among others, over her infatuation. Hysterical and unable to withstand their pressures, she agreed in the winter of 1783, while living in Argyll Street, to terminate the affair. GP left England to visit his parents and stifle further gossip.
3. Probably erased at some later date was the deceptive signature H: L: Piozzi. HLT had wished SJ to believe that the marriage was consummated so that he would no longer interfere.
4. HLT, in London on the 16th, had been there since the 12th. The letter may have been written earlier and left behind in Bath with orders that it be posted on the 16th. Or it may have been written in London and enclosed in another letter to friends in Bath—like Frances and George James—who did the actual posting. The obvious reason for this deception is that HLT did not wish SJ to know that she was in London and unmarried; above all else, she wished to avoid an encounter with him. See Clifford, pp. 228–29.

TO FANNY BURNEY

Saturday
[18 July 1784]

Indeed my dearest you can scarce imagine how *very* little I think about *what* the Guardians say; they none of them say any thing to me good or bad, except Dr. Johnson, who wrote me an affectionate Letter: Miss Thrale complains that they use *her* very roughly, and I should be sorry beyond endurance, but that I may be sure she may leave their Tyranny when she chuses.[1] Mr. Cator and I must have some Money settling——[2] The other Gentleman's Approbation of my Conduct is of little Consequence to my Happiness,[3] which depends wholly on the health and continued Attachment of my Husband.

He is however very far from well, I recover faster by far; and with regard to Reputation, mine can be no better protected than by his Honour; which has I believe no equal. The newspapers say not a Syllable about us, We wait for Mr. Greenland to finish our Parchments, and then shall be married in every requisite Form.

The dear Bath Folks long for us back again—Lord Dudley sends me a Thousand Compliments and *Love* as he calls it to the *Angel Gabriele*.

Lord Conyngham *was* Mr. Burt<on> when you and I were at Bath together, and we often met him at Mrs. Lambarts. I live *here* quite for the Purposes of Business, and see no Company of Course but my Piozzi and his Friends; who will I hope always be mine. Mr. Borghi is a Man of very extraordinary Accomplishments, very considerable Understanding, and very pleasing Conversation: his Wife is pretty, and modest, and gentle in her Manners. Young Bartolozzi[4] who lives with 'em is uncommonly agreeable, and I should be strangely fastidious indeed, if I did not take unaffected Delight in the Company of my new Associates.

We dined at Mr. Greenland's the other Day——why not? he gave me a gallant Dinner and a private Concert where Piozzi sung with the young Ladies, and all went sweetly and smoothly—or I thought so. The Storms are past I hope, but if more are gathering—let them spare his Head, whom I prefer so much to my own, and take or leave us *together,* at least. To those who have experienced like me the pangs of Separation, few things are difficult to endure, when assisted by mutual Support.

Let me always have your Kindness, and believe me ever / most tenderly yours / H: L: T.

Text: Peyraud Collection. *Address:* To / Miss Burney / at William Lockes' Esq: / Norbury Park / near Leatherhead / Surrey.

1. On 7 July HLT had commiserated with Q as a fellow victim, as one *"accustomed to Tyranny, of the Tyrannies practised on you, who have been ever unaccustom'd"* (*Queeney Letters,* p. 157). Q could be legally liberated only on her twenty-first birthday, 17 September 1785.
2. Upon the death of HT, Cator had assumed management of HLT's financial affairs and was to be a constant irritant.
3. That is, Crutchley.
4. Gaetano Stefano Bartolozzi (1757–1821), engraver and musician, son of Francesco.

TO HESTER MARIA THRALE

[London] Friday
July [23, 1784][1]

My sweet Girls are too charming, too tender, too kind for the—Ah! I won't say another Word;—somebody stops our Letters, I am *sure* of it; for Miss Nicholson says you have written—& God knows your hands have I never seen since Susan's Letter dated—Oh Dear! I can't find it just now, but it was above a Week ago. I have an infinite deal to say, if I thought I might write *freely,* but if the Guardians are to see my Stuff how can I divert you as I wish?[2] M^r^ H: Cotton knows his way to the Post Office perfectly too—to my Knowledge: so I am afraid on *that* side—I enclose this to Miss [Sarah Ann] Nicholson who will direct it to our amiable Miss Jane.

Tell me but that I may write *safely* and I will write fully, & largely, and as you would like—but receiving no Acc[ts] from any of you so long; (& I sent such *heaps of Stuff,* two Whalleian Letters in one Day,) that I wondered—Adieu! & God bless you, & depend on the Friendship & Fondness of Your own / H: L: T.

My last told a droll story of Miss Hudson—I shall know that you received the Letter, if you remember that Circumstance. Direct to Bath.

Text: Queeney Letters, p. 169. *Address: To Miss Thrale, at her House, / West Street, Brighthelmstone, Sussex.*

1. HLT misdated the letter, 25 July; Friday, which is probably correct, fell on the 23d.
2. HLT's fears were relieved by Q's letter of 27 July.

TO FANNY BURNEY

Bath
Sunday 25: July 1784.

Wish me Joy my dearest Miss Burney, and let the Time of Circumspection and alarm be over *now:* that in the Face of God and the whole Christian World, Catholick, and Protestant, my Piozzi and myself are at length happily I thank heaven, as well as irrevocably united.

When Mr. Morgan declared in St. James's Church today that those who *then* said nothing against our Marriage should *forever after* hold their peace, I felt my Heart warmed with the Consolation of having at last publicly declared a Choice made on the most virtuous and disinterested Principles on both Sides, as the Conduct of my Husband has evinced more than once during the whole of this long-delayed Transaction. Wish me Joy then generously and like a Friend, and be not more severe than our gracious Sovereign himself, who has been heard to speak very partially of a little Subject no ways deserving so high an honour. Mr. James gave me away; you know how I loved him before, and today's Business makes him truly dear to us both. Adieu charming Burney! and be not sorry to see your Letter signed by the beloved and long desired Name of / Your Affectionate / H: L: Piozzi.

Text: Berg Collection, no. 1784, folder 4.

TO HESTER MARIA THRALE

Bath, Sunday Morning,
25 July, 1784

You are very generous my lovely Hester in saying it does not teize but comfort you to hear of my Happiness: now then let me tell you that this morning it was

Mrs Piozzi ~~Thrale~~ to Miss F. Burney ~~No~~ (96) Bath – Sunday 25: July 1784.

Wish me Joy my dearest Miss Burney, and let the Time of Circumspection and alarm be over now: that in the Face of God and the whole Christian World, Catholick, and Protestant, my Piozzi and myself are at length happily I thank heaven, as well as irrevocably united.

When Mr Morgan declared in St James's Church today that those who then s:d nothing against our Marriage should hereafter hold their peace, I felt my Heart warm'd with the Consolation of having at last publicly declared a Choice made on the most virtuous and disinterested Principles on both Sides, as the Conduct of my Husband has evinced more than once during the whole of this long:delay'd Transaction. Wish me Joy then generously and like a Friend, & be not more severe than our gracious Sovereign himself, who has been heard to speak very partially of a little Subject no ways deserving so high an honour.] [Mr James gave me away, you know how I loved him before, and today's Business makes him truly dear to us both. Adieu

has written very

H: L: Piozzi.

"Wish me Joy my dearest Miss Burney. . . ." Hester Lynch Piozzi's letter, Bath, 25 July 1784. *(Reproduced from the Henry W. and Albert A. Berg Collection by permission of the New York Public Library: Astor, Lenox and Tilden Foundations.)*

compleated, and that in the face of God and the whole Christian World *Catholick* and *Protestant* I was two hours ago irrevocably united to the Man of my Heart—chosen from amongst all his Sex to love honour and obey with chearfulness & Delight—Oh, with how much Delight! If I loved him before we lived so continually together, how certainly have his Manners and Conduct towards me since his return rivetted my Regard! The Catholick Gentleman who married us took to me most kindly,[1] & we talked Controversy together much to his approbation & my Credit—I shall do very well among my new Associates, & have brought dear Madame Borghi to shew her Bath & give her some of the Water for her Bile. Her Husband gave her leave kindly enough, & she is a comfortable Creature—pretty, and sick, and gentle spirited as can be. My dear Piozzi trembled so violently during the Ceremony, that I was half sorry for him; When however we were pronounced *one* in the name of the Holy Trinity & declared *inseparable* by mortal Man, he recovered *his* Spirits to a Degree of Transport; & is now gone to the Bell-Tree House to thank God in his own Way: I dare not go to Church for fear of being stared at, but in every Room when I have been on my Knees *for* this Felicity, will I bless God for giving it to my innocent & fervent Prayers.

Well! it was Time to recover, for our Physician is dead—and *so is my Enmity.* Like Zanga I scorn to prey on Carcasses:[2] poor Dr Dobson dyed this morning while I was wedded to an honest Man whom he had the Impudence to say was come home so ill, and nerve-shaken by anxiety, that he *would not answer Mrs Thrale's Purpose* whose Health required a *Man.* Beastly & unjust Dr Dobson! all the People here say he died of an evil conscience—God forgive the Wretch! he is gone to answer for all; Mrs Vanbrugh reproved him most sharply for speaking so of me, whom She said was an honour to her sex. Oh but the King! King George the third told his Librarian[3] that Mrs. Thrale had made an *odd* Choice, but he doubted not it was a *wise* one, as She was one of the *best* as well as one of the most accomplish'd Women in England; & that He should be sorry Mr Piozzi carried her out of his Dominions, tho' it was natural he should be proud of his Prize—he would not deserve her else—Oh yes, & the King said how I had written a Letter to Dr Johnson in vindication of the Step I had taken, which made Dr Johnson cry—that's true enough too:—and so Mr James says *'I Knocked him down with a Feather,'* & some say I drew *Iron Tears down Pluto's Cheeks,*[4] and some say *even Butchers wept* &c.[5] I always *thought* I could manage with Charles well enough, but dear Fanny Burney wonders he softened so soon[6]—you shall see the whole Correspondence some Time. I'll write to Susan & Sophy & Miss Nicholson tomorrow—mean Time thank her for her Purse & tell her I have not yet Leisure to love her as I ought. Tomorrow I sign my Will with all due Form—[7] Oh what a disinterested! what a noble Heart has the Man to whom I was this day united. Adieu! & love us all you can.

Text: Queeney Letters, pp. 170–71. *Address: To Miss Thrale, at her House, / West Street, Brighthelmstone, Sussex.*

1. Richard Smith (1725–1808), a secular priest, had been born near London of Catholic parents. He entered the English College at Lisbon on 2 April 1738. In September 1741 he

was sent to Rome where he matriculated at the English College. He was not confirmed until 12 January 1743, receiving his first tonsure in 1747. He was ordained in Rome on 1 February 1750 and left for England on 13 April. See Godfrey Anstruther, *The Seminary Priests. A Dictionary of the Secular Clergy of England and Wales, 1558–1850* (Ware: Saint Edmund's College; Durham: Upshaw College, [1969–]); *Liber Ruber Venerabilis Collegii Anglorum de Urbe,* ed. Wilfrid Kelly, with Olivia Littledale, Silvia Roxburgh, and Irene Vaughan (London: Privately printed for the Catholic Record Society by John Whitehead and Son, 1943), pp. 197–98.

2. Zanga in Edward Young's *The Revenge* (1721) is a captive Moor. Vengefully and triumphantly, even as he is about to be led to his execution, he declaims (end of act 5):

> So is my Enmity.
> I war not with the Dust: the Great, the Proud,
> The Conqueror of *Africk* was my Foe.
> A Lyon preys not upon Carcasses. . . .

3. Sir Frederick Augusta Barnard (1743–1830), F.R.S., F.S.A., presumed to be the natural son of Frederick Louis (1707–51), Prince of Wales.

4. From Milton, *Il Penseroso,* line 107.

5. John Gay, *Beggar's Opera* 1.1. air 12; see also *Thraliana* 1:46.

6. See CB's letter of congratulation to HLP, dated 30 July. As early as 23 May, he had known about the impending marriage and "behaved with the utmost propriety" (*Thraliana* 1:594).

7. HLP's will written in 1784 is missing. Others, which are accessible, are dated 4 September 1793 (Princeton University Library), 19 April 1813 (Ry. Ch. 1258), 19 April 1814 (Pierpont Morgan Library, MA 322), 29 March 1816 (Ry. Ch. 1259).

ELIZABETH MONTAGU[1] TO ELIZABETH HANDCOCK VESEY

[25] July 1784

My dear Friend[2]

Mrs. Thrales marriage has taken such horrible possession of my mind I cannot advert to any other subject. I am sorry and feel the worst kind of sorrow that which is blinded with shame. Sorrow lies in state on the Tomb of the Dead, in the regions of melancholly, it preserves a certain dignity and fears not to meet the eye which casts a look of pity on it, but when one <laments> and weeps over the disgrace of a Friend bitter are the sensations and as the cause of ones grief is an object of contempt and scorn one cannot disburthen the heart by communicating its sufferings but shuts it up with all its poisonous and baleful qualities. I am myself convinced that the poor Woman is mad and indeed have long suspected her mind was disordered. She was the best Mother, the best Wife, the best friend, the most amiable member of Society. She gave the most prudent attentions to her Husbands business during his long state of imbecility and after his death, till she had an opportunity of disposing well of the great Brewery.[3] I bring in my verdict lunacy in this affair. I am heartily grieved for Miss Burney,[4] and Doctor Johnson,[5] female delicacy, and male wisdom, will be much shocked, and they have both a very sincere attachment to their friends, and a delicate sense of honour. I respected Mrs. Thrale, and was proud of the honour she did to the human and female character in fulfilling all the domestick duties and cultivating her mind with whatever might adorn it, I would give much to make every one think of her as mad, the best and wisest are liable to lunacy. If she is not considered in that light she must <throw> a disgrace of her sex. My spirits are so sunk by all this I must have recourse to a noble subject to raise them. I set before my imagination our Queen coming into the drawing room attended by Lady Harcourt,[6] Thank me my dear Friend for offering to your contemplation what will reinstate your ideas of female purity dignity and excellence: and drive away the Marmiton Cupids,[7] the base plebean loves, which wait on some soft hearted Dames to the great debasement of their character and the honour of the Sex. . . . I am ever most affectionately / Yours / E. M.[8]

Text: Huntington Library. Montagu MSS 3583.

1. Elizabeth Montagu's initial impression of HLT is summed up in a letter to James Beattie on 12 April 1776: "Her uncommon endowments and love of literature expose her to the illiberal jests of the ignorant and idle, but her life is rational, usefull, decent" (Clifford, p. 151). But by 5 November 1784, the *Morning Herald* had been able to hoard sufficient gossip to report: "Mrs. Montague's select literary *quartetto,* which she termed the *Blue Stocking Club,* from their wearing hose of that color on their first day of meeting, is now totally annihilated by the strange *amorous* propensities of Mesdames *Macaulay* and *Thrale,* and the chagrin which the unlooked for frailty of the latter has invincibly riveted on the mind of Dr. Johnson!" See also HLT to FB, 30 June, n. 9; Hyde, p. 114; *Thraliana* 1:495. For Catharine Macaulay (1731–91), see *Boswell's Johnson* 1:447–48, 3:46.

2. Elizabeth (Handcock) Vesey, née Vesey (ca. 1715–91), was also a leading Bluestocking. Her second husband, Agmondesham Vesey (1718–85), was M.P. for Harristown (county Kildare) and Kinsale (county Cork); accountant-general of Ireland. Associated with the Johnson circle, he belonged to The Club.

3. Upon the suggestion of Charles Scrase (1709–92), her legal adviser, and with SJ's agreement, HLT had sold the brewery for £135,000 to be paid to her over four years. The purchasers were John Perkins, his brother-in-law Sylvanus Bevan, and two rich Quakers, David Barclay and his nephew Robert Barclay (the "principal negotiant"). The four men had equal shares, HLT lending money to Perkins for his contribution. On 31 May 1781, less than two months after HT's death, the articles of sale for the brewery were signed. For the final details of this transaction, see John Field to HLP, 28 December 1791, n. 2.

For Scrase, see HLP to Q, 25 February 1785 (*Queeney Letters,* p. 193) and 4 June 1785; for Perkins and the Barclays, John Field to HLP, 28 December 1791, nn. 2 and 3; for Bevan, *Thraliana* 1:499 n. 2; Clifford, p. 203 n. 1. See also Hyde, passim.

4. For FB's dismay, see her "French Exercise Book III" (Berg), *Journals and Letters* 7:537–38:

"Mais tout cela me revennoit à cette heure dans l'esprit,—et tout d'un coup mille choses et mille que je n'avois pas *pesé* dans le tems se presentoient a *mes souvenirs.* Ce seroit sans fin de vous les reciter, mais l'un venoit si vîte à l'aide de l'autre, que la verité sembloit me percer les yeux comme si c'étoit par un *eclaire.* C'est donc comme cela! m'en ai'je? C'est . . . . . Piozzi!!!—!—Je vous fais grace de mes commentaires, de mes chagrins, je puis dire de ma honte—car Je l'avois aimée et honorée à un point d'avoir cru impossible *une pareille oublie, une pareille sacrifice fait à toutes* ses devoirs *pour* l'indulgence d'une passion si peu respectable, si étrange, si extraordinaire! . . . Enfin, c'étoit un tems bien triste pour moi, de toutes manières. . . . mais, bientot après, elle *avouat* le tout à Mlle. Thrale: qui egalement froide et haute *de nature la reçu* avec une espèce de sangfroid *etonnante.*"

5. The marriage was a continuing torment to SJ. As late as November he told FB: "I drive [HLP] quite from my mind. If I meet with one of her letters, I burn it instantly. I have burnt all I can find. I never speak of her, and I desire never to hear of her more. I

drive her, as I said, wholly from my mind" (*Diary and Letters* 2:274); cf. Chapman, *Notes and Queries* 185 (1943):133–34.

6. Elizabeth Venables-Vernon (1746–1826) in 1765 married her cousin George Simon Harcourt (1736–1809), second earl Harcourt (1777). Countess Harcourt was a close friend of Queen Charlotte, her confidante, and a lady-in-waiting.

7. Kitchen scullions.

8. This was one of the earliest of Mrs. Montagu's letters to various friends on HLT's marriage, and the answers were equally intemperate.

Mrs. Vesey, for example, in an undated letter (Huntington, MO 6351), wrote: ". . . you must accept Mrs. Thrales Marriage with Piety. Her daughter has told Her She could never acknowledge such a Father and She and her three Sisters have taken refuge with their guardian at Brighthelmstone. She has cut down all the Trees upon the Estate in Wales, would have carried her Daughters abroad if the Trustees had consented. . . . The Bridegroom very black, low, and mean. . . . She has wrote to Doctor Johnson upon this occasion and desired he would not censure what She has done. He burst into Tears. I wish we could read His answer."

Sarah Scott (née Robinson, 1723–95) wrote to Mrs. Vesey on 25 July (Huntington, MO 5411): "This is a year for imprudent marriages. I gave you an erroneous account of Mrs. Thrale. Piozzi it seems was in holy orders. She gave him 2,000 *l*. a year ago with which he went abroad, it is supposed to purchase a Dispensation, and is but lately returned. . . . As soon as the friends of the family learnt her fixed purpose they informed her the children must not remain with her and fetched them for Brighthelmstone, where they were under the care of a person little older than Miss Thrale."

From Mrs. Scott to Mrs. Montagu, 23 August (Huntington, MO 5414): ". . . Dr. Johnson says he did not think there had been so abandoned a Woman in the World."

The ladies continued their self-righteous vitriol (Huntington, MO 5415, 5 September [1784]), Mrs. Montagu sharing hers with Leonard Smelt (ca. 1719–1800) and his wife Jane, née Campbell (d. 1790) (Huntington, MO 5040, 20 December 1784): "The news will inform you that Living Poets need not fear Dr. Johnson should wish their memoirs after they are no longer able to refute calumny, I hear he dyed with great piety and resignation; and indeed he had many virtues; and perhaps ill health and nervous circumstances gave him a peevish censorious turn. I was afraid Mrs Thrales imprudent marriage shortened his life. Her letters to her Friends from abroad were full of her felicity, it is said accounts are now come that she is confined in a Convent at Milan. Her Husband says she is insane, he is the only Person in the World who can say it with ill grace."

ELIZABETH MONTAGU TO ELIZABETH CARTER[1]

July 25 [1784]

. . . Mrs. Thrale is undoubtedly married to Signor Piozzi,[2] at which I am still more grieved than astonished. She has very uncommon parts, but certainly never appeared a Person of sound understanding. Who ever possesses that Blessing never is guilty of absurd conduct or doing any thing which the World calls strange. . . . Miss Burney and Dr. Johnson have been much afflicted on account of Mrs. Thrales indiscretion, and indeed I pity them both, but what misery may in time await the poor Woman herself one cannot guess. Piozzi has bought an estate in Italy with her money. There she will probably weep out the rest of her days for bitter must be her reflections when her passions subside and give place to reason. . . . / Yours / E. Montagu.

Text: Huntington Library. Montagu MSS 3572.

1. Elizabeth Carter (1717–1806), Greek scholar and poet, was a friend of SJ, the Bluestockings, and HLT, who once playfully mocked her store of "useful knowledge" (*Thraliana* 1:331).

2. Mrs. Montagu's letter was precipitated by one from Elizabeth Carter, dated from Deal, 19 July:

"From an authority which seems too good, I am informed that Mrs. Thrale is by this time Signora Piozzi, and that her daughters have chosen another guardian. Is it true? I am sorry if it is, but not surprized; and she always seemed to be a genius of that eccentric kind, which is mighty apt to be accompanied by 'a plentiful lack' of common sense." See *Letters from Mrs. Elizabeth Carter to Mrs. Montagu, between the Years 1755 and 1800*, ed. the Reverend Montagu Pennington, 3 vols. in 1 (London: F. C. and J. Rivington, 1817), 3:215, 221.

FANNY BURNEY AND SUSANNA PHILLIPS TO DR. CHARLES BURNEY

Norbury Park
26: July, 1784

As to poor Mrs. Thrale—she only keeps retired till she finds who will seek her; she has no intention at all of *concealment*, but merely of present obscurity. There have been difficulties about the ecclesiastical Court that have delayed the marriage, and I do not believe it to be yet over.[1] The moment the Ceremony has been performed in the Romish Chapel in Town, they are to go to Bath, and be remarried at her Parish Church. This she has written to me.[2] Mr. Selwyn need be under no apprehensions, for she is arranging her affairs for settling them all, honourably and honestly, before she changes her name.[3] She was at No. 30, Berner's Street, Oxford Road, when she wrote; but pray give the Direction to no one; as she would not be interrupted in her retreat, unless by *You*—which would be a *joyful* interruption, I know; though she does not mention it; and means to leave every body to themselves.—Poor unhappy Mrs. Thrale! What a delusion she has to awake from!—alas!— . . . / adieu most dear Sir / Your F. B. and S. E. P.—

Text: Barrett, Eg. 2690.19. (The ellipsis indicates an omitted conclusion that refers briefly to the kindness of Mrs. Walsingham, a visit to Mrs. Garrick, and the Burneys's friendship with the Lockes.)
Address: Dr. Burney / St. Martin's Street / Leicester Fields / London.
Postmark: 26 JY.

1. FB had not yet received HLP's letter of 25 July.

2. See HLT to FB, 12 July.

3. Charles Selwin, or Selwyn (1715–94), retired banker of Down Hall, Essex. Apparently he was the "gentleman who had acquired a fortune of four thousand a year in trade, but was absolutely miserable, because he could not talk in company." Selwin had been a frequent visitor at Streatham and a possible HLT suitor. FB in 1779 was attracted to him,

not "for brilliancy, talents, wit, person, nor youth, since he is possessed of none of these; but the fact is, he appears to me uncommonly good, full of humanity, generosity, delicacy, and benevolence." See *Diary and Letters* 1:240, 5:254; *Boswell's Johnson* 4:83; *Thraliana* 1:530 n. 5, 535.

HLP trusted Selwin as a friend. According to FB, however, who saw him in 1792, "He still visits, occasionally, at Streatham—but he says the place—the inhabitants, the visitors, the way of life, are all so totally changed, it would make me most melancholy again to tread those boards" (*Journals and Letters* 1:155).

HESTER MARIA THRALE TO HESTER LYNCH PIOZZI

Brighton
27: July 1784.

I don't at all wonder dearest Madam at your being shy of writing, when you have an Idea, either of the Letters being lost—or of my reading them to the guardians, nothing can so effectually destroy Confidence, for though one seldom writes about Matters of great Importance yet to have it all canvassed over by those who are *sure* to judge unfavourably, is so very offensive, that a Correspondence upon such Terms must I am sure give you more Pain than Pleasure.[1]

No one has however I assure you, ever read your Letters but myself—I sometimes read Passages of them to the Girls before Miss Nicolson—but to that you have I dare say no Objection.

All your Letters have come perfectly safe, and nothing but my Folly would have given you any Reason to suspect the contrary. You have by this Time got all our Letters I suppose, I sent a great Packet in a Frank, with Miss Nicolson's Purse—May I say that I wish you would just write her a Line or two? It would delight her much, and she is more kind to us than I had the smallest Reason to expect. When your last Letter came, I lamented for want of Franks, and she, immediately it seems wrote to her Sister and got me some to you.[2] Only think how polite! But I hear that after the first of August the Priviledge of Franking ceases[3]—so we shall write away whilst it lasts. May I trouble you [to] send the enclosed to poor Hudson[4] and to believe me / your ever-affectionate / and dutiful Servant / H: M: Thrale.

Text: Ry. 553.1.

1. This is Q's response to her mother's letter [23 July].
2. Sarah Nicolson induced her employer Charles François Dumergue to secure the franks from one of his powerful clients.
3. Although there was pending legislation to do away with a much-abused privilege, franks were not abolished in 1784. Their value was, however, curtailed by the mandate that they be dated by the M.P. who supplied them and that they be used on that date alone. See *Encyclopaedia Britannica*, 3d ed. (1797), s. v. "Franked letters."
4. According to HLP (4 March 1786), the Bath seamstress "is out of all Hope, while her Madness is not enough to call help about her, and her Folly sufficient to drive every Friend away! You are exceedingly good not to forsake her" (HLP to Q, in *Queeney Letters*, p. 220). The enclosure was probably bank notes or a draft.

1

3382
3

I don't at all wonder dearest
Madam at your being shy of writing, when
you have an Idea, either of the Letters
being lost– or of my reading them to the
Guardians, nothing can so effectually destroy Confidence, for though one seldom
writes about Matters of great Importance
yet to have it all canvassed over by
those who are *sure* to judge unfavoura-
-bly, is so very offensive, that a Corres-
-pondence upon such Terms must I
am sure give you more Pain than Pleasure.
No one has however I assure you
ever read your Letters but myself– I
sometimes read Passages of them to the

"I don't at all wonder dearest Madam of your being shy of writing. . . ." Queeney Thrale's letter to Hester Lynch Piozzi, Brighton, 27 July 1784. *(Reproduced by permission of the John Rylands University Library of Manchester [Ry. 553.1])*

DR. CHARLES BURNEY TO HESTER LYNCH PIOZZI

Friday Night
30: July 1784.

Dear Madam

If my wishes for your felicity should seem to arrive late, I hope you will not imagine that I was slow in forming them; but ascribe my silence to the true cause: my not being certain that the Event had taken place. For till this evening that I saw it announced, seemingly with authority, in my own paper, the Morning Chronicle,[1] I had nothing but slight and uncertain rumour to depend on. Fanny is still at Mr. Lock's, and I have been shut up in the *Spidery* scribling in the utmost hurry an account of the late Commemoration of Handel,[2] for immediate publication, so that I gain but little information from mixing with the world, and still less from news-papers, into which I have hardly time to look once in a week. This it seems necessary to say in apology to you, dear Madam, and my friend, Mr. Piozzi, to whom I most heartily wish every species of happiness which this world can allow.

I fear Mr. P. is displeased with me for not writing to him at Milan in answer to the Letter with which he favoured me from that City early last Winter;[3] but you can explain to him my situation, and the eternal hurry of my Life; which so far from affording me sufficient time for my friends and for social happiness, scarcely allows me leisure to support existence by the necessary aliments of sleep and food. I was mortified to hear of his arrival in England, from any one but himself. Make my Peace with him, dear Madam, I entreat you, and prevail with him to partake of the assurance of my esteem and regard jointly with yourself.

I had not time to thank you for your last Letter, or the agreable Visit it procured me from Mr. Lysons, who is a charming young Man. I had the honour of sending to you, by him, a *proof print* from Bartolozzi's engraving of me from your picture by Sir Joshua.[4] It will not be published or presented to any one else till my last volume comes out; an event not yet within my ken.[5] Bartolozzi has the picture still; but is to return it to Sir Joshua and your orders for its future disposal will be instantly and implicitly obeyed.

I beg you will present my best Compliments of congratulation to Mr. Piozzi, and ever regard me as your most obliged and affectionate Servant / Charles Burney.

Text: Ry. 545.12.

1. "On Sunday last, and not before, was married at St. James's-church, Bath, Gabriel Piozzi, Esq.; of that parish, to Mrs. Thrale, widow of Henry Thrale, Esq.; of St. Saviour, Southwark" (*Morning Chronicle*, 30 July).

2. CB's contribution to the choral celebration was *An Account of the Musical Performances in Westminster-Abbey, and the Pantheon, May 26th, 27th, 29th; and June the 3d, and 5th, 1784. In Commemoration of Handel* (London: Printed for the Benefit of the Musical Fund, and sold by T. Payne and Son and G. Robinson, 1785). See Lonsdale, pp. 283–84, 500.

3. The letter is missing.

4. See HLT to Q, 14 July. The Reynolds portrait of CB had been commissioned by HT for the Streatham library. It filled the "last chasm in the chain of Streatham worthies." HLT had met Bartolozzi in London on 13 July. See *Thraliana* 2:611 n. 1; Hyde, p. 180; *Queeney Letters*, p. 161; Hayward 2:170–80.

5. At the time CB accepted the commission to write the *Account* of the Handel commemoration, he had been working on *A General History of Music*. In the face of numerous interruptions, he had published vol. 1 in 1776 and vol. 2 in 1782. The "last volume" was to become 3 and 4 in the spring of 1789 (Lonsdale, pp. 316–41).

TO DR. CHARLES BURNEY

Bath
Monday 2: August [1784][1]

The Compliments of Congratulation which we have received from many friends—from most indeed; have been less dear to both of us than the kind Letter which came this Moment to my hands from dear Dr. Burney. I long however for the good Wishes <of your> amiable Daughter more than I can express; my own Daughters write very kindly, and the Inhabitants of this Place which I shall love as long as I live——stifle us with tenderness and Civility. Business however will call us from hence in a few days when I shall at least have to make me amends—The pleasure of saying with how much Sincerity I am ever Dear Dr. Burney's / most Affectionate and faithful Servant / H: L: Piozzi.

Volti subito

Le rendo mille grazie delle sue cortesi attenzioni, e <per essere> certo della stima, ed amicizia, che ho sempre avuto per Lei, e spero che in avvenire ancore saranno sempre le stesse. Io sono contento della mia scielta, e ringrazio ogni momento Iddio Supremo d'avermi dato una compagna sì amabile, forse difficile a poterne ritrovare un'altra simile. Oggi otto sarò di ritorno in Londra, e spero d'avere il piacere di riverirla, ed assicurarla della mia vera e sincera amicizia, che ho avuto per Lei e che avrò sempre in avvenire; e sono con pienna stima, e rispetto / di Lei / Suo Umilissimo . . . Servitore / Gabriele Piozzi.

Text: Yale University Library. With a note by GP.

1. The Piozzis had come to Bath by the 24th or 25th of July, spending a little more than two weeks there. They returned to London on 11 August in order to prepare for their extended European honeymoon. They conferred with Cator and their bankers. In addition GP "bespoke a magnificent carriage capable of containing every possible accommodation [including a small harpsichord], and begged me to take tea enough and books enough." But he allowed only an English Bible. "[R]eflect," he urged, "that you are not travelling as you ought to be, like a Protestant lady of quality, but as the wife of a native, an acknowledged Papist, and one determined to remain so" (Hayward 2:63).

TO FANNY BURNEY[1]

Bath
Fryday 6: August 1784.

Dear Miss Burney
I not only thought you unkind, but I think so still:[2] True Tenderness does not express herself ambiguously: If I have, as you say, *deserved* my Husband's Affection, I will take Care not to rely on *past Merits,* as many Women are apt to do; but will make myself a pleasing Companion if possible, and so sincere a Friend that every Action of my Life shall convince him that my Heart holds no Fellowship with those who refuse him the Esteem due to his Character and Conduct.

I am sorry for Mrs. Phillips's bad State of Health, She is in the right to try Continental Air:[3]—Your kind Father has written very sweetly to his ever Affectionate / H: L: Piozzi.

Text: Berg Collection, no. 1784, folder 4. *Address:* Miss Burney at Norbury Park / near Leatherhead / Surrey. *Postmark:* BATH; AU 7.

1. HLP's disillusionment with FB grew slowly and did not reach a conclusion until after 25 July. By August she was labeled with some justice as one of the "Mischief-makers," having acted as a double agent who supported Q's opposition to the wedding and HLT's desire for GP. By 13 August, all friendship between the two was over, FB now fixed in the older woman's mind as the "aimable traitresse" who had betrayed their relationship and alienated her daughters. Yet despite resentment over such "false & cruel" behavior, HLP on 3 September was to regret that she had "to leave London without seeing Miss Burney." See *Thraliana* 2:612; Hemlow, pp. 171–82; Clifford, pp. 213, 216–17, 222–25; *Journals and Letters* 7:521.

2. FB's letter, which triggered HLP's present angry response, is missing. Its contents, however, are suggested by the former's "French Exercise Book III," *Journals and Letters* 7:543:

"Le Jour même de ce Marriage à jamais étonnant Elle m'ecrivit, pour me faire part de son bonheur, et pour me demander mes felicitations. Cela *m'étoit* trop. Je n'ai vu *ce* fin de tant de surpris, de chagrins, d'efforts inutiles, qu'avec la douleur la plus vive, *et affecter* de la joie m'auroit été aussi impossible que *de la* sentir. Je répondis tristement à sa demande, et quoique toujours avec affection et tendresse, car je *l'aimai* de tout mon coeur, je n'avois pas la force, ou plutôt l'hipocrisie, de lui faire des felicitations quelconques."

3. Susanna Phillips and her husband had decided she should go to Boulogne for a change of air, a plan that agitated FB: "But must it be to the Continent?—the division by sea—how could I cross it were you ill? . . . You certainly have been well in various parts of England: Ipswich, Twickenham, Norbury,—all shew the nation is not against you, only the clay soil" (*Diary and Letters* 2:265).

FANNY BURNEY TO HESTER LYNCH PIOZZI

Norbury Park,
August 10, 1784

When my wondering eyes first looked over the letter I received last night,[1] my mind instantly dictated a high-spirited vindication of the consistency, integrity, and faithfulness of the friendship thus abruptly reproached and cast away. But a sleepless night gave me leisure to recollect that you were ever as generous as precipitate, and that your own heart would do justice to mine, in the cooler judgment of future reflection. Committing myself, therefore, to that period, I determined simply to assure you, that if my last letter hurt either you or Mr. Piozzi, I am no less sorry than surprised; and that if it offended you, I sincerely beg your pardon.

Not to that time, however, can I wait to acknowledge the pain an accusation so unexpected has caused me, nor the heartfelt satisfaction with which I shall receive, when you are able to write it, a softer renewal of regard.[2]

May heaven direct and bless you! / F. B.

Text: Diary and Letters of Madame d'Arblay 2:265–66.

1. This was HLP's letter of 6 August, which FB read as "a letter of *reproach* for my want of cordiality! ! !" FB described her response as "a Letter of ice" in which "I flung myself upon her memory for my vindication, but I desired to close our correspondence by those letters of exquisite kindness which had preceded all but the last: or to resume it upon the same terms." After HLP's "very friendly answer" of 13 August, FB replied "in kind . . . but I have never heard from her since!—never" (to Q, May 1813, in *Queeney Letters*, p. 116). See also *Journals and Letters* 7:544–45.
2. FB interpreted the perfunctory note of 13 August as being more conciliatory than it was. As far as HLP was concerned, her intimacy with FB was ended. Recalling the correspondence as late as 14 May 1813, she admitted to JSPS: "When Connections are once broken, 'tis a foolish Thing to splice and mend; They never can . . . unite again as before" (Ry. 587.184).

TO FANNY BURNEY

Welbeck Street, No. 33 Cavendish Square
Friday, August 13, 1784

Give yourself no serious concern, sweetest Burney. All is well, and I am too happy myself, to make a friend otherwise; quiet your kind heart immediately, and love my husband if you love his and your / H. L. Piozzi

Text: Diary and Letters of Madame d'Arblay 2:266.

TO HESTER MARIA THRALE

Wellbeck Street
Tuesday 17: Aug. [1784]

I feel infinitely obliged by my charming Tit's present and Letter which Miss Nicholson[1] brought me yesterday Evening with a hundred kisses & kind Words. She really seems to have a true & tender Regard for *you* whose *generous* Behaviour & polite Treatment She spoke of as it deserv'd; I adore her for it, and shall ever love those best who behave to my dearest Queeney with most respect.

Miss Burney seems to have managed with less adroitness on this Occasion than one expected:[2] She has been unmeaningly particular in never writing or naming Mr Piozzi's Name for these 18 Months, & at last with as little Necessity, has obliged herself to spell it *for the first Time* in the Act of *begging his Pardon.* bad Management sure!

I have got a pretty little House here for three Guineas a Week,[3] & a Man who keeps us in a continual Laugh: poor John may go home to his *Wife of Bath* who it seems has been arrested in his Absence,[4] he cannot regret being turned off more than does dear Miss Nicholson.

I am very unhappy my Love about the loss of our Letters, Mr Cator will be obliging enough to take Care of this: but what on Earth became of a large Packet? Bills, Rec^ts^ and a long Series of Money: Matters which I sent in a Cover directed and freed by Lord Dudley[5] from Bath to Brighthelmstone: four Franks likewise directed to me I enclosed in another of his Covers—do tell if ever they came to hand—I am quite uneasy about them.—

Well! I am absolutely quite ashamed to write the Word *uneasy,* so happy is my Heart, & so comfortable is my Life: God give me Grace to remember *him* in a State of Ease who did not forget *me* when in a State of Affliction. Had it not been for Miss Burney's Interposition with you, I might it seems have been happy long ago: but I forgive her from my Soul: let us however not encourage Mischief-makers now we are parted, for there are enough who will take up the employment. As for me, the People who do not respect my Husband and my Daughters according to their *Merit,* or at least according to their *Character,* shall never be treated as Friends or even Companions by me, whose Duty as a Wife is to keep up the Dignity of him who is dearer to me than myself, and whose Affection as a Mother will not suffer me to hear those spoken slightly of, to whose Accomplishments I have myself contributed.

God bless you in every House you inhabit, my sweet Hester, & God bless that House for your Sake;[6] however inimical it may be to / Your / H: L: Piozzi.

I am grown so fat & look so much better Miss Nicholson scarce knew me—yet I am not recovered—this last nervous Fit has been worse than you would believe: it fell on the Muscles of the Bladder, and plagued me cruelly, but 'tis over now, and the Terror is gone away too.

Peggy Rice[7] has been here, for her ten Guineas I guess, but I referred her to you for whom I have paid various Sums to the Amount of 37£ odd Shillings I think, If you have not got the Acc[t] I must make it out anew—pray where shall I send your Clothes? they are all here, & safe.

I wrote Miss Nicholson as long a Letter as this, & She never got it: Sophy too has missed one of my Scrawls—I shall grow like Hudson anon, and fancy we are surrounded with Enemies.

Write me word that at least *this* comes safe, & write quickly *do*. The Straw Tea-Chest is so much more beautiful than anything I can make, that it only makes me ashamed—it is however the happiest accompanyment to a Dejeuné of *Blue* Imitation of Antique at Wedgwood's;[8] so that one would think you knew it was the *very thing* we wanted.

I have received the kindest & most tender Congratulations this moment from poor Miss Owen;[9] See how *early* Friendships last! She & Stricky were my first Intimates—may it be just so with you & dear Miss Nicholson.

Text: Queeney Letters, pp. 178–80. *Address: Miss Thrale, at John Cator's Esq[r]/ Beckenham place, Kent.*

1. See HLT to FB, 2 June, n. 2; and to Q [15 July], n. 3.
2. While overtly accusing FB of unscrupulous conduct, HLP spares Q, whose good will she wanted.
3. Welbeck Street, Cavendish Square. The Piozzis lived at No. 33 after the marriage and before the honeymoon journey abroad.
4. The Piozzi servants, John and Mary Johnson. In the *French Journals* (12 September), HLP alludes to a letter from George James "telling me of many Treacheries [the debts, doubtless] acted by the Maid I have so long confided in, and at last brought away from England with me, mistaking her for a treasure" (p. 198).
5. Lord Dudley, no longer M.P., probably procured the franks from his half-brother William Ward (1750–1823), M.P. for Worcester (1780–88), who was to become third viscount Dudley and Ward and eighth baron Ward (1788).
6. Q was now living with the Cators in Beckenham, Kent.
7. Margaret Rice, HLT's maid, had a dream in 1781 that Q would marry Crutchley (*Thraliana* 1:515).
8. Josiah Wedgwood (1730–95), master potter of Staffordshire, created ceramic ware notable for both artistry and chic. He built a village, Etruria, for his kilns and for himself a mansion, Etruria Hall. Much of the Wedgwood attraction derives from its imaginative imitations of Greek art, e.g., of Etruscan vases. See *Queeney Letters*, pp. 180, 183; *Thraliana* 2:714, 908 n. 3.
9. Margaret Owen (1743–1816), HLP's distant relative from Shrewsbury and Montgomeryshire, was CMT's godmother. At one time (7 January 1777) HLT speculated, "Miss Owen is very likely to be my Successor" as the second Mrs. Thrale (Hyde, p. 175). This speculation did not affect their friendship.

TO HESTER MARIA THRALE

[Paris] Tuesday
14: Sept[r] 1784

Well Dearest Tit! here am I at Paris, thinking how to fulfill my Promise from Montreuil,[1]—& make you up an entertaining Letter: what shall I tell you of this

Town or the Road to it that you do not already know? Shall I tell you how all the Gentlemen of these Provinces have got our Rage for planting long Walks of Lombardy Poplars?—and how their Chateaux look like Macbeth's Castle at Dunsinane when the Soldiers bring each a Bough to make good the Prophecy of Birnam Forest?[2] Shall I tell you of a comical French Maid who attended us at one of the wretched Inns we passed through, when complaining of our Courier's insolence 'Il Parle sur le haut Ton Mademoiselle' (says we) 'mais il a le Coeur bon.' 'Ouy-da Monsieur' (replied the Damsel) 'mais c'est le Ton qui fait le Chanson.'[3] We live à L'Hotel Luxembourg just by where we lived before:[4] have a sweet Apartment & elegant Accommodations. Mr Piozzi is gone out to visit Goldoni the Author of the Comedies we used to read together, I shall be glad to see Goldoni.[5] Chantilly Palace[6] looked more lovely than ever, the Waterfalls seemed *so* comfortable, & the Carp *so* tame: when I saw the Butterflies Hector & Achilles in the Prince's Cabinet,[7] I thought of young Lysons. Paris will afford me but little that is new to *you* except that they are grown more elegant since we were here—The Tea Cups they provide one are of Sève or Tournay China, & the Butter is sent to Table in Iced Water as well as the Wine. Our Apartments are cheap & charming, and they hang their Rooms with Paper now as we do, only richer Patterns; in imitation of the fine Tissues they abound in.—You remember hearing how the Duc de Chartres[8] disobliged people by cutting down those fine old Trees which were such an Ornament to the City: but he has made 'em amends now, by converting the *Parc* as they called it into a Place of Diversion with Tents, Fountains, &c. where you walk, & chat, & drink Lemonade: all built round with Shops it is, under an elegant Colonade, as if Lincoln's Inn Fields was ornamented with regular Arches down the four Sides, while the Middle should be divided into Walks—& spotted here & there with Pavilions full of People who come for this *Conversazione al Fresco.* Hats à L'Anglais seem the Mark of Distinction for Women of Fashion & elegant Manners—nobody under a certain Rank dares put one on: they wear them very large, often transparent, and always without Caps: Long Black Clokes of thin Gauze are the Ton in the public Walks, and no Trains at all, but the *Robe* just touches the Ground. A Town so very full of People and all so apparently *idle,* is no unobservable Contrast to our London, where even the Maid Servant who sits by a Soldier's Side in St. James's Park—pretending to buy Milk for her Master the Linen drapers little Boy—looks hurried as she listens to the rough Courtship of her Sweetheart; and wipes her Face, & wishes to be at home; & wipes her Face again, but can't get the Anxiety off of it. *Here* nobody seems to be *expected* to be busy;[9] all sit, & chat, and call for Ice to cool them, tho' no appearance of Heat or Haste is discernible in their Countenances or Manner: The Servant lifts himself and his rich Laced Coat leisurely up the Derriere of his tranquil Lady's Equipage, and taking out his Snuffbox looks as if he would never cease to wonder at the Fatigue supported by our dapper Footmen, whose Agility in leaping at the Leathers while the Cock Tail Nags[10] fly on upon full speed, is the Admiration of all the straight-comb'd Nymphs in the Neighbourhood. Here all the Horses are heavy, with long Manes & Tails; Coloured Ornaments, and sleek Skins, like those we use in England for Waggons or for Drays. 'Tis fit indeed *some* Animals should remain as God made them, the Men & Women are at an Immeasurable Distance. but, Adieu! here is a long Letter, & little in it;—how glad should I be tho' to see *your* hand was the Letter still less! Something tells my Heart you are not well, tho' 'tis not your not writing: but you looked ill when I saw you last, as if there was a Fit of the Worms coming on. Oh pray, for God's Sake take Care of your health: *Non est vivere* (you know,) *sed valere Vita.*[11]

Farewell, and God bless you, and all you love for your sake—when one is able to say *that,* the Affection is true, & the Friendship sincere: the Family you live with, demands and deserves my best Wishes.

I am with the utmost Esteem & Fidelity / Your ever Affectionate / H: L: P.

Text: Queeney Letters, pp. 186–88. *Address: A Mademoiselle, / Mademoiselle Thrale, chez Monsieur Cator / sur la Terrace Royale, Adelphi, Londres.*

1. The travelers had arrived in Dover on 4 September. For the remainder of the month their itinerary was as follows: Calais, the 7th; Montreuil by way of Boulogne, the 9th; Montreuil to Amiens and then to Chantilly, the 11th; Paris, the 11th until the 25th. See *French Journals,* pp. 191–207; *Observations* 1:1–24; *Thraliana* 2:613.
2. *Macbeth* 4.1.92–93; 5.6; 5.8.30.
3. See *Observations* 1:8; *French Journals,* p. 196.
4. In 1775 the Thrales had lived within walking distance of the Luxembourg Gardens and Gallery. In 1784 the Piozzis' "Lodging (in the Quartier d'Angleterre) is elegant & comfortable, but here is a burning Sun that even the Italians shrink from, & that tans one's Skin to a Parchment" (*French Journals,* pp. 197, and passim).
5. Carlo Goldoni (1707–93), Italian dramatist. "Goldoni dined here one day, and we struck Fire vastly well; he is . . . extremely garrulous; the Italians talk a great deal, but he out talked 'em all" (*Thraliana* 2:614; cf. *French Journals,* pp. 207–8; *Observations* 1:19–20).
6. Cf. HLT and SJ in the *French Journals* (pp. 150–51, 186–87) and *Observations* (1:10–11). The history of the château begins in medieval times. Built on a grand scale, and fortresslike, it had been prior to the Revolution the residence of Louis-Joseph de Bourbon (1736–1818), eighth prince of Condé.
7. See HLP to SL, 17 September.
8. Louis-Philippe-Joseph de Bourbon (1747–93); duc de Montpensier, from birth until 1752; duc de Chartres, 1752–85; duc d'Orléans, 1785–93 (known as Philippe Égalité). HLP repeats the anecdote about the trees in *Observations* 1:13, and *French Journals,* p. 198. See also HLP to LC, 4 December 1793.
9. "The French are really a contented race of mortals;—precluded almost from possibility of adventure, the low Parisian leads a gentle humble life, nor envies that greatness he never can obtain. . . . I feel well-inclined to respect the peaceful tenor of a life, which likes not to be broken in upon, for the sake of obtaining riches, which when gotten must end only in the pleasure of counting them" (*Observations* 1:13–14).
10. Cock tail: a tail that has been docked, leaving a stump erect like a cock's tail.
11. "Non est vivere, sed valere vita est" (Martial's *Epigrams* 6.70.15).

TO SAMUEL LYSONS

Paris
Fryday 17: September 1784.

Dear Mr. Lysons

Though I hear by our Friend Mr. James that you are still at Bath, yet I make use of your own Direction, as it is always safest to follow Rules exactly, when people are very distant from each other. Was I writing to a Person who I thought regardless of *me*, and only desirous of my *Letters*, I would not begin by saying how well and how happy I find myself, but if that were not the first thing *you* wished to hear, I would not write to you at all. The second is how, and what, and where, &c: and what do you see with most Pleasure? and so forth. Why then absolutely I think the Prince of Bourbon's Cabinet afforded me as much Pleasure as anything; and that because it put us in Mind of *you*, and we cried out Lord! if Mr. Lysons did but see these beautiful Butterflies! and here's Hector I remember *him* I'm sure—and Achilles with the broad blue Stripe down his Wing—and Beau Paris and all![1] Mr. James will tell you that all this is at Chantilly, where the Waterfalls are so fine, and the Fish so tame.

Well! but this Moment brings me your kind Letter, and assures me I am not forgotten. Mercy on me! What Wonders Mrs. James has written:[2] God bless you speak to every body you know, and protest that *I* owe nothing; as for the Debts incurred by Johnson, her Husband must see to *them*——Let us however get rid of the dirty House in Duke Street:[3] I had no Letters from Phillips[4] or Coward[5] while at London, but whoever writes now I shall get the Intelligence safe enough.

I'm glad you are sitting for your Picture——The Portrait[6] of Lysons Earl of Tetbury[7] High Chancellor of England *in his Youth* will be of *amazing* Value two hundred Years hence. Mean Time tell me some News do of what you hear and see, and do, and study: We find it so very hot we dare not venture the Suffocation of a Theatre: but out-door Diversions so swarm about this gay Town, that there is no need except to put your Head out of Doors, and you see every thing *qui respire le Plaisir a Paris, comme l'Opulence a Londres.* Assure yourself my dear Sir, and assure my Bath Friends, that 'tis equally out of the Power of *both* to drive from my Mind those who have so long and kindly contributed to its Relief: I shall be very studious to execute all your Commissions, but that odious Customhouse! that Foe to friendly Intercourse! how shall we charm or stupefy that ever wakeful Dragon!——Tell Mrs. James that they seized my Flannel Petticoats (altho' made up) which I had provided for Winter Wear[8]—and upon Muslins and *Dimitties—no nunc dimitties* said they, but detained all they could find.[9]

Well! now am I a professed Traveller, and what shall I tell to divert you of my Travels: Dr. Johnson says (you know) that whoever would entertain another by his Remarks—must make the subject of them *Human Life.*[10] Mr. Whalley[11] would with equal Confidence assert no doubt, that the Voyager should be particularly attentive to the *Scenery* of the places he passes thro': for both speak of what would most entertain *them.* I think *you* would wish to hear a little of each; to be told that the Vines clustering up the Apple Trees and mingling their Fruits, fill one's Eye with Elegance and one's heart with Comfort as one drives along the splendid Avenues which constitute the Approach to this prodigious City, and are *called* the high Road to it for ten or twenty miles——that your Friends *Io* and *Brassica* flutter about the Tuillerie Gardens among the Two legged and less simply coloured Butterflies, every Evening; that tho' this Town seems in some Respects bigger than London; ill built and crowded to a most disagreeable Excess, the Air seems always fresh, and the Bats flie about the Streets as if we all lived in the Fields. Nothing indeed is a greater proof of the purity of the Air here, than the healthiness of the Inhabitants; in Spite of Dirt, Poverty, and Pressure of one Family against another, in Houses *eight* Story high, and Streets so narrow that every Noise is echoed and detained below, in such a manner as to stun a Person who has lived 15 Months in the tranquil City of Bath: which is to our Town here, like a new Shilling shining from the Mint, compared to a Hundred Pounds worth of old—but good Half Pence, with here and there a bright Broad Piece of Portugal Gold[12] among them: for you have heard with Truth that the Palaces at Paris are magnificent:——and for the rest I refer you to every peny Book, which can tell you better than I, all that I have to tell; except that I am with unalterable Regard and real Esteem / Dear Mr. Lysons's / Faithful and Affectionate Servant / H: L: Piozzi.

My Husband sends you a thousand Compliments——You must now direct to *Lyons* but write soon—or if you write late—direct to *Turin.*

Text: Hyde Collection. *Address:* A Monsieur / Monsieur Samuel Lysons / John Jeffries's Esqr. / Bath.[13] *Postmark:* 23 SE [1784]; 25 SE [1784].

1. Hector and Achilles (and in her final paragraph, *Io* and *Brassica*). An avid collector, SL responded from Bath 27 September: "I had the satisfaction of receiving your very kind letter yesterday, and have read it over with pleasure I know not how many times, that I and my Butterflies should be so honoured with your remembrance is too flattering a reflexion, and raises me at least one Inch in my own opinion every time I think of it" (Ry. 552.1).

2. The letters of SL and Mrs. James are missing.

3. "With regard to the house in Duke Street [HLT's residence in Bath]—I suppose Mr. Piozzi properly authorized some person in London to transact his business in general, by some such person the last quarter Rent of that house now due should be paid, and then any one authorized so to do by a letter from Mr. P. or his Attorney in London may let it for all or some part of the remaining time—otherwise Phillips who is a very troublesome fellow will most probably give the tenant some uneasiness. I wish he would agree to take the lease on reasonable terms, it would be best to write to your attorney in London to settle with him" (SL to HLP, 27 September).

4. George Phillips owned several houses in Duke Street. According to the "St. James's Parish Burial Records" (Bath) at the C.R.O., Somerset, he was buried in the churchyard on 20 February 1803. His wife Eliza was also buried in the churchyard, on 2 January 1810.

5. See HLT to Q [28 June].

6. The portrait was probably by George James. Subsequent portraits of SL were executed by Thomas Lawrence, W. J. Newton, and George Dance the younger.

7. Reporting to HLP that he expected to leave Bath by 24 October after nearly eight

years to continue the study of law in London, SL added that "nothing of consequence is to be done except in Capitals." He noted playfully: "There are no opportunities [in Bath] of becoming *Lord High Chancellor* and *Earl of Tetbury*" (27 September). Tetbury was a small town near Rodmarton, where SL was born.

8. HLP had violated import restrictions on certain textiles. Flannel, dimity, and muslin had a common source in cotton. "My republican spirit . . . boiled up a little last Monday, when I had to petition Mons. de Calonne for the restoration of some trifles detained in the custom-house at Calais." Despite his courtesy, she was humiliated by "the drudgery of running from subaltern to subaltern, intreating, in pathetic terms, the remission of a law which is at last either just or unjust . . ." (*Observations* 1:23).

9. A pun on *nunc dimittis,* one of the standard canticles of evening prayer in the Anglican service. It is rendered in Luke 2:29: "Lord, now lettest thou thy servant depart in peace, according to thy word." See Bacon, Essay 2, "Of Death."

10. "He that would travel for the entertainment of others, should remember that the great object of remark is human life" (*Idler* 97). While journeying in Scotland (21 September 1773), SJ had made a corollary observation, that we travel "to regulate imagination by reality, and instead of thinking how things may be, to see them as they are" (*Letters* 1:139). See also SJ to SAT, 9 September 1783 (Chapman 3:69); HLP to Parsons, 5 February 1787.

11. The Reverend Thomas Sedgwick Whalley (1746–1828), nonresident pastor of Hagsworthingham, near Spilsby, Lincs., prebendary of Wells, poet, traveler, and friend of SS and Hannah More. TSW, who lived in the center house of the Royal Crescent, was prominent in Bath society when HLT met him in 1780. By his marriage to the widow Elizabeth Sherwood, née Jones (ca. 1740–1801), he acquired wealth and an estate in Burrington Parish, Somerset. There, at a cost of almost sixty thousand pounds, he built Mendip Lodge overlooking the Bristol Channel.

12. Important gold mines were discovered in Brazil (ca. 1693) during the reign of Pedro II (1683–1706; b. 1648); the subsequent gold coinage of Portugal became famous for its quality and profusion.

13. John Jefferys (fl. 1750–92) was the Bath attorney to whom SL was apprenticed in June 1780. According to the Bath directory (1792), Jefferys' address was the Crescent.

TO SAMUEL LYSONS

Turin
19: October [1784].

Your Letter Dear Mr. Lysons was the first Thing I found after my Passage of the Mountains; and my desire to oblige you by complying with your Request, was naturally the second Sensation.[1] I have enquired out Dr. Allioni,[2] and shall have leave to see his Collection tomorrow; my Letter shall lie open till I can give you an Account of my Success.

Meantime you ask me what I think of Savoy and its Alps! Shall I protest to you that I have not yet arranged the Ideas with which they crowded my Mind; and that although I have now been here six days staring every Instant at some Work of *Art,* the least of which would serve for a Wonder in England—my Eyes turn perpetually towards those glorious Productions of *Nature,* and I half scorn to think of any thing but them. Why what Monkeys were we all at last to titter at Mr. Whalley's Descriptions?[3] Those four Days Journey from Pont Bon Voisin to

Novalesa[4] would be enough I should think to make a Coxcomb of Dr. Johnson, or a Pedant of Mr. James.

We often wished for your Company, and said how you would sit upon this Rock and that Rock taking Views of the Country: I jumped out of the Coach myself at one Place to drink at a beautiful Cascade that came foaming down the Side of the Hill all tufted with various coloured Greens, where I followed *Hyale* among the Bushes (the yellow Butterfly with brown-edged Wings) but could not catch her. This City is the most symmetrical, the most delicate, and the most tranquill I have ever seen——London is dirty, and Bath heavy compared with it:——'Tis like a Model of a Town exhibited in white Wax for a Show; I did not know till now that the Metropolis of a Nation could be a *pretty Thing*.

But I do not wish for you here; I wish you fast shut up with Piles of Lawbooks all the week to dig Fame and Fortune out of Black Letters, and blacker Recitals of Injury Fraud and Ruin: then to taste fresh Air at Sheene[5] from Saturday to Monday in the more pleasing Contemplation of Gods Works unperverted by Man.

We are going to Alexandria, Genoa, and Pavia, and then to Milan for the Winter; as Mr. Piozzi finds Friends every where to delay us; and I hate Hurry and Fatigue, it takes away all one's Attention. Lyons was a delightful Place to me, and we were *so* feasted and adored there by my Husband's old Acquaintance:[6] The Duke and Duchess of Cumberland[7] too paid us a Thousand caressing Civilities where we met with 'em; and we had no means of musical Parties neither. The Prince of Sisterna[8] came yesterday to visit Mr. Piozzi, and present me the Key of his Box at the Opera for the Time we stay at Turin[9]——Here's Honour and Glory for you! When Miss Thrale hears of it all—*She will write perhaps:* The other two are very kind and affectionate.

My Health and Spirits mend every day thank God, and my husband's Kindness makes me amends for all I suffered to obtain him. We mean to go quietly forward in the Spring, but there is no Joke at all in passing the Appenines at Christmas, so you will only have Accounts of the North of Italy from me this Year: Let me add how much more magnificent the Rhône appeared to me than the Po—and then lay by my Paper till after my Visit to Dr. Allioni.

Well! I have seen the good old Man and his Collection, but could not coax him out of any thing really curious—and as for Trash one would not be plagued with *them*. The Specimens of petrified Wood and Marbles of this Country are exceedingly fine indeed, and I longed to buy, or change, or procure them for you by some method: The Fossil Fish in Slate too are admirable, and there is one flat Stone with a Fish in it, so perfect on both Sides that it seems a Cameo and Intaglio. I will not rest however till I can obtain you something. He is good natured and communicative, and will publish his Book upon Botany next January,[10] but being nearly blind the Pleasure once produced to him is lost, and he means to sell all his Rareties together——The Hortus Siccus I fancy is a very good one, but you know how little a way my *Skill* reaches in such matters.—

I was glad to see Atlas and Antenor again tho.

God bless you, and be very wise, and very good, and very happy, and do not forget your Mother's preachments, nor those of your ever sincere and faithful / H: L: Piozzi.

Give my Love to the dear Jameses—and accept my husbands Compliments.

Direct to Milan, and write very soon, and a long Letter; few People love you better than I do——for few People know you as well. / Adieu!

Text: Hyde Collection. *Address:* A Monsieur / Monsieur Samuel Lysons chez le Reverend / Monsieur S: Peach / a East Sheene / près de Richmond / en Surrey / proche de Londres. *Postmark:* <   >.

1. From Bath, 27 September (Ry. 552.1), SL wrote: "Apropos of the *dulce,* I had almost forgot to tell you of these Italian fossils which I threatened to tell you about—There are in many parts of Italy particularly about Sienna fossil shells composed of a substance resembling jasper or agate—and at Monte Bolce and other places near Verona are found fossil plants and fish in a kind of slate."

2. Carlo Allioni (1728–1804), a native of Turin (the "Piedmontese Linnaeus"), was a physician and author of treatises on medical subjects, zoology, paleontology, botany. SL described him as one who "has a very fine collection of natural Curiosities particularly of the productions of Piedmont and Savoy" and who "could tell you how and where [such] fossils are to be procured, and then if a small specimen or two of each can be got without much trouble, I shall be much obliged to you for them."

The remains of Allioni's fossil collection, which came largely from Monte Bolca, have been deposited in the seminary at Chieri.

3. TSW's travel accounts were characterized by florid, exuberant, and egocentric descriptions. See, e.g., his "Three Excursions in Savoy and France, 1783, 1784," in Wickham 1:43–230.

4. For HLP's "immediate sensation" of Beauvoisin, see *Observations* 1:36–41. She was less impressed by Novalesa, the town where the Piozzis "stopped . . . upon entering Piedmont. . . . For compensation of danger, ease should be administered; but one's quiet is here so disturbed by insects, and polluted by dirt, that one recollects the conduct of the Lapland rein-deer, who seeks the summit of the hill at the hazard of his life, to avoid those gnats which sting him to madness in the valley" (*Observations* 1:43).

5. SL was visiting his maternal uncle Samuel Peach (1746–1803). An alumnus of Oxford, he received his B.A. in 1766 and his M.A. in 1769. He had served as chaplain to the duke of Cumberland, was rector of Compton Beauchamp, Berks., and resided at East Sheen (near Richmond).

6. See *Observations* 1:32–33.

7. Henry Frederick (1745–90), duke of Cumberland and Strathearn, brother of George III, married Anne Horton, née Luttrell (1742/43–1808). See *Observations* 1:33; *French Journals,* p. 213; *Thraliana* 2:614.

8. The city-state of Cisterna d'Asti became a principality by papal sanction in the seventeenth century. The ruling family were the Dal Pozzos. The Prince della Cisterna to whom HLP refers is Bonifacio Dal Pozzo (1712–99). He was succeeded by his son (whom HLP also knew) Claudio Gerolamo (1759–1832).

9. "Model of Elegance, exact Turin! where Italian hospitality first consoled, and Italian arts first repaid, the fatigues of my journey: how shall I bear to leave my new-obtained acquaintance? how shall I consent to quit this lovely city? where, from the box put into my possession by the Prince de la Cisterna, I first saw an Italian opera acted in an Italian theatre" (*Observations* 1:45; *Thraliana* 2:614).

10. That is, [Carolus Allionus], *Flora Pedemontana, sive enumeratio methodica stirpium indigenarum Pedemontii,* 3 vols. (Turin, 1785), fol.

TO SAMUEL LYSONS

Milan
7: December 1784.

I thank you very kindly Dear Mr. Lysons for *your* Attention which I value exceedingly, and beg you to continue: The Attention and Politeness with which I am treated here is really prodigious, I did not expect any Thing like it.

What shall I tell you to compensate for the Length and Good nature of your last Letter?[1] I must begin with Genoa I believe, and rejoyce that my Paper is long and wide if I propose to describe either its Elegance or Splendour: The Entrance of the City so justly called *la Superba* or the Magnificence of the Gulph it overlooks and appears to command. Oh if one was Enthusiastically fond of natural Beauties one certainly should never quit the Bocchetta of Genoa,[2] where the Clouds veil the Hill, and the Strawberry Trees growing wild like our Furze Bushes help to adorn it; where Balm and Rosemary perfume the Road, and fill the little Ditches that in England are deformed by Nettles, Thistles &c. (not one of which have I seen since I left France;) where Standard Fig Trees spread their great Leaves, and hold out their delicious Fruits like Oaks and Acorns in our Country—while Oranges and Lemons flourish over every Wall that encloses a Pleasure Ground belonging to the numberless Palaces scattered up and down for a few Miles round the City.

Two Days ago I received a Box of Roses and Carnations from thence—all of which blew out in the open Air, at this Time of the Year when the People on the other Side the Strand can scarcely see the scarlet Pocket Books which shine in your Landlord's Shop Window for Fog I trow.[3] *Poor Sammy!* said your Mother[4] when first you described your Situation to *her* I'm sure; *if he should lose either his Health or his Disposition to Virtue in that nasty Town I should wish he had never seen it, let him grow as rich and as fortunate as he will.* You know I used to preach to you like your Mother, and press you to lose no Ground in the great Race by following *Golden Apples:*[5] I still continue to take the Same Liberty, and often fancy a young Man committed so to the wide World like a fine Picture painted in Enamel and put into the Furnace——from whence if it comes out with the Likeness *fixed* and the Colours *firm,* all agree to admire and strive to possess it:——if they run!!——but my Sermon is at an End, and we will begin a new Subject.

Mr. Piozzi is much pleased with your Letter which I translated my best; and bids me send you a Copy of a Sonnet[6] written in my Praise already, as I have made no Verses myself, and as you will like these better than any I should have written——every body here says they are very good ones—give a Copy of them to dear Mr. James who reads this Language as well as his own—or nearly.

Al Merito Impareggiabile dell'Ornatissima Signora Donna Ester Thrale Inglese, condotta Sposa in Milano del Signor Don Gabriele Piozzi

Sonetto

D'Insubria il Genio, lieto oltre l'usato,
  Per le vie di Milan giva sclamando;

Agli Affanni si dia eterno bando,
Che un raro Don dal Cielo a noi vien dato.

Infelice Israel saria pur stato,
Se dell'empio Amano al fatal Commando,
Sospeso de'Persi impazienti il Brando,
La bella Ebrea non avesse ostato.

Nuova Estera dall'Anglia a noi qui scese
Per mano di Gabriel cui l'Alma Imene
Avvinse, già d'Amore un Tempo accese.

Ah! fia sempre che con tal Donna a Lato
Lo Sposo e Milan gioiscan d'un Bene,
Cui non osi turbar avverso Fato.—

No don't put *this* in the Newspapers; for if you do, I will never write to you another Word while I live, and send the same charge to Mr. James; for I have been too much persecuted in England by publick notice[7] and if one cannot trust *any* Friend with one's Vanity 'tis *very* hard: The Truth is I *do* send few Letters to England: who is there that have not been busily spiteful, or spitefully busy about our Affairs except yourself? Mr. Seward perhaps meant—and I believe he did—more to divert himself, than to offend me by the ludicrous and contemptuous Manner with which he thought proper to treat a Connection which has made the happiness of my life;[8] but though I value his Virtues exceedingly, and think Society both benefited and blest by his long Continuance as a Member of it——you would not blame my putting an End to the Correspondence which produced me such Letters as I received from him this Time Twelve month and ever since that Time till I left Bath in August last if you saw 'em. I correspond constantly and copiously with such of my Daughters as are willing to answer my Letters, and I have at last received one cold Scrap from the eldest,[9] which I instantly and tenderly replied to.[10]

Dear Sir Lucas Pepys who saved my Life, before I came to Bath, where the Waters and your Friendship preserved it—assisted by Mr. James's amiable Family, and uncommon Talents sweetened by cordial Kindness—has never been neglected, and I shall write to him again in a day or two. Mrs. Lewis[11] too and Miss Nicholson have had Accounts of my Health for I found *them* disinterestedly attached to me——Those who led the Stream, or watched which way it ran that they might follow it, were not I suppose desirous of my Correspondence; and till they are so, shall not be troubled with it. I ventured a Letter to Dr. Lort[12] tho' by the Abate Bocchetti,[13] who wanted recommendatory Letters to Learned Men; since I received yours it pleases me that I *did* write to him, but I had no heart of it at the Time.

Adieu my dear Friend, and continue your partial Regard for me, who have for you a true and affectionate Esteem; let me hear what, and how, and where, and when: and believe me ever most faithfully your Friend and Obedient Servant / H: L: Piozzi.

My husband sends you his kind Compliments. He studies English while you work at the Italian, so the Conversation will do excellently when you meet next. I dined at the Minister's o'Tuesday, and he called all the wise Men round me with great Politeness indeed——You must like the new Venetian Resident[14] when he comes to England as in a few Months he will, for his Partiality to us as well as his agreable Qualities. Once more keep me *out* of the Newspapers if you possibly can: They have given me many a miserable hour and my worst Enemies many a merry one——but I have not deserved public Persecution, and am very happy to live in a place where one is free from unmerited Insolence such as London abounds with.

Illic Credulitas—illic temerarius Error &c.[15]

God bless you, and may you *conquer* the many headed Monster which I could never *charm* to Silence. Farewell! My next Letter shall talk of the Libraries and Botanical Gardens, and twenty other clever Things here at Milan; and I mean to go to Pavia, and Padua on purpose to find something worth your Acceptance which may not disgrace your Collection, but such Things must be carried, not sent. Write to me very soon, I wish you a comfortable Christmas, and a happy Beginning of the Year 1785. Do not neglect Dr. Johnson,[16] you will never see any other Mortal either so wise or so good——I keep his Picture in my Chamber, and his Words on my chimney; the Germans who study English here all talk of his Writings—but the Italians are all for Dr. Young[17]—They treat Pope as a Spinozy.[18]

Text: Hyde Collection. *Address:* A Monsieur / Monsieur Samuel Lysons chez the Reverend / Mr. S. Peach at / East Sheene / near Richmond / in Surrey / près de Londres / Angleterre. *Postmark:* 20 DE; 21 DE.

1. Perhaps the one written from Bath, 27 September, but it is more likely an allusion to a later letter (one now missing that described his London lodgings).
2. The Piozzis traveled from Novi through Bocchetta, a pass in the Ligurian Apennines some dozen miles northwest of Genoa, at an altitude of about twenty-five hundred feet. For an extended description of Genoa, see *Observations* 1:57–65.
3. SL's landlord, who crafted ladies' bags or pocket books, was John Godwin (fl. 1780–91), at 167 Strand. SL was to reside there for at least two years (Ry. 552.6).
4. See HLT to Q, 1 July, n. 10.
5. Hippomanes (or Melanion) was given three of the golden apples of the Hesperides by Aphrodite. When he dropped them, Atalanta stopped to pick them up and so lost the race.
6. The sonnet is by Abate Giuseppe Bossi (d. 1798), a Milanese ecclesiastic, and is recorded in *Thraliana*, 27 November (2:618–19; cf. 670).
7. As early as November 1782, HLT complained that "There is no Mercy for me on this Island. . . . one Day the paper rings wth my Marriage to Johnson, one Day to Crutchley; one Day to Seward" (*Thraliana* 1:547).

After the marriage, newspaper slurs abounded. See, e.g., the *Morning Herald*, 20 December: "Signor Piozzi, by his return to Venice with his English bride, has convinced his country-men, that although the shrill voice [of] Pacchierotti has done much in this country, yet there was amongst the Italian singers, one, whose *pipe* was able to accomplish more!"

8. See HLT to FB, 30 June.
9. Even FB conceded of the reserved Q: "Elle étoit froide de nature, peu demonstrative, ou plutôt glaciale" ("French Exercise Book III," *Journals and Letters* 7:530).

10. Probably HLP to Q, 19 November. See *Queeney Letters,* pp. 189–90.

11. Charlotte Lewis, née Cotterell (d. 1796), of Richmond, Surrey, and Carmarthenshire, widow of John (1717–83), dean of Ossory (1755–83). An early friend of SJ, she was also close to HLT during the troubled period preceding the marriage to GP. See P.R.O., Prob. 11/1280/514, proved 7 October 1796.

12. Michael Lort (1725–90), clergyman and antiquary, with an M.A. (1750) and D.D. (1780) from Cambridge, was elected F.S.A. (1755); F.R.S. (1766). From 1759 to 1771, he was regius professor of Greek at Cambridge; from 1779 to 1783, domestic chaplain to Archbishop Cornwallis, having become in 1771 rector of Saint Matthew's, Friday Street, London, and in 1780 having been appointed to the prebendal stall of Tottenham in Saint Paul's Cathedral.

13. Abate Lodovico Maria Buchetti, or Bucchetti (1747–1804). "[A] Jesuit far from home & without any Power is a most delightful Companion—talkative, insinuating, penetrating & informed" (*Thraliana* 2:678). HLP first met him in Paris, September 1784 (*French Journals,* p. 202).

14. John Strange (1732–99), diplomat and antiquary. A fellow commoner of Clare Hall, Cambridge (B.A. 1753, M.A. 1755), independently wealthy, he traveled extensively in France and Italy. In November 1773 (or 1774), he was appointed British Resident at Venice. He retained the post until 1788, meanwhile continuing his archaeological studies. See *GM* 69, pt.1 (1799): 348; *Repertorium,* p. 180. For the death of his wife at Venice, see *GM* 53, pt.1 (1783): 540.

15. Ovid, *Metamorphoses* 12.59.

16. SL wrote from East Sheen on 29 December (Ry. 552.2): "As bad news is seldom tardy in its course, you must have heard 'ere now that the world is at last deprived of the example and abilities of Dr. Johnson—I often called at his house during his illness, twice by appointment, but he was always too ill to be seen—".

This may have been the first report of SJ's death on 13 December to reach her.

17. Edward Young (1683–1765) was an Oxonian who became a dramatist, a poet, a chaplain to the king, and ultimately rector of Welwyn (1730). Italian readers particularly admired *The Complaint, or Night Thoughts on Life, Death, and Immortality* (1742–45).

18. Alexander Pope (1688–1744), as the author of *An Essay on Man* (1733–34), would be likened to Baruch (Benedictus) Spinoza (1632–77), whose *Tractatus theologico-politicus* (1670) and *Ethica* (1677) influenced Pope's own theodicy.

TO HESTER MARIA THRALE

Milan,
5 January 1785

I received your obliging Letter last night my Dearest, and hasten to thank you for it:—but as there is thirteen Yards Depth of Snow on some of the Alps, one may reasonably wonder how any of them are passable, and of Course how any Correspondence can be carried on. Mrs Hawkesworth's Name is so very respectable I wonder not that your Intention of passing some Time with her should be approved of;[1] indeed I never knew you propose an imprudent Plan, and am sorry you have been so teized—The Year in which however Liberty will certainly come, is commenced at last; and I congratulate you very sincerely on its near Prospect and quick Approach. Your Picture arrived last Week,[2] with our other little Matters from England: it is the much admired Ornament of my pretty Dressing room, where I have the Satisfaction to hear the Praises of your Person

Henry Thrale's Brewery, Southwark. A drawing by Dorothy Collins. *(Reproduced from* **Boswell's Life of Johnson,** *ed. Roger Ingpen [1925], by permission of George Bayntun [publisher], Bath; and The Henry E. Huntington Library and Art Gallery.)*

from all who visit us; & the Italian Language never seems so easy to me—as when I add the just Praises of that uncommon Merit which is acknowledged by many, but best known to myself.

What shall I tell to divert you! we used to say that Theatrical News was your Passion: well then! the Theatre is of a surprising Capacity, Beauty, & elegance of Proportion:[3] the manner of enjoying its Pleasures just such as you have always heard, the Lady having a Box where She entertains Company as if at home, with Ices, &c. prepared in the back Room belonging to it. You may however by forbearing to light up your Candles, sit and hear the Music uninterrupted, for that is *being denied* as we say in London. There is however this Year little Temptation to such Amusement, for the Opera is complained of as very bad, & though we have *two* first Women, everybody despises them both. They act Goldoni's & other Comedies at the little Theatre which is larger than our best in the Haymarket, but the Court seldom goes thither, and others neglect it of Course.[4] Vienna is I find the Place where Acting is studied; they exhibit Shakespeare's Tragedies and the Ladies caress the great Performers as Mrs Siddons was caress'd in England—we have a great many German Noblemen here in Consequence of this Town's being under the Dominion of the Emperor;[5] they almost all speak & study English, and were very happy to see the little Shade of Mrs Siddons which I carry always in my Pocket. Apropos the brown & blue Butterfly which you worked for my Satchell when dear Sophy was sick is still in *good Preservation:* but the Bullfinch & Grapes are admired by all Beholders—I am *so* sorry that I lost that Raffle for Hudson's Chairs! The Public Library here is very magnificent, & well stocked with English Books. I was always vexed about Dr Johnson's suffering poor Young to be so treated in the Lives you know;[6] but I am more sorry now because of the Foreigners, who all reverenced him before, & called him the Christian Poet. We have a Pliny here printed at Parma in 1418 very beautiful, and a Livy printed at Milan within the same Century.[7]

I write to you about literary Matters, concluding you will not lose your Taste for them: I never saw any Place where Knowledge did *not* confer Distinction, but the Town I am now in has an Appetite for learned Conversation beyond all I have ever seen hitherto: perhaps that may be one Reason for their excessive Partiality to your ever Affectionate & Faithful / H: L: Piozzi.

Text: Queeney Letters, pp. 191–92. *Address: A Mademoiselle / Mademoiselle Thrale chez Mr Cator, / Royal Terrace, Adelphi, Londres, Angleterre.*

1. A chaperone for whom Q considered leaving the Cators. Apparently the plan came to nothing. By April Q was settled in the West Street house at Brighton. See HLP to Q, 4 June 1785, n. 23.

2. Either Sir Joshua Reynolds's portrait of Q (Bowood House) or a watercolor of her, when she was seventeen, by an unknown artist (Four Oaks Farm). See Hyde, pp. 191, 229.

3. The Teatro della Scala (1776–78), ". . . a receptacle so capacious to contain four thousand people, a place of entrance so commodious to receive them, a show so princely, so very magnificent to entertain them, must be sought in vain out of Italy." See *Observations* 1:87–89 for further particulars. After the San Carlo Theatre of Naples, La Scala was the largest in Europe. It is situated in the piazza near the church of Santa Maria della Scala.

4. Both La Scala and the nearby much smaller Teatro della Canobbiana (or Cannobbiana) were intended to replace the Ducal Theatre, destroyed by fire in 1776. The Canobbiana was opened in 1779 and until its destruction in 1885 occupied the site of an ancient school established by one P. Canobbia. It was a popular setting for operas, comedies, and ballets.

5. From the death of Francesco Sforza (1401–66), duke of Milan (1450–66)—and the end of his house in 1535—until the War of the Spanish Succession, Milan was a dependency of the Spanish Crown. In 1706 an Austrian army took possession of the city and the dominion of the Austrian Habsburgs was confirmed (except for brief interludes) until the Napoleonic campaign of 1796. At the present time it was ruled by Joseph II (1741–90), Holy Roman Emperor.

6. SJ's biography of Young consists almost wholly of a memoir by the Reverend Sir Herbert Croft (1751–1816), a friend of the poet's son Frederick (b. ca. 1732). As HLP knew, SJ was lukewarm about Young's aesthetic talents. Too bored to write his own essay, SJ made deep cuts in Croft's and would not have been "sorry to see it yet shorter." Croft, furthermore, had undertaken to improve a spotty public image of the young man associated with the character of Lorenzo in *Night Thoughts*. Implicitly the elder Young is drawn with chinks—especially paternal ones—in his moral armor. Such praise as Croft bestows and SJ accommodates is grudging. See *English Poets* 3:361–99; *Thraliana* 1:174, 208; *Boswell's Johnson* 4:59.

7. In *Observations* 1:76, HLP wrote about "A Livy, printed here in 1418 . . . and a Pliny of the Parma press, dated 1472. . . ."

TO SAMUEL LYSONS

Milan
20: January 1785.

I thank you very kindly Dear Mr. Lysons for the agreable Letter which last night's post brought to my hands;[1] your friendship has ever been most disinterested, and if God grants me a Continuance of Life and Health, I shall make you my personal Acknowledgments in two Year's Time; for all the People in London say that Mr. Piozzi has shut me up in a Convent.[2] *This News I had from Mr. James*.

I wish they would enquire of those best known here: The Minister Count Wiltzeck[3] has shewn us many Distinctions, and we are visited by the first Families in Milan. The Venetian Resident will however, be soon sent to the Court of London, and give a faithful Account of us I am sure, to *all their obliging Enquiries*.

The Favours which I have been most eager to accept however, are literary ones: and we are kindly indulged with our Choice of Books from the public Library, where I have seen a variety of Things that would have pleased you exceedingly. 13 Volumes of Psalms in MSS written by the Friars of a lately suppressed Convent, and illuminated—Oh! far beyond all my Powers of Description. One can *only* admire when things are so *very* perfect in their Kind. We have here a Pliny printed at Parma in 1418 very fine, and a Livy printed at Milan about the same Date in high preservation——The famous Sexto Quinto Bible as 'tis called, and the same called in and reprinted purged and most exceeding scarce:[4] Tis a glorious Library in short, well kept and well disposed by an Intelligent and learned Man,[5] who means to visit England in a Year or two; and is well known by Correspondence to Herschall,[6] Maskelyne[7] &c. as Professor of Astronomy.

I shall get some nice Fossills for you thro' his means, and be a greater favourite than the Lady of the fifty Denarij.[8]

How comfortable a House for you is that of the Dear Pepyses![9] to whom I am, much obliged; as I shall one Day perhaps have an Opportunity of showing, when *Separation shall be made between Friends and Enemies!*

Ask Mr. Pepys do whether there is any Truth in the article we read here Journal Encyclopedique for last December about his Friend the famous Lord Lyttelton——how he wrote some Arguments for Suicide which perswaded a Man to murder himself.[10] I suppose 'tis like their saying Mr. Piozzi has sold my Joynture and locked me up——but they should let the Dead alone, the Living may defend themselves.

What you say of the *Seleucidæ* is curious enough, but 'tis a Subject I would rather hear than speak of; they have none of them written to me yet.[11]

Our Gothick Cathedral is a most awful Pile indeed—as big as any two of the English Churches I verily think; the People here are impatient and ashamed that tis not yet finished—but to me there is an additional Sublimity in the Idea that tho' they have been working at it so many Ages——one hardly can hope that it ever will be finished, yet still the Expectation of *more* without which nothing Satisfies—is kept alive.[12]

I will write to Dr. Lort by the Post, he is a Man whose esteem I am proud of.[13]

The Prose Tale in Mrs. Williams's Miscellanies will make that Book very valuable:[14] I wish you would get *me* all the Anecdotes you can of the *early* and *late* Parts of a Life, the *middle* of which no one knows as well as myself, nor *half* as well:[15] Do not however proclaim either your Intentions or my own, which are scarcely settled yet;[16] I shall tell Sir *Lucas* Pepys in confidence, as I keep no Corner of my heart from *him:* and you may sh[ew] *him* my Letters at any Time if you like it. I meant to enclose you some Verses, translated by me from an Italian Sonnet written on an Air Balloon sent up here at Milan,[17] but there is no Room in *your* Letter, so I shall put them into *his.*

Adieu my dear Mr. Lysons, and may God bless you with Fame and Fortune such as was ever prophesied you by Your / Affectionate and Faithful Servant / H: L: Piozzi.

My Husband desires his Compliments—

I cannot think how to direct to Dr. Lort—ask him when you see him do, and ask if Mrs. Cowley the Author is related to John Gay the Contemporary of Pope, Swift &c.——Our People here have a high Esteem of her, and her Plays are acted at Vienna I believe.[18]

Your sweet Drawing of Bath hangs in my Dressing Room, and is admired by every one; I recollect many past Scenes when I look on it——most of 'em very melancholy ones indeed:— I hope I am grateful for the Change, I scarcely can be enough so. Mr. James is very good however, and so is dear Mrs. Lewis; I love Bath for *your* Sakes, as miserably as I lived there.[19]

Adieu Dear Mr. Lysons and continue your kindness to Mr. Piozzi and his H: L: P.

Text: Hyde Collection. *Address:* A Monsieur / Monsieur Samuel Lysons / chez le Rev: Monsieur S. Peach / a East Sheen / near Mortlake / Surrey / Angleterre. *Postmark* <   >

1. SL wrote from East Sheen on 29 December 1784 (Ry. 552.2).

2. One of the slanderers was Elizabeth Montagu; see Montagu to Vesey [25] July 1784, n. 8. For several months the rumor persisted in London social circles and newspapers. The *Morning Post* for 4 March 1785, for example, asserted that "*Signora Piozzi,* late Mrs. Thrale, is at present immured in Italy by her husband, who having possessed himself of about 30,000£ of her cash, is striving with use of it, to dissipate the remains of her affection!" See Clifford, p. 240 and n. 3; and HLP to SL, 7 December 1784.

3. Heinrich Wilhelm Wilczek (1710–87), Austrian minister to Milan, whose "Civilities have made [HLP] all the Fashion" and an object of the "most flattering attentions" (*Thraliana* 2:620, 635 n. 2; see also *Observations* 1:137).

4. *Biblia Sacra Vulgatae Editionis. (Sixti Quinti Pont. Max. jussu recognita atque edita.)* This was the revised edition of the Vulgate published in 1592: the first edition was issued in 1590 under the authority of Pope Sixtus V. It is commonly known as the "Clementine edition" because of a further revision authorized by Pope Clement VIII (1592–1605), born Ippolito Aldobrandini (1536–1605).

5. Apparently Baron Anton von Cronthal [Kronthal] (fl. 1755–96), librarian of the Brera Palace, who "gave [HLP] free Access to the public Library" ("Harvard Piozziana" 2:27–28).

6. William (Friedrich Wilhelm) Herschel (1738–1822), knighted (1816), German-born mathematician, musician, and founder of sidereal astronomy. HLP was aware of Herschel by at least 31 November 1783; see *Letters* 2:336–37.

7. Nevil Maskelyne (1732–1811), fifth English astronomer royal (1765), was a graduate of Trinity College, Cambridge, a fellow of the college (1756), M.A. (1757), D.D. (1777), and F.R.S. (1758). He achieved fame as director of the Royal Observatory and founder of the *Nautical Almanac.*

8. SL had written on 29 December: "My collection of medals has lately received great additions—A Lady at whose house I supped last week gave me fifty Roman denarii" (silver coins often mentioned in the New Testament).

9. HLP's response to SL's comment: "Last Wednesday I dined at Master Pepys's—Mrs. Ord was there and a Mrs. Buller, a lady who I am told reads Greek—I liked the Pepys's much and wish Wimpole Street a little nearer to my Lodgings—." For her feelings about the Pepyses, see her letter to SL, 26 February, n. 9.

10. Known as "the good Lord Lyttelton," George Lyttelton (1709–73), first baron (1756). As a literary figure he is known for the *Dialogues of the Dead* (1760).

HLP refers to the article in *Journal Encyclopédique ou Universel* (Liége et Bouillon: Par une Société de Gens de lettres, 1756–93):

"*Anecdote Angloise*

"Les *Lettres persanes* de Mylord Lyttelton sont un ouvrage de sa jeunesse. Il avoit eu l'imprudence de rassembler dans une de ces lettres tous les sophismes qui tendent à justifier le suicide. Peu de tems après leur publication, quelqu'un lui écrivit pour le remercier d'avoir recueilli ces argumens, parce qu'ils l'avoient décidé à se donner la mort; & se tua en effet. Le jeune auteur, en proie au remords le plus vif, courut aussi-tôt chez son libraire, fit retrancher la lettre funeste de tous les exemplaires qui lui restoient, & se hâta d'en substituer une dont les principes étoient absolument opposés; mais le coup avoit porté, & l'on assure qu'il ne se le pardonna jamais" (8, pt. 2 [1784]: 332).

11. The Seleucidae, a wry allusion to the three eldest Thrale girls, were descendants of a warlike dynasty founded by the Macedonian Seleucus Nicator (d. 280 B.C.), King of Syria. Yet HLP responds on 5 January to a letter of Q.

12. Construction of the cathedral went on between 1386 and 1813. HLP thought "the Duomo, first in all Europe of the Gothic race; whose solemn sadness and gloomy dignity make it a most magnificent cathedral" (*Observations* 1:77).

13. HLP's letter to Michael Lort is missing as is the one of 22 March, but—among a variety of subjects—she had asked him to call upon Dr. William Adams (1706–89), SJ's Pembroke College friend (and master there) for anecdotes. Lort responded apologetically on 28 May (Ry. 544.3): ". . . I learn that [Adams] has little or nothing of any consequence to communicate."

14. SL informed HLP on 29 December: "With great difficulty I have procured a Copy of Mrs. Williams's Miscellanies—and admire the translation from Boileau exceedingly."

The allusion is to *Miscellanies in Prose and Verse* (1766), compiled by SJ's friend Anna Williams (1706–83).

The reference to Boileau gratified HLP, who had contributed the "Epistle of Boileau to his Gardener" along with her well-received poem "The Three Warnings." SJ had provided "The Fountains: A Fairy Tale," which HLT had transcribed for him. In time she was to translate it into Italian (Ry. 654) and to dramatize it as "The Two Fountains" (1789). See Clifford, p. 61.

15. HLP had anticipated a biographical account of SJ, and after his death on 13 December was importuned to produce one. Her intentions were complicated by residence in Italy and by awareness of much biographical activity in England. SL advised her 25 February (Ry. 552.3):

"I fear Anecdotes of the early part of Johnson's life will not be very easily procured, tho' Sir John Hawkins who is writing the life which is to be prefixed to the Edition of his works, says that he has materials sufficient to fill an octavo volume, what he has will of course be kept 'close' till the publication, several others of the Doctor's friends, they say, intend publishing their scraps separate, Mr. T: Tyers whom you might probably know has sent his to the Gentleman's magazine for December. . . . It contains a curious string of Anecdotes brought strangely together and without any method, indeed just such a thing as I should have expected from *him*." SL went on to mention a number of letters and notes from SJ to John Nichols regarding the *English Poets*.

By 15 April SL could report that "the Bishop of Peterborough . . . was much pleased when I told him of your intentions, he thinks it will not be worth while for you to give yourself much trouble in collecting early or late anecdotes of Johnson, for which you must depend on the Memory of others, as they will not be expected in your account of him and as those you have, will be infinitely more interesting than any other Period of his life could be expected to furnish" (Ry. 552.4).

See "A Biographical Sketch of Dr. Samuel Johnson," *GM* 54, pt. 2 (1784): 899–911, signed "T. T."" and "Original Letters from Dr. Johnson," *GM* 55, pt. 1 (1785): 3–11.

16. HLP's initial caution reflects awareness of public satiety. The *Morning Chronicle and London Advertiser* reported on 1 January: "The articles entitled Dr. Johnson, and signed *Bolt Court*, are purposely omitted, it having been pretty intelligibly whispered to the Printer, that the Public have for some days past said *'something too much of this!'* when they have seen any articles on the subject."

Undaunted, however, she began to compile her own anecdotes, asking SL in March to have her project announced in the newspapers. As we have seen, she solicited his help as well as Dr. Lort's in gathering more anecdotes; she was in time to call upon Dr. Pepys also.

17. This was reproduced in *Thraliana* 2:626–27; *Florence Miscellany*, p. 59.

18. According to SL, Dr. Lort "says he shall be extremely happy in receiving a Letter from Milan, a Direction to him in Saville Row will be sufficient—He does not know whether Mrs. Cowley is related to Gay" (Ry. 552.3).

HLP's guess was well founded. Hannah Cowley, née Parkhouse (1743–1809), a popular dramatist and poet, was originally from Devon. Her paternal grandmother was a cousin of John Gay.

19. HLT on 28 March 1783 reported having rented a house at Bath; but she delayed moving because of the illness of her two youngest daughters, Henrietta (d. 18 April in Streatham) and CMT. By 14 April—and except for a brief visit to Streatham (20–23)—she

had settled at Bath with her "three [eldest] Daughters, three Maids, and a Man." For more than a year (including a month's sojourn at Weymouth in August), she was separated from GP, the subject of gossip and of filial suspicion (*Thraliana* 1:560–64; Hyde, pp. 237–38).

TO SAMUEL LYSONS

Milan
25: February 1785.

Dear Sir—

Our Friend Mr. Bartolozzi, (Son to the great Engraver)[1] passing through this Town; I take the Opportunity to send you your Fossills, which I hope and verily believe are exceedingly valuable:[2]

The Professor of Natural History[3] here gave them to me, from his own private Collection, and stripping himself trusted to his Correspondent for a fresh Supply.

We are going to Venice after Easter, whither you must direct your Answer: mean Time continue your kindness to me, and if you hear any false Reports—(all ill reports of us *are* false ones I assure you:)—strangle them instantly.[4] My Husband deserves the Esteem of every one, as well as the entire Love and Fidelity of his Wife—who is ever with true Regard / dear Mr. Lysons's / Faithful and Obedient Servant / H: L: Piozzi.

Mr. Piozzi sends his Compliments and hopes you'll be pleased with your Slates: At Naples we shall pick up something else perhaps.

Text: Hyde Collection. *Address:* To / Samuel Lysons Esqr. at Godwin's / Pocket Book Shop No. 167 over against / The New Church in / The Strand / with a Box. / London.

1. HLP refers to Francesco's son Gaetano. See HLT to FB [18 July 1784], n. 4.

On the twenty-fifth also, in *Thraliana* (2:632), HLP wrote: "Young Bartolozzi has been here in his way to England . . . he will give a good Acc[t] of us to the envious Italians resident in England; & I sent by him a little Box of Trash to please Susan & Sophy— . . ."

2. SL eventually received his fossils, writing to HLP, 15 April (Ry. 552.4): "I called on Mr. Bartolozzi yesterday and agree with you in thinking him a very agreeable young man, he desired his Compliments to you and Mr. P. as did Mad. Borghi."

3. HLP identifies the professor of natural history as Baron Cronthal: "very clever—an ex Jesuit and an Infidel" (*Thraliana* 2:664 n. 2; Clifford, p. 238).

4. Although SL ostensibly continued as HLP's friend, his attitude was equivocal. Instead of "strangling" hostile reports of the Piozzis, he scoured newspapers and journals, pasting into a scrapbook from 1785 to ca. 1788 any derogatory bit of biographical detail, any negative review of HLP's early work. When she learned about the scrapbook (now in Special Collections, Columbia University Library), she hoped that it might be destroyed.

TO SAMUEL LYSONS

Milan
26: February 1785.

Dear Mr. Lysons.

I write this Letter by *the Post,* to tell you that I wrote you one yesterday by a private Hand; Young Bartolozzi, Son to our great Engraver: who is returning to England after visiting his Friends in Italy, and promised to take Care of your Fossills, and deliver them Safe into your own hand. I directed him to Godwin's Pocket-Book Shop and said nothing of Country Residence; but if he does not bring them to *you,* the Place to find *him* is at Mr. Borghi's No 5: John Street Oxford Road.[1]

My Notion and hope is that you will like your Petrefactions; they are Fish preserved in Slates very curious. Baron Cronthal the great Naturalist gave them to me, out of his own private Collection, with an Account of whence they came, on the Paper that contains them. I hope to pick up other Rareties in the Course of my Travels, and bring them you myself; but was impatient to send these, having found so good an Opportunity: as I can rely on Mr. Bartolozzi's Regard both for me, and for every Branch of Knowledge.

Do write to us at Venice, and tell that they are come safe, and mind the Date of this Letter *do,* and say which came first the Friend or the Post, for he proposes travelling Day and Night, and outstripping the Letter Carrier if possible——God send him safe thro' the Snows of Savoy, there was a Waggon lost on the Tyrolese Hills t'other day.

And now dear Sir how shall I fill my Paper, and give you an Equivalent for your fourteen Pence? Shall I tell you of a Play I saw some Time ago acted by Fryars in their Convent before Lent began?[2] Or shall I tell you of an Oratorio we went to Yesterday where the Crowd hindered us from breathing, and the Noise from hearing, tho' performed in a Church of vast Capacity?[3] Shall I tell you of the Carnival Masqueraders, which in Merriment and Multitude exceeded any thing I ever saw?[4] Shall I lament the coldness of the Weather,[5] or rejoyce in the Warmth of Affection every day shewn me by my kind Husband? while his Friends pay me all possible Respect, and try to make me regret leaving a Place where I have lived very happily: but the Name of Venice is *so* attractive, and there is a fine Collection of Natural Curiosities to be seen at Verona, so that I shall set out again very chearfully the Week after Easter: so much the more so, as Mr. Piozzi's Health is always best upon the Road; though Bartolozzi says he never looked nor sung so well in His Life.

Tell me Something of Home *do;* how the People tear Mrs. Siddons in Pieces, and why they tear her:[6] How the Executors and Mr. Boswell quarrel over the Remains of poor Dr. Johnson. I saw something of it in an English Newspaper one Day, but it only served to whet, not gratify Curiosity; the Particulars must come from you.[7] The Booksellers have written to me for Materials or Letters, but I told them truly enough that I had left most of my Papers in England, and could do nothing till my return.[8]

When you see Sir Lucas Pepys and his Brother present my best regards.[9] I long to return chiefly that I may express the Esteem and Gratitude I feel for that Family; but nothing will I send by *private hands* till I hear your little Box is safe arrived. Some Trifles I trusted a Man with for my little Girls—or rather great Girls at Kensington never reached them; so I am somewhat shy of venturing Presents across the Water——You must however accept your little Fish, I hope they will swim very well. Here have I been writing on the fourth Side of the paper I swear—and took it for the 3*d*. What shall I do now? You will have to pay double Postage perhaps, (but I hope not;) for hearing that my husband sends you his Compliments and that I am Dear Sir / Your Affectionate Friend / and humble Servant / H: L: Piozzi.

Text: Hyde Collection.

1. After waiting until 14 April for his fossils, SL found them and Bartolozzi at the residence of Aloisio Borghi (SL to HLP, 15 April, Ry. 552.4).
2. A trifling performance by the monks of Saint Victor at Milan. She thought much of it gross and infantile, although she enjoyed the sentimental interludes (*Thraliana* 2:631; *Observations* 1:79–83).
3. On 27 February HLP noted in *Thraliana* 2:632 that she had attended Metastasio's *Passione* in Saint Celso's Church and was shocked by a castrato's representation of Saint Peter. See also *Observations* 1:84–85.
4. For her detailed impressions, see *Observations* 1:95–96.
5. The cold continued until April, at times with heavy snow (*Observations* 1:92).
6. Throughout the autumn of 1784, the newspapers had viciously accused SS of exploiting benefit performances for the ailing actors William Brereton (1751–87) and West Digges (ca. 1720–86). Both in time exonerated her; and further testimonies to her kindness and generosity were circulated by the actor Charles Lee Lewes (1740–1803) and her husband William Siddons (1744–1808). She endured the slander, although at one point threatening to retire from the theater.

The affair is summarized by Manvell, pp. 107–15. For journalistic outcries, see appendix 1.

7. HLP's response to SL: "[SJ's] Executors are Sir Joshua Reynolds, Sir John Hawkins and Dr. Scott—he died worth above two Thousand pounds, a great part of which he has left to his black servant Frank—No less than Six persons have engaged to write his life Sir J. Hawkins, Dr. Kippis, Mr. Davies and Mr. Boswell are of the Number. I suppose you have been or will be applied to for Anecdotes of him" (SL to HLP, 29 December 1784; Ry. 552.2).
8. HLP had already received a letter (Yale University Library) from James Robson (1733–1806) of New Bond Street, dated 28 January:

"Madam

"Will you pardon an old acquaintance for intruding a Moment upon Your time and attention; An Affair of some concern and consequence to the World at large, (at least the litterary part of it) is deeply interested in Your Friendship and kindness upon the present sollicitation: You must have heard that the good and great Doctor Johnson, Your old faithful Friend and Companion, is now no more: The World have unanimously called for an elegant Edition of all his Works, and it is now the business of the Booksellers to endeavour to do Justice to his memory: As one interested in the publication, I take the liberty to sollicit Your help and assistance with Materials which may by chance, or other wise, have fallen into Your possession: His long residence at Your Villa, as well as at Your House in Town, it is presumed must have produced many original scraps, both in Verse and prose, and perhaps many valuable Letters, to so valuable a Patroness:—We wish not to lose one Morsel of this immortal Man: Deign then, Dear Madam, to contribute Your assistance upon this important business; The World will have it, that you have a *Portfolio* repleat with *Johnsoniana*. . . . his Executors give their Assistance and Sanction to the Edition. . . ."

9. HLP's attitude toward Sir Lucas and his brother William Weller Pepys (1741–1825), cr. baronet (1801), master in chancery, was not as friendly as she intimated to SL. Three years earlier she had been pointedly resentful of their "spying" and gossiping. Although willing to solicit Sir Lucas's help with the *Anecdotes,* she continued to smart. "The Pepyses," she remarked in 1790, "have used me very ill—I hope they find out too, that I do not care." See *Thraliana* 1:526–27, 2:770–71; Hayward 1:304.

TO SAMUEL LYSONS

Milan
22: March 1785.

I feel much obliged by your Letter dear Mr. Lysons, but between your own Dilatoriness and that of the Post, I thought it would never have reached me. You and I are fortunately situated for the accumulation of new Ideas. I see something every Day which I never saw before; the last Image imprinted on my Mind is that of the Cardinal Prince D'Orini,[1] who most condescendingly, and unexpectedly paid us a Visit as he passed thro' the Town. We had a little Concert in our best Room, and about thirty Friends; who all stood up astonished at the Entrance of the Cardinal, while he kissed Mr. Piozzi, and blessed him in a Manner equally venerable and graceful; and turning to me said he hoped the Milanese Nobility knew the Respect that was due to so much Merit &c.

He came again next Morning at Breakfast Time, sate with us two Hours I believe, invited us at our Return to spend a Week with him at his Palace, in the Monte di Briança; and parted from us, leaving me his Benediction, tho' my Faith was not totally the same as his own he said, but that I had given an Example at Milan of that Morality which it was the Business of all Religions to enforce.

So cry mercy Mr. and Mrs. Piozzi! We will now if you please talk a little about England— I am sorry you came so late into Dr. Johnson's Acquaintance;[2] *you* might have got some Advice to write down if that Journey from Bath to London had not been prolonged so. My Book is getting forward, and will run well enough among the rest; the Letters I have of Dr. Johnson's are two hundred at least I dare say, and some of those from Skie are delightful:[3] they will carry my little Volume upon their Back quite easily.

Do you know who Dr. Taylor[4] gives his Anecdotes to? Mr. Johnson bid me once ask *him* for Memoirs if I was the survivor, and so I would, but I am afraid of a Refusal; as I guess Sir John Hawkins is already in possession of all that Dr. Taylor has to bestow. There lives however at Birmingham a Surgeon Mr. Edmund Hector,[5] whom likewise Mr. Johnson referred me to: he once saw Mr. Thrale and me, and perhaps would be more kind, and more likely to relate such Things as I wish to hear.——Could you go between us? and coax him out of some Intelligence——The Story of the Duck is incomparable.[6] Sir Lucas Pepys advised me not to declare to private Friends alone, but to publicly advertise my Intentions of writing Anecdotes concerning Dr. Johnson,[7] you will therefore see it proclaimed in all the papers I hope.

This Post carries a Letter to dear Dr. Lort, for whom I always had a very great Regard: you are lucky indeed in making such an Acquaintance as the Bishop of Peterboro'.[8] Surely you and I shall dream of Red Caps and Lawn Sleeves now every night.

Have you had your little Fish? I hear they are *flying Fish*, having already passed the Alps, as I understand by a Letter from Bartolozzino who carries them, and whom you will find an extremely pleasing, companionable young Man.

I am glad you have been to see pretty Tetbury; the Writers of the next Generation will be examining that Neighbourhood for Anecdotes of *your* early Days, and then *I* shall come in for having in the year 1784 prophesied your future Glories.

What shall I tell you to divert you? About Milan nothing;—about the Milanese but little: The other Italians reckon them fat and heavy, and say there can be no Vivacity in a Country that is famous only for its Butter and Cheese. The Language is offensive to one's Ears, and all the People speak it; even those of the first Fashion complain that it puts them in Subjection as they phrase it to speak Italian. All this however the Bishop of Peterborough and Mr. Seward can tell you as well as myself. That the Women are very pretty it were better hear[d] from them; that they are kind to me I half wonder at, yet 'tis true: and some protest that they shall cry for *dispetto* when we leave the Country.

Farewell, and continue me *your* kindness, and let no Tumults of Business or Pleasure make you forget your early Friends. One sees Instances of long and strong Attachments in these *idle* Countries, difficult to be matched in *busy* ones where constancy is considered as a Joke, and Love and Hatred are equally *out of the Question. Here's much to do with* Hate and more with Love as Juliet says,[9] and the people stab one another in the Streets of Italy for Causes that would not induce an Englishman to cross the way.

Be assured Dear Sir that the more I think of your present, and future Occupations, the more I am flattered that you will continue to remember with Regard Your / truly faithful affectionate / H: L: Piozzi.

My Husband sends his best Compliments. Adieu, and do write soon, or I shall be run from Venice to Pisa and you must direct thither.

Text: Hyde Collection. *Address:* A Monsieur / Monsieur Sam: Lysons chez le Rev: / Monsieur / S: Peach / East Sheene / near / Mortlake / Surrey / Angleterre. *Postmark* < >.

1. Angelo Maria Durini (1725–96), poet, and patron of the arts. Titular archbishop of Ancyra, he was made a cardinal in 1776. See *Observations* 1:284; *Thraliana* 2:635, 637.

SL responded, 15 April (Ry. 552.4): "I am delighted with your account of the Cardinal and his liberality of sentiment, how different a reception have you experienced from *that* prophecied by the Bathonian and London Scandal Mongers, I believe they are all silenced 'ere this, unless Baretti perhaps may still pour forth his torrent of abuse, which he has done, I believe more than any other, because he says you used his friend Meci so ill. He told every one here, that he had written circular letters to Italy to abuse you, but I believe he was not credited."

For references to Mecci and Baretti, see HLP to SL, 27 July 1785 and 23 August [17]88; to Sophia Byron, 2 and 8 June 1788.

2. SL had made his first visit to SJ on 26 June 1784. Thereafter SJ was too ill to receive him. SL on 15 April "regret[ted] having seen so little of Dr. Johnson, as from the little I did see I think we should have agreed very well."

3. Accompanied by JB, SJ was at Skye from 2 September 1773 to 3 October. See *Boswell's Johnson* 5:147–284.

4. John Taylor (1711–88), a native of Ashbourne, Derbyshire, was a fellow student with SJ at Lichfield Grammar School and a lifelong friend. He studied at Christ Church College, Oxford (1729), but left without taking a degree. Sometime after 1736 he was ordained and then (1742, 1752) attained the degrees of B.A., M.A., LL.B., LL.D. His preferments included the living of Market Bosworth, Leics., and a prebendal stall at Westminster. Taylor provided details for *Boswell's Johnson* (passim; see also Chapman, passim).

5. John Hawkins (1719–89), knighted (1772), was SJ's authorized biographer.

Edmund Hector (1708–94), a Birmingham surgeon, a Lichfield schoolmate, and a long-standing friend of SJ, was another of JB's sources.

In the letter of 15 April, SL wrote: "Sir Lucas . . . has I suppose told you that Mr. Hector has given his Anecdotes to Boswell—Mr. Seward has a large collection of Johnsoniana which have been perused by Kippis and squeezed again by Hawkins, if any drops remain they are he says very much at your service. . . ."

6. As SL told it (25 February): "There is just arrived from Litchfield an epitaph written by him at five years old on a Duck—'Here lies poor Duck, which Samuel Johnson trod on. If it had liv'd it had been more luck for then there had been an odd one.' " See *Anecdotes*, p. 11, and *Poems*, p. 354.

7. Encouraged by SL's energetic support, HLP soon broached the subject to an enthusiastic Thomas Cadell, the bookseller (7 June, below), and the project was launched.

8. John Hinchliffe (1731–94), bishop of Peterborough (1769); master of Trinity College, Cambridge (1768–88); orator and preacher. He was an acquaintance of the Thrale years and a member of The Club. SL had written on 25 February: "I dined about a fortnight ago at the Bishop of Peterborough's—Dr. L[ort] and Mr. Seward were there. The Bishop I met a few days before at Mr. Walpole's, where he very obligingly recollected me and gave me a pressing invitation to his house, which I certainly shall not neglect, as he is a man whom I admire very much, he has since paid me a visit" (Ry. 552.3).

9. Romeo (rather than Juliet) said: "Here's much to do with hate, but more with love" (1.1.175).

TO HESTER MARIA THRALE

Venice,
22 April, 1785

I arrived here last Saturday, & found every thing that was delightful, among the rest your charming chatty Letter; which *could* only have been *Kinder,* more agreeable or entertaining it could not have been: I will make you all the Amends I am able. We came hither through Cremona, Mantua, Verona & Padua,[1] at each of which Towns we stopt for two or three Days, & delivered Letters of Recommendation, & received Civilities; particularly a private Concert prepared for us at the House of a very pleasing Couple who live at Mantua, & are intimate with some of our kind Milanese that wished to prolong our obligations to them. An agreable Countess there took a great fancy to me, & told me how She taught her little Children—but I really do make myself a favrite with the Italian Ladies surprizingly, one Reason is perhaps because they soon see I wish not to rob 'em of their Male Admirers. The Women of Fashion all over the North of Italy go without Caps old as well as young, & dress their Hair fantastically with Flowers &c never thinking of Fashions, & studying only how best to set off their Charms. The great Gyants however painted by Giulio Romano[2] at this Town will be remembered by me after the prettiest Ladies are forgotten. the Pictures here are all known in England I believe, but nothing can give one a just Idea of them except the Sight. Verona is an exquisite Spot, I hated ever to leave it, tho' fatigued to death with posting up & down to see the Antiques, Amphitheatre &c. at Vicenza we were entertained by the Nobleman whose beautiful Villa built by Palladio[3] was the Model of Meriworth Castle;[4] there is indeed no Difference in their *form,* but a great deal in their Situation & Furniture. At *Padua la dotta*[5] I had Letters for the Astronomical professor,[6] who shewed us every Attention in His Power, & took us up to his Observatory whence we saw *such* a prospect. The beautiful Brenta[7] then brought us hither in a Barge, and Mr Piozzi's Forte piano[8] never sounded so sweet I think as on that Water, which is used to the Freightage of Musick; and is adorned with Palaces on its Sides that put one in Mind of Pococurante's Villa.[9] Just as the Sun set, we came in View of Venice.

& now's the Time that if a Poet
Shined in Description he might show it;[10]

for here are literally

Palladian Walls, Venetian Doors,
Grotesco Roofs, & Stucco Floors:[11]

but as I never now speak my own Language except to My Maid, I am more in the way of resembling Mr Johnson's Madman, who in order to attain perfection said if you remember that it was sufficient to pronounce the Word *bel, bel, bel, bel, bel:*[12] and *this* Word occurs so often in *this* Country that I shall soon arrive at the State he wished for. Well! where shall I begin in praising this lovely Place? Head-Quarters of Beauty, Elegance, & pleasure as it is. With my own Lodgings I think I will begin, which consist of a Magnificent Gallery, Drawing Room, Bedchamber & Balcony on the Grand Canal: the view of which exceeds all that Painting can express,

or youthful Poets fancy when in Love.[13]

in fact no Description gives one adequate Ideas of the Splendour and Gayety of Venice[14] and as to St. Mark's Place, it was half an hour that I had stood in it before I once *thought* of Apollo's brazen Horses,[15] so much was I struck by the general Effect of the whole. The Steeds are however worthy of all that has been said of 'em, and look half sensible of the Applause they so justly receive, but *every* thing here takes pains to delight the Imagination, every Shop disposes its Goods in a manner unknown to London or Paris, whose *Foire St Ovide*[16] is a faint Imitation of Venice's everyday Diversions. Here is Musick[17] either in Gondolas rowing up & down, or on the *Lido* as they call a great Flagd Walk by the Seaside, all Evening: here are Theatres and Coffeehouses, & *Casinos* and every *Convenience* for every Vice that can be nam'd. A Young Man here whom we knew at Milan—Mr Parsons of the Sussex Militia[18] confesses that he had not an Idea of such Luxury, of such Licentiousness till he came to Venice

> Where eas'd of Fleets the Adriatic Main
> Wafts the smooth Eunuch and enamour'd Swain.[19]

A propos to the former you may be sure of *Marchese* next Winter;[20] and you may be sure that he will astonish England as he has done Italy, who crowd about him as if he was a Thing drop'd from the Moon. In fact *his* Excellence is not like that of Mrs Siddons, the excellence of others, push'd to perfection in *him:* his Excellence is like that of the Man who about 30 Years ago stood on his Head on the Top of the Monument on Fish Street hill,[21] & then came down flying on a rope into Fleet Street—He had no *Imitators* however, & those who try to do what Marchese does will as effectually, tho' figuratively break their Necks. The *Pastry Cook* Sadler & his Expedition made me laugh heartily;[22] had I only read it in the Newspaper, I should have thought it a *Puff.* The *Pig's* abilities are however more respectable, because they are attended with Success.[23] The Robbers you speak of are very proper Fruit for the deadly *Nevergreen,* but what is done to those who steal Kisses in *your* Country! I believe it is considered here as mere petty Larceny. Did not Doctor Johnson say once that Macbeth w^d make a good Pantomime?, & don't you remember how angry Mr Murphy was at the Remark?[24] Surely these Dancers will make all Words superfluous, and *Discourse will* (as Gratiano says) *become commendable in none but Parrots:*[25] I saw the Story of Don John or the Libertine exhibited *in Ballo* at Lodi,[26] & fairly ran away from the Theatre; as I had somewhat too much of little *Shepherd's* Notions about me, to think an impenitent Sinner going to Hell quite a good Subject for a Dance.[27] Mr Piozzi took me the other Day to a Church, where there was a *Concerto Spirituale*[28] performed all by Women, some of which were good Violin Players, some had Bass Voices, & he commended the French-Horn which one would think impossible for a Female Mouth to manage: it was a Conservatorio I understood, and is I believe mentioned in Dr Burney's Travels. The famous Picture of our Saviour's first Miracle at the Marriage in Cana of Galilee, which contains the Portraits of Titian, Tintoret, and Paulo Veronese,[29]—a Copy of which you once saw at Old Scarlet, the Optician's, who sold it for 100£—cannot be seen by Women, as it is in a Refectory belonging to a rigid Convent, Mr Piozzi and Mr Parsons went *in* this Morning to look at it, & left me on the *out*side of the Wall; as I wear the Dress of the Venetian Ladies now, a Black Zendeletto[30] & Petticoat; I am no longer stared at as a Foreigner. My female Friends tell me how becoming it is & I am myself delighted with my Appearance—in Black Shadow.—Now you live so much at Brighthelmstone you perhaps see Dr Delap[31] often, do tell me how he does: few Men in England have given me more Pleasure unmingled with *any* Offence than Dr Delap. I therefore reflect on his past Friendship with great Esteem & Tenderness, & hope he continues it to me; for few People love him as well.

You are happy in Mr Scrase's Society; his knowledge is such, & such his Attachment to your Father's Family, that every day will strengthen that Regard for him wch may, if you pay him the Attention his Merit & Wisdom deserves, in some Measures alleviate his Pains, & smooth his Bed in Sickness. Sophy tells me poor Kipping is sick;[32] *God bless my Soul Ma'am, why now these Things will sometimes—but if the Dr would come down indeed,* but then *the Time o' Year & that—& besides now you know Ma'am the Dr God bless him—but he is just the same as ever for the matter of that. &c.*

Poor Kip! I hope he will recover.

Do go & look in some great Mapbook & see how distant *your* Sea is from *our* Sea; I shall think myself nearer England when at Naples: here however we eat after the mode of Great Britain exactly—for the first Time since I left Dover, as the Innkeeper is used to our Customs. We shall wait till the Ascension is past, & then go slowly to Florence, where I shall hope to find a Letter from you directed to the Banker's—or no, no, tis better the old way, *Poste restant.* Adieu my dearest Hester, be good & wise—of those there is no Doubt nor Danger—but be healthy, & happy; & merry, & kind: for that will delight yourself, and all your Friends, and particularly your Affecte / H: L: Piozzi.

Here is a sweet Lady that writes incomparably—a Countess Rosenberg[33] who has all the *blues* about her, so we are in no want of *Conversation spirituelle,* her French Comedy of *le Prejugé à la mode* is charming, & She is writing a Novel that will be translated into English.[34] Have you seen the *Tableau d'Angleterre?*[35] 'tis all the Ton in Italy.

Adieu; direct to Florence, Poste restante.

Text: Queeney Letters, pp. 196–200. *Address: A Mademoiselle / Mademoiselle Hester Maria Thrale / in West Street, Brighthelmstone, Sussex, Londres, Angleterre.*

1. See *Observations* 1:112–49.

2. Giulio Romano (ca. 1499–1546), painter and architect. Roman-born and apprenticed in his youth to Raphael, he settled in Mantua about 1524. "The Fall of the Giants" (Sala dei Giganti) in the Palazzo del Te, probably his most memorable fresco, is a powerful conception of a collapsing universe, inspired by Ovid. "The giants could scarcely have been more amazed at Jupiter's thunder, than [HLP] was at their painted fall" (*Observations* 1:120).

3. Andrea Palladio (1508–80), architect, who was born in Padua and died in Vicenza.

4. "The property of Lord le Despencer, [Merriworth Castle] is an elegant structure, designed by Colin Campbell [for John Fane and completed in 1723], in imitation of a house in Italy, built by the famous Palladio. It is a square, extending sixty-eight feet, and has four porticoes of the Ionic order. In the middle is a semicircular dome, which has two shells. . . . The rooms are in general small, but . . . fitted up in a very costly manner." See G. A. Cooke, *Walks through Kent; containing a Topographical and Statistical Description of the County* (London: Sherwood, Neely, and Jones, 1819), p. 263. See also Thomas Philipot, *Villare Cantianum; or, Kent Surveyed and Illustrated,* 2d ed. ([1659] Lynn: 1776); *Observations* 1:136.

5. See *Observations* 1:137–38.

6. Abate Giuseppe Toaldo (1719–98) was professor of astronomy at the University of Padua and director of the observatory (the *Specola*), whose construction he had supervised in 1769. Toaldo was a member of the College of Philosophy and Theology and author of *Della vera influenza degli astri, delle stagioni, e mutazioni di tempo, saggio meteorologico . . .* (Padua, 1770).

The Piozzis carried letters of introduction to Toaldo from John Strange, the Venetian Resident (*Observations* 1:143).

7. The Brenta River rises in the Alpine lakes of Caldonazzo and flows down through the Venetian plain to the Adriatic Sea.

8. See HLP to CB, 2 August [1784], n. 1.

9. Describing the beauties of the environment and architecture along the Brenta, HLP—allowing for Gallic ignorance of Italian sentiment and values—supposed them "best described by Monsieur de Voltaire, whose Pococurante the Venetian senator in Candide [chap. 25] that possesses all delights in his villa upon the banks of the Brenta, is a very lively portrait . . ." (*Observations* 1:222).

10. Pope, *Imitations of Horace,* Satire 2.6.187–88.

11. Ibid., 191–92.

12. ". . . a well order'd Mind shd Keep Hypotheses out, with Diligence, or one may grow like the Man Johnson told of, that found every thing was O or L. & ran about crying Bel! Bel! Bel! A mad Mr Nelme he was, I think."

"L. D. Nelme, who wrote *An Essay towards an Investigation of the Origin and Elements of Language and Letters* (1772). In it, he expounded the universality of O, which was the symbol of the boundary of sight, or the horizon, and of I (not L), which was the symbol of extent or altitude" (*Thraliana* 2:1033 and n. 2; see also, *Queeney Letters,* p. 257 n.).

13. Nicholas Rowe, *The Fair Penitent* (1703), 3.1.

14. *Observations* 1:150–230.

15. *Observations* 1:151–52, 157.

16. HLP first visited the Foire Saint Ovide in 1775. See her *French Journals,* p. 92; and cf. *Observations* 1:179. The fair was held in an open place, dominated by an equestrian statue of Louis XV, that was surrounded by shops and booths. These were destroyed by fire in 1777, the statue razed by order of the revolutionary government in 1792.

17. CB observed: ". . . upon the *Piazza di S. Marco,* I heard a great number of vagrant musicians, some in bands, accompanying one or two voices; sometimes a single voice and guitar; and sometimes two or three guitars together. Indeed it is not to be wondered at, that the street-music here is generally neglected, as people are almost stunned with it at every corner. . . ." *The Present State of Music in France and Italy* (London: T. Becket, 1771), pp. 143–44.

18. William Parsons (fl. 1764–1807) was a member of the coterie that published verses in the London *World* (1784–85) while residing in Florence. He met the Piozzis at the theater in Milan and became a major contributor to the *Florence Miscellany,* writing thirty-one of the English poems. He was also the author of *A Poetical Tour, in the Years 1784, 1785, and 1786. By a Member of the Arcadian Society at Rome* (London: J. Robson and W. Clarke, 1787). See HLP to SL, 27 July 1785; *Thraliana* 2:631–34; Clifford, passim; and the unflattering article in *DNB.*

19. Pope, *The Dunciad* 4.309–10.

20. Luigi (Lodovico Marchesini) Marchesi (1755–1829), a male soprano and one of the last of the castrati, was among Italy's most admired singers. CB, on the other hand, "did not much like" Marchesini, who made his debut in Rome in 1773–74 and in London in 1788. See *The Present State of Music,* p. 96.

21. The Monument is the doric column designed by Christopher Wren and erected (1671–77) as a memorial of the Great Fire (2–7 September 1666). It is situated on Fish Street Hill (also known as New Fish Street), which, running from East Cheap Street to Lower Thames Street, afforded the principal access to the old London Bridge. Fish Street Hill was once noted for its rowdy atmosphere.

22. James Sadler, a balloonist, who attempted several ascents in 1784 and 1785. Lansdowne (*Queeney Letters*, p. 198 n. 2) suggests that it may have been Sadler who nearly drowned in the sinking of an "aquatic balloon." Somewhat more laughable were two incidents in which the hapless Sadler's balloon took flight without him. See *GM* 55, pt. 1 (1785): 315, 480–81.

23. See *Boswell's Johnson* 4:373, 547–48; *GM* 55, pt. 1 (1785): 413–14.

"Learned" animals, popular attractions in London at least as early as 1750, had been so advertised: e.g., "Le Chien Savant," a "Sapient Pig," as well as an educated bullfinch, goose, etc. See DL, *Collecteana* (British Library, advertisements, 1661–1840, in 5 vols.), 2:73–96; Joseph Strutt, [*Glig-gamena, Angel Đeod*, or] *The Sports and Pastimes of the People of England*. . . . ed. William Hone ([1801]; London: Chatto and Windus, 1898), 3.6.339.

24. SJ believed that acting, even as fine as Garrick's, could not adequately represent the emotions verbalized in great tragedy. When JB said of the actor (19 October 1769), that he had " 'brought Shakespeare into notice,' " SJ retorted: " 'Sir, to allow that, would be to lampoon the age. Many of Shakespear's plays are the worse for being acted: Macbeth, for instance' " (*Boswell's Johnson* 2:92).

SJ's hostility to the creative gap between dramatist and actor becomes apparent in the riposte to Garrick: " 'Prithee, do not talk of feelings, Punch has no feelings.' " Arthur Murphy adds: "This seems to have been his settled opinion; admirable as Garrick's imitation of nature always was, Johnson thought it no better than mere mimickry" (Murphy's "Essay on Johnson's Life and Genius," *Johns. Misc.* 1:457; cf. 2:248, 317).

SJ defined "pantomime" as "The power of universal mimicry," but also as the action of a "buffoon" or "harlequin."

25. It is Lorenzo who says: "I think the best grace of wit will shortly turn into silence, and discourse grow commendable in none only but parrots" (*Merchant of Venice* 3.5.44–46).

26. The first night after leaving Milan (ca. 9 April), en route to Venice, the travelers stopped at Lodi, southeast of Milan. They attended the opera and saw "a new dramatic dance, made upon the story of Don John, or the Libertine; a tale which, whether true or false, fact or fable, has furnished every Christian country in the world, I believe, with some subject of representation. . . . I have at least *half a notion* that the horrible history is *half true;* if so, it is surely very gross to represent it by dancing" (*Observations* 1:113–14).

27. Probably the Reverend Thomas Shephard (1757–1843), only son of the Reverend Thomas Shephard (1716–96), for whom he has sometimes been mistaken as vicar of Speen and rector of Woodhay, Berks. Born in Hungerford, the younger Shephard attended Eton College (1770–73) and was further educated at Brasenose College, Oxford (B.A., 1778) and Cambridge (M.A., 1782; D.D., 1828). For several years he ran the boys' school at Enborne where JSPS was to be a pupil. He married Anne Parke Goddard (d. pre-1829), by whom he had three daughters and a son.

In his will (a copy, D/EX 360/17, is at the C.R.O., Berkshire; proved in the Prerogative Court of Canterbury 29 August 1843), Shephard describes himself as a clerk, a doctor of divinity, and a resident of Crux Easton, Hants.

28. CB recorded that (in Paris, Thursday, 14 Fête Dieu: Corpus Christi Day) he "went to the *Concert Spirituel*, the only public amusement allowed on these great festivals. It is a grand concert performed in the great hall of the Louvre, in which the vocal consists of detached pieces of church music in Latin" (*The Present State of Music*, p. 23).

29. Paolo Veronese (Caliari or Cagliari, 1528–88) was commissioned in 1562 to paint the "Marriage at Cana," the first of his great banqueting scenes, for the refectory of the convent of San Giorgio Maggiore. In addition to his own portrait, Veronese included those of the painters Titian and Tintoretto. Among other historical characters were Eleanor of Austria, her bridegroom Don Alfonso d'Avalos, Francis I of France, Emperor Charles V, Queen Mary of England, the Sultan Soliman I. See *Observations* 1:171–72. ("The Marriage of Cana" was removed to the Louvre in 1799.)

30. For a description, see *Observations* 1:184.

31. A family friend of the Thrales, the Reverend John Delap, was a minor dramatist. See HLP to Charlotte Lewis, 8 December 1790, n. 6.

32. Henry Kipping (1726–85), a Brighton surgeon and apothecary who had helped to treat Ralph Thrale. See Hyde, pp. 122–23, 125; *Thraliana* 1:410.

33. Born in Venice, Giustina (Justine) Frances Antonia Wynne (ca. 1732–91) was the eldest of six children born to Sir Richard Wynne (d. 1751) and Anna, née Gazini (1713–80). Justine married in 1761 Philip Joseph (1691–1765), Count Orsini-Rosenberg, Austrian ambassador to Venice (1754–64). The countess was recognized for her literary salons and publications, although her taste and style in both were deemed questionable.

Her best known works are: *Della dimora de' conti del Nord in Venezia* (1782); *Pièces morales et sentimentales* (1785); *Il Trionfo de' gondolieri* (1786); *Alticchiero illustrato* (1787).

For her association with Giacomo Casanova, see the latter's *History of My Life*, trans. Willard R. Trask, 12 vols. in 6 (New York: Harcourt Brace & World, 1966), 3:172, 5:171 ff.

34. According to Parsons in his *Poetical Tour*, pp. 41–42, she "was then meditating a Novel on a very interesting occurrence in the Venetian History——It is the story of the unfortunate Foscarini, who was condemned and strangled by a sentence of the Senate, in the year 1602, on a suspicion of his being concerned in a conspiracy against the Republic, which was set on foot by the Spanish Ambassador."

There is no evidence that the novel ever went beyond an idea.

35. The *Tableau* in 1784 made no noise in London, whence SL wrote on 20 May: "I have never so much as heard of [it], nor has any one to whom I have mentioned it" (Ry. 552.5).

By 1785 it was translated as *A Picture of England for the Year 1780, continued by the Editor till the Year 1783*. The unfavorable notice in the *English Review* (6 [1785]: 460–65) begins: "This publication appears with an air of mystery: the title page neither informs us by whom, nor where it was printed. In this the author was prudent: no reputation was to be gained by publickly acknowledging this offspring of rancorous malignity."

TO SAMUEL LYSONS

Venice.
30: April 1785.

You are very lazy, indeed, Dear Mr. Lysons, to take a short bit of Paper, and write to a Friend a Thousand Miles off as if it was a Letter sent by the Hampstead Hurry[1] to fetch a Turbot up the Hill for a Dinner at the Long Room:[2] but I will scold no more, for Joy that you like your Playthings; it vexes me you missed Bartolozzino as we call him, he is an amiable young Man, and You would have had a Hundred Things in common, besides talking about me. Never was I so mortified at my own worthlessness, as since I have seen myself in Venice, unable to make *one* Sketch of the various Beauties which present themselves: you are quite right though to cast your Eyes on Cannaletti's Views[3] when you have a Mind of a little Chat with Mr. and Mrs. Piozzi, as they lodge upon the *grand Canal*[4] a good Way below the Rialto;[5] among, and over against such beautiful Palaces as Palladio and Sansovino[6] who built them could alone have imagined. Oh! *Do* talk to Sir Lucas Pepys about the Piazza St. Marco, and ask him if he was as much enchanted with the Architecture there as I am? Had his Brother ever seen it as I did the other Evening, the Moon rising out of the Sea on one Side, the Setting Sun gilding the Horses which once drew Apollo's Chariot on the other; Men and Women gayly chatting up and down the Squares, while Musick and Merriment resound from the Shops and Coffeehouses that crowd the Arcades—

—he would (as I did) have fancied himself in a Theatre. The Churches and Paintings are all known by heart to all the people You frequent, so I shall not teize you with Descriptions that every *Venezia illustrata* can produce; but confess that the general Effect has something inexpressibly striking, and from a Tower that I mounted yesterday the little Islands scattered about the Lagoon looked like Faery Cities formed in Water by the Touch of some Magical Wand.

At Verona as we came hither I was little less than transported to see an old Roman Ampitheatre kept in such elegant Preservation that they used it for the Purpose of a Ball Feast the other day as the Emperor passed through;[7] by the other day I mean the time when he was journeying about, a few years ago.

At *Padua la dotta* I enquired about Mr. San Giorgio but could not find him; Bozza of Verona[8] has a very fine Collection of petrified Fish, most of which are the natural Produce of the pacifick Ocean, the accidental produce of Mountains here in the Venetian State about sixty or seventy Miles from *any* Sea, but nearest to the *Adriatick*, where such Creatures as flying Fish were never seen, and he has some quite perfect: now if these are not Proofs, and all but living Evidences of the Deluge, what Things will be ever acknowledged as such?[9] In this age of Infidelity indeed the strongest Witnesses to the Truth of Sacred Writ will be brought in Question, and I found the Professor of Astronomy at Padua considered such a Specimen as a mere Lusus Naturae. How happy you are dear Sir to be thrown at your first Launch on the Ocean of this wide World not into *deep* Water only, but *clear* too: the Company of Mr. Pepys, Dr. Lort, and the Bishop of Peterborough! whose true Christian Faith, and steady Principles of Morality are valued by me far above their Conversation Talents, which however are as rare to be found as petrified Fish;——and dear Dr. Lort was dug out of the Welch Mountains you know.[10]

My Book is in very pretty forwardness, but the Letters I have in England are my best Possessions. A propos the Papers said that Sir John Hawkins has had his House burned down, is it true?[11]—Pray enquire for a Letter which *I know* Dr. Johnson wrote to Mr. Barnard the King's Librarian[12] when he was in Italy looking for curious books: the Subject was wholly Literary and Controversial, and would be most interesting to the Publick; I would give any thing almost to obtain a Copy *now,* and there was a Time when I might have taken twenty Copies. Do not you be as negligent of *your* Opportunities of Improvement, one always repents such Negligence in the End. No End to my Preachments you'll say, but you always gave me Permission to preach to you, so I am at least a Licenziata.

The French People fly further than the English still I find, or propose at least to fly further; they tell me Montgolfier meant to look for the North East Passage from his Balloon:[13] In the mean Time as Things come to perfection apace, I shall hope for aerial Visits from English Friends in a *Diligence* till every Gentleman keeps his own Machine. I knew, and always said, you would like Miss Burney, *every* body likes her I believe: The Cambridges[14] will be a very agreeable house to you, it was cleverly done to get into it, but you *do* make your way delightfully, and will make your early Friends proud of you many a long Year hence I am confident. Tell me about the Irish Bill, I do not understand a Syllable of it; what do the Irish people want? and what does Mr. Pitt refuse? You are in a Nation where every one has a Right to think and to talk about Religion and Government, *do pray* let me who live under other Regulations, hear what you think and say.[15]

Miss Thrale has written to me from Brighthelmstone,[16] and Susan and Sophy have thanked me for a little Box I sent at the same Time as yours, with Female Trifles in it: Mr. Piozzi is so good as to send them some Token of our Existence and Regard by every Opportunity, and the Venetian Resident will be good-natured, and carry some thing I am sure; but then He will not get to London these ten Months. I hope you will all like him when he comes among you, and I rather think it, he is a Man of an active Mind and soft Manners; what is there in this World I wonder, unattainable by the old Maxim well persisted in—of *suaviter in modo, fortiter in Re.*[17] Very few Things I do think.

This Place does not agree with me, I have never been the least indisposed since I left Dover till now, and I have never been right well since I entered Venice; we shall leave it as soon as the Show of the Bucentoro is over.[18] You must direct to *Florence* and pray write soon and tell me of the Weather, it is very extraordinarily cold here they say.

'Tis very odd, but all the Places bring some Scenes of Shakespeare to my Mind: my Head ran more on Romeo than on Virgil at Mantua and Verona, and here when I go to hear the Cause pleaded by the eloquent Venetian Advocates, fair Portia and Dr. Bellario of Padua meet my Imagination in every long Wig and Black Gown that I see.[19]

Send me word how much you pay for this Letter; it is *but one sheet* you see, but tell me the Truth what they make you pay for it.

You have heard of the Casinos a hundred times.[20] Here are some for every purpose; We frequent a *blue* one, where there is very agreable and very Literary Conversation on Tuesday and Fryday Evenings: a Demi-English Lady Countess of Rosenberg who has published a great many Things in French generally presides there. Tell me if the *Tableau d'Angleterre* makes a noise in London: it is thoroughly *tasted* on the Continent. Give my kindest Words to all who still remember me with Esteem and Tenderness: and accept Mr. Piozzi's Compliments with those of your Affectionate Friend and Servant / H: L: Piozzi.

Write me a long, kind letter to Florence directly——I love to receive your Letters.

Text: The original, somewhat mutilated, in the Hyde Collection, and emended by the printed version in *Bentley's Miscellany* 28 (1850): 169–71. *Address:* A Monsieur / Monsieur Samuel Lysons chez le Rev. Monsieur S. Peach / East Sheene / near Mortlake / Surrey / près de / Londres. Angleterre. *Postmark:* <   >.

1. A witticism adapted to "hurry-curry," the fashionable curricle.

2. The Long Room, part of the much-frequented spa and pleasuregrounds at Hampstead, was famous as well for its drinking and dining accommodations. Concerts and dances were held in the Great Room, assemblies in the Long Room. See Fanny Burney's *Evelina*, ed. E. A. Bloom with L. D. Bloom (London: Oxford University Press, 1968; reprint 1982), p. 179 n. 2, p. 428.

3. Antonio Canaletto, or Giovanni Antonio Canal (1697–1768), began his artistic career with theatrical decorations. After 1719 he turned to the antiquities of Rome. He also portrayed the street scenes of his native Venice, as well as of London during a visit (1746–48). He was probably the first artist to use the *camera lucida.* The Piozzis purchased a total of eight paintings by Canaletto. See *Observations* 1:150, 171; HLP to SL, 11 May 1786; and 5 September 1794.

4. See *Observations* 1:174–75.

5. In *Observations* 1:172–73, she describes "the Rialto, said to be the finest single arch in Europe . . . but so dirtily kept, and deformed with mean shops" that it elicits disgust.

6. Jacopo (Tatti) Sansovino (1486–1570), sculptor and architect. He was a pupil of Andrea Sansovino (Andrea Contucci, ca. 1460–1529), a native of Monte San Savino.

Jacopo followed Andrea to Rome ca. 1503 and took the teacher's name. He came into his own after 1527, when he moved to Venice. There he became a leading figure and a friend of such as Titian and Pietro Aretino. His architectural achievements include: Palazzo della Zecca (1536); Palazzo Corner (Ca' Grande, 1532); San Francesco delle Vigna (1534); Libreria Vecchia di San Marco (1537–54); Scuola Nuova di Santa Maria Valverde delle Misericorde (1532–63). As a sculptor, he executed the Scala dei Giganti (Doges' Palace courtyard, 1554).

He was appointed protomaestro of San Marco (1529), with the culmination of his career the bronze sacristy doors (1563) of the cathedral.

7. See *Observations* 1:121.

8. Paolo Antonio Sangiorgio (1748–1816) at Milan and Vincenzo Bozza (fl. 1735–95) at Verona—both apothecaries—were recommended by SL on 27 September 1784 as collectors of fossil fish (Ry. 522.1).

Bozza has been described as "apothicaire et chymiste distingué," by Joseph Jérôme le Française de Lalande in his *Voyage en Italie,* as cited by Herbert Barrows, ed., *Observations* (Ann Arbor: University of Michigan Press, 1967), p. 426. Bozza's discovery of southern fish preserved in slate in a mountain near Verona (a discovery that interested HLP) is described in his *Delle Acque Marziali ne' monti Veronese di Roverè di vele novellamente scoperti* (Verona: L'Erede di Agostino Carattoni, 1767).

Sangiorgio was professor of pharmaceutical chemistry at the Ospedale Maggiore di Milano (1783–98); professor of chemistry, botany, and natural history at the *lycea* of Brera and San Allesandrio (1806–16); author of, e.g., *La farmacia descritta secondo i moderni principi di Lavoisier,* 5 vols. (Milan, 1804–6). See Antonio Esposito Vitolo, "Di Giannambrogio et Paolo Sangiorgio, Speziali Milanesi," in *Castalia* 5–6 (1950): 233–37.

9. *Observations* 1:134–35; 2:195. Such details are repeated in *British Synonymy* under "Rare, Curious, Unfrequent, Scarce, Seldom Found" (2:192–93).

10. Lort was born in mountainous Pembrokeshire.

11. SL responded on 20 May (Ry. 552.5): "Sir John Hawkins's house was certainly burnt down and he lost almost every thing in it, but all Dr. Johnson's papers were saved. It is said that Sir John ran a great risk in getting at them."

The fire occurred in Sir John's house in Queen Square, Westminster, on 23 February. Thereafter he resided in Broad Sanctuary, Westminster. Although he saved the Johnsoniana, most of his personal possessions, library, drawings, and prints went up in flames. See B. H. Davis, *A Proof of Eminence: The Life of Sir John Hawkins* (Bloomington: Indiana University Press, 1973), pp. 338–39.

12. SJ's letter to Barnard (28 May 1768) was unavailable to both JB and HLP. See *Boswell's Johnson* 2:33 n. 4; Chapman 1:214–19; Clifford, p. 256, and his "Further Letters of the Johnson Circle," *Bulletin of the John Rylands Library* 20 (1936): 276–77.

13. The Montgolfier brothers—Joseph-Michel (1740–1810) and Jacques-Étienne (1745–99)—invented the hot-air balloon (the "Montgolfier"), which became the first manned flight vehicle on 21 November 1783.

14. FB's meeting with SL must have occurred at the Twickenham home of Richard Owen Cambridge.

15. Creating a new committee for trade, the prime minister William Pitt the younger

(1759–1806) charged it to help settle Ireland's financial troubles. Subsequently he brought before the Irish parliament a bill intended "to fuse the economies [of England and Ireland] . . . by admitting Ireland into the whole colonial trade and by adopting a system of trade" that would be favorable to it. Economic concessions were expected and, with modifications, accepted by the Irish parliament. The English manufacturers, prompted by Josiah Wedgwood, protested that their own interests were being threatened. In attempting to appease the English, Pitt succeeded only in alienating the Irish and thus guaranteeing the death of his scheme. See Watson, pp. 276–78.

The Irish bill confused many. SL wrote on 20 May: "You say you do not understand a syllable about the Irish affairs—If you did it were more I believe than most of us do here. . . . It is intended I believe to grant the Irish great Commercial advantages, and I suppose we are to have some thing in return—but the thing is far from being settled. . . ."

16. Sometime between 25 February and 22 April, Q had moved with ST and SAT to the house on West Street.

17. "Gentle in manner, vigorous in performance." A familiar maxim, attributable equally to Sophist and Jesuit philosophy. In more modern times it persists, e.g., in Chesterfield's letters to his son (4 February 1751) and *Thraliana* 1:137, 2:1081.

18. From Bucentaur: the old Venetian state barge. The Bucentoro refers to an annual ceremony of the "wedding of the sea" on Ascension Day, symbolizing Venetian sea power. The ritual continued for centuries until 1798, when the French destroyed the last bucentaur. See *Observations* 1:186–92; also William Parsons, "On Seeing the Doge's Marriage with the Adriatic," *Poetical Tour,* pp. 43–44: "Take subject Ocean my accustom'd vow, / And this the mark of my eternal sway." This is Parsons's version of the Doge's address: "Desponsamus te, mare, in signum perpetui dominii." Cf. Howell 1:70–71; William Shenstone, "Rural Elegance," lines 78–82.

19. Portia is disguised as Balthazar, the representative of the renowned advocate Bellario (*Merchant of Venice* 4.1.).

20. The casinos were small apartments over the cafés in Saint Mark's Square and the Procuratie. They were generally frequented by fashionable Venetians for music, chat, or dancing.

TO HESTER MARIA THRALE

Florence, 4 June, 1785

It was here that I received & read with infinite Pleasure my dear Hester's delightful Letter of the 16th of May; but *my* Letter will talk of nothing but the lovely City and State of Venice which I left with regret[1]—& almost with Tears, so amiable are its Inhabitants and so affectionate their Treatment of me—we have however promised to return to them. I saw the Ceremony of the Bucentoro sure enough, & saw it from the Galley of a noble Venetian who rowed us about as if he had no other Employment than our Diversion,[2] which to prolong beyond the Morng Show he added Tickets for his Ball at Night, & gave me Liberty to bring any English Friends I might think proper. Mrs Welldon,[3] a tall Daughter of Ld Conyngham's, who was so civil to Mr Piozzi & me at Bath when we first married, claimed my Acquaintance, so we went about together very much, & *set off each other's Figure* to no small Advantage.[4] His Excellency Bragadin however took only *us* in the Evening to the Corso, where every body goes in Gondolas, and a kind of Regatta is made by the Watermen's reciprocal Efforts to pass each other, as at a Horse Race by Jockeys;[5] whose Dress is not very different, except that the Gondoliers wear a Sash of Pink upon White or blue upon Brown according to the Owner's Taste—& this, with the Addition of a very few gay Barks belonging to the Captains of Galleys, constitutes the Evening Entertainment till 'tis Time to dress for the Ball.

The Barge *we* sate in like a burnish'd Throne &c. but it did not *burn* upon the Water, for no gilding is allowed: it was all blue & White exquisitely elegant though; with Canopy and eight Gondoliers of the same Colour, the Family Arms flying in a large Flag from the Stern: do you not think we were envied & admired enough? Mr. Palmer said I *looked like Cleopatra upon the Cydnus.*[6]—You remember Mr Palmer, & his kind Behaviour when your Father was ill at Brighthelmstone,[7] he is very kind still I think. The *Trè Rè Magi* did not make any *Giro* this Year, but I saw a fine Procession round St Mark's Place on St Mark's Day,[8] when we sate up by the brazen Horses to look at it, and I handled the Steed which once drew the Car of Apollo—

But you bid me tell you about the Conversations, which were very pleasing, & very literary; there is a *blue* Casino belonging to Guerini[9] one of the first Statesmen of Venice, where the countess Rosenburgh—a most accomplished Lady—presides: to this Eccellenza the Venetian Resident at Milan gave us Letters and we had as much Belles Lettres as could be wished: the Italian Nobility of that Republick are at an immeasurable Distance from the State of Ignorance we represent them; and they quote *Clarissa,* and repeat Pope's Essays, and the Chevalier Pindemonte[10] is busy now translating my *Three Warnings:* I have imitated an Ode of his in Praise of England much to his Satisfaction,[11] which you would like vastly I do think, but it is such an enormous Length that the People in your Country will perhaps be *Stuffo* of it: I will however try its Fate in some Newspaper or Magazine one of these Days. The dear old Scaligers[12] repose very magnificently at Verona, & very foolish they were to prefer Nobility to Talents, by which alone they are at present remembered either in Italy, France or England. The Tomb of Anternor & Shrine of St Anthony[13] at Padua were made more interesting to me by the charming Contessina Ferres,[14] a *nobile Tedesca,* to whom the German Minister at Milan recommended us;[15] and who took upon her to amuse and inform me of everything that Place could produce: We went with her to the Theatre, were introduced by her to the Abate Cesarotti,[16] and all the people worth knowing—She made a *Conversatione scelta* of 30 or 40 Gentlemen & Ladies of the first Rank, and kissed me most affectionately at parting with promises of perpetual Correspondence. Another sweet Lady of a Venetian Senator, with whom and her little Boy I left much of my heart; has already written to me, & shews I am not forgotten.

It was at the Pieta that we heard the Girls play on French Horns &c. but we, like Dr Burney—preferred the Mendicants.[17]

You will not have Marchesi at last; the Empress of Russia *will* have him: his Salary from her is 1500 Guineas a Year with a House, an Equipage and two Benefits—all this for three Years certain:[18] it is in *Compass* that he is so wonderful, & in the Sudden & surprising Transitions from the lowest Notes to the highest, without ever being out of Tune—It is really a very astonishing exertion of a Power never before possessed, and it was exceedingly agreeable to hear him *once;* but as Dr Johnson used to say, *one cannot be an April Fool twice by the same Trick.*

The next Song in the Book as the Hawkers phrase it, must be about Bologna; which I did not like; tho' my Connoisseurship was fully gratified[19]—but we were just come from Venice, and few places will do after *that.* The Weather was complained of there as intolerably hot by all but me who keep my Cotton Stockings still on; so every body went into the Country, and we took Shelter here in the Apennines, the passage of which was exquisitely pleasant indeed, and perfectly cool. It was very pretty to see the places of which one has been always reading & hearing so; and I looked with particular Pleasure on the places whence the pale Moon

—the Tuscan Artist views
At evening from the Top of Fesole
Or in Valdarno to descry new Lands,
Rivers or Mountains on her spotty Globe.[20]

We are now absolutely in that beautiful Valley, the identical Mountain within our Sight, and the fine River rolling under our Window. I see as yet no Resemblance of Florence to Bath in any one Respect, but then I have seen nothing of it yet at all, as we came last Night very late from Bologna, where the King of Naples's Arrival[21] detained us so long, & whence we were too happy to be at length dismissed: though the Vines clustring round every great Tree, the Rosemary perfuming every little Ditch, and the Hedges all filled with Honeysuckles & Sweet Briar, might have contented any One who was not spoiled like me—but

Non omnes Arbusta juvant, humilesque Myricae[22]

and perpetual Indulgence at Home & flattery abroad has made me capricious, so I scorn'd *Bologna la grassa. This* appears a lovely Town indeed from our Lodgings which are exceeding handsome at an Englishman's; & the people of the house very attentive, and Cold Baths at next door, & all things cool and comfortable about us: when you write again direct to Florence, & do let it be soon. I am very glad Miss Dickens[23] has done so well, and that dear Mr Scrase is happy in his young Folks;[24] give a kind Word from me to Mr Kipping. Is poor Presto alive still?[25] I have not seen one pretty dog in my Travels, the Race of Dutch Mastiffs or *Pugs* extinct in England or nearly so, are the fashionable Favourites of the Ladies at Padua; & I suppose Garrick's Farce of *Lethe* will be exhibited soon to ridicule 'em for it:[26] as they translate every thing from our Stage, and performed Romeo & Juliet the other Night while I was there under the Name of *Tragedia Veronese.*[27]

Your Dream is nearly come true about my handwriting being grown little like that of my husband, but if one *will* crowd a heap of Stuff into one Sheet of Paper, one *must* write small, and 'tis ill worth the while to send empty Letters across Seas & Mountains. My next shall contain the Description of Florence: purchase it dear Tit by a long Acc^t^ of something, or of nothing, or of the King's Birthday:[28]—

mean Time God bless you, and carry a *merry Face* and a chearful Heart too—Why not? Tell Sir Lucas Pepys that nobody out of his own Family loves him as well as his obliged Friend & Y[r] Affec[te] Mother H: L: P.

Text: Queeney Letters, pp. 201–5. *Address: A Mademoiselle / Mademoiselle Hester Maria Thrale / In West Street, Brighthelmstone, Sussex, Londres, Angleterre.*

1. The Piozzis left Venice on 26 May. They went to Ferrara and Bologna before arriving at Florence shortly before 4 June. There they stayed until 12 September, when they traveled to Lucca and Pisa. *Observations* 1:231–68, 268–332, 332–51.

2. Francesco Maria Bragadin, whose ancestry may be traced to at least the fifteenth century, was a Venetian senator and a prominent member of the Quarantie. He was born at Parenzo, 28 October 1753, to Giacomo and Anna Maria, née Donà. See Archivio di Stato Venezia, M. Barbaro, "Arbori de Patritii veneti," MSS, vol. 3, ca. 156. See also *Thraliana* 2:654; *Observations* 1:186–87.

3. The daughter of Lord and Lady Conyngham, Ellena, or Helen (d. 1815), had married in 1777 Stewart Weldon (1751–1829), a student of Trinity College, Dublin, and Oxford; M.P. for Ennis, 1783–90.

4. An acquaintance wrote in 1758: "I am sorry to hear Miss Salusbury is so short, but hope she has not done growing." Even as an adult, she was less than five feet tall (Clifford, pp. 23, 160).

5. See *Observations* 1:187.

6. Shakespeare's *Antony and Cleopatra* 2.2. 191–97.

7. A "Mr. Palmer who *squints*" had met the Thrales at Brighton in the autumn of 1777. See HLT's letter to CB, 6 November 1777 (Yale University Library) cited in Constance Hill, *The House in St. Martin's Street* (London and New York: John Lane, 1907), p. 189. He was either Joseph Palmer (1749–1829), a nephew of Sir Joshua Reynolds, or Robert Palmer (d. 1787), an attorney of Great Russell Street, Bloomsbury Square, and an agent of the duke of Bedford.

8. 23 April (*Observations* 1:154–55).

9. Angelo Querini (1721–96) served from 1758 to 1760 as a counsel for the state of Venice, i.e., avogador di comun. (See Archivio di Stato Venezia, "Segretario alle Voci," regg. 29, 30.) A member of the reformist movement, he was arrested in 1761 for contempt of the Consiglio dei Dieci and imprisoned until 1763. Traveling widely in Europe, he visited Voltaire at Ferney in 1777. His country villa at Altachiaro, near Padua, was often a meeting place for Italian intellectuals.

From 1782 to 1796 he lived in Rome. In the latter year, when he was named censore di stato Venezia, he returned to Venice and died there on 29 December.

For further information about Querini, see the following: Girolamo Festari, *Descrizione del viaggio nella Svizzera fatto da A. Querini nel 1777* (Venice, 1835); F. C. Lane, *Venice—A Maritime Republic* (Baltimore: Johns Hopkins University Press, 1973); A. Dal Piero, "Angelo Querini e la correzione dei Consiglio dei X nel 1761–62," *Ateneo Veneto* 19 (1896): 280–303 and 358–63; L. Ottolenghi, "L'arresto e la relegazione di Angelo Querini," *Archivio Veneto* 15 (1898): 99–145; B. Brunelli Bonetti, "Un riformatore mancato: Angelo Querini," *Archivio Veneto* 48–49 (1952): 185–200; Girolamo Dandolo, *La caduta della Repubblica di Venezia ed i suoi ultimi cinquant'anni* (Venice, 1855), 1:175–80; Marino Berengo, *La società veneta alla fine del settecento* (Florence, 1956), pp. 8–9. See also *Observations* 1:179; *Thraliana* 2:654.

10. Ippolito Pindemonte (1753–1828) befriended the Della Cruscans and contributed to the *Florence Miscellany.*

Many years later (4 June 1817) Byron described him to John Murray: "To-day, Pindemonte the celebrated poet of Verona—called on me—he is a little thin man—with acute and pleasing features—his address good & gentle—his appearance altogether very philosophical—his age about sixty—or more—he is one of their best going. . . . He enquired about his old Cruscan friends Parsons—Greatheed—Mrs. Piozzi—and Merry—all of whom he had known in his youth.—I gave him as bad an account of them as I could—answering . . . that they were 'all gone dead,'—& damned by a satire more than twenty years ago—that the name of their extinguisher was Gifford—that they were but a sad set of scribes after all—& no great things in any other way." See *Byron's Letters and Journals,* ed. Leslie A. Marchand, 12 vols. (Cambridge: The Belknap Press of Harvard University Press, 1973–82), 5 (1816–17): 233–34.

11. In *Gibilterra Salvata* (1783), Pindemonte celebrated England's long (1779–83) struggle with the French and Spanish for the possession of Gibraltar.

The poem concluded with a "Hymn to Calliope," which was printed in the *Florence Miscellany* (pp. 14–18) and followed by HLP's translation (pp. 19–23).

The Three Warnings was often reprinted and anthologized, but we find no record of a translation by Pindemonte or one in German, as she claimed. Clifford (p. 61 n. 3) accepts HLP's assertion.

12. Scaliger is the Latinized name of the Della Scala family of Verona. HLP refers to the two scholars, father and son (whose descent from the Della Scala family is suspect).

Julius Caesar Scaliger (1484–1558) was for many years involved with the activity of the court and the duke of Ferrara. He had planned to take holy orders, aspiring to become a cardinal and even a pope. In his last thirty-two years, he gave himself over to the study of philosophy, science, and the classics.

Joseph Justus Scaliger (1540–1609) was almost totally devoted to scholarly activity. He published in 1594 *Epistola de vetustate et splendore gentis Scaligerae et J. C. Scaligeri vita.*

13. The inhabitants of Padua claim fabulous descent from the Trojan counselor Antenor, whose relics they identified in a large stone sarcophagus exhumed in 1274.

In Padua's basilica, commonly called Il Santo, the bones of Saint Anthony rest in a chapel ornamented with carved marbles, the work of such sculptors as Jacopo Sansovino.

14. Maria-Leopoldina, née Starhemberg (fl. 1757–1800), married on 24 November 1778 conte Giovanni Giuseppe Ferri of Padua. (See Archivio di Stato Venezia, "I. R. Commissione Araldica," b. 53.) On 7 March 1793, she was anonymously accused of allowing suspected Jansenists and Freemasons to conduct meetings in her house. Nothing came of the charge (Archivio degli Inquisitori di Stato, b. 70, letter to Padua, 7 March 1793). See *Observations* 1:137–38.

15. Count Wilczek (HLP to SL, 20 January, n. 3).

16. Abate Melchiorre (Melchior) Cesarotti (1730–1808), ecclesiastic, poet, and translator. HLP admired his *Poesie di Ossian* (1763).

17. From *The Present State of Music:* "This city is famous for its *conservatorios* or musical schools, of which it has four, the *Ospidale della Pietà,* the *Mendicanti,* the *Incurabile,* and the *Ospidaletto a S. Giovanni e Paula,* at each of which there is a performance every Saturday and Sunday evening, as well as on great festivals. I went to that of the *Pietà,* the evening after my arrival, Saturday, August 4. . . . [T]he performers, both vocal and instrumental, are all girls; the organ, violins, flutes, violoncellos, and even French horns, are supplied by these females" (p. 139).

"In the afternoon of the same day I went to the hospital *de' Mendicanti,* for orphan girls, who are taught to sing and play, and on Sundays and festivals they sing divine service in chorus. . . . The girls here I thought accompanied the voices better than at the *Pietà*" (pp. 141–42).

18. In the summer of 1785, Marchesi set out for Russia with Giuseppe Sarti (1729–1802), whose opera *Giulio Sabino* he sang in Vienna on 4 August and Warsaw on 25 August. In Saint Petersburg he was given a three-year contract but remained only through the autumn season of 1786.

19. It seemed to HLP "at first sight a very sorrowful town [that] has a general air of melancholy." She thought it scenically boring as well. On the other hand, she admired the Caraccis (Carraccis), a family of Bolognese painters who were important for the Italian Seicento: Lodovico (1555–1619), Agostino (1557–1602), Annibale (1560–1609), Antonio (1583–1618). See *Observations* 1:248–68; "Harvard Piozziana" 2:48–50.

20. *Paradise Lost* 1.288–91.

21. Ferdinando (1751–1825), third son of Carlos III of Spain. When only eight, he became Ferdinando IV, king of Naples and Sicily, and from 8 December 1816 was styled Ferdinando I, ruler of the Kingdom of the Two Sicilies. He married (1768) Maria Carolina Luisa Giuseppa Giovanna Antonia (1752–1814), tenth daughter of Franz I, Holy Roman Emperor, and Maria Theresa, queen of Hungary and Bohemia, archduchess of Austria. For Ferdinando's arrival in Bologna and the attendant festivities, see *Observations* 1:266–67.

22. Virgil, *Eclogues* 4.2.

23. Not yet of age, Q at the West Street house was the charge of Miss Dickins, probably the sister of Anthony Dickins (b. 1734; originally of Broadway, Worcs.), who had married Sarah Scrase.

24. Charles Scrase had in May 1771 purchased property in Brighton.

In June 1742, he had married Sarah, née Turnour. They had two daughters: Elizabeth, who married William Smith, of London and died without issue; Sarah (Sally), who married Anthony Dickins and had several children.

For HLT's admiration of Scrase, see *Letters* 2:34; cf. *Queeney Letters*, p. 193.

25. Originally Harry's dog and a family favorite, Presto was taken to Brighton, where he died (*Thraliana* 1:226 and n. 2).

26. *Lethe, or Aesop in the Shades* opened at the Drury Lane on 15 April 1740 and was performed intermittently until 1789.

27. According to *Observations* (1:225–26), HLP missed by one evening the Italian performance of *Romeo and Juliet (Tragedia Veronese).* Cf. *Anecdotes*, p. 282.

28. George III was born 4 June 1738.

TO THOMAS CADELL

Florence
7: June 1785.

Sir

As you were at once the Bookseller and Friend of Doctor Johnson, who always spoke of your Character in the kindest Terms;[1] I could wish you likewise to be the Publisher of some Anecdotes concerning the last twenty Years of his Life, collected by me during the many Days I had Opportunity to spend in his instructive Company; and digested into Method since I heard of his Death.[2] As I have a large Collection of his Letters in England,[3] besides some Verses known only to myself;[4] I wish to delay printing till we can make two or three little Volumes not unacceptable perhaps to the public, but I desire my Intention to be notified for obvious Reasons; and if you approve of my Scheme, should wish it to be immediately advertised.[5]

My Return cannot be in less than 12 Months,[6] and we may be detained still longer, as our Intention is to complete the Tour of Italy; but the Book is in forwardness,[7] and has been seen by many English and Italian Friends.

I beg you to direct your Answer *here* Poste restant and am / Sir Your most humble Servant / Hester: L: Piozzi—

Text: Hyde Collection. *Address:* A Monsieur / Monsieur T. Cadell / Libraire / Strand / Londres / Angleterre. *Postmark:* JU 2 < > "received the 26th June."

1. Thomas Cadell (1742–1802), bookseller, publisher, and "Printer to the Royal Academy." Associated with the publication of the works of Robertson, Gibbon, Blackstone, he impressed SJ with his "liberality" (Chapman 2:412) and his rank as the "primary agent in London" (ibid. 3:367). From 1770 onward, alone or collaboratively, Cadell published *The False Alarm* (1770), *Thoughts on the Late Transactions respecting Falkland's Islands* (1771), *The Patriot* (1774), *Taxation no Tyranny* (1775), *Political Tracts* (1776, the four political pamphlets), the *Dictionary,* 4th ed. (1773), *A Journey to the Western Islands of Scotland* (1775), *Prefaces, Biographical and Critical, to the Works of the English Poets* (1779–81), the *Idler,* collected 4th ed. (1783), *Prayers and Meditations* (1785).

2. HLP's choice of Cadell as publisher of the *Anecdotes* was also prompted by preliminary negotiations between SL and the bookseller. On 20 May, SL had written: "Mr. Cadel is very desirous of being the publisher of your work and I wish on every account that you may employ him as such, not only as being the first Bookseller in London, but a very sensible man, and of a much more liberal mind than falls to the share of all Booksellers" (Ry. 552. 5).

Cadell responded affirmatively 28 June.

3. Besides the "two hundred at least" (HLP to SL, 22 March) she later calculated some "forty Letters of Johnson's in the old Trunk which may *very well* be printed; some of them exceedingly long ones, and of the *best sort*" (HLP to SL, [15 April 1787]). Additionally, so Charles Selwin had informed her (29 April 1785): "Sir Joshua Reynolds has in his hands all your Letters to Dr. Johnson that were found amongst his papers, and wishes to know what you would have done with them" (Ry. 556.167). By 30 August, if not sooner, the letters had been turned over to Cator "in a sealed Parcel or Box agreeable to your Desire" (Ry. 566.168).

4. These were Latin "Verses addressed to Dr. Lawrence, composed by Dr. Johnson, as he lay confined with an Inflamed Eye" and eight "Metres" of Boethius's *De Consolatione Philosophiae.* They became the concluding matter (2:415–24) of the *Letters.* HLP was proprietary because the poems represented an overt literary association: she had translated the Lawrence lines and alternated with SJ in translating Boethius (see her prefatory statement, 1:vi).

Apart from the anticipated volumes of *Letters,* the *Anecdotes* was to become an important primary source for SJ's poems. See *Poems,* passim.

5. For an acknowledgment of this request, see Cadell to HLP, 28 June and n. 1.

6. The Piozzis did not return to London until 10 March 1787.

7. By 21 September, HLP could advise SL that the *Anecdotes* had been completed, and Cadell on 20 October that the manuscript was to be dispatched from Leghorn. SL, writing on 12 October, congratulated her: "I am very glad you have finished the Anecdotes, and think you are quite in the right to send them before you, the earlier they can be published in the year, the better I should think, I hope they will meet with the favorable reception from the public, which I am sure they will deserve" (Ry. 552.6).

Three days after publication of the *Anecdotes,* SL reported that "the whole Edition of a thousand, sold off in *less* time, I believe than [Fielding's] Amelia" (28 March 1786; Ry. 552.9).

The first impression of *Amelia* (18 December 1751), consisting of five thousand copies, sold out so quickly that a second of three thousand appeared within a week.

SL alludes to SJ's comment, as recorded in *Anecdotes* (pp. 221–22), that *Amelia* was "perhaps the only book, which being printed off betimes one morning, a new edition was called for before night."

See Wilbur L. Cross, *The History of Henry Fielding,* 3 vols. ([1918]; New York: Russell and Russell, 1963), 2:304–5; *Thraliana* 1:247.

Your faithful and
affectionate humble servant
James Boswell

James Boswell, ca. 1793. A sketch by Sir Thomas Lawrence. ***(Reproduced by permission of the National Portrait Gallery.)***

TO SAMUEL LYSONS

Florence
14: June 1785.

Dear Mr. Lysons—

I thank you very kindly for the Letter I found here last Week and shall be too happy to see your hand-writing again at Pisa when I arrive at that Place.

It was exceeding friendly in you to tell me about the Spitfire Wits,[1] and nothing can prove the Regard I pay to your good Counsel so completely as the Method I immediately took by writing to Mr. Cadell and offering him the Anecdotes. He will probably shew you my Letter, perhaps publish it; in order to convince the World that 'tis *no Joke* at all; and that they must wait till they have read, before they begin to ridicule it.

Mean Time I have sent Sir Lucas Pepys an Ode written by the Chevalier Pindemonte a noble Venetian in praise of England, with my Translation over against it: so People may see *I am at Liberty* to write *something*, and may undertake the Memoirs of Dr. Johnson as well as anything else.[2]

Mr. Colman[3] is right enough in his Conjectures I dare say, but those who had a true Knowledge of our great Man's Mind will remember that he preferred Veracity to Interest, Affection, or Resentment; nor suffered Partiality or prejudice to warp him from the *Truth*—let Mr. Boswell *be sure* to keep that Example in View;[4] his old Friend often recommended it to him.

It will be a sad Thing for me when you go into Wales,[5] the Letters will never reach you there; and you will not write upon your Journey perhaps, and so our Correspondence will fade away, and that will be a Loss to both; for I shall desire most earnestly to hear what you think of my native Country, which at least affords good Food for a Fossillist: So indeed does Italy, and I was a Blockhead not to make myself more conversant in such Matters before I set out, I will however bring you some nice Playthings home with me.

The Great Duke's Gallery puts one out of Breath with Admiration;[6] tho' I was just come from Bologna too, and had seen the Caracci School shining away at that Town in all its Glory. Here however we lodge on the Banks of the *Arno*, and see the full Moon shining over *Fesole*[7] opposite the Window of our common sitting Room: We walk every Evening in a Wood full of Nightingales, where Oaks, and Olives, and Firs of a prodigious Size form an impenetrable Shade; where Pheasants fill the Underwood, and Blackbirds whistle on the Branches:—where the tall Cypress overtopping every Tree looks like Charlotte Clavering[8] among the Beauties at St. James's, and realizes the Virgilian Simile of

lenta solent inter Viburna Cupressi.—[9]

Was I ever so pedantic or so poetical in my Life before? Scarcely ever, but 'tis stupidity not to feel Enthusiasm here; and besides the moment one returns to sober Senses again, the Image of charming Venice returns with its sweet Society, and friendly Conversation, scarcely to be equalled for kindness, Literature, and Vivacity.

Count Mannucci[10] however, a Tuscan Nobleman who was intimate in England with Mr. Thrale, at Paris with Mr. Piozzi; does all in his Power to make us amends, introduces us to Literary Acquaintance, and carried me to the Academy[11] last Thursday, where I heard the famous Giannetti[12] pronounce a Eulogium on Captain Cook:[13] very fine indeed! and the tender-Hearted Italians wiped their Eyes at the Relation of his Death. This Giannetti is the only Improvisatore in Europe who makes his Verses and *recites* them offhand—the others all sing, and depend on the Time given by the Tune or Chant for the Invention of fresh Rhimes and Matter.

The Heat here is *furious* now, and no Rain at all; and every body is shocked, and fears of future Distress alarm them exceedingly. I am sorry that the same Apprehensions are well founded in other Countries, for by that means each will be deprived of help from another: 'tis very odd to feel the Sun So troublesome and See the Snow so plain at the same Time as I do while I am writing.

I knew the friendship of the two Brothers Pepys would be exceedingly delightful to you: Lady Rothes[14] is one of the best, as well as one of the most agreeable Women I know. The World was against her once on Account of her second Marriage without knowing why; but She has had the good Fortune to see her Choice approved at last by Family Friends and Acquaintance and I have no doubt but I shall enjoy the same Consolation for the same Reason, because my husband deserves every Day more than I could ever have done for him, had I as Portia says been

Trebled twenty Times myself.[15]

Poor Soul he has got the Gout now, and I am writing by his Bedside: we went o'walking last Night very late, and saw the Phosphorus Fly sparkling in the Hedges and Ditches, that they seemed all illuminated as if with Fireworks; I never saw such a Phænomenon, and was exceedingly pleased with it.[16]

The Libraries here are magnificent, and full of valuable Manuscripts— A Chaldaic Bible of inestimable worth and ornamented with Profusion of gilding, Figures &c. is greatly esteemed, and many Commentators have written very wisely upon it. A Manuscript Livy too of surprizing Elegance and neatness, took much of our Attention; but I was most pleased with Petrarch's Latin Letters in his own pretty handwriting.—[17]

The Gems here seem likewise a very rich Collection but I am not yet a Lapidary worth a pin; I will learn something about these Matters however before I see you again.

Mean time make my best Compliments to Dr. Lort[18] [and] to the kind Friends in Wimpole[19] and Upper Brook Street;[20] and when the Bishop of Peterboro' remembers *me,* let him be assured that I do not forget *him.*

I am ever Dear Mr. Lysons / Yours most sincerely / H: L: Piozzi.

My husband sends his Compliments. Write very soon again, and direct still to *Florence.* I wish we could see Barnard's letter.

Text: Hyde Collection. *Address:* A Monsieur / Monsieur Sam: Lysons chez le Reverend / Monsieur Sam: Peach / a Sheene près de / Surrey / proche de / Londres / Angleterre. *Postmark:* 29 JU.

1. Apparently an allusion to HLP's rival biographers and anecdotists. At her request, SL had advertised in the *St. James's Chronicle* for 14–16 April her intention to memorialize SJ. On 20 May SL had written: "I believe some of Johnson's Biographers are by no means pleased that you should be added to their number—Many ill natured things have been said and a paragraph inserted in the papers to tell the world that it could not be your advertizement as you was not at present sufficiently at liberty to be the author of it."

2. HLP's refutation not only of the "Spitfire Wits" but of the persistent gossip that she was immured in a convent.

3. SL sought anecdotes from SJ's acquaintances, among them George Colman the elder (1732–94), dramatist and theatrical manager, who probably suggested or stated his misgivings that the biographers would not portray SJ's frailties (recalling, no doubt, SJ's insistence on biographical veracity and wholeness: *Rambler* 60 and *Boswell's Johnson*, passim).

Including HLP among "the futile tribe" of biographers who capitalized on fame, Colman versified:

At length—Job's patience it would tire—
Brew'd on my lees, comes Thrale's *Entire*,
Straining to draw my picture;
For She a common-place book kept,
Johnson at Streatham dined and slept,
And who shall contradict her?

Thrale, lost 'mongst *Fidlers* and *Sopranos*,
With them play *Fortes* and *Pianos*,
Adagio and *Allegro!*
I lov'd Thrale's widow and Thrale's wife;
But now, believe, to write my life
I'd rather trust my negro.

From "A Posthumous Work of S. Johnson. An Ode. April 15, 1786," *Johnsoniana; or, Supplement to Boswell* [ed. John W. Croker] (London: John Murray, 1836), p. 476, stanzas 7 and 8. See also Clifford, pp. 256, 273.

4. Having just learned from SL that "Boswell intends publishing his Hebridian Tour with anecdotes very soon" (Ry. 552.5), HLP intimates that her competitor has forgotten SJ's insistence on biographical truthfulness and his fear that veracity might be distorted for narrative sensationalism. This, ironically, was JB's attitude toward her (Clifford, p. 256).

The *Tour* was published before "22 Sept. the day George III was to receive a copy" (*Walpole Correspondence* 25:634 n. 38). For details of publication, see "Preface," *Boswell's Journal of a Tour to the Hebrides with Samuel Johnson, LL.D., 1773*, ed. Frederick A. Pottle and Charles H. Bennett ([1936]; New York, Toronto, London: McGraw-Hill, 1962).

5. SL had told her on 20 May: "In about two months I intend making an excursion into North Wales, and then I shall shew you some drawings of places which you may have seen." For the scope of the walking tour with DL, see HLP to SL, 4 November, n. 2.

6. Leopold II (1747–92), Holy Roman Emperor (1790–92) after being grand duke of Tuscany as Leopold I (1765–90). The gallery in Florence contained works by Titian, Guido, Raphael, and a variety of Greek statuary. See *Observations* 1:299–305. The gallery was celebrated by Parsons in the "Epistle to the Marquis Ippolito Pindemonte," *Florence Miscellany*, p. 28.

7. Fiesole in Tuscany, near Florence, on a hill overlooking the Val d'Arno.

8. Charlotte (1759–1841), second daughter of lieutenant general John Clavering (1722–77) and Lady Diana, née West, daughter of the first earl De la Warr. On 28 April 1783, she married Sir Thomas Brooke-Pechell (1753–1826). She died 23 October at Hampton Court Palace. See *GM* 119, pt. 2 (1841): 665.

9. "Verum haec tantum alias inter caput extulit urbes, / quantum lenta solent inter viburna cupressi," in *Eclogues* 1.24–25; see also *Thraliana* 1:439.

10. Son of conte Jacopo Mannucci, Giovanni Tommaso was born in the Montisi Castle, Peinza, on 4 July 1750 and died 19 December 1814. Connected with the Florentine court as private secretary to its cabinet, he was to ask for and obtain on 3 October 1805 admission to the nobility of Florence. (See Archivio di Stato Firenze, Ceramelli Papiani 2966; Giustificazioni di Nobilità, 79 ins. 9.)

Of the meeting with Mannucci in 1785, HLP later wrote to JSPS: "[The Count] was an old Acquaintance of *mine:* Mr. Thrale picked him up at Paris in 1774 [actually 1775] and invited him to Streatham Park, where he resided with us a Month or two and made Court to Miss Owen. . . . The good natured Nobleman however having been told that Piozzi was come to Florence with a rich Wife from England &c. made haste to wait on him—Wish him Joy &c.—They talked awhile in my Dressing Room whilst I was in an Inner Apartment. The Count asking particularly for *Mrs. Thrale* and whether She was married again or no, Your Uncle evading his Questions: till I rushed in: and Manucci exclaimed in French—Ah Madame! quel coup de Theatre!!" ("Harvard Piozziana" 2:55–56).

11. The original institution was the Accademia della Crusca founded in Florence in 1586, but abolished by Grand Duke Leopold on 7 July 1783 to stifle suspected political opposition. Subsequently he founded his own Accademia Fiorentina (*Thraliana* 2:643 n. 3).

12. Michelangelo Gianetti (1743–96), physician and scholar, who delivered the "Elogio del Capitano Giacomo Cook." See *Observations* 1:274–75.

"In a Day or Two we all went to The great Public Library, where Eulogiums were pronounced from a Sort of Pulpit to the Memory of departed Merit. The Liberal Spirited Professor pronounced a fine one in honour of our Circumnavigator Captain Cook——and The tears came into my Eyes—a Doctor in his Robe asked what could make me cry so.—Did I know the Man? Oh I replied in Metastasio's Words

Che questo Pianto mio
Tutto non è Dolor. . . .

"Surely said I

Tis not Grief alone or Fear,
Swells the Eye or Prompts the Tear. . . ."

("Harvard Piozziana" 2:51–52)

(HLP misquoted *Demetrio* 2.12. 480–87.)

13. Captain James Cook (1728–79), explorer and navigator, was killed by Hawaiian natives during an unsuccessful voyage to discover a passage to the Pacific Ocean from the northwest coast of North America. The occasion of the eulogy was the publication in 1784 (2d ed., 1785) of *A Voyage to the Pacific Ocean. Undertaken by the Command of His Majesty, for making Discoveries in the Northern Hemisphere. . . . Performed under the Direction of Captains Cook, Clerke, and Gore, in His Majesty's Ships the Resolution and Discovery. In the Years 1776, 1777, 1778, 1779, and 1780. 3 vols. Vols. 1st and 2d written by Captain James Cook, F.R.S. Vol. 3d, by Captain James King LL.D. and F.S.R. . . .* (London: Printed by W. and A. Strahan, for G. Nicol, and T. Cadell, 1784).

14. Jane Elizabeth, née Leslie (1750–1810), daughter of John (d. 1767), tenth earl of Rothes, and Hannah, née Howard (d. 1761). In time to be *suo jure* Countess of Rothes, she had married in 1766 George Raymond Evelyn (d. 1770), and in 1772 Lucas Pepys.

15. *Merchant of Venice* 3.2.154.

16. For her detailed account, consult *Observations* 1:307–9; and Robert Merry's "Ode to Summer," the *Florence Miscellany*, pp. 109–11.

17. HLP saw these treasures at the Laurentian Library where she was taken by Count Mannucci and where she met Angelo Maria Bandini (1726–1803), historian, bibliographer, and director of the Laurentian Library from 1756. See *British Synonymy* 1:62; *Observations* 1:280. Cf. the brief account of the Laurentian's holdings in Joseph Spence, *Observations, Anecdotes and Characters of Books and Men*, ed. James M. Osborn, 2 vols. (Oxford: Clarendon Press, 1966), no. 1510.

18. Dr. Lort lived in Savile Row.

19. William Weller Pepys lived in Wimpole Street.

20. Sir Lucas Pepys and the countess of Rothes lived at 37 Upper Brook Street.

FROM THOMAS CADELL TO HESTER LYNCH PIOZZI

28: June 1785.

Madam!

Your very acceptable favour of the 7th of June I received, and beg leave to return you only grateful acknowledgements for the preference you are pleased to give me as the Publisher of your Anecdotes of my excellent Friend Dr. Johnson. I heartily approve of your intention of giving three Volumes of Anecdotes, Letters and Verses. I am convinced the publication will be highly acceptable to the Public, and I shall esteem it an honour to be engaged in any way most agreeable to you. Permit me however to suggest that the work should not be delayed if possible longer than next Winter, as you will be convinced that such a publication will be more sought after while the remembrance of Dr. Johnson is recent upon the public. If you should agree with me in expediting the publication perhaps it may be possible to convey to you your Collection of Letters &c. by which means you will be able to compleat the Work so as to publish early in the next Spring. In the mean time I have followed your directions in notifying your Intention, and have also inserted an Advertisement according to the form I send; and which I hope will meet with your approbation.[1] I wished to consult you upon the form of the Advertisement previously to its being inserted but did not think myself authorised to wait for the return of the Post as your orders were express to advertise *immediately.* Any alteration you wish to make may be adopted in future. The Book shall be elegantly printed, and I flatter myself my conduct in this Transaction will be such as to meet with your approbation, as I am truly ambitious to prove myself to be with great respect, Madam, / Your obliged and most faithful / and Humble Servant / T. Cadell.

Text: Ry. 554.17.

1. "Preparing for the press and will be published / with all possible Expedition / Anecdotes of the late Samuel Johnson LLD / during the last twenty years of his Life / By Mrs. Hester L. Piozzi / To which will be added A Collection of Letters and Verses / never before published. / Printed for T. Cadell in the Strand."

TO THOMAS CADELL

Florence
18: July 1785.

I am favoured with your Letter, and pleased with the advertisement, but it will be impossible to print the Letters and Verses till my Return to England as they are all locked up with other Papers in the Bank, nor should I chuse to put the Key (which is now at Milan) in any one's Hand except my own. If you will have the Anecdotes and print them first, I believe the Venetian Resident would be kind enough to carry them for me, as he is much Mr. Piozzi's Friend and mine; and will be in London the first or second Month of next Year at latest—perhaps somewhat sooner,[1] but if that should be the Case I am willing to double my diligence, and we may publish the two other Volumes when I get back.[2] Let me know your determination, and remember the Reliance I have made on your honour in leaving the whole to be transacted by you in the Absence of Sir / Your most humble Servant / Hester: Lynch Piozzi.

Text: Bodleian MSS Montagu d. 19, fol. 85. *Address:* Mr. T. Cadell / Bookseller / Strand / London / Angleterre.

1. The manuscript was not carried by John Strange but (20 September) was sent through the post from Leghorn to London. On 31 December, Michael Lort wrote that her memoirs were still quarantined in the Thames and that "all the world is impatient to see them in print" (Ry. 544.5). On 28 January the *Morning Herald* announced the arrival of the manuscript at Cadell's and that it contained "many curious particulars of the life of Dr. Johnson for the last twenty-five years." Throughout February, the printers rushed the publication of the *Anecdotes,* which finally reached the bookstalls on 25 March.
2. That is, the *Letters,* which appeared in March 1788.

TO HESTER MARIA THRALE

Florence,
26 July, 1785

Dear Hester,
Surprize & Concern are my present Reasons for writing; what can be become of dear Susan & Sophy? who never write themselves, & of whom you say not a Syllable, tho' Mr Cator's last Letters tell me they are under your Care.[1] Why do you my sweetest Girl, write so coldly and so queerly? & why do you hinder your Sisters from writing at all? is it because I am married to Mr Piozzi? that Reason (as Shakespear says) *is somewhat musty;*[2] for we yesterday celebrated our Wedding's Anniversary with a Dinner and Concert, to which not only all the Italian Nobility, but all our own now here,—were happy in contributing both Gaiety & Splendour. The Prince Corsini,[3] & his Brother the Cardinal[4] honoured us with their Company, & paid Mr. Piozzi every possible Attention. Lord & Lady

Cowper[5] who are reckon'd difficult to *many*, are kind to *us:* Ld Pembroke[6] & Mr Parsons of the Sussex Militia live in the house, & dine with us on other days, besides *Gala* ones; while Mr & Mrs Greatheed,[7] (whose family you cannot but know;)[8] are our constant and partial Friends; I think we have never been three Days apart since the Acquaintance began. Yesterday's Celebration assembled them all, *cum multis aliis*,[9] and dear Count Mannucci express'd his Tenderness to my Husband in the sweetest & sincerest Terms: I shew'd him that part of your Letter which mentions *him*, & the passage relating to Presto, whom you think it so odd that I should remember; though he does not doubt your recollecting his Spaniel Thames, that he used to call his *Hoond;* She is still alive, but exactly in the same Case with poor old Pet. His sisters are charming Women,[10] & their female Friends to whom I was introduced at his country house, are very pleasing. We have the offer of three different Boxes at the Opera every Night,—& may chuse our Company among the first Houses in Florence: the beautiful Marchioness Pocci[11] even brings her *Daughters to our* House, a favour which is never done where there is not great Intimacy & great Esteem—but She took to me from a particular Circumstance: the first time I saw *her* Children, I suddenly burst into Tears from the Thoughts of my own; dear lovely Sophy especially, who I fancied like her Theresina. When *every* body then is thus goodnatured to me, when *every* body expresses a just sense of Mr Piozzi's Merit, and seeing his Value pays him a proper Respect—why should you be the only Person to stand out? the only Person not pleased to see your Mother happy, and well treated. Be contented however to let your Sisters shew the Regard they owe us, and bid them send a Kind Letter directly to their & your / Affectionate Mother and / Guardian / H: L: Piozzi.

I have seen the Book you speak of or Extracts from it—Anecdotes are almost always pleasing, & yours of the Prince delights everybody,[12] but I want Anecdotes of Susan & Sophy.

I forgot the Music—Miss Davies is the first Singer in Italy & so acknowledged by the Conoscenti:[13] We have only Tenors & Women supportable. Do you know Mr Biddulph's fine Seat in Sussex?[14] He is one of our Coterie: Be another yourself dearest Tit, the Company will not disgrace you—in short treat us as We are treated by others every way your *Equal* at least, or do not continue any longer a Correspondence in which enters neither Confidence, nor Respect; neither Affection nor the appearance of it on *your* Side, while *my Heart* is full of them all.

Text: Queeney Letters, pp. 210–11. *Address: A Mademoiselle / Mademoiselle Hester Maria Thrale / in West Street, Brighthelmstone, Sussex, Londres, Angleterre.*

1. Cator informed HLP on 8 July that the younger Thrale girls were going to join Q in Brighton (*Thraliana* 2:612 n. 1). "The bond between the 'Miss Thrales' was very close, and everyone thought of Queeney as Johnson had—as head of the family" (Hyde, p. 250).

Bolstered by the fact that she would soon be of age, Q was more self-possessed than usual. On 26 August (Ry. 602.1), HLP learned from Cator: "Miss Thrale has wrote me she does not intend to come from Brighton till November, but I have told her she had better come when she is of Age and all her Fortune will be ready for her, so she must do as she pleases, as for Susan and Sophia [who had been visiting the Cators] I wonder they have not wrote as we talk of you with respect and I recommend them to be attentive to write you as well as in every thing else, and by their Conversation I thought they did."

2. "Ay, sir, but 'While the grass grows'—the proverb is something musty" (*Hamlet* 3.2.343–44).

3. Bartolomeo di Filippo Corsini (ca. 1729–92) succeeded his father as commander of the noble papal guard, a hereditary honor. He resigned the post, however, when he decided to return to Florence. A court favorite, he was appointed by Emperor Joseph II as ambassador extraordinaire to the sacred college, which assembled in conclave in 1775 to choose a successor to Clement XIV. For that function he received the order of the Tonson d'Oro.

4. Andrea Maria Corsini (1734 or 1735–95). At only twenty-four he was elected cardinal's deacon by Pope Clement XIII. Thereafter he was cardinal's priest of Santa Maria at Merulana, prefect of the justice records, bishop of Sabina, and vicar of Rome.

5. George Nassau Clavering-Cowper (1738–89), third earl Cowper (1764), inherited the estates of his grandfather Henry d'Auverquerque (ca. 1672–1754), the earl of Grantham. Accorded an unusual honor, Lord Cowper was created by Joseph II at Vienna in 1778 a prince of Milan in the Holy Roman Empire. He died in Florence but was buried in England at the family estate at Hertingfordbury.

He had married Hannah Anne Gore (1758–1826) in Florence on 2 June 1775. A onetime mistress of the Grand Duke Leopold, she also had an affair with Robert Merry. She was to die at her villa "del Cipresso" near Florence and to be buried at Leghorn.

About 1811, HLP recalled that "Lord and Lady Cowper . . . visited and caressed us" ("Harvard Piozziana" 2:52).

6. Henry Herbert (1734–94), tenth earl of Pembroke and seventh of Montgomery (1751), lieutenant general in the army with the colonelcy of the First Regiment of Dragoons. In 1756 he married Elizabeth, née Spencer (1737–1831), second daughter of Charles, third duke of Marlborough.

7. Bertie Greatheed (1759 or 1760–1826), of Guy's Cliffe, Warwickshire, married his cousin Ann Greatheed (1748–ca. 1822). Her parents were Marmaduke (d. 1762) of Saint George Basseterre, West Indies, and Anne, née Wilson, of Saint Christopher, West Indies.

HLP first met the Greatheeds in Florence in June 1785 where Bertie, one of the Della Cruscans, became a contributor to the *Florence Miscellany.* The friendship continued after the Piozzis returned to England. A dilettante with radical political sympathies, Bertie wrote a blank verse tragedy *The Regent* (produced in 1788), with an epilogue by HLP.

8. Bertie Greatheed was the son of Samuel (d. 1765), who in 1747 married Lady Mary, née Bertie (d. 1774), eldest daughter of Peregrine (1686–1742), second duke of Ancaster (1723), and Jane, née Brownlow (d. 1736). Samuel was a Whig M.P. for Coventry (1747–61). In 1750 he had bought the estate at Guy's Cliffe (which he had previously rented). The immediate founder of the Bertie family fortunes seems to have been John, who emigrated to the West Indies, eventually settling at Saint Mary Cayon, Saint Kitts, and holding the office of chief justice from 1721 to 1727.

See Bertie Greatheed, *An Englishman in Paris,* ed. J. P. T. Bury and J. C. Barry ([1803]; London: Geoffrey Bles, 1953).

9. An abridgment of a line familiar to pupils who had studied in the *Propria quae maribus . . .* of *The Eton Latin Grammar.* The full line, signifying a summation, reads *Cum multis aliis, quae nunc perscribere longum est.* It may be rendered, "With many other matters, which it would just now be too tedious to state." See HLP to SL, 1 March 1786, n. 8.

10. According to Rosamaria Maglietta of Montisi, a descendant of Giovanni Tommaso Mannucci, HLP erroneously mentions "sisters." Genealogical records and the M.I. in the Church of the Madonna, Montisi, indicate that there was but one sister, buried in this church, "morta nel 1813 all' etá di 60 anni."

11. Conte Francesco di Piergiovanni Pocci (1744–68), of Viterbo, married in 1763 Margherita di Carletti (fl. 1745–1800), a member of a noble family, residents of Montepulciana. In 1779 she was named "dama della Croce Stellata" by Empress Maria Theresa. As a

widow, the marchesa Pocci was responsible for the education and care of her four children: Piergiovanni (b. 1765), Fabrizio (b. 1766), Marianna (b. 1767), Francesco (b. 1768).

12. The daily newspapers had in the Prince of Wales a constant source of rumor and gossip. Recently, as one of the more blatant examples, he had been badgering an embarrassed monarch for permission to travel abroad. Fox, who had influence with the prince, was called to Saint James and urged to prevail with him to "give over all thoughts of a foreign tour, by representing to him the impressions it would give the publick mind, of his imbibing notions incompatible with the constitution of the Empire he would one day be called upon to govern." (Meanwhile, in ironic contradiction, Prince Edward—like other brothers before him—was preparing for the jaunt denied the Prince of Wales.) See the *Morning Chronicle and London Advertiser,* 7, 18, and 25 May 1785; Christopher Hibbert, *George IV, Prince of Wales, 1762–1811* (New York, Evanston, San Francisco, London: Harper and Row, 1972), chaps. 3 and 4.

George Augustus Frederick, Prince of Wales (1762–1820), was to become King George IV (1820–30). Edward Augustus (1767–1820) was the duke of Kent.

13. Cecilia Davies (ca. 1753–1836), an operatic soprano who had made an impressive reputation in France, Italy, and Vienna (1768–73), as well as in England, came back to Florence (1784–85) with her sister. The English colony, apprised of their financial difficulties, enabled their return home. Cecilia performed in England until 1791, but her final years were saddened by poverty and neglect. See Highfill and *Thraliana* 1:463.

Her sister Marianne (1744–ca. 1816) was also an accomplished musician (harpsichord, flute), although less acclaimed.

14. John Biddulph (d. 1835) of Biddulph, Staffs., and Burton Park in Sussex, succeeded his father Charles (d. 1784). His mother was Elizabeth, née Bedingfeld (d. 1763). The Biddulphs claimed a Saxon origin for both their name and their family.

According to E. V. Lucas, less enthusiastic than HLP, "Two miles due south from Petworth is Burton Park, a modest sandy pleasaunce, with some beautiful deer, an ugly house, and a church for the waistcoat pocket." See his *Highways and Byways in Sussex* (London: Macmillan, 1921), p. 107.

TO SAMUEL LYSONS

Firenze
27: July 1785.

Dear Mr. Lysons—

You deserve long Letters indeed, you are so good-natured, in writing often and kindly——Miss Thrale does just the reverse——but I will not let anything vex me when I have so much with which I ought to be pleased.

We celebrated our Wedding's Anniversary two Days ago with a magnificent Dinner and Concert—at which The Prince Corsini and his Brother the Cardinal did us the honour of assisting, and wished us Joy in the tenderest and politest Terms. Lord and Lady Cowper, Lord Pembroke, and *all* the English indeed doat on my Husband, and shew us every possible Attention——Mr. and Mrs. Greathead—(whose Family you cannot but know) are our constant and partial Friends; we have never been three Days apart since our Acquaintance began, and they love one another at five years end——just as we do now I think, who hope to follow their Example for half a Century at least, and then we shall be a Show—like the learned Pig.—

I will not teize Mr. Barnard about *his* Letter, when I have so many of my own; nor will I fret in the Month of August about what you writ in the Month of April concerning the Trick Mr. Seward has served me; giving the Anecdotes to others which he originally had I suppose from me, and I am sure of it[1]——a Basta! as the Italians say; I have always honoured his Virtues, respected his Abilities, and lamented his Health, too much to take amiss that futile and unkind Behavior which he has thought proper to shew in every Transaction betwixt him and me, his earnestness, perhaps his Necessity to be doing Something, is his best Excuse.

Mecci[2] and Baretti[3] are *Par nobile fratrum,*[4] my Money has often relieved their Necessities, and Charity always precludes Ill Will.—

Florence is the loveliest City I ever yet saw, standing *on dry Ground;* but perhaps I said that before——I say it all Day long.

I have been playing the Baby, and writing Nonsense to divert our English friends here, who do the same thing themselves; and swear they will print the Collection, and call it an Arno Miscellany;[5] Mr. Parsons, and Mr. Merry[6] are exceeding clever, so is Mr. Greathead, and we have no Critics to maul us, so we laugh in Peace.[7]

I am glad you have sent your Butterflies to the Exhibition; Mr. Piozzi is always wishing to make you up a little Recueil of this Country['s] Insects, but I am sure you have them all already. The Cigales are loud and troublesome and very ugly; and the Spiders and Gnats bite one terribly——If the *Tarantula* attacks *me* however, the Cure is at hand you know.[8]

What will you say to *my* Country I wonder; you will climb Snowdon and find it a very respectable Mountain——That which faces us in this moment one of the beautiful Appenines, is not higher; nor does the Snow lie so long on it——the Clouds repose however very majestically on its Top.

I went to a Horse Race yesterday.[9] You have heard how the Italians drive their Horses down a long Street without Riders, and so they do: yet is their management of Horses in general here not to be despised, but imitated; nor could Astley[10] and all his Rivals exhibit Instances of greater Command than is shewn in the Streets and Theatres of Italy every Day.

A triumphal Car was brought on the Stage t'other Night, filled with Dancers and Pageantry; and drawn by four beautiful Chesnut Horses with white Manes and Tails all harnessed a'Breast; they drove round the Stage with the utmost Grace and steadiness, turning the Car just at the Lamps of the Orchestra, during the distracted and various Noises of Gongs, Trumpets, Drums, and applauding Multitudes which they seemed wholly to disregard, as well as the Boards that shook under them at every Step, quietly drawing up at the Back of the Scene and standing like Statues for the Dancers to dance before them——They were borrowed of a Nobleman in the Town, who often drives them himself on such Occasions in a fancy dress.[11]

What else shall I tell you? That the People here lie a Bed all Day and sit up all Night——even the Shopkeepers shut up their Windows and go to Rest at

Noon.[12] The Ponte della Trinita said to be the most beautiful Bridge in Europe,[13] is our public Walk till twelve o'Clock; and if you are recreant even then, and steal home to Sleep as we did last Night, you are instantly pursued and waked with a Concert under your Window. Mr. Piozzi called me up at about two this Morning to be serenaded, and I assure you that the Moonlight, the River, and the Heat, give charms to *their* Musick, which ours in England has no Possibility of receiving.

Lord Cork's Letters have just been lent me;[14] I think he has left nothing unsaid about Florence, but the manners are changed as to *Dress*, all the Gentlemen go in Frocks, and are more to be complained of as Slovenly than finical— The Word Cicisbeo is out of Fashion and Cavalier Servente substituted in its stead—[15] The Custom is adopted still by all, but despised and even abhorred I think; it is difficult to express the Esteem and Fondness shewn by the Florentines of both Sexes to Mrs. Greathead and myself for the Sincere Love we bear to our amiable Husbands—*che bel Esempio! che care Inglesine! che Copie felice!* resounds from every Mouth. Oh for Candour and liberality of Sentiment, for honest Praise and kind Construction of Words and Actions Italy is the place, nor have they an Idea of pretending to approve what they really do not like: Affectation is not the Growth of this Country, and when you have their Applause you may be sure of their Esteem.

Adieu dear Mr. Lysons and write again very soon to your Obliged and Faithful Friend / H: L: Piozzi.

My husband sends his Compliments. Our Concert was so admired, our Wedding Dinner so crowded with English and Tuscan *Nobiltà*, that he says we shall give a little Musick in our own house every Tuesday Evening. / Addio!

Text: Hyde Collection. *Address:* A Monsieur / Monsieur Sam: Lysons chez le Reverend / Monsieur S: Peach / a East Sheene / near Richmond / Surrey. / Angleterre. *Postmark:* AU 14.

1. HLP's response to SL's information (15 April, Ry. 552.4) that most of Seward's Johnsoniana had already been used by the nonconformist clergyman and biographer, Dr. Andrew Kippis (1725–95), and Sir John Hawkins.

2. Francesco Mecci (fl. 1740–91), an Italian scrivener and teacher, was a close friend of Baretti and GP in England; he had witnessed the HLT-GP marriage, 23 July. In *Thraliana* (1:600, 2 July 1784), however, HLT had described Mecci as "a faithless treacherous Fellow" and (2:616, 27 November) "a Bosom Serpent." He may have revealed that HLT paid him to be a guardian who would have assured GP's chastity in Italy, 1783–84. At least, this version of the GP-Mecci friendship appears in Baretti's "Stricture the Third," *European Magazine* 14 (1788): 89–99.

According to "Mr. Gabriel Piozzi's Account, 1784–92" (Drummond's Bank, Charing Cross), fifty pounds (£12.10 a quarter) was paid to Mecci annually from 3 July 1788 to 7 October 1791.

3. Giuseppe Marc' Antonio Baretti (1719–89), an Italian writer, was urged in 1773 by SJ to teach Q modern languages. He agreed on condition that he could come and go as he pleased. Prompting his agreement was his belief that HT, in addition to paying him a stipend, would give him gifts and a pension when his employment ended. See Lacy Collison-Morley, *Giuseppe Baretti* (London: John Murray, 1909), p. 237.

Described by SL as the most tenacious of "the Bathonian and London Scandal Mongers" (15 April), Baretti disapproved of HLT's maternal conduct and her second marriage. He was, she wrote many years later, "A Man who made it his Boast to live by Defiance of the Country which protected, and the Friends who supported him. Independent in his Spirit, unbending in his Opinions—Insulting when offended—*Polite* tho' not *obliging* when flattered and truckled to——and caressive to Inferiors who acknowledged his Superiority. Full of general Information and so adroit at learning Modern Languages—No Nation knew him to be a Foreigner" ("Harvard Piozziana" 1:121; see also HLP to Sophia Byron, 2 June [1788]).

4. Horace, *Satires* 2.3.243.

5. The *Florence Miscellany* was originally to be called the *Arno Miscellany.* The latter title, however, had been preempted by a Florentine group known as the *OZIOSI,* who published fugitive pieces in 1784. Bertie Greatheed, William Parsons, and Robert Merry all contributed to the *Arno Miscellany.*

6. Robert Merry (1755–98), dilettante dramatist and poet. Having come from a good family and attended Harrow and Christ's College, Cambridge, he bought a commission in the Horse Guards. He soon tired of military life and joined the English colony at Florence. There he competed with the Grand Duke Leopold for Countess Cowper and began the Della Cruscan fad after an exchange of poems with Hannah Cowley. Along with other English visitors, he was the Piozzis' "fellow-lodger" at Mr. Meghitt's English Inn. See W. N. Hargreaves-Mawdsley, *The English Della Cruscans and their Time, 1783–1828* (The Hague: Martinus Nijhoff, 1967); Clifford, "Robert Merry—A Pre-Byronic Hero," *Bulletin of the John Rylands Library* 27 (1942): 74–96; *Observations* 1:275; *British Synonymy* 2:277–78. See also *Thraliana* 2:643 n. 3.

7. HLP's optimism about the "critics" was premature. The following spring, for instance, Walpole wrote to Horace Mann: "I have very lately been lent a volume of poems composed and printed at Florence, in which another of our ex-heroines, Mrs. Piozzi, has a considerable share. . . . The present is a plump octavo, and if you have not sent me a copy by your nephew, I should be glad if you could get one for me—not for the merit of the verses, which are moderate enough, and faint imitations of our good poets; but for a short and sensible and genteel preface by La Piozza, from whom I have just seen a very clever letter to Mrs. Montagu to disavow a jackanapes, who has lately made a noise here, one Boswell, by anecdotes on Dr. Johnson—in a day or two we expect another collection by the same signora."

He described the contributors as a "constellation of *ignes-fatui* [who] have flattered one another as if they were real stars," but he "could not find the only name I expected to see—yours." Indignant at such a failure of gratitude, he grumbled, "if you send me the book, I think I will burn all but the preface" (*Walpole Correspondence* 25:633–35).

8. A playful allusion to the tarantella, a Neapolitan folk dance, that at one time was believed to be a specific against tarantula bites. See Steele, *Tatler* 47, and John Brand, *Observations on the Popular Antiquities of Great Britain*, 3 vols. ([1777]; New York: AMS Press, 1970), 3:381.

9. For a description of "the *concurrenti* without riders," see *Observations* 1:285–86.

10. Philip Astley (1742–1814), equestrian performer and theatrical manager, well known in Dublin, London, and Paris.

11. The nobleman was conte Francesco Alamanno de Pazzi (fl. 1740–90). See *Observations* 1:290–91. The event was a ballet, *Il Cid,* by Sacchini.

12. For a description of Florentine idleness, see *Observations* 1:298–99, and passim.

13. "It was made [1570] by *Ammanati,* a celebrated *Florentine* sculptor and architect, the old bridge having been carried away by an inundation in the year 1557. The arches of it, after a rise of a few feet from the place where they spring, are turned in the form of a cycloid; a particularity which, they say, no other bridge in the world has. It is all of a fine white marble, and there are four statues of the same representing the four seasons, two placed at each end of the bridge." See Boyle's *Letters from Italy,* p. 75.

The Bridge of the Holy Trinity was destroyed in World War II but reconstructed from the original design of Bartolomeo Ammannati (1511–92), the builders utilizing whatever fragments could be found.

14. John Boyle (1707–62), fifth earl of Cork and Orrery in Ireland and Baron Boyle of Marston in England (1753), author of *Letters from Italy, in the Years 1754 and 1755*, published from the originals with explanatory notes and a biographical preface, by John Duncombe (London: B. White, 1773).

15. Synonymous terms, the *cicisibo* or *cavalier servente* satisfied the strict social code of Italian society. Generally, either a humble relative or a male equally above suspicion, he acted as an escort in the absence of the husband. HLP's *cavalier servente* was Domenico Palazzi (1735–1800) "(a tottring Old Priest of fourscore Years old). . . . My old coughing Canonico (proud as a Peacock) entered on his Office" ("Harvard Piozziana" 2:32).

Not all such relationships, however, were as chaste as HLP's. Consider the broader interpretation conveyed by Nicholas Owen Smythe from Florence to his father Nicholas Smythe, 12 December 1788 (Ry. 569.12): "All the Women of Fashion at the Masquerade go about without their Husbands, and if they like the figure of any Man, they go up and ask him to take them home. . . ."

For a biographical account of Palazzi, see HLP to Q, 28 January 1795, n. 11.

TO LORD COWPER

Leghorn
Tuesday 4: September 1785.

My Lord—

Intrusion is a common Tax upon politeness, and your obliging Behavior towards me, has given me Courage in some Measure to renew My Visit in the person of those who I think will be most welcome to a Man of your Lordship's refined Taste and Liberality of Sentiment.

This Letter will be presented by three [of] the most eminent Musical Professors in Italy—perhaps in Europe—they are in the Service of the Duchess of Parma, who permits them to make this little Journey for their Pleasure and Advantage:[1] and Mr. Piozzi who heard 'em in this Town with Astonishment and Delight, could not help being earnest that your Lordship and dear Lady Cowper should share the Pleasure which such superior Powers as theirs can alone bestow. No Praises can equal the Merit you will find in their Performance, nor have they need of any Recommendation; it is much more *my own* Interest through their means to keep alive in your Lordship's remembrance those Civilities which on our part will never be forgotten, and which you were pleased kindly to show during our Residence at Florence[2] to my Husband, and to / Your Lordship's and dear Lady Cowper's / ever Obliged and Obedient / humble Servant / Hester: Lynch Piozzi.

After taking the Baths of Pisa in our Way for a Week, we shall go on to Rome if your Lordship should wish to honour us with your Commands.

Text: C.R.O., Hertfordshire. *Address:* Right Honourable / Earl Cowper / Florence.

1. The duchess of Parma was Maria Amelia (1746–1804), daughter of Maria Theresa. In 1769 she had married Ferdinando (1751–1802), duke of Parma (1765–1802).

The "Musical Professors" may be among the following: Giuseppe Colla (1731–1806), since 1 May 1766 *maestro di cappella* at the court of Duke Ferdinando. From 1780 to 1806, he was concert leader of the Teatro Ducale. Composer of cantatas, operas, and perhaps sacred music, he had taught Ferdinando and, after 1785, his son Lodovico (1773–1803).

The others could have been "Signor Poncini . . . composer to the great church . . . [or] Signor Ferrara, brother to the famous violin player, who is a remarkable fine performer on the violoncello . . . [or] Signora Roger, a great harpischord player, who was mistress to the prince of Asturias, [all of whom were] in pension at the court of Parma" (Burney, *The Present State of Music*, p. 385).

Signor Ferrara [*sic*] was Carlo Ferrari (ca. 1710 or 1730–1780 or 1789), a cello virtuoso who had established his reputation in Parma.

His brother, Domenico Ferrari (1722–80), was a violin virtuoso and composer who spent the early part of his career in the Württemberg court at Stuttgart. In his later years he resided in Paris.

2. The Piozzis were in Florence from 15 June to 12 September. Lord and Lady Cowper were present at their wedding anniversary. According to HLP in *Observations* (1:275–76), the Cowpers "contribute to make the society at this place more pleasing than can be imagined; while English hospitality softens down the stateliness of Tuscan manners."

TO HESTER MARIA THRALE

Pisa, Saturday
17 September 1785

My Dear Hester
I received your Letter at Florence, & one from each of your Sisters, in Consequence of my Lamentations—they protest it was nobody's fault but their own that I remained 12 Weeks without hearing of 'em, and when you say it was not yours, I hold myself bound to believe it. That My Name should never be named among you, is too probable for me to doubt; but I must assure you in Confidence that the Ladies *did* do me the favour to write very fondly & familiarly after our parting, & indeed till I left Milan[1] I had perpetual Letters from them, begging me to return, & perswading Mr Piozzi to bring me back. *This* is my Excuse for having written fondly & familiarly to them: and when you consider the Matter over, you will see that in my Situation I can do nothing so proper as to take up the *Ton* of my Correspondents; as they write to *me* (be they who they will) I write to *them*, and it is the surest way I can think on not to tread awry. My last Letter to you somewhat transgressed the Rule; fright and Uneasiness at their utter & unprovoked Silence, must excuse it.

It is now more than Time to wish you Joy,[2] which I do from the bottom of my heart: you may say this Morning

Sento che L'Alma è sciolta;
Non sogno questa Volta
Non sogno Libertà.[3]

I thought I should at least have been got to Leghorn, & given you an imaginary Meeting in the Sea on your Birthday, but the English Families at Florence were so fond of my husband, & he passed his Time so pleasantly among them, that I believe nothing but my Illness would have got us away. One of the Scirocco Winds however seized me on one side, & confined me to my Bed & Room with a Fever, such as I have never experienced, for above a Week.[4] Dear Mrs Greatheed waited on me with excessive tenderness; and tho' She liked my Company very much, readily consented to my changing an Air which agreed so ill with my health. My Appetite began to return by the Time I got to Lucca, and I sent word to the Friends at Florence, as if it was a prodigious Event. After the Rains our Physicians say Asses Milk will be wholesome, but no herbs can spring up yet for their Food, the Heat & Droughth are so furious. Should I recover by Seabathing &c, we shall go on to Rome in Autumn after the Sun has lost some of his Power, & *there* I shall hope to receive a Letter from you, who must begin to tell some News, and always remain assured that none will be so pleasing as a good acc^t^ of that Health, which alone gives Enjoyment of anything this World can bestow. Dear, lovely Tit, do not neglect your health; indeed—& I can now speak by Experience, there is nothing on Earth so valuable. Have I ever told you that we were all Verse-mad at Florence, so by dint of Compliments to myself, & to my Husband wch had a still greater Effect on me, they coaxed me to make some Stuff, and so we printed it alltogether, theirs & mine; & call'd it the *Florence Miscellany:* I shall may be send some Copies to England, & Mr Cator will give you one.[5] We have been living of late much like the Travellers Ld Chesterfield talks of, who keep all together—and tittering at the Natives when they *see* them—do nothing but *Huzza for old England;*[6] to compleat the Resemblance, I have been this Morning to look at the *leaning Tower:* don't you remember a Paper he wrote in the *World* laughing at the English People's remark on the leaning Tower of Pisa?[7] Well! but you would like to see the Pillars which support the Cathedral here, & to know that they were brought from the Temple of Diana when that was destroyed:[8] and you would like to see the Tomb of Algarotti, who to do himself the greatest possible honor, ordered that he should be recorded on his Monument as the Disciple of *Newton.*[9] and you would like the magnificent Cloisters all painted by old Cimabue with the History of the Old Testament—and many other Things.[10] What you would not like, are the Gnats, Bugs, Spiders, Scorpions, & Serpents which keep one in perpetual Terror.[11] But I have not mentioned the sweet Republick of Lucca, with *Libertas* written up at every Turn:[12] it lies in the middle of Tuscany, like a Parenthesis in a Sentence, but I sh^d^ be sorry it were *left out.* We went to the Opera there; they had a very pleasing Soprano *Bedini,*[13] and that whispering Miss Morigi[14] whom you remember in London was 1st woman, but the Theatre is so little at Lucca She is heard well enough.

Robinelli[15] is a sort of Favourite at Florence, because his Voice is so particular: a heavy Contralto approaching to a Tenor—don't laugh out, but I protest he put me in Mind of Mathews the Butcher at Bath. Pray give my Service to Mr Gibbs of Brighthelmstone[16] and to Nancy Smith—*if they will own me:* I hope her little Anna Maria is alive and well.[17] I have scarcely left Room I see for the Initials of a Name which you profess so much to *abhor,* but of which the Possession is regarded as an honour by / Your H: L: P.

God bless you & adieu! I am really very ill now.

Text: Queeney Letters, pp. 212–14. *Address: A Mademoiselle / Mademoiselle Hester Maria Thrale / in West Street, Brighthelmstone, Sussex, Londres, Angleterre.*

1. The Piozzis had left Milan ca. 6 April, after five months' residence.
2. HLP was writing on Q's twenty-first birthday.
3. Metastasio, "La Libertà" (1733), lines 6–8.
4. See William Parsons, "Ode on the Siroc," *Florence Miscellany,* pp. 126–28 and n.: "The Siroc is a south-east wind, the same as the Latin Syrus, which is much dreaded by the Italians, on account of its oppressive heat, and the extraordinary melancholy it occasions." See also his *Poetical Tour,* pp. 155–58.
5. Cator's role as distributor of the *Florence Miscellany* is further apparent in letters from HLP to SL, 4 November, and in those to her from George James, 23 February 1786 (Ry. 555.107) and from Dr. Lort, 5 March 1786 (Ry. 544.6). HLP had sent to Cator's Adelphi residence eight copies, but two had been "lost and damaged," as James reported.
6. Philip Dormer Stanhope (1694–1773), fourth earl of Chesterfield (1726), essayist, statesman.

In the *World* (no. 29, 19 July 1753) Chesterfield satirizes chauvinistic young Englishmen, "smart Bucks" who patronize English coffeehouses, dine together, carouse together, go sightseeing together. Speaking no Italian, they are contemptuous of the natives, who speak no English. When "[w]e saw the Pope go by t'other day in a procession . . . we resolved to assert the honour of old England; so we neither bowed nor pulled off our hats to the old rogue."

7. Succinctly, in the same essay, Chesterfield describes, through the persona of a letter writer, English reaction to the "steeple of Pisa . . . the oddest thing I ever saw in my life; it stands all awry; I wonder it does not tumble down." For HLP's account, see *Observations* 1:342–43.
8. Near the ancient Ionian city of Ephesus a temple (the Artemisium) was dedicated (430–420 B.C.) in honor of Diana (Artemis). It was destroyed by fire on the night in 356 B.C. when Alexander the Great was born. Twenty years later he ordered its reconstruction as a monument to himself, and the project was carried out by his architect Dinocrates in collaboration with the sculptor Scopas. The vast structure, one of the seven wonders of the world, was supported by some one hundred twenty-seven columns, each about sixty feet high. The shrine, ruined by the Goths in 262 A.D., was completely dismantled after the Roman Emperor Theodosius I (ca. 346–95) ordered the pagan temples closed ca. 392. See *Observations* 1:342, 423; Bayle 3:59a, b; 4:405b; 5:553b.
9. Conte Francesco Algarotti (1712–64), Italian philosopher and connoisseur of arts and sciences. The author of a popular treatise on Newtonian optics, *Il Newtonianismo per le dame; ovvero dialoghi sopora la luce e i colori* (Naples, 1737), he died in Pisa on 3 May. On his monument over the tomb ordered by Frederick the Great (1712–86) is the inscription: "Algarotto, Ovidii æmulo, Neutonii discipulo Fridericus rex." His own, more modest epitaph, was: "Hic jacet Algarottus non omnis" (*Queeney Letters,* p. 214 n. 1).
10. Giovanni Cimabue (fl. 1251–1302), a Florentine painter. The reference is probably to his earliest known works, the Joseph mosaics: *Joseph Sold into Egypt* and the *Lament of Joseph's Parents,* in the cupola mosaics of the Florence baptistery.
11. For the stings and bites that plagued HLP in Pisa, see *Observations* 1:348–49.
12. "I was wonderfully solicitous to obtain some of their [Luccan] coin, which carries on it the image of no *earthly* prince; but his head only who came to redeem us from general slavery on the one side, *Jesus Christ;* on the other, the word *Libertas*" (*Observations* 1:339; 332–41). Howell describes Lucca "as a Partridge under a Faulcon's Wings" (1:92).
13. Possibly a dancing member of the opera company at King's Theatre (fl. 1787–ca. 93) and the wife of Carlo Francesco Badini (fl. 1770–93), a librettist also associated with King's at this time. For alternative consideration: Haydn in *The First London Notebook* (1792)

mentions a female singer named Badini among the musical persons he had encountered (see Highfill).

14. Margherita Morigi (fl. 1780–90) made her London debut at King's Theatre on 14 November 1782 in *Medonte* (1777), by Giuseppe Sarti. She sang in the opera several times until 28 June 1783.

CB professed astonishment "not by the powers she *had*, but by those she *wanted;* for it was hardly possible to account for such a singer having been recommended, or thought of, for the first woman of a serious opera, or indeed of *any* opera. She was not only much limited in her taste, style, and knowledge, but in total want of voice. In recitative she had not one musical tone; and in her songs the greatest efforts she made amounted to little more than a shriek. . . . She was young, had a pretty figure, and, with teeth, would have been handsome" (*A General History of Music, from the Earliest Ages to the Present Period . . .*, 4 vols. [London: Printed for the author, 1776–89], 4:514–15).

HLP also had heard "the Girl who whispered it" in London, and then again in Florence (*Queeney Letters*, 15 June, p. 207). Despite CB's harsh judgment, Signora Morigi was to make other London appearances, in 1786 and 1788.

15. Giovanni Battista Rubinelli [Robinelli] (1753–1829), of Brescia. An alto, he performed in the leading opera houses of Europe from 1771 to 1800, and at King's in 1786 and 1787.

16. William Gibbs, a butcher, owned an establishment identified as "Gibbs Slaughter House and Ground" in Middle Street, Brighton. See the "Brighton Land Tax Assessments," 1785, C.R.O., East Sussex.

17. A garbled reference to Mary Smith (d. 1805), HT's cousin-in-law, whose eighth child (b. 1772) was named after Anna Maria Thrale (1768–70). See "Baptisms, St. Michael's Parish," C.R.O., Hertfordshire.

TO SAMUEL LYSONS

Leghorn
21: September 1785.

Dear Mr. Lysons—
It is from this place that I reply to the kind Letter which followed me hither from Florence, where one of the Scirocco Winds seized me Suddenly when I had often laughed at those that talked of its Effects—and gave me a Fever which kept me to my Bed and Room ten days. You never felt such a feel as that Strange Wind gives, blowing hot upon one like the Steam of a boyling Kettle; but Change of Place has restored my Appetite, and I intend to grow fat again now. The kind English Friends in the house with whom we lived, did all in their power to sooth me, and pacify my Husband, whose anxious Tenderness for his troublesome Wife increased that Esteem which every body feels for him wherever we go.

He and all his British Friends went on a party to Vallombrosa, on a Visit that is to the Convent there. They came back pleased with the Scenery but saying that Milton was mistaken when he talked of the Autumnal Leaves falling thick, for the Wood is entirely composed of Evergreens.[1] Two or three of our Gentlemen were disposed to be poetical, and drew me in of Course to make some mock Etruscan, or Wedgewood's Ware Verses in *Etruria;* but you would rather hear of my working hard at the Anecdotes, which yesterday I finished; and have this moment set a Man to copy them over for the Press, while Mr. Piozzi seeks for a Captain here at Leghorn, to carry them Safe to England.

Our plan is to go from hence as soon as the Rains have fallen to Sienna, Rome, and Naples—but it is I see a real hazard of one's Health to travel in these intolerable Heats; to which when you add the Bites of Animals, whose Venom is scarce credible, you will not condemn us for taking Matters quietly. Cadell will have his little Book to print in Spring, or even earlier if he chuses; the two Volumes of Letters and Verses may very well wait till my return:——People will see by this, that I am *alive and at Liberty.*[2] You must give me *your* Opinion of it freely, and openly, and truly; and tell me what others say, who do not wish me as well.

Doctor Lort is very kind, and I shall tell him tomorrow that I think so——how curious! that he and you should be visiting poor dear old Bachygraig, just while I am ranging over Italy: the Account you have given me of dear Mrs. Myddelton's tender Remembrance[3] pleases me almost as much as the Thoughts of my Nova-Scotia Fortune;[4] one's first Possession should be the hearts of one's Friends. I have however written to Mr. Cator concerning it, and hope it may end in something of real Value. My Father used to talk with Delight of a Place he called *Dunk Cove,* and joke me many Years ago about my American Estate, when he little thought of the Disturbances which have lately distracted that beautiful Country.

But you would rather hear about the little peaceable Republic of Lucca than the thirteen States of America; and it is so very tranquil, fertile, and elegant; that I could write about it with Pleasure till my Paper would reach from one End of its faery State to the other. The word *Libertas* shining in gold Letters on every Wall and Door delighted me much. The Doge who is changed once a Quarter,[5] and his pretty little Senators *so* respectable, and so respected. The exquisite Beauty of their Territory which seems a mere pleasure Ground walled in by the Appenines, the Pride of the Republican Peasants compared with the Meekness of all the Country People I have hitherto seen upon the Continent; their elegant Arsenal, their Sumsuary Laws which oblige them all to a Uniformity of Dress, their Theatre so small, yet so decorated; and the Appearance of the Prince at the Playhouse at once so venerated and so beloved, was quite a pleasing Spectacle. You will see I am quite in Love with the Lucchesi but not without Reason——No Man has been murdered in Lucca since any one can remember, no Man has been hanged for Robbing these forty Years, and if I was to be hanged tomorrow for so doing I *would* commend the dear little Lucchesi.—

Well! but here we are at Leghorn,[6] which is a Place of no small entertainment in its way: like Noah's Ark, it contains all manner of Creatures, but *un*like that here are all Religions, Dresses, Customs and Languages. Armenian Christians, Greek Church, Turks, Jews,——and even the poor *Church of England* are all established at Leghorn; shame to our Ministers that keep no Chapel in any other Town of Italy, while the Merchants and Captains of Ships who report hither, have provided decent Conveniencies at their own Expense for serving God in their own way.

What else shall I tell you? nothing more I think this Time, but that you must direct to Rome now, or to Naples, or both; but certainly to Rome, and that you must accept our kindest Compliments, and continue us your Regard and Esteem; and tell us if we can oblige you any way, and *how.*

I don't fancy I ever mentioned to you that Lord Cowper keeps a very fine Collection of natural Curiosities, and a Man of some Eminence to look after them—besides Telescopes, Microscopes, Globes &c. in a very princely Style I assure you. We saw some Experiments in Electricity and Astronomy very well carried through, and he has a Room for Chymistry very nicely furnished indeed.

Farewell my dear Sir, and do not forget / Your faithful Friend and Servant / H: L: Piozzi.

My husband sends his compliments.

Text: Hyde Collection. *Address:* A Monsieur / Monsieur Samuel Lysons / chez le Reverend / Mr. S. Peach / a East Sheene / near Mortlake / Surrey. / Angleterre.

1. GP's companions were Parsons and Biddulph.

HLP refers to Milton's simile of the fallen angels, "Thick as autumnal leaves that strow the brooks / In Vallombrosa," in *Paradise Lost* 1.302–3. In the *Observations* 1:323, she concluded the simile to be botanically correct.

See also Parsons' poem "Vallombrosa" in the *Florence Miscellany,* pp. 173–87, and in the *Poetical Tour,* pp. 84 ff.

2. HLP continued to repudiate London gossip that she was confined and unable to write the *Anecdotes.* On 20 May Dr. Lort had reiterated the innuendoes: he had seen "a paragraph positively asserting that the advertisement [of the *Anecdotes*] in your name was a fictional one; though most likely the paragraph writer knew to the contrary and may have some interest in making the public believe otherwise—However your letter [now missing] made me look out for the Advertisement and there I was pleased to find in a postscript . . . that you had announced your intention of returning to England" (Ry. 544.3).

3. Mary Myddelton, née Butler (d. 1792) of Gwaynynog, Flintshire. SL replied on 12 October that "Mrs. Myddelton says she hopes to see you [at Gwaynynog]" (Ry. 552.6).

4. HLP's father, John Salusbury (1707–62), had reluctantly gone to Nova Scotia twice as registrar of the new colony, first in the summer of 1749 and then in the late spring or early summer of 1752. The Piozzis, beginning to suspect that he had acquired land in or near Halifax, asked their attorney in 1785 to attempt establishing a property claim. They tried again in 1790. For the nature of the property, including Dunk Cove, and its disposition, see HLP's letters to Jonathan Sterns, or Stearns (30 October 1790), and to Hugh Griffith (11 February and 28 March 1791). See also Ronald Rompkey, ed. *Expeditions of Honour: The Journal of John Salusbury in Halifax, Nova Scotia, 1749–53* (Newark: University of Delaware Press; London and Toronto: Associated University Presses, 1982).

5. In *Observations* (1:334), HLP reports: "A Doge, whom they call the *Principe,* is elected every two months; and is assisted by ten senators in the administration of justice."

6. See *Observations* 1:351–61.

TO THOMAS CADELL

Sienna
20: October 1785.

Sir—

I finished my Anecdotes of Dr. Johnson at Florence;[1] and taking them with me to Leghorn, got a clean Transcript made there, such as I hope will do for you to print from: though there may be some Errors, perhaps many—which have escaped me; as I am wholly unused to the Business of sending Manuscripts to the press——and must rely on You to get everything done properly, when it comes into your hands.

We left the Book with Mr. Otto Franck Banker at Leghorn, who promised to send it to London by the Ship Piedmont Joel Forster Captain.[2] It was sealed up and directed to you, and Mr. Otto Franck gave me his Word you should receive it safely the Moment the Vessel arrives at its Place of Destination.

I thought it useless to write to you before now, and indeed I have been ill and have not thought of writing to anybody: when you shall be pleased to answer this Letter, it must be to Naples that you direct;[3] and it is there too that I hope to be told of the Manuscript coming safe to your hands.

I have the fullest Confidence of your doing every thing for our mutual Honour and Advantage and have only to wish that the Book may be well received.

I am Sir / Your most humble Servant / Hester Lynch Piozzi.

Mr. Otto Franck consigns our Manuscript to Mess: John and Francis Baring and Company.[4] It is to them therefore that you must make Application, if it does not come to you without sending for.

We left Leghorn the 6th of this Month.[5]

Text: Hyde Collection. *Address:* A Monsieur / Monsieur Thomas Cadell / Bookseller / The Strand / London / Angleterre. Postmark < >.

1. On 20 September. See HLP to Cadell, 18 July, n. 1.
2. The *Piedmont*, commanded by Joel Foster, was to arrive at Dover on 25 November (*Public Advertiser*, 28 November; *Observations* 1:361).

Delivery to Cadell, however, was delayed until some time in late January 1786. On 7 February (Ry. 552.7), SL stated: ". . . the arrival of your Book, which was so long, performing Quarantine, and in the Warehouse, that I began to fear it would never arrive, and the Papers began to be witty about it—I was sitting with Cadell when it was brought to him and had a peep at it, all that I saw, I can assure you surpassed my expectations, great as they were, the preface is I think delightful, and the Ease and Elegance of the Style charming. . . . Cadell says it may be out the latter end of this month—" (it was not to appear until 25 March).

3. The Piozzis were to arrive at Naples on 10 December (*Observations* 2:1).
4. At this time the Barings were located at 6 Mincing Lane, London. Founded by Sir Francis Baring (1740–1810), a director of the East India Co. and M.P., the firm of shipping agents was to become a prosperous banking house.
5. The Piozzis went onto Bagni di Pisa, Sienna, and Rome.

TO SAMUEL LYSONS

Rome
4: November 1785.

Dear Mr. Lysons
Among all the surprising Edifices that surround me, none has excited as much Wonder—and I'm afraid I might add as much *Delight,* as the View of poor dear old Bachygraig, drawn by the partial hand of a kind Friend.[1] Your pedestrian Tour[2] was well imagined and well executed; it could however scarcely have been effected in any Climate but our own, the Heats and Colds of Italy would be grievously unfavourable to such a Project, and a Man might be disabled from any future Undertaking, if he resolved to walk 400 Miles *here*. The Myddeltons are a comfortable Family; I love them much, and shall be glad to see Mr. Piozzi and myself among them.[3]

You ask me if Rome answers my Expectations;[4] I answer *No* as far as relates to the external Appearance of ancient Buildings which Piranesi gives one so pompous an Idea of——yet I cannot say that everything he represents, is not *exactly* represented;[5] but you know the Art and the *Artifices* of Drawing well enough to be sensible that keeping down mean Objects is tantamount to exalting great ones—and he judiciously leads one's Attention away from the disgusting Sight of that Wretchedness and dirt, which is here every where mingled with the Monuments of ancient Magnificence.

In Ecclesiastical Splendour however, and modern Dignity, in the elegance and number of their Churches and Palaces; in the richness of their Marbles, and disposition of their Ornaments, I find all my Imagination transcended at every Step. The reigning Sovereign[6] has made such Additions to the Vatican, and built such beautiful Repositories for the Statues which attract the Notice of Travellers, as evince his Taste and his Generosity: To shew at the same Time that he does not neglect the useful for the elegant, there has been lately made a very good Road to and from his Capital; where I would he could arrive at regulating the police a little, but horrible Crimes are connived at by Justice, as far as I can observe in all the Italian States; and the facility of Escape even from those slight Punishments which *would* be inflicted if they waited for them,——presupposes a people much less inclined to instant Gratification, than are easily found in hot Climates.

What Mr. Coxe[7] observes of the Country round this great City, is I fancy strictly true in Winter:——*We* found it arid, desolate, harsh, and so full of noxious Vapour, (tho' they told us the Malaria was at an End;)[8] that I saw a Flame look nearly globular in the Night; and smelt a Stink which as Trinculo says, *much offended my kingly Nostrils*[9]——The Weather is however exceedingly favorable for us who run about incessantly seeing Sights which dazzle one with their Splendour, and as to *Country,* the look of these Environs shocked one more as we came hither from Tuscany, which is quite a Terrestrial Paradise: so like our first Parents when they were expelled we almost wept to see the Ground covered with Thistles.

What else shall I tell you about? of the beautiful Fountains which water this wonderful Town, or the filthy creatures which I am always wishing to be washed in them? But every thing is either mean or magnificent in the deepest extreme——a Connoisseur would say they were all like Rembrant's Pictures composed of the strongest Lights and darkest Shadows possible: you do well to examine our Land of Mediocrities before you come hither; from whence Mr. Piozzi says he shall be glad to return to clean Rooms, neat Workmanship, and good common Sense.—

This last Article reminds me of dear Dr. Johnson. I was very sorry indeed to hear of his useless Prayers for the Dead:[10] which as the prophet David says—*it cost more to redeem their Souls, so that we must let that alone for ever.*[11] Mean Time I wish *my* Anecdotes may be found less trivial than Boswell's: I always hoped that even Trifles belonging to Johnson would be welcome to the public, or what will become of my Book?——Did the Executors publish those Prayers and Meditations? or how came they printed?—do tell for I am earnest to hear.[12]

Somebody said poor Tom Davies the Bookseller was dead, is it true?[13] Let me know what is wanting of your Roman Denarii and they shall be supplied if possible——We are going to Naples whither you must direct Poste restant; but shall return hither for the Lent and holy Week.[14] Mean Time I have not been idle in examining the few Things one could look at in so short a Moment as a Month, and when I see poor old Rome destroyed by the Goths in so surprizing a Manner, I can't help recollecting the Story that Smeathman tells of an Elephant eaten by Ants.[15]

How glad I am that the dear Bath Folks are all so well and prosperous! Mr. Morgan[16] did me the greatest favour I ever received, and it would be ungrateful not to love him.

Will you have a pretty Book as a Present? Mr. Parsons, Mr. Greathead, Mr. Merry, and myself—(who had the least share:) diverted ourselves with writing Verses while we lived together at Florence, and got 'em printed——but very imperfectly as you may suppose; and I have sent a few Copies to England; of which I beg you to accept one; you must call on Mr. Cator for it. He lives in the Adelphi you know. They made me write the Preface and find the Motto[17]——but some of the Verses are very good ones indeed, and I hope you will say so, as I think exceeding highly of Merry's poetical Powers.

No room for another word. Accept my Husband's Compliments with those of / Yours most faithfully / H: L: Piozzi.

Had you a Letter from me dated Leghorn?

Text: Hyde Collection. *Address:* A Monsieur / Monsieur Samuel Lysons No. 167 / Mr. Godwin's a / Pocket Book Shop in / The Strand / London / Angleterre.[18]

1. The Salusbury family estate, located in the parish of Tremeirchion, Flintshire. It consisted in 1772 of eleven fields and "Tenements," in all some 605 acres valued at £512 11*s.* 6*d.* in annual rents. In addition to money, each tenant had to provide the owner (HT) with "2 Fat Hens at Shrovetide, 6 Chickens at Whitsuntide, 2 Days Reaping in Harvest and the Carriage of a Load of Coles. . . . 1 Pew for Servants before the Reading Desk, two Benches on the South side behind the Church Door" (Ry. Ch. 1014). Bachygraig was built by Richard Clough, second husband of Katheryn of Berain.

It was described by SJ as "an old house, built 1567, in an uncommon and incommodious form" (*A Journey into North Wales in the Year 1774*, in *Boswell's Johnson* 5:436); more objectively by Thomas Pennant (*A Tour in Wales*, 2 vols. [(1778–81); London, 1784], 2:22–23). In a letter of 12 October (Ry. 552.6) SL hopes that HLP "will think the little drawing of your Welsh Mansion worth your acceptance which I have sketched on the opposite side." The sketch is missing, but for an interesting contemporary view (by S. Hooper, 1776), see Broadley, facing p. 182, and Hyde, p. 99. The original house has long since vanished, although some of the adjoining buildings are still in use.

2. Also on 12 October, SL reported that he and DL "walked from Liverpool to [Gwaynynog] thro' Chester and Holywell, we afterwards continued our pedestrian route thro' St. Asaph, Rhudllan, Abergelley (where we spent an evening with Dr. and Mrs. Lort), Conway, Beaumaris, Bangor, Carnarvon, from whence we went to Snowdon. . . . and proceeded thro' Bethhelert, Festinog, Dolgelley, Welsh Pool and Montgomery, into Shropshire and thro' Worcestershire to this place [Rodmarton], having then compleated a tour of above five hundred Miles, four of which we walked in a little more than a Month."

3. John Myddelton (1724–92) was born in Denbigh, matriculated at Oriel College, Oxford, in March 1742/43, and studied at Lincoln's Inn in 1745. He held various positions in the Denbigh corporation, including that of burgess. Long active in the Denbighshire militia, he was now its colonel. By 1787 he was deputy steward of the lordship of Denbigh. He entertained SJ and the Thrales at Gwaynynog in August 1774 and memorialized SJ with an urn in the deer park that the latter had frequented. See *A Journey into North Wales* 5:443, 452–53 and n. 1; *Boswell's Johnson* 4:421 n. 1. For Myddelton's wife, see HLP to SL, 21 September, n. 3.

4. For HLP's impressions of Rome, see *Observations* 1:377–437; 2:94–149.

5. Giambattista Piranesi (1720–78), Italian architect and engraver, was known for his prints of Roman ruins. In the 1740s he began to execute a series of 135 "Vedute di Roma" (1748–78) and ca. 1745, another series of plates, "Carceri d'invenzione." Piranesi drew the plans for rebuilding the church of Santa Maria del Priorato on the Aventine Hill (1764–65).

6. Pope Pius VI (1775–99), born Giovanni Angelo Braschi (1717–99).

7. In the letter of 12 October, SL referred to "Mr. Coxe who is lately returned from Italy [tear] tho' Rome itself is a very magnificent place, yet the Country round it is extremely unpleasant, indeed he called it I believe a black Bog."

The brother of the historian William (1747–1828), George Coxe (ca. 1758–1844) was one of the English visitors in Rome when the Piozzis were there. He had traveled in Europe as a tutor, and—ordained in 1783—later held livings in Ireland; Withcall, Lincs.; and at Saint Michael's, Winchester.

8. "These are sad desolated scenes indeed, though this is not the season for *mal' aria* neither, which, it is said, begins in May, and ends with September" (*Observations* 1:378).

9. Her refinement of "Monster, I do smell all horse-piss, at which my nose is in great indignation" (*The Tempest* 4.1.199–200).

10. HLP alludes to *Prayers and Meditations*, which had been published in 1785.

She had not seen the volume, but from SL (12 October) learned that "The Publication of Dr. J's Meditations and Diary has been universally condemned—among the prayers is one on the Rambler—when his Eye was restored—and a Thanksgiving for the comforts and advantages he received from Hen: Thrale Esq.—In his Diary he constantly purposes to rise earlier in the morning—on Easter day at church 'to pray for Tetty and the rest' he frequently afterwards speaks of his deceased wife Tetty with great affection."

According to one censorious reviewer, the prayers "were evidently composed for the Doctor's own use, and not designed for the public eye. In several of them there is a penitential cast, and mere common place expressions. They should never have seen the light. It is remarkable, that the *Doctor* has offered up prayers for deceased friends, which is somewhat superstitious, and indefensible upon protestant principles" (*Daily Universal Register*, 12 September).

See also *Diaries, Prayers, and Annals* 1:50, 79.

11. See Ps. 49:8.

12. The *Prayers and Meditations* was so designated by SJ, who turned the collection over

to the Reverend George Strahan (1744–1824) shortly before his death (*Boswell's Johnson* 4:376 and n. 4).

13. Thomas Davies, an actor turned bookseller, provided the location for the meeting between SJ and JB on 16 May 1763 (*Boswell's Johnson* 1:390–91). For his obituary, see HLP to SL, 31 December, n. 4.

14. Lent began on 1 March 1786; Holy Week ran from 10 April to Easter Sunday, the sixteenth.

15. Henry Smeathman (d. 1786), author of "Some Account of the Termites which are found in Africa and other Hot Climates. In a letter . . . to Sir Joseph Banks, Bart. F.R.S." This paper was read on 15 February 1781 and printed in the *Philosophical Transactions of the Royal Society* 71, pt. 1 (1781): 139–92. Smeathman describes the insects as "rapacious" (169) and asserts that "nothing less hard than metal or stone can escape their destructive jaws" (142). The story, although it does not appear in the "Account," is reported in *Observations* (1:127) as having been told to HLP by Smeathman. See also *GM* 51, pt. 2 (1781): 526, and 56, pt. 2 (1786): 620.

The image of elephants being devoured by ants was not uncommon. See, e.g., "Thoughts of Bishop Horne," as cited by William Jones, *Memoirs of the Life, Studies, and Writings of . . . George Horne* (London: G. G. and J. Robinson, 1795), p. 240.

16. See HLT to Q, 15 July [1784], n. 7.

17. There are two mottoes on the title page of the *Florence Miscellany:*

> Cur non, Mopse, boni quoniam convenimus ambo,
> Tu calamos inflare levis, ego dicere versus,
> Hic corulis mixtas inter considimus ulmos?
>
> Virgil [*Eclogue* 5.1–3]
>
> Nunc opus est leviore lyra.
>
> Ovid [*Metamorphoses* 10.152]

18. SL wrote from Rodmarton, 12 October: ". . . I small remain another Year at the same Lodgings, in which I have hitherto been. You may direct to me at Mr. Godwin's, No. 167 Strand, as I shall then receive your Letters sooner than at present." Previously she had been addressing SL's letters to the residence of his uncle, the Reverend Samuel Peach, at East Sheen.

TO THOMAS CADELL

Naples, 26: *December* 1785.

Sir,—I wrote to you from Sienna last October,—I forget the day,—and told you in that letter that the Anecdotes of Dr. Johnson were sent from Leghorn to London in the ship Piedmont, or Prince of Piedmont, Joel Forster commander, consigned to Mr. Otto Franck, banker at Leghorn, to Mess. John and Francis Baring and Compy. London. Never having had any answer to this letter, nor any account of the book's arrival, I am afraid there has been some mistake or accident;[1] and earnestly beg your answer by return of post, directed to Mr. Thomas Jenkins, banker, at Rome,[2] as he will be sure to forward it to, / Sir, your most humble servant / Hester L. Piozzi.

Text: GM, n.s., 37 (1852): 136.

1. See HLP to Cadell, 20 October, n. 2.

Two similarly named ships sailed regularly between Leghorn and various English coastal ports. One was the *Prince of Piedmont*, commanded by a Captain Stevenson, and sighted off Gravesend on 3 November. The other ship, which in fact carried the manuscript, was the *Piedmont*.

2. The prominent banker Thomas Jenkins (1722–98) was also a painter and dealer in antiquities. HLP was indebted to him for receiving letters sent to her and for "general kindness and hospitality to all his country-folks, who find a certain friend in him; and if they please, a very competent instructor" (*Observations* 1:397).

See also Joseph Gorani, *Mémoires secrets et critiques des Cours, des Gouvernemens, et des Moeurs des Principaux États de L'Italie.* 3 vols. ([1793]; Londres, 1794), 2:26–28.

TO SAMUEL LYSONS

Naples
31: December 1785.[1]

Dear Mr. Lysons

Your Letter tells me numberless Things which I was earnest to be informed of, but nothing that has pleased me so much as what relates to yourself; of whom I long ago formed the greatest hopes from my Knowledge of your Talents and Virtues. They will be rewarded with Fame and Fortune I doubt not. You live in a Country where Merit is never neglected and where no Man perishes obscurely but by his own Fault—unless some Singular Accident intervenes.

The more I see of other Nations the more I respect my own; which while I compared it (like a Novice) with the Ideas I had formed of Perfection, I justly despised: but now, drawing the Comparison with other States and other Climates; I love, honour, and esteem. You will wonder when I commend the Temperature of its Air so loudly lamented by most People, but if its not particularly salubrious, it is at least not pestiferous like the Environs of Rome, sullenly unwholesome as about the Bagni di Pisa, or impregnated as here with fiery Particles, and Mineral Exhalations that hourly threaten the Lives of the Possessors, while they fructify the Land, and ripen the Fruit to a Perfection unknown in our Country, and only to be imitated by artifice [and] Care.

We have been entertained by a very beautiful Eruption [of] Mount Vesuvius—which on the Night of our Arrival flamed away so a[s] to be easily seen 35 Miles off;[2] and there was a prodigious Storm at Sea besides, with the most horrible Lightning I ever saw—and the *bluest*. I suppose it takes that peculiar Hue from the Quantities of Vitriol drawn up into the Clouds that surround us; but it has an Appearance to me totally new and striking. The Thunder here too [is] singularly loud and awful, and in the Night we sometimes hear the sighing of the Mountain with Sensations not difficult to imagine, but far from easy to explain. While I write this the Sea rages with a Violence I never saw surpassed unless 'twas once upon the Coast of Sussex,——and as our Apartment is gloriously s[itu]ated and commands a complete View of the Bay—the Island of Caprea and Vesuvius which is worth all the rest; I never want [for] Amusement nor much seek those of

Society—tho' the Ven[etian] and Swedish Ministers[3] have been excessively kind, and here are English Families too that I like vastly. Mr. Piozzi al[ways] finds Friends among my Countrymen and prefers their Acquain[tance] to that of the Italians [in the] Town we reside at.

Your account of poor Davies gives me Concern,[4] and all the Play-goers will grieve about Henderson:[5] I wish I had been to the Theatre last Night that I might have told you how we act King Lear at Naples, but perhaps there may Offer another Opportunity;[6] Miss Brunton's Father was a favourite at Bath I remember,[7] and reckoned a Scholar and a Man of Sense— I hope She will do well but would not wish dear Siddons to lose an Inch of Ground.

I have read poor old Bellamy's Narrative since I was here, and wish to know if She is likely to end her Days comfortably by means of her Book?[8] *My* Book about Johnson was left in the Hands of Otto Franck a Banker at Leghorn who promised to put it among his own Things consigning it to Mess: John and Francis Baring and Co. London. Of all this I wrote word to Cadell from Sienna, telling him at the same Time the name of the Ship which was Piedmont, or Prince of Piedmont Joel Foster Commander; but to my Letter no Return has been made, so I don't know what to think,[9] and sincerely wish you would be kind enough to go to Cadell, and ask him whether he ever has had either Book or Letter on the Subject, for I am in some Anxiety about it.

Mr. Boswell did me very great Injustice in saying I could not get through Mrs. Montagu's Performance,[10] for the Elegance and Erudition of which I hope I am [n]ot wholly without Taste or Cognizance; and as for Dr. Johnson, [he] had to my certain Knowledge a true Respect for her Abilities, [an]d a very great Regard and Esteem of her general Character. It is hard upon me that I am not at home to defend myself, [b]ut Mr. Boswell is well qualified to be witty on the *Dead* and the *Distant*.

You will get the Florence Miscellany [sa]fe I dare say; Mr. Cator had a List of Names sent him from [R]ome the same Day that I wrote to you, and it is very odd that [so]me Letters should be lost and others come to hand when sent by [the] same Courier.[11] Your Observation on his Manners is a very [ ] to be sure. Do write again soon, and direct to Mr. Jenkins [ ] at Rome; he will be sur[e to] have, and to forward the Letters.

[The] best amends I can make for your agreeable Correspondence is to tell you wha[t I see] and how I like it——Why then absolutely the sight of the Theatre overwhelmed with Lava at Herculaneum,[12] the Bread left baked, the Meat put upon the dishes, the Wine petrified in the Decanters, the impression of a Fool in the Act of escaping, and of a Female who being confined to her Bed could not try to escape, but has left the print of her Person—and *light*——in the hot Liquid which suddenly surrounded her—excited in me Ideas which will not be easily erased. —Oh there is no Comparison between one's Sensations at home and those one feels at Naples.

Royalty demolished, and Empire destroyed;—Power unlimited once, now changed to a childish display of empty splendour; and Riches *heaped up* as the Scripture says, *without knowing who was to gather them*[13] are the Images with which Rome impresses one's Imagination——but *here* the Business comes closer to our own Bosom. The Shopkeepers killed by a sudden Burst of Fire from the neighbouring Mountain——while some of the Wares they sold were left standing on the Shelves——Soldiers stifled in the Guard Room, and Babies in the Cradle——*these* are the Things to strike [and] terrify those who examine them: the Mind shudders more at read[ing] Lillo's Fatal Curiosity[14] than at all the Heroic Tragedies writt[en] by Dryden, Thomson or dear Dr. Young: for we cannot all be Kings and Heroes; but we are all Men and Women, and may [be] seduced by Poverty to Guilt—or betrayed to Danger by a refined Curiosity: I am sure too that those who live *her*[*e*] may *very easily* be swallowed up by an Earthquake, so ought to lead good Lives: for there is a constant *Warning*, a *Beacon* kept blazing to assure us of Heaven's Vengeance on some future Day.

'Tis said however that the People here are not *better* but rather *worse* than in other Nations; that fair *Parthenope*[15] as She still retains her Power to allure Travellers, retains likewise her Inclination and skill to pick their Bones most neatly: and my Husband complains that we are cheated in all our [dealings] with the [ ] Inhabitants.

But 'tis Time to release and [ ] my Christmas wis[hes] New Year and many [ ] shall [ ] in various Comforts.

Tell me if ever you had a Letter from me [at] Leghorn? and whether Dr. Lort ever had his from the same Place?[16] I [have] my Reasons for asking. Tell me of the Pepyses, and tell me of Florence Miscellany when it arrives. It was sent in a Ship called the Roman Emperor—Hamstroom Commander from Leghorn.[17]

God bless you dear Sir, and accept my Husband's best Compliments and Wishes, with those of Your Old and faithful Friend / H: L: Piozzi.

I will take care about the Coins never fear.[18]

Text: Hyde Collection. *Address:* A Monsieur / Monsieur Samuel Lysons chez le Reverend / Mr. S. Peach / a East Sheene / near Mortlake / Surrey / près de / Londres / Angleterre.

1. SL did not receive this letter until 5 February 1786 "at Sheen, I believe it arrived there the 2d of this month, so that it was more than a Month on the road—" (7 February, Ry. 552.7).

2. For this event, which coincided with their arrival in Naples on 10 December, and impressions of their stay there, see *Observations* 2:1–86.

3. For the Venetian minister John Strange, see HLP to SL, 7 December 1784; the Swedish minister was Wilhelm André (fl. 1746–95), "consul and agent" to Sicily. See *Repertorium*, p. 416; *Observations* 2:52.

4. On 5 May 1785 "in Russel-str. Covent Garden, in his 75th year, [died] Mr. Thomas Davies, bookseller; a man of uncommon strength of mind, and who prided himself in being through life 'a companion of his superiors.'" Apparently he suffered from cancer. The last time he was visited by the writer of this *GM* account, he "wore the appearance of a spectre; and, sensible of his approaching end, took a solemn valediction. . . . Mr. Davies was buried, by his own desire, in the vault of St. Paul, Covent-Garden," See *GM* 55, pt. 1 (1785): 404.

5. John Henderson (1747–85), the "Bath Roscius." He began his acting career in Bath under the name of Courtney and was acclaimed for his Shakespearean roles. His popularity continued when he came to London (ca. 1777) and evoked the jealousy of Garrick

(whom he could mimic). He was encouraged in his career by Charles Macklin (ca. 1697–1797) and Richard Brinsley Sheridan (1751–1816) and acted opposite SS. It was perhaps Henderson who provided entertainment "at a Birthday held in the Summer House at Streatham." See *Queeney Letters,* p. 220; *Thraliana* 1:518.

6. Under an entry of 20 January 1786 (*Observations* 2:73), HLP noted: ". . . *il Rè Lear è le sue tre Figlie* are advertised, and I am sick tonight and cannot go."

7. John Brunton (1741–1822), a native of Norwich, acted mostly in Bath and Bristol, in important secondary roles. His daughter Anne (1769–1808) made her London debut on 17 October 1785 in the Covent Garden Theatre as Horatia in *The Roman Father* (by William Whitehead, 1750), competing with SS, who was then performing at the Drury Lane Theatre. Father and daughter joined in *The Grecian Daughter* (by Arthur Murphy, 1772), 28 October, but bad notices drove him back to the provincial theaters.

8. *An Apology for the Life of George Anne Bellamy, late of Covent-Garden Theatre, written by herself* [probably by Alexander Bicknell], 5 vols. (London: Printed for the author, by the Literary Society, at the Logographic Press, 1785). An Irish-born actress (ca. 1731–88), she was the natural daughter of the diplomat James O'Hara (1690–1773), cr. Baron Kilmaine (1722) and second baron Tyrawley (1724). After an appearance in the pantomime *Harlequin Barber* (1741), she made her professional debut (1742) as Miss Prue in Congreve's *Love for Love.* Favored by the aristocracy, she rose rapidly in public notice. In her final years she was in poor health and probably impoverished. SL observed on 7 February 1786 (Ry. 552.7): "Mrs. Bellamy's Book did her little service, for tho', by that and her Benefit, she got enough to have lived comfortably with, yet I believe she has been for some time as bad as ever in her Circumstances."

9. HLP did not receive Cadell's letter of 24 January 1786 (Ry. 892.3) until some time in February.

10. In the *Tour to the Hebrides,* JB purports to quote SJ on Elizabeth Montagu's *Essay on the Writings and Genius of Shakespeare* (1769), a defense of the dramatist against Voltaire: ". . . neither I, nor [Topham] Beauclerk, nor Mrs. Thrale, could get through it" (*Boswell's Johnson* 5:245). As a mutual friend of the two women, Lucas Pepys alluded on 15 December (Ry. 536.27) to the sleepless hours suffered by the "Queen of the Blues" because of JB's sneer. See also Michael Lort to HLP, 31 December (Ry. 544.5) for a similar comment.

Subsequently, on 7 February, SL relayed a request from Sir Lucas and the bishop of Peterborough for HLP's reaction to the offending passage. He added: "It was a shameful thing in Boswell to mention so many foolish things relating to living persons. . . . *Bozzy* (as he says Johnson called him) is *unique*" (Ry. 552.7).

An annoyed HLP thereupon drafted a postscript, dated "Naples Feb. 10, 1786," that she authorized Sir Lucas to append to the *Anecdotes.* This, as he informed her on 28 March (Ry. 892.5), had been executed and the postscript appeared thus:

"Since the foregoing went to the press, having seen a passage from Mr. Boswell's Tour to the Hebrides, in which it is said, that *I could not get through Mrs. Montagu's Essay on Shakespeare,* I do not delay a moment to declare, that, on the contrary, I have always commended it myself, and heard it commended by every one else. . . ."

For the hostile reaction of Edmond Malone and JB to the postscript, see *Boswell: The English Experiment 1785–1789,* ed. Irma S. Lustig and Frederick A Pottle (New York, Toronto, and London: McGraw-Hill, 1986), pp. 54, 59 and n. 4.

11. The letter to Cator is missing, but he obviously received it. Dr. Lort on 5 March 1786 (Ry. 544.6) acknowledged receipt of the *Florence Miscellany* "which Mr. Lysons brought me from Mr. [Cator]."

12. See *Observations* 2:34–35.

13. See Ps. 39:6.

14. *The Fatal Curiosity* (published 1736), by George Lillo (1693–1739), deals with the unwitting murder of a son by his own father.

15. In Greek mythology Parthenope was a siren who threw herself into the sea because her singing did not entice Odysseus. Her body was washed up on the shore of Naples. Parthenope is the ancient name for that city.

16. SL received a letter from HLP dated Leghorn, 21 September, but her letter to Dr. Lort is missing.

17. The *Roman Emperor* arrived at Deal on a Thursday, 17 February 1786. By 20 February it was outward bound for Charlestown. The command perhaps changed, for the captain is identified as "Kerr." See the *London Chronicle*, 17–19 and 19–22 February.

18. See HLP to SL on 20 January and 4 November 1785. He had written on 12 October of that same year: "During your stay at Rome I shall probably trouble you with my wants in a series of Roman Denarii. I wish to compleat that series as it may be done with greater ease than any other, probably you might there without much trouble supply some of my Deficiencies."

THOMAS CADELL TO HESTER LYNCH PIOZZI

London
24: January 1786.

I am to acknowledge the receipt of two of your Letters, and should have wrote you in answer to the one dated October 20th but my mind was then so distressed that I was wholly incapable of attending to any thing but the painful illness of a Beloved Wife.[1] Her dissolution has deprived me of the best of Women—my Children of the most tender and affectionate of mothers.[2] I must request your pardon for being thus particular on my own concerns. A few hours before I received your Letter of the 26th of December I was very anxious to get possession of the M.S. I sent repeatedly but could not get it out of the Kings Warehouse. I had hardly read your last Letter when the M.S. was delivered to me, and without loss of time I sent for Mr. Strahan to put the press going.[3] Two modes of printing were proposed. One in two Volumes the size of the Sentimental Journey[4]—the other one handsome Volume according to the inclosed specimens, and this I determined upon as being, in my opinion, the most respectable. I print 1000 Copies of the first Edition and shall retail it at 4s. in boards or 5s. bound. The difficulty in printing will be to have the Latin, French, Italian and Spanish correct. We will do our utmost to procure your and the publicks approbation. You will doubtless make some presents—may I request the favour of a List that they may be sent previous to the publication. Our friend Mr. Lysons mentioned that perhaps you might wish to take notice of some part of Mr. Boswell's curious publication[5]—if so it may be done by way of Postscript. Mr. Lysons is in daily expectation of having the pleasure of a Letter from you. As we now draw near publication may it not be proper for us to explain the Terms of publication. I mean this in case of any Accident to myself that you may have no trouble with my Executors. Permit me, Madam, to request that you will either name a price for the property or if more agreeable we will divide the profits. I mean that I shall advance for paper, print &c.—after these are repaid to account to you for the moiety of the profits of this and future Editions.[6] The latter mode I have followed with Mr. Gibbon, Bishop Lowth, Adam Smith, Hay<ley> and many other of my capital Authors. I will make no Apology for troubling you on this subject as in matters of Business being explicit is the way to promote a durable connection.

I remain with great respect, Madam, / Your most Humble Servant / T. *Cadell*.

Text: Ry. 892.3.

1. The daughter of Thomas Jones of the Strand, Elizabeth had married Cadell on 1 April 1769. She had died on 31 December (*GM* 56, pt. 1 [1786]: 83) and was buried in a vault in the Eltham Church where Cadell was also to be buried. See his will, signed with a codicil, 15 June 1802; proved 22 April 1803 (P.R.O., Prob. 11/1390/342).

2. The Cadells had two children. Joanna (d. 1829) was to marry Dr. Charles Lucas Edridge (1764–1826), rector of Shipdham, Norfolk (1804–26), and chaplain to George III. (She would bring to the marriage initially twenty thousand pounds and after the death of Cadell another thirty-nine thousand.) See the will of Dr. Edridge, proved 9 March 1826 (P.R.O., Prob. 11/1709/148). The other Cadell child was Thomas (1773–1836), who conducted his father's business in partnership with William Davies (d. 1820) from 1793 until the latter's death, and thereafter in his own name.

3. The youngest son of William Strahan (1715–85), printer and publisher, Andrew (ca. 1749–1831) successfully carried on his father's business. He became one of the joint patentees as printer to His Majesty, was M.P. successively for Newport, Wareham, Carlow, Aldeburgh, and New Romney (1796–1820).

4. Laurence Sterne's *A Sentimental Journey* appeared in 1768 in two volumes, octavo; the *Anecdotes* was produced as a single octavo volume.

5. JB's *Tour to the Hebrides* was much criticized upon publication (see *Boswell's Johnson* 5:3, 259 n. 1). SL (12 October 1785) told HLP: "I have just read part of it but had hardly patience to proceed, the Egotisms are so frequent and disgusting and he mentions so many trifling and absurd occurrences, and so many sayings of Johnson unworthy of being recorded. . . ."

According to Lort, 31 December 1785 (Ry. 544.5): "Mr. E. Burke fell hard upon [JB] for the absurdities in that performance. . . . John Wilkes told Boswell that he had wounded Johnson with his pocket pistol and was about to dispatch him with his blunderbuss when it should be let off."

See Clifford, p. 259, for other comments on JB's performance.

6. HLP chose "the latter mode" (17 February). The sum she received has been stated variously as £130 and £150 (Clifford, pp. 263–64 n. 3; "Harvard Piozziana" 2:72). But see HLP to JF, 24 October 1815. She recalled receiving £300 (Hayward 2:305).

TO THOMAS CADELL

Naples, 17: *February* 1786.

Sir,—I am much obliged to you for the letter just now sent me from Rome by Mr. Jenkins, dated 24 of January and feel sincerely mortified at the thoughts of having plagued you when your spirits were depressed by a recent misfortune. Be assured, my good Sir, that I am perfectly satisfied to settle our pecuniary affairs in the manner you say other people do;—dividing the profits equitably between us, when print and paper are paid. The book will be larger than I thought for; I enclose you a list of friends who must have each of them one. Mr. Lysons is very goodnatured, and if the letter I wrote him the 31st of last December comes safe, he will have my thanks in it for his kind friendship; but I have never seen Mr. Boswell's publication, nor should have known a word of its contents, had not two or three correspondents told me very lately that he had said some strange thing about Mrs. Montagu's Essay on Shakespeare, and laid to my charge concerning it expressions which I never used. My distance from all possibility of defending myself will perhaps invite attacks; but if I was weak enough to let such arrows poyson my peace, I should be very imprudent indeed to engage as Mr. Cadell's correspondent, and obedient servant, / Hester L. Piozzi.

Please to direct as before, to the care of Mr. Jenkins, at Rome.

Bishop of Peterborough. Mrs. Montague. Dr. Michael Lort. Saville-row. Mr. Samuel Lysons. Mr. George James, Oxford-row. Bath. Mrs. Lewis,[1] at Mrs. Codrington's, Albemarle-street.[2] Sir Lucas Pepys, Bart. Dr. Delap, Lewes, Sussex. Mr. Richard Tidy, Brighthelmstone.[3] Mr. Cator, Adelphi. Dr. Parker, St. James's.[4] Charles Selwin, Esq. Manchester-square.[5] Mr. Henry Johnson:—will call for it,[6] Count Turconi, *Paris*, if possible.[7] Charles Jackson, Esq. of the Post-office.[8] Sir Philip Jennings Clerke, Bart. Miss Jane Nicholson, No. 110, Bond-street.[9] 4 to Mr. Lysons. 1 Mr. Peach.[10] Count Turconi lives at No. 24, Rue de Sautier, Paris.

Text: GM, n.s., 37 (1852): 136–37.

1. "Mrs. Lewis has left [33] Albermarle Street; and is now at No. 15 Prince's Street, Hanover Square" (SL to HLP, 21 June 1786, Ry. 552.11).
2. Sarah, née Capper (d. 29 August 1806), the widow of John Archibald Codrington (d. 1759), of Chingford Hatch, Essex. Charlotte Lewis had been a guest of Sarah Codrington who, according to *Boyle's Court Guide*, lived at 33 Albemarle Street.
3. Richard Tidy (d. 1789), a Brighton friend of the Thrale years, and of FB. See *Queeney Letters*, pp. 133, 136; C.R.O., East Sussex.
4. See HLT to FB, 20 May 1784, n. 2.
5. See FB and Susanna Phillips to CB, 26 July 1784.
6. Perhaps Henry Johnson (1748–1835), cr. Baronet (1818): an army officer who was in action at the Battle of New Ross (5 June 1798).
7. Count Turconi had entertained the Piozzis in Paris on Q's birthday in 1784. "[H]e is a Milanese Nobleman, but chuses to inhabit Paris, and enjoy that Liberty which no Place but a populous City can afford: he politely offer'd us his Seat in the Neighbourhood of Milan to reside in" (*French Journals*, p. 201). See *Thraliana* 2:613–14.
8. Charles Jackson (d. 1798) of Gerard Street, Soho, was comptroller of the General Post Office's foreign office (at an annual salary of £150), ca. 1767–90 (see the *Royal Kalendar*). He had obliged HLT in 1783 by forwarding mail to GP that she neglected to send prepaid. He also assured the delivery of SAT's letters to the Continent. See Hayward 2:54; *Thraliana* 1:566 n. 3; *Queeney Letters*, p. 234; "Harvard Piozziana" 2:16; P.R.O., Prob. 11/1308/413; *GM* 68, pt. 1 (1798): 543.
9. SL on 21 April (Ry. 552.10) informed HLP that "Cadell's people could not find out Miss Nicolson's Lodging in Bond street." But on 21 June (Ry. 552.11) he reported seeing her at No. 118, New Bond St. "She seemed much pleased at hearing of you, having she said, written you many letters to Milan during the last twelvemonth, and not knowing that you were not there now she sends you her love, and desiring you will accept her thanks for your Book, which I carried her." See HLP to SL, 26 May and [5] July 1786.
10. See HLP to SL, 19 October [1784], n. 5.

TO SAMUEL LYSONS

Rome
1: March *1786*.

Dear Mr. Lysons.
Your very kind and friendly Letter[1] met me here the moment of my return yesterday and very glad was I to see it. But what would you have me do about this extraordinary Stroke of Mr. Boswell's?[2] I have written to Sir Lucas Pepys, to Dr. Lort, to Mrs. Montagu herself, and to Cadell about it—and I have not yet half expressed the degree of Pain it has given me. The News you send me of the Bishop of Peterborough's continued partiality is best capable of making me some Amends;[3] nobody's Esteem is more valuable in itself, and I have at least the Merit of valuing it as it deserves.

If the poor Book had sunk at Sea many Witticisms would have been produced to be sure, and now it is safe arrived, they must be witty on its Dulness: if I am out of the Possibility of Self defence, I am at least sheltered from hearing the Storm patter on my paper Umbrella and so the Old Precept is obeyed *When the Winds rise worship the Echo*.[4] Doctor Johnson said in Kelly's Prologue you know *The House may hiss—the Poet cannot hear.*[5] But I am glad at my heart that you like what you have seen, and hope the Florence Miscellany will divert you too, there are some very pretty Lines in it.

I will try to get the Print for Mr. Seward,[6] whom I have always been studious to oblige, and ready to applaud: both for such Virtues as benefit Mankind, and for such Talents as adorn it. His contemptuous Behavior towards me, and the additional Vexation his Conduct gave me when I was little able to endure more Pain, proves little except that he was disposed to be merry when I was very sad:—he will perhaps never serve anybody else so, and 'twere better not. *Veniamo ad altro* as the Italians say. After seeing some curious Cameos at Naples particularly one of a *beardless Jupiter,* it came into my Head at Terracina that Anxur was a Noun both Masculine and Neuter because *Jupiter Anxurus*[7] was worshipped there——*Et genus Anxurquod dat utrumque* Says the old Grammar you know; do ask some wise Man if that was the real Reason: there is a Line in Virgil somewhere too about this shorn Jupiter but I can't find it.[8]

The Elysian Fields afforded me very small Speculation; everything about Naples was better than the Elysian Fields. I was loth to leave that delicious Spot for all the Shows of Rome; nothing in Italy yet so fine as Venice and Naples for general and immediate Appearance, but the Curiosities of *this* Place never tire, and those *do:* I saw an English Lady who has lived eight Years here; and says it is not enough.[9]

Apropos that Lady is a Person of surprizing Endowments, and Erudition much too deep for me to pretend praising it as I ought. Her Power over the French Language in particular is such as few Natives possess, and had I known her before my Book went out, She says She should have liked to translate it——I regret exceedingly that we made Acquaintance only at Naples for many reasons; we had great Talk about Dr. Johnson who was her Mother's Friend;[10] her Father was Captain Knight, made Sir Joseph when the King went Aboard his Ship at Portsmouth.[11]

Oh! you have got our little Book of Verses written in Tuscany safe by now; for Miss Thrale has thanked me for hers, and says She likes the preface. Write to me soon do, and tell me all the news: Miss Brunton is set up as a Rival to Siddons I hear, but sure that won't do.—How droll it must be to see Mrs. Abingdon act *Scrub!*[12] Our theatres here, where so little is represented, are the most Splendid Places Imagination can conceive, while England has not a Playhouse fit for Strollers: I wonder that among all your Luxuries in London there is never a tolerable Theatre.

Well! our diversions finished last night, and it was very comical and very curious to see the Gentlemen and Ladies drive up and down the Streets throwing Sugarplumbs at the Mob, and calling out *E morto il Carnavale* with lighted Candles or showy Lanthorns in the Coaches to make Sport. The Town was gayly illuminated indeed, and if one had not felt some English Fears of overturning in that prodigious Confusion, one might have laughed very heartily. Today We saw the Ceremonies of Ash Wednesday in St. Peter's Church, and propose working hard these forty Days to see some of the most curious Wonders of Rome.

St. Peter's Church is a perpetual Wonder, and when one hears and knows that with all its Appurtenances, Courts &c. it equals in Size the whole City of Turin[13] one begins wondering all over again I think. Adieu Dear Sir, and on this good St. David's Day[14] remember your Welch Friends; and her who claims the first Place among them / Your truly Affectionate Servant / H: L: Piozzi.

My Husband sends his best Compliments.

Text: Hyde Collection. *Address:* A Monsieur / Monsieur Samuel Lysons / chez le Rev. Monsieur S. Peach / at East Sheene / near Mortlake / Surrey / by London, Angleterre. *Postmark:* [MR] 2; MR 18.

1. SL's letter was dated 7 February (Ry. 552.7).
2. That is, the contretemps concerning Mrs. Montagu's *Essay on Shakespeare.*
3. SL reported 7 February that Bishop Hinchliffe wished HLP to refute JB's slur about Mrs. Montagu's *Essay.*
4. The author of *Tatler* 214 (probably Addison, according to Donald F. Bond) alludes to "a most pleasing Apothegm of *Pythagoras: When the Winds,* says he, *rise, worship the Eccho.* . . . By the Winds in this Apothegm, are meant State-Hurricanes and popular Tumults. When these rise, says he, worship the Eccho; that is, withdraw your self from the Multitude into Deserts, Woods, Solitudes, or the like Retirements, which are the usual Habitations of the Eccho."

Bond attributes the Pythagorean quotation to André Dacier, *The Life of Pythagoras, with his Symbols and Golden Verses* (London: Jacob Tonson, 1707), pp. 125–26. See *The Tatler,* ed. Bond, 3 vols. (Oxford: Clarendon Press, 1987), 3:124–27. See also a letter of Pope to Sir William Trumbull, 16 December 1715; and SJ, *Rambler* 117.

5. SJ had written the prologue in conjunction with a benefit performance (29 May 1777) for the widow and children of Hugh Kelly (1739–77), author of *A Word to the Wise* (1770): "Forbear to hiss—the poet cannot hear" (line 18). See *Poems,* p. 291; *Boswell's Johnson* 3:113–14.
6. SL had written on 7 February: "Mr. Seward says that he should be much obliged to

you, if you would get him a print of Cardinal Passionée who was Librarian to one of the Popes, I forget which—I do verily believe that no one here wishes you better than Seward does, and I am sure no one speaks of you at all times—with greater regard, or seems more interested in your welfare."

Domenico Passionei (1682–1761), cardinal and secretary of briefs in the Vatican during the papacy of Clement XIII (d. 1769). See Pastor 37:21–22.

For the ambivalent relationship between HLP and Seward, see her letter of 30 June 1784 to FB, n. 3; also *Thraliana* 1:576 n. 3; *Queeney Letters*, p. 70.

7. Anxurus, a Roman divinity, was worshipped in groves near Anxur (later Tarracina and then Terracina). He was believed to be a youthful Jupiter, hence the inscription on a medal struck in his honor by the consul Caius Vibius Pansa (d. 43 B.C.): "imago barbata, sed intonsa." (The name appears on various coins as Anxur and Axur.) A temple dedicated to Jupiter was also at Terracina.

8. The "old grammar" was by William Lily (ca. 1468–1522) combined with a work by Charles Hoole (1610–67). In chap. 5, par. 2, "Of the General Rules of Proper Names," Anxur is parsed as 'both of the Masculine and Neuter gender."

Lily's text was *De Generibus Nominum, ac Verborum Præteritis et Supinis, Regulæ. . . . Opus Recognitium ad Adauctum cum Nominum ac Verborum Interpretamentis, per Rituissi, Scholæ Paulinæ Præceptoris* (London, ca. 1520).

Subsequently, the more familiar designation became *Propria quæ Maribus, quæ Genus, and As in Præsenti, Englished and Explayned* [from *De Generibus Nominum . . . Regulæ*] . . . By Charles Hoole (1650). It also bore the title in some editions of *Grammatica Latina* (London, 1670); *The Latine Grammar,* as in the 3d ed. (London: Printed by Thomas Mabb for Henry Mortlock and Thomas Basset, 1659); see pp. 28–29, and *An Introduction to the Latin Tongue, for the Use of Youth* [*Eton Latin Grammar*] (Eton: J. Pote and Thomas Pote; [London], 1758), p. 57.

For a fuller account, see HLP's *Observations* 2:88–90, in which she also quotes from the *Aeneid*, 7.799–800: ("Circeumque jugum, queis Jupiter Anxuris arvis / praesidet"); *Thraliana* 2:647.

9. Ellis Cornelia Knight (1757–1837), author of *Dinarbas*, an "imitation" of *Rasselas*, or a supplement to it. For her "surprizing Endowments," see *Thraliana* 2:775, 776, 779.

10. Her "strange old drunken Mother" (*Thraliana* 2:779) was Phillipina Knight, née Deane (1727–99). See her anecdotes of SJ in *Johns. Misc.* 2:171–76; also *Boswell's Johnson* 5:514–15.

11. Joseph Knight (d. 1775), rear admiral of the White. When knighted on 24 June 1773, he was described as "captain of the *Ocean*, senior captain in the fleet at Spithead." See also *Boswell's Johnson* 1:378 n. 1.

12. SL had mentioned on 7 February that he would attend a performance of Farquhar's *The Beaux' Stratagem* the following Friday (10 February). The low-comedy role of Scrub was to be played by Frances Abington, née Barton (1737–1815), a leading comedy actress.

13. See *Observations* 1:430.

14. The date of this letter, 1 March, is the anniversary of Saint David, the fifth or sixth century patron saint of Wales who led the Welsh to victory over the Saxons. (In Welsh, Taffy or Tavy, as in *Henry V* 4.7.103.)

TO THOMAS CADELL

Rome
3: March 1786.

Mr. Cadell
Sir.

Having heard repeatedly from various Acquaintance that Mr. Boswell has thought fit to prejudice me in the Minds of the Publick and of Mrs. Montagu by giving them to understand that I disliked her Book, or Words to that Effect: I earnestly beg you will contradict the Report in whatever manner you think most efficacious, and assure the Town of my Esteem for the distinguished Talents of that Lady, which can only be exceeded by my Veneration of her Character.

I am Sir / Your Obedient Servant / H: L: Piozzi.

Be pleased to send the Anecdotes of Dr. Johnson's Life very finely bound to Sam: Whitbread Esqr. Portman Square[1] and write in the first Leaf of it—From the Author

Text: Hyde Collection. *Address:* A Monsieur / Monsieur Thomas Cadell / Libraire / The Strand / London / Angleterre. *Postmark:* MR 21.

1. Samuel Whitbread (1720–96), affluent landowner and brewer, HT's business rival, and M.P. for Bedford (1768–96). His first marriage (1758) was with Harriot, née Hayton (1735–64), by whom he had a son, Samuel, and two daughters, Harriot and Emma Maria Elizabeth. A second marriage (1769), with Lady Mary, née Cornwallis (d. 1770), produced a daughter, Mary (1770–ca. 1858). HLT thought Whitbread was in love with her. See Hyde, p. 206; *Thraliana* 1:547.

TO HESTER MARIA THALE

Rome,
4 March, 1786

My Dear Hester

I received yours of the 7 of Feb: here from the hand of Mr Jenkins,[1] & find it is better for every body to direct our Letters to him, as we are liable to lose them else. I am very apprehensive that mine to you from Naples written the 16 of January missed its Passage[2]—it was a *very long one,* and thanked you for that you sent me in Octr which never arrived till three Months after its date: & I not knowing the N^o^ of your House in Wimpole Street, wrote at Random; instead of directing to Mr Cator as I ought to have done—do tell if you ever received it, & in the mean Time think where I shall begin now I have a Fancy to amuse you with some Accounts of Rome & Naples. The first and greatest Thing then which I have seen since I left England, that which has given more new Ideas to my Mind

Hester Lynch Piozzi, ca. 1785, by an unknown Italian artist. *(Reproduced by permission of the National Portrait Gallery.)*

I mean, and most Employment to those Ideas I had before, is unquestionably Mount Vesuvius;[3] & now we are returned to Rome, and to our old Business of examining Churches & Palaces, I feel still more perswaded of the superiority:—because one View of the Eruption covered with its River of Fire every Image obtained at Rome; while Guido[4] and Guercino,[5] Michael Angelo[6] and Bernini[7] do nothing towards making me forget delightful & astonishing Naples. The best *Day* I have spent for the Acquisition of Materials to think upon in future—was that spent at Pompeia & Portici; which last you know, now contains the Curiosities dug up from the Subterranean City, & [from a] pretty Country House a few Miles off, discovered very lately: where every thing was found exactly as it stood when the Shower of Pumice Stones (for there was little Lava *there*) entirely covered it as with a Crust—to keep it one w^d^ think for our present Inspection & Warning.

Oh! tis a wonderful Place sure enough, and it would be *in me* the grossest Affectation not to admire it incessantly; there are however some who even disdain to be pleased or surprised with the Sight or Effects of Vesuvius, but I am not desirous to be upon the List. Shall we now talk of the Theatres all thro' Italy? those of Milan & Turin please me best;[8] but the Masquerade was most *riant* at Florence I think, & most splendid here at Rome.[9] The People at Naples did not correspond with the vastness of the Building, which is so *very* large, so *very* rich in decorations, and so *very* perfectly proportioned to *itself,* that neither Actors nor Spectators, nor the Throng that when there is no Opera crowds into it by way of making *Festa di Ballo*[10]—bear any degree of Comparison with the *Place* they are assembled in. Roncaglia[11] & Morichelli[12] however acted the Olimpiade[13] so well that like Sr Hugh Evans *'Mercy on me! I had great dispositions to cry'*.[14] The Music was not approved tho', and I was myself conceited enough to think I could find that Paësiello was out of his Walk,[15] which is elegant Buffo rather than serious Composition—Your Singer's Name is *Babini,*[16] and he is called a good Tenor here—the agreable Soprano who pleas'd us at Lucca was *Bedini*[17] of the old Tenducci School.[18] Rubinelli set off for London last Night after being stunned with Applauses here in this Town,[19] said to be the *nicest* in all Italy: the Pleasure he gave *me* was from his utter Want of all Affectation, so that he at least gives to his *very fine voice, very fair play;* but the Truth is good Singers are scarce! Marchese is gone to Russia[20] & poor Morichelli (whom I like vastly) does not go to England this winter—so you have got all we have for you.

The Paintings & Sculpture here at Rome are really more in Number & Excellence than one could form any notion of;[21] it was said by Vopiscus you remember that there were more statues than Men at Rome in his Time;[22] and as the People are daily popping their heads under Ground, & the Statues peeping theirs above Ground,—I fancy they now nearly double the Number of the Inhabitants. Never was more Attention paid to polite Arts than now, when the Sovereign[23] puts himself to enormous Expences on their Acc^t^ providing Repositories for the Busts of old Emperors, which the Emperors themselves might have inhabited—I never saw anything so gloriously fine as the Vatican Palace, Library &c.[24] and tho' you have probably heard and read it often times before, it is always [a] new Surprise to one when the Thought recurs, that St Peter's Church with all its Appurtenances, Courts, Colonnades &c, equals in Extent & Capacity the whole City of Turin. I am glad you liked my Preface in the *Florence Miscellany*[25]—but perhaps you think we *sung the sweets of Arno's Vale*[26] but little better than Henderson at a Birthday held in the Summer House at Streatham—Well! who can help it! there really are some good Lines amongst us too; and Mr Merry's *Viaggio & Dimora* I thought enchanting at the Time.[27]

The pretty Greek's good Fortune delights me, with Patience every thing comes about one sees; I hope they will be very happy at last.[28] Poor Hudson is out of all Hope, while her Madness is not enough to call help about her, & her Folly is sufficient to drive every Friend away![29] You are exceedingly good not to forsake her. Bath has been a Scene of many Wonders lately, or Fame has not left off her old Trick of lying: I am grieved for poor Anne Fitzherbert.[30]

What else have we to talk about? Painting has not had its Share perhaps in a letter like this, not only from Italy but from Rome: the Truth is one sees hands here which never are seen in England, & I passed two Mornings in looking at the pictures of Sasso Ferrato[31] and Andrea Mantegna,[32] Names which I used to know only in Books: the Works of Guido *Reni* as the Italians always call him however, give one the real, & true, & unaffected Delight which that Art can afford—and as Goldsmith used to say the way to set up for a Conoscente was to talk a great deal about *Pietro Perugino*.[33] I assure you that in that Merit I have already made many advances. Affectation after all (tho' many People may bring it home with 'em) is certainly no Plant of this Country's Growth: the Folks here live and die quite their own way, & not having any Taste of ridiculing others, or any fear of being ridiculed, behave naturally, & never pretend to be sorry when sad, or insensible when really diverted. So much for Character. What is left of my Paper will not serve to give the slightest Idea of our Ecclesiastical Splendors—let it just suffice to thank you for your Letters and to desire the next may be sent as the last was under Cover to Jenkins & directed to / Yr truly Affecte H: L: Piozzi.

Text: Queeney Letters, pp. 218–21. *Address: A Mademoiselle, / Mademoiselle Thrale, / No. 60 Wimpole Street, Cavendish Square, London, Angleterre.*

1. See HLP to Cadell, 26 December 1785, n. 2.
2. Actually 17 January. See *Queeney Letters*, pp. 215–17.
3. See HLP to SL, 31 December 1785, n. 2; *Observations* 2:1–6.
4. Guido Reni (1575–1642), painter and engraver of the Bolognese school. He was influenced by the anti-Mannerist techniques of the Carracci family and was important for his religious and poetic frescoes. One of his most celebrated paintings is *Phoebus and the Hours, preceded by Aurora* in the Borghese garden house (now the Palazzo Rospigliosi). See *Observations* 1:249–52, 413–15.
5. Guercino was the professional name of Giovanni Francesco Barbieri (1591–1666). Also influenced by the Carraccis, he executed religious frescoes in Bologna and Rome. Among his best known works are the Aurora fresco for the Casino of Villa Ludovisi and the *Burial . . . of Saint Petronilla* (Capitoline Museum, Rome).
6. See HLP to SL, 11 May 1786, n. 14; *Observations* 1:428, 2:103.
7. Son of the Florentine sculptor Pietro, Giovanni Lorenzo Bernini (1598–1680) was a sculptor, architect, and painter, a leading exponent of the baroque tradition. He was appointed in 1629 architect of Saint Peter's Cathedral (among other ecclesiastical assign-

ments), working under the patronage of Cardinal Scipione Borghese and Popes Urban VIII and Alexander VII. See *Thraliana* 2:737, 779; *Observations* 1:428.

8. For the Teatro della Scala and Teatro della Canobbiana at Milan, see HLP to Q, 5 January 1785, nn. 3 and 4.

From the seventeenth to the eighteenth centuries, Turin had become increasingly a cultural center in northern Italy. Its highly regarded theaters, attracting companies of *commedia dell'arte* performers, were especially popular for their musical entertainments. In HLP's day the Teatro Carignano (ca. 1752) provided a stage for plays and operas; the Teatro Regio (since 1738) for musical performances. See HLP to SL, 19 October [1784], n. 9; *Observations* 1:45.

9. See HLP to SL, 1 March.; *Observations* 2:96.

10. See HLP to SL, 30 April 1785; *Observations* 2:96.

11. Francesco Roncaglia (fl. 1747–81) was one of the principal operatic singers of the London season (1777–78). He "had an elegant face and figure; a sweet toned [soprano] voice; a chaste and well disciplined style of singing; hazarded nothing, and was always in tune. . . . Both his voice and shake were feeble; and of the three great requisites of a complete stage singer, pathos, grace, and execution . . . *cantabile*, *graziosa*, and *bravura*, he was in perfect possession of only the second. As his voice is merely a *voce di camera*, his singing in a room, when confined to the *graziosa*, leaves nothing to wish." See CB, *A General History of Music* 4:508, 514.

12. Anna (Reggio Emilia) Morichelli-Bosello (1759–1800), a soprano who performed in Saint Petersburg and London (1794–96), as well as in Italy. See *Observations* 1:113.

13. The opera *L'Olimpiade* (1733), with music by Antonio Caldara (ca. 1670–1736) and libretto by Metastasio (see HLT to Q, 4 July [1784], n. 1).

14. The Welsh parson in *The Merry Wives of Windsor.* Immediately after saying "Mercy on me! I have a great disposition to cry" (3.1.21), he bursts into song.

15. Giovanni Paisiello or Paesiello (1740–1816), a Neapolitan composer who began singing at the age of five in a Jesuit school at Taranto and studied music in the Conservatorio di Sant' Onofrio (1754–63) in Naples. After eight years in Saint Petersburg at the invitation of the Empress Catherine, he became (despite republican sympathies) *maestro di cappella* to Ferdinando IV. During a long career, he wrote approximately one hundred operas and an equal number of other musical compositions, all notable for simplicity and grace.

16. Mateo Babbini (1754–1816) was a "tenor, whose voice was sweet, though not powerful, had an elegant and pleasing style of singing. It is easy to imagine that his voice *had* been better; and not difficult to discover, though his taste was modern, and many of his *riffioramenti* refined and judicious, that his graces were sometimes redundant, and his manner affected. His importance was much diminished when he sung with the Mara, and after the arrival of Rubinelli [in England], he sunk into insignificance" (*A General History of Music* 4:524, 526).

17. See HLP to Q, 17 September 1785, n. 13.

18. Giusto Ferdinando Tenducci (ca. 1736–ca. 1800), castrato tenor and composer. After a promising start in Venice and Naples, he came to London in 1758, singing for two seasons at King's Theatre. Although he performed often, he never achieved significant status as an operatic singer.

19. See HLP to Q, 17 September 1785, n. 15. See also CB's enthusiastic appraisal in *A General History of Music* 4:524–26.

20. Marchesi had gone to Russia the previous summer. See HLP to Q, 22 April, n. 20; 4 June, n. 18, both letters in 1785.

21. See HLP to SL, 4 November 1785; *Observations* 2:98–112.

22. Flavius Vopiscus (fl. 290–316), a Sicilian-born historian, was one of the six "Scriptores Historiae Augustae." He wrote nearly a dozen biographies of eminent personages, including those of Aurelian, Tacitus, and the four tyrants (Firmus, Saturninus, Proculus, Bonosus). See *Observations* 1:431, and *The Scriptores Historiae Augustae,* 3 vols., trans. David Magie (London and New York: William Heinemann and G. P. Putnam's Sons, 1922–32). See especially the life of Tacitus, 3:295–333.

23. That is, Pius VI, as in HLP to SL, 4 November 1785, n. 6.

24. See *Observations* 2:98–112.

25. See also HLP to SL, 27 July 1785, n. 7; 25 March 1786, n. 5.

26. A reference to a line ("More clear than bright, less sweet than plain") that was part of a stanza carelessly omitted from HLP's "La Partenza" (p. 209). See HLP to SL, 25 March.

27. "La Viaggio" and "La Dimora" (pp. 196–211).

28. The "pretty Greek" is Sophia Streatfeild, or Streatfield (HLP to Q, 25 November 1786, n. 9) for whom HLP anticipates a union with the Reverend William Vyse (1742–1816), canon residentiary of Lichfield (1772), chancellor of that diocese (1798–1816); rector of Saint Mary's, Lambeth (1774). But Vyse would not or could not terminate an unhappy marriage and Sophia, usually attractive to men, died unmarried. Nevertheless, out of an estate of three thousand pounds he left her five hundred pounds for a mourning ring and a token of his "sincere regard" (P.R.O., Prob. 11/1581/342, proved 12 June 1816). See *Thraliana* 2:682, 803 n. 5; Hayward 1:118–19.

29. See HLT to Q [28 June 1784], n. 4.

30. Defying the Act of Settlement (1701) and the Marriage Act (1772), the Prince of Wales had on 15 December 1785 married the twice-widowed Maria Anne Fitzherbert, née Smythe (1756–1837) in a private Anglican ceremony. Mrs. Fitzherbert was a commoner and a Catholic. Although invalid and never acknowledged, the marriage was an open secret, and the couple lived together intermittently for several years.

HLP's response to the gossip conveyed by Q was probably more dramatic than real. If HLP experienced "grief," it was because of her dislike of the prince's behavior that now tainted his bride. Furthermore, the scandalmongering aimed at Mrs. Fitzherbert was painfully similar to that which she herself continued to endure.

For the public innuendoes regarding the prince's marriage to Mrs. Fitzherbert, see, e.g., the *Daily Universal Register,* 6 January 1786; and for a full account of the affair, see Christopher Hibbert, *George IV: Prince of Wales 1762–1811*, pp. 44–59.

31. The Italian painter Giovanni Battista Salvi (1609–85), known as Sassoferrato (after his birthplace in Ancona province), studied with Domenichino and is recognized for his sentimentalized madonnas in the style of Raphael.

32. A painter and engraver of Isola di Carturo, Andrea Mantegna (ca. 1431–1506) executed a number of his religious frescoes and chapel ornamentations in Padua (many destroyed in World War II) and Mantua. One of his celebrated small-scale works, "The Circumcision" (ca. 1460–70), hangs in the Uffizi. He was probably called to Rome by Innocent VIII about 1488 to decorate the pope's private chapel in the Belvedere.

33. As Lansdowne comments: "The art of cognoscence was acquired, according to Goldsmith, by a strict adherence to two rules: 'the one to observe that the picture might have been better if the painter had taken more pains; and the other to praise the works of Pietro Perugino' " (*Vicar of Wakefield,* chap. 20). See *Queeney Letters,* p. 221 n.

Familiarly known as Perugino (after his native Perugia), this Umbrian artist of religious subjects is Pietro di Cristoforo Vannucci (ca. 1445–ca. 1523).

TO SAMUEL LYSONS

Rome
25: March 1786.

Dear Mr. Lysons—
I received your Letter of the 3d. but *two Hours* ago,—and tho' not a little fatigued with seeing the functions of the Day, I sit down to thank you most sincerely for

your active and diligent Friendship in making the Alteration and the *Application* concerning Johnson's Anecdotes.[1]

It was so wise and so well-thought to consult with the Bishop and Sir Lucas Pepys; and Dr. Lort was so good and charming to translate the Epitaph: Oh pray thank them all, and say how much I love them, how much I feel obliged to them, and how kindly I take their Interposition——till I have Time to tell them so myself. Why my Shoulders would have ached for a Year with the Blows I should have received!——and justly, there's the Astonishment; for I protest to you I thought I had *seen* that Mr. Boswell returned thanks for the impudent Letter of the 8th of January: and very angry I was naturally enough; but one gets the Papers here so irregularly—and in short I made a gross Mistake, and have been happy enough to light on true Friends who were sufficiently interested in my Welfare to correct me: I only wish long to deserve, and long to retain their regard.

The Florence Miscellany too is printed with a hundred Faults; but I had no Time to mend them, as I left Florence very ill, and Mr. Parsons did not take good Care.[2] In the Partenza[3] there is a necessary Couplet quite left out:—it should run thus

Since parting then on Arno's Shore
We part perhaps to meet no more;
Let these last Lines some Truths contain
More clear than bright, less sweet than plain.
Thou first—&c.——

The simple Sonnet about an English Watch[4] too is imperfect; they have printed it

Touch'd by thy magic *hand*

instead of——

Touch'd by thy magic Wand

for Hand comes in the Line that rhymes to it. How good-natured it would be in you to correct these Passages in any of the books you can pick up; if I had not been sick they should have been sent right at least, but I'm glad you are pleased with the Preface.[5]

Nothing was ever more pretty, comical, and sparkling than the Verses about Mr. Boswell which you tell me are Dr. Walcot's;[6] but upon my honour the World is very rigorous, for if Boswell was Plutarch, nothing but the *Sayings* of Johnson could he record——like Arabella's maid in the Female Quixote we should all be at a Loss to keep a register of *his Actions* for even her ladyship's Smiles might be mentioned as She suggests—but dear Dr. Johnson did not afford us many of *them.*[7] Is Mrs. Montagu convinced of my Respect, and of Mr. Boswell's flippancy![8] I hope so.

Do your best my Dear Sir to keep alive the unmerited but highly-valued Tenderness of all my Friends for their and your / greatly Obliged / and ever grateful / H: L: Piozzi.

My Husband sends his best Respects and Compliments to all who love his Wife——I feel exactly so to all who love my Husband.

Text: The Carl H. Pforzheimer Library. *Address:* A Monsieur / Monsieur Samuel Lysons / chez the Rev. Mr. S. Peach / at East Sheene / near Mortlake / Surrey / by London. *Postmark:* < > 5; AP 14.

1. SL had commented on 3 March (Ry. 552.8):

"One thing [in the *Anecdotes*] struck me, as a mistake, I mean the part wherein Mr. Boswell's Letter to the St. James's Chronicle is mentioned. I lost no time; but searched immediately at all the Coffee houses for the Papers in question, but without success, however and my anxiety for the welfare of your little Volume, would not let me rest 'till I had seen them; which I did at last with some difficulty at the stamp office—and here I found the fact was as I feared, in the Letter to that Paper of the 8th of [January] in which *you* are so grossly insulted, not a *syllable* is mentioned of *Mr. Boswell,* and in that of the 11th of January in which Mr. Boswell is so flattered, and for *which* of course he returns the letter of thanks of the 18th of January, *your* name is not mentioned, or alluded to, so that it is very probable that Mr. Boswell might never have seen the paper of 8th of January. Having satisfied myself with regard to these points, I was very well convinced that the Book must not come out with such an error, the consequences of which could not but have been very unpleasant, but *what* was to be done, it was just ready for publication, and a delay of six weeks would have been very improper, and no one here was authorised to make any correction—however I made extracts of all the principal matters, with the dates from the St. James's Chronicle and consulted Sir Lucas Pepys, the Bishop of Peterborough and Dr. Lort, who were all unanimously of opinion that the necessity of the Case above was such that we must run the hazard of incurring your displeasure by doing so bold a thing as leaving out the whole passage, and filling up the vacancy with a Translation of the Epitaph which Dr. Lort was so good as to make."

The excised passage is cited by Clifford, pp. 262–63.

2. Despite proof errors, journals and newspapers did not stress the faults. Parsons was to brag later in the year that "we make a brilliant appearance in the European Magazine, which the Editors have also enriched with an Engraving and Memoirs of yourself,—a distinction which they seem not to judge the rest of us worthy of" (to HLP, 1 October, Ry. 558.17). For the fame of the *Miscellany,* see the *European Magazine* 9 (1786): 121–22, 203–4, 286, 362–63; the *London Chronicle,* 14–16 February, 30 May–1 June 1786; *GM* 57, pt. 1 (1787): 257–58; Clifford, p. 253.

3. "La Partenza," by HLP, pp. 209–11.

4. HLP's "Translation of an Italian Sonnet upon an English Watch," p. 62.

5. That the preface outshone the rest of the *Florence Miscellany* was a generally shared opinion. See, e.g., Walpole's comment, in HLP to SL, 27 July 1785, n. 7.

6. *A Poetical and Congratulatory Epistle to James Boswell Esq. on his Journal of a Tour to the Hebrides with the Celebrated Dr. Johnson by Peter Pindar, Esq.* (Dublin: Colles, White, Byrne, M'Kenzie, Marchbank, and Moore, 1786). SL (3 March) quoted forty-two specimen lines.

John Wolcot (1738–1819), M.D. (1767) and clergyman (1769), emerged as Peter Pindar about 1782 and as author of "Bozzy and Piozzi, or the British Biographers" (1786).

7. See the satiric antiromance *The Female Quixote, or The Adventures of Arabella,* 2 vols. (London: A. Millar, 1752), by Charlotte Lennox (1720–1804). The allusion is to "Some curious Instructions for relating an History (vol. 1, bk. 3, chap. 5). Lucy, Arabella's maid, has been ordered to detail of her mistress's life, every incident, word, thought, "Change of Countenance . . . for these Ten Years past."

A modern commentator, Duncan Isles, adduces in an appendix: "When she was writing" the novel, "Mrs. Lennox was fortunate in receiving both literary and practical assistance from Samuel Johnson and Samuel Richardson" (*The Female Quixote,* ed. Margaret Dalziel [London, New York, Toronto: Oxford University Press, 1970], p. 418).

8. For Mrs. Montagu's response, see HLP to SL, 11 May, n. 5.

TO THOMAS CADELL

Rome, 28th March, 1786.

Sir,—I hasten to tell you that I am perfectly pleased and contented with the alteration made by my worthy and amiable friends in the Anecdotes of Johnson's Life. Whatever is done by Sir Lucas Pepys is certainly well done, and I am happy in the thoughts of his having interested himself about it. Mr. Lysons was very judicious and very kind in going to the Bishop of Peterboro and him and Dr. Lort for advice. There is no better to be had in this world, I believe; and it is my desire that they should be always consulted about any future transactions of the same sort relating to, / Sir, your most obedient servant / H. L. Piozzi.

Direct to Venice, at Algarotti's,[1] a banker there; and tell Mr. Lysons to do so.

Text: GM, n.s., 37 (1852): 232.

1. A letter from Jean Gore to Bonomo Algarotti (Ry. 601.13), dated 24 March 1785 from London: "Monsieur / Un de nos amis nous ayant priés de lui fournir une Lettre de Credit en faveur de Monsieur Gabriel Piozzi qui est actuellement a Milan avec Madame Son Epouse d'ou il Se propose de passer a Venise pour y faire un Sejour de quelques Mois; En consequence Nous vous prions de lui Compter jusqu'a la Concurrence de la Valeur de Mille Livres Sterling, contre Ses Traittes Sur Monsieur Jean Cator, a la place Adelphi, a Londres qui aura Soin d'acceuillir ses Traittes. S'il arrivoit qu'il ne fit pas usage de toute la Susdite Somme a Venise, Nous vous prions de lui fournir des Lettres de Credit pour le reste de la Somme, pour vos Amis de Naples ou toute autre place ou il pourra passer en pratiquant la meme Methode pour leurs rembourcements qu'il est mention cy dessus.

"Nous avons l'honneur detre avec une parfaite Consideration / Monsieur / Vostres humbles & tres / obeissants Serviteurs / Jean Gore & Co."

On the cover sheet: "Monsieur / Monsieur Bonomo Algarotti / a Venise."

TO LORD COWPER

Rome
7: April 1786.

My Lord[1]

While the Florentines are reflecting on the Loss they are so soon to feel from your Absence, and while the English exult in the Thoughts of your speedy Return; I am principally interested to desire that Lord Cowper to whom I have so many Obligations, may not leave Italy without receiving my best Acknowledgments; and sincerest good Wishes for his future Happiness under another Sky. Every one is curiously earnest to hear how your Lordship will like England after spending so many Years at so great a Distance: for my own part I have no doubt of your being at least contented in a Country, where you will see so many People happy in that Rank of Life whose Comforts your Lordship's beneficent Hand has *here* been ever studious to increase:—and I remember that Mr. Miller the famous

Botanist[2] once shewed me a Tree, which having been transplanted in its Youth, and brought back to the native Soil after an Absence of more than twenty Years; regained its Spirit of Vegetation, and shot up to a considerable height.

I have the honour to be / My Lord / Your Lordship's much Obliged / and truly Obedient Honourable Servant / H: L: Piozzi.

My Husband begs your Lordship and Lady Cowper will do him the honour to accept with mine, his best Respects and Wishes.——We leave Rome immediately after Easter, and mean to be at Venice for the Ascension[3]—if your Lordship should have any Commands.—

Text: C.R.O., Hertfordshire.

1. By 5 September Lord and Lady Cowper were returning to Florence. See Sir Horace Mann to Walpole in the *Walpole Correspondence* 25:660.
2. Philip Miller (1691–1771), gardener and prolific author of treatises on botanical subjects.
3. The Piozzis were in Venice by 11 May. See HLP to Q in the *Queeney Letters,* pp. 222–24; to SL, 11 May. For another celebration of Ascension Day, see HLP to SL, 30 April 1785, n. 18, and *Observations* 1:189–92.

TO SAMUEL LYSONS

Venice
11: May 1786.

Dear Mr. Lysons

You have been a very kind and a very active Friend to me indeed, and I only beg you will add to your other favors that of believing me grateful, till you find me so.

Two Letters from you dated on the 28th of March the other the 21:st of April, saluted me at my Arrival here: and nothing can exceed my Sense of the Public's generous Approbation;[1] for Curiosity might easily have sold the first Edition of any Book about Dr. Johnson, but the other Copies must have owed their Reception to kinder Motives.[2]

Will you ask if Mr. Selwin had a Volume sent him? But Mistakes *will* be made in all little Matters of Ceremony when the Writer is at so great a Distance, they must be considered as *Errata* of which I wonder there are so few.[3] It would be very kind of you to make Cadell send me two or three of them to Lyons directed to Monsieur Sipolina.[4] When I publish the Letters, there will be an Opportunity given of correcting past Errors, and till then I shall hold a most flegmatick Silence to all that may be said.

Mrs. Montagu has written to me very sweetly,[5] but the bad Roads and good Company kept us So long on the Way between Rome and Venice, that I never got her Letter till Yesterday.

We were paid however for coming through Loretto, Ancona, &c. by the Sight of a Country which in Beauty, Riches and disposition of Parts exceeds all I ever saw[6]—Oh! vastly superior to the Neapolitan State, which is so talked of as full of Situations peculiarly striking. The Adriatick Sea is delicious to drive by; and I shall attend to her annual Marriage *this* Year, and keep her Weddingday with still more Interest in her Happiness than I did *last*.[7]

I wish you were taking Views of this lovely City with us all: Mr. and Mrs. Greatheed, Mr. Shard,[8] Mr. Chappelow[9] and ourselves came down the Brenta in a Bark together three Days ago—with Music, and cold Chickens, and Cyprus Wine; and here <we> met Mr. and Mrs. Whalley of the Crescent at Bath,[10] and we live in a most delightful Society indeed. Mr. Piozzi is *so* kind to us all in this his charming Country; and it is *so* hard to tell whether the English or the Venetians love him best. Dr. Lort[11] knows Mr. Chappelow intimately, so does the Bishop I believe: dear Mr. Coxe met us again at Bologna, but his ill Health is a drawback upon all our Comforts.

We bought few Things at Rome, but I shall shew you one Canaletti which one *must* love because tis the best Representation of *Piazza St. Marco*, which after all we have seen still holds the first Place in my heart, for Elegance and Architecture;[12] and I thought yesterday that Tintoret's Paradise[13] here in the great Hall looked very well after Michael Angelo's last Judgment.[14]

If you think me partial, remember that my Husband is a Subject of Venice;—and excuse me. The Weather has not been particularly good, heavy Rains with hot Winds and little Sun: but the Country is really fine as long as it lasts, and when one is once fixed in this Town for a Month, one regrets neither Bird, Beast, nor Flower, but contents oneself with the Court of Amphitrite,[15] and lives in the Water till it becomes one's native Element. You will soon hear all I say confirmed by our amiable Friend Mr. Parsons, who will be in London this Autumn, and seek for your Friendship and Acquaintance: The Florence Miscellany will introduce You to his Character, and all our clever People will like him I am sure. The dear Greatheeds will not be long neither before they join the Coterie——but we have all Switzerland to travel over, which they have already seen, and keep firing our Imaginations about it So, that I am half afraid of meeting with a Disappointment. What a foolish thing it is for People not to learn drawing in their Youth! and how much happier You painters are in a fine Country than any of us! I hope the Exhibition is brilliant this Year,[16] and that your Views will be liked as they deserve.

Tell me all the news dear Mr. Lysons, but you really are *very* good in writing so often, and I should do nothing but thank you, if I was not sure you would rather hear twenty other Things.

Direct now to Monsieur Bonet Banker at Milan, and believe me with the truest Regard. Your ever faithful and Affectionate Friend / and Obliged Servant. / H: L: Piozzi.

My husband sends his Compliments.

Text: Huntington Library MSS 6925. *Address:* A Monsieur / Monsieur Sam: Lysons / chez le Reverend Monsieur S: Peach / at East Sheene / near Mortlake / Surrey / by London / Angleterre. *Postmark:* MA 29.

1. As advertised, e.g., in the *General Evening Post,* 25–28 March: "This Day was published, Elegantly printed in One Volume, small Octavo, Price Four Shillings in Boards. Anecdotes of the late Samuel Johnson, LL.D. during the last Twenty Years of his Life. By Hester Lynch Piozzi. Printed for T. Cadell, in the Strand."

The *Anecdotes,* according to SL on 28 March (Ry. 552.9), "was published last Saturday, [the 25th] Lady day," with gratifying success (HLP to Cadell, 7 June 1785, n. 7). "[I]t is generally very much admired—A Paper of this Morning says 'this delightful little Book, which, in the little the Editor had to do, in connecting narrative, and incidental observation, there is enough to shew a power of mind and neatness of expression'. . . indeed I have as yet seen no paper which says anything against it. . . . I have heard no one speak of it, without saying, that it was a very entertaining work, and written in a very pleasing style. . . . I was told that your Book is to be attacked by those who *call* themselves Johnson's *friends,* for not having done him Justice, but I should like to ask, whether they could themselves truly represent his manners as *amiable.* You have, I am sure, borne ample testimony of his Virtues."

Dr. Lort informed her on 1 May (Ry. 544.7): "Most of the Images and illustrations are exceedingly happy, beautiful, and just. One of the best of our reviews, *the English* just now published and come to my hand says—of the nine Lives of this Giant in Learning, which have been presented to the public Mrs. Piozzis . . . is *the best.*" Lort nevertheless took exception to her opinion that SJ "was great beyond Human comprehension and *good* beyond the imitation of perishable Beings." See the *English Review* 7 (1786): 254–59; cf. *Anecdotes,* pp. 297–304.

Less critical, George James on 14 June (Ry. 555.108) delighted "in the way every body goes on admiring you and your pretty book—and says how nicely You have cooked your Ragout of Elephant—that you have given all the Flavor of the Substance—without the Rankness and Heaviness of the Beast—and done with such pure clean Hands too—whereas Boswell has *pawed* his Scotch Collops about so—that they stink of himself to such a degree that they turn every body's stomack."

Cadell on 31 August (Ry. 554.19) admitted "that several Criticisms have appeared, some of them favourable and others severe—the latter evidently written by some of Johnson's indiscreet friends who foolishly suppose the Anecdotes have done injury to his memory. But their abuses have done us but little prejudice as the Sale continues."

2. On 21 April (Ry. 552.10) SL wrote: "The *fourth* Edition of your Anecdotes is now printing, with all speed, the third being nearly sold off, which is more than I believe was ever done in so short a space of time, but it is indeed a very great favourite. . . . Those who do find fault, rather attack the subject of it, than the language, for even the Newspaper Criticks allow the merit of that." See also "Harvard Piozziana" 2:72.

3. SL to HLP, 3 March (Ry. 552.8): "If you should wish to make any alteration, it may be done in a second Edition and I see there are one or two Errata which I shall point out to Cadell, before a second comes out, I shall expect the first to be sold in a week" (see HLP to Cadell, 7 June 1785, n. 7; 20 May 1786, n. 1). Errata slips were inserted in the second or third editions as well as in the fourth. See *Anecdotes,* ed. Arthur Sherbo (London, New York, Toronto: Oxford University Press, 1974), pp. xv, 163.

4. A banker in Lyons, whose firm was Venetian.

5. In a letter of 28 March (Ry. 551.2) Mrs. Montagu shifted guilt from HLP to JB: "[T]he kind partiality you had always shewn for me gave me some right to flatter myself, it would have influenced your judgment and taste, so far as to have prevented any severe censure of my essay, and the mortification I should have felt in the sentence you were said to have passed upon it, was mitigated by the very moderate degree of credit I give to all Mr. Boswell has ascribed to or reported of Dr. Johnson, for thó it can not be supposed he would [utter] any wilfull falsehood, yet poor man! he is so often in that condition in which Men are said to see double, the hearing in the same circumstances may probably be no less disordered.

"Your Anecdotes of Dr. Johnson my dear Madam are very different from Mr. Boswells. Yours do honour to the subject, the Writer, and harm to no one; He indeed tells the World that *Mr. Boswell* thought highly of Dr. Johnson, but all he relates of him tends to diminish the Worlds esteem of his friend, and raise many particular enemies to his memory, but they must be malicious enemies indeed, who are not more vexed and angry at the disgrace he has thrown upon his deceased friend than at any reflections or censures he had made him the instrument to throw upon others."

Charlotte Lewis confided to HLP on 8 May (Ry. 556.127): "Mrs. M. is monstrously proud of your letter and shews it every where."

6. See *Observations* 2:150–89.

7. For the Bucentoro, see HLP to SL, 30 April 1785, n. 18.

8. Charles Shard (1756–1814), a large landholder in Winkfield, Berks., with a town house in Fitzroy Square. By his first wife, Sarah, née Gillie (f1. 1765–1805), whom he married in 1787, he had a son, Charles (b. 1791), and a daughter, Sarah. His second wife was Sarah, née Stout (d. post-1814). See his will, P.R.O., Prob. 11/1552/94, proved 21 February 1814; and HLP's letter to LC, 13 February 1787, n. 4.

9. Leonard Chappelow (1744–1820), classical scholar, naturalist (F.R.S., 1792), amateur poet, was to become a close friend and prolific correspondent of HLP. A native of Roydon, Norfolk, LC attended Trinity College, Cambridge (B.A., 1766; M.A., 1769). He was ordained deacon in 1766 and priest in 1768. One of his pastorates (1791–1820) was to be at Teddington, Middlesex, near Streatham, and he was soon to serve as chaplain to Sir Henry Bridgeman (1725–1800), first baron Bradford (1794) of Weston Park, Salop. For many years LC's London address ("Mousetrap Hall," probably after *Hamlet* 3.2.237) was at 12 Hill Street, Berkeley Square, his "rus in urbe." See *Thraliana* 2, passim; *Queeney Letters*, p. 223; LC to HLP, 4 July 1786 (Ry. 562.1).

On the way to Venice in mid-April, the Piozzi carriage had broken down in the Apennines just as Shard and LC arrived on the scene and were able to assist the travelers (Clifford, p. 278).

10. See HLP to SL, 17 September 1784.

11. For Michael Lort, now librarian of Lambeth Palace, see HLP to SL, 7 December 1784.

12. For the Canaletto bought by HLP, see her letter to SL, 30 April 1785, n. 3. She continued to make art purchases in Rome and especially in Venice where she acquired an original sketch of Guido Reni's *Aurora* and additional works by Canaletto, Salviati, Domenichino, Amigoni, and Bassano. See Clifford, p. 279 and n. 1; *Observations* 2:189.

13. The *Paradise* (1588), said to be the largest picture in existence, was one of the last major works of Tintoretto. It was commissioned for the Doge's Palace.

14. *The Last Judgment* (1536–41) of Michelangelo (Michelangnioli) di Lodovico Buonarroti-Simoni (1475–1564). The famous fresco on the wall behind the altar in the Sistine Chapel portrays Christ angrily pronouncing his curse on the damned.

15. Venice, supposedly rising out of the sea, becomes allusively the court of Amphitrite, a mythological goddess and queen of the sea.

16. From the *Daily Universal Register*, 29 April: "This day will be celebrated in the Exhibition-Room the Annual Festival of the Royal Academy, to which the Prince of Wales and most of the nobility are invited. . . ."

Reynolds exhibited thirteen portraits, all "executed . . . in his best manner." But SL's offering—"a Welsh view, [the west end of] Valle Crucis abbey" went unnoticed by major newspapers. See SL to HLP, 21 April (Ry. 552.10).

TO THOMAS CADELL

Venice 20: May 1786.

Mrs. Piozzi sends her Compliments to Mr. Cadell, and tho' She has not heard from *him* about the little Book's Success,[1] desires him to be assured that he is the only Friend from whom She has *not* heard of it; as every Post brings her very flattering Accounts of its Reception.

Whatever Money comes to her Share, (and she concludes they are getting rich apace now:) must be paid in to Mess: Drummonds and Co.[2] in her Name, and she begs that Mr. Cadell will present to Charles Shard Esqr. and to the Rev. Mr. L. Chappelow of Hill Street Berkeley Square—each a Copy of the Book elegantly bound—

—She has another Favor to beg, which is that he will send her three Copies to Lyons, directing to Monsieur Sepolina as she wrote Mr. Lysons word two or three Days ago.[3]

Text: Hyde Collection. *Address:* Mr. T: Cadell.

1. The commercial success of the *Anecdotes* is described by Cadell to HLP, 8 May 1786 (Ry. 554.18): "I am to acknowledge the rest of your Letters particularly that of the 17th of [February 1786]. Permit me to return you my grateful acknowledgments for the liberal manner you have accepted my Terms of publication, and I trust you will have no cause to repent your confidence. I should have wrote before but our active and intelligent Friend Mr Lysons promised to supply my place [as he did on 28 March and on 21 June] by giving you the most early information of the success of your publication—It has indeed been very great, and the Sale more rapid than any Book I ever published since my being engaged in Business. I must own at the same time that I have consulted the reputation of the Work more than our profit for I preferred having second, third, and fourth Editions upon the Title page to printing a numerous Edition at first—If indeed I had cast off three or four thousand at once the profit would have been more considerable, but as a length of time must have elapsed before I could have advertised even a second Edition the World would have concluded that the Sale was not so extensive. I therefore printed one thousand Copies of the first Edition—these were sold off in a few hours—within the week I had a second Edition of a thousand Copies ready. The Sale of these were equally rapid—In two days I had a third Edition of 500 Copies and at the same time set about preparing for a fourth if the demand continued—the Demand did continue, and I had the fourth Edition of one thousand Copies ready for publication as soon as the third was sold off. The fourth is now selling, and I have little doubt but I shall be obliged speedily to announce a fifth edition." The fourth edition was the last printed in HLP's lifetime except for one issued in Dublin (1786).
2. The bankers Robert and Henry Drummond and Co., No. 49 Charing Cross.
3. See HLP to LC, 1 September, n. 19.

TO SAMUEL LYSONS

Venice
26: May 1786.

Dear Mr. Lysons.—

I write again so soon for the pleasure of writing I think, and of receiving your Letters; which have always contained those same partial Praises, and kind Invitations to return home, which are now confirmed by the Voice of the generous Public, to whom I shall ever confess my very uncommon Obligations.

Cadell says he never yet published a Book the Sale of which was so rapid, and that Rapidity of so long Continuance: I suppose the fifth Edition will meet me at our Return.

But my dear Mrs. Lewis never writes to me, and I am afraid She is ill, or something[1]——I certainly ordered *her* a Copy; if She has not yet had it, do carry her one to Mrs. Codrington's[2] house in Albemarle Street, and learn how She does, and let me know.

Miss Jane Nicholson is lost too; I wish you would ask after her at No. 104 Dumergue's in Bond Street where her Sister lodges.

I am most exceedingly sensible to your Good nature and Friendship and very sure you will do me these two or three little favors quite chearfully.

Give my Compliments to Mr. Murphy,[3] and tell him to direct his Letter under Cover to Monsieur Bonet Banker at Milan. I am always happy to hear he is well, and have always wished for more of his Conversation than I could ever obtain even through Mr. Thrale's Interest, who loved him with a sincere Affection indeed: and never shall those Friends be forgotten or neglected by me who have shared the Tenderness or deserved the Esteem of my *Husbands*.

These amiable Venetians seek to detain me among *them* by paying Mr. Piozzi every possible, every respectful Attention; it is certainly the *only* way for *any* Set of People to detain me; but my Desire of seeing him caressed by my own Country will draw me away from this in a short Time now.

Tell Sir Lucas Pepys how I love him and all that belongs to him. Dr. Lort had a long Scrawl from me a Week before you will get this,[4] and I have no Secrets from the Bishop of Peterborough, whom I wished to make my Confessor the Year I spent at Bath when you and I first got acquainted——but I could not find one Moment's Opportunity.

The Book's being printed so many Times, and always falsely in so many Places is vexatious enough to be sure; we will remedy all that at my return: but these poor Anecdotes have been published as Philidor is said to make his Moves at Chess, whilst he himself is playing on the Fiddle in another Room.[5]

Adieu my dear Sir, and do write very often and very kindly to your truly Affectionate Friend / and faithful Servant / H: L: Piozzi.

The Weather is prodigious hot already—we drink cold Lemonade all Morning—hot Chocolate or Coffee at Midnight, *so* queer! A Thousand Compliments to Mrs. Hinchliffe and to Mrs. Boscawen if you know her:[6] I am never sure whether you visit her or no. I am exceeding proud of Dr. Douglas's Praises.[7] Mr. Stephens[8] knew Johnson by heart I'm sure, and his Approbation of the Portrait is a strong Proof of its Resemblance. / Adieu!

Text: Hyde Collection. *Address:* A Monsieur / Monsieur Sam: Lysons chez Le Rev: Mr. S. Peach / at East Sheene / near Mortlake / in Surrey / Angleterre.

1. For Charlotte Lewis, see HLP to SL, 7 December 1784, n. 11. Mrs. Lewis was indeed ill, "confined," as she wrote to HLP on 8 May, "a second time for six weeks" (Ry. 556.127). SL would report on 21 June (Ry. 552.11) that she "just got the better of a severe illness,

which prevented her writing to you, tho' she seems far from well now, she said she should write, if possible by this post—."

2. See HLP to Cadell, 17 February, n. 2.

3. Arthur Murphy (1727–1805). The dramatist, actor, editor, and lawyer, "whose Intimacy with Mr. Thrale had been of many Years standing," introduced SJ to the Thrales probably on Wednesday, 9 January 1765 (*Thraliana* 1:158–59 n. 5). Murphy remained loyal to HLP, accepted GP, and helped them both with their legal and domestic problems.

4. HLP's letters to Michael Lort are missing, although on 24 July he acknowledged two of them, dated at Venice 16 May and 4 June (Ry. 544.8).

5. François-André Danican, known as Philidor (1726–95), composed comic operas, dramatic ensembles, and religious music. He was a chess master, author of the classic *Analyse des échecs* (1749). A frequent visitor to England, he was to be arrested in London in 1793 and placed on the list of émigrés. He died there, separated from his family.

6. HLP is responding to specific praise of the *Anecdotes* reported to her by SL on 28 March. "The Bishop of Peterborough, and Mrs. Hinchcliffe, desire me to thank you for your book, and the amusement it has afforded them—Mrs. H. told me too, that Mrs. Boscawen admires it very much—Mr. Stephens [Steevens] told me today, that if there were twenty Books written on the subject, he was sure no one would be so great a favourite as this—Seward read it thro', as soon as it was published, he speaks very handsomely of it, and says he will vouch for its accuracy. . . ."

Elizabeth Hinchliffe, née Crewe (d. 1826), was the wife of the Bishop and sister of baron Crewe of Crewe.

Frances Boscawen, née Glanville (1719–1805), was the widow of Edward Boscawen (1711–61), M.P. for Truro (1742–61) and admiral of the Blue (1758–61).

7. John Douglas (1721–1807) took his Oxford B.A. in 1740, M.A. in 1743, and D.D. in 1758. He was ordained deacon in 1744 and priest three years later. Early in his ecclesiastical career, he enjoyed the patronage of William Pulteney (1684–1764), earl of Bath (1742). Douglas was to become bishop of Carlisle (1787), dean of Windsor (1788), and bishop of Salisbury (1791).

Elected F.R.S. and F.S.A. (1778), he was appointed a trustee of the British Museum in March 1787. As a literary figure he is best known for his edition (1763) of the *State Letters . . . and Diary* of Henry, second earl of Clarendon. See also *Boswell's Johnson* 1:407, for Douglas's association with SJ.

8. While she basked in presumed flattery, HLP was ignorant of the malice aimed at her by George Steevens (1736–1800), Shakespearean editor and scholar. Resorting to anonymous public attack on her and praise of Boswell in the *St. James's Chronicle* (8 and 11 January 1785), he "set two of his acquaintances at each other's throats." For the incident and its near-unfortunate effect on the *Anecdotes,* see James L. Clifford, "The Printing of Mrs. Piozzi's Anecdotes of Dr. Johnson," *Bulletin of the John Rylands Library* 20, no. 1 (January 1936): 157–72.

Steevens met SJ in 1765, the two men drawn together by their interest in Shakespeare. SJ tolerated Steevens's idiosyncracies, and nominated him for membership in The Club (1774) and in the Essex Head Club (1783). For their association and for various interpretations of Steevens's sarcasm and perversity, see *Boswell's Johnson,* passim; Nichols' *Literary Anecdotes* 2:650–53; *Anecdotes,* ed. Sherbo, p. xi; Hyde, *The Impossible Friendship,* pp. 103–4.

TO SAMUEL LYSONS

Milan
[5] July 1786.[1]

Dear Mr. Lysons—

I am vastly obliged to you for your friendly Letter of the 21: of June,[2] which I received soon after my arrival to this Place: The Journey from Venice hither has been very hot and fatiguing, but it was worth all the Cost to see how differently the Amphitheatre at Verona looked after the Sight of the Colosseo at Rome.[3] Bozza's Collection will be always an astonishing Thing; but we will keep that Subject to *talk* about when we meet.

If I really had the Assurance to fancy that I or my Book were seriously *wanted* and *called for,* either by Country, or Countrymen; Mr. Piozzi would willingly go home with me this Autumn, and it might yet be published (I mean the Letters from Johnson) before the World was quite wearied from variety of Publications; but in the mean Time we are making Parties for the Isole Borromeo,[4] and talking of Switzerland as Mr. Coxe has told you.

Well! what one *has* seen is certain, what one *is to see* uncertain; So I must tell you that the Correggios at Parma even surpassed my Expectation: nothing is more completely what it pretends to be than the St. Girolamo, and the Madonna della Scudella.[5]

The State of Venice is however most agreable to inhabit of all Italy in my Mind: Verona is a heavenly Situation,[6] the Society delightful, the Air wholesome, the Antiquities entertaining and respectable; while Nature has been lavish in her Gifts, and beautified its Environs with unequal and various Elegance, as Palladio[7] has enriched her Streets with all the Charms of Proportion and Variety.

You will think presently that I am like Romeo who says

There is no World without Verona's Walls:[8]

but I still remember that England claims my first and fondest Regard, which is really now very much strengthened by its kind Reception of the first Attempt I ever made to obtain *public* Notice, or deserve *public* Applause.

If Cadell would send me some Copies I should be very much obliged to him[9]——'Tis like living without a Looking-Glass never to see one's own Book so.

You shall be sure of your Pearls,[10] but it won't be today nor tomorrow that you will receive 'em. I hear with Pleasure that your Drawings were admired;[11] South Wales will afford fresh Objects of Curiosity[12]—and how pretty it would be if we should all meet at Bath for the Christmas Holydays——My Husband has not felt a cold Day so long—nor no more have I——that it would be a new Sensation to us; but I believe not an unwholesome one.

Tell Sir Lucas Pepys that I take it very unkind of him never to mention my health, and I am always trying to force some Enquiries from him by one Lamentation or another—and not a Word will he say.

Miss Nicholson's never having had my Letters, nor I hers, is amazing; we thought She was gone to France; and She it seems imagined us still at Milan.[13]

Ask Mr. Coxe if you see him again, whether Mr. Davis is come to England?[14] I sent some Roman Pearl by him to our Daughters at Kensington, and never have heard of their safe Arrival.

You will be very happy at Cambridge——Oh pray present our best Respects, Regards and Compliments to my partial Friends there: The Bishop and Mrs. Hinchliffe are among those I most love and honour——Why does not Dr. Lort write to me? I am a teizing Correspondent to *him.* Never have I had a Sight of the Epitaph he translated:[15] tis a great Plague really not to see how the Book looks; when do you think one may expect it?

Adieu dear Sir, and assure yourself of the continued Kindness of my kind Husband, who loves with his whole heart those who shew real Esteem of your Obliged and faithful / H: L: Piozzi.

Text: Hyde Collection. *Address:* A Monsieur / Monsieur Sam Lysons chez le / Rev: Mr. S. Peach / at East Sheene / near Mortlake / Surrey / by London / Angleterre. *Postmark:* JY 21.

1. Although HLP dated this letter 6 July, the Italian postmark is 5 [July]. It was marked JY 21 in England (see cover).

2. The twenty-first was also the day on which the Piozzis had returned to Milan, after leaving Venice on 10 June (*Observations* 2:204).

3. See *Observations* 2:194–95.

4. Giberto Borromeo (1751–1837) was one of the sixty *decurioni* and chamberlain to the Holy Roman Emperor. By 1812 he was created *conte del Regno d'Italia* and two years later was asked to take part in the *Reggenza Provvisoria di Governo.* He was a cavalier of the Order of the Toson d'Oro and of the SS. Annunziata.

He turned his palace over to the Piozzis and as HLP wrote to Q on 9 August, "left us King and Queen of the Isola bella. Guess you if we made Lago Maggiore resound? . . . Johnson said the place at our first Arrival looked so like a scene at the Opera instead of reality. . . . There is however no want of Solidity: the Palace & Garden are founded on a Rock, & ten Terraces covered thick so as to hide any appearance of Wall, rise in a Pyramidal Form to the Water; displaying Lemons, Cedrati &c. in such abundant such *re*dundant Superfluity—that all one reads of the Hesperides falls short of its Beauty—The House is best described by Johnson in his *Rassellas*" (*Queeney Letters,* pp. 228–29; cf. *Observations* 2:218–24; "Description of a Palace in a Valley," *Rasselas,* chap. 1.

5. See *Observations* 2:200–201. The artist, Antonio Allegri (ca. 1494–1534), was known as Correggio after his birthplace. Many of his religious paintings in Parma belong to the period of 1522 to 1530. One of them, the *Madonna della Scodella,* is an altarpiece in the Parma Galleria. The *Madonna del Gerolama* at the time of this letter was in the Palazzo Ducale.

A number of Correggio's works have not survived, but among those that HLP perhaps saw in the Galleria Nationale of San Giovanni Evangelista were the *Martyrdom of the Four Saints* (Placido, Flavia, Eutychius, Victorinus) and the *Deposition.* Also in San Giovanni Evangelista were the frescoes, the *Ascension of Christ* and the *Coronation of the Virgin;* and in the Duomo, *Assumption of the Virgin.*

For a full account of the *œuvre,* see Cecil Gould, *The Paintings of Correggio* (Ithaca: Cornell University Press, 1976).

6. *Observations* 2:194–97

7. See HLP to Q, 22 April 1785, n. 3.

8. *Romeo and Juliet* 3.3.17.

9. Copies directed to Mr. Sipolina at Lyons were sent on 27 July. Presumably Cadell intended that HLP's copies should then be forwarded to her from France. He could not find speedier "modes of conveyance" than the Paris diligence. See SL to HLP, 31 July (Ry. 552.12).

10. On behalf of his "very good friend," the wife of the Reverend William Dickson (1745–1804), bishop of Down and Connor (1784), SL had requested "some strings of the finest Roman Pearl, to make a pair of Bracelets, and to go four times round the neck." They were not to be had in England or France (SL to HLP, 21 June).

11. The report about SL's Welsh drawings probably came from Q (*Queeney Letters,* p. 224; see also HLP to SL, 11 May, n. 16).

12. SL had mentioned his projected tour to South Wales on 21 June. On 13 September he wrote from Rodmarton: "I am just returned from a short Tour I made with my Brother into Monmouthshire and Glamorganshire, both which Counties are very pleasant, and

furnished some employment for the pencil; we saw the famous bridge of one Arch over the River Taffe and the great Castle of Caerphilly and some others of the wonders of South Wales, but nothing to make us think it by any means so interesting a Country, as that which we saw last Summer" (Hyde Collection).

13. See HLP to Cadell, 17 February, n. 9.

14. No Mr. Davis, bearing gifts to her daughters, appears in the corespondence with Q at this time. ST and SAT were at Kensington Square under the care of Mrs. Murray. Q was at her Wimpole Street residence in Cavendish Square. CMT had been removed from the Ray-Fry school in Streatham to one in Queen Square. See HLP to Parsons, 4 August, n. 4.

15. In the *Anecdotes* (pp. 134–35) Dr. Lort translated SJ's Latin epitaph for HT as a substitute for an omitted passage (HLP to SL, 25 March, n. 1).

TO THE REVEREND LEONARD CHAPPELOW

Varese[1]
3: August 1786.

Dear Sir—
I really never saw any thing so friendly and good natured as your Letters,[2] which came both together to this Place, where we have been making *Villeggiatura*[3] forsooth; and flashing away a Week at a Time among the more than enchanted Islands of Lago maggiore, where Count Borromeo lent us his Palace, and you need not doubt but we made it echo with Musick—the best Band in Italy——how Mr. Shard would have been delighted! said my husband! I think <said> I, *this* would have made Mr. Chappelow for<get> Mouse-Trap hall.[4] We have been to Lug<ano> too, so who says we don't see Switzerland?[5] I am sure nothing it contains can exceed the natural Beauties this last Month has presented to my View. Living in the Country too is so very comfortable after running from great Town to great Town for a Twelve month together, and we have a charming Society about us, Marquisses and Monsignori—who can be merry without making Ridicule one of another——and that is no small Consolation when one has lived in the World, and is weary of winking and tittering; and lampooning, and being lampooned.

Dr. Walcott is a new Name to me, who is he dear Sir, and what is his Profession?[6]

I am glad you like our pretty Daughters, but have some Idea that 'tis the youngest *you* are particularly partial [to. Sophia] is possibly taller than Susanna, [and] that might mislead you.[7]

Mr. Piozzi in the midst of Luxuries cheaply purchased, and Prospects of Health and Abundance; sighs for a clean Floor, a neat Breakfast, Tables that will stand fast, and Windows that will open and shut; desires to see again at London the English Friends who loved him at Venice and Bologna,and to find himself in the neighbourhood of Cavendish Square where he used to visit a certain Lady now his Affectionate Wife / and Dear Mr. Chappelow's / most Obliged and Faithful Servant / H: L: Piozzi.

I will remember the Sannazarius[8]—but you never told me the Bookseller's Name,[9]—Is there anything else I can bring that you would like?—Oh *do* write again and tell me. We come home the German Way for Variety, my Husband has already passed Mount Cenis seven Times:[10] he tells me I have not said half enough of kind Things from *him*, either to Mr. Shard or you.

Text: Ry. 559.2. *Address:* A Monsieur / Monsieur The Rev: Leonard Chappelow / Hill Street / Berkeley Square / London / Angleterre. *Postmark:* AU 18.

1. A community northwest of Milan, where the Piozzis had spent six weeks (*Queeney Letters*, pp. 228–31).
2. HLP is responding to LC's letters of 4 and 11 July (Ry. 562.1, 2).
3. A country holiday.
4. At this time Shard was LC's guest at his London residence.
5. Lugano, on the Swiss-Italian border, lies between Lake Maggiore and Lake Como, hence quite near the Piozzis' summer retreat.
6. In the letter of 4 July, LC disdainfully mentioned "a curious publication by Peter Pindar called Bozzi against Piozzi" that he had not seen except for "a miserable extract . . . in the English review." On 11 July he identified the author as "a Dr. Wolcott, who has published other *fooleries*."

HLP had forgotten that SL had introduced her to the name of the satirist (see her letter to SL, 25 March, n. 6).

7. LC reported (4 July) that recently "Mr. Shard called on me—away we went—to Kensington Square [the Honorable Mrs. Murray's school] and visited 2 most agreeable Young Ladies—The Eyes of the Youngest sparkled with joy when we mentioned you, and an agreeable smile of self satisfaction and complacency diffused itself over the countenance of the Elder.—They are 2 very different Characters, different are their features, but both I am sure Good Girls, with good hearts.—Tis unnecessary to tell you the purport of our half hours conversation—general observations in consequence of a comparison made between old England and the continent.—We asked after Miss Thrale, who they said was quite well.—"

Shard on 11 July (Ry. 892.7) noted: "Mr. C. has hardly recovered the Impression the Eyes of the Youngest Lady made upon him and I was equally struck with the mild and pleasing behaviour of your favorite Sophy."

8. Jacopo Sannazaro (Sannazar) (1458–1530), a Neapolitan best known for his *Arcadia* (1502, emended 1504), a series of verse eclogues connected by prose narrative. Diversified in his literary activities, he also wrote Petrarchan *canzoniere*, piscatory eclogues, elegies, epigrams, etc. Suggestive of his varied interests is: *Actii Synceri de partu Virginis . . . de morte Christi Domini . . . Ecloguæ Piscatoriæ. . . . Salices . . . Elegiæ. . . . Odæ . . . . Epigrammata. . . . Petri Bembi hymnus in Divum Stephanum. Eiusdem Benacus. Gabrielis Altili epithalamion. Io. Cottæ Veronensis carmina. Io. Mutii Aurelii Mantuani hymnus in D. Io. Bapt. Eiusdem elegia ad Leonem x Pont Max.* (Venice: Per Ioannem Antonium & Fratres de Sabio, 1530).

LC had complained (4 July): "I hunted all over Italy for the Quarto Edition of Sannazario published at Padua, *apud Cominum*—and found it at Milan but the Bookseller asked me 5 times more than twas worth.—The price is 6 or 7 shillings English.—If you can get it for me and keep it till you come I shall be much obliged to you—but tis a lumbering piece of Business for you to be plagued with.—Set your feet upon it in the Coach—I know they do not reach to the bottom; so that you will have a poetical pedestal.—I thought to have found it at Turin—or I would not have passed it at Milan."

9. The work in question and its publisher are: *Jacobi, sive Actii Synceri Sannazarii neapolitani, viri patricii, Poemata, ex antiquis editionibus accuratissime descripta. Accessit ejusdem vita, J.A. Vulpio auctore, item G. Altilii, et H. Fascitelli Carmina nonnulla* (Padua: Josephus Cominus, 1719).
10. See *Queeney Letters*, p. 230.

TO MR. WILLIAM PARSONS

Varese
4: August *1786*.

Your very friendly and agreable Letter[1] followed us to this charming Place, where Mr. Piozzi has taken me a Country House for the hot weeks, and we have already spent a *Month* of the Time in great Gaiety, and some little Splendour too with our Beds all filled by Milanese Friends—Marquisses and Monsignori;—who wrote Verses on our Wedding day,[2] and praised with unaffected Good humour that Happiness they all appeared willing to increase.

Your kind Count Borromeo put his Faery Palace and the whole Isola Bella into my husband's Hands for a Week; so we carried thither a Band of nine [of] the best Musicians in Italy, and made Lago Maggiore echo with our French Horns &c.[3] I think their Effect on that Water by Moonlight was something singularly fine indeed—few Efforts made by Man to give Temporary Pleasure ever succeeded in equal Degree—for the Weather was exquisite and the Company willing to *be* pleased, and *confess* themselves so: You have often heard me praise the Italians for being clear of all Fastidiousness and all Affectation, and you will therefore the more readily believe me when I assure you that Mr. Piozzi in the midst of Olive Yards and Orange Groves, with a Country round him unrivalled in Beauty and glowing with natural Riches—sighs for the Conveniencies and cleanly Comforts of Great Britain, and refuses daily Offers of deserted Palaces, or suppressed Convents which near this lovely Spot might be purchased for a *mere nothing*—in hopes of sharing your Friendship with that of dear Mr. and Mrs. Greatheed this next Spring in the populous Neighbourhood of New Bond Street or Cavendish Square.

I hope you will carry *my* kind Love and my *Husband's* to our pretty Daughters at Mrs. Murray's house—The *Honourable* Mr. Murray in Kensington Square;[4]—They will be happy to see Mr. Parsons; of whom I have written to them so often, and so much—and with whom by Virtue of the Florence Miscellany, they are already well acquainted. A propòs you must not wonder at the Tricks you tell me of, played by Authors, Booksellers &c. It *is the way* with the English you know to make every thing as publick as the Sun—I think it most surprizing the Event did not happen before now.[5] Every Man that writes even an Epigram with us is called out to the *Colosseo* presently, and must stand his Tryal at the *Bocca della Veritá*. Do tell me dear Mr. Merry's Success,[6] and how the World receives Paulina's Story.[7] Let me know likewise something of Lord and Lady Cowper.

All I said of Benincasa's Death was false it seems, he was given over by his Doctors, and left for dead but recovered—and all *goes on as before*.[8]

Dear Sir Adieu, accept my Husband's kindest Regards and believe me ever / Your much Obliged / and faithful Servant / H: L: Piozzi.

Direct to Ami Bonet as usual, and excuse my saying nothing about your recent Loss[9]—for what *can* one ever say to a Friend on such a Subject?

Text: N.L.W., 13936C. *Address:* A Monsieur / Monsieur William Parsons Esq. / chez Messrs. Griffiths, Fry, and Robinson Bankers / in London / Angleterre. *Postmark:* AU 18.

1. Parsons had written to HLP on 8 July from Bern.

2. An ebullient HLP described for Q the social ambience of Varese: the "true Italian *Villeggiatura* . . . is . . . an extremely delicious, I might say an extremely luxurious Thing:—*as we managed it*—with a full Table of Friends never fewer than *15* at a Time to dinner. . . . The Marquess of Araciel's Verses to Mr Piozzi on our Wedding Day were found so clever by the rest of the Company that they persuaded him to print & put his Name to 'em. . . ." (*Queeney Letters,* p. 228).

Marchese Giuseppe de Araciel (fl. 1731–98), imperial chamberlain, was of Spanish extraction; the family was elevated to the marquessate (1712) and granted a fiefdom in the state of Milan (1722). He was invested in 1761 with the rights and privileges of a *Patrizio Milanese.* The connection with the Piozzis, of long standing, began when he befriended the youthful GP, who had left home to avoid training for the priesthood (*Thraliana,* passim; Clifford, p. 238 n. 1).

The poem, "Cantata Epitalamica," a copy of which is in the Berg Collection, is dated "Varese 25 Luglio 1786 . . . In attestato di vera stima ed amicizia Il Marchese de Araciel Ciamberlano di S.M.I.R.A." It was privately printed in Milan.

3. See *Observations* 2:226.

4. According to *Boyle's Court Guide,* Mrs. Murray lived at 8 Kensington Square. The former Sarah Maese (1744–1811), she had married in 1783 William (d. 25 December 1786), a Royal Navy Captain and brother of John, fourth earl of Dunmore. Mrs. Murray conducted the school at Kensington Square that SAT and ST attended. In 1798 she traveled with Q to Scotland, publishing in the next year *A Companion and Useful Guide to the Beauties of Scotland.* On 1 November 1802 she married George Aust, undersecretary of state for foreign affairs.

On 8 August, Cator wrote (Ry. 602.3), "Susan and Sophia are now with us at Beckenham place . . . Cecilia is now at Mrs. Stephenson in Queen Square School as it was thought she did not advance so much as she ought at Streatham, Miss Thrale is at Brighton." See *Thraliana* 2:679 n. 5; HLP to Q, 7 July 1787.

CMT was attending a "fashionable boarding-school kept by the Misses Stevenson at two houses in Queen Square [Bloomsbury]. In 1786 the number of young ladies in their charge was 220 and the fee over a hundred guineas." Among the pupils was to be JB's daughter Veronica. See *Boswell: The English Experiment 1785–1789,* pp. 224–25 and n. 5; HLP to Q, 7 July 1787.

5. Parsons confirmed in October (Ry. 558.17) that the *Florence Miscellany* had been pirated in the *European Magazine* (February–June). The *London Chronicle,* likewise, had extracted freely from it. At least the collaborators were getting the recognition for which they hungered.

6. Merry, temporarily in England, was negotiating for publication of "Paulina's Story." Cadell, contrary to expectation, had declined it, and Merry finally came to terms with James Robson.

7. *Paulina: or, the Russian Daughter,* in two books of heroic couplets, had been printed in Florence, 1786, but Robson, who was associated in the London publication with William Clarke (fl. 1750–87), delayed publication until early in 1787. The extravagantly mannered, melodramatic poem had at the time pleased HLP and others in her circle, but its readers in England were more critical. For HLP's appraisal of the poem, see *Thraliana* 2:682, and of the style, *British Synonymy* 2:277–78.

8. Bartolommeo Benincasa (1748–1816), a native of Modena and descendant of a noble family, was an eminent political writer, translator, belletrist, dramatist, traveler. In Vienna he met Countess Orsini-Rosenberg and thereafter was to collaborate with her in a number of literary ventures until her death in 1791. He flourished as a journalist during the Napoleonic period, becoming secretary to the commission of public instruction in Italy

and vice-director of the Theatres Royal. His later works include *Lettere di Yorick e di Elisa* and a collection, *Il Romanziere Inglese,* both published in Milan in 1815.

9. HLP's allusion to the death of Parsons's mother in Sussex.

TO SAMUEL LYSONS

Milan
15: August 1786.

Dear Mr. Lysons

You are just setting out on *your* Summer Excursion I see, when we are returning from *ours:*[1] Since I wrote last the Heat grew so intense, that to shelter me from its ill effects Mr. Piozzi kindly procured me a Country House about 45 miles off in the Varesotto where the Grison Alps covered with eternal Snow, refresh the Air; and the beautiful Lakes with that astonishing Verdure that for ever adorns their Sides, cures the effect made upon ones Eyes by the dazzling of the Sun in less shaded, and less lovely Situations. Oh! nothing I have hitherto seen at all equals or comes near the Lago Maggiore, with its enchanted Island and Palace; which inspired by a Politeness peculiar to himself, Count Borromeo put into our possession for a Week—and we made it resound with Musick and Merriment having carried out from Milan a Band of nine Performers to divert us on the Water——and I do think that the Effect of the French Horns by Moonlight, with the View of our Faery Dominion rising as by Magic out of the Lake, was a Scene no Theatre can pretend to represent.

A Barge full of Noble Friends who favored us for five Weeks with their Company at Varese though used to the Delights of this glorious Climate confessed they had never been so entertained before. Every Art has indeed been tried by our Acquaintance here, all of the first Rank: to detain Mr. Piozzi among them; and I will allow that such Temptations are very near irresistible——You cannot figure yourself the cheapness with which one might hire or purchase here Places so beautiful, that in England no Money would be thought enough for them.

My Husband is however not only willing, but desirous to move Northward;[2] and proposes to himself no small Consolation in that Country where good Talents and good Conduct are respected beyond Birth and Fortune, as Miss Burney's well-deserved Preferment can evince, better than any thing I can say upon the Subject.[3]

In Consequence of this Resolution we return to dear Verona the End of next Month,[4] and there you must direct *Poste Restant:* from thence over the Tyrol into Germany that one may see something of the Rhine, and the Danube; and breaking the Winter by passing a Month or two at Vienna, come home with the New Year, and publish our Letters when the *Town* is at *full,* to say nothing of the *Moon.*[5]

You are very good natured to send me some News, and I am very happy to see you so sedulously bent on Success in your Profession:[6] tis exceedingly commendable indeed, and nothing will be able to stand against Virtue, Genius, and Application united.

We used to laugh about *my Lord Tetbury,*[7] but as Shakespeare says

Jesters do oft prove Prophets.[8]

Let me hear some good of the dear Jameses; when you are at Bath tell them how sincerely their Happiness as well as your own is desired by my kind Husband and / Your sincerely Obliged / Friend and faithful Servant / H: L: Piozzi.

Write soon, or we shall be run from Verona again; and after the *next* Letter you must be kind enough to direct to *Vienna* Post restant——but let me find one Letter at *Verona* pray do.

Addio!

Text: Hyde Collection. *Address:* A Monsieur / Monsieur Samuel Lysons / to be left / at The Post Office / Cirencester / Gloucestershire / Angleterre. *Postmark:* SE 4; BRISTOL.

1. SL had informed HLP on 21 June (Ry. 552.11) that he intended going to Gloucester the first week in August, to remain about three months, with some journeys into South Wales, Bath, and Worcester.

2. About to leave Italy in mid-September, HLP had mixed feelings. She resented the gossip that swirled about her name in England and she did "not *now* as formerly feel a *fondness* for England: Esteem and Preference over evry other Place is all that's left." Recognizing the Italians as "rascally," she nonetheless discerned their approval of her and was "half sorry" to leave them (*Thraliana* 2:662).

HLP's uneasiness about her return may have been prompted by newspaper slurs. See, for example, the *General Evening Post* (4 May 1786): "We hear that Madam Piozzi, with her *cara sposa,* will soon return to England—when she intends to have him naturalized, and take the name of her ancestors; how far the name and family of Salusbury may be enriched or ennobled by such an alliance and union, she certainly can best explain to the public." The notice was possibly written by JB (*The English Experiment, 1785–1789,* p. 62 and n. 3). His informant would be SL.

3. HLP had learned from SL's letter of 31 July (Ry. 552.12): "Miss Burney is lately appointed Dresser [i.e., second keeper of the robes] to the Queen . . . the salary is 200£ a year but the attendance is so constant, I am told, as to render it by no means a pleasant situation; it was given without any application having been made for it—."

4. For the final months of the Piozzis' European travels, see *Observations* 2:259–65.

5. SL had reassured HLP (31 July) that there would be a demand for SJ's correspondence: "I talked with Dr. Lort about the publication of the Letters, and told him what Cadell said on that subject, he thinks you should not publish them 'till after . . . Hawkins's Edition of [SJ's] Works, unless you wish them to be serviceable to the Knight, in his compilations—By the way, no great matters are expected from this promised piece of Biography—."

6. An ambiguous remark, since SL's legal and antiquarian interests ran parallel to his social aspirations. He not only cultivated important friendships but planned to take a "comfortable Set of Chambers for three years" at No. 17 Clifford's Inn, preparatory to commencing "Special Pleader below the Bar at Christmas, or as <soon> as any one chooses to employ me" (Hyde Collection, 13 September 1786).

7. See HLP to SL, 17 September 1784, n. 7.

8. *King Lear* 5.3.71. Cf. *Thraliana* 2:713.

TO THE REVEREND LEONARD CHAPPELOW

Milan
1: September 1786.

Dear Mr. Chappelow—
Your two friendly Letters which followed us to Varese,[1] deserve [at] least two Letters in return; and this I am writing now, is rendered necessary by our new Resolution of passing some part of the bad Weather at *Vienna* where we hope to hear from you who were kind enough to promise us a Packet of domestic News. Let us always hear of your health and Mr. Shard's, in which we are sincerely interested. I have got you a lovely Sannazarius;[2] which I *fished* for, not unskillfully, nor unsatisfactorily—whoever sets their feet upon it, it were better for them that they touched the *Torpedo.* I shall go to Pavia[3] before we leave Lombardy to see the Tomb of Boethius if possible:[4] You and I love the Poets of the middle Ages,[5] and when we were at Bergamo this last Week, passing the Fair Time[6] at the Marquiss of Araciel's Palace, (who by the way entertained us most splendidly;) I looked at the Church,[7] and thought how that mixture of Gothic and Grecian Architecture resembled the Verses of our *mezzi Secoli* Men: A propòs, or perhaps mal apropòs—I find Marcellus Palingenius was only the Anagram of the Man's Name who wrote the Poem called the Zodiack,[8] and who was not born at Ferrara, tho' he always lived there, while the Duchess gave him her Protection.[9] *Yea, and all this did I know before* Juliet says;[10] but you did not know where to direct, till I said it must be to Messieurs Fries and Company Bankers at Vienna;[11] which being neither my husband's Country nor my own, I care not how much Fog and Frost there is in it; nor how much he curses it, and comparing that Climate with this, how much this carries away the Preference; and London will look quite brilliant after the Towns in Germany, (at least by Candlelight:) and Sun there will be none when we arrive that's certain; but Spring will be within hopes at least; and then to revive our recollection of the Prospect from those beautiful Mountains of Bergamo, we must drive to Windsor I think, which alone has any Chance to come up with it. I shall for ever say that no Man in his Circumstances but himself would have left Milan this Winter; but he is better than good, and loves his English Wife and English Friends better than all the Distinctions which Fortune can give, in a Country where all naturally look on *his,* with a mixture of Wonder, Envy and Respect.

What is become of our amiable Friends Mr. and Mrs. Greatheed?[12] She wrote me the tenderest Letter imaginable from Lausanne[13]—then flew to England upon particular Business and I have heard of her no more: I know She is incapable of forgetting those She once loved, and am therefore uneasy lest Something has befallen the Child[14]——do Dear Sir favour me with a Line about that sweet Family when you write to Vienna.

Tell Mr. Shard and Dr. Lort our Resolution to see *Josephus secundus*[15] [and] that if they are good humoured enough to write, we may get their Letters. If Vi[n]cenzo Bozza's[16] heart is not petrified like his Fish, I shall bring home the first of those Gentlemen an Opal from Verona yet——as I sent him a present of

Derby Fossills[17] that we had here at Milan by Mr. Lawless[18] six Weeks ago, and he has thanked me most vehemently.

Cadell has never sent the Books yet, or I have never received 'em.[19] 'Tis very disagreable to be the *only* Person who has not read Johnson's Anecdotes. I scolded him terribly for serving Mr. Shard as he did, it vexed me so.[20]

Adieu dear Sir, and pray for our safe Passage over the Tyrolese Alps with our Paduan Wheels[21]—for the Friends who took Care of us among the Appenines are now safe at home——and I wish we had your Man Pietro for Courier[22] with all my heart and Soul / Ever Your much Obliged Servant / H: L: Piozzi

Text: Ry. 559.3. *Address:* A Monsieur / Monsieur the Rev: Leonard Chappelow / at his House in / Hill Street / Berkeley Square / London / Angleterre. *Postmark:* SE <21>.

1. See HLP to LC, 3 August. She alludes to his letters of 4 and 11 July (Ry. 562.1, 2).

2. LC, on 15 October (Ry. 562.3), was to acknowledge her "kindness in procuring for me Sannazarius, alias the Torpedo. I know you think him a Dull Dog, and wont suffer yourself to be benumbed with him in capacity of a foot stool. . . . my Letter is so stupid, that you must suppose that I have stolen [Dame Dullness's] footstool, which is the true Torpedo." Cf. SJ on Sannazarius in *Rambler* 36.

Sannazarius had a certain vogue among the Della Cruscan set. See Parsons, "Epistle from Naples, to Bertie Greatheed Esq. at Rome," in *Poetical Tour,* pp. 145–46; and HLP's eulogistic lines in a long poem descriptive of Naples ("Harvard Piozziana" 2:74).

3. The Piozzis left Milan for Pavia and Verona on 22 September (*Observations* 2:258).

4. Anicius Manlius Severinus Boethius (ca. 480–524), Roman philosopher. See *Observations* 2:251, for a statement about his tomb in "a chapel dedicated to St. Austin in St. Peter's Church at Pavia," a tomb built "four hundred and seventy-two years after his death, with an epitaph preserved by Pere Mabillon, but now no longer legible."

5. HLP regarded Boethius highly. About 1765, she and SJ began verse translations of Boethius's "Metres." She rendered about six, he three, and they collaborated on perhaps as many as five others. See Clifford, pp. 57–58 and n. 5; HLP to SL, 9 September 1787, n. 11.

6. The fair, housed in a building constructed ca. 1740, took place between the end of August and early September. For HLP the "fair at Bergamo differs little from a fair in England, except that these cattle are whiter and ours larger" (*Observations* 2:242).

7. The earliest church on the site of the cathedral of Milan (Piazza del Duomo) was created in 390. The foundation of the cathedral was begun in 1386 under Gian Galeazzeo Visconti (ca. 1351–1402), duke of Milan. The entire structure was completed only in 1805–13, by order of Napoleon. One of the largest medieval churches in Europe, it is richly ornamented, its mixed Gothic style reflecting the architectural designs and trends of several centuries.

"The exterior is a gleaming mass of white marble with lofty traceried windows, panelled buttresses, flying buttresses and pinnacles crowned with statues, the whole wrought into a soaring design of lace-like intricacy." Sir Banister Fletcher, *A History of Architecture,* 18th ed., rev. by J. C. Palmes (New York: Charles Scribner's Sons, 1975), p. 736.

8. Marcellus Palingenius, pseudonym for Pietro Angelo Manzolli (ca. 1500–43) of Ferrara: *Zodiacus Vitae, Pulcherrimum Opus . . . Marcelli Palengenii Stellati Poetae ad . . . Ferrariæ Ducem Herculem Secundum, Foeliciter Incipit* (Venice, ca. 1531). Also cited as *Zodiacus Vitae, hoc est, de Hominis Vita, Studio, ac Moribus Optimè Instituendis, Libri Duodecem [and XII]* (Basel, 1543; 1548).

The *Zodiacus Vitae,* a didactic poem patterned after the signs of the zodiac on the subject of human happiness, combines metaphysical speculation with satirical attacks on ecclesiastical hypocrisy. The Vatican denounced it as immoral and heretical. The Inquisition ordered it placed on the *Index* (1559); earlier the author's body had been exhumed and burned. For Pope Paul IV's *Index,* see *Die Indices Librorum Prohibitorum des Sechzehnten Jahrhunderts,* coll. and ed. Fr. Heinrich Reusch (1886; Nieuwkoop: B. De Graaf, 1961), p. 197.

HLT had read the first two books of the *Zodiacus Vitae* in 1767 with SJ (*Thraliana* 2:864).

9. Renée of France (1510–75), second daughter of Louis XII and Anne of Brittany, married Ercole II (1508–59), successor to the duchy of Ferrara. Her court became a rendezvous for men of letters and a sanctuary for persecuted French Protestants. After the duke's death she returned to her duchy of Montargis, converting it into a center of Protestant propaganda. For this she suffered harassment by Catholic troops during the religious wars.

10. *Romeo and Juliet* 2.5.46. Cf. HLT to SJ, *Letters* 2:184; *Observations* 2:384.

11. Virtually the national bank of Austria, it was founded in 1766 by Johann Fries (1719–85), scion of an Austrian banking family with roots in Switzerland. The current head was Josef Graf Fries (ca. 1763–88).

12. On 15 October, LC informed HLP: "Mr. Greatheed and Family I met in London Streets a few days after my arrival—I was astonished to see them. Mr. G. had been indisposed, but Mr. Shard who called upon them with better success than I did, told me he was much better—I saw him but once, they staid not long in Town" (Ry. 562.3).

13. The letter is missing.

14. The only child of the Greatheeds was Bertie (1781–1804). He was to become an amateur painter of considerable talent. Acording to LC, "Their Dear little Boy was quite well."

15. See HLP to Q, 5 January 1785, n. 5.

16. See HLP to SL, 30 April 1785, n. 8.

17. LC "was Indeed delighted with the [petrified] Fish at Verona.—I bought an odd one.—Mr. Shard a considerable number.—" (LC to HLP, 4 July).

18. Robert Lawless (1763–86), with whom the Piozzis "made Acquaintance . . . at Naples, Venice, and Milan, died at Nice; & never reached *his* Home" (*Thraliana* 2:678).

He was the son of Nicholas Lawless (1733–99) and Margaret, née Browne (1748–95). The elder Lawless, a prosperous Irish merchant and landowner, had been created a baronet [Ireland] in 1776 and was to be raised to the peerage as Baron Cloncurry (1789).

19. According to LC: "You cannot I think as yet have had your books from Cadel.—If I am not mistaken, they were to be sent to Lyons" (15 October).

20. While acknowledging receipt of the *Anecdotes,* Shard also complained of Cadell: "I could not help scolding the *Person who gave it me* a little, for giving me an unbound Book when I know you had ordered me one bound, for you read me the Letter in which you was so obliging as to give the order—he denied it and said Mr. Chappelow's alone was ordered bound—he however told me that altho it was not his orders I should have one bound—which I refused, giving him to understand the real truth, that it was the gift first and then the Book" (11 July, Ry. 892.7). He did, nevertheless, receive a bound copy (HLP to LC, 9 October 1787).

21. An allusion to the first meeting of the Piozzis and LC when the Piozzis' carriage broke down on a mountain road.

22. On 15 October, LC responded: "You want my man Pietro for a Courier—he is not displeased with England—but at Learning the Language—he is quite a Torpedo. I believe I shall soon get him a return Master.—When you see Joseph secundus you may hire him, he often acts as his own Courier, and why not as Yours?—Josephus 2dus with *his Long Train* of Titles will make a Noble Figure Flying before the Bird of Paradise."

TO SAMUEL LYSONS

Milan
20: September 1786.

Dear Mr. Lysons.

I write just as I am leaving Milan to enclose Cardinal Passioneus's Head which you desired: for the Answer to my last Letter I have some slight hopes of finding it at Verona, but you must now direct to *Vienna*, and tell all my Friends to send their kind Words to the same Place.

Cadell tells me how kind you are,[1] but so have you always been.

The Pearls *should* have come here before now, and then I *should* have carried them with me——but Care shall be taken that you get them somehow.[2]

I can add no more, being between Nest and Wing so; one is half crazed with Packing.

Adieu accept my husband's best Regards with those Dear Sir yours sincerely / H: L: Piozzi.

Send me the News of the World to Vienna.

Text: Hyde Collection.

1. On 8 May (Ry. 554.18), Cadell had written: "I should have wrote before but our active and intelligent friend Mr. Lysons promised to supply my place by giving you the most early information of the success of your publication."
2. See HLP to SL, [5] July, n. 10.

TO HESTER MARIA THRALE

Verona
27 Sept[r], 1786[1]

From this last and most lovely of all the Italian States & Towns I begin a letter to my dear Hester; from whom I had some hopes of hearing even to the Utmost moment of my Stay at Milan: As the disappointment however might possibly arise from your own distance, being possibly at Brighthelmston or even further off still—I write just as if you had written to me,[2] and tell you of our Jaunt to Bergamo, where we spent a Week at the Palace of the Marquiss of Araciel which he had not visited for many years, till he was resolved to show me the Beauties of that wonderful Prospect which is exceeded only by Windsor Terrace, & scarcely by that. We had a temporary Theatre; Oh what a pretty Plaything! and they sung Guglielmi's fine Terzetto to divert us![3] I warrant you have it at every Concert room in England by now—*and vote it a Bore* by this Time; it is very delightful however after the 100th Repetition. So would not be the Verses and Lamentations of our too partial Milanese Friends whose sincere Concern for our Departure c[d]

Gabriel Piozzi, ca. 1785, by an unknown Italian artist. *(Reproduced by permission of Viscountess Eccles, the Hyde Collection, Four Oaks Farm, Somerville, New Jersey.)*

only be softned by frequent promises of Correspondence & Return: we are got away tho' to gay, cheerful, charming Verona: and I have already received Visits from all our Venetian Ladies who have Country houses here.[4]

The Countess Mosconi[5] (celebrated in your Florence Miscellany)[6] made Mr Piozzi and I pass the first Evening we came at her Conversation; where Abate Bertola[7] made Improviso Verses to my husband's Accompanyment, in a way quite different from the Tuscan Fashion—I will try to describe it. One Friend sits down to the Harpsichord, & three or four of the Company sing two Lines of any well known tune song in parts to a slow Tune by way of Chorus—for Example

Spargo in vano i miei lamenti,
Ni ritrovo il Caro Ben.

The Poet makes one, or two, or three Strophes expressive of his Search for the Lady, and when he wants Time for further Invention concludes with that part of the Air which corresponds to the *first* of these Lines, when the Chorus repeating 'em again forms the Rhyme, and gives him a temporary Suspension: I don't know whether you understand me, but I am sure that I could do it myself, so as to content a partial audience of Intimates by dint of familiarity with a Language I have now spoken so long. The worst is want of *Voice;* when they make Verses round a Table after Dinner, *my* Stuff seldom fails of being applauded—We had a great deal on't at Varese.[8]

But I am more in earnest about the Petrefactions found in Monte Bolca just by here, than about all the Poetry possible: I shall really bring home some Specimens of great Value[9]—the People are so excessively kind, they make me quite ashamed; and when I read *my Name* this Morning in ye Musaeum written up in Gold Letters: *Ornamento d' Inghilterra Grazia d' Italia: dei Tesori della Natura Interprete, Custode, e Dispensatrice,* I was fairly overwhelmed, and could not say one Word. At Vienna however whither we are now going I shall know nobody, so I can get Time to cure my Sauciness before I come back to my own Country. We pass the Tyrolese Alps this Time for ye sake of varying Matters, & seeing new Modes of Life: My last Letter[10] told you that such were our Intentions, & described to you the beauties of Lago Maggiore; but I have a Notion it never came to hand because you had perhaps left Wimpole Street where I directed it, and so all the fine Acc^ts^ of the Isola bella, the Music upon the Lakes &c, was lost, to y^r^ much Affliction.

Rats half the manuscript have eat
Dire Hunger which we all regret![11]

My *serious* Vexation about it was & is, that through foolish Management I lost your Answer, which I beg'd might be sent to Mr Bonet at Milan: it is my present Request that you will give me the satisfaction of hearing you are well at *Vienna; Mess: Fries & Co Bankers* take Care of all our Correspondence. We wished you many returns of the 17th of Sep^r^: Monsignor Schiaffinati[12] bowed to the Picture[13] very genteely when he took the Glass in his Hand.

I was looking at myself the other day, & thought I w^d^ tell you what a motley

Creature I was become: for my Riding Habit was bought at *Rome* I recollected; my Hat & Shirt at *Naples;* my Shoes at *Padua,* my Stockings at *Brescia,* my Ruffles at *Genoa,* one of my Petticoats at *Milan,* & the rest of my dress in *England.* We sate for our Pictures at Rome[14] as I said I would—but such *Objects!* mine particularly, that I have done nothing but beg they might be burned ever since; as a Red-haired old Hag in a white Bedgown, is neither 'Ornamento' of *one* Country, nor 'Grazia' of *another.* If you had been at Home when dear Mrs Greatheed called at No. 60,[15] and tried so hard for Admittance: you would have received a more favourable Resemblance of me than any Painting could give, from her kind & friendly Description—Adieu my dear, I enclose this Letter to Mr Cator,[16] who will take Care it does not lie unreceived at the Office as probably the last is now doing: tho' Mr Jackson's good nature has been all along astonishing:[17] for without him Susan's Letters w^d^ never have reached us at all. Once more Adieu: & expect the Congratulations of the New Year 1787 from Yours most affectionately, / H: L: Piozzi.

Text: Queeney Letters, pp. 232–34. *Address: Addressed to Brighton (substituted for 60 Wimpole Street).*

1. A belated birthday letter to Q.
2. Q apparently had last written on 17 June (*Queeney Letters,* p. 230).
3. Pietro Alessandro Guglielmi (1728–1804), prolific composer of operas, oratorios, cantatas, chamber music, etc. From 1767–72 he was in London, connected with King's Theatre. Active thereafter in Venice, Rome, Turin, Milan, and Naples, he was appointed by Pope Pius VI in 1793 *maestro di cappella* of Saint Peter's.
4. *Observations* 2:259.
5. Elisabetta Mosconi Contarini (1752–1807). Intimately a part of Italy's cultural life, the contessa was to edit *Saggio di Poesie campestri, del Cavalier Pindemonte* (Parma, 1788). She is mentioned frequently in the letters of Pindemonte; see Nicola Francesco Cimmino, *Ippolito Pindemonte e il suo tempo,* 2 vols. (Rome: Edizione Abete, 1968).
6. In William Parsons's "Epistle to the Marquis Ippolito Pindemonte at Verona," dated "Florence 24. July 1785," there is on p. 27 the following reference to Mosconi:

> Round female brows when living laurels twine,
> Broader they spread and more a resplendent shine;
> . . . a Mosconi's thine!

Cf. *Observations* 2:264; Parsons, *Poetical Tour,* p. 50.

Q probably received her copy of the *Florence Miscellany* from Cator toward the end of 1785. See HLP to Q, 17 September 1785.

7. Abate [Severino] Aurelio Bertòla de Giorgi (1753–98), born in Rimini of a noble family, was a gifted poetic improviser. As a secular priest he held the chair of universal history at the University of Pavia in 1784.

His chief literary works are: *Operette in verso e in prosa,* 3 vols. (Bassano, 1785–89); *Poesie,* 3 vols. (Pisa, 1798); *Alcune operette in prosa di A. de G. B.,* ed. B. Gamba (Venice, 1829); *Poesie di Ticofilo Cimerio* [pseudonym] (Cremona, 1782); *Tre notti di PP. Clemente XIV* (ca. 1775). He also wrote poetic fables; HLP translated one that dealt with the meeting of a lizard and a crocodile (*Thraliana* 2:668–69; *Observations* 2:262–63).

8. *Observations* 2:218, 226.
9. For the collection of Vincenzo Bozza at Verona, see HLP to SL, 30 April 1785, nn. 8 and 9. ("Bolca" is misprinted "Bolea" in *Queeney Letters,* p. 233.)
10. 9 August, *Queeney Letters,* pp. 228–31.

11. Matthew Prior, *Alma; or the Progress of the Mind*, lines 5–6.

12. Monsignor conte Gaspare Schiaffinati (1738–1826), the son of Carlo and Margherita, née Pandini. At one time *canonico ordinario* of the cathedral of Milan, he became *canonico* on 21 June 1785. No further records of his ecclesiastical life are known. See *Memorie Storiche della Diocesi di Milano* (Milan: Biblioteca Ambrosiana, 1954), 1:54; and *Milano Sacro Almanacco per L'Anno 1826*, p. 55.

13. For Q's portrait, which arrived in Milan at the close of 1784, see HLP to Q, 5 January 1785.

14. The portraits, by an unknown artist, appear in Hyde, pp. 248–49; see also *Queeney Letters*, p. 237. That of GP is at Four Oaks Farm; that of HLP is in the National Portrait Gallery. Both are reproduced in this volume, pp. 186, 213.

15. The Wimpole Street house, which Q had rented since coming of age.

16. Correspondence to Q, as to her sisters, was often addressed to the Cator residence, either at Beckenham Place, Kent, or Royal Terrace, Adelphi, London.

17. Charles Jackson, "Comptroller of the Foreign Post Office." See HLP to Cadell, 17 February 1786, n. 8.

TO SAMUEL LYSONS

Vienna 8: November 1786.[1]

Dear Mr. Lysons.—
While you are lamenting the Rainy Weather which keeps you within doors, and the Fog which takes away all Taste of going out——how little do you think of the bitter Frosts and Snow that whiten all our Prospects, and while they whet our desire of returning home, impede our Progress; and render it very Serious in the Eyes of these good Germans, who kindly wish to detain us among them the whole Winter.

The Streets *are* narrow, and I suppose dirty, when 'tis less violently cold than now;[2] the Men all walk out clothed in Wolfskins, and the Danube looks willing to swell when the Frost shall be willing to break.

The sweet Veronese sent me your Letter hither and I hope to have *but* one More from you *this* January; You will please to direct that to *Brusselles*.

We will promise to be very diverting Companions at our Return, when I hope you will be among the first to say *Welcome home Dear Mr. Piozzi. I see your Wife is grown fat in your Country; let us keep her so now She's come back to her own.*

If I said a Word of the Fossil Fish that we carry in the Coach, or of the petrified Wood—I might be jealous that it was *them* you came to see, so not a Word shall I tell.

My Book is sent for to put up in this publick Library they tell me; it has had very great honors paid it indeed both in England and abroad: but Cadell never sent the promised Copies to Lyons, or they never received it there.

I am glad you are settling in Chambers, and say with Sincerity God give you good Luck. My Expectations are very high, and will not I dare swear be disappointed.

Tell all my true Friends that I love them exceedingly; and that my Husband proves his Love towards me in every possible Indulgence of my Taste and even of my Caprice——poor Johnson has been sick here— Oh how kind he has shewn himself to her on my Account. If I had not been in Love with him before, I would begin now.

But you would rather hear about Baron Borne[3] who has found the Secret of Amalgamation:[4] well: he is sicker than Johnson——the Quicksilver has seized him,[5] and he looks like the poor Wretches that used to be sent from the Mines near Bristol to recover at Bath by dint of the hot Water:——His Company is pleasing however, if his Print had any resemblance I would bring it you.

Adieu! these nasty Stoves suffocate but do not warm one—my Husband wishes for a good Coal Fire / so does / Your Affectionate Friend and Servant / H: L: Piozzi.

Text: Hyde Collection. *Address:* A Monsieur / Monsieur Sam: Lysons / chez Le Rev: Mr. S: Peach / at East Sheene / near Mortlake / Surrey/ Angleterre. *Postmark:* <DE> 2.

1. HLP's response to SL's letter of 13 September sent to Verona whence it was forwarded to Vienna.

The Piozzis had journeyed in easy stages since leaving northern Italy late in September, their travels across the Alps taking them to Trent, Innsbruck, Munich, Salzburg. By 28 October they were in Vienna. See *Queeney Letters,* p. 235; *Observations* 2:266–87.

2. For HLP's impressions of Vienna, see *Observations* 2:287–315 (specifically 2:310). She is answering SL's question, "I shall like to hear whether the Streets there are as narrow as Lady Mary Wortley describes them. . . ." See *The Complete Letters of Lady Mary Wortley Montagu,* ed. Robert Halsband, 3 vols. (Oxford: Clarendon Press, 1965–67), 1:259–60 (8 September, o.s., [1716]).

3. Actually, *Edler* (a lower order of nobility than baron) Ignaz von Born (1742–91), born at Karlsburg in Transylvania, was a onetime Jesuit priest and satirist, who had been called to Vienna in 1776 by Maria Theresa to classify the collections of natural history in the state museums. In Vienna he became the center of a learned and literary circle.

4. Born was primarily a mineralogist, noted for his successful experiments in metallurgy, and principally in the process of amalgamation. "The use of quicksilver in extracting the noble metals from their ores, was not a discovery of the Baron's, nor of the century in which he lived; yet he extended so far its application in metallurgy, as to form a brilliant epoch in this most important art. After he had at great expence made many private experiments, and was convinced of the utility of his method, he laid before the Emperor an account of his discovery. . . . he published, by order of the Emperor, his *Treatise on the Process of Amalgamation.*" See *AR* 39 (1797): 386–87.

5. According to the above article in *AR,* "It was at Felso-Banya where he met with [his illness]. . . . He descended here into a mine where fire was used to detach the ore, to observe the efficacy of this means, too soon after the fire had been extinguished, and whilst the mine was full of arsenical vapours raised by the heat" (p. 384). As a result of this accident his health was seriously impaired.

TO THE REVEREND LEONARD CHAPPELOW

Vienna
8: November 1786.

A Thousand Thanks to my very kind Friend Mr. Chappelow for his charming Letter,[1] so full of Humour, and *Good*-Humour—one must be a true *Torpedo* not to have a proper Taste for it. Well! we are so far advanced of our Journey, but here is the terriblest Weather you ever saw, to fright one from going forward; and the most agreeable Society imaginable to keep one a little back.

The <Viennese> Ambassador is excessively polite to us indeed—Mr. Piozzi dined with him Yesterday among the first Company of Vienna, and Sir Robert Murray Keith is as friendly to me as I could any way expect.[2]

These dear Germans who ought, and who do in fact excell in Chymistry, Natural History, and almost every Branch of useful Knowledge; are all mad after the Belles Lettres, and care for no Praises but what are given to their Poetry and Musick. But *optat Ephippia Bos* you know,[3] and the World has been always absurd in the Same Way. I long to see Mr. Cowper's Performances, and am astonished to find him already known among the Literati in this Town:[4] but they are very well acquainted with our Literature; of which no greater Proof can be given, than their having read Extracts of Johnson's Life in our Reviews &c. I have an agreable Intimacy here with two Ladies in whose House the famous Metastasio lived and died;[5] and they tell me pretty Anecdotes about him,—Anecdotes of the Emperor are so very numerous that one must a little doubt their Authenticity, but 'tis pleasing in the mean Time to hear them.[6] That the Sorrows of Werter is not only a Book originally written in German, but a Story literally true, is what I can best assure you:[7] Count Bruhl[8] who married Lady Egremont[9] is the Person who translated it into English.

I wish to give you more Amusement, but tis not easy to do so: Baron Borne, who has sacrificed his Health and risqued his Life for the Advancement of Natural History would be an agreeable Companion to my dear Mr. Chappelow, and I am sorry to think you are so unlikely ever to meet. Here is a Mr. Hawkins whom you knew at Cambridge[10] that has made good use of his Time in the Study of Fossills and Mineralogy: this is the place for such Things you know and I wish I could procure you any Specimens—Custom house Imposition[11] and Mortifying Circumstances however of many Sorts, (in that way) keep me from wishing to divert myself by adding more lumber to my Travelling Stock.—Mr. Piozzi gave me a Dog[12] this Morning indeed, because he did not find two English Women plague enough for him; and Johnson has been sick these three Days to mend matters too. Do pray write to Brussells whither if we are not lost in the Snow we shall at length arrive; and make haste to London, to confirm the kind Welcome you promise from Old and kind Friends to my Dear worthy Husband and to / Your Sincere humble / Servant / H: L: Piozzi.

Text: Ry. 559.4. *Address:* A Monsieur / Monsieur Le Rev: Leonard Chappelow / chez / Sir Henry Bridgeman / Bart. / Staffordshire / Angleterre. *Postmark:* NO 21.

1. From Diss in Norfolk, 15 October (Ry. 562.3).
2. Sir Robert Murray Keith (1730–95), lieutenant general (1781) and diplomat. In November 1772 he was posted to Vienna, where his father (Robert, d. 1774) had once been British minister, and where he himself represented British interests as envoy and minister plenipotentiary for the next twenty years. For his diplomatic posts, see *Repertorium*, pp. 157, 159, 165, 172; for his obituary, see *The Times*, 25 June 1795.
3. Horace, *Epistles* 1.14.43; *Observations* 2:300. The Horatian line served as the motto of *Rambler* 116.

4. On 15 October LC reported to HLP: "Oh what a Poet has unfolded himself—in full bloom—as beautiful as the Creeping Ceres. Like the aloe bitter and sweet.—Surprised us all in a moment." He went on to compare William Cowper favorably with Thomson and Pope. LC's enthusiasm was generated by *The Task*, published July 1785 (2d ed., 1786).

5. For a more detailed account, see HLP to Q, 25 November 1786. According to Lansdowne (p. 238 n. 1), the ladies were Marianna Martines (1745–1812) and her sister Antonia, "daughter[s] of a Papal official in Vienna, in whose house Metastasio lived from 1730 till his death in 1782," and to whom he made substantial bequests.

6. The eccentric behavior and decisions of Joseph II prompted a constant flow of anecdotes. HLP was to publish her own "Sketch of the Character of the Emperor" (*World*, 25 July 1789), which is virtually identical with the account in *Observations* (2:295–99). She emphasizes the ruler's austere personal habits and accessibility to his subjects. See also *Thraliana* 2:649–50.

7. *Die Leiden des Jungen Werthers* (1774), by Johann Wolfgang von Goethe (1749-1832), an epistolary romance based on autobiographical incidents.

8. The learned and congenial Hans Moritz [Count John Maurice] (1736–1809), Graf von Brühl zu Martinskirch, Knight of the White Eagle and ambassador extraordinary to the court of Saint James from the elector of Saxony (1764). He was to become a permanent London resident. See *GM* 79, pt. 1 (1809): 186.

The translation of *Werther* alluded to is probably the anonymous one of 1786, published in London by J. Parsons. Goethe and Brühl were friends, but we have seen no evidence that Brühl was the translator. See *Goethes Briefe*, ed. Karl Robert Mandelkow, 4 vols. (Hamburg: Christian Wegner Verlag, 1962), 1:395.

9. Brühl had married in 1767 Alicia Maria (1729–94), the daughter of George Carpenter (d. 1749), second baron Carpenter of Killaghy, and widow of Charles Wyndham (1710–63), second earl of Egremont (1750).

10. Probably a John Hawkins, who matriculated at Trinity Hall, Michaelmas term, 1762. LC was a student at the same college during that period.

11. HLP wrote to Q immediately after arriving in Vienna: "The Custom House Officers are a terrible Scourge to us, we have been completely stript here not only *to* the Skin, but *of* the Skin; for they have seized all my Furs" (28 October, *Queeney Letters*, p. 237). For the resolution of this annoyance, see HLP to Keith, 15 March 1787, and his response of 22 April (Ry. 892.10).

12. The Spitzberger lapdog, Flo (d. 1797), a male spaniel recently presented by the prince of Liechtenstein from a new litter, and destined to become a favorite of the Piozzis. See Clifford, p. 286; *Thraliana* 2:940 n. 6.

TO HESTER MARIA THRALE

Prague,
25 Nov., 1786

My dear Hester,

You will now read a letter with a Date which I flatter myself is wholly new to you,[1] and all the Folly is in my writing before I know any thing at all of the Place; but we will if you please talk about Vienna & about the Road from thence hither before we say a word of *John Huss* and his Companion the first Reformers.[2] In my last I said that you must not then expect Acc^{ts} of the Society, because we had not then presented our Recommendations: which however introduced us to one House for the Entrance into which I would willingly have bought Tickets at a high Price—The Lady having been bred up by the famous Abate Metastasio, who lived in her Father's House fifty Years, and died while She stood at his Bedside. He has instructed her so completely, that She has been received as a Professor in the Academy of Berlin, & likewise of Bologna: She has composed much sacred Musick which is highly thought of by her Countryfolks—with whom a slight or superficial Knowledge of the Art is not sufficient to obtain Applause—and She has set his favorite Cantatas so as not only [to] content but enchant the good old Man, who adored her and her Sister as if they were his Guardian Angels,—& who expired leaving them that were already rich, all he possest in the World. We were shown his Books & pictures you may be sure; & of his Operas he lived to see the 63^d Edition, A Thing scarcely to be credited. The Queen of France presented him a Set with the Royal Arms upon each Vol: most splendidly adorned three Months before his Death. I will enclose this Letter to Mr Cator—tis ye first I ever was Fool enough to fancy of Importance to *anybody,* but whatever relates to a man of Metastasio's Consequence, it would be a Pity to lose: I had an Avidity to gather up little Anecdotes of his private Life, that they were the more willing to indulge, & endure from me, as my Book about Dr Johnson is in ev'ry Body's hands at Munich & Vienna, & they are translating it away—as if it was the finest Thing in the World.[3]

When one goes to an Evening Conversation in Germany, Chocolate is presented one with Cream to put in the Cup: that Cream kept hot in a Silver Vase, & another Vase with more Chocolate to mix—very comfortable Stuff to me, but the Italians cry *Porcheria.*[4] I remember a Venetian Lady saying to my Husband who was speaking in Praise of English Elegance: that it was hardly possible that Nation should be very delicate—when She had herself seen a Lord sowce Cream into his Coffee, which says She 'you must acknowledge to be a very odious Trick'—Such are the various Manners one meets wth when travelling from one Country to another. You would perhaps however hear more willingly somewhat of the *Materials,* and to describe with due Commendations the Library & Arsenal of Vienna would be a pleasing Employment, if I could find Leisure & Paper. The Belvedere Palace too is gloriously fine,[5] the Pictures disposed—for Show & for Instruction—not for Pleasure, as one finds 'em in the Roman Villas, but a Room to a School—Titians & Tintorets for example in one apartment, Raphael & Michael Angelo in another, wth the Flemish & Dutch Masters all apart. But we are now going thro' Frost & Snow, thro' the most dreadful Roads in Europe, to see the Dresden Gallery;[6] where all the Correggios carried from Parma can alone be found. That charming Painter will perhaps cost me dear at last—I suffered a great deal from the Heat last June, to get a good View of his sweet Performances there; & now in spite of Furs & Flannels we expect to be half killed with Cold.[7] Sir John Sinclair kindly wrote to beg we would take another Road, this from Prague to Dresden was so *very* dangerous:[8] but what signifies a little Danger when Curiosity is strong? & when we are together to live or die, & no Reason to think anybody at home violently interested about our personal safety:—We shall carry our Dog by Turns—so I shall write again from Dresden if we get there: if not, why Susan & Sophy will look divinely in Mourning—but all my Crape that I bro't from Bologna is torne away by the Emperor's Custom House Officers. Sir Robt Murray Keith was as kind as possible about it, that he was—but we were too late in our Application, so all was lost.

The Friends we left at Milan & Verona have no Idea that we mean to run hazards, we suffered them to think we meant to pass all the Winter at Vienna, or we should never have got away. This Language is a great Torment to *us,* but I somehow think Mrs Dobson or Miss S: Streatfield,[9] or any of the people who study *Chaucer,* & read him familiarly, would not be much at a Loss: and I have found out here why Count Manucci called old Thames his *Hoond* so comically, they cry *Sheen Hoond* at all these Places, when they see Mr Piozzi & I caressing our little Dog.[10] In Bohemia tis very curious to see Ladies dress'd in Pink & Silver Caps with Tassells to them, trimmed with Furs, and they say the Women of Quality here in fair Weather drawn on Sledges make a splendid Appearance: but here is the most horrible Weather ever seen, so no Sights of that sort come in our way hitherto.

A Letter from you at Brussells would be the finest Sight to *me* that could be shown; and if it please God to protect us forward as he has done hitherto, we shall be there in six or seven Weeks:[11] let me hope to find you have not wholly forgotten / Your Affectionate Mother / H: L: Piozzi.

The last Time I had the Happiness to see Sophia's handwriting was at Rome.

Text: Queeney Letters, pp. 238–41. *Address: A Mademoiselle, / Miss Hester Maria Thrale / at her House No. 60 Wimpole Street, Cavendish Square, / London, Angleterre.*

1. The Piozzis had left Vienna on 23 November, arriving in Prague the next day (*Observations* 2:313, 316).

2. John Huss (ca. 1369–1415), the Bohemian martyr who, excommunicated along with his followers, was tried for heresy and burned at the stake.

His "heretical companion" was Jerome of Prague (ca. 1370–1416), who likewise was martyred for reformist activities. See *Observations* 2:319.

3. We have seen no record of the translated *Anecdotes.*

4. See *Observations* 2:315.

5. The imposing *Gartenpalais,* i.e., the Belvedere palace, erected in Vienna for Prince Eugene of Savoy (1663–1736) between 1714 and 1723 by Johann Lukas von Hildebrandt (1668–1745), the foremost architect of the age in Austria.

6. HLP paid homage to the rich exhibitions in *Observations* 2:330–33.

7. The travelers were to leave Prague on 30 November, arriving in Dresden on 4 December (*Observations* 2:323–24).

8. The roads between Prague and Dresden were as perilous and uncomfortable as he had warned. See *Observations* 2:324–25; *Queeney Letters,* pp. 242–44.

John Sinclair (1754–1835), of Ulbster and Thurso Castle, Caithness, M.P. for Caithness and Lostwithiel since 1780, was seeking distraction in European travels (1786–87) after the death in 1785 of his first wife, Sarah, née Maitland. Created baronet in February 1786, he was to have a long and distinguished political career.

9. Sophia Streatfeild, or Streatfield (1754–1835), of Chiddingstone, Kent, whom HLT first met in Brighton in 1777. Sophia's sexual charms (which had entrapped HT, among others) were well known to HLT, who nevertheless regarded her as a friend and praised her learning, especially her language skills. See *Thraliana* 1:323–24, 376; "Harvard Piozziana" 1:108.

10. Mannucci (HLP to SL, 14 June 1785, n. 10) was given to language blunders and mispronunciations. Cf. *Thraliana* 1:157; HLP to Q, 26 July 1785. HLP also observes in *British Synonymy* (1:286): "Foreigners . . . are apt to call every dog they see a *Hoond,* which is the transcendental word for that animal in High Dutch, as I have been told."

11. They arrived in early February, prior to the fifth. See Clifford, p. 290; *Queeney Letters,* pp. 245–47.

TO SAMUEL LYSONS

Prague in Bohemia
29: November: 1786.

What will you give dear Mr. Lysons for a Letter with this Date? Does it not look very wild somehow? and so here we are sure enough at the original Source of Reformation, at the Camp of the King of Prussia,[1] at the Scene of poor Prince Palatine's Miseries:[2] by the Side of a Bridge justly famous for its Size and Convenience;[3] and in the midst of Weather so hideous, and Roads so terrifying, that no people but ourselves would venture forward almost.— My *tenderest* Friends however need not apprehend my being put in a *Convent* here in Germany, for the Emperor has taken them all away:[4] when we made a Party to see Presburg in Hungary,[5] we were within 40 Posts of the Turkish Dominions;—— and *there*, my *Beauty* might have occasioned some Hazards of a *Seraglio*.

Well now for all I joke about my Beauty, You will see a *better Face put upon Things* than when we parted at Bath, that you will; mean time you want to hear how the People live at Vienna? Why they live five, or six, or seven Families all in one House; every one shutting his Apartment, or Set of Apartments out from the others, by a great Iron door, or Grate; so that the Approach to each Habitation seems like a Prison or a Nunnery. How they get to one anothers Houses is difficult, for the Streets are miserably narrow, and dirty; crowded besides with four wheeled Carts, and cutters of Wood, which incommode Passengers more than all the rest: but the People are pleasing enough when one gets at 'em. It is at *Prague* of all places that one eats best, and sleeps softest of any Town we have yet experienced:[6] so where I hoped for Diversion abroad, I found to my much Amazement excessive great Comfort at Home; perhaps those intolerable Inns we have passed through to get hither, may make us still more delighted with our present Lodging. I fancy we shall take England for Italy at our return, so beautiful will Whitehall and even the Horse Guards look after German Architecture: and the Theatres here and at Vienna! What Things they are!

The Rivers, Forests, and Furs of such Animals as reside in them, are the real Glories of this Country: such Fish it is impossible to see out of smaller Streams, and a little Severn Salmon on Mr. Hancock's Board at Bath[7] would hardly venture to measure against a *Danube Carp.* If we 'scape the Precipice between here and Dresden, and if we do not make food for the Eels in the Elbe which runs under it, I will write again *one* other Letter, to tell of the *Notte of Coreggio;*[8] and so crawl on to Brussells thro' Leipsig, Cassel, and Cologn——not Hanover and Amsterdam:[9] our Coach will hardly hold out more frisks,[10] and one grows tired of seeing—The Library, and the Musæum, and the same Stuff over again at every Place.

Mr. Murphy used to say when we asked him to go with us to look at some Gentleman's Seat I remember—No do let me alone (says he) I'll describe it to you when you come home just as exact. Accordingly when we returned he was ready to rec<eive us.> And *Well* (says he,) *You ran up a Flight of Stone Stairs did not <you;> turned into an Egyptian Hall; then thro' a magnificent <corridor> to the Picture Gallery——the Library is in the other Wing <&c.>*

I begin now to be of his Mind, and think it would [be] a comfortable Thing to sit quiet and stir the Fire, a Pleasure we never enjoy for the Stoves here warm, but do not divert one, and the double Windows teize me to death, I can never get a good Look <o>ut in the Street,—there is such a Ceremony with our curious Casements.

My Husband is going out on foot and promises to carry this Le<tter> himself to the post, an Offer I will not decline for if on<e> leaves 'em to others I see they never go.——Adieu then Dear Sir / You have now the *Pragmatic* Sanction[11] added / to every other Reason for believing me your sincerely / Obliged Friend and humble Servant / H: L: Piozzi.

Answer this to Brussells and God bless you.

Text: Hyde Collection. *Address:* A Monsieur / Monsieur Sam: Lysons chez Monsr: / Le Rev: / S: Peach at / East Sheene / near Mortlake / Surrey. / Angleterre.

1. In 1744 the "great" Frederick II of Prussia seized Prague after destroying a large part of it. The occupation lasted only a short time, but in 1757, at the beginning of the Seven Years' War, Frederick again besieged the city. In June of the same year, however, the Austrian victory at Kolin forced the Prussians to end the siege and leave a virtually devastated Prague.

2. HLP alludes to Karl Theodor (1724–99), Kurfürst von Pfalz-Baiern (1742), elector of the Palatinate (Pfalz) since 1777, on the death of Maximilian III. On 26 November 1741 Prague was assaulted by an army of Bavarians, French, and Saxons, who supported the regal claims of Karl Theodor. Although he was crowned king of Bohemia in Saint Vitus's Cathedral on 17 December 1741, he kept his throne for less than a year.

3. Probably the Charles Bridge, constructed in 1357 under the aegis of Charles, or Karl IV (1316–78), Holy Roman Emperor and king of Bohemia. The bridge connected the parts of Prague lying on either side of the Moldau (or Vlatava) River, a tributary of the Elbe.

4. HLP's exaggeration alludes to "Josephism" or the emperor's sweeping edict of 1781—the "Patent of Tolerance"—that nationalized the Catholic Church. For example, more than seven hundred of the church's 2,163 religious houses in the Austrian territories were closed, including many of the contemplative orders. The millions of florins obtained from the confiscation of monastic property were applied to education, poor relief, and increased clerical stipends. See, e.g., Owen Chadwick, *The Popes and European Revolution* (Oxford: Clarendon Press, 1981), pp. 250–51, 411–17, and passim.

5. The expedition (1 November) was cancelled because of HLP's illness (*Observations* 2:290–92).

6. The typical English traveler, HLP was attracted to amenities in Prague that had "a less foreign aspect than almost any where else" (*Observations* 2:316).

7. Either Samuel Hancock of West Gate Street or Benjamin Hancock of Trim Street. Both were Bath apothecaries who kept lodging houses.

8. In the Dresden Gallery (*Observations* 2:330–31).

9. The Piozzis went to Hanover, and thence to Brussels, Antwerp, and Lille (*Observations* 2:370–84).

10. The coach needed repairs by the time the Piozzis reached Dresden, where they remained until 1 January. Only then had they recovered from fatigue. With the vehicle and spirits "once more repaired," they set out for Berlin (*Observations* 2:349).

11. At the beginning of the eighteenth century, fears arose that the male line of the Habsburgs might become extinct with Karl VI (1685–1740), Holy Roman Emperor (1711–40). In 1713, therefore, he promulgated a Pragmatic Sanction to insure the rights of a direct female succession—specifically that of his daughter Maria Theresa—against possible claims by more distant relatives. The estates of Bohemia approved the female succession in 1720, thus acknowledging the indivisibility of the Habsburg realm.

TO WILLIAM PARSONS

Dresden
8: December 1786.

Dear Sir—
Your obliging Letter followed us hither,[1] but the Date shews that it has been a long Time on the Road. I never found it till Monday last. It was particularly pleasing to read your Account of my Daughters, which indeed agrees with that of all the others I receive:[2] Mrs. Greatheed probably never had my Acknowledgments for *her* Civilities of the same kind, as She gave me no Direction where to write: They are very charming People, and very sincere in their Attachments; I earnestly desire their Happiness whether in Town or Country.

Our Journey thro' the Empire has answered exceedingly well; but I liked many Towns in it better than the Capital:

Munich is delightful,[3] and the strong Contrast between German and Italian Taste is very entertaining—no Wonder those Nations like one another so little, their Notions of Excellence are different on every Subject, and tis beyond Measure curious to pass the Tyrol and see Manners so diametrically opposite presented before one in three days travelling only.

The Women on *our* Side of those Mountains shew nothing but their Face, and scarcely more than their Nose: the Ladies all speak many Languages, and value themselves on literary Accomplishments which they display in a Manner that our English Gentlemen would hardly suffer from their Wives and Daughters lest Pedantry should be the Cry——So wide are the Ways of the Viennese Dames from those of your charming Venetians—but here the Musick is learned, the Painting deeply studied, the Workmanship finished to the utmost nicety, and the Conversation correct to minuteness. I however who profess to like the good Parts of every Place and Country, find a great deal in Germany to divert me upon the whole; nor can I think it necessary indeed for an Admirer of Shakespeare or Salvator Rosa, to renounce the reading Terence's Plays, or looking at the Miniatures of Gerard Dow.[4]

The Gallery here at Dresden is an amazing—a dazzling Collection, and I do not now regret leaving Modena unlooked at, as all her best Rareties have been transplanted here.

We have a good Opera too, and Mr. Piozzi finds the Music very pleasing to him. I suppose if one carried home even a Tea Cup of this charming Porcelane,[5] one should lose it at Dover, as I did all my Clothes at Vienna thanks to the Black Eagle:[6] but no Torment ever equalled the vile Roads between Prague and this Place——too bad for Language to lament or to describe, so I will say nothing about 'em: Bohemia is a better Country than Hungary though, for we have had a Stroke even at *that;* and it was not unamusing to see the Scenes of modern Battles, and the Ruins of modern Ambition,[7] after having with you examined the Theatre of ancient Phrenzy, and seen the sad Remains of Mankind's wolvish Spirit to devour their weaker Fellow Creatures in every Age and Nation.

The chief Pleasure is however still to come, and I hope to find it in chatting comfortably with our Friends in England; my Husband will be willing to be pleased there I am sure, it is natural for me to desire that he may be so, as whatever he likes best, will be ever the Choice of Dear Sir / Your much Obliged Friend / and Obedient Servant / H: L: Piozzi.

Accept a Thousand Compliments and Wishes of a merry Christmas which I shall be very happy to keep here in a Protestant Country, for tho' my *Lord Peter* and I agree very well, yet I am glad to see *Brother Martin* again to be sure.[8]

Take Care of your Health Dear Sir and keep these Feavers at a Distance: now you have lost your Mother you should get you a pretty Wife: so God bless you and Adieu: if you are very good natured you will direct to Brussells where we shall be towards the end of January—

Mr. Piozzi fait bien les Compliments a Mr. Parsons and shall be very glad to see you again in England.

Text: Hyde Collection. *Address:* A Monsieur / Monsieur Guilliaume Parsons Esqr. / chez Messrs: Griffiths Fry and / Robinson Banquiers / London / Angleterre. *Postmark:* DE 22.

1. His letter of 1 October 1786 (Ry. 558.17).
2. HLP had received news of the girls from LC, Shard, and Cator. Parsons had written: "I must not omit to tell you that I a few days ago did myself the honor of paying a visit to the Miss Thrales at Kensington, they appear to me charming unaffected girls, and I cannot but congratulate you on your having such daughters, and on your happy prospect of seeing them again so soon."
3. *Observations* 2:273–82.
4. Salvatore Rosa (1615–73), Italian baroque painter, is noted for his vast historical canvases, while Gerard (or Gerrit) Dow (Dou or Douw) (1613–75), Dutch realist, is best known for his miniatures and meticulous detail of local scenes and types (*Observations* 2:293–94).
5. *Observations* 2:326.
6. Officials of the Austrian customs.
7. Throughout much of the century, Bohemia had been a battleground for such major conflicts as the Wars of the Austrian and Bavarian Successions and the Seven Years' War.
8. HLP's borrowing of the allegory in Swift's *A Tale of a Tub* to evince her allegiance to the Church of England. Cf. *Observations* 2:327, 347.

TO SAMUEL LYSONS

Brussells
3: February 1787

Dear Mr. Lysons.

After a very long Journey as you know, and if one had a mind to multiply Wonders—a very serious one at this Season; I found sincere Comfort in your three agreable Letters.

What you tell me of Mr. Murphy's friendly remembrance flatters and pleases me: those who loved my Husbands shall always be loved by me, that's certain; and Dr. Lort is very kind too, and writes very sweetly.

Every one agrees in sending us back to Antwerp; we mean to be there next Monday to dinner if possible:[1] the Dusseldorp Gallery answered very well[2]—— but 'tis not the *Dresden* one to be sure.

Potzdam, Berlin, and Sans Soucy exceeded all my Imagination, perhaps more than any thing I have seen at all; for of every other famous Town or Palace I had screwed up my Fancy very high—but had no Notion of the Magnificence, Taste, and Splendour united by the King of Prussia in his Dwelling House.[3]

Did not I write to you from Saxony to say how we passed the Precipice between Lowositz and Aussig? half on Foot and half in the Carriages of the Country; having floated our own Coach down the Elbe to save its utter Ruin, and leave it at least in a *mendable* State which with less good management would have been impracticable, as those Roads have certainly been getting worse every day since Lady Mary Wortly passed them; or her Husband would not have been asleep I believe, nor the postillions neither.[4]

All was forgot however when we saw the Elector's Treasures,[5] and the Pictures of Correggio, worth more in my Mind than the Green Diamond and the Onyx together.

After Berlin the most striking Thing was our King's arms and Livery and Picture found in a Country little resembling his British Dominions,[6] God knows, for a more melancholy Place than Hanover—except Brunswick did I never see:[7] had the English Mob a Notion how welcome 15000£ must be to such Princely People in so poor a State they would have been more generous[8]—but John does run a Head before he knows at who, and is sorry when he has done *tossing* an innocent Person.

The Story of Mr. Bowes and Lady Strathmore is a very disgraceful one, and I'm sorry it ever happened:[9] All the Foreigners wonder as they do at the Histories of highway Robberies—and say 'Tis very strange that the Laws of a Country like England do not prevent such Outrages and the diffusion of Gazettes and Newspapers to distant Nations is really not a desirable Circumstance; every little ridiculous Incident is by that means displayed before all Europe, and canvassed over by those who never could have taken any Interest in it if they had known the original beginning. Not that I think slightly of these Crimes against Heaven and against Society; but if People will play such Tricks, 'tis better not publish them to others who can't mend them. And now Adieu Dear Sir, and be glad to see us when we come to the Hôtel Royal in Pallmall which I trust will be before St. David's Day.

Mean Time and ever believe me / Much your Affectionate Friend and Servant &c. / H: L: Piozzi.

My Husband sends you a Thousand Compliments——No Letter from Mr. James here—tis the 1st Time he has failed to write in Answer to mine from Dresden—tell him I say so, and that we love him dearly.

Text: Hyde Collection. *Address:* A Monsieur / Monsieur Sam: Lysons chez / The

Rev: Mr. S: Peach / at East Sheene / near Mortlake / Surrey. / Angleterre. *Postmark:* FE 6.

1. That is, 5 February; but on that date HLP was still writing letters from Brussels and anticipating a party at the Whalleys on the 8th.

HLP was to find Antwerp "a dismal heavy looking town . . . melancholy" and deserted (*Observations* 2:380).

2. See *Queeney Letters*, p. 246. For a contemporary account of the Düsseldorf gallery, see *The Autobiography of Colonel John Trumbull: Patriot-Artist, 1756–1843*, ed. Theodore Sizer (New Haven: Yale University Press, 1953), pp. 136–39.

3. See *Observations* 2:350–63. Sans Souci at Potsdam was the residence of Frederick the Great. He died there on 17 August 1786. See HLP to SL, 9 September 1787.

4. *Observations* 2:324–25. HLP had read Lady Mary Wortley Montagu's graphic account (21 November [1716]) of the dangers to be encountered while passing along "the frightfull Precipices that divide Bohemia from Saxony" (*Montagu Letters* 1:281–82).

5. See *Observations* 2:334–36; *Queeney Letters*, p. 242.

6. See *Observations* 2:366–67.

7. *Observations* 2:363–69.

8. HLP alludes to British opposition to the Hanoverians between 1720 and 1750, specifically to a British fear of "their King's desire of enriching his Electoral dominions . . . with their good guineas" (*Observations* 2:369).

9. Mary Eleanor, née Bowes (1749–1800), was the widow of John Lyon, afterward Bowes (1737–76), seventh earl of Strathmore and Kinghorne (1753). In 1777 she married Andrew Robinson Stoney, afterward Bowes (1747–1810). She left him in February 1785, but in November 1786 he had her abducted. Upon regaining her liberty, the countess won a much publicized divorce suit (3 March 1789). Stoney-Bowes lived out his final twenty-three years within the "Rules" of the King's Bench Prison. See, e.g., the *Public Advertiser* (20 May 1788) for the publicity generated by the case.

Several years later, when reading *Spectator* 423, HLP wrote in her copy of the periodical: "I believe poor Lady Strathmore was caught by Mr. Bowes in this sort of way. One Fellow (like Greyhounds in a Leash) ran and turned her into the Mouth of another who was slipped at her to advantage" (6:166).

MR. WILLIAM PARSONS

Brussells
5: February 1787

Dear Mr. Parsons—

Your Letter is so kind, and your good Opinion so flattering, that I will not wait to pay you personal Acknowledgments, but tell you at once how sensible my Husband and myself are to your valuable Friendship.

Mr. Merry lodges in our Hôtel here, and we talk of you and dear Mr. and Mrs. Greatheed by the Hour. The Whalleys too help to make our Time pass very agreably;[1] I always loved 'em, and they are grown more amiable now than ever.

You will say we shall never cross the Water, while Matters are made so pleasing to us on this Side it; and that my Love for my native Land resembles that of the Irishman for his Mistress when he cries out—*Ah my pretty Sheelah! was I once within 40 Miles of thy Face, I would never desire to be nearer it as long as I live.*[2]

All this we disclaim, and will soon return, and chat over the Wonders We have seen since Dresden; among which the most striking are the Glories of Potzdam, the Elegance of Sans Soucy, and the Horrors of a Drive thro' Westphalia. The Weather was however strangely delightful all the Way; and I found no Difference at all from the Dozen Degrees of Latitude in which we passed this Winter and the last, except that in the North there is no Thunder and Lightning.

Mr. Revely's Accounts of Egypt have perhaps enflamed your Curiosity, as they have mine; I met him at Rome one Evening I remember, and regretted the Moment when we were obliged to quit the Company. His Explanation of the Sphinx is learned, elegant and new.[3]

I should be sorry however that You were to set out again o'Travelling; the End of Labour is Rest; and the Intention of gleaning up Ideas in distant Regions, is only to benefit home by their Dispersion, or enable a Man to endure home by their Combination.[4] If the last Flight don't answer—You must out once more—but resolving always at least to *write* your Travels: for no one should rob his native Country of those Talents, which owe their Cultivation to the Soil in which they were originally dropt.

You will however have probably pitched upon a Companion before we get back, and forget all rambling Fancies.

Whatever you decide, *our* earnest Wishes for your Happiness will always attend you, and *we* shall always consider that Day as a lucky one in which we first met in my Box at Milan.[5]

Adieu then Dear Sir for a few Weeks, or rather days, and accept my Husband's sincerest Regard and Compliments with those of / Your Obliged Friend / and faithful humble Servant / H: L: Piozzi.

We shall have Time to receive a Letter here if you are kind enough to write one.

Text: N.L.W., 11060D. *Address:* A Monsieur / Monsieur William Parsons Esq. / At Messrs: Griffiths, Fry and / Robinson Bankers in / London / Angleterre. *Postmark:* FE 10.

1. "Here are Crowds of English here—we wait for a fine Assembly at Mrs Whalley's Thursday [8 February]" (*Queeney Letters*, p. 246).
2. The same joke appears in HLT to SJ, 11 November 1778 (*Letters* 2:31).
3. Willey Reveley (d. 1799) accompanied the antiquary Sir Richard Worsley (1751–1805) as "architect and draftsman" on a tour through Italy, Greece, and Egypt (1784–89). Reveley and Parsons knew and communicated with each other. Parsons acquired further accounts of Egypt and of the Sphinx's meaning, many of which he probably related to HLP.
4. Cf. HLP to SL, 17 September 1784, n. 10.
5. HLP to Q, 22 April 1785, n. 18.

Sarah Siddons, 1787. Chalk drawing by John Downman. *(Reproduced by permission of the National Portrait Gallery.)*

TO THE REVEREND LEONARD CHAPPELOW

Brussells
13: February 1787

What a gay, pretty, pleasing Letter was that I found here from our kind Friend Mr. Chappelow![1] tho' the honestest Man in the World will some Times as you see play the *Guineadropper*——and that don't answer in any Way. You *might* know that *Hearts* are chiefly of English Growth, and People here have no Value for 'em. The Banker says 'tis a foolish Thing, and that the Fellow wants no Money, and Twenty such Stories. I suppose you have been told that *Mr. Howard* is considered as crazy on the Continent;[2] then give your Money to some poor deserving Countryman at *home*,[3] and think no more of this Man——*He is at Brussells*.

So Mr. Shard is going to be married;[4] I wish him happy from my Heart, and hope he knows what will make him so. We shall come home soon now, and give *him Joy*, if he will give *us leave:* will you do me the Honour to tell him what I say?

Our Journey has been exceeding long, but no ways tedious; The Gallery and Treasures of Dresden paid for the bad Roads we were plagued with to get thither: and the Civilities we received there, made me not sorry that the Coach wanted a Month's residence to put it in repair.

Berlin and Potsdam were the next Scenes exhibited by our magic Lanthorn of perpetual Motion: and could hardly fail to excite many serious Reflexions. At *this* place I have read some of your Friend Mr. Cowper's Poems, with sincere Delight to think that there is in the World so good a Man, who writes so well, now Johnson has left it.

You are very droll and very kind in your Concern for my Maid—She is better thank God, but I shall be happier when She is once at home with her Husband.

Mine sends you a Thousand Compliments and wishes for the pleasure of telling you personally how sincerely you are beloved and respected by him and by Dear Sir Your Obliged and faithful Servant / H: L: Piozzi.

I hope we shall be at the Royal Hotel, Pallmall upon St. Taffy's day.

Text: Ry. 559.5. *Address:* A Monsieur / Monsieur The Reverend / Mr. Leonard Chappelow / at his House in Hill Street / Berkeley Square / London / Angleterre. *Postmark:* FE 19.

1. LC's letter (missing) was written in January and sent to Brussels. In this response HLP refers to points he had introduced on 15 October 1786 (Ry. 562.3).

2. John Howard (ca. 1726–90), philanthropist and reformer who traveled throughout Europe inspecting and seeking to improve prison and hospital conditions.

According to LC, "we are all statue mad.—so many hundreds are subscribed, that I verily believe Mr. Howard (who was at Naples when you was there) will have erected to his memory a Statue which would make St. Carlo at The Boromean Isles look not much bigger than a Mandrake." The statue was eventually erected in Saint Paul's Cathedral.

3. HLP believed in homespun charity, supporting the gentry's faith in such as Thomas Gilbert (1720–98), poor-law reformer.

Like HLP, LC had applauded "those people of property who spend at least half if not all their time at a distance from the Capital, and are continually meeting in order to mend the

Morals of, and provide for the maintenance of the Poor. A Grand reform will soon take place under the direction of Parliament which has passed a preliminary Act obliging every parish in England to give an Account how their poor are maintained. . . . Mr. Gilbert is the man, to whom I believe this Kingdom will in future be more indebted than to any other individual that ever existed" (15 October).

4. Charles Shard in 1787 was to marry Sarah, née Gillie.

TO HESTER MARIA THRALE

Hotel Royal, Pallmall
Sunday Morn[g] [March 11, 1787]

My dear Hester will see by the Date of this that we are arrived, but upon my Honour to the very worst Hotel I have been at in any Capital City of Europe;[1] & we have seen above a Dozen: I told one of the Women so two Minutes ago, & She replied *Indeed my Lady and everybody that comes to the House says the same Thing*.

You may be sure we shall get into some ready furnished Habitation even today if possible,[2] & I hope the Confusion & Hurry we are now in, will serve me as an Excuse for not being able before tomorrow[3] to assure you personally how much & how Affect[ly] I am / Your / H: L: Piozzi.

Text: Queeney Letters, p. 248. *Address: Miss Thrale, N[o] 30 Lower Grosv[r] Street*.

1. Although expecting to arrive on 1 March, the travelers did not reach London until Saturday, the 10th. HLP wrote to Q the following morning. Soon the Piozzis began to renew friendships, attend theatrical performances, and plunge into social activities.

2. The Hotel Royal was still the Piozzis' address on 24 March, but on the 27th the *World* reported: "Mrs. *Piozzi* has taken a house in Hanover-square [on the south side, at the corner of Saint George's Street]. Mrs. *Piozzi*, if not again admitted to the *Blue-Stockings*, will probably establish a similar meeting of her own. The intervals of Conversation to be relieved [by] Music." As HLP recalled, they "opened" the residence "with music, cards, &c. . . . The World, as it is called, appeared good-humoured, and we were soon followed, respected and admired" (Clifford, p. 294; Hyde, p. 251 n. 18; Hayward 1:305–6; *Queeney Letters*, p. 249).

3. "The [three eldest] lady-daughters" called formally at the hotel. They "behaved with cold civility, and asked what I thought of *their* decision concerning Cecilia, then at school. No reply was made, or a gentle one; but she was the first cause of contention among us. The lawyers gave her into my care, and we took her home to our new habitation" (Hayward 1:305).

TO SIR ROBERT MURRAY KEITH

London
15: March 1787

Sir—
It shocks me to be troublesome to you about such trifles, but after the Indulgence I received from you when I mentioned it last November at Vienna[1] I will hope at

least to escape Blame. The people at the Custom house at Franckenmarch[2] seized some Furs of mine which though very old and much worne, were of particular Value to me partly because they were my Mother's. I lost at the same Time a Satten Gown half made up which had been bought in the Emperor's own Dominions[3]—some Crape to make me a Cap upon the Journey, and three Hanks of thread that my Maid worked with. For this supposed Offence Mr. Piozzi paid 15 Zecchines[4]——and we were repeatedly promised Restitution: if you Sir should happen to recollect any thing of so unimportant a Transaction, you will likewise recollect your own politeness in *protesting* that my Trifles should be restored; in hope of which we waited day after day at Vienna, till the Rain came and spoiled the Roads already very bad between that Town and Dresden.[5] Count Fries[6] has since let us know that the things *did* come back *sometime* to Vienna, and that he forwarded them as we begged he would to Danot, Banker at Brussells[7]—but they were stopt again at the Frontiers (for want of an Ambassadors Protection) and are at Vienna again. Mr. Piozzi hoped to see his Money at least; but I believe *that* too is contraband, for the Abate [Trents] writes us word that without the Goods we cannot see the Guineas.

I now take the Liberty to beg for the Honour of your Instructions——what we ought to do, and what we ought to hope, and what we ought to pay—for having carried to Vienna an old Fur Petticoat purchased in this Town just 30 Years ago, and half worne out before it came to the Possession of / Sir / Your very Obedient / and very humble Servant / H: L: Piozzi.—

Text: Brit. Mus. Add. MSS 35,538.70. Hardwicke Papers, vol. 190.

1. The incident occurred in late October (*Queeney Letters,* p. 237). Sir Robert responded from Vienna, 22 April (Ry. 892.10):

"I was very sorry to learn by your favour of the 15th of March, that So many fresh Obstacles had arisen to prevent your receiving the Furs &c. which had been detained at the Custom house on the Imperial Frontier. The fault seems to have rested, in a great measure, with the person to whom that Commission was intrusted by Mr. Piozzi at the time of your departure from hence.

"Immediately after the receipt of your Letter I renewed my application to have the goods delivered into my hands. I obtained this, and have (a week ago), given them in Charge to the Earl of Crawfurd who is returning to England, and who will deliver them carefully at your house in London. The fifteen ducats (which were deposited) will either be paid into the hands of Lord Crawfurd, or restored to your Bankers Messieurs Fries, of which they will give you Notice."

2. Frankenmarkt, a small market town, in Upper Austria.

3. In 1787 Joseph II was the Habsburg-Lorraine ruler of the Holy Roman Empire, whose borders encircled an area consisting of Germany, Austria, Bohemia, Moravia, the Austrian Netherlands, and the northern tip of Italy.

4. Zecchin (or zechine), formerly a Venetian and Turkish gold coin.

5. See HLP's letters in November; *Observations* 2:324–25.

6. See HLP to LC, 1 September 1786, n. 11.

7. Daniel Danoot (1710–89), a prominent Belgian banker. See *GM,* pt. 1 (1789): 577.

TO HESTER MARIA THRALE

Royal Hotel
24: March 1787

My dear Hester—

You have perhaps already heard from others what I ought to tell you first: that my Letters written by Dr. Johnson are loudly claimed by the Public,[1] and that I shall print 'em directly. What shall I do with the dear Name of *Queeney?* Scratch it out, and put Miss T—— in I believe.[2] It occurs very often, but always mentioned with Tenderness and Respect. Tell me *what you would have* me do, and assure *your*self that nothing is more precious to me than your Approbation,[3] which I still venture to assure *my own self* shall at length be most fully obtained by / Your truly Affectionate / H: L: Piozzi.

I write this to leave if you are not at home.[4]

Text: Ry. 533.8.

1. Even before her arrival in London, the *World* on 9 March had reported, albeit inaccurately, that "Mrs. Piozzi brings with her the collection of *Sam Johnson's Letters* &c. in much readiness." Cadell, one of her first visitors at the Royal Hotel, "came to make his Bargain for Johnson's Letters—for which he gave £500 *sur le Champ.*" To this she agreed. On the morning of 21 March, as Dr. Lort told Bishop Percy—quoting HLP—she had retrieved from the bank " 'Johnson's Correspondence' amongst other papers, which she means forthwith to commit to the press." See Clifford, p. 295 n. 3; Hayward 1:298; *Queeney Letters,* p. 249; "Harvard Piozziana" 2:96.

2. Although other names were eradicated, those of Queeney or Hester (however SJ designated Q) were allowed to stand.

3. This note may be HLP's implicit request for Q's hoard of SJ letters—over thirty in all. Q not only refused but objected to the publication of the edition. SAT, however, relinquished five and ST one, all the SJ letters in their possession.

4. Although Q was at home, HLP had second thoughts or—more likely—quarreled with her and retained this letter of request.

After publication of the correspondence, the *Morning Post* (25 March 1788) announced that Q held letters "from the Rambler, infinitely superior to those of her Mother . . . but *Miss Thrale* with a resolution that does honour to her delicacy, however unfortunate it may be for the Public, has declared that these *Testimonies of confidence* shall never see the light."

For HLP's interpretation of Q's refusal to share, see *Thraliana* 2:680.

TO SAMUEL LYSONS

Holy Thursday [5 April 1787]
Hanover *Square*

Dear Mr. Lysons—[1]

I have found about forty Letters of Johnson's in the old Trunk which may *very well* be printed; some of them exceedingly long ones, and of the *best sort*. I read two or three to Mr. Cadell, and he liked them vastly, but will not abate of *mine*,[2] and for the sake of his partiality I am now resolved to be patiently tyed to the Stake, and if we can find six or seven tolerable ones for each Volume, he shall have them, but let me look them over *once again*.[3]

No need to *expunge* with Salt of Lemons all the Names I have crossed—let the Initials stand: 'tis enough that I do not name them out; Civility is all I owe them, and my Attention not to offend is shewn by the Dash.[4]

The Preface is written,[5] and when I get the Verses from Dr. Lort[6] I will not be dilatory, for I have got a nice little Writing Room, and a very Gentleman-like Man to deal with in Mr. Cadell.

Marquess Trotti[7] and Mr. Colle[8] carry my Commendation to the dear Jameses. When shall you get to Bath I wonder:[9] Write at least once again to your Obliged / and faithful Servant / H: L: Piozzi.

Text: Hyde Collection. *Address:* To / Samuel Lysons Esqr: / at Rodmarton / near / Cirencester. *Postmark:* 6 AP.

1. SL acted as editorial adviser, helping HLP to choose and arrange the correspondence, to erase names and occasionally paragraphs prior to publication. With his approval, for example, she deleted from SJ's letter of 19 June 1775 a paragraph praising JB's unpublished Hebridean journal and characterizing him as "a very fine fellow." See Clifford, pp. 299–301, 318–19; Chapman 2:47. In *Review of English Studies* (22 [1946]: 17–28), Chapman would not "suspect" HLP's editing "in general. She seems to have been at the worst, indifferent honest."

Despite his efforts on her behalf, SL's loyalties were untrustworthy. On 12 April 1788, thus, he visited JB and "filled up" for him "a great many of the blanks in Dr. Johnson's *Letters to Mrs. Piozzi.*" See *Boswell: The English Experiment 1785–1789*, p. 209.

2. SJ had saved over one hundred of HLT's letters. In 1785 Reynolds, as executor, turned them over to Cator in a sealed parcel for safekeeping (Clifford, p. 297).

3. Uneasy about public response to her own letters, HLP hesitated about a week before deciding to draw upon them as a method of filling out the two volumes of *Letters:* she included twelve in the first and fifteen in the second.

4. Names—readily identifiable—are often retained. Sometimes only the first initial of the surname is kept, as "Mr M——" in Letter 100. At other times names are indicated by a series of asterisks with no other clue. Again in Letter 100: "but yesterday I had I know not how much kiss of Mrs. Abington, and very good looks from Miss ***** the maid of honour." Or as in Letter 115: "Mrs. Cobb is to come to Miss Porter's this afternoon. Miss A——comes little near me." See Chapman, "Piozzi on Thrale," *Notes and Queries* 185 (1943): 242–47.

For *Letters* with the blanks and asterisks filled in by HLP (along with other marginalia), see the Rothschild copy, Wren Library, Trinity College, Cambridge.

5. The preface to *Letters* (pp. i–vi) justifies the printing of a private correspondence.

6. Possibly HLP hoped that he would translate the thirty-six lines of Latin "Verses addressed to Dr. Lawrence, composed by Dr. Johnson, as he lay confined with an inflamed Eye" (2:415–16). Once before, at a critical stage in the publication of the *Anecdotes*, Dr. Lort had come to HLP's rescue by translating SJ's Latin epitaph on HT. In the end, however, she produced her own translation of the verses to Lawrence (2:416–18). See also HLP to Cadell, 7 June 1785, n. 4.

7. Lorenzo Galeazzo Trotti (b. 1759), member of a noble Milanese family, obtained the title of *marchese* officially in 1817. HLP had met Trotti and his tutor, the Abbé Buchetti, in Paris in September 1784 and in Munich in October 1786. See French Journals, p. 202; "Harvard Piozziana" 2:91; also HLP to PSW, 28 July [1791], n. 1; 15 October 1791, n. 2.

8. Francesco Maria Colle (1744–1815), an antiquarian and writer associated with Padua.
9. SL spent many of his youthful years in Bath, where he attended the grammar school and began his legal studies. His uncle, Daniel Lysons (1727–1800), elected in 1780 a physician of the Bath General Hospital, lived at 3 Paragon Buildings. Not until 1784 did SL leave the city for London.

TO SAMUEL LYSONS

Hanover Square, Thursday
12th April 1787

Dear Mr. Lysons,

Do not dispirit us, all will do very well; and we will have lines enough; I have a great deal to tell you which I should not quite like to write.[1] Come on Tuesday morning, do, at nine o'clock, and bring all the letters, and let us have a good sitting to them; wherever the names can carry displeasure, we will dash them. Miss Thrale refused her assistance, but we will do without, and very well too. Adieu! till Tuesday morning, and accept the thanks of / Your much obliged and faithful, / H. L. Piozzi.

Text: Bentley's Miscellany 28 (1850): 541. *Address:* to Samuel Lysons, Esq. / at the Rev. Mr. S. Peach's House, / at East Sheene, near Mortlake, Surrey.

1. HLP had by now accumulated about four hundred SJ letters. Several were short, treating of his health and therapy; and they would—as she and SL assumed—flatten interest in the collection. Partly to offset this limitation, she chose her own letters to SJ with an eye toward lively revision and amplification. Thus she made the tone of some more literary, and in others she inserted anecdotes and incidents from *Thraliana*. Throughout the twenty-eight HLT letters, she substituted words and corrected grammar.

TO SAMUEL LYSONS

Hanover Square
Monday 23 April [1787]

What can be become of two other Letters where my Unkle is mentioned?[1] They should come in before the account of his having willed away the Estate;[2] you may remember I made you take them: they spoke of his *Stagnation of unactive Kindness,*[3] and you once wished to reject them, but repented and accepted them.

Where are they?

Will you dine here o'Wensday next, and shall I ever see Mr. Cadell again? Tomorrow is a Children's Ball, and I am devoted to Cecilia.

Text: Hyde Collection. *Address:* Sam: Lysons Esqr. / Cliffords Inn.

1. These are dated, from SJ, 24 and 29 October 1772: *Letters* 1:56–57, 59; Chapman 1:284–86.

2. HLP refers to the fact that Sir Thomas Salusbury left his Hertfordshire estate, which she had long expected to inherit, to his second wife, Sarah. For SJ's correspondence on this matter, see 3 and 12 November 1773: *Letters* 1:194–203; Chapman 1:384–90. In that of the 12th, SJ urged resignation. "Be alone as little as you can; when you are alone, do not suffer your thoughts to dwell on what you might have done, to prevent this disappointment. You perhaps could not have done what you imagine, or might have done it without effect."

3. SJ to HLT, 24 October: "When you wrote the letter which you call injudicious, I told you that it would bring no money, but I do not see how, in that tumult of distress, you could have forborn it, without appearing to be too tender of your own personal connections, and to place your unkle above your family. You did what then seemed best, and are therefore not so reasonable as I wish my mistress to be, in imputing to yourself any unpleasing consequences. Your unkle, when he knows that you do not want, and mean not to disturb him, will probably subside in silence to his former stagnation of unactive kindness."

Sir Thomas Salusbury (1708–73), LL.D., knighted 18 November 1751, was a judge of the High Court of the Admiralty. He had married, first, Anna Maria Penrice (1718–59); and then (1763) Sarah King, née Burrows (ca. 1721–1804).

For HLP's interpretation of her "Expectations" from Sir Thomas and her frustration "at the Instigation of his Lady," see *Thraliana* 1:54. See also Clifford, pp. 25 ff.; "Harvard Piozziana" 1:2–3; Hayward 2:10, 16–18, 19, and Sir Thomas's will, P.R.O., Prob. 11/992/447, proved 11 November 1773.

TO SIR ROBERT MURRAY KEITH

Hanover Square
15: June 1787—

Sir

I have the Honour to thank you at the same Time for your obliging Letter and for the care you have been pleased to shew that I should receive the Trifles seized at Franckenmarch: Lord Crawford did not fail in his troublesome Commission to bring them me perfectly safe,[1] and I have now no other Concern than how to express my Sense of your Politeness. To detain you any longer with Acknowledgments and Apologies would be however only giving you fresh Trouble, and a new Opportunity of shewing how patiently your spirit of serving a Countrywoman can endure Intrusions from Sir Robert Murray Keith's extremely Obliged / and very Obedient Servant / Hester L: Piozzi

Text: Brit. Mus. Add. MSS 35,538.227. Hardwicke Papers, vol. 190.

1. George Lindsay-Crawford (1758–1808), twenty-second earl of Crawford (1781). See HLP to Sir Robert Murray Keith, 15 March 1787, n. 1.

TO HESTER MARIA THRALE

Bath
7: July 1787

Dear Miss Thrale,[1]
I have very few Letters from you, and this last is an odd one. I had no Notion till I read it, that Cecilia was either generally unhealthy, or at this Time particularly ill: when we parted She made no Complaints: and Mrs. Stevenson—under whose Care I am told *You* placed her, said She was perfectly well. If London however disagrees with her—why is She there? I left her in the Country at Mrs Ray and Fry's School Streatham,[2] where She enjoyed the Air of her *native Place* and if you removed her thence, on pretence of Improvements which you now say are Trifling Matters at so early an Age—it will be found necessary perhaps some Day for you to produce your Authority for so doing.

That I am her Mother and Guardian appears by her Father's Will, which expresses that no Marriage made by her while under Age shall be held legal if it has not my Consent:[3] and it is no longer ago than last Month, that I was called with Mr Piozzi to the Chambers of an Attorney to sign Settlements and Papers relative to her Fortune. Now as you did not appear that Day in the Character of Parent or Guardian, I conceive the Laws of England do not consider you as such;[4] and I must add, that to bathe a lean growing Girl of large Expectations, whom *you* say is unhealthy—in the Sea, without more and nearer Medical Advice than the Isle of Wight would afford—seems somewhat a rash Step when taken by a young and single Lady who cannot pretend to the smallest Degree of Legal Power over the Child's Person. Your proposed Removal of her to some other School is in the same Strain—*We intend* &c. the Expression I acknowledge to be Kingly, but we do not feel a like disposition to recognise the Authority[5]—as I have the Happiness to be hers as well as / Your Affectionate Mother / H: L: Piozzi.

Text: Queeney Letters, pp. 250–51.

1. A response to Q's "strange Letter thanking me for my *polite Attentions* to Cæcilia, but observing that they were superfluous, for that *She* intended removing her from the School She is in, to another *further from me;* and that She should take her immediately away to the Isle of Wight" (*Thraliana* 2:685).

2. CMT had attended a girls' school, Russell House, at Streatham, run by Sarah Ray and Eliza Maria Fry between 1777 and 1801.

Sarah Ray (1722–1814) was the wife of Richard Ray (d. 1795), a wealthy "wood mason"; churchwarden of Saint Leonard's in Streatham, 1786–93; collector and assessor of taxes there. Their son Robert (d. 1837) was a barrister and trusted friend of the Piozzis. See HLP to PSW, 7 November 1792; "Streatham Land Taxes" and "Register Book of Burials, 1754–1812" (C.R.O., Surrey, Kingston upon Thames); also P.R.O., Prob. 11/1889/43 for Robert Ray's will, signed 22 June 1837, proved 1 January and 7 February 1838.

Eliza Maria Fry in October 1788 married Thomas Sainsbury, alderman of the ward of Billingsgate; sheriff of London (1780); lord mayor (1786). He died 10 May 1795 at Newcourt House, Devon, she on 14 December 1800. See *GM* 65, pt.1 (1795): 445; *GM* 70, pt.2 (1800):

1297. For Sainsbury's will, see P.R.O., Prob. 11/1262/409, proved 3 June 1795; HLP to Charlotte Lewis, 30 May 1791.

3. HT's will stipulates that CMT was to have the interest, dividends, and profits on her portion (twenty thousand pounds) of his estate if she attained twenty-one years, or if she married (prior to that age) with maternal consent.

4. During HLP's absence on the Continent, Q had constituted herself guardian of all her sisters.

5. Q replied to HLP's letter with comparable anger. HLP believed Q's reply "must . . . have been dictated by *Baretti* and so it probably was: it would have been scarce justifiable to send such a one to the last Woman who was hanged" (*Thraliana* 2:685–86). With this exchange of letters began an estrangement of six years.

TO SAMUEL LYSONS

Portsmouth
July 17th, 1787

Dear Mr. Lysons,

We have passed a very pleasant month driving about England, which I think grows more beautiful every day; so do Mr. James's children, who bid me give you a thousand compliments. I shall expect a world of news in return for my lean accounts of Stourhead, Wilton, Southampton, &c.[1] Pray do pick me up whatever can most interest me in particular, and bring it with you on Friday evening to Hanover Square, where we hope to arrive after seeing Payne's Hill, &c.[2] No signs of poor "Paulina's Adventures" in the "Monthly Review:"[3] I do think she is used very ill.[4]

Mr. Piozzi sends his kind regards, and bids you observe that he is always better than his word, and always comes home some little time before he is expected.

I am very sincerely yours, &c. / H. L. Piozzi.

Text: Bentley's Miscellany 28 (1850): 542. *Address:* Samuel Lysons, Esq. No. 17, Clifford's Inn, London.

1. The Piozzis spent a part of June and July on their first English "Tour . . . round by Bath, Salisbury, Southampton &c. We set dear Mrs Lewis down at Reading . . . and carried Count Martenengo a Venetian Nobleman about to see Sights: particularly the Shipping at Portsmouth which we English are justly proud of" (*Thraliana* 2:685).

The "Venetian Nobleman" was Giovanni Ettore Martinéngo Colleoni (1754–1830), of Brescia, who with the advent of Bonaparte was to have an active political career.

2. Painshill Park, an estate on the river Mole, near Church Cobham, Surrey. The grounds contain a lake of thirty acres.

3. See HLP to Parsons, 4 August 1786, nn. 6, 7.

4. When Merry left Florence in the spring of 1787, he found favor among London literary coteries and a market in the *World* for his verse. Yet the very people who were at first amused by him were soon disaffected, and his work (with the possible exception of the poem "Diversity") was not reviewed seriously. Still loyal in 1787, HLP was to break with Merry in January 1789. No longer tied by friendship, she could be objective about

the poetry of this "foolish Fellow" (*Thraliana* 2:741), his superabundance of "ornamented diction" and intellectual vapidity. See *British Synonymy* 2:277–78.

TO SOPHIA BYRON

Buxton Baths[1]
Tuesday 4: September 1787

Your beautiful Purse my dearest Mrs. Byron[2] has followed us quite hither,[3] bringing with it a sweet Proof of your obliging Remembrance, and I hope of your Health—for I am as earnest to know you are well, as to feel that you are kind. We have past some agreable Weeks at Guy's Cliffe[4] the seat of our Friends the Greatheeds, and from there have wandered about to see various places—Hagley,[5] Leasowes,[6] Keddlestone,[7] Chatsworth,[8] and a long *Et Cætera.*[9] Matlock[10] detained us longer than we intended, because we had the luck to find very pleasant Acquaintance,[11] but I have no heart of this Place from the first View of it: tho' the Buildings are splendid on the outside to what I left them 15 Years ago,[12] yet the Rooms seem calculated for Barracks only, or Apartments for Strolling Players. Well! the shorter Time we spend here, the sooner we shall get *to* Wales,[13] and *from* Wales; and the sooner we shall come home to see our dear Mrs. Byron, who I hope will be settled in Bolton Row[14] and glad to make comfortable chatting parties before Xmas. Mean Time do prevail on Yourself and write me a sweet Letter *a L'ordinaire* and direct To Bertie Greatheed's *Esq. Guy's Cliffe near Warwick;* we shall call there going back.[15]

Mr. Piozzi likes England vastly, and Cecilia seems a very dapper Traveller, She delights in Variety as most young Folks do—and we have shewed her a great deal in this little Tour.

I wish You would send me some News of Your Children or my Children, none of whom I know one Word about.[16]

Adieu and remember how much your Tenderness is felt, and esteemed, and desired by My kind Husband and by Your ever Affectionate / H: L: Piozzi.

Text: Ry. 546.1.

1. Buxton in Derbyshire, the highest town in England, at the center of the Peak District, is renowned for its climate and mineral waters. See *Thraliana* 2:690.
2. See HLT to Q [15 July 1784], n. 5.
3. The purpose of this journey, which took them as far as North Wales, was to gather new material for the second volume of *Letters.*
4. In Warwickshire (*Thraliana* 2:688).
5. Hagley Park was the seat of the Lytteltons. When HLT first saw the estate on 17 September 1774, she agreed that it was "indeed the beautiful spot it has been called. The house is spacious enough, well-decorated with pictures, and eminent for its commodiousness and disposition of the rooms" (*Welsh Tour,* p. 211).
6. In *Thraliana* (2:689) HLP described Leasowes as "charming beyond Expression . . . the retreat of a poor but tasteful Poet," i.e., William Shenstone (1714–63). In 1774 she had been more explicit, confessing "that if one had to chuse among all the places one has seen

the Leasowes should be the choice to inhabit oneself, while Keddlestone or Hagley should be reserved for the gardener to show on a Sunday to travelling fools and starers" (*Welsh Tour,* p. 213).

7. HLT had visited Kedleston Hall, Derbyshire, on 19 July 1774. The ostentatious structure (ca. 1760–70) was the residence of Nathaniel Curzon (1726–1804), cr. Baron Scarsdale (1761). It was designed by Matthew Brettingham (1725–1803) and James Paine (1717–89), completed by Robert Adam (1728–92) and his younger brother James (d. 1794). See *Welsh Tour,* pp. 173–74; Howard Colvin, *A Biographical Dictionary of British Architects* (London: John Murray, 1978), p. 52.

8. Chatsworth House, the principal seat of the dukes of Devonshire, stands close to the river Derwent. Begun in 1687, it is situated in an extensive park, elaborately landscaped, and replete with fine works of art. HLT in 1774 had been displeased with the artificiality of the estate, which to her was no more than a collection of amusing "bawbles" (*Welsh Tour,* p. 166).

9. This was essentially the route followed by the Thrales, Q, and SJ, as they made their way toward North Wales from July to September 1774.

10. Matlock Bath, Derbyshire, overlooks the narrow and precipitous gorge of the Derwent. Surrounded by cliffs and woods, it derives its name from three medicinal springs that became well known toward the close of the seventeenth century.

11. The Reverend Sandford Hardcastle (1742–88), rector of Adel, Yorks., who in 1780 married Sarah, née Delaval (1742–1821), dowager countess of Mexborough.

12. For Matlock on 13 July 1774, see the *Welsh Tour,* pp. 166–67.

13. The Piozzis and CMT reached Wales about mid-September, happy to be in their "own Country again" (*Thraliana* 2:691).

14. Mrs. Byron's will, proved 3 February 1791 and 28 June 1792, identifies her residence as "Bolton Row, Parish of St. George, Hanover Square" (P.R.O., Prob. 11/1201/54).

15. Despite the absence of the Greatheeds, the Piozzis on their way back to London stopped at Guy's Cliffe, where they remained until an ailing GP recovered his health (*Thraliana* 2:691).

16. Sophia Byron had nine children, of whom two are known to have died in infancy. Present at Admiral Byron's funeral in 1786 were John (1756–91), father of the poet and known as "Mad Jack"; George Anson (1758–93), captain in the Royal Navy. Her daughters included: Augusta Barbara Charlotte (d. 1824), now married to a naval officer, Christopher Parker (1761–1804); Juliana Elizabeth (d. 1788) married first to her cousin William Byron (d. 1776), and secondly to Sir Robert Wilmot (ca. 1752–1834); Sophia Maria; Frances (d. 1823), married to an army officer, Charles Leigh (ca. 1740–1815).

TO SAMUEL LYSONS

Manchester
Sunday 9: September 1787

Dear Mr. Lysons

You must forgive me for not writing sooner, we have been rambling about and I lost your Letter; the best way will be to direct this to London. Mr. Greatheed is sorry you could not come to Guy's Cliffe where he will always be happy in seeing you he says, but 'tis likely enough you may have met in Town before now, for he went up in Consequence of my urgent Advice to promote the bringing forward his Tragedy which is a very likely one to please the Publick, and should not be kept concealed.[1] In our Return home we shall call again at his charming Seat in

Warwickshire, and thither I would have you direct your Answer to this Letter. It was a great Gratification to me the being shewed Shakespear's Tomb, after seeing those of Virgil, Raphael, and the King of Prussia.[2] Since we were in that part of the World I have not been idle in endeavouring to swell Cadell's 2nd Volume for him,[3] with Matter less trifling than familiar Nonsense scribbled by myself a Dozen Years ago with little Notion of printing it heaven knows; and how the public will receive my Letters, tis certain I tremble to think: but the Promises and Anecdotes picked up at Lichfield[4] and Ashbourne[5] give me some hopes of making everybody amends.

Mr. Piozzi has been very well diverted in his little Tour, and likes Hagley Park vastly as a fine Specimen of English Taste, and Chatsworth house as a good Imitation of Italian Magnificence: but I have seen few Things superior to Warwick Castle[6] in the old Way, and Keddlestone in the new. The dear Leasowes are always delightful, and our British Alphæus and Arethusa's Marriage in Mr. Port's Garden at Ilam is singularly curious.[7] You would never have the Pencil out of your hand was you to perambulate Derbyshire, and surely Matlock by Moonlight is a first Rate View for a painter.

We met Mr. Parsons at Buxton, he esteems you much, and desires to cultivate your acquaintance; do not neglect him. This is a rich and populous and thriving Town: what did the people lament about so? And why did they say they were all o'ruining?

> Ungrateful Britain! dost thou call it *Ruin*
> To live as we do?——[8]

I find every place in a State of Improvement beyond my Expectation all over England; and Buxton is so fine I had not the least Recollection on't. The Report is that the Duke of Devonshire[9] has found a Silver Mine in the Mountains——that would indeed be a fine Thing. Farewell Dear Sir, we are going on to Liverpool, Chester, Flint, Denbigh and dear Bachŷgraig; then back thro' Wrexham, Shrewsbury &c. to Warwickshire again——and then to Town: Where all shall be settled for our *Spring Publication*.[10] Mean Time accept Mr. Piozzi's best Compliments with those of your faithful Friend / and Obedient Servant / H: L: Piozzi.

Let me find a Letter from you at Guy's Cliffe.

Text: Folger Library. *Address:* To / Samuel Lysons Esq. / Cirencester / Glocestershire. *Postmark:* MANCHESTER; SE 12 87.

1. *The Regent,* a forthcoming play in blank verse, with an epilogue by HLP. Despite her enthusiasm it did not open at Drury Lane until 29 March 1788. Thereafter it enjoyed only a modest success, with eight intermittent performances until 27 May 1788 and publication ca. 20 May *(Public Advertiser).* See HLP to LC, 9 October, n. 1; to Ann Greatheed, 2 April [1788], nn. 1 and 2.

2. A continuation of her "sepulchral tour."

Shakespeare's body lies under the chancel of Stratford's Holy Trinity church. On the chancel wall, as part of the monument, is a bust by Gheerart Janssen (Gerard Johnson). For a full description of the monument and the bust, see E. K. Chambers, *William*

Shakespeare: A Study of Facts and Problems, 2 vols. (Oxford: Clarendon Press, 1930), 1:90–91, 182–83.

Virgil's remains were transferred from Brundisium to Naples, which had been his favorite residence, and interred near the road from Naples to Puteoli (Pozzuoli).

Raphael [Raffaello] Santi or Sanzio (1483–1520) is buried under the dome of the Pantheon at Rome, beside an altar endowed by him with an annual chantry. On the wall is a plain slab with a Latin inscription by his friend Cardinal Pietro Bembo (1470–1547).

Frederick the Great is interred at Sans Souci. His "corpse, no longer animated by ambition, rests quietly in an unornamented silver coffin, placed in a sort of closet above ground . . . beside [the bodies] of his father and the great elector, as he is still justly called" (*Observations* 2:357; see HLP to SL, 3 February 1787).

3. This is HLP's response to a letter from SL, dated from Rodmarton 16 August 1787. "The first volume of the Letters was finished before I came away, except about half a dozen pages, and a good fairly printed volume it makes, tho' when bound it will not be so <thick> as you suppose.—how they will be able to fill up a second I do not know, unless you should be so fortunate, which I hope you will, as to procure some of these Litchfield Letters—Mr. Strahan's people think that with a good deal of what they call *driving out* . . . it is possible that the remainder including the verses may make about three hundred and fifty pages—but it will not I fear look very handsome, to have the second Volume printed so much more loosely than the first—you will say *so I comforted*" (Ry. 552.13). See n. 10.

4. Anna Seward (1742–1809), the Lichfield poet, agreed to help HLP find additional SJ letters, particularly those to his friend Hill Boothby between 1755 and 1756. They had been promised to JB but were not yet secured by him. Miss Seward applied to Sir Brooke Boothby for the privilege of transcribing the letters written to his sister. On 3 August 1787, she described to HLP her negotiations:

"The Hour in which I received your thrice welcome letter from Ashbourn, saw me at Sir Brooke Boothby's, vainly endeavoring to obtain his consent that you should have Doctor Johnson's letters to his late Sister immediately. . . .

"Sir Brooke persisted that, being his Son's property, he could not think himself intitled to sign their passport to you. I applied to him, imaging they might be left in his possession, the day you quitted Lichfield. He fancied his Son had taken them with him to France, and promised to give me a direction to him in a few days. This direction arrived last night; and I mean, by tomorrow's post, to urge Mr. Boothby to send me, as soon as possible, his consent that you should transcribe them. You shall hear from me immediately on my receiving an answer from Mr. Boothby. There can be no good reason why he should refuse at my earnest request what a few weeks past he voluntarily offered" (Ry. 565.1).

The only letter readily promised HLP during the Lichfield visit was a copy of one to Joseph Simpson (1721–ca.73), the son of an early friend of SJ. It was given by Simpson's cousin, Mary Adey (1742–1830), who said that since she had supplied JB with a copy earlier, she saw no reason to deny one to HLP. See Hyde, *The Impossible Friendship*, p. 122; Mary Adey to HLP, 29 October 1787 (Ry. 892.14); Clifford, pp. 308–10.

The principals, other than Anna Seward, are Hill Boothby (1708–56); her brother Brooke Boothby (1710–89), fifth baronet (1787); and her nephew Brooke Boothby (1744–1824), sixth baronet. The SJ-Boothby correspondence is at the John Rylands Library.

5. At Ashbourne, Derbyshire, HLP met Dr. John Taylor. He made her no "Promises" although he possessed papers written by SJ and held on deposit the letters to Hill Boothby. On 19 September, Anna Seward wrote: "I will not delay a single hour after I have received [Boothby's] assent, to transmit it to yourself, and to Doctor Taylor; but all is likely, in future, to be discord between *him*, and the Boothby's. He accuses Mr. Boothby of having forfeited his word in an affair, which the Doctor believes material to the good of the little Town he lives in. Since Mr. B[oothby] went abroad letters have mutually passed on this subject which will be laid up, *not* in *lavender*, but in wormwood" (Ry. 565.2).

Not until 13 October did Dr. Taylor forward the Boothby letters to HLP, with a caveat: "Dr. Johnson's Mental Powers and extreme good Heart, all Men very well know, and his

Enemies acknowledge; but I shall be greatly grieved to see the ridiculous Vanities and fulsome Weakness's which he always betrayed in his Conversation and Address with his amiable female friends exposed; and I cannot forbear to entreat you to change your Resolution about printing these Letters" (Ry. 892.13).

6. Warwick Castle stands high above the Avon. While the battlemented walls and towers are of the fourteenth and fifteenth centuries, its interior was largely commissioned by Fulke Greville (1554–1628), first baron Brooke (1621), who was granted the castle in 1604 by King James I. When HLP saw the castle, it was surrounded by a splendid park and garden. In a greenhouse is the marble "Warwick vase" of the fourth century B.C. that once belonged to Hadrian's villa at Tivoli, Italy. For a description, see *The Antiquities of Warwick and Warwick Castle; extracted from Sir W[illiam] D[ugdale's] Antiquities of Warwickshire. To which is added . . . a detail of the Earl of Leicester's arrival at Warwick . . . in the Year 1751. And also an account of Queen Elizabeth's reception in Warwick, in 1572* (Warwick, 1786).

7. John Port, formerly Sparrow (d. 1807). HLP's metaphoric joke relates to the Greek myth in which the river Alphaeus joins the fountain of Arethusa at Syracuse. The British version occurs near Ilam, Staffs., at the conjunction of the Manifold and Dove rivers. See *Welsh Tour,* p. 165.

8. A play on lines spoken by Lothario in Rowe's *The Fair Penitent* 4.1: "Unjust *Calista!* dost call it ruin / To love as we have done. . . ."

9. See HLT to FB, [24] June 1784, n. 3. He had spent large sums of money on the improvement of Buxton. For example, he underwrote the building of the Doric-styled Crescent during 1780–86. The silver mine to which HLP refers was probably associated with Diamond Hill, so named for the quartz crystals in its rocks.

10. *Letters* was published 8 March 1788. Its second volume had been expanded not only by the Boothby correspondence (pp. 391–400) and the letter to Joseph Simpson (pp. 402–4), but by further anecdotes (pp. 378–90), five letters to Francesco Sastres (pp. 405–12), and one to Charlotte Cotterell, later Lewis (pp. 400–402). Also included in this volume as an expedient afterthought were SJ's Latin verses to Dr. Thomas Lawrence (1711–83), HLP's translation of them, and SJ's and her joint translation of the "Metres" of Boethius (pp. 415–24). See *Poems,* pp. 257–63, 275–77.

TO THE REVEREND LEONARD CHAPPELOW

Hanover Square
Tuesday 9: October 1787

Your Spies dear Sir are always watching I fancy for Opportunities that their Employer may do Acts of Politeness——this last was a very *sweet* one, at least when you did it; but Mr. Piozzi was detained by a little Fever in Warwickshire and we never got to London till late last Night. I wish you were in Hill Street, for I have much to say about literary Stuff, and no body in Town to talk to except dear Mr. Greatheed, whose Head is full of his own new Tragedy, which will fill everybody's Mouth too when it once appears.

Our Tour has been a very fine one, somewhat too long perhaps; for nothing will do when drawn out into too much length. Let me remember my own Precept while writing, and not be too tedious in sending the sincere Thanks and Compliments of my Husband and myself for so very charming an offer. The Truth is we make a little Dinner for Mr. and Mrs. Greatheed and *Mrs. Siddons* (you understand me—and I must not speak out, because the Secret is not my own but a Friend's—) next Week;[1] and shall be glad of a pretty Thing for so pretty a purpose. How your Spies found *that* out I cannot imagine, but they are dear vigilant Creatures that's plain.

Where does Mr. Shard live?[2] And where shall I send his Book?[3] that good Man will hate me at last, and I'm sure I love him dearly.

Here is no War coming sure[4]——the Country is so beautiful and so cultivated now, and if they press our Men and send 'em fighting—Oh I cannot bear the Thoughts of such a Thing. and all for what?

Let us break off here and let me assure you of Mr. Piozzi's best respects with those of Dear Sir Your much Obliged and faithful / H: L: Piozzi.

What is Diss in Norfolk?[5] I do not know to direct.

Text: Ry. 559.6.

1. The dinner grew out of Murphy's advice to HLP on 3 September: "You will be so good as to present my Compliments to Mr. Greatheed, and assure him that whatever I can do, I shall most chearfully contribute. Your grand Question is what is to be done with the piece? Considering the present Managers of the Theatre, I am afraid I cannot solve your difficulty. If there be a Leading female Character, you know that nobody can do it justice but Mrs. Siddons. With her my acquaintance is very slender. You know her, I believe. . . . Now if in the course of the winter, you can contrive to make her one of your party, when I am to have the pleasure of seeing Mr. Greatheed at your house, it may be possible to interest Her in the Business" (Yale University Library).

The dinner was arranged for the 12th. But no stratagems were necessary. The actress agreed to take the female lead because she had lived in 1771–72 with the dramatist's mother, Lady Mary, as a maid-companion. Despite her misgivings about the play, SS even persuaded John Philip Kemble to take a major role, and together they energetically advertised the coming production. See *Thraliana* 2:693.

2. See HLP to SL, 11 May 1786, n. 8.

3. See HLP to LC, 1 September 1786.

4. In September 1787, a Prussian army, supported by England, destroyed the power of the pro-French "Patriot" party in the United Provinces and returned the Stadholder, Willem V (whose wife was of Prussian royalty), to his former power. This was followed by the signature of an Anglo-Prussian convention early in October. HLP correctly intuited that events such as these were harbingers of further military diplomacy: of Anglo-Dutch and Prusso-Dutch treaties of alliance on 15 April 1788 and, more important, of a defensive alliance between Prussia and Britain on 13 August 1788.

See HLP to LC, 7 January 1795, n. 8.

5. A market town in Norfolk on the river Waveney, some twenty miles southwest of Norwich. LC was rector at Royden, near Diss (1777–1820).

TO SAMUEL LYSONS

Wednesday Night
[ca. 10: October 1787][1]

I enclose you some trifling Letters from Johnson——and some too melancholy for me to endure the reading of—They are on my dear Son's Death:[2] if your

Heart is as hard as that *Alexander's* we talk so much of in our Letters,[3] *You* perhaps may like them.

Write me word what you do with *my* Stuff, and pray take care to scratch Names out. Yours is a very serious Trust, and tho' you live to be Lord Tetbury, you will never again have the heart of any one so completely in your hand to rummage every Sorrow out, as you now have that of your / humble Servant / H: L: Piozzi.

It comes in my head seeing these Letters from me dated Bath, that I must have a Heap from him somewhere which we have not yet looked over: when I have a quiet Moment I'll Search again——and then if we find enough of *his* mine may be excused.

Text: Hyde Collection. *Address:* Mr. Sam: Lysons.

1. Arriving in London late Monday night, 8 October, HLP wrote to SL in all likelihood on the 10th, i.e., the "Wednesday Night" which she hastily dated her letter.

2. Henry Salusbury Thrale, aged nine years and one month, died on 23 March 1776 and was buried in Saint Leonard's Church, Streatham, on 28 March.

SJ wrote a consolatory letter on the 25th, and the still grieving HLT replied on 3 May (*Letters* 1:307–9, 316–19). See also Hyde, pp. 151–53.

3. Thomas Alexander (fl. 1748–90), "the chymist in Long Acre," had accused HT of fraud and threatened legal action. In the role of a go-between, HLT had sought SJ's counsel. See their correspondence between 9 and 16 March 1773 (*Letters* 1:74–75; Chapman 1:308–12); Hyde, p. 60; Clifford, p. 97.

TO SOPHIA BYRON

Hanover Square
11: October 1787

My dearest Mrs. Byron

Must believe me when I assure her that I have not been 48 Hours in possession of the kind Letter I begged, and was so truly happy to receive. Mr. Piozzi was taken ill of a Feaver at Shrewsbury,[1] and we drove on to Guy's Cliffe in one Day—which increased it—The Letters which amounted to 15 Mrs. Greatheed had carried to London with *her,* who had been unexpectedly called thither, and detained. *We* remained in Warwickshire, but desired her to keep them for us against we should get to Hanover Square, where I thank God we are at last arrived——but shall stay only to finish my Book-Business with Cadell,[2] and then to Bath for the gloomy days before Xmas, which your Friendship will comfort, and your Conversation enliven.

I am glad to hear so favourable an Account of your Health: our Tour was a delightful one,[3] and you can scarce think how happy it made me to see dear Wales again; and to find my Husband so caressed by my oldest Friends—he is satisfied with *My* Country, and in Love with its Mountains and Castles; more resembling Lombardy to be sure than any part of England does—and so Lady Carlisle[4] would say too.

She has filled Mr. James with Admiration of her Talents; *his* Letter which I opened after yours, contains nothing but Praises of her Conversation. Our old Acquaintance Murphy however dines with us tomorrow, and then we shall drink *your* Health, and say sweet Things of Mrs. Byron who does well to love *me* who have never ceased to *love her.*

My Misses are cold and cruel, and so their Sweethearts say as well as their Mother: I wish some of them were once well married.[5] Cecilia is not like them, either in their good or ill Qualities, I hope you will think her improved when we come to Bath. I would put her to school if any thing was taught at a School:[6] but a mere Roost for Ignorance to perch upon, and put its Head under its Wing for years together——is too great a Waste of life which for ought we know may be short:——and should not sure be artificially curtailed. There are other Reasons too, which we will talk over when we meet, for you now see only one Side of the Question.

It was Cator's Mother not his Wife who died while we were away[7]—Well! here's Chat enough for the present: My Husband sends you his best Respects, so does Cecilia——Adieu, and remain assured of my Affectionate Regard. My dear Mrs. B. has no truer Friend yet than her faithful Servant / H: L: Piozzi.

Text: Ry. 546.2.

1. See *Thraliana* 2:691; and HLP to Sophia Byron, 4 September. The Piozzis had stopped at Shrewsbury to visit HLP's cousin Margaret Owen.
2. See *Thraliana* 2:694. Editorial details concerning the *Letters* were completed by the last week in October.
3. See *Thraliana* 2:690–91.
4. Margaret Caroline, née Leveson-Gower (1753–1824), daughter of the first marquess of Stafford. She had married Frederick Howard (1748–1825), eighth earl of Carlisle, in 1770.

Of the relationship between the Howards and the Byrons: Isabella (d. 1795), sister of Sophia Byron's husband, had married on 8 June 1743 Henry Howard (d. 1758), seventh earl of Carlisle (1738). Their son Frederick was Sophia's nephew and Lady Margaret Caroline her niece.

5. HLP alludes to the three eldest daughters, of whom two approached marriage gingerly and one not at all. ST was to marry Henry Merrik [Merrick] Hoare (1770–1856) on 13 August 1807. Q, after a courtship of sixteen years, married on 10 January 1808 Admiral George Keith Elphinstone (1746–1823), cr. Baron Keith (1797 [Ireland]; 1801) and Viscount Keith (1814). SAT had a brief affair with a married artist, William Frederick Wells (1746–1836), but remained unwed. See Hyde, pp. 271–76.
6. Not only did HLP quarrel with Q over the school CMT was to attend, but she feared the loss of her youngest child's affection if they parted. For a time CMT was educated at home, because HLP—as self-styled Niobe—found it "so very comfortable to have *one* at least saved out of *twelve*" (*Thraliana* 2:686).
7. Mary Cator (d. 26 August 1787). The daughter of John Brough, she had married on 11 February 1728 John Cator the elder (d. 1763) of Ross, Herefs., and Bromley, Kent.

Cator's wife was Mary, née Collinson (d. 1804).

TO THE REVEREND LEONARD CHAPPELOW

Hanover Square
Thursday 18: October [1787]

Dear Sir
The eating of your delightful *Birds* will be to me by no means the best part of the Pleasure——a Feather in one's Cap is always desirable you know, and these are quite *Shining* ones. In short you are amazingly good and kind, and your Praises shall be ever said and sung by Mr. Piozzi and myself—who are I think no Gluttons neither, except of Friendship; and yours is particularly desirable.

When I asked what was Diss in Norfolk, I little thought it was the Residence of all the excellent *two legged* Creatures that can be named. Our Peacock however shall be the Dinner of some Foreigners; a Venetian Count and Countess very handsome and very rich, who are upon their Travels thro' England, France, and Germany.[1] People begin now to adopt your Notions and mine, that Great Britain is at last a Glorious Country after seeing all that Europe has to shew: may this secret Expedition by its Success render her still more so![2]

With your good help I hope we shall get dear Mr. Greatheed's Play upon the Stage after Xmas——when it is once there, all the Difficulty will be *to get Places.* But I had more need be thinking of *my own* Stuff, and beg Mercy for those Letters of Mrs. *Thrale's* which are mingled among Dr. Johnson's. Oh do come and help them along a little for the Regard you kindly bear to Mrs. *Piozzi.*[3] We are going to Bath for a while, and I shall leave my Work all done ready for Cadell to do his best with.[4] He may think himself happy that Mr. Boothby has given me Johnson's letters to his Aunt——but there is in the World a Treasure I could *not* get, very valuable indeed; in the Possession of Dr. Taylor of Ashburne, over whom I have vainly tried every possible Influence. He is stopt by scruples only, not Unkindness: he would not give it I believe to any mortal Man.

Adieu Dear Sir and direct your next kind Letter here, after the 1st of November Bath will be the Abode for some Weeks of your Ever Obliged and faithful humble Servant / H: L: Piozzi.

My Husband is ashamed of these Packets of Eateables, but bids me give ten Thousand Compliments and Thanks.

Text: Ry. 559.7. *Postmark:* 19 OC. 87.

1. Conte Giacomo di Francesco Maria Carrara (1742–1810) and his wife whom the Piozzis met in Venice and found "agreeable enough" (*Thraliana* 2:654).

2. From the *Daily Universal Register,* 17 October:

"Rear Admiral Sir Edmund Affleck, who commanded the fourth division on the ever-memorable 12th of April, 1782, will hoist his flag on board his old and favourite ship the Bedford . . . that ship having orders to get in immediate readiness to receive him and suite. Her destination, it is whispered, will be to the East Indies [to quell a potential uprising there]."

The rumor was untrue and Affleck (ca. 1723–88), rear admiral of the Blue since 1784, did not sail.

3. HLP's implicit admission that she planned to rewrite still more of her letters to SJ. An examination of the watermarks reveals that she probably revised several at this time. See Clifford, p. 311.

4. HLP and GP arrived in Bath shortly before or on 5 November. The *Letters* was therefore press ready before the end of October. See also *Thraliana* 2:694.

TO SAMUEL LYSONS

Monday noon [22 or 29 October 1787][1]

I am ashamed to plague you so my Dear Sir, but my Papers are ready before I hoped, and if you could come either to Dinner, or directly after Dinner *today* it would do nicely.

We have here 2000 *good Lines*, fairly and *more* than fairly counted; besides my own Letters, and a pretty long Preface and all the Verses.

Tomorrow Morning at nine o'Clock I *depend* on your Friendship and Company if not this Evening. Adieu much yours / H: L: Piozzi.

Text: Hyde Collection. *Address:* Mr. S: Lysons / No. 17——or No. 11 / Clifford's Inn.

1. On 18 October HLP had written LC that she had nearly finished editing the *Letters*, that she intended leaving it for Cadell and departing for Bath by 1 November. Since this letter is dated Monday, it could have been written either 22 or 29 October.

TO SAMUEL LYSONS

Alfred Street *Bath*
17: November 1787

Dear Mr. Lysons—

I was glad to see your Letter and am much pleased with the Contents; but do not let your Health suffer by your Diligence;[1] he who would gain too much is apt to lose some other way: I am happy that Business flows in so fast however.

Mr. Coxe is kind in remembering us,[2] his Brother looks very well this Year;[3] the Bishop of Peterboro' will surely have some great Compensation.[4]

The Authors of the World are vastly civil,[5] but I have not yet been able to get a Sight of the Paragraph.[6]

Miss Lees are charming Women, and appear to deserve their very uncommon Success.[7]

With regard to my own Book if no one thinks more about it than I have done since I saw you, Woe betide Cadell! If anybody has *stolen* a Letter of mine, they will add little to their Guilt, tho' much to their Shame by publishing it.[8]

Bath is a beautiful Town,[9] but I cannot quite agree with those who would make me believe it a great City neither, while I can readily walk from one End to the other, and back again.

The Jameses are well, and kind, and handsome; and send their Love to you with Mr. Piozzi's Compliments and those of Dear Sir / Your faithful Servant / H: L: Piozzi.

Text: Hyde Collection. *Address:* Samuel Lysons Esqr. / No. [17] Cliffords Inn / London. *Postmark:* <   >.

1. SL entered the Inner Temple in 1784 and served under Robert Walton (d. ca. 1794), a pleader before the King's Bench and Common Pleas. In 1787 SL began his practice as a special pleader.

2. See HLP to SL, 4 November 1785, n. 7.

3. The widely traveled William Coxe was at this time vicar at Kingston upon Thames (1787–88).

For his recent publication, see HLT to Q, 1 July 1784, n. 5.

4. On the basis of Bath rumor and SL's gossip, HLP was able to predict an "advance" for Bishop Hinchliffe.

Vocal in the Lords, he had annoyed the government with his liberalism. To speed his removal as master of Trinity College, Cambridge, a post that he had held since 1768, the authorities offered him (and he accepted) in September 1788 the rich deanery of Durham on condition that he resign the mastership.

5. The *World,* a daily newspaper, was started on 1 January 1787 by Edward Topham (1751–1820), and it ended on 30 June 1794. He was aided in its direction by Miles Peter Andrews (d. 1814) and Charles Este (1752–1829).

HLP received extensive and favorable notices in the *World,* largely through the friendship of Este, whose varied career included acting and the study of medicine. In October 1776 he was ordained deacon and, in December priest; but soon he turned to journalism. See his biography, *My Own Life* (London, 1787), pp. 4–17; *The Fulham Papers in the Lambeth Palace Library,* a catalog compiled by William Wilson Manross (Oxford: Clarendon Press, 1965), 38:11, 41; HLP to Sophia Byron, 3 August [1789]. For Este's will, see P.R.O., Prob. 11/1765/23, proved 28 January 1830.

6. The paragraph was a puff for the forthcoming *Letters,* followed by another for JB, under the rubric "Coming Books," 15 November:

"Mrs. Piozzi is dear to elegance and taste. Her work, as exquisite as *Johnson*'s genius can make it, is in such forwardness, as to be out, with the *Laurel,* &c. at Christmas. With Johnson's Letters, we hope she will not be sparing of her own.

"Mr. Boswell too, who knows from his former successes, the high tide in the Calendar, goes auspiciously into the Press, when Mrs. *Piozzi* comes out of it. This work will be a Quarto, divided into thirds. One, the *Letters* of Johnson. One, the Maxims and Bon-Mots of Johnson.—One, a *Biography* of this transcendental man."

7. The four Miss Lees, Bath residents, were Charlotte (fl. 1748–1800), Sophia (1750–1824), Harriet (1757–1851), and Anna (ca. 1760–1805).

The author of *The Recess* (1783–85), a historical novel in three volumes, Sophia conducted "Mesdames Lees, Ladies Boarding School, Belvidere House, Lansdown Road." (The school was to close in 1803.) Their quarters had been described by George James to HLP, 14 June 1786 (Ry. 555.108): ". . . a most sweet situation it is and an excellent house for their purpose—besides large rooms for their business they will have ten good bed chamber[s] and every other convenience. They are worthy—clever Women—*and thrive* and deserve it."

Harriet Lee was the most literary of the sisters. In 1786 she had published *The Errors of Innocence,* a novel in five volumes; her comedy *The New Peerage* had opened at the Drury

Lane on 10 November 1787, where it was to be performed on nine nights (prologue by Richard Cumberland).

For Charlotte, see HLP to PSP, 30 January 1793, n. 10; and for Anna, HLP to LC, 14 November 1805.

8. An allusion to her chatty letter to SJ (28 April 1780) that began "I had a very kind letter from you yesterday, dear Sir, with a most circumstantial date." It was published in *Boswell's Johnson* 3:421–23. Cryptically in the margin of her 1816 edition, she commented: "This is the famous Letter with which Mr. Boswell threatened us all so; He bought it of Francis the Black for half a Crown to have a little Teizing in his Power" (3:456). See also Chapman 2:349–50.

9. Cf. *Thraliana* 2:697.

TO SAMUEL LYSONS

Bath Thursday
6: December 1787

Dear Mr. Lysons.

I received your Letter at the same Moment one came from Mrs. Greatheed;[1] pray do me the Favour to wait on those amiable and worthy Friends and carry them my best Compliments. They live in Holles Street Cav: Square No. 4.—

If Dr. Lort does not make haste to mend in London, it would be wise to come hither, where there is comfortable Society, and good Accommodation, and Assistance for ill Health——no Place like pretty Bath, and you know I always said so.[2]

Mrs. James says She must have more particulars from you before She can execute your Commission:[3] her good Husband and mine are both a little Gouty just now, but they *hop* after charming Miss Lee, and court her very prettily not with *Dance* indeed, but with *Song*.[4]

I will write to Dr. Farmer[5] with all my Heart, if it will do the Book any Good; as to Mr. Cator's Name I am perfectly indifferent about it to be sure; but it may as well stand.

I will try to get the Letter you speak of, but it was from you that I heard of it for the first Time.[6]

Accept our best Compliments Dear Sir, and present them to Dr. Lort. Mr. Murphy's Inaccessibility[7] will save us a Copy, for I trust all the Contributors, and *sub* Contributors will have somewhat like a natural Right to be presented with the Book—of which doubtless Mr. Cadell is well aware.

Adieu and believe / me your sincere humble servant / H: L: Piozzi.

Text: Hyde Collection. *Address:* Sam: Lysons Esqr. / No. 17 / Cliffords Inn / London. *Postmark:* DE < >.

1. Both letters are missing.

2. A "croaker" by self-admission, HLP worried about the seemingly fragile health of any friend. She had first met Dr. Lort as early as 1775 at Streatham Park, and the years since then proved his loyalty and friendship. She was grateful for his correspondence while she and GP were abroad, for his welcome in March 1787, and above all for his help

in the production of the *Anecdotes*. See *Thraliana* 2:787 for the value she placed on their association.

3. An allusion to a portrait of HLT begun some time after 1780, when George James had settled in Bath. But he did not complete it for several years. Writing to HLP on 23 May 1788, he reminded her: "When you was here last you gave us reason to hope you would come this way again about this time of the Year. . . . we will get you a shady house—so cool and so pleasant and then I could finish my picture so pretty and then we would have a print made of it to put before your next publication" (Ry. 555.112).

SL must have hoped the print could be used in the *Letters*. Failing that, it could appear in the "next publication," the *Observations*, about which HLP was already thinking.

James completed the portrait after 1 July 1788, when the Piozzis briefly visited Bath on their way to Exmouth. It has, however, never been reproduced, and its location today is unknown. See HLP to SL, 18 July [17]88, n. 6.

4. Harriet Lee.

5. Dr. Richard Farmer (1735–97), master of Emmanuel College, Cambridge. HLP wrote in vain, for Edmond Malone (1741–1812) had already procured SJ's letters to Farmer for *Boswell's Johnson* (2:114; 3:427).

6. HLP did not know where to turn for the letter. On Friday the 24th [Aug. 1787] she had written from the Swan Inn to Francis Barber (ca. 1745–1801), SJ's "faithful servant," for "the favour of seeing [him] some Time today if not very inconvenient" (Hyde Collection). During their visit he said nothing about the letter or its sale. In fact, the letter was already JB's.

7. An HLP circumlocution. Because Arthur Murphy anticipated his own work, *An Essay on the Life and Genius of Samuel Johnson, LL.D.* (1792), he contributed neither anecdotes nor letters to HLP.

TO THOMAS CADELL

Hanover Square, Wednesday,
23rd. January [1788].

Mrs. Piozzi sends her compliments and her preface to Mr. Cadell, and begs that he will neither say nor think that her negligence delays the publication.[1]

Text: Bentley's Miscellany 28 (1850): 522. *Address:* Mr. Cadell, Bookseller, Strand.

1. HLP had reported to SL [5 April 1787] and n. 5, completion of the preface to *Letters* but delayed more than nine months before sending it to Cadell. Abetted by SL, she took further time to revise her own letters and to search for additional correspondence from SJ to others. About the beginning of May 1787 work on the edition was therefore put aside for a time.

TO SAMUEL LYSONS

31: January [1788]

Dear Mr. Lysons

I recollect a gross Mistake in the printed Sheet you showed me this Morning—it was in a Letter of my own from Bath, in which *Torquato Tasso* is mentioned, and the Reply he made to one who asked him what use he made of his philosophy.[1]

Do me the favour to let me have that Sheet again, and believe me much your Obliged Servant / H: L: P.

Mrs. Siddons is charming.[2]

Text: Hyde Collection. *Address:* Sam: Lysons Esq. / No. 17. Cliffords Inn.

1. On Good Friday, 18 April 1783, HLT had learned that the four-year-old Harriet (Henrietta Sophia) had died; and she feared the imminent death of an ailing CMT. Terrified, she repeated Cator's admonition that she "must'nt sit *philosophically* at Bath, but come to London . . . to see them buried I believe [as Harriet was at Saint Leonard's Church].—I am already so altered that the people here don't know me—my *Philosophy* has not therefore benefited my Complexion at least—but like Tasso one should learn from it to bear with *them.* (Ry. 540.108; Chapman 3:14).

So she had written to SJ that night (with an addendum on the 19th). But in the published version she emended her statement to read: "Was it not Torquato Tasso who was asked once what use he made of his *philosophy?* and did he not reply thus? *I have learned from it to endure your malice?* It ought to have been my answer to [Cator's] epistle of to-day" (*Letters* 2:253–54).

2. SS agreed to play Dianora in *The Regent*, but rehearsals were not yet begun, and the "Play [was] in no sense advanced" since HLP's planning dinner in October (*Thraliana* 2:705). See SS to TSW, 1 September 1787 (Wickham 2:18–20); HLP to LC, 9 October 1787, n. 1.

TO ELIZABETH LAMBART

Hanover Square
Tuesday 19: February *1788*

My sweet Mrs. Lambart's[1] kind Letter was received only Yesterday; I had flattered myself you were coming up to Chelsea, and then We should have met often——dear Mrs. Byron too was in great hopes of seeing you soon—but this Panick Terror about your Son[2] has carried you away, and now God knows whether we shall get a Bit of your Company all Summer. Why will [you] suffer such Fears to overwhelm the Heart of a General's Lady? Mr. Lambart will get well, when he sits quiet for a few Weeks: his Youth will easily overcome such Shocks, while the Power of Vegetation is yet strong, and active to recover harder Blows than he has yet received—What says our Dear Mr. Hay[3] to him? was it he who sent him to Bristol?[4] I trust so.

Mrs. Lewis will be grievously disappointed; She was expecting you at Reading in your Way up,[5] and I had written to beg of her not to delay you there too long. You do not do Justice to poor dear Mrs. Lewis, she esteems you greatly and though her Mind has not the bright Shine upon it which you require in those who have the Happiness to please you; it is very elegant, pure and tranquil: and polished quite to smoothness——tho' without the *Speenham Land* Varnish.[6]

I hope the Letters of Dr. Johnson now very soon to be published,[7] will amuse

Samuel Johnson, ca. 1778, the Streatham portrait. Painted by Sir Joshua Reynolds. ***(Reproduced by permission of the Tate Gallery.)***

your Care; and Sooth your Sorrow into a pleasing Remembrance only of our dear Sir Philip,[8] whose Memory I shall ever cherish as of a very true, tender, and partial Friend. Miss Dodd[9] visits me very kindly, but we have not met. I know not where to send proper Enquiries after Lady Jennings and Miss.[10]

Adieu dear Madam and assure yourself of my kind Husband's Respectful good Wishes united with the sincerest Regard of your / Affectionate and faithful old Friend / and humble Servant / H: L: Piozzi.

Text: Ry. 550.21.

1. For Elizabeth Lambart, widow of General Hamilton Lambart, see HLT to Q [27 June 1784], n. 10.

2. Edward Hamilton Lambart had been suffering from pleurisy. Mrs. Lambart's concern was aggravated by the deaths of her other young children: Charles (d. 1773) and Elizabeth (d. 1783). See the M.I. in the Bath Abbey chapel to the right of the high altar on the south wall; also HLT to Q, 29 June, n. 2; to FB, 30 June 1784, n. 7.

3. Alexander Hay (1732–1801) is listed in the Bath directories as an apothecary. He had begun his practice in that city at least as early as 1778 on the North Parade. By 1784 he had moved to 3 Bladud's Buildings (Walcot parish) where he remained until his death. From 1801 his practice was to be carried on by his son George Edward (1778–1844) at the same address.

4. That is, Bristol Hotwells, at this time a spa considered effective for treating respiratory ailments.

5. Charlotte Lewis now resided at Reading to be near her sister Frances Cotterell Ewing (as identified in Mrs. Lewis's will: HLP to SL, 7 December 1784, n. 11). HLP had last seen her friend during the first week of January, when the Piozzis were returning to Hanover Square from Bath. At that time HLP "miscarried of a daughter" in Mrs. Lewis's house. "Oh how that Event did vex me!—*Ten* times more than it vexed my Husband, to whom it certainly was More Important—but he seemed never to regret *his* Loss. . . . It was a mortifying Circumstance" ("Harvard Piozziana" 2:100; cf. *Thraliana* 2:704).

6. HLP calls ironic attention to a town near Newbury in Berkshire, notorious for the economic distress suffered by its rural poor in the wake of the enclosure movement. Adverse conditions there would soon give rise to reformation of the poor laws, through the so-called Speenhamland System (1795).

7. The sheets for the two volumes were printed by February. But at that time the Warren Hastings trial was distracting attention from literary ventures. The *World* (3 March) explained that "amongst other effects of the Trial it has delayed the publication of Mrs. Piozzi's Letters—nobody had then time to read" (cf. *Thraliana* 2:709).

Not until Saturday, 8 March, were the *Letters* published. Cadell printed two thousand copies, of which eleven hundred had been sold before publication (*Thraliana* 2:711).

8. Sir Philip Jennings Clerke had died on 14 January. See HLT to FB, 30 June 1784, n. 6.

9. In 1789 (probably March) Edward Hamilton Lambart was to marry his affluent cousin Frances Dodd (1755–ca. 1854), daughter of the late John Dodd (1717–82) of Swallowfield, M.P. for Reading and lieutenant colonel of the Berkshire Militia. See *Thraliana* 2:748–49; *Eton College Register, 1698–1752; GM* 52 (1782): 95, and 59, pt.1 (1789): 371; *Walpole Correspondence,* to William Cole, 2:299–300.

10. Lady Jennings was Anne (ca. 1724–97), daughter of the late Colonel Richard Thompson of Jamaica and Coley Park, Reading, and the widow of Sir Philip. The "Miss" is Diana Jennings, Mrs. Lambart's only sister.

TO ANN GREATHEED[a]

Wednesday
2: [April 1788]

For God's Sake tell me what can be the Matter with the Dear Siddons's: something seriously dreadful I fear: Will it affect the Tragedy tomorrow?[1] Pray let me know that I may inform my Friends.

We are full of Care and Grief for this Affair and its possible Consequences—— How near is Misfortune to Triumph: and yet My dear Mr. and Mrs. Greatheed are *so good:*

Oh write directly, and *pray pray* come this Evening at seven o'Clock and tell particulars. / Ever Your H: L: P.

Text: Yale University Library. *Address:* No. 80 / Pall Mall.

1. *The Regent* was first presented at the Drury Lane on 29 March 1788 with SS, John Philip Kemble, and William Barrymore (1759–1830) in the leading roles.

By the morning of 2 April HLP had received SS's letter reporting her "Indisposition" and need to withdraw from the play after only two performances.

TO ANN GREATHEED[b]

Hanover Square
2: April [1788]

I'm glad it's no worse after all, Siddons's Letter terrified me:[1] This is only a *Hitch* in the Business which will end in still more Triumph and Delight——'Tis the little Murmur repeated.[2] Do not be saddened, but bring Mr. and Miss Greatheed,[3] and beg them to excuse separate Cards——come early, and receive all the Consolation that true Friendship and Sympathy can give—from Your truly Affectionate / H: L: Piozzi.

It was not *that* Mrs. Hamilton to whom I was engaged for tomorrow.[4] I saw the Merrys today. Come before 7: and let us be as happy as we can: all will go well at last.

Text: Yale University Library. *Address:* No. 80 / Pallmall.

1. By now HLP had learned that SS had "lost a live child"—Elizabeth Ann, aged six— and suffered a miscarriage. See *Thraliana* 2:714; Manvell, p. 141.

Notwithstanding such difficulties, *The Regent* was reopened on 26 April. On 27 May, it was again "unavoidably deferred . . . on Account of the sudden and severe Indisposition of Barrymore." During the summer, the play was to enjoy a brief Dublin revival: see the *World*, 4 and 8 July; the *Morning Post*, 5 July.

2. HLP, who was present, recorded that the play opened "with prodigious Eclat"

despite misgivings about the near-violence of the fifth act. From hearsay evidence, she concluded that "the Play . . . was more crowded & more applauded the 2d Night than the first." See *Thraliana* 2:713.

The blank verse tragedy was for the most part well received. According to *The Times*, 5 May, "The Regent, on Saturday evening, proved what fine writing and fine acting will do—even in May: The House was remarkably brilliant, and at the latter account—crouded." On 20 May, the day of publication, the *Public Advertiser* announced that *The Regent* was "Now performing with Universal Applause." And the *Critical Review* (13 [1788]: 324) pointed out: ". . . so many years have elapsed since any thing like a tolerable tragedy has appeared, that it is with peculiar pleasure we hail the present production. The Regent, tho' very far from a faultless piece, tho' there are several great inconsistencies in the constitution of the plot, and harsh quaintnesses in the diction, yet professes so much of the genuine spirit of the *effera vis animi*, as to raise it far above the orb of its compeers."

3. Brother of Ann Greatheed, Richard Wilson Greatheed (1749–1832) studied medicine in the West Indies before coming to England to practice. At the time of his death, he resided in Nottingham Street, London. See P.R.O., Prob. 11/1806/634 (proved 31 October 1832); HLP to Q, 26 July 1785, n. 7.

Bertie's aunt, Mary Greatheed (d. 1790), now living at Guy's Cliffe, was buried in the parish church of Saint Mary's, "in the Borough of Warwick in the county of Warwick" (P.R.O., Prob. 11/1192/241; proved 29 May 1790).

4. HLP intended a visit to Rachel Hamilton, née Daniel (d. 1805), that did not materialize: on Thursday, 3 April, HLP noted in her "Pocket Book," "Nothing but Disappointments." The two ladies met only on 7 April, when "Mrs. Hamilton [came] to Supper" (Ry. 616.2).

For the Hamilton family, see HLP to Sophia Byron, 2 June [1788], n. 5.

TO ANN GREATHEED

Written late o'Thursday Night
[10: April 1788][1]

My dear Mrs. Greatheed: I can live no longer without some Account how your poor Husband's Health does.[2] Our sweet Siddons will mend now every day, and get about again, but he must try to be chearful mean Time—indeed he must.

Mrs. Hamilton has written the sweetest Letter in the World: every body is sorry, and I think every body kind. No real Damage will be done at last[3]—only a Fright, and a Vexation. The dear generous Publick will make ample Compensation, see if it will not: all I ever said about this Play came true remember and I now say All will End well and happily as the Tragedy does—the happier for our previous Alarm. Write 3 Lines of Comfort however / to your Affectionate / H: L: P.

My Husband says nothing about *Mondaccio* and *Maladet*.

You know we called today when you were out.

Text: Yale University Library. *Address:* Mrs. Greatheed / No. 80 / Pallmall.

1. HLP wrote on Thursday, 10 April, before visiting Bertie Greatheed the following Sunday. See HLP's "Pocket Book" for 1788 (Ry. 616.2). She brought him a new prologue and epilogue to celebrate *The Regent*'s reopening. But they were "shelfed" by SS and Kemble (*Thraliana* 2:693, 715).

2. Greatheed was so discouraged that he never again wrote for the theater.

3. HLP correctly anticipated a majority of favorable reviews for *The Regent*. She also relied on Greatheed's many friends to support the production. When the play reopened on 26 April she was there and again on Saturday, 17 May. According to *The Times* (19 May), "A very brilliant shew of company graced this theatre on Saturday evening, in compliment and for the benefit of the author. . . . Most of Mr. Greatheed's friends were at the theatre."

TO SOPHIA BYRON

Monday 2: June [1788]

My sweetest Mrs. Byron

has ever experienced the Vicissitudes and varieties of Life in an uncommon Degree: I am more glad of the new Friend[1] almost than enraged at the *Old Enemies.*[2] Have you seen how *I* am treated by that unextinguishable Viper Baretti?[3] who like Aaron the Moor in Shakespear's Titus Andronicus, digs up people's dead Friends, and sets them at their doors——*even when their Sorrows are almost forgot.*[4]

Mean Time new acquaintance are kind as you say—and we past a sweet parting Night at the Hamilton's[5]——poor dear Siddons however looks like very death.[6]

Mr. Bridgeman *is* married,[7] and the Cake came from *them,* perhaps Lady J. Russel's Illness makes 'em deny it.[8]

Be as well as ever you can my charming Friend, and never forget how you are adored by my Husband, loved and esteemed by your Obliged and faithful / and Affectionate / H: L: Piozzi.

Do you see a House advertised as if on purpose for us in last Saturday's Paper at Exmouth? And do you [see] a Man advertising to find his Mother? how very unlike our Misses he must have been formed.

Text: Ry. 546.3.

1. HLP alluded to the *English Review* (11 [1788]: 352–60), which had at least qualified praise for the *Letters.*

2. Among the "old enemies" was the *Morning Post* (14 March), which accused HLP of converting "her private epistles into hard *cash;* so that every letter sent her by Dr. Johnson had a *double value*—the *value* of *informing,* and the value of a *bank note.*"

Another "enemy" was the *Original Star & Grand Weekly Advertiser* for 7 May 1788: "Here then we behold *friendship* sacrificed to *vanity,* and the weak ambition of becoming the topick of publick conversation prevailing over the most sacred ties. If obligations of the most valuable nature were ever conferred on the Doctor by Mrs. Piozzi, they are all cancelled by this false step."

For other hostile reactions, see Clifford, pp. 314–21.

3. The first of Baretti's three "Strictures" had appeared in the *European Magazine* for May. Like the others that were to be published in June and August, it was a personal assault, although purportedly "On Signora Piozzi's Publication of Dr. Johnson's Letters." He mocked the second marriage of "La Piozzi, as my fiddling countrymen now term her . . . [who] in the great wisdom of her concupiscence . . . has degraded herself into the wife of an Italian singing master." Baretti accused her of denigrating SJ by the greedily motivated publication of a trivial correspondence. She was, further, an unfeeling mother who nearly killed Q by urging her to take *"tin-pills"* against medical advice.

For the "Strictures," see the *European Magazine* 13:313–17, 393–99; 14:89–99.

4. *Titus Andronicus* 5.1.135–40.

5. The Hamiltons consisted of the Reverend Frederick (Frederic) Hamilton (1728–1811), vicar of Wellingborough, Northants., archdeacon of Raphoe (1757–72). He was the second son of Archibald Hamilton (1673–1754), who was in turn the seventh and youngest son of William Douglas (1634–94), third duke of Hamilton (1660). In 1757 Frederick Hamilton had married Rachel Daniel (d. 1805). They had two daughters and one son: Jane (d. 1810), who in 1798 married Joseph George Holman (1764–1817), the actor; an elder daughter Elizabeth (d. 1846), the wife of John Stratford (d. 1823), third earl of Aldborough (1801); Robert, who died unmarried in 1809. See Hamilton's will: P.R.O., Prob. 11/1520/1241. For Robert Hamilton, *GM* 79, pt.2 (1809): 1179.

6. Between January and the end of May, she had performed such demanding roles as Cordelia in *King Lear;* Chelonice in Hannah Cowley's *Fate of Sparta;* Kate in Garrick's adaptation of *The Taming of the Shrew;* Dianora in *The Regent;* and Cleopatra in Dryden's *All for Love.* But what most altered her appearance at this time were the personal tragedies of early April.

7. Orlando Bridgeman (1762–1825) had married on 29 May Lucy Elizabeth (1766–1844), daughter and coheir of George Byng (1740–1812), fourth viscount Torrington (1750). Bridgeman became second baron Bradford (1800), cr. viscount Newport and earl of Bradford (1815).

8. Georgiana Elizabeth, née Byng (d. 1801), was the daughter of the fourth viscount Torrington. On 21 March 1786 she had become the wife of John Russell (1766–1839), afterwards sixth duke of Bedford.

TO SOPHIA BYRON

Reading
8: June 1788.

My dearest Mrs. Byron's sweet Letter followed me here, and filled me with real Concern, in which I have two true Sympathizers, for both my husband and Mrs. Lewis are sincerely affected with your Story.[1] When Mr. and Mrs. Byron and their dear Children arrive, you will get Comfort sure: pray make them for your sake accept our best Regards.[2]

We are going on to Bath when this kind Lady will let us; and then to Exmouth[3] where I mean to shut myself up and mind my Book—May it *but* please![4] from your tender Partiality I shall rely on one Pleasure——that of pleasing you by it, for though the *Ground* is *beaten* very much to be sure——if one keeps to *Windward* (a'nt it) the Dust need not quite blind one from seeing and distinguishing some new Objects on the Way.[5]

Mean Time do write me word how you get thro' *your* Difficulties; *mine* don't

Frances Burney (Mme d'Arblay), ca. 1784–85. Painted by E. F. Burney. *(Reproduced by permission of the National Portrait Gallery.)*

hurt me much, yet why should I *affect* to appear *unaffected?* when a Person of the Name of Burney is supposed to delight in publishing Libels against me written by a Man whom I so studied to oblige as I did for a year together, that spiteful Mr. Baretti.

When Burney and Baretti threat one so[6]—from what friendly Offices can one ever more expect the return of Kindness?[7]

Adieu my dear and continue to love us both——you are among those whose Affection I could not bear to part with. Tell Mrs. Lambart that I will write to her when a Moment can be stolen—but let her remember that I have with me for the constant Occupation of my Thoughts a Husband, a Child, and a Book. / Ever and Ever Yours / H: L: Piozzi.

The Man and Maid are like other Men and Maids, only a little handsomer.

Text: Ry. 546.4.

1. Mrs. Byron's second daughter, Juliana Elizabeth, had died on 15 March at Osmaston, Derbyshire, the family seat of her husband, Sir Robert Wilmot (HLP to Sophia Byron, 4 September 1787, n. 16). Mrs. Byron never recovered from her grief (*Thraliana* 2:739).

2. Mrs. Byron's younger son, George Anson, and his wife Henrietta Charlotte, née Dallas (d. 1793), had been married in 1780. They had a daughter, Julia Maria (d. 1858), and were at this time planning a move from the Continent to Bath.

3. After stopovers at Reading and Bath, the Piozzis were to make a "coasting Journey" to Exmouth, where they resided from the end of June until late in October (*Thraliana* 2:718–20).

4. The basis of *Observations* was two folio notebooks, the journals in which HLP recorded facts and impressions during the course of her Italian and German travels, 1784–87 (Ry. 618). Then, during two months in Exmouth, she elaborated these details in seven notebooks, essentially the rough draft of *Observations* (Ry. 619). The final stage, which occupied her until about 10 November (*Thraliana* 2:719–20), was a fair copy for the printer in three volumes (Ry. 620–22).

5. HLP's variation on the proverb "He that blows in the dust fills his eyes with dust" (Tilley, D648).

6. Until HLP died, she erroneously believed the younger Charles Burney was editor of the *European Magazine* who contracted for Baretti's "Strictures."

Charles Burney, Jr. (1757–1817), a classical scholar, was at this time a schoolmaster at Hammersmith (1786–93), having received his M.A. from Aberdeen in 1781. In 1808 he was to receive an M.A. from Cambridge and to be ordained priest. By 1810, while directing a school at Greenwich, he became chaplain to George III and by 1811 held several livings simultaneously, favoring the vicarage of Saint Paul's, Deptford.

See HLP to Sophia Byron, 8 June [1789], n. 7.

7. A veiled allusion to HLP's break with her eldest daughters.

TO SOPHIA BYRON

Exeter
24: June 1788.

My dear Mrs. Byron

This is to give my sweet Friend notice that today we take possession of our Palace—alias Cottage by the Seaside; where if I can but be diligent in proportion to my good Intentions, I will try to get you some Amusement for a future hour. Mean Time do not forget to tell me everything interesting *from* yourself and *of* yourself. My husband went to the post yesterday for Letters from Mrs. Byron he said, and came back disappointed because there were none. You used to be more punctual. Sure no harm has happened: calm my Anxiety dear Madam, and write soon, pray do. From this Midsummer day to Michaelmas Day you must direct to me at Mr. Cumming's, Strand, Exmouth, Devon. where we hope to save Money, but it will not be by living at the Inn in this City;[1] for Salthill is more reasonable in its Prices.[2]

Well! 'tis Time to talk of something else; and do tell me what that Report meant, if it meant any thing—that Miss Thrale was to marry Coxe——The Writer of that Name is abroad,[3] and Hippisley Coxe[4] is dead they say——I suppose Queeney gave him one of my *Tin Pills.*[5]

The poor old Duchess of Montrose too![6] I long to hear how She died, and whether She reached 100 or no. Remember we are out of the World and wish to hear what goes forward in it.

Farewell dearest Madam once more, and remember your distant but ever obliged and / faithful / H: L: Piozzi.

My Husband and Cecilia join in best Compliments and Respects. We have been dawdling away our Time at Bath to get here on Midsummer day.

Text: Ry. 546.5.

1. George Cummings (fl. 1765–90) owned a cottage called Whiterows on the Strand, which was then and is now Exmouth's main street. Whiterows, which the Piozzis occupied, was but one house away from the costly Globe Hotel, owned in 1788 by William Pomeroy (C.R.O., Devon).

2. HLP's joking reference to a tradition once associated with an Eton festival, the "Montem." Every third year, on Whit-Tuesday, the scholars would gather at a mound near Slough to collect "salt money" from passersby. See Brand 1:432–41.

3. William Coxe. See HLP to SL, 4 November 1785, n. 7; 17 November 1787, n. 3.

4. John Hippisley Coxe (1743–82) grew up in Stone Easton, Somerset. On 4 May 1759 he had been admitted to Lincoln's Inn. However, he decided against the study of law and instead matriculated (1760) at Trinity College, Cambridge. After receiving his B.A. in 1764, he resided at Downside, near Bath, until his death in January 1782.

5. HLP's wry designation for one of Baretti's assaults upon her in the first of his "Strictures."

Tin pills were made of the powdered metal. "Take of tin, six pounds. Melt it in an iron vessel, and stir it with an iron rod until a powder floats on the surface. Take off the powder, and when cold, pass it through a sieve." The pills were popularly prescribed as an antihysteric, antihectic, and as a purge for worms. See *Encyclopaedia Britannica*, 3d ed., s. v. "Pharmacy."

6. Lucy (b. 1717), a daughter of John Manners (1676–1721), second duke of Rutland (1711), married on 28 October 1742 William Graham (1712–90), third duke of Montrose (1742). She died on 18 June, aged seventy-one.

TO THE REVEREND LEONARD CHAPPELOW

Exmouth, Devon
28: June 1788.

Dear Mr. Chappelow

I feel half angry, and quite afflicted that you never write to us: in Revenge this Letter to ask how and what you do, will cost you eight Pence I suppose, by coursing after you from Hill Street to Norfolk, and back again.

Do write, or you shall have more eight pences to pay—and tell me if you recollect the name of the very very old Church at Padua, whose Walls were covered with Cimabue's Pictures——and we said they were like Dante's poetry.[1] And do tell me if it's true that the Harebell, that red Weed which grows in all our Hedges,[2] is peculiar to England or no; and whether you think there was ever a Weeping Willow on the Banks of the Brenta——I say there was none.[3]

This is a heavenly Country, but a wretched Town; just such a place as I wanted to sit down quiet in: and wish for your Knowledge of Botany. But if I ever do live in the Country as much as my Wish leads me to it, Natural History shall be made amends, for I will study nothing else.

My Husband sends you his Love and Compliments. He rides, and walks, and I think looks exceeding well; Cecilia grows too fast——Oh *do tell* if you know anything of her eldest Sister; the World will have it She marries Mr. Coxe——I thought he was abroad with young Portman;[4] tell me for Pity if you know anything, for one cannot help being anxious, / I am ever with the truest esteem / Dear Sir / Your Faithful and Obliged / Servant / H: L: Piozzi.

P.S. Questo luogho è solitario ma fà bene dopo li rumori della gran dominante, e se il nostro amico Mr. Chapelow voleva, veniva qui a passar qualche tempo con noi, abbiamo una bella casa, e vi è una cameretta in piena libertà, si mangia poco in quantità, e non si muore di fame, io quasi mi lusingho di vederlo, ma se siamo privi di questo piacere, almeno non ci privi delle sue nuove, che ci sono sempre carissime. Addio.

Text: Ry. 559.8. With a postscript by GP. *Postmark:* JU 30 88, JY 2 88.

1. "The beautiful church of Santa Giustina, the ancient church adorned by Cimabue, Giotto, &c. where you fancy yourself on a sudden transported to Dante's *Paradiso*" (*Observations* 1:224; HLP to Q, 17 September 1785, n. 10).

There are, however, no known Cimabue paintings in Santa Giustina. HLP probably meant the series of Cimabue's paintings (since destroyed by fire) in Padua's Carmine Church, which she visited.

2. Both harebell and foxglove are marked by bell-shaped flowers, the former bright blue, growing on English heaths and pastures. Foxglove also grows easily in England, but its colors range from purple to purple crimson. HLP acknowledged confusing the two flowers when she wrote to LC, 13 August 1788.

3. LC assured HLP that there were no willows along the Brenta. She therefore "longed to see the weeping willow planted along this elegant stream; but the Venetians like to see nothing weep I fancy" (*Observations* 2:183).

4. In 1788 the Reverend William Coxe was abroad with Henry Berkeley Portman (ca. 1768–1803), the first son of Henry William Portman, of Orchard Portman, Somerset, and of Bryanston, Devon. See *GM* 73, pt.1 (1803): 294.

TO SOPHIA BYRON

Exmouth, Devon
Sunday 29: June 1788.

My sweetest Mrs. Byron!

And how glad I was to see your dear Hand again! our Heads were filled with silly presagings, no Mortal can guess why; so I wrote to enquire of Mrs. Lewis—who was tolerably sure *not* to know.

Of all Evils I least apprehended those of drowning or starving—and indeed such odd Disasters are rather good Things to talk about afterwards, than any real Evils. My Fear was, lest Care should be likely to drown you, and the Lawyers to leave you no Appetite.[1] Do pray tell me the Result of all, the Moment it is known to yourself. We had just such a Mad shower as you describe while I was last at Bath[2]——so violent, that coming up Stall Street, and meeting the Torrent accumulated at the Corner of Paragon Buildings, by all that poured down Lansdown hill; I really felt a momentary Terror lest the Chairmen should be taken off their Feet before I could reach York House[3]——and while I looked at the River, my Head grew giddy, so excessively rapid was its Motion. Here however we are in a State of almost too perfect Tranquillity—Who would ever think my dear Mrs. Byron a native of these Western Counties[4] where I am told that 'tis never very hot, nor very cold; that it never thunders and never snows: I could scarce have imagined so quiet and steady a Climate; our View is beautiful, just as you say, opposite Star Cross,[5] and looking on Powderham Castle,[6] nothing can be lovelier when the Setting Sun gilds our elegant *Lake* for it does not look like Sea from these Windows at all, but when one takes a short Walk, more Extent is opened to the Eye. Ours is a thatched *Palace,* the rest are *Huts*——and God knows we are in more danger of Fire than Water, for touch us with a Candle, and our *City* would be burned down in ten Minutes I'm perswaded.

Mr. Piozzi is very nervous, but the Air agrees with his Voice so, that the increase of its Compass is to me almost miraculous: Your pretty Nest of Nightingales too! little half-fledged Warblers! how I should like to hear them.[7] I thank God for the Comfort My dear friend is at least likely to have in that Branch of her Family.

God preserve the Chancellor![8] and God save the King![9] but those who are made ill by eating Strawberries or even Turtle, were not very well before I have a Notion.[10] The old Duchess who hung on the Tree till She dropt withered off,[11] was not so easily affected by Trifles I dare say.

Mean Time I do not labour so as to hurt myself I assure you: ten pages o'Day of long folio paper is all I pretend to, and on Sundays *you see how I rest my weary fingers.*[12] Mr. Este and two or three other Friends spirited me up to this Folly—— if it does not succeed I shall fall hard upon *them*, how very agreable that Mr. Este is! do you see him often at Mr. Hamilton's?—they were beginning to love one another when we left London and I hope for all their Sakes they are much together now, and you with them.

Here is *no Society at all:*[13] so one ought to read and write and sing for no Pretence can be made of wanting Time. Cecilia seems weary enough of herself and her Companions; but we shall have a fine Visit to make on Fryday, for lady Duntze and her three Daughters came Yesterday to court Acquaintance, and invite us to their House 12 Miles off.[14]

Farewell! my Husband is coming home from his solitary Ride, I will go and tell *him* now I have no Paper left to tell *you* how much I am / Yours and his affectionate H: L: P.

Text: Ry. 546.6.

1. Having dissipated most of the fortune of his second wife, Catherine, née Gordon (1765–1811), since their marriage in 1785, "Mad Jack" returned from France with her prior to the birth of George Gordon. The victims of John's profligacy were Catherine and his mother, both of whom were being dunned persistently by the lawyers of his numerous creditors. See HLP to Sophia Byron, 4 September 1787, n. 16.

2. For a vivid account, see *GM* 58, pt.2 (1788): 652–53.

3. The York House and Hotel, located in the York Building on George Street, was known for its hospitality and, as described in *The New Prose Bath Guide* (1778), was "an excellent Hotel, the Only House of Reception, which is situated in an open airy Part of the city" (p. 62). See also HLP to PSW, 11 February 1791.

4. Mrs. Byron was born in Carhayes, Cornwall.

5. Starcross, a watering place on the Exe estuary, is a ferry station for Exmouth.

6. Powderham Castle, an ancient Norman edifice, was in 1788 the seat of the earl of Devon.

7. Mrs. Byron's grandchildren in 1788: John's Augusta (1784–1851) and George Gordon (1788–1824); George Anson's Julia Maria (ca. 1785–1858); Frances Leigh's George (d. 1850); Juliana Elizabeth Wilmot's Robert John (1784–1841); and Augusta Barbara Charlotte Parker's Peter (1786–1814) and Margaret (ca. 1787–1802).

8. Edward Thurlow (1731–1806), first baron Thurlow of Ashfield, Suffolk (1778), Baron Thurlow of Thurlow, Suffolk (1792). As lord high chancellor, he presided over the lengthy trial of Warren Hastings, beginning on 13 February.

9. In early June George III, in addition to a bilious attack, suffered the first symptoms of a mental disorder for which he was urged to try the Cheltenham waters. The symptoms were not alleviated by early autumn when SS, visiting Windsor, was handed by the monarch a sheet of paper that was blank except for his name. She reported the event "to the Queen, who was duly grateful for this dignified proof of her discretion" (Campbell 2:128–29). See also Jesse 3:32–34; Olwen Hedley, *Queen Charlotte* (London: John Murray, 1975), p. 140.

10. HLP faults William Wilberforce (1759–1833), who by 1787 had become nominal leader of those M.P.'s advocating abolition. Despite her cynicism, he was dangerously ill

in the winter and spring of 1788. He recuperated slowly in Bath, while Pitt was leading the debate in the Commons, begun 9 May, on the slave trade (Stanhope 1:369).

11. HLP's allusion to the recently deceased duchess of Montrose.

12. HLP was at this time writing the *Observations*.

13. Or at least, as she commented unenthusiastically, "What there is to be *had*—we *have it*" (*Thraliana* 2:718). Those whom she identified were:

"The Staffords from New Norfolk Street," i.e., Edward Smith [or Smythe] Stafford (1747–1802), originally of Maine in Ireland, an army colonel, and high sheriff, county Louth; his first wife Frances, née Palmer (d. 1790). They had been married on 25 July 1776; she was the niece of Elizabeth Stanley, née Hesketh (1694–1776), countess of Derby. See *AR*, "Chronicle," 19 (1776): 210.

"Ld Huntingdon"—*styled* Lord [Francis] Hastings (1728/29–89) until 1746, when he became tenth earl of Huntingdon. Among other honors, he had served as bearer of the sword of state at the coronation of George III (22 September 1761) and as lord lieutenant of the West Riding of Yorkshire (1762–65).

"Lady Betty Cobbe and her daughter"—Elizabeth Cobbe, née Beresford (d. 1806), was the daughter of the seventh earl of Tyrone. In 1755 she had married Colonel Thomas Cobbe (1733–1814), M.P. for Newbridge, county Dublin. Their daughter was Catherine, who in 1788 would marry Henry Pelham (1759–97), second son of the first earl of Chichester. For the marriage of Thomas Cobbe and Lady Elizabeth, see the *Appendix to the Twenty-Sixth Report of the Deputy Keeper of the Public Records and Keeper of the State Papers in Ireland* (1895), p. 166 (P.R.O., Ireland).

"Mrs Gould," also of the Exmouth set, was probably Mary, née Stillman (fl. 1770–92), the wife of Nicholas Gould (1745–1823), of Frome Bellet, Dorset, and Milbourne, St. Andrews.

14. Frances (d. 1801), daughter of the late Samuel Lewis, "an eminent merchant of Tiverton," was the wife of John Duntze (ca. 1735–95), "respectable merchant of Exeter," whose seat was at Rockbere, Devon. They were married in March 1757 and had three sons (John, James Nicholas, and Samuel Lewis), and three daughters (Frances, now married to John Burridge Chalwith; Charlotte Lewis, and Elizabeth).

Created baronet (8 November 1774), Sir John was M.P. for Tiverton (1768–95).

See his will, P.R.O., Prob. 11/1257/157, proved at London 13 March 1795; *GM* 60, pt.1 (1790): 474–75, and 65, pt.1 (1795): 174–75; *AR*, "Chronicle," 37 (1795): 53.

TO SAMUEL LYSONS

Exmouth
9: July *1788*.

Dear Mr. *Lysons*

This is a very quiet Place, and from it I write to you for News, as we see little, except The Tide coming in and going out; and hear little except that there will be an Assize Ball such a Day at Exeter, and all the pretty Lasses will be there. Sir John Duntze and his Family are our best Country Neighbours, but 12 Miles is a long way to drive; Mr. and Mrs. Stafford of New Norfolk Street live here in the Town, and of Course are our kindest and most conversible Companions, as here is nobody else *but* them however if I remain idle, that Idleness will be without Excuse, for something must be done even in one's own Defence.

Do not let me lose your Correspondence, but tell me something, *any* thing you find interesting and give my Loving Compliments as the ordinary People *here* say, to your good Brother. Tell me above all what the truly wise, and learned, and Rational people (Dr. Lort for example) think of the Pamphlet giving an account of the Devil's Exploits at Bristol.[1]

Direct to Mr. Cummings House, Exmouth, accept Mr. Piozzi's Compliments and Cecilia's / and believe me Dear Sir / Your faithful Friend and / Obedient Servant / H: L: Piozzi.

Text: Hyde Collection. *Address:* To / Sam: Lysons Esq. / No. 17 Clifford's Inn / London. *Postmark:* JY 11 88.

1. The incident occurred on 13 June in Temple Church, Bristol, when the Reverend Joseph Easterbrook, vicar of the Temple, tried to exorcise George Lukins, a tailor of Yatton. The tailor "was violently convulsed upon the exorcists [thirteen in all] singing a hymn, and the voices of various invisible agents proceeded from his mouth uttering horrible Blasphemies—a 'Te deum to the Devil' being sung by the demons in different voices whilst the ministers engaged in prayer." After a two hours' struggle the devil departed and the patient was delivered. See *Sarah Farley's Journal,* 21 June. The exorcists were ridiculed by one Samuel Norman, a surgeon of Yatton, "who stated that Lukins . . . a clever ventriloquist, had begun his imposture in 1770 by alleging, in the course of fits of howling and leaping, that he was bewitched, and had from time to time renewed his exhibitions of pretended torture" (John Latimer, *The Annals of Bristol in the Eighteenth Century* [1893; reprint, Bristol: George's, 1970], pp. 483–84).

The pamphlet read by HLP is one of the following, all printed in Bristol in 1788: *Appeal to the public respecting G. L., called the Yatton demoniac,* by Joseph Easterbrook; *Great apostle unmask'd; or, a reply to Mr. Easterbrook's appeal, in defence of his demoniac, G. L.,* by Samuel Norman; *Authentic Anecdotes of G. L., the Yatton demoniac, etc.,* by Samuel Norman; *Narrative of the extraordinary case of G. L., who was possessed of evil spirits for near eighteen years; also, an account of his remarkable deliverance in the Vestry-Room, of Temple Church, in the city of Bristol . . . with Mr. Easterbrook's letter, annex'd, authenticating the particulars which occurred at Temple-Church.*

See also a review of Norman's *Authentic Anecdotes,* in the *English Review* 13 (1789): 228.

TO SOPHIA BYRON

[Exmouth]
Sunday 13: [July 1788.]

My dear my kind Mrs. Byron was very friendly and obliging in saying that now at least *half* her heart was at rest: The Furniture will follow, and then all will be settled and the Tormentors—tormented in their Turn.[1] Let your Health be now your only Care; for your Son's sake[2] and mine, who loved you always—and will love you for ever. London in the Summer is a cheap Place, without being a dull one; *some* Society you are morally certain of, and that a less laboured one than in Winter: People are more *en Corset* in hot Weather, and tell their Thoughts with less reserve. The Hamilton's House is to me a charming one, their Partialities are strong, and we have a large Share I know. My Husband is delighted beyond Measure at Your Triumph,[3] and bids me tell you that he is to have Leave of Absence as soon as the 25: of this Month is over[4] and then he will come and see you. Poor Soul! I am really grieved for him, here is not even the distant Hope of a

Companion for him, and *I* am always employed. The Visit to Rockby[5] was charming; I had not seen an old English Baronet in his Country Seat so long, it renovated my Youth, and sent me back to the Year 1760, when I lived just the same life as Miss Duntzes do now I suppose;[6] for they were all preparing to enjoy the Assize Ball at Exeter next Tuesday, and made us promise to be of the Party—so then I shall be able to tell you whose Feathers were highest, whose Gown was best trimmed &c.

Here have been long-continued heavy Rains, and we now wish for bright Weather to ripen and carry our Corn. Mr. Piozzi laughs at my facility of accommodating myself to every Place: *here* I bathe and write, (by the by the 1st Volume[7] is done) and go to Bed at 10 o'Clock, and comb my Hair clean out of the Powder, washing it every Morning in the Sea and on Sundays tell my Friends at a Distance how I love them. Let me dear Madam hear from you very often, and continue to love your amiable Namesake Miss Weston: She has Sincerity, Good humor, and Conversation-Talents all in a very eminent Degree.[8] I will write to her one of these Days: Apropós Mrs. Lambart will no longer have Reason to regret my Neglect of *her* old and las<ting> Friendship. Poor Mrs. Lewis is in Agonies over her Daughter—without Reason I earnestly pray, for the Loss would kill her, and She has surely suffered enough[9]—and may be permitted to dye in Peace.—

I have like you got rid of *half* my Cares by finishing the 1st Volume but 'tis neither copied nor corrected, and what's left to do is the hardest Work; but if Mr. Piozzi leaves me I will be *double diligent*. Pray be kind to him and remember he is quite the dearest Part of Your ever Obliged and Affectionate / H: L: P.

Is Mr. Hamilton *Honorable* from being Son to Lord Archibald?

Text: Ry. 546.7.

1. Sophia Byron was relieved that the John Byrons had decided to settle at Aberdeen. The "Tormentors" were John's creditors. In all likelihood the furniture did not follow them to Aberdeen since Catherine was forced to live in lodgings with her infant.
2. George Anson Byron.
3. See HLP to Sophia Bryon, 21 October 1788.
4. Following the anniversary of their wedding, GP was "to go for a Week's Business & Pleasure to London" (*Thraliana* 2:718).
5. Lord Duntze lived at Rockbere, Devon.
6. As HLS she had spent long periods at various landed estates: Offley Place; her grandmother's in East Hyde; Llewenny in Flintshire; Combermere Abbey in Cheshire. (The last two belonged to Mrs. Salusbury's brother, Sir Robert Cotton.)
7. Of *Observations*.
8. PSW (1752–1827) was known by 1785, at least to Anna Seward, as the "graceful and eloquent Miss Weston," a leader of "ingenious and charming females at Ludlow, in Shropshire." She resided with a widowed mother, but they had little in common. PSW's literary pretensions were distant from her mother's interest in domestic chores and gossip. In 1788 they moved from Ludlow to Queen Square, Westminster, not far from the Piozzis at Hanover Square. PSW occupied herself in part by being governess to a "young charge." See *Seward Letters* 1:82, 256.
9. Charlotte Lewis was greatly concerned about the health of her only daughter, Sarah. See HLP to Sophia Byron, 1 September [1789].

TO SAMUEL LYSONS

Exmouth
18: July [17]88.

I thank you very kindly dear Mr. Lysons for the friendly Letters I received from you to day: the Writer of the enclosed was very judicious as well as very good natured about the Newspaper Letter——He did just as I could have wished him to do.——Who in the World is he?[1]

You will have fine Diversion in your County this Year——find some Way to get your Glocestershire drawings seen by the King when he is upon the Spot; he knows what good Drawings are fast enough. I hope he will not lose the Sight of Bath and Bristol: nor Hagley Park, nor Warwick Castle: What a Holyday Summer he has got this year![2]

I wish that nasty Impostor may get the punishment he deserves—but what is bad enough for him?[3] Dr. and Mrs. Lort are going abroad it seems,[4] and every body is taking their Flight to someplace: London will be a Desart, yet I think Mr. Piozzi has a Mind to try whether it will not afford something better than Exmouth at worst.——He has a fortnights Furlow out and home and will bring me some News back I hope, and I shall shew him if I have been diligent the while.

Adieu, and pray write to me, you see the World considers us as Friends, do not let it be mistaken.

The Assize Ball at Exeter shewed us an Acquaintance of yours, a Mr. Hollwell[5]—we like him much.

Farewell my good Sir, and love the Jameses, they never forget you; and Mr. James has made a very fine Portrait[6] indeed of / Your faithful / Friend and Obedient Servant / H: L: P.

Text: Hyde Collection. *Address:* Samuel Lysons Esqr. / No. 17: / Cliffords Inn / London. *Postmark:* JY 19 88.

1. The *Morning Herald* (30 June) printed "Gregory's" attack on *The Regent*. He "found it in language, in poetry,—in plot, more vulgar, more languid, and more inartificial, than the most contemptible production of any" of the works of "*Gibbon, More,* [and] *Pratt.*" On 7 July in the same paper, Gregory was answered by "C.": "It becomes every Critic . . . to exhibit to public view not only the dark and faulty shades of a piece upon which he professes to animadvert, but, if such there are, its beauties and excellencies also. . . . I trust it will appear unnecessary for me to endeavour to make manifest, what is already strongly impressed on the minds of every liberal reader and spectator, viz. that in this play, there are some blemishes, and many beauties—the whole plot is managed with great art,—and exhibits the finer passions in an eminent degree; a finer display of the horrors of a base and guilty soul, depicted in the character of Manuel, perhaps modern times have not produced."

2. On 12 July George III went to Cheltenham for the waters. His absence from Windsor (lasting until mid-August) included visits to ecclesiastical and noble dignitaries in the neighborhoods of Gloucester and Worcester.

3. George Lukins.

4. The plan of the Lorts to visit Italy was not carried out (see his letter to HLP, 11 July 1788; Ry. 544.10).

5. William Holwell (1726–98), M.D. and B.D. He was presented to the vicarage of Thornbury, Glos., by Christ Church, Oxford, in 1762; appointed prebendary of Exeter in 1776. At one time chaplain to George III, he was an occasional writer on classical subjects.

6. The portrait was only recently completed; see HLP to SL, 6 December 1787, n. 3. The portrait of HLP—"the dear Lady in the *Green Hat*"—was still at the James's on 7 April 1789. PSW "always kiss[ed her] Hand" to it when she visited, and admired it as "a very *strong* Likeness" (Ry. 566.3).

TO SOPHIA BYRON

Exmouth
Monday 11: August [1788].

My dearest Mrs. Byron

I have got my Husband home again after his fortnight's Absence, the first we have ever experienced for more than 12 Hours in our four Years Union—and very glad was I to see him indeed, and he looks *so* well too—You were all excessively good to him. He tells me you have kindly accepted the Key of my Furs:[1] they are the most valuable of my weareable Possessions, and I am particularly choice of them as I told him, so to do a very clever thing I think he has put 'em in a damp Closet, when I had left them in the Wardrobe in our own Bedchamber, bidding Sibylla[2] make a Fire there from Time to Time.

What a kind sweet Letter you have written me![3] and what a nice Thing it is to have a partial Husband and Friends who think better of me than I deserve! may the publick but continue *their* generous Partiality![4]

I do nothing now, but rejoice, and be idle, and ask Questions of what does Mrs. Byron say? and how does She look?[5] and when will She be easy in her Mind and tranquil and happy? and what will Mr. Farquahar[6] do for that poor Man[7] &c.

Mr. Piozzi went to see poor Mrs. Lewis too, and brought me word how She was; Cecilia thinks Lord Huntingdon[8] would beat her over a Race Ground, but by these late Accounts of her Improvements I think *She* would have the better.

How comfortable it will be to Mrs. Lambart to be near you! would you were here! but tis impossible I find. Edward would recover with this soft Air perhaps too,[9] and here are pretty drives: Mr. Piozzi is enchanted with Miss Kitty Beaver[10] and he loves Miss Weston, and every body *we* love; and that is *so* sweet of him!

I cannot make a Scholar of Cecilia, I never shall;[11] tis impossible, but there are Scholars enough in the World without her: She has many good Qualities——among her bad ones a Spirit of total Idleness is the worst.

Your Namesake Miss Weston! how She has fought for Knowledge against every Disadvantage! and how those fight against knowledge who might gain it with Ease: tis curious observing this World——but I do think whatever is obtained with difficulty grows precious in Proportion.

How did I get your dear Friendship?

The Book I have really not *read* yet, only *written,*[12] which sounds odd, but *so it is.* I shall now read, correct and copy it over——beginning next Thursday at soonest, for just now I hate the sight of it.

You will like the description of Naples best: but there will be great Censure upon the whole, *that* I expect and shall willingly compound for. The first thing for a Book is to be *read,* the second to be *praised,* the third to be criticized[13]—— but the irremediable Misfortune is——*to be forgotten.*[14] Edward will get thro' the *Pleurisy* by the same Rule, and dye quietly of the succeeding Consumption, if he *does* dye.——

Adieu, and God bless you. My Husband can give me no other Direction to Miss Weston tho' he was at her House, except that She lives near Mr. Towneley[15] who has the fine Collection of antique Statues; is not that a true Italian Idea!

Once more Farewell, and love / Your truly Affectionate / and Obliged / H: L: Piozzi.

Miss Weston says she is going to Margate, perhaps that Direction will do.

Text: Ry. 546.8.

1. See HLP to Sir Robert Murray Keith, 15 March 1787; and Sir Robert to HLP, 22 April 1787 (Ry. 892.10).

2. Aptly ironic nickname for Mary Johnson, the servant who had accompanied the Piozzis to Europe and now looked after the Hanover Square residence. Like the Sibylla of classical legend, she was thus a wanderer, although more officious than prophetic. Cf. *Thraliana* 2:743.

3. The letter is missing.

4. Perhaps HLP overstates public "Partiality." Cadell had printed two thousand copies of the *Letters,* and, while the initial sale was rapid (see HLP to Mrs. Lambart, 19 February, n. 7), he had no need to publish a second edition.

Several newspapers and journals in 1788 commented favorably upon the *Letters: World* (18 March); *GM* 58, pt. 1: 233–34; *English Review* 11:352; and *Monthly Review* 78:324–31. In the last periodical the article was Murphy's and he concludes:

"We have made very few quotations from Mrs. Thrale's Letters, but in justice to that lady we must say, that they are written with elegance and vivacity, and that they exhibit a mind enriched with literature, and provided with a plentiful store of images. Our business was chiefly with Johnson; and after seeing him struggle with illness and morbid melancholy, it refreshes our imagination to hear him say, almost at the close of life, 'Attention and respect give pleasure, however late, or however useless. But they are not useless, even when they are late: it is reasonable to rejoice, as the day declines, to find that it has been spent with the approbation of mankind.' " See *Letters,* 31 December 1783, 2:343.

5. HLP asked for the sake of politeness; she knew the answer. "Mrs Byron has lost all Face, but retains that elegance of Form & Manner—that still strikes you with the Idea of a decay'd Belle, a Lady of Quality more battered by Sickness than subdued by Age. . . . Byron was *born* a Woman of Fashion" (*Thraliana* 2:734).

6. Possibly the doctor Walter Farquhar (1738–1819) referred to in Mrs. Byron's will as "my friend Mr. Farquhar." He had retained his connections in Aberdeen, where he had been a student, and through them could have helped John Byron. See HLP to Sophia Byron, 11 September 1789, n. 2.

7. John Byron by this time had followed his wife and child to Aberdeen and settled there in lodgings apart from them. HLP used the epithet "poor" as a term of contempt. She had been informed two years before by Mrs. Lewis that Jack was a "scape grace . . . who has behaved in a most shocking manner to his mother," that he "goes on as much like a Rascal [as ever]" (Ry. 556.127). See also HLP to Sophia Byron, 13 [July], n. 1.

8. What made Lord Huntingdon so attractive to HLP was his ability to "please—nay *charm* in Conversation at 60 years old, with a worne out Person which had never been better than *bearable* even in his Youth. Were his Powers the gift of Nature or of art." See her marginalia in *Spectator* 4:170.

9. Edward Hamilton Lambart; see HLP to Elizabeth Lambart, 19 February.

10. HLP was to be long fascinated by the six surviving children of the Reverend James Beaver (d. 1777) and his wife Jane, née Skeeler. He had been curate of Lewknor, Oxon, for seventeen years. In the summer of 1777, shortly after being presented to the living of Monk Silver in Somerset, he died suddenly. Mrs. Beaver was left with the responsibility of educating the children.

Here HLP refers to Catherine (1763–1801), who on 11 September 1794 was to marry Dr. John Gillies (1747–1836), historian and classical scholar. For the birth and baptismal dates of Catherine Beaver, see "Lewknor Parish Records, Register of Baptisms" (Bodleian MSS D. D. Par Lewknor d. l.).

11. HLP attributed CMT's dullness to a severe case of whooping cough and measles contracted in 1783. See *Thraliana* 2:721, 798.

12. *Thraliana* 2:719.

13. This was to be the order of Elizabeth Carter's comments in a letter to Mrs. Montagu, written at Deal on 5 October 1789: "[*Observations*] is writ with spirit, acuteness, and much sensible observation. The style is sometimes elegant, sometimes colloquial and vulgar, and strangely careless in the grammatical part, which one should not expect from the writer's classical knowledge, which is very considerable, and which she applies very happily in many parts of her work. She sometimes puts me out of humour, by her being so vexatiously desultory. . . . One circumstance is highly to her honor, that she always mentions religion with the deepest reverence, and piety of expression" (*Letters from Mrs. Elizabeth Carter to Mrs. Montagu* 3:314–15).

14. An axiomatic borrowing from SJ.

15. Charles Towneley, or Townley (1737–1805), the elder brother of Cecilia Strickland, lived at 7 Park Street (Queen Anne's Gate). An aesthete, he traveled to Rome, Florence, Sicily and, until ca. 1780, collected antiquities. In 1786 he became a member of the Society of Dilettanti and in 1791 a trustee of the British Museum, which in 1805 purchased his marbles and terra cottas for twenty thousand pounds; his bronzes, coins, gems, and drawings in 1814 for over eight thousand pounds.

TO THE REVEREND LEONARD CHAPPELOW

Exmouth
13: August 1788.

Dear Mr. Chappelow[1]

You are very comical and very kind, and very much am I obliged to you: but why do you date your Letters so that no Direction can be obtained where you are but the Post Mark: I should have written forty Times before now, had I guessed where to send my true Thanks for the sweet Hanover Square Visits, and the droll Letter about my *Yellow* Complaints[2] and *Cis* with her Flagellations[3]——Oh dear!

I believe you think a little whipping would not have been ill bestowed upon the *Mother Plant*. My Husband is come home safe and kind, and says Mr. Chappelow *é vero Amico*, and I must write to him somewhere. I wish he was nearer I know, to look over my MS: and pick some *Weeds* out, as he is a good Botanist. Mean Time let me tell you 'twill make a very respectable Figure as to Quantity.

The Mistake of *Fox* Glove for *Hare* bell was worthy a Westminster Elector; but your Account of the weeping Willow was the Thing I wanted.

Much obliged, much obliged—In the mean time will you accept this French Epigram upon a Violet presented to a Lady in return for some of your Botanical Favours. I do not think 'tis universally known.

Modeste en ma Couleur, modeste en mon sejour,
  Franche de L'ambition, Je me couche sous L'herbe,
Mais si sur votre Front Je dois briller un Jour,
  La plus humble des Fleurs sera la plus Superbe.[4]

Adieu, and pray dear Sir *date* your charming Letters[5] if you would have them answered by your much / Obliged and faithful Servant / H: H: Piozzi.

My Husband and Daughter send a hundred Compliments.

Text: Ry. 559.9.

1. HLP responds to a missing letter in which LC answered questions she had asked on 28 June.

2. HLP was ailing from what she would describe as melancholy, whose symptoms were jaundice (often called "the yellows") and stomach disorder. See HLP to Sophia Byron, 4 September; *Thraliana* 2:720.

3. At Exmouth HLP tutored CMT, an indifferent, restless pupil. Equally impatient, HLP apparently disciplined the eleven-year-old child and was later remorseful.

4. The epigram upon the violet was written by Jean Desmarets de Saint-Sorlin (1595–1676), man of letters and first chancellor of the Académie Française. For HLP's explanation of the poem's origin, see *British Synonymy* 1:388–89. She herself found the quatrain quoted and its origin explained in *Ménagiana* 3:57, in *Ana, ou Collection de Bon Mots,* 10 vols., comp. Charles G. T. Garnier and C. J. F. Beaucousin (?) (Amsterdam and Paris: chez Visse, 1789–[99]).

5. HLP is recalling SJ's frequent admonition that she had failed to date correspondence (e.g., *Letters* 2:101, 112, 370).

TO SOPHIA BYRON

Exmouth
Wednesday[1]
[20: August 1788.]

My dearest Mrs. Byron

This last was indeed a melancholy Letter, and sadly did it grieve both Mr. Piozzi and myself;[2] I wish we were nearer you tho' my company is good for little just now as the Book takes me up a great deal of Time, and if it was not for a pretty little Coterie that we live in all Evening, I should stupefy myself with hard work; for I want to rid my hands on't: and I made more than a Week's Holydays when my Husband first came home. It will vex me to leave this Place: Lord Huntingdon's Company is charming, and we dine with one another once o'Week: Sir Harry Heron is with him who seems to know you.[3] Here are some pleasing Women too, but Pleasure never comes any more than Kindness from the People one has a Right to think likely to bestow it. I have but one old Acquaintance here and She does nothing for me.

Has poor Mrs. Lambart had my Letter yet? do tell her that I love her; and wish her well. Ask her if She is acquainted with Mrs. Stafford——there is I believe an intimate Connection between her and Mrs. Colleton.[4]

We will come to London early this Year, in November I hope; and go out of Town the last Week in May at latest, to settle our Welch Affairs a little[5]——my kind husband talks of building a Cottage there, and then we shall have *one house* of *our own*.[6]

Mean Time let me see you often at any which I inhabit, Streatham will soon be empty to receive us, and then we will coax you out of much of your Company: Mr. Steele *can* stay in it but 15 or 16 Months more.[7]

Adieu and be chearful and continue me your Kind Friendship and assure yourself of one of the earliest Copies of the Book which now takes up all the *Time*, but not all the *Thoughts* of / Your ever Affectionate H: L: P.

Is poor Edward alive—and *where* is he? My Husband says I never thank you for your kind Care of my Furs——though dear is my *Coat* I have always heard—but dearer still *My Skin*. My Skins have been much honoured by your sweetly kind and polite Attention: dear *dear* Madam take Care of your Health and blunt down Sensibility a little: for 'tis a too warm Heart, makes hot the Palms of your white Hands I know.

Mr. Piozzi says your Hairdresser is a Hero for finding good Servants; we shall want his Assistance when we come to London. Can he pick us up a good Cook and Housekeeper and a good Valet who can dress Men and Women?

Text: Ry. 546.9.

1. GP had returned to Exmouth by 8 August, and HLP did not work on the *Observations* for at least a week thereafter, i.e., until the 15th or 16th. The Wednesday closest to the latter date was the 20th.

2. Sophia Byron continued to mourn the recent deaths of her husband and second daughter. Moreover, she could not adjust to John Byron's unpredictable behavior.

3. HLP writes Harry in error for Sir Richard Heron (1726–1805). Nearly of an age, the two men were partial to Ireland, Lord Huntingdon because of his Irish antecedents and Sir Richard because of his service as lord lieutenant of Ireland (1777–80).

Admitted to Lincoln's Inn on 30 January 1748/49, Heron held a number of other important posts: commissioner of bankruptcy (1751); remembrancer in the exchequer (1754); M. P. For Lisburn [Ireland] (1766–83); privy councillor [Ireland] (1777). He was cr. baronet on 25 July 1778. He married Jane (Thompson), née Hall (1723–1814).

4. Frances, née Jennings (d. 12 April 1821), had become on 30 March 1754 the second wife of James Edward Colleton (ca. 1709–90), of Haines Hill, Berks., M. P. for Lostwithiel (1747–68) and Saint Mawes (1772–74). She was the only daughter of Sir Philip Jennings Clerke and niece of Mrs. Lambart.

5. Leaving Exmouth in September, the Piozzis went on to Bath. In early December they were again established at Hanover Square, remaining until 3 June 1789, when they traveled by slow stages to Edinburgh. They did not arrive in Denbigh until nearly September. See Clifford, pp. 341–51.

6. Of HLP's various properties—Crowmarsh in Oxfordshire, Bachygraig in Flintshire, an estate in Carnarvonshire, Streatham Park in Surrey—only the future Brynbella was the house she would regard as hers and GP's.

7. Streatham Park had been leased to Thomas Steele (d. 1802), beginning 10 October 1786, for three hundred pounds annually. See Cator to HLP, 8 August 1786 (Ry. 602.3); also, for the agreement with Steele, see Ry. 602.4 and 22. Steele was preparing to leave Streatham by 1 April 1790 (Cator to HLP, Ry. 602.7), and in May the Piozzis returned "for *Good* as the Phrase is" (*Thraliana* 2:767).

TO SAMUEL LYSONS

Exmouth
23: August [17]88.

Dear Mr. Lysons

You are very friendly and good natured, and I thank you for your agreable Letter. This will find you in a most interesting Spot, among the People one loves best in the World[1]——but I told a Man to day that I would have no more to do with *You now,* because you were so loved by every body else: See what a fine thing it is at last to be an honest Man with a good sharp Wit——such a person may really do just what he pleases with Mankind—they esteem him so.

Mr. Hutton[2] introduced himself to me as a friend of Mr. Lysons; I will carry *his Trumpet* for him: and sound his praises willingly, for he has admirable Society Talents—good Talk, good Taste, and good Breeding.

The Hamiltons are Enchanters—and as such just now I trust are properly placed——*in a Castle.* I hear Lord Warwick is improving his Park and if so, that Place will have no equal in my Mind—the Entrance, and Court where the Antique stands, has a natural Superiority to all I have seen yet.[3]

Poets do oft prove Prophets.[4] Mr. Pope has been such in two Instances very strikingly—that you mention, which I am right glad of; and that in Windsor Forest—where he says—

The Time shall come, when free as Seas or Wind,
Unbounded Thames shall flow for all Mankind,
When the *freed Indians* in their *native Groves*
&c. &c.[5]

All the succeeding Verses are prophetical—the Time *is* come thank God. Prior was a *Seer* too I think: He says the Women shall turn Writers for the Stage if you remember, and adds

Your *Time* poor Souls—they'll take your *Fame*, your Money,
Female third Nights shall come so *thick upon ye.*
&c.[6]

Mrs. Inchbald[7] and the Lees[8] say He was a *very true prophet*. Well! adieu: give my dear Love to the dear Creatures you are surrounded by—

Flo takes it very ill You never enquire for him—so *gentle* so *kind* a Friend as he is! He has been sick this Summer, but is happily recovered; and snaps, and barks, and bites as prettily as ever.[9]

Farewell—and take my Counsel another Time: Mr. Hutton said it was a very wise one—to shew the King your drawings.[10]

Mr. Este is a true Friend and a charming Companion;[11] how happy he and you made my Husband that Day at Dinner! I long for London Season that may hold us all together as Johnson says;[12] though we have now a sweet Society here: and when I fall in Love next, it shall be with Lord Huntingdon, who is a most agreeable Man indeed:—and I regret living so many Years without making his Acquaintance.

He dotes on My Husband and admires Della Crusca,[13] quotes Verses from the Regent. Is not he a Man of true Taste and sound Judgment and likely to be so in the Eyes / of Yours and Yours Sincerely / H: L: Piozzi.

It was the heat of the Summer exalted Baretti's Venom so——I am told *all* the Vipers sting terribly this Year.[14]

He'll cool with the weather you'll see.

Text: Hyde Collection. *Address:* Sam: Lysons Esqr. / Guy's Cliffe.

1. SL was visiting the Greatheeds at Guy's Cliffe.
2. James Hutton (1715–95), Moravian leader in England, sometimes referred to as the founder of that church there. Among his important acquaintances were John Wesley, King George, Queen Charlotte, Benjamin Franklin, CB, etc.
3. George Greville (1746–1816), second earl Brooke of Warwick Castle, earl of Warwick (1773), had "bought the Tachbrook estate, 2,500 acres, adjoining the park of Warwick Castle," and made it a part of the ornamental grounds surrounding the castle. See HLP to SL, 9 September 1787, n. 6.
4. HLP's variation of Shakespeare's "Jesters do oft prove prophets" (*King Lear* 5.3.71). See also HLP to SL, 15 August 1786, n. 8.
5. HLP has combined lines 397–98 and 409, slightly misquoting the last: "Till the freed Indians in their native Groves." See also *Thraliana* 2:713 for this and the above quotation.
6. Matthew Prior's epilogue to *Lucius* (1717), by Mary de la Riviere Manley (1663–

1724), lines 44–45: "Your Time, poor Souls! we'll take your very Money; / Female Third Days shall come so thick upon Ye."

7. Elizabeth Inchbald, née Simpson (1753–1821). An actress between 1772 and 1789, she began to assume stature as a dramatist by 1782. Also author of two popular prose romances—*A Simple Story* (1791) and *Nature and Art* (1796)—she was well paid for most of her literary work.

8. Harriet and Sophia Lee.

9. See HLP to LC, 8 November 1786, n. 12.

10. Hutton, who had access to the king, could have arranged a showing of SL's drawings before the royal family.

11. Charles Este and Robert Merry had gone to Paris in May. There Este "had preached before the Ambassador" (*Morning Post,* 2 June). By August he, unlike Merry, had returned to England where he continued to court HLP. See, e.g., his letters to her, postmarked 29 August and 12 November 1788 (Ry. 555.66, 67).

12. See SJ to HLT, 3 December 1781 (*Letters* 2:229).

13. Merry's pseudonym extended to his coterie, the Della Cruscans. See HLP to SL, 27 July 1785, n. 6.

14. Among the other "vipers," HLP would include Charles Burney, Jr.; writers for the *Morning Post* (in March, April, and June); the anonymous authors of "The Quintessence of Johnson's Letters to Mrs. Piozzi," a doggerel satire, in Broadley, pp. 116–18; and "In Bozzum et Piozzam," Latin verses (*GM* 58, pt. 1 [1788]: 65); James Sayers (or Sayer), for his caricature, *Frontispiece for the Second Edition of Dr. Johnson's Letters* (described in *European Magazine* 13 [1788]: 248).

TO SOPHIA BYRON

Exmouth
1: September 1788.

You have a charming heart my sweet Friend, and are excessively good to all who want your Help. Poor dear Mrs. Lambart is very sensible of your kind Attentions——keep her alive till Spring, for all our sakes; and then I will contribute my Share. She is very jealous of me She says, and I know Mrs. Lewis is the Object, but that is not fair; when She cannot tell my Obligations to *her* at a Time that is dreadful to me to reflect upon.——

15 Months spent at Bath in a Situation my Nerves will not yet bear to recollect, tho' *sometime* I may perhaps *try* to talk to you and Mrs. Lambart of my Sufferings, which Mrs. Lewis only at that Time alleviated by her gentle Friendship, and Mr. James the Painter by his sprightly Wit:[1] though neither of them guessed *to what Extent* I suffered, nor how grievously my Sorrows were aggravated by a variety of concurring Circumstances—especially in the *Money way,* which entangled and embittered my Life;[2] and now nothing shall hinder my *loving her,* and *liking* and *thanking* him; as long as I live.

She is very vexed at present that I won't go to Weymouth, but I will go nowhere till my Work is done;[3] and then we will come home and settle snug for the Winter in Hanover Square, and tell old Stories, and thank God who has given me a calm pleasant Evening after a Noon-day Storm that had very near destroyed me.

——May such peaceful Hours at length be the desired Portion of my Dear Mrs. Byron! and I have a great Trust in Providence that they will be; whilst every *black Lady* and white-faced Fellow who is sick and sorrowful, has Cause to bless you daily, and pray for your Happiness.

Will you do Mr. Piozzi the honour to put this Letter into the Post Office for him, with a Shilling to frank it forward? His Letters to his Father[4] and Brother[5] have been often lost, when at a distance for want of that friendly Care.

Grosset is a nice Man: our new Cook should go to Market and take Care of all Kitchen Matters, while Bryant has Charge of the Table Linnen &c. and is a sort of nominal Housekeeper. Mrs. Cook must not be affronted neither if I sometimes go to Market myself; nor insist on other privileges than having a Girl under her. But one should like a notable Woman who could do little French Dishes for my Master prettily, for tho' an excellent Englishman in many Respects, a great boyled Leg of Mutton spinning out with Gravy, has *no Charms for him*. Now I don't want a fine 20£ or 30£ a year Cook, one whit the more for that:—*they* do nothing as ever I see but spend 20£ or 30£ o'year more in wanton Folly; *We* want such a Woman as *you* kept, to make little dainty Messes for the Admiral.

My Furs if they were once more endued with Life, would lay down their Ferocity, and pur round you like Cats and Kittens: as I shall do when we meet in London to thank you for all the tender partiality shewn / to your most Affectionate / and Obliged / H: L: Piozzi.

I shewed Mr. Piozzi the passage about *Cookey:* he says She must be capable of dressing a good Dinner, or sending up an elegant Supper &c. If dear Mrs. L. is gone you'll send the enclosed after her.[6]

Text: Ry. 546.10.

1. At Bath in 1783 and 1784, often ill and distraught because of GP, HLT was intimate with "The James Family & Mrs Lewis . . . the only People I am free with—yet I can't bear to tell even them the Truth" (*Thraliana* 1:595 n. 1).
2. In 1782 Lady Salusbury found a long-forgotten mortgage drawn by Sir Thomas against a loan for Bachygraig. When she threatened to seize the property, HLT agreed to pay seventy-five hundred pounds. She soon arranged a mortgage of seven thousand pounds in favor of her daughters to cover her "loan" from them. Seemingly misled by Crutchley and Cator's details of her financial affairs, she was reduced to penny-pinching. HLT did not learn that her money worries were needless until she met Greenland in the early summer of 1784. See her letter to Q [27 June] 1784, n. 6; and *Queeney Letters*, p. 60.
3. Preparation of *Observations* for the press.
4. Domenico Piozzi (ca. 1717–97), of Brescia.
5. Giovanni Batiste (Giambattista) Piozzi (fl. 1742–1813), of Brescia.
6. The enclosure for Mrs. Lewis is missing.

TO SOPHIA BYRON

Exmouth
4: September 1788.

My sweetest Mrs. Byron

You are an admirable Paintress; and I have a high Opinion of Whitehorne[1] from your Description—so has Mr. Piozzi; but 'tis like a Russian Marriage, to take and engage a Man one has never seen: When we are at Bath perchance we may meet, and like one another, and perchance Flood—our present *Perruchiere* may there be tempted to many a naughty Trick, that will harden our too-kind hearts against him: for at present he behaves well; and poor Fellow, his Faults are chiefly those of sudden Impulse, for the Intention is never bad I think—but an Irishman who loves Drink and Company—what can it end in? We give him 30 Guineas a Year, and so we did Cæsar.[2]

I have been ill tho'; not Ill to confine *me*, but suddenly seized, so as to fright my Master into a nervous Trembling. Waking in the Night with a strange Obstruction in the Stomach and Bowels, which would not do their Office at first, and made me faint away: all was well before Morning tho; and I am only very *sore* from the violence which they used to themselves, as soon as they found their Ability. Bath Water will set *all to rights,* that has been a *little to Wrongs* I trust.

My fair Daughters have been seen at Bath I hear; Is it not silly to feel delighted that they are well and happy? who wish me no good I am sure either of Health or any other Enjoyment——as they have done their utmost to deprive me of all:[3] Yet glad I am at my Heart——for after every thing is said they *are* my Children—at least *Mr. Thrale's* to whom I owe many Obligations.

I am glad Mrs. Lambart does not go with her Son, and so I dare swear is *He:* Young Men and their Mothers seems a strange sort of Connection to run about the World together, and that Mother unhealthy too! She is best and safest where She is.

Adieu my dearest Friend and accept the truest and tenderest Thanks / of your truest and tenderest H: L: Piozzi.

Text: Ry. 546.11.

1. Whitehorne was the valet Mrs. Byron secured for the Piozzis. He entered into their service on 1 December in London. See HLP to Sophia Byron, 10 (n. 1) and 14 September; 31 October (Ry. 546.17).

2. For the valet Flood, see HLP to Sophia Byron, 10 September, n. 1; 14 September. For the biblical allusion to Caesar, see Matt. 22:21.

3. A motif of HLP's letters at this time. See TSW to HLP on 3 April: "That naughty Queeny! What an amiable and pretty dear it *once* was! Will it never be so again! Will its crabbedness, and sourness, and disobedience, and petulant obstinacy never pass away! I trust in God they *will,* and then Queeny Hester will be restored to your Arms, and Heart with renewed Grace, and Glory. . . . And the *other* perverse Dears! But *they* are only Satellites to the Elder Planet, and moving in the attraction of her Sphere, will follow her wherever she goes, turn at her influence, and sparkle as she commands" (Ry.564.4).

TO THOMAS CADELL

Exmouth
7: September [17]88.

Mrs. Piozzi sends her Compliments to Mr. Cadell, She is much hurt to find that Mr. Myddleton never had the Books She begged might be sent to him directed thus.

For John Myddleton Esqr. Gwaynŷnog near Denbigh N: Wales.[1] If Mr. Cadell sent them She wishes earnestly to know by what Carriage, that proper Enquiry may be made; if he did not——desires the favour that they may go directly. It was a Copy of Johnson's Letters, that She ordered for Mr. Myddleton; another for Mrs. Browne Brock Street Bath.[2] Quere whether *those* were ever sent or no.

Mrs. Piozzi mentioned her Intention *to pay for 'em* and had no Doubt but they were gone long ago: till a Letter from Wales let her know the contrary—They must both be *bound* Copies, and forwarded now immediately.—if Mrs. Browne has not got hers yet, Mrs. Piozzi will be ashamed to look her in the Face next Month.

[In a different hand:] Sent as Ordered 20th of June

Text: Bodleian MS Montagu d. 9, fol. 152. *Address:* Mr. T. Cadell / Bookseller / Strand / London. *Postmark:* SE 9 88.

1. See HLP to SL, 4 November 1785, n. 3.
2. According to the "Walcot Parish Rate Book" for the years 1784 through 1788 a "Mrs. Sus: Browne" lived in Brock Street (Guildhall, Bath).

TO SOPHIA BYRON

Exmouth
10: September 1788.

My dearest Mrs. Byron—

You are very good, and like all very good People are very much plagued: our Man Flood told me last Night he would not wait upon a heap of Children: Mr. Piozzi had kindly invited half a Dozen pretty little Girls the Daughters of our Acquaintance here to drink Tea and make a little Dance with Cecilia Thrale: We *must* change him; my dear Master is too kind and gentle, and spoils every body——so he says—do I. It will be charming to meet Whitehorn[1] at Bath and I hope He will not measure Age nor Size of those he is to wait upon: he may be happy with us if he *will*.

I am very sorry, but not surprized at your Spasms; how should you be well my sweet Friend, and fretted as you are?[2] Go to Brompton,[3] and do not mind the

Expence; what can 50£ more or less be to those you leave behind? Think of yourself only—and of them who love you best; among which, number me and my Husband as long as we all shall live.

The Duke of Manchester[4] was a mighty poor weak Creature, and where much is not given &c.[5] I am more shocked at the Duchess of Kingston[6]—She had more Knowledge Sense and Education. Bath will be vastly benefited by Her Death.

Comfort dear Mrs. Lambart, and love her, I wish her most sincerely well, and shall be glad when *we three meet again.*[7]

Mr. Piozzi says a sharp notable Woman who would have his Interest at heart would save her Wages—if it was even 30£ a Year.[8] Chuse for us Dear Madam, and love us, and accept the kindest Compliments / and Wishes of your / H: L: P.

Do you ever call in Hanover Square dearest Madam? Oh do bid Sibylla look About her if you do—for we will come home in November.

Adieu—I *ought* to be writing out my Book, which never will be done by then, if Mr. Piozzi takes me from my Business every Minute so: poor Mrs. Lewis is as poor as a Church Mouse,[9] but I always advise her to spend all on *herself,* as I do *you*.

Text: Ry. 546.12. *Postmark:* SE 13 88.

1. Despite what HLP says here, she did not alter her original plans. Flood remained in the Piozzis' service while they visited Bath. He surrendered his place to Whitehorne only when they arrived at Hanover Square.
2. According to HLP's implicit diagnosis, Mrs. Byron's spasms were precipitated by a nervous condition. Except for George Anson, who maintained cordial relations with his mother, Mrs. Byron continued to be ignored by her daughters and to be plagued by the problems of "Mad Jack."
3. Probably in Yorkshire, about seven miles from Scarborough, then a health resort.
4. George Montagu (1737–88), fourth duke of Manchester (1762), Whig M.P. for Huntingdonshire (1761–62). Although one of the lords of the Opposition, he made no great figure in politics. Yet he became master of the horse (1780), lord chamberlain of the household (1782–83), and ambassador to Paris (1783). In 1783 he supported the coalition of Fox and North. On 2 September, he died of a chill caught while watching a cricket match.
5. Cf. Luke 12:48: "For unto whomsoever much is given, of him shall be much required."
6. Augustus John Hervey (1724–79), sixth earl of Bristol (1775), had married in 1744 Elizabeth Chudleigh (1720–88), whose father had been governor of Chelsea Hospital. She served as maid of honor to the Princess of Wales in 1743. Early in 1769 Hervey had divorced her *a mensâ et thoro,* an ecclesiastical decree that she thought annulled her marriage. On 8 March 1769 she married Evelyn Pierrepont (1711–73), second duke of Kingston (1715). She was tried for bigamy, 15 to 22 April 1776, before the House of Lords and found guilty. Pleading the privilege of a peeress, she escaped sentence and left England. She died at the château of Sainte-Assize, near Fontainebleau, 26 August.
7. "When shall we three meet again?" (*Macbeth* 1.1.1).
8. The new cook destined for Hanover Square.
9. HLP assumed that Charlotte Lewis had been left penniless by her husband John. Actually he knew that her private resources were ample for the care of their two children. He therefore left the greater portion of his estate to the children of his first marriage. See P.R.O., Prob. 11/1106/367, proved 5 July 1783 in London.

TO SOPHIA BYRON

Exmouth
Sunday 14: September [1788]

My dearest Mrs. Byron's

Letter is very kind, and very droll; and Miss Sibylla's Behaviour very extraordinary. She never sate beside a Woman of Quality till that Day I trust, and was willing to say she had done so once before She died.

I have got the most violent of all violent Colds; Eyes Nose &c. tormenting me so that I can hardly speak or write, or see or hear, but it will run away in three Days I hope—Mean time Mr. Piozzi won't let me work at my Book—and without working how will it be done?

Let Whitehorne wait for us in London dearest Madam; Bath is a Place to spoil any Servant in the World——but over Flood I do defy its Power: he is finished ready to their Hands: I am sorry for the Man because he is ignorant, and handsome-looking; and quite a wild Irishman, who would be good perhaps, were there no Temptations to be wicked——Insolence however is not to be borne from a Servant: and we have agreed to part, and I am very glad a decent Successor is coming. Mr. Piozzi will be very kind to him if he is soft-mouthed and civil, and even *pretends* to have one's Interest at heart.

My Maid is so like my eldest Daughter in Person, and cold heartedness, you would laugh.

God bless my dear Friend, and send her safe to her little Place at Brompton, and restore her Health for the Happiness of many—none more affectionately interested tho' than her infinitely obliged / and faithful Servant / H: L: P.

Mr. Piozzi is very angry I say no civil Things for *him* he says—but my Pocket handkerchief claims all my present Attention. I do hope Bath will strengthen me, and do me good: My health is not quite what it has been.

Text: Ry. 546.13.

TO SAMUEL LYSONS

Exmouth
16: September [17]88.

Dear Mr. Lysons.

I thank you for your Letter and direct to Guy's Cliffe as naturally as if you were an Inhabitant. I have been far from well: a Cold, a Fever——a deal of Plague——I began to think you would have had a Stroke at the Thraliana soon;[1] but mean to put it off now again, and recover by Dint of Bath Water if possible, and get hardened there for the Winter. My Master was worse frighted than I.

Do you know Mr. Noguier?[2] He is a very sensible pleasing Man, and seems to like us much; his *Taste* is good of Course.

Lord Huntingdon is demydivine, and whoever sees him sit down to shilling Whist at our little Thatched house Coterie,[3] may learn that Delicacy does not consist in Fastidiousness and Difficulty of being pleased; for no Man has a more Elegant Mind than he——and no living Creature has more Good humour I am perswaded.

We shall leave this Place (if Life and Health go well and nothing worse befalls us) tomorrow sennight, 24: September[4]—see something of Devonshire, Dartmouth, Plymouth, &c. and then to Bath, for six or seven Weeks Water, which I hope will keep me alive for a comfortable Winter in Hanover Square.

My Husband sends you his best Compliments and hopes to see you often there so does / Your very sincere / &c. / H: L: Piozzi.

I wish Seward[5] and Miss Streatfield[6] would make a Match of it at last—There would then be a Collar of *S S S.*

Text: Hyde Collection. *Address:* Mr. Lysons. Direct to the *Post Office Bath.*

1. Accompanying the cold or preceding it was a bout of depression that made HLP fear her death. Since at this time she planned to make SL her literary executor, she implies his responsibility for the destiny of *Thraliana.*

2. John Anthony Noguier, Esq. (1763–1814), of No. 3 Figtree-court, Inner Temple. His name first appears in the "Lists of Council" in 1792. SL described him as "an agreeable man, and a brother Special pleader. I dare say you recollect him, he met you at Exmouth" (14 November 1788; Ry. 552.15). See also HLP to SL, 15 November [1788]; *GM* 84, pt. 2 (1814): 87.

3. HLP's joking analogy of her social set with such as the Dilettanti Society that met regularly at the Thatched House Tavern, No. 75 Saint James Street, until the building's demolition in 1843. The society was formed in 1743 by admirers of classical art for the exchange of information and opinions, the encouragement of good taste and the arts in England. See Wheatley 1:504–5; *Tatler* 65; *Rambler* 15.

4. On 6 October, the Piozzis were to occupy a rented house on Bennet Street, Bath (*Thraliana* 2:720).

5. For William Seward, see HLT to Q [27 June 1784], n. 8. Although HLP had long been aware of his attraction to Streatfield, she also knew that he felt no deep or lasting attachment (*Thraliana* 1:224, 497 n. 2).

6. Sophia Streatfield's ability to attract and repel men baffled HLP, who had long wished to marry her off. At Condover Park, as late as 6 June 1812, HLP "said 'then you knew Sophy Streatfield,' Mrs. Pemberton replied in the affirmative—Mrs. Piozzi then said 'Did you know her in all her beauty? she was a pretty creature. . . . You know all the married men were dying for her.' She then ran over my Lord this and Sir that, and a number of names ending with, 'and Mr. Thrale.' . . . After Mrs. Piozzi was gone Mrs. Pemberton told me that Mr. Thrale was so attached to this girl that he used his Wife very ill upon her account, that he had her in the house, and that in his last illness he would take nothing but from her hands." From the "Diary" of Katherine Plymley, MS 567 / Book 92, C.R.O., Salop.

Much earlier than this, when reading *Spectator* 241, which described parted lovers agreeing "to offer up a certain prayer for each other," HLP had written in the margin of her copy: "This Trick was imitated by Mr. Thrale and Sophy Streatfield, as the Lady herself told me, after he died——how truly I know not" (3:421).

TO SOPHIA BYRON

London Inn Exeter
Thursday 25: September [1788]

I wish my dear Mrs. Byron saw me with all my Papers for the *Book Stuff* and the People coming in every Moment, and the Dog flying at 'em, and Cecilia's Task to look over; and My sullen Maid with *Ma'am this Guinea won't pass,* and my husband crying Come, shut away this Work *do,* and write to dear Mrs. Byron: I think you would say, What a different Life do my Cat and I lead at Brompton! Well! but really I am sorry for poor Mrs. Lambart; your Character of her is a just one—but her Love of the Speaking Figure as you comically say, does not proceed from natural Inclination so much as from an embarrassed Mind, poor Soul! which seeks to relieve itself by Talk, that for a Moment at least drives Thought and Care away. Her Son will ruin her I much fear; but She adores him, and would like no one the better for saying a Word against her ill-placed Fondness.

That seems to be the true Difference between maternal Affection and every other Sort of Love. Ill usage extinguishes Friendship, it cures Passion, it annihilates Esteem; but does nothing towards the Abatement of parental Fondness: of which no Person can be a better Judge than you or I dear Madam——Well! I hear my young Ladies are gone into Wales, what can that Frisk be for? was it because we were coming within ten Miles of them?

Direct now to Bennet Street Bath and believe me ever Dearest Madam your faithful / and Obliged Servant / H: L: Piozzi.

If I do not work at copying over this Book however, you will never get it to read.[1] My Husband sends a Million of the kindest Words in the softest Language. We are going to see Mount Edgecumbe, Dartmouth &c. and then to Bath: our Lodgings begin on the 6th.

Let us find a sweet Letter from you there.—

Mr. Piozzi is enraged with Sybylla, Miss Weston has sent a Spaniel for Cecilia to Hanover Square. I hope my cross Letter to the Lady who keeps the house, will not be revenged on poor Fidelle. I am sorry for Edward.[2]

Text: Ry. 546.14.

1. By 10 November, in Bath, she could record: "I *have* finished my Book, and hope it will please the Publick," although she expected little of "the three cruel Misses" (*Thraliana* 2:720).

2. Edward Hamilton Lambart felt compelled to leave England, whether to regain his health or to avoid the consequences of a scrape. This scheme was abetted by Mrs. Byron, to whom HLP wrote on 31 October (Ry. 546.17), that the plan "of saving poor Edward's Life is a noble one, but if he is destined to spend it in India or the Madera Islands—I greatly fear his forgetting his Benefactress, as those are no good Places to learn Virtue, however they may benefit Health."

TO SOPHIA BYRON

Bennet Street, Bath
Tuesday 7: [October 1788]

My charming Mrs. Byron's Letter was the first I opened of a Hundred that we found here; your Whitehorn will be the Comfort of our Lives if he turns out good, for Flood is never sober for a Day together; and his Hand shakes, and he cannot dress one after drinking so, and we are at our Wits End with him——and yet he is very *agreable* somehow, and we are as sorry for his Ruin, as for our own Inconvenience. The Maid is sober, and decent, and does no harm, and one *hates her* She is so *dis*agreeable: don't you know how all that feels exactly? Well! here are we once more at pretty Bath where I have passed the most happy and the most miserable of all possible Hours——and I do love the Place passionately and the Waters gratefully.

Mr. Hay[1] is always Your humble servant; he is sorry for poor Mrs. Lambart, but says all is her own fault: for my Part, I have no doubt but her Anxiety *in earnest* is totally occasioned by the Character and Conduct of her Son, though She may *talk* of any strange things to drive Time and Thought away. Poor Soul! I fear all will not end well with her.

My Notion is that we have picked up a Cook *here* that we *know* can dress Meat, because she lives with a Friend at whose House we have dined more than once, and who speaks highly of her *other* good Qualities.

This Town fills apace, if Captain Byron does not come soon, and secure a House, he may be disappointed of finding one to his Mind,[2] tho' the Buildings encrease every day.

I never heard of Miss Anguish till now: 'tis a very odd Name——but She will change, or rather sink it advantageously, if this Report is true: Let us remember however that the great End of being a Duchess is making one's Child a Duke;——and She misses that inevitably.[3]

God bless you my dear Friend and continue me your Kindness, and lay in a Stock of health for the Winter——My Work is not done yet remember. There does not remain less than 400 Octavo printed Pages——that is—what will make 400 Pages when printed in Octavo, to copy out *now.*

Is not that a vast deal? Mr. Piozzi says never had Man so diligent a Wife—and never had any one so amiable and so obliging a Friend as Dear Mrs. Byron has been to him and to her ever equally / Sincere and Affectionate / H: L: P.

Text: Ry. 546.15. *Address:* Hon: Mrs. Byron / No. 3 Prospect Row / Brompton. *Postmark:* OC 9 88; BATH.

1. See HLP to Elizabeth Lambart, 19 February, n. 3.
2. George Anson and Henrietta Byron sought a house in Bath and awaited the birth of George Anson, Jr. (8 March 1789), who was to become seventh baron Byron in 1824.
3. On 11 October Catherine Anguish (1764–1837) became the second wife of Francis Godolphin Osborne (1750/51–99), fifth duke of Leeds (1789). She was an accomplished musician. As the duchess of Leeds she was to have two children: Sidney Godolphin

(1789–1861) and Catherine Anne Sarah (1798–1878). HLP recognized that George William Frederick Osborne (1775–1838), the elder son of the duke's first marriage, would be the sixth duke.

Mrs. Byron was interested in the duke's marriage because his first wife Amelia, née Darcy, *suo jure* Baroness Conyers (1754–84), whom he divorced May 1779, had married John Byron, 9 June 1779.

TO SOPHIA BYRON

Bennet Street
21: October 1788.

My dear Mrs. Byron

Should not have gone so long uncongratulated for an Event which pleased me so much as her Son's Preferment, and I might say Preference shewed by Lord Chatham[1]——but that my Husband has been *half sick*, and I have been *wholly* employed. This nasty Book! but if People drop in every Moment so, how can I finish it? and if I shut them out, they are affronted.

Mr. Piozzi gets tired of Bath, he is an ungrateful Creature; There is no Place where one lives so *well* for so little Money, no Place where so many Beauties meet, no Place where there are such Combinations of Gayety and such Opportunities of Snugness. Town and Country, Health and Society are to be found at Bath, which is now improved beyond my Power of praising it.

How happy for us who fix in London that you did not think of it as I do!—were I Mrs. Byron or even Mrs. Lambart, Bath should be my Residence.

Did I ever tell you that poor Flo had swallowed a Pin? such a Narration looks as if this Place afforded little News, but in Truth I have heard of no Event as interesting to *me:* Mr. Hay is very goodnatured about it, but he is ever kind to Man and Beast.

I *hope* I have got a decent Welch Cook, and I *hope* that I have some *Hopes* of an upper Maid: my present Lady has seen Mr. Piozzi ill, and me agitated, without ever asking even *How does he do?* and that is *too* disagreeable. She is very decent, and very Philosophical, and very well-looking—and may suit somebody: but Natives of North Wales or the Venetian State can not bear such slow minded, stronghearted Things, about Them.

Do not say Piozzi has been sick tho', for he is very well again—nothing wanting but a little Gout in the Toes, and we have it *now.* If you see dear Miss Weston tell her Mr. Whalley wrote me the prettiest Letter I ever saw six Weeks ago, and I have never answered *that.*[2] She will then forgive my apparent neglect of *hers* which really does not proceed from want of one's Esteem. The Puppy She so kindly gave Cecilia is dead I find.

Miss Anguish is of a Baron's Family neither old nor young:[3] The Osborns are nothing very sublime as to Antiquity you know:[4] I am contented She should be Duchess of Leeds.

Do write again and let me if possible be <daily> more and more Your Obliged as I am your Affectionate / Servant / H: L: Piozzi.

I shall get my Work done in a Month now, and then home to rest——Oh how glad I shall be! I will enjoy the Time till Publication in Peace and Comfort.

Text: Ry. 546.16.

1. In July 1788, John Pitt (1756–1835), second earl of Chatham (1778), joined the ministry of his younger brother William (1759–1806), then prime minister. Lord Chatham as first lord of the Admiralty had invited Captain Byron to be one of his aides.
2. HLP probably answered TSW's missing letter on 5 January [1789].
3. Catherine Osborne, now duchess of Leeds, was the daughter of Thomas Anguish (d. 1785), accountant general of the court of chancery. See *GM* 56, pt. 1 (1786): 83.
The Anguishes were connected through marriage with the Allins of Somerleyton in Suffolk, a line of baronets created in 1699 with Richard Anguish, otherwise Allin (d. 1725), and extinct in 1794. The manor of Somerleyton and various other estates of Sir Thomas Allin (d. 1794), fourth baronet (1770), came to the Reverend George Anguish (1764–1843), prebendary of Norwich Cathedral, and finally to his nephew, Lord Sydney Godolphin Osborne, son of the duke of Leeds by his second wife Catherine. See the Reverend A. Suckling, *The History and Antiquities of the County of Suffolk,* 2 vols. (London: John Weale, 1846–48), 2:44–45.
4. The first Osborne to be made a baronet was Edward (1596–1647) in 1620. His son, Thomas (d. 1712), was created first duke of Leeds on 4 May 1694.

TO THOMAS CADELL

Bennet St. Bath
Fryday, 14: *November* 1788.

Mr. Cadell,
Sir,—this is a letter of business. I have finished the book of observations and reflections made in the course of my journey thro' France, Italy, and Germany, and if you have a mind to purchase the MS. I make you the first offer of it. Here, if compliments had any connection with business, I would invest a thousand, and they should be very kind ones too; but 'tis better to tell you the size and price of the book. My calculations bring it to a thousand pages of letter-press, like Dr. Moore's;[1] or you might print it in three small volumes to go with the Anecdotes.[2] Be that as it will. The price at a word (as the advertisers say of their horse) is 500 guineas, and 12 copies to give away; though I will not like them, warrant it free from blemishes. No creature has looked over the papers but Lord Huntingdon, and he likes them exceedingly. Direct your answer here, if you write immediately; if not, send the letter, under cover, to Mrs. Lewis, London St. Reading, Berks;[3] and believe me, / Dear Sir, your faithful humble Servant / H. L. Piozzi.

Text: GM, n.s., 37 (1852): 232–33.

1. John Moore (1729–1802), M.D. and man of letters. HLP uses Dr. Moore as a model because of two works published by Strahan and Cadell: *A View of Society and Manners in France, Switzerland, and Germany* (1779), and *A View of Society and Manners in Italy* (1781). Each, consisting of two volumes, had great popular success.
2. The *Observations* appeared in two octavo volumes of about four hundred pages each.
3. The Piozzis were to leave Bath for London on 24 November with a brief stopover at Mrs. Lewis's in Reading (Clifford, p. 342 n. 1).

TO SAMUEL LYSONS

Saturday
15: November [1788]

Dear Mr. Lysons

You are very right at last, and have written it seems like a good young Man, but I never had the Letter. Miss Lee will tell me how poor dear Mr. Greatheed does *now,*[1] for she was called into Warwickshire three days ago, and loves the very Idea of Guy's Cliffe.

We have Places for Diamond's Regent on Tuesday next—[2] our Party Major Ross's amiable Lady and Daughter,[3] and Miss Harington.[4] Tonight—Supper at charming Mrs. Hartley's;[5] Wensday the Concert, Thursday—a Musical Party at Doctor Harington's;[6] Fryday Miss Lee's;[7] Saturday we have an Engagement of long Standing with the Lights[8] and Luders,[9] where Cards and Supper, and everything agreable may be expected.——Could Miss Jenny in the Journey to London[10] give in a better filled-up Account?——I have made Cadell an Offer of my Book.[11] The kind Kembles, Siddonses &c. are among those we are really panting to see: I admire them *in* their Profession, and I love them *out* of their Profession[12]——and with regard to their Partiality for *us,* I reply with Benedick that *if 'tis no addition to their Wit 'tis surely no argument of their want on't: for we have a true Regard for them.*[13]

If this delightful Weather continues, Mr. Angerstein's obliging Invitation will surely be thankfully accepted[14]——*How sweet in the Woodlands*[15] comes naturally to People who have been at *Bath* you know. That Song, nor its Writer and Composer Dr. Harington, will ever grow old or unfashionable.

The Gentleman whose Name you can't remember, that liked our Company at Exmouth—is Mr. Noguier I hope:—for we liked his exceedingly. You say nothing of your Brother who if he has forgot our Name is a *false* Prophet *Daniel.*[16]

The King will get well again I'll warrant him, why should he not?[17] he has every body's Prayers; and the Disorder you mention is curable enough: Twenty People get well of it. How does your Friend Seward?[18] *he* was very bad here at Bath. We go to Mrs. Lewis at Reading in our way home next Monday Sennight——Till then you may perceive there is enough for us to do. / Ever yours Sincerely / H: L: Piozzi.

My husband sends best Compliments.

Text: Hyde Collection. *Address:* Sam: Lysons Esqr. / No. 17 / Cliffords Inn / London. *Postmark:* BATH NO 17 88.

1. According to SL, "Greatheed I find has been quite ill since I left them with a Rheumatism or some such thing caught in looking at Shakespear's Tomb when he was very much heated with riding—but as he has been out on a visit since I conclude that he is recovered" (to HLP, 14 November 1788; Ry. 552.15).

2. William Wyatt Dimond (d. 1812) began to act at Drury Lane in 1772. By 1774–75 he was already associated with the Theatre Royal, Bath. The association—as actor-manager and after 1801 as manager—continued until his death. He was particularly adept in "genteel Comedy," according to *Felix Farley's Bristol Journal.* See Highfill.

On 18 November, Dimond played the leading role in *The Regent* (*Bath Journal,* 17 November).

3. Major David Ross (d. 1805), formerly of Exmouth; his wife Elizabeth (d. 1808); their daughter Mary Ann, who was to become the wife of the Reverend Samuel Blacker. The Rosses were settled at Bath by 1792, residing at 8 Circus.

See Guildhall, Bath, for the document of 8 December 1792 by the "Association for preserving Liberty, Property, and the Constitution of Great Britain, against Republicans and Levellers" (signed by Ross among others); "Walcot Parish Poor Rates, 1800–1807"; P.R.O., Prob. 6/184, for the administration of Elizabeth Ross, 14 May 1808.

4. The eldest daughter of Dr. Henry Harington, Susanna Isabella (1762–1835) was to marry the Reverend Josiah Thomas (1760–1820) in 1794. See Henry Harington's will, P.R.O., Prob. 11/1577/81, proved 23 February 1816.

Thomas, a Cantabrigian, was ordained deacon in 1782 and priest in 1784, serving parishes in Cornwall, Somerset, Wiltshire, and Bath. He was to become a prebendary of Wells (1798) and archdeacon of Bath as well as vicar of Christ Church, Bath (1817–20). See *GM* 90, pt. 1 (1820): 565–66.

5. A courtesy title for the crippled Mary Hartley (ca. 1738–1803). The unmarried woman shared a house with her half-brother David Hartley (ca. 1730–1813), financial expert and M.P. for Kingston-upon-Hull (1774–80, 1782–84). The house was located on Belvedere and Guinea Lane, Bath.

To HLT's annoyance, Seward jested on the "mortification" of Mary Hartley's leg, which "dropt off." See *Thraliana* 1:576.

6. Henry Harington (1727–1816) was born at Kelston, Somerset. He received his B.A. (1749) and M.A. (1752) from Queen's College, Oxford. He took his M.D. in 1762. In 1771 he moved to Bath where he practiced medicine and devoted his leisure to musical composition and the Bath Harmonic Society, which he founded. He served as physician to the duke of York and as alderman, magistrate, and mayor of Bath. See *GM* 86, pt. 1 (1816): 185–86.

7. See HLP to SL, 17 November 1787, n. 7.

8. The Lights were a large and prominent Somerset family. HLP may be here alluding to John (fl. 1739–1800) and Ann (1742–89) Light, whose son John was baptized in the Bath Abbey ("Bath Abbey Register, Christenings 1767," C.R.O., Somerset).

9. The barrister and legal writer Alexander Luders (1756–1819), and his wife Sarah (d. 1806), of Claverton Street. They were members of a well-known Bath family. See "Lyncombe and Widcombe Burial Registers," C.R.O., Somerset.

10. A character in *The Provok'd Husband, or a Journey to London,* a comedy by Sir John Vanbrugh and completed by Colley Cibber. It was first produced in 1728.

11. The *Observations* was to be published about 4 June 1789, by Strahan and Cadell.

12. On 8 December 1787, John Philip Kemble had married Priscilla, née Hopkins (1758–1854). The daughter of Drury Lane prompter William Hopkins and the actress Elizabeth,

she was the widow of the actor William Brereton (1751–February 87), whom she had married in 1777.

HLP is responding to SL's account: "The Siddons are here [in London] and charming they are, the little girl is quite recovered [from scarlet fever], and her mother acts as delightfully as ever—and Mr. Kemble is an excellent Manager of Drury Lane and talks much of you, and says he should like to head a party to meet you on the road and escort you into Town" (14 November; Ry. 552.15). He had become manager of the Drury Lane in October and in November mounted *King Henry the Eighth* as a splendid pageant with SS as Katherine and himself in the dual roles of Cromwell and Griffith.

13. HLP alters Benedick's lines (2.3.233–35) in *Much Ado about Nothing* to match her feelings: ". . . by my troth, it is no addition to her wit, nor no great argument of her folly, for I will be horribly in love with her."

14. SL had reported to her on 14 November: "I spent last Sunday at Mr. Angerstein's at Woodland's, they hope to see you and Mr. P. there before they leave it—it is a charming place.

John Julius Angerstein (1735–1823), merchant, philanthropist, and art collector, owned a villa, "Woodlands," at Blackheath, and another residence in London at 102 Pall Mall. Probably at Woodlands with him at this time were his son John (ca. 1773–1858) and his daughter Juliana (1772–1846). His wife Anna, née Muilman (Crokatt), had died in 1783.

15. Harington's compositions, whether secular or sacred, were melodic. Particularly popular in his own lifetime was the duet "How sweet in the woodlands."

16. The brother of SL, Daniel (1762–1834) was graduated from Saint Mary Hall, Oxford, B.A. (1782) and M.A. (1785). Taking orders, he was in 1784 and for several years thereafter curate of Mortlake and Putney in Surrey. For his later career, see HLP to SL, 14 July [1790].

17. According to SL (14 November): "Nothing is so much talked of here, you may suppose as the King—There is now certainly no danger of Death but what is much worse I think, a confirmed madness. Parliament is expected to meet next Wednesday, and if there is then no prospect of a change in his disorder, a regency it is thought will certainly be appointed—as it is an Event unparalleled in our History, it employs I suppose the attention of those who are concerned in it to continue how these things are to be brought about. . . ." Within a week, on 20 November, SL predicted: ". . . for tho' you have such sanguine expectations of the King's recovery—the like do not appear to be entertained here, for if there is any alteration in him it is daily for the worse" (Ry. 552.16). See *Thraliana* 2:721–24.

18. According to SL (20 November), "Seward is in London and vastly well. His illness was I have always under[stood] in consequence of fever—now this [has passed]."

TO THOMAS CADELL

Hanover Square
Monday 15: December 1788.

Mrs. Piozzi presents her Compliments, and thinks it right to tell Mr. Cadell that the more She consults her own heart, or her Friends, the more She remains determined to Abide by her original proposals as most honourable and least troublesome to herself.[1]

Text: Hyde Collection.

1. See the letter to Cadell, dated 14 November, in which she spells out her suggestions for publication.

TO THOMAS CADELL

Fryday
19: December 1788.

Mrs. Piozzi returns her kind Compliments to Mr. Cadell, and confides the Manuscript to his Hands, with the most perfect reliance on his Honour and Discretion.[1]

Text: Yale University Library.

1. Financial records exchanged between HLP and Cadell with regard to the *Observations* are missing.

TO GEORGE COLMAN, THE YOUNGER

Hanover Square
[1788 or 1789]

Sir

Among the many Liberties taken with your Time and Patience, you will scarcely expect to suffer any from me who never had the honour of passing but one Day in your Company and that at my own House many Years ago:[1] but slight Reasons must operate when strong ones cannot be found, and when a poor deserving Friend is in want of help. I think your Humanity and Tenderness will pardon the Intrusion for the Motive's Sake.

Mr. Tagnuoli has shewed his great Skill in Languages by writing an English Comedy,[2] and his little Skill in matters of common Life by chusing me out to present it to Mr. Colman——yet could I not deny so harmless and at the same Time so ingenious a man his request—and I have besides some odly-founded hope that you will not refuse mine when I protest that whatever Support and Protection you kindly resolve to afford his Play will be considered as a very kind and a lasting obligation by Sir . . .

Text: Ry. 533.9; an unsigned draft in the hand of HLP.

1. The draft, when rewritten, was intended for George Colman, the younger (1762–1836), dramatist and acting manager of the Haymarket since his father's paralytic stroke in 1785. HLP presumed on her association with the elder Colman that had begun as early as August 1768.
2. For a possible identification, see HLP to Charlotte Lewis, 20 September [17]89, n. 2.

TO THE REVEREND THOMAS SEDGWICK WHALLEY

Hanover Square
5: January [1789]

My dear Sir

Will you forgive an old Friend's long Silence?[1] It should be compensated by an infinite Quantity of new Chat, were we nearer to each other; but never was any ill Luck like ours, which has separated us so oddly, and sent us up and down in the manner of Buckets at a Well. Miss Sage[2] will tell you how little Amusement here is stirring for the young and Gay, and I can assure you that Literary Subjects were never so little talked of in London since I can recollect the place.

——One thick Political Gloom[3] covers us just now—*Art after Art goes out,—and all is Night.*[4] Della Crusca's fine Poem called Diversity breaks thro' however, and flashes with transient Lustre gleaming across the Mist from Time to Time:[5] And Mrs. Siddons unites all Parties in *her* Favour twice o'Week.[6] Poor dear Mr. Greatheed meantime! *his* Play and Profits all put by, what Patience he must have![7] but his Mind is like your own. May you enjoy many happy returns of this Season Dear Sir, and do rejoyce with me that 88 is past: those two Figures have already brought Confusion and temporary Distress upon this Island twice before[8]——but Calamity never comes from the Quarter whence 'tis looked for—so I suppose 1988 will be a comfortable Year, as the People then will be prepared to expect Evil.

Miss Seward has a Right to be angry and I hope is a little so with me for not writing;[9] make my Peace in a sweet Letter of yours to her——and then I will close in with the best Apologies that can be found, for I want one of her long charming critical Letters sadly; and have not deserved one at all: procure me that unmerited Pleasure do my kind Mr. Whalley and believe me with the sincerest Esteem and truest Attachment Your Obliged and / faithful Servant / H: L: [P.]

My Husband sends his kindest Compliments and Wishes to Mrs. Whalley and all your Family.——

Text: Berg Collection+. *Address:* Rev: Mr. Whalley / Royal Crescent / Bath. *Postmark:* JA 5 89.

1. TSW had last written to HLP in September 1788 and she "never answered." See her letter to Sophia Byron, 21 October, n. 2.

2. Frances (Fanny) Elizabeth Sage (fl. 1772–1830)—attractive and musically talented—was the eldest daughter of Isaac (d. 1818), once a member of the East India Company, and Elizabeth Sage, née Whalley (1745–78), both of Thornhill, Dorset, and Gatton, Surrey. When Mrs. Sage, TSW's favorite sister, died, Fanny succeeded her in his affections. See the Sage M.I. at Wells Cathedral; the will of Isaac Sage, proved 2 March 1818, P.R.O., Prob. 11/1602/145.

3. George III was mentally ill, and the nature of the Regency was being debated in parliament. Should it be, as Charles Fox advocated for the Prince of Wales, unrestricted? Or should it be, as Pitt recommended, limited by parliament? On 19 January Pitt's resolutions carried.

4. Pope's *Dunciad* 4.640.

5. *Diversity*, published in 1788, was Merry's "frigid and elaborate ode." See *Monthly Review* 80 (1789): 529–32. HLP thought it "very fine," yet substanceless and destined to failure (*Thraliana* 2:726).

6. Between 25 November 1788 and 5 January 1789, SS played Queen Katherine, in *King Henry the Eighth*; Jane Shore; Lady Randolph, in *Douglas*. In this period she often repeated her role in *King Henry the Eighth*.

7. With the Regency a strong possibility, Bertie Greatheed's play seemed doomed. He himself lamented: ". . . as my Regent is a villain, the play cannot be acted. Mrs. Siddons took that tragedy to Windsor to read it to the Royal Family when one of the King's first paroxysms came on, and she was prevented." See *An Englishman in Paris*, p. xii; *Thraliana* 2:725.

8. The Spanish Armada that threatened England in the summer of 1588 was routed in a major British naval victory. In 1688 the bloodless, "glorious" revolution took place, with the Catholic James II exiled and the Protestant William and Mary brought to the English throne.

9. Anna Seward wrote to TSW on 27 November 1788, and he did not respond. She then sent him a scolding letter, which he had received only recently and reported to HLP, also remiss in her correspondence with Anna Seward. For the source of HLP's indebtedness, see her letter to SL, 9 September 1787, n. 4.

Apparently, HLP sent a letter of apology before the end of January to Miss Seward, who on 13 February replied without animus (*Seward Letters* 2:242–44).

TO PENELOPE SOPHIA WESTON

[London]
Fryday 3: April [1789]

My Dear Miss Weston

It was very good of you to write at last, but I thought the Letter long in coming. Mrs. James laments seeing so little of you; as for the charming Whalleys, I mind their Silence but little; as a Corner of the Heart is my chief Aim, and that I beg you to keep warm for us. Make my best and kindest Compliments to Miss Lees, and say that after Robertson's History,[1] and your Namesake's Recess,[2] I thought so little more could be done for Mary,[3] that no Accounts of Mr. St. John's Success have hitherto been able to draw me in *her Cause* to Drury Lane.[4] We were there last night tho'; and I have scarcely slept since, for the strong Agitation into which Southerne and Siddons together threw me last night. 'Tis an odd Thing, but I never saw the old Tragedy of Isabella represented before in any Place, or by any People whatever.[5]

Well! you are a clever Lady sure enough, so to secure for me a Window on the most joyful Occasion ever known in England;[6] I thank you most sincerely, and am impatient for the day, but we must have dear Miss Weston in London on *Wednesday*, for our Concert which is to be 22nd of April.

Mrs. Byron has been—not ill, but dying:[7] She is now convalescent, and calls people about her, we meet many Friends there tonight, particularly the beloved Greatheeds who had not the audience deserved by such a Performance as his inimitable Regent the Evening it was acted for his own Benefit.[8] 'Twill be a Stock Play no less for that however: such Merit is not left unregarded here, nor unrewarded neither, and it's Day *will* come I have no doubt.

Farewell my lovely Friend, and if you can't be fond of Bath, pray love London and best of any body in London / Your Affectionate / H: L: P.

My Husband sends You a thousand Compliments and Cis. The Ode was mangled and altered so, that I hardly knew it myself.[9]

P.S. your Dear P. Sigh the [precious] moment to see you again in Hanover Square, I must tell you the truth, that you are a *Charmante* Lady, and every Body are in Love with you, but not so much of me, but my love is sincere, the same it is with the Charming Sid: and I can assure you last Night I cried on the Tragedy, she is an [extraordinary] Women; come, come to see your friends.

Text: Yale University Library. With a postscript by GP. *Address:* Miss Weston / No. 7: / Milsom Street / Bath. *Postmark:* AP 3 89.

1. William Robertson (1721–93), a royal chaplain in Scotland, principal of Edinburgh University, and moderator of the general assembly. He published a two-volume *History of Scotland during the Reigns of Queen Mary and of King James VI till his Accession to the crown of England*, 11th ed. (1759; London: Thomas Cadell, 1787).
2. Sophia Lee's successful historical novel *The Recess, or a Tale of other Times*, in 3 vols. See HLP to Samuel Lysons, 17 November 1787, n. 7.
3. *Mary* (i.e., *Mary Queen of Scots*), a tragedy in five acts by John St. John, was first produced at the Drury Lane on 21 March 1789 with SS as Mary and John Philip Kemble as Norfolk. SS also spoke the epilogue.
4. John St. John (ca. 1746–93), a sometime playwright and pamphleteer, was the third son of John (d. 1749), second viscount St. John. Made a member of the bar in 1770, St. John was also M.P. in three parliaments (1773–84). From 1775 until 1784 he was surveyor general to the land revenues of the crown, publishing in 1787 *Observations on the Land Revenue of the Crown*.
5. The dramatist Thomas Southerne [also Southern] (1660–1746) wrote *The Fatal Marriage, or the Innocent Adultery* (1694). It was slightly altered and revived in 1757 by David Garrick as *Isabella; or, the Fatal Marriage*. In the title role of the Garrick version, SS, who first played it in the 1782–83 season, achieved one of her most popular triumphs.
6. The 23rd of April was a day of Thanksgiving for George III's recovery. HLP watched a grand procession headed by the royal family. It assembled before the House of Commons and terminated at Saint Paul's for divine services (*The Times*, 24 April). For HLP's pleasure on the occasion, see *Thraliana* 2:742.

According to PSW's letter (30 March), she planned to accompany the Piozzis to "Mr. Bells, at the British Library in the Strand, where we are secure of a Window, to see the procession pass by to St. Pauls" (Ry. 566.2).

7. See HLP's gloomy account in *Thraliana* 2:739.
8. HLP alludes to the second benefit performance of *The Regent*, played on Tuesday, 17 March, at the Drury Lane. (The first benefit night was 26 April 1788, almost a month after its initial showing on 29 March.)
9. HLP's poem "For the Public Advertiser [12 March]. Ode on the Rejoicings for the King's Providential Recovery." It was also published in the *St. James's Chronicle* (10–12 March) and the *World* (11 March). The "Ode" consists of eight six-line stanzas and is a paean to the "Sov'reign's Health" and its miraculous restoration. Typical is the last stanza:

While vibrating, through every vein
Beneficence extends the strain,
The roofs, responsive ring!
Heav'n hears well pleas'd, resolv'd to bless
And as a Pledge of Happiness
See God has sav'd our King.

TO SOPHIA BYRON

Ferry Bridge
Sunday Morning
8: June [1789.][1]

Dearest Mrs. Byron

will receive the Answer to her kind note dated Ferry bridge in Yorkshire[2] where a good Inn and a pretty Situation makes all the Amends it can, for distance from the Sun, which seems to have wholly left us, and here we sit shivering over a Fire on the 7th or 8th of June.

Have you been ever clear of Mrs. Hayes's Company I wonder, since you lost that of her quondam Mistress?[3] 'Twas odd enough you should so hit upon her Name however, She *is* Black-Eyed *Susan*[4] sure enough; and the best and *civillest* Reason I can give for parting with her is her ill Health, on which 6 Guineas were expended in six Months between Doctor and Apothecary, let alone the Trouble taken by House Maids—neglect of Duty on her Account &c., &c., &c.

I trust London has not yet left off talking of the Marquis del Campo's Gala,[5] we read of it in the Newspapers with Wonder, and indeed Lord Fife[6] told us a good deal when he called so kindly with Letters of Recommendation to Edinburgh the Day we set out.

But 'tis Time to Answer your Friend's Charge about Johnson's Letters:[7] I resolved while abroad to publish them, and wrote word so to London from Florence I remember:[8] when we arrived at Vienna a Year and four Months after, the Librarian there reproached me for not having kept my Word;[9] and when we replied that we must go home first, he said *pray then make haste and be gone.*[10]

I remember no Counsel either asked or given after our Arrival in England about the matter, Sir William Ashhurst said in Conversation one Day at Guy's Cliffe, I hope Mrs. Piozzi will publish *every Scrap* sent her by Dr. Johnson: so you see I had the *Judge's Advice* in good Time![11] It was ill worth the while consulting about such a truly unimportant Correspondence to be sure but the World had a Fancy to see how Johnson wrote upon frivolous Subjects,—and now it is seen that he did it better than anyone else. Dr. Young told us long ago that

Triflers not even in trifling can excel,
'Tis Solid Bodies only polish well.[12]

Giuseppe Baretti, 1773. Painted by James Barry. *(Reproduced by permission of John Murray [publisher], London.)*

Adieu Dear Madam here is a great deal upon a frivolous Subject enough God knows, excuse it for the Affectionate partiality you feel towards / Your H: L: Piozzi.

Text: Ry. 546.18.

1. This is one of HLP's first letters describing a journey, begun on 3 June, that was to take her, GP, and CMT as far north as Scotland. For the itinerary, see *Thraliana* 2:749 n. 2 and "Journey Book," Ry. 623.

2. "Ferry Bridge where I sit writing in a Bow Window, is a beautiful situation, and the Road from Doncaster hither completely smooth and even, exhibiting both on the right and left hand numberless Seats, Parks &c. laid out very tastefully indeed, and uniting the merits of both Nations by combining German Solidity and neatness with English Skill in disposition of the Ground. Bavaria itself shews no handsomer Gates, no firmer Pales, no better formed Fences than this part of Yorkshire produces. . . . Stone Buildings much encrease the Air of Opulence and Comfort that breathes thro' this County, a Lady once told me she thought a Brick House resembled a Bob Wig, and I thought there was something pretty as well as whimsical in the Idea" ("Journey Book").

3. Susan Hayes was formerly a servant of the Piozzis, "coveted" by Sophia Byron. See *Thraliana* 2:746.

4. An ironic hit at Susan Hayes. See John Gay's popular, sentimental ballad, "Sweet William's Farewell to Black-Ey'd Susan," in *Poetry and Prose,* ed. Vinton A. Dearing with Charles E. Beckwith, 2 vols. (Oxford: Clarendon Press, 1974), 1:249–51, 2:596–97).

5. Don Bernardo, marquis del Campo (d. 1800), for several years Spanish ambassador to England. According to rumor, he was the natural son of General Richard Wall (1694–1778) and a woman named Field. The marquis had won the gratitude of George III by virtue of "extraordinary politeness and presence of mind" in 1786 when Margaret Nicholson threatened "his Majesty's sacred life" at Windsor. See *GM* 56, pt. 2 (1786): 708–9; 70, pt. 1 (1800): 488–89.

Early in June, according to *AR* 31 (1789): 254, "the Marquis del Campo gave his promised Fête, at Ranelagh, in compliment to the Queen of England, on his Majesty's recovery." About two thousand guests attended.

6. James Duff (1729–1809), second earl Fife, &c. (Ireland, 1763). He was M.P. for Banffshire (1754–84) and Elginshire (1784–90). He was created a peer of Great Britain in 1790 as baron of Fife, Fifeshire. A shrewd businessman, he nearly doubled the family fortune and was acclaimed for the agricultural improvement of his vast estate.

7. FB, a close friend of Mrs. Byron, questioned the propriety of publishing SJ's correspondence. HLP "has given all—every word—and thinks that, perhaps, a justice to Doctor Johnson, which, in fact, is the greatest injury to his memory" (*Diary and Letters* 4:12).

FB's disapproval of the *Letters* further nurtured HLP's belief that her former protégée, as intimated by Lord Fife, was associated with her brother Charles in publishing Baretti's "Strictures" in the *European Magazine.*

See HLP to Sophia Byron, 8 June 1788; to Q, 25 March 1811; *Thraliana* 2:719, 916; Hayward 2:70–71; Clifford, p. 323.

8. See HLP to Cadell, 7 June 1785.

9. The Johnson enthusiast in Vienna was identified by HLP in *Observations* (2:304) as the Abbé Denys, i.e., Michael Denis (1729–1800), Jesuit poet and librarian at the Garelli'sche Bibliothek (ca. 1761) and (in 1784) director of the Hofbibliothek in Vienna.

While HLP was in Florence, she had considered publishing the *Letters* but did not undertake the venture until, in Rome, she "received Letters from Mr. Lysons, crying *Wonder* about my Anecdotes of Dr. Johnson. . . . Booksellers wrote to me to request they might publish our Correspondence, and Mr. Piozzi permitted me to say We should be at home in a Year or Two, and look out the Doctor's Letters" ("Harvard Piozziana" 2:72).

10. Cf. *Macbeth* 3.4.117–18.
11. Sir William Henry Ashurst or Ashhurst (1725–1807), judge on the King's Bench. Highly regarded as a lawyer, he was twice one of the commissioners entrusted with the great seal: 9 April–23 December 1783; 15 June 1792–28 January 1793.
12. *Love of Fame*, Satire 3, lines 215–16. For "trifling" read "trifles."

TO PENELOPE SOPHIA WESTON

Scarborough
Thursday 11: June 1789

Dear Miss Weston

You bid me write and charged me to give you some *Commands*—but as the Children say, I like *Questions* better:[1] How do you do? and how does dear Mrs. Byron do? and how does Major Barry do?[2] and which among you ever thinks of Us? *All,* if you are not *Ingrates* in the French phrase.

We like our Journey so far exceeding well, but 'tis as cold as October, and just that Wintry feel upon the Air; a Northern Summer is *cold Sport* to be sure, but Castle Howard is a fine place, and the Sea bathing at this Town particularly good.[3]

What Difference between Scarbro' and Exmouth. Yet is this Bay by no means without its Beauties—but they are more of Features than Complexion.

Now for the Commands. Poor Cecilia languishes for news of her Phillis, and the Maids at home forget, or know not how to write word that She is alive and well: will Dear Miss Weston if She ever walks towards Hanover Square, be kind enough to call? and ask for the poor little Spaniel.[4] I shall get an early Letter by the Bargain, and if She brings four Puppies, Major Barry is to have one: I shall write to him very soon.

Tell me all the News—of the *Blue Coat Boys* particularly, *poor little Charity Children* as they are:[5] and keep your passion warm for my Master, and continue to love / Your Affectionate / H: L: Piozzi.

We have got a nice Lodging on the Cliff, very pleasant; but you had better direct to the post office. [In GP's hand] and in the same time pray d'ont forget some fine Linens for the Master of Hanover Square.

Text: Princeton University Library. With a postscript by GP. *Address:* Miss Weston / Queen Square / Westminster. *Postmark:* JU 15 89.

1. "Questions and Commands" is a children's game in which a "commander" orders one of his or her subjects, upon pain of penalty, to answer a question satisfactorily.
2. Ultimately a colonel in the army (1793), Henry Barry (1750–1822) served during the American Revolution as aide-de-camp and private secretary to Baron Rawdon (*later* Rawdon-Hastings). For a short time thereafter he was posted to India. Although he remained in the army until 1794, he was well known in English literary and scientific circles by 1789.

For Rawdon, see HLP to Barry, 19 October, n. 4.

3. According to HLP's "Journey Book": "Meantime the Wind howls like the End of October in Sussex and this is the 12: of June: our Bay at Scarboro' is beautiful. . . . [T]he Sea here is bluer—of a more Cærulean Colour somehow than we find it in less cold Latitudes. . . . Our old Castle here has nothing remarkable but its Age; it was built in the Roman Time; and the Gothick Arches of it are modern.——What more can be said about Scarborough? That it was the first place which invited People to bathe in the Sea, and taste a Pleasure we English can now scarce Exist without, but which is Luxury not fourscore Years old I believe, even in our Country, and no other Inhabitants of Europe have taken Delight as yet to follow our Example and seek Health united with innocent and natural Recreation by dipping in the Ocean's beneficial Waters that surround this Island replete with Advantages derived from its Vicinity."

Castle Howard is the seat of the Carlisle family in Yorkshire.

4. Phillis, now pregnant, was the family's "little favourite red & white Spaniel" (*Thraliana* 2:838). Other friends were similarly charged to report "news" of Phillis. See LC to HLP, 18 June (Ry. 562.4); HLP to SL, 8 July; to PSW, 10 July.

5. The Blue Coat School, i.e., Christ's Hospital, Newgate Street. Founded by Edward VI in 1553 for "poor fatherless children and others," the school took its name from the pupils' uniform—a blue coat or gown set off by a red leather girdle, yellow stockings, a clergyman's neckband, and a saucer-shaped black cap.

HLP was interested not only in the education of charity school boys but also in a custom that in July (before the term's end) allowed the "Grecians" or head boys to deliver a series of speeches and orations before the mayor, corporation, and governors.

TO SAMUEL LYSONS

Edinburgh[1]
8: July 1789.

Dear Mr. Lysons—

I felt much Pleasure from your Letter, and thought it so long since I had seen your hand writing, that I read it with great Avidity. You do me sad wrong however about poor Omai, he was no small favourite of mine, and I feel more interested concerning the War with Bolabola than you think for[2]——Two Islands quarreling for the Possession of a German Organ and Puppet Show——

——Omai's[3] best and most valuable Effects as I remember—would make an Excellent Subject for a mock Heroic Poem, and beat *La Secchia rapita* out of Doors.[4]

Are the French fighting and squabbling for any thing that will answer better? I question it: Truth is, my Knowlege of their Government and Grounds of their Revolt is so small, that I cannot think to any purpose on the Subject:[5] but my Heart tells me all will end in *Air:* because Anarchy *naturally* finishes in Despotism, and Despotism in a Country long accustomed to Monarchical Government, *naturally* drops into the hands of a King.[6]

We arrived here only last night having loitered at Durham to admire its beautiful Environs too long perhaps—but I know not who could have left them sooner. The approach to this Capital did not much please me, but its Magnificence when arrived makes ample Compensation, and I see that *my* Intention will be answered, for all has an Appearance totally *new* to *me:* tis no more like London—than Naples is. Here is Description enough for the first Letter I think, we shall not present our Recommendations till tomorrow,[7] for I am as tired as a *Dog,* and the Comparison runs most happily; even *Flo* is much fatigued, and rejoyces in the elegant Accommodations of *Walker's Hotel:* where you must be so kind to direct again very soon, and tell me something good of dear Dr. Lort,[8] in whose Happiness I am much interested.

Cecilia bears her Journey like a Stout Girl, but her Heart sighs after Phillis; do ask at Hanover Square if the poor little Creature is alive and well, and her Puppies safe in the Straw. The Servants at home have been very negligent in not writing, or I would not give you the Trouble—but tis *so* near Clifford Street, and Saville Row, where I am sure you go very often.

I am glad the Book swims poor Thing[9]—what does Doctor Lort say of it? Yet he would have written himself I fear, had it much pleased him.[10]

The Opera House will never be Rebuilt on the Spot sure, we must have a fine Theatre *now* for shame;[11] and if they once erect a large one for the exhibiting *Italian* Dramas,—John Bull will begin talking about Shakespear and Siddons, and so we shall get another good Playhouse by the Bargain.

Adieu dear Sir, and send another kind and long Letter full of News very soon to your faithful and obedient Servant / H: L: Piozzi.

Remember we are 380 Miles off.

Text: Folger Library. *Address:* Sam: Lysons Esq. / No. 17 Clifford's Inn / London. *Postmark:* JY 10 89.

1. According to HLP's "Journey Book":

"Nothing can strike one more than the Magnificence of Edinburgh new Town, or surprize one more than that so little should hitherto have been said of it by English Men, who might be naturally proud methinks that Foreigners can find few Places to oppose to the *Second* City of Great Britain. Truth is, the general Appearance resembles no other Town I have run over; and of all other Towns perhaps least resembles London.

"Houses eleven Stories high, of excellent Stone; a Pons sine Flumine which joins one Part of the Town to the other, with Habitations under it and a sort of Greenplace wild enough where the Women bleach Linen, milk Cows, &c. have a strange Look, while George Street, Princes Street, and Queen Street, each a Mile long and not inferior to Portland Place in general Splendour of Appearance with the new Assembly Rooms of an exquisite Doric Architecture give an Air of Dignity unrivalled by any City I have seen yet, as each terminates with a striking View either of the Country, the Castle or the Sea."

2. HLP inaccurately remembers the warfare in the Society Islands, in this case between Ulietea and Bola Bola (also Bora Bora or Porapora). The former, of which Omai was a native, was conquered by warriors of Bola Bola (pre-1769) and was "in some measure under the dominion of Opoony," king of Bola Bola. See *The Journals of Captain James Cook on his Voyages of Discovery,* ed. J. C. Beaglehole, 4 vols. and a portfolio (Cambridge: The University Press for the Hakluyt Society, 1955–74), 2:232–33.

3. Omai (d. ca. 1780) was brought to England by Captain Cook and lived there between 1774 and 1776. SJ, who met Omai at Streatham, was impressed by his elegant behavior. In the margin of *Boswell's Johnson* (1816 ed.), HLP wrote: "When Omai played at Chess and Backgammon with Baretti, everybody admired at the Savage's good Breeding,

and at the European's impatient Spirit" (3:9). For Captain Cook, see HLP to SL, 14 June 1785, n. 13.

4. The mock epic (1622), by Alessandro Tassoni (1565–1635). The twelve cantos in octaves narrate a struggle between the cities of Bologna and Modena over possession of a bucket.

5. HLP alluded to such events as the bread and corn riots between March and July in 1789 throughout France. Rebellion against grain shortages and rising bread costs was expressed in destruction of country estates, bread seizure, and refusal to pay the *octroi*, or king's taxes.

The most important political event was the formation on 17 June of the National Assembly, which sat despite royal repudiation. On 27 June Louis rescinded his initial order and commanded the nobility to join the National Assembly, which on 2 July became the Constituent Assembly to deal with constitutional reform.

Also in June a secret society, formed by soldiers of the Gardes Françaises, was pledged to disobey all orders directed against the National Assembly. When several of its members were discovered and imprisoned in the Abbaye, a mob on 30 June freed them.

6. HLP was prophetic. Life in France in the summer of 1789 was anarchic. The violence of the subsequent revolution was a cause of the Robespierre dictatorship in the summer of 1793, which ended with his execution on 28 July 1794. With the coup d'etat of 9 and 10 November 1799, the five-year-old Directory yielded to Bonaparte's despotic tenure as first consul and (by 18 May 1804) emperor of all France. On 6 April 1814, at Fontainebleau, he abdicated. On 3 May, Louis XVIII entered Paris, and the Bourbon monarchy was restored.

7. Lord Fife and Dr. Moore had given the Piozzis letters of introduction to various Edinburgh families. The former's carried the weight of the peerage and the doctor's the authority of not only Scottish birth but of influential native associations. He had practiced medicine in Glasgow from about 1751 to 1772, receiving his M.D. in 1770 from the university there. In 1772 he traveled on the Continent as tutor-physician (for five years) to Douglas Hamilton (1756–99), eighth duke of Hamilton and fifth duke of Brandon (1769).

See HLP to Cadell, 14 November 1788, n. 1; to Sophia Byron, 8 June [1789], n. 6; *Thraliana* 2:749.

8. A letter (Ry. 544.10) from Lort, written 11 July in London, crossed HLP's to SL. In it Lort described his concern over the "Rumors of famine and civil war which seem prepared to scourge" France; he wrote further of his recollections of Scarborough and of his interest in the *Observations*.

9. The *Observations*, published about 4 June, was to go through English and Irish editions in 1789, a German translation with an introduction and annotations by Georg Forster in 1790.

The chief objections to the work were HLP's pretentiousness and, paradoxically, her use of colloquialisms. Hannah More wrote to Elizabeth Montagu on 7 July: ". . . I have finished Madam Piozzi and found in almost every page amusement and disgust; very sprightly and shining passages debased by the most vulgar colloquial barbarisms; much wit spoilt by much affectation; some learning rendered disgusting by insufferable pedantry" (Huntington Library, Montagu MSS 3997). See the *European Magazine* 16 (1789): 332–34 for similar criticism.

But not all were hostile. On 18 June LC reassured HLP. "I have read the first Volume with infinite delight, as most every one else, and at present can only say that Anticipation is more than rewarded.—I have not seen one Person whom as a Critic I could examine; indeed The Town is almost empty. . . . [One] coupled your Book with Zelucco, Dr. Moores and spoke handsomely of both—but his account was a hasty sketch—and he promised in a future Critique to be more diffuse. One Observation I can most conscientiously make, which is this—should anyone say to me, that 'twas a desultory Publication, I shall immediately reply—Twas intended to be so—for to read 20 pages and hear Mrs. P. talk for 20 minutes is the same thing" (Ry. 562.4).

10. "And now for your Book," Lort wrote on 11 July, "I do assure you that as far as my observation extends it meets with as favorable a reception as you could wish or expect; I shall not content myself with reading it once over but a second time and a third and a 4th when I enter on my travels."

On 12 January 1790 (Ry. 554.12), Lort was to write of the *Observations:* "Having said so much of your book, I am tempted to go a little further and give you the good and the bad I have said of it in a letter to Seward and his reply. 'I have been again reading Mrs. P's travels and really think them much superior to most modern books of this class. The excellent observations and uncommon beauties which struck me on the first perusal made me overlook those Specks and blots which I find since have so disquieted the minor critics. Some colloquial barbarisms and awkward words and phrases which occur so often have been eagerly fastened on and held up to view by her enemies and cannot be defended by her friends; These might be removed by a single dash of the pen not only without injury but with advantage to the pages. . . .' In answer to this Mr. S. says 'Of Mrs P's travels you seem to think as I did when I gave my opinion to Cadell; they are written I think with more plenitude of observation and with greater compass of knowledge than any modern travels into Italy.' "

11. The opera house in the Haymarket was known variously as the Haymarket Opera House, the Queen's Theatre, the King's Theatre, and Her Majesty's Theatre. Built and established by Vanbrugh, it opened in 1705 and was destroyed by fire on 17 June 1789. The first stone for its replacement was to be laid on 3 April 1790. See Wheatley 2:199.

TO PENELOPE SOPHIA WESTON

Edinburgh
10: July 1789.

And so you will not write again—no, *that* you will not, Dear Miss Weston—with all your mock Humility—till Mrs. Piozzi answers the last Letter, and begs another.

Well! so She *does* then: I never was good at *pouting* when a Miss; and after fifteen years are gone, one Should know the Value of Life better than to *pout* any part of it away. Write me A pretty Letter then directly, like a good Girl; and tell me all the News. The emptier London is, the more figure a little News will make, as a short Woman shows best at Ranelagh[1] when there is not much Company.

Echoes are best heard too when there are few People to break the Sound you know, so let the Travelling Trunks, Hat Boxes and Imperials that pass over Westminster Bridge every Day at this Time of the Year, be no Excuse for your not writing.

We have had a good Journey, and the Weather cannot be finer; a Northern Latitude is charming in July, and the long Days here at Edinburgh delightful[2]—but no Days are long enough to admire its Situation or new Buildings, the Symmetrical Beauties of which last quite exceed my Expectations, while the Romantic Magnificence of the first is such as gives no Notion at all of the other—so I like Scotland vastly; and as we have Engagements for every Day, one should be ungrateful not to like the Scotch too—but for that my heart was always equally disposed.

I shall thank Dr. Moore for his Letters on Saturday after we have had the honor to sup on Fryday Night with Lord Advocate[3] as soon as the Concert is ended.

Say a kind Word for me to Miss Williams,[4] and do not let Mrs. Byron have a Notion I neglect her, but She wants a long descriptive Letter, and must of Course wait till I have got her one ready—I am now making up my Cap for Company.

Poor Cecilia's too tender heart frets about Phillis; She has an Idea the little Thing is dead bringing her Puppies—and I am sure I would not lose Flo's eldest Son or Daughter for their Little Weight in Gold—the Father is grown *Thin* and *light* with his Journey, but barks and snaps as becomingly as ever.

I am much flattered with finding my Book read here, and every body talks about *Zeluco*,[5] but I hope no one more than myself, or with more true Esteem of its Author.

Come now, write soon, and direct to Walker's Hotel Edinburgh,—so God bless you, and never fail to remember with Kindness, our Dear Master and your own / Affectionate Servant / H: L: Piozzi.

Text: Princeton University Library. *Address:* To / Miss Weston / Queen Square / Westminster. *Postmark:* JY 13 89.

1. A fashionable center for entertainment in Chelsea, designed by the architect William Jones (d. 1757) and constructed in 1742. It was razed in 1805. An orchestra situated in the large covered rotunda (a shelter not available in the rival Vauxhall) provided music. The favorite pastimes, however, were promenading around the spacious room and supping in the boxes. The Thrales had frequented the resort, sometimes with SJ, who admired it. See *Boswell's Johnson*, passim; Clifford, p. 128; Hyde, p. 180; Wheatley 3:147–48.

Cf. Rowlandson's depiction of high life at Vauxhall. Among the figures seen in a supper box, M. Dorothy George has noted SJ, JB, Goldsmith, "and reputedly Mrs. Thrale." See *Hogarth to Cruikshank: Social Change in Graphic Satire* (New York: Walker and Co., 1967), p. 77 and plate 4.

2. Even before arriving at Edinburgh, the Piozzis required "a fire every Evening, and should not find it disagreeable at Noonday: but if we are not regaled with the Produce of a hot Sun, his long Duration makes some Amends—one can see to read without Candles at 10 o'Clock at Night, and between two and three in the Morning he gilds the Horizon again" ("Journey Book").

3. The lord advocate, like the attorney general in England, prosecuted and defended all causes concerned with the national interest. In 1789 he was Robert Dundas (1758–1819), of Arniston.

4. Helen Maria Williams (1762–1827), a recent acquaintance, is known for her analyses of French politics from 1790 to 1819. She wrote a volume of poems (1786), in which she included a laudatory epistle to Dr. Moore, her physician during a serious illness. In 1788 she visited France. Not long thereafter she was to become a permanent French resident, supporting Girondist principles but repudiating those of Robespierre. For her subsequent career and relationship with HLP, see passim.

5. In 1789 John Moore had published his first novel, *Zeluco: Various Views of Human Nature, taken from Life and Manners, Foreign and Domestic*, 2 vols. (London: Strahan and Cadell). As a moral exemplum of "Happiness, Prosperity, Success, etc.," Zeluco is "conducted through two octavo volumes, every page of which shews him Successful in all his projects, yet failing of happiness in each, only because his plans were never dictated by virtue" (*British Synonymy* 1:270).

TO SOPHIA BYRON

Edinburgh
Saturday 11: July 1789.

My dear Mrs. Byron

deserves the best Letter that ever was written, for her good Taste and Judgement in desiring to hear about Edinburgh and Dublin, rather as She says than about Lisbon or Madrid—because they interest a rational English Reader much more nearly. Well now! and what do you expect me to tell you of this Country—I dare say you expect, as I certainly did too—a second hand London set in a Second-hand England—something worse because of the Climate—but very *like.* Not a Bit on't. Edinburgh resembles no Place I have seen yet——or if any Place, not that you are living in at present above all.

Mountains high enough to be seen at fifty Miles Distance—a Castle of venerable Dignity upon one of them, and Arthur's Seat upon the other, are our *nearest* Objects; while a Broad Arm of the Sea dividing us from the Hills of Fifeshire, which gilt every Evening by the Setting Sun—form a delightful View at some Distance from the Town; gives Ideas of romantic Antiquity and surly Greatness not easily to be matched or rivalled.[1] Mean Time the new City all Symmetry and exactness, every Street crossing the other at right Angles——and looking like a Cork Model when one views it from the Hill; promises the pleasures of Society very favourably, and so far as I have been concerned, pays all it promises. We had a charming Dinner at a very agreeable House yesterday, a showy and chearful Supper at another last Night, and our Engagements give us Hope of many more.[2] In short I like the Country and the people prodigiously, and am willing, nay happy to tell them so.——But 'tis like commending the musical Powers of a sweet Female Friend we are intimate with in London[3] to her own Mother——She can always do it *so much better herself,* that it takes off one's keenness a little, and may be reasonably allowed so to do: Hopelessness of Succeeding will cure one's Passion for anything, and when I praise the Scots I find too many Rivals springing up round me, that *by long Use* are attained to more Perfection in the art.

Now for some London Chat. After seeing Hatfield House[4] however, and Burleigh House,[5] 'tis a shame to say pray who are the Cecils you talk about? Yet I really do not know; but by your Account the Gallant has the worst of the Adventure.[6] Was not the Father of this Lord Bolingbroke for many Years a complete Lunatic?[7] I think so; the Lady's Maiden Name I never heard or have forgotten—who did he marry? They must all be very young People.

Are you thinking of the French Government at all? It takes up Attention reasonably enough: some will have it that they are going to be free now, and *then* how they will eat us up! for Freedom was all they wanted. Well! the English are always hated somehow by every other Nation, go where one will: yet I think their Money enriches many, and their Knowledge illuminates some. They hate themselves however, and are always listening after remote Subjects of Discontent and Causes of Apprehension without any good Grounds *this* Time I do believe.

We shall stay here till this Day fortnight, so now dear sweet Soul pray write: and remember we are 400 Miles off. Glasgow, Loch Lomond, &c. will be taken in our Road thro' Dumfries to Carlisle——Look at your Map, and you will find we shall visit both East and West of the Island this Time.

Were you ever much a Reader of Johnson's Tour to the Hebrides? Tis one of his first Rate Performances——I look it over now every day with double Delight. Oh how the Scotch do detest him!![8] Accept all our very best Compliments and Adieu; and / love your / H: L: P.

Text: Ry. 546.19. *Address:* The Hon: Mrs. Byron / Bolton Row / Berkeley Square / London. *Postmark:* JY 11; JY 12; JY 15 89; JULY < >

1. Boldly elevated in the center of Edinburgh sits the twelfth-century castle; to the east rises Calton Hill; and to the southeast, the hill of Arthur's Seat, shaped like a resting lion, overlooks Edinburgh. On the west side of Arthur's Seat are Salisbury Crags, forming a crescent of steep cliffs. Toward the north the land slopes gradually to the Firth of Forth and the port of Leith; while the south is punctuated by a series of hills: Liberton, Blackford, Braid, and Craiglock.

2. Among those whom the Piozzis met in Edinburgh were Samuel Rogers (1763–1855), poet and art collector; Dr. Moore; Robert Cullen (d. 1810), Scottish judge and periodical essayist; William Robertson: either the historian (1721–93), or the deputy keeper of the records of Scotland (1740–1803); the Reverend Hugh Blair (1718–1800), poet and critic; Alexander Campbell (1764–1824), musician and miscellaneous writer; Thomas Erskine (1750–1823), lord chancellor; perhaps Adam Smith (1723–90). See Clifford, pp. 348–49.

3. Jane Hamilton. Of her musical ability, the *World* on 23 June 1788 had commented: "Miss Hamilton's singing at Richmond House was with Reason applauded—Marchesi has pronounced her the best Amateur he has heard." See HLP to Sophia Byron, 2 June [1788], n. 5.

4. Hatfield House (parts of it dating from as early as the fifteenth century) in Hertfordshire belongs to the Cecils, the marquesses of Salisbury.

5. William Cecil (1520 or 1521–98), cr. Baron Burghley (1571), was Queen Elizabeth's chief minister. Apart from his political expertise, he was an enthusiastic builder. The one monument of his architectural skill, yet extant, is Burghley House at Stamford Baron, Leics.

6. The young "Gallant" was George Richard St. John (1761–1824), third viscount Bolingbroke (1787). He had married first in 1783 Charlotte, née Collins (d. 1803), daughter of his tutor. He was separated from her, and during her lifetime—probably in 1789—he went through a form of marriage with the Austrian Isabella Charlotte Antoinette Sophia (d. 1848), Baroness Hompesch. In 1804 the two were legally married.

7. Frederick St. John (1734–87), second viscount Bolingbroke (1751), third viscount St. John (1749), was for the last six years of his life deranged. In 1757 he had married Lady Diana, née Spencer (1734–1808), whom he divorced in 1768. The cause was *crim. con.* [i.e., criminal conversation] with Topham Beauclerk (1739–80), whom she married on 12 March, a few days after the divorce decree.

8. In 1773 SJ undertook a journey with JB to the Scottish Highlands and the Hebrides. SJ recorded his adventure in the *Journey to the Western Islands of Scotland* (1775); JB's view of the same experience is his *Journal of a Tour to the Hebrides* (1785).

According to JB in April 1775, "I had brought with me a great bundle of Scotch newspapers in which his *Journey to the Western Islands* was attacked in every mode; and I read a great part of them to him, knowing they would afford him entertainment." See *Boswell's Johnson* 2:363; 5:273, 471.

TO THE REVEREND LEONARD CHAPPELOW

Edinburgh
12: July 1789.

Dear Mr. Chappelow

Your very kind and very friendly Letter came safe to Scarborough,[1] I wish we had one from you here—for 400 Miles is a long Distance from the Fountain Head of Intelligence, which takes many Colours before it can arrive at the Frith of Forth—notwithstanding the diligence of our Mail Coaches.

Though I direct to London my Heart tells me you are at Diss in Norfolk attentive to the Duties and studious of the Comforts of a quiet Country Life. We are admiring the Romantic Magnificence of Scotch Scenery, which I did not expect to have found so near the Capital; but here are gallant Mountains worthy of any Country——and in the Town noble Streets, worthy of any City—'Tis quite a new Picture for the Mind, and I am exceedingly glad to have seen it——my Fear was of a second hand London, but Edinburgh is perhaps more like Paris or Potzdam than it is to anything we possess in the Southern Parts of our Island.[2] That the Environs of Durham should look like our own dear Country; so sweet, so cultivated, so elegantly disposed, so rich and fertile too: while a Nation so near keeps no Trace of resemblance, is really very odd: but we are going forward through Glasgow to Loch Lomond, Inverary &c. and I really now hope for more Amusement in our Journey than once I counted on. Carlton Hill had been enough, had one seen only that—and we shall see much more.

Mean Time Mrs. Jordan is coming,[3] so we shall have her to talk about instead of the French. Many People perswade themselves that they are becoming a free Nation, and that the Loss of our Liberty is to follow the obtaining of theirs, I don't know how soon: My Fears do not reach so far, but it will be right for England to pay Debts and extend Commerce I think, while France is too much disturbed to interrupt her.

Farewell dear Sir and do not forget us. Mr. Piozzi joins in sincerest Compliments with / Your obliged and Faithful / humble Servant / H: L: Piozzi.

Text: Ry. 559.10.

1. LC's letter from London, dated 18 June (Ry. 562.4).

2. In her "Journey Book" (Ry. 623), HLP wrote: "Mean Time the old Town . . . has a Parisian Look; and puts one in mind of Rue St. Honoré: especially as the Bakers and other little Shopkeepers take the French Method of painting the Wares they sell in ill drawn and worse Coloured Figures upon the Wall, which leaves an Impression of Dirt and Meanness not pleasing to an English Eye. The poor Women too have much of the French Manner by what I can observe; go like them without Hats, and carry their Baskets &c. on their Backs, slung like gypsie Children, not in their hands as we see People of the same Rank in London——add to this their Notion of living numberless Families in one House, and carrying the stairs to the Door without Passage or Hall, which you find on a first Floor where there are likewise Antichambers for servants to wait as in Italy or France. . . . Yet in the midst of all the Splendor, one sees the Continental Taste of mixing Misery with their Magnificence, and the moment you are out of a fine Street or Square there are old tumbling down Cottages to offend your Eyes, or Houses where the Grass literally grows

out of the Thatch——Beggars too with Ulcers, Nakedness, and every kind of disgusting deformity follow one about as in the South of France, and devoured themselves by Vermin, threaten Infection while they ask for alms. . . . The Love of Dirt is another Continental Taste, and their Attachment to it can surely be with difficulty denied while they continue building fine Places, and polluting them with Nastiness that shocks an English Reader even to think of. . . . The Scots have never turned their Thoughts towards making a Common Sewer, nor ever considered Cleanliness an Ornament, much less a *necessary* of Life. Every thing most odious is brought and thrown out before the owners door at 10 o'Clock of an Evening without Shame or Sorrow—Carts being provided to carry it off before Morning, leaving only the Smell behind—as not a Privy is yet used in Edinburgh."

3. Dorothea (or Dorothy) Jordan (1761–1816) began her acting career in Dublin (1779) and made her London debut at the Drury Lane Theatre, 18 October 1785. As a comic actress she had few equals: she "seems to speak with all her soul; her voice, pregnant with melody, delights the ear with a peculiar and exquisite fulness and with an emphasis that appears the result of perfect conviction" (Leigh Hunt, "Comedy," *Dramatic Essays*, ed. William Archer and Robert W. Lowe [London: Walter Scott, 1894], p. 80).

TO SAMUEL LYSONS

Edinburgh
Tuesday
21: July [1789]

Dear Mr. Lysons—

I wish Cadell had sent my Money to Drummond's before he left London, but I warrant he forbore only before he felt that it was too little for such a Book;[1]——so means to do something handsome just at *Harvest* Season, and the *Genteel Thing* is the *Genteel Thing* at any Time, as Goldsmith's Bear-leader says in the Play.[2]

Dear Phillis's happy Delivery has been most kindly announced by all our Friends, *you* have however been most obligingly attentive to describe her Progeny—they cannot chuse but be Beauties.

Mean Time everybody is talking of Famine and Bloodshed, and filling each other's Heads, and their own Mouths with most tremendous Uproar[3]——but mind what I say, and remember I was right about the King's Illness,[4] and told you all along how it would end.

My Notion then is *strictly* this.

I do believe that less than ten Years will scarcely suffice to quiet the Storm which these Commotions have excited in France: that the present Sovereign will have much to suffer, but that if the little Dauphin turns out a Youth of good Parts, and personal Accomplishments,—the French will have fatigued themselves with their own violent Exertions just by the Time that his Merit or Figure will strike them; and by the Year 1800 Louis Charles shall receive the voluntary Homage of his adoring Subjects, and restored to even more than Hereditary Influence and Power,—shall lead them where he pleases—mais *tousjours a la Victoire Monsieur.*[5]

Meantime let our dear Mr. Pitt recover from his Gout,[6] extend our Commerce, establish our Credit, discharge our Debts: and we will envy no Nation's Glory, nor desire a Continuance of its Distress.

How like you my Prophecy? Mrs. Siddons always says What a good *Hoper* I am.

Dear Doctor Lort is very kind, his friendly Letter came safe a Week ago.[7] Will you not shew your Mother a little of the Town now She is so near?

This Place would be *too* delightful was it clean, 'tis exceedingly seducing to me in its present State, and the People so *very* agreeable! But we set out Westward on Thursday next, make Glasgow our Head Quarters, and leaving our Coach there, scramble about in the Carriages of the Country to see Sights, Loch Lomond, Glencroe, and Inverary. Lord Fife has sent his Nephew *Macduff's* Representative to court us Northward;[8] but 170 Miles rough road is no Joke, and tho' I do suppose *Their* Plantations are the finest, here are so many, and so fine Plantations nearer, that one cannot resolve to go so far. Besides I long to be in Wales and have a little Chat with the dear Greatheeds so Adieu! and write to *Glasgow* and let us not *burst in Ignorance:*[9] accept our Compliments and believe me ever Dear Sir your obliged and faithful / Servant / H: L: Piozzi.

Text: Yale University Library. *Address:* To / Sam: Lysons Esq. / No. 17: / Cliffords Inn / London. *Postmark:* JY 24 89.

1. The financial agreement for publishing *Observations* is unknown, but—as this letter makes evident—HLP did not receive the five hundred guineas demanded (14 November 1788).

2. *She Stoops to Conquer,* act 1, in the alehouse dialogue following Tony Lumpkin's song.

3. HLP refers to the fall of the Bastille, the murder of its governor, de Launey, and others there. The success of the revolution in Paris encouraged other cities and towns to take similar action. Yet the events of 14 July did not create the peasant revolution. They did, however, cause riots against feudal lords to spread: "manorial archives were burned, walls and fences were pulled down, and seigneurial hunting and fishing rights ignored. The peasants were doing what they expected the Assembly to sanction." See Stuart Andrews, *Eighteenth-Century Europe: The 1680s to 1815* (London: Longmans, 1965), pp. 281–82.

4. See HLP to SL, 15 November 1788, n. 17; but cf. hers to TSW, 5 January 1789, n. 3. HLP must have remembered particularly the national jubilation that accompanied the announcement that on 10 March the king's physicians had withdrawn from Kew. See the celebratory description by Sir Nathaniel William Wraxall (1751–1831) in *The Historical and the Posthumous Memoirs . . . 1772–1784,* ed. Henry B. Wheatley, 5 vols. (London: Bickers and Son, 1884), 3:369–70.

The *World* of 11 March described the Piozzi house in Hanover Square as being "alight—from the roof to the area. With a Transparence in the Heart of the building—God Save the King."

5. Louis-Charles (1785–95), dauphin of France and later (1793–95) Louis XVII, did not have the happy fate HLP predicted. On 3 July 1793, he was to be taken from the queen and imprisoned in "that part of the Tower which Louis XVI. had previously occupied." He became ill in February 1795 and died of an infection attributed to "the miseries he endured in his confinement, the horrible nature of his food and the filth amid which he was intentionally forced to live by his tormenters." See Madame Campan, *Memoirs of the Court of Marie Antoinette,* 2 vols. (London: H. S. Nichols, 1895), 2:266, 275–77.

6. At this time William Pitt the younger was first lord of the treasury and chancellor of the exchequer (1783–1801, 1804–6). On 14 July he described in a letter to his mother some of the symptoms of a malady that was to trouble him until his death. See Stanhope 2:38;

John Ehrman, *The Younger Pitt: The Years of Acclaim* (New York: Dutton, 1969), p. 595; HLP to SL, 30 April 1785, n. 15.

7. Dr. Lort's letter, dated 11 July 1789 (Ry. 544.10), is cited in hers to SL, 8 July, n. 10.

8. James Duff (1776–1857), fourth earl Fife (1811), styled Viscount Macduff (1809–11). He was to distinguish himself during the Peninsular War, having volunteered his services; he attained the rank of major general in the Spanish army. Created Baron Fife, 28 April 1827, he was the last to bear that title.

9. See *Hamlet* 1.4.46.

TO SOPHIA BYRON

Glasgow
Monday 3: August [1789]

Dearest Mrs. Byron

Why did you suffer part of my Letter to be printed in a publick Newspaper?—That is the way to hinder all Confidence of Communication; when every thing one does, and every thing one says is suddenly presented (with all its Imperfections on its Head) before a Public to whom no one owes more Gratitude, or feels more respect than I do——People will think it was with my Consent perhaps, while God knows I have no Intention to fatigue their partiality *so*. Let us have no more such Tricks played; it was unkind in Mr. Este too, but I have fewer Claims on his Good nature than on yours.[1]

Well! we will wrangle no longer, but begin telling about the Highlands;—beautiful Inverary, and horrible Glencroe. 'Tis an astonishing Country after all, and perfectly well worth seeing: but it would have been inconvenient to have gone further, and our Fatigues would have been ill repaid they told us if we made less than 226 Miles: which I could not bear the Thoughts of dragging poor Cecilia over, for mere barren Curiosity. After sweet Lough Lomond, so soft and delicate at one End of it, so stern and majestic at the other, what can be wished of Scenery? either gaily Pastoral or gloomily Magnificent? We have had the finest possible Weather, and made a whole Weeks Tour of 120 Miles only, taking Time not only to *see* but to *enjoy* the various Beauties of a Place so pleasing.

Miss Weston has not written, nor dear Mrs. Lambart, no harm is come to *her* I hope, and yet 'tis odd She is so silent, after worrying for Letters from *us*.

But these Frenchmen! these frantic Fools! May their Madness be of short duration I pray God—when one reads of their Cruelties, and reflects on that Theatre of Gayety and Good humour—Paris—made a Scene of Sorrow and Bloodshed in this dreadful Manner—how one ought to Thank God that has removed the black Storm from over *our* apparently devoted Heads, and suffered it to break just near enough to impress us forcibly with the Idea of our *own* Deliverance. I can add nothing just now, and think of nothing but the newspaper, which hourly brings new Horrors, I hope exaggerated:—yet private Letters confirming public Accounts what can be said!!! nothing by me but that I am my dear Mrs. Byron / ever yours / H: L: Piozzi.

Direct to the Post Office Liverpool.
Mr. Este is an Acquaintance made by me since our last Return to England you know; but I suppose he has had a Wife many Years,[2] as he has brought his Sons as old as Cecilia with him to our House more than once if I remember right.—One of them is very particularly handsome.[3]

When will your poor Heart cease fluttering so? I am sincerely sorry for your Persecutions[4]—Tell me Things mend in the Letter directed to Liverpool.

I begin to long now to get Thither, and when I found a Rash upon my Skin this Morning was glad we went no further into the Highlands.

Text: Ry. 546.20. *Address:* Hon: Mrs. Byron / Bolton Row / near Berkeley Square / London. *Postmark:* GLAS<GOW>; AU 7 89.

1. For some time the *World* had been following HLP's travels northward. On 9 July it reported: "Mrs. Piozzi, who, as Johnson said of Gray [*English Poets* 3:428], writes so well of her travels, that we wish her to travel most of her life, is now about to enter Scotland—from Scotland she passes to the Lakes, and from them thro' Wales." See also the same newspaper for 29 and 30 July. For "Imperfections," see *Hamlet*, 1.5.79.

When Sophia Byron received HLP's letter from Edinburgh, dated 11 July, she showed it to Este, for on 31 July the *World* announced:

"Mrs. Piozzi is gone to Glasgow. As any remark of an observer so elegant, will be curious and gratifying, we are happy in the memorandum of what she says of *Edinburgh;* and what do you expect to find it? I suppose, a sort of *second-hand town*—in a sort of *second-hand* country." Cf. HLP to Sophia Byron, 11 July; to PSW, 22 August.

2. Little is known about Este's first wife, Dorothy (or Dorothea), née Lambton. She predeceased him by several years, and he sired a large second family in Antigua on a plantation called Fosters. When Este died in the spring of 1829, he left his property to his wife, Mary, and six underaged children. In his will there is no mention of a prior marriage or of earlier children. The document was signed 26 March 1829 at Government House in Antigua and proved in London on 28 January 1830. See P.R.O., Prob. 11/1765/23; also HLP to SL, 17 November 1787; and D. Este to HLP (ca. December 1791), from Saint George's Row, Hyde Park (Ry. 555.69).

3. The handsome son was Michael Lambton Este (1779–1864), who was to become a distinguished physician in London. See Charles Este to HLP, 24 June 1793, n. 2.

There were two other Este sons: Charles Lambton, a future banker in Paris; and Thomas. See HLP to LC, 1 May 1802, n. 5. For Este's daughter, see HLP to LC, 1 May 1802.

4. Although Sophia Byron's letter is missing, she undoubtedly wrote about her son John, who imposed his money problems on her. Probably for this reason, on 10 July at Bath, she added a codicil to her will that omitted any mention of "Mad Jack" and his family.

TO SAMUEL LYSONS

Keswick
Thursday 13: August [1789]

Dear Mr. Lysons

I received your agreeable Letter at Glasgow, but am glad I did not answer it from there, because my writing would perhaps have resembled the place—not in

Loftiness but in dullness of regularity, and gloomy seriousness of Style: I was glad to leave Glasgow, where I found much Merit but no Attraction:[1] Some Gentlemen's Seats in the neighbourhood however were charming,[2] and the Inhabitants *so* amiable they would have made any Place delightful.

Of Scotland and its various Excellencies we took leave a Week ago——I saw the Cathedral at Carlisle with double Pleasure:[3] but so sweetly do the Beauties of this lovely County encrease upon one at every Step that we shall find it difficult to get out of Cumberland I am sure.

As a proof we stopt two Days at Penrith for the sake of seeing Ullswater, the English Lake of Lugano,[4] and last Night was spent upon Derwentwater[5] the Miniature of Lago Maggiore, with its pretty little Islands, one covered with Wood, and one adorned with a Summer House so neat and so delicate.[6]

This is the place where if a Poet
Shin'd in Description he might show it.[7]

I have read none of their Descriptions, but have a Notion from our Talkers that the word *aweful* comes in oftener than I should use it. *My* Eye see nothing but Amenity; contrasted, or rather contracted, and held together by High Grounds of peculiar Beauty, thrown about as if on purpose to fascinate the Sight, while it follows their flying Shadows.

I suppose the Black Lead Mine[8] has exhausted itself in drawing the sweet Landschapes that surround it——Ovid would have expressed such a sentiment very neatly, and he is the true Poet to write Verses on the Meres of Cumberland.[9]

Tomorrow we drive forward to Winander:[10] some Ladies from this House are climbing Skiddaw now;[11] but I like better to see it capt with a light Cloud, which courts Imagination to encrease its height; than by running up to its Top give myself a convincing Proof that it *is* not, nor *cannot* be *very* high: I trust No *Ladies* would have dreamed of attempting the respectable Heights that hang over the Expanse of Loch Lomond[12]—but I certainly began wrong by looking at the Alps first—Savoy, Scotland and Westmoreland: why tis Milton, Thompson, and Waller.

Will you have any more pedantry? Or is this enough for one Dose? Pray who is my enemy that writes in the British Review?[13] You told me one Enemy's name and I forgot it again; which Review does *he* write in? or are they both the same Man?

Adieu and direct to Liverpool: accept Mr. Piozzi's Compliments with those of your faithful Servant / H: L: Piozzi.

[On cover sheet:] I have written to scold Mr. Este, the Truth is I felt very angry.

Text: Pierpont Morgan Library MA 322. *Address:* Samuel Lysons Esq. / Rodmarton near / Cirencester. *Postmark:* KESWICK PM 17 89.

1. Arriving in Glasgow on 25 July, the Piozzis visited for almost two weeks. HLP found it perhaps first "among the second Rate Cities of Europe. 'Tis larger than Dresden I think, and the Situation finer than Munich; Streets more spacious, Houses of greater

Dignity and exhibits a larger Portion of Regularity than the best of them all—Berlin alone excepted. While a very elegantly planted Walk upon the Banks of Clyde amuses the Inhabitants, and two Stone Bridges of considerable Merit as mere Fabrics, and of Beauty as mere Objects, attract a Traveller's Notice. . . . yet how sincerely do I wish myself at Salisbury or Nottingham! Oxford or Ousely Bridge! Tho' Candour must confess that we have here Colonades to walk under as at Bologna, that the streets are paved after the foreign Manner, and better than in London, that the College is very handsome, and that the Cathedral would have been so too, but for the violating hand of hasty and rapacious Reform. For the Absence of Cleanliness indeed Uniformity or even Grandeur hardly make amends and I have now found a most discreditable Reason why Passengers walk up the Coach way so in Edinburgh and Glasgow,—'tis because People used to throw Ordure &c. out of the Windows, and Foot folks rationally enough chose those rather than to hazard being run over" ("Journey Book").

2. E.g., Douglas Castle in Lanarkshire, the seat of Alexander Home, afterwards Ramey-Home (1769–1841), tenth earl of Home (1786); and the summer residence of the eighth duke of Hamilton.

3. HLP was intrigued by the varying styles, the successive centuries of architectural devotion that had gone into the cathedral. Begun ca. 1130 under the aegis of Henry I, construction went on fitfully for at least two centuries. Scottish parliamentarians destroyed a major part of the nave between 1645 and 1652. The principal material is red sandstone, but the surviving Norman portions are of dark gray stone, possibly reused from the Roman wall.

4. "Ullswater is a lovely Mere too, headed by high Grounds thrown about it as if on purpose to be described not painted; a sweetly planted Hill at its foot—Hay Makers and comfortable Cottages filling the foreground on every Side—Lago Lugano half in the Swiss, half in the Milanese Dominions is like Ullswater for size and Beauty but the Town renders it more respectable" ("Journey Book").

5. A deep lake in Cumberland in the northern part of the Lake District, surrounded by mountains that in their turn are surrounded by still taller peaks. The lake is notable also for its wooded shores and numerous islands.

6. Among Derwentwater's islands are Saint Herbert's Isle, named after a religious mentioned by Bede; the illusionary "Floating Island"; Derwent Isle, about six acres in extent, the site of a fine house with lawns, gardens, and great trees.

7. Pope's *Imitations of Horace*, Satires 2.6.189–90.

8. The black lead mine was at the head of Lake Borrowdale, in south Cumberland, about five miles from Keswick.

9. Ovid was born at Sulmo (now Sulmona) in a picturesque region among the lakes and mountains of the Abruzzi. The beauties of his birthplace quickened a love of nature, which he describes evocatively, as in the *Tristia*.

10. HLP means Windermere (as Winandermere in the Lake District is known), the largest lake in England; or the town of the same name, which provides a superb view of the lake.

11. A mountain in the center of Cumberland, on the east side of Bassenthwaite Water, about three miles north of Keswick, reaches an altitude of over three thousand feet.

12. In Dunbartonshire and Stirlingshire, it is the largest loch in Scotland and attains a depth of about six hundred feet. It is almost entirely surrounded by ranges of lofty hills, culminating in Ben Lomond, which rises on the eastern side to an altitude of almost thirty-two hundred feet.

13. HLP's reference to the *British Review* is cryptic. She may have meant the subtitle, the *London Review*, of the *European Magazine* or a periodical named the *English Review*.

In his letter now missing, SL perhaps mentioned that he had advance information about notices in either of these periodicals. In the *European Magazine* 16 (1789): 332, there is an unflattering notice of *Observations:*

"Beauties and defects are so closely intermingled in almost every page of this desultory and heterogeneous performance, that the acutest powers of criticism might find it an arduous and perhaps impractical task entirely to decompose them. Sentences, the harmonious and accurate structure of which would certainly not discredit the pen of a Johnson or a Gibbon, are frequently surrounded by a context crowded with familiar phrases and vulgar idioms, while sentiments and descriptions equally elegant and spirited are contrasted with penurious thoughts and impotent reflections. It would however be uncandid to conceal, that many of the defective parts of this work appear to be rather the result of negligence, and the affectation of an easy, playful, and familiar stile, than an ignorance of the art of composition."

In the *English Review* 14 (1789): 385–86, *The Sentimental Mother* is not unfavorably noticed, and HLP is named as the possible "monster," or unnatural mother. Attributed to Baretti, the play calls ironic attention to her in the subtitle: ". . . a comedy, in five acts; the legacy of an old friend, and his last moral lesson to Mrs. Hester Lynch Thrale, now Mrs. Hetser [*sic*] Lynch Piozzi."

TO SOPHIA BYRON

Liverpool[1]
19: August 1789

Peace peace dearest Mrs. Byron——and don't think any more of such *Three penny* Afflictions: I wrote to scold Mr. Este,[2] and am perswaded he will never play me those paltry Tricks again: *very* paltry Tricks they are, *to be sure;* yet not worth serious fretting, or eager Quarelling about. We have been detained from this Place longer than was our Intention by the renewed Kindnesses of an old Friend you must have heard me speak of many Years ago: Mrs. Strickland of Sizergh in Westmorland, who was one of my *earliest* Intimates; her Maiden Name *Townley:*[3] her Grandmother Lady Phillippa Standish Daughter to the old Duke of Norfolk.[4] She was in France with Mr. Thrale and me in the Year 1773 I think—but various Accidents have kept us long asunder.[5] The first Thing I heard at Kendal however, was that She had taken Pains to waylay, and carry us to her House instead of the Inn, so with her, and her Son who is married to Sir John Lawson's Daughter a pretty pleasing Girl whom Mr. Piozzi and I had met with at Brussells in our Way to England;[6] we have been living this last Week, and are now half killed with the Heat, tho' travelling as slowly as possible.

What a Harvest here is! and what charming Weather to carry it in! I am so good a Lover of my Country that neither the beautiful Lakes, nor the nice Diversions they afford of rowing—Dipping, driving by the Side of 'em &c. could give me more solid Pleasure than the Sight of this brilliant Sun, and the Effect it has upon every body's Comforts at a Time when other Nations are so terribly distressed too, and Corn was just going to rise violently even in England—but we are always saved from Ruin at the *very Moment*.

Mean while poor Mrs. Strickland whom I left in high Health has lost the use of all her Limbs—so far worse than Mrs. Lewis that She can neither walk nor stand, and Miss Weston writes me Word that Sir Joshua Reynolds is going quite blind[7]——He and I never much loved one another,[8] but I am sincerely grieved——He has now got *two of his Warnings* poor Fellow! you know how deaf he was long ago.[9] What Age can Sir Joshua be of I am thinking;[10] hard upon Seventy sure, but you know better than I.

Tell me some thing pretty dearest Madam and direct it to The Post Office Denbigh N. Wales.

We are now at Liverpool where Daniel—once my ladyship's Butler comes to see us, and asks for Mrs. Byron: he married the Housemaid, pretty Nancy we called her, and has little Sophias and Cecilias by the Score. The Kembles[11] will I trust do so too in an Hour for we have not been here longer.

Accept my Husband's respectful and my own Affectionate Compliments and believe me / Ever Yours / H: L: P.

Text: Ry. 546.21.

1. HLP enjoyed Liverpool where the docks were "so magnificent, the Streets so large, so splendid with richly furnished Shops all Day so luminous with well ranged Lamps all Night—so clean tho' so crouded, so comfortable tho' splendid—so decent tho' unavoidably noisy. Viva Liverpool!" ("Journey Book").
2. The letter of rebuke is missing.
3. For Cecilia Strickland, see HLT to Q, 3 July [1784], n. 1.
4. See HLT to Q, 3 July [1784], n. 4.
5. The year was 1775. See *French Journals,* pp. 56–64 and passim.
6. The elder son of Charles Strickland and Cecilia was Thomas. On 24 February 1789, he had married Anastasia Maria (1769–1807), the eldest daughter of John Lawson (1744–1811), fifth baronet (1781) of Brough Hall, in Catterick, Yorks., and Elizabeth, née Scarisbrick (1749–1801). See HLT to Q, 3 July [1784], n. 2.
7. Joshua Reynolds (1723–92), knighted (1769). As he painted a portrait, Sir Joshua's eyesight suddenly failed. He first noted the event on 13 July 1789. Within ten weeks he had lost the sight of one eye. He suffered from *Amaurosis*—gutta serena—a disease of the optic nerve, which in his case progressed so slowly that he never became blind.
8. HLP admired him as a great painter and sociable man but was uncomfortable that, like Voltaire's Pococurante, he could not be pleased (*Thraliana* 1:382).
9. After three years of study on the Continent, Reynolds returned to London on 16 October 1752 with two physical defects: a scar on his lip from a riding accident at Minorca and deafness brought on by the cold of the Vatican while he was studying Raphael.

HLP alludes obliquely to her poem "Three Warnings," which she had contributed to Anna Williams's *Miscellany* (1766). The pertinent lines, uttered by "Death," are:

> If you are lame, and deaf, and blind,
> You've had your three sufficient warnings.

See HLP to Q, 4 June 1785, n. 11.

10. In 1789 he was sixty-six.
11. See HLT to Q, 14 July [1784], n. 3; HLP to SL, 15 November [1788], n. 12.

In her "Journey Book" HLP wrote: "Our Friends the Kembles help to make [Liverpool] pleasant and here are no drawbacks. We have a mighty pretty Theatre and Lord Derby's Park at Knowesley served for a Day's Amusement well enough."

TO PENELOPE SOPHIA WESTON

Liverpool
Saturday
22: August [1789]

So dear Miss Weston and her Hanover Square Friends have shared all the Delights that *Water* can give this hot Weather—

While a River or a Sea
Was to us a Dish of Tea &c.[1]

Mean Time I do not tell you 'twas judiciously managed to run from Lago Maggiore to Loch Lomond, and finish with the Cumberland Meres; any more than it would be wisely done to put Milton into the Hands of a young Beginner, and when good Taste was obtained—lay Thomson's charming Seasons on the Desk;[2] then make your Pupil close his Studies with Waller's Poem on the Summer Islands.[3]

Beg of Major Barry to make my Peace with his Country men; some one told me the other day they were offended at a Passage in the Journey thro' Italy; and I should be very sorry on one Side my Head, and much flattered on the other—— *That they should think it worth their while.*[4]

Mrs. Byron is justly enough enraged with Mr. Este; I shall leave her to punish him: his Offence to *me* was free from ill meaning I am perswaded——but it was a very paltry Trick, and its Consequences will cure him of ever playing such another.

We spent a sweet Day at Drumphillin near Glasgow, in Consequence of Dr. Moore's attentive Kindness;[5] and even from that charming Spot continued to see the majestic Mountain which attracted all my Admiration, and which still keeps possession of my Heart:[6] I took *my* last leave of it from the Duke of Hamilton's Summer house, but at a Distance of seventy or eighty Miles it may be discerned.[7]

If you ask me what single Object has most impressed my Mind in this Journey of 800 Miles round the Island,—I shall reply *Ben Lomond.*

After our Business in Wales is finally settled, we shall go *Bath-wards* by Shrewsbury; I think 'tis best follow the Severn on to Gloucester: have not I heard Mr. Whalley and you tell Wonders of the Scenery about Ludlow? That part of England must be very fine which effaces the Ideas of Softness and Amenity excited by the Views round Keswick, but do when you write, say whether the Wenlock and Bridgnorth, or the Ludlow and Bishop's Castle road are likeliest to please us—my Heart votes for this last I think; besides I *have* seen Worcester, and Hereford will be new to me.

If I promised you an Account of Glasgow I did a foolish Thing; What *account* can one give of a very fine, oldfashioned, regularly-built, Continental-looking Town? full as Naples, yet solemn as [Turano][8]—after Glasgow too every thing looks *so* Little. I think Mr. Piozzi must write the Account of *this* Town; he is all Day upon the Docks, and all night at the Theatre: both are crowded, yet both are *clean;* the Streets embellished with showy Shops all Day, and lighted up like Oxford Road all Night. A Harbour full of Ships: a chearful, opulent, commodious City.

Have you had enough for a Dose? And will you give all our Compliments to all our Friends. And will you love my Husband and Cecilia / and Your Affectionate Servant / H: L: P.

Direct to The Post Office Denbigh / N: Wales.

Text: Princeton University Library. *Address:* To / Miss Weston / Queen's Square / *Westminster. Postmark:* LIVERPOOL AU 24 89.

1. From William Shenstone (1714–63), "The Rape of the Trap." See *A Collection of Poems in Six Volumes by Several Hands* (1748; London: Printed by J. Hughs, for J. Dodsley, in Pall-Mall, 1765), 5:43.

2. *The Seasons,* a poem in blank verse, consists of four books, one for each season, with a concluding hymn. Written by James Thomson (1700–1748), it was published in 1726–30.

3. Edmund Waller (1606–87) wrote "The Battle of the Summer Islands" in three cantos. It was first printed with his collected poems (1645).

4. In *Observations* (2:125), HLP mocked Irish taste in art:

"We have just been to see [the pope's] gardens; they are poor things enough; and the device of representing Vulcan's cave with the Cyclops in *water*-works, was more worthy of Ireland than Rome!"

Major Barry was of Irish descent and after 1794 lived for long periods in Ireland.

5. HLP refers to his letters of introduction, one of which procured a visit to the Hamilton summer house.

6. From the duke of Hamilton's summer estate, HLP "took [her] parting look of Ben Lomond a Mountain so high as to be easily seen from thence, a Distance of fifty or sixty Miles at least: and so handsome as to make it difficult for any Object to obliterate the Idea" ("Journey Book").

7. Of this house, called Châtellerault, opposite Cadzow Castle, HLP wrote: "Hamilton Park is like many another Park, so is the house; but there are Vandykes in it which have no Rivals nearer than Wilton, and one Rubens which has no superior even at Antwerp.

. . . The Duke's Woods, Walks, &c. are delightful: Oaks of prodigious Dignity indeed to very great age contradict the Speech made about Scotland's having no Tree in it planted before the Union; these are at least 3 or 400 Years old, and very fine ones of their Kind" ("Journey Book").

8. HLP recalls the area around the Turano, a tributary of the Nera. It joins the larger stream a few miles below the waterfall at Terni.

TO PENELOPE SOPHIA WESTON

Denbigh Tuesday
1: September [1789]

Dear Miss Weston

I thank you for your Invitation to pretty Ludlow, and shall let you know when we are likely to arrive there that all possible Advantage may be taken of your friendly hints. Mr. Knight is an old Acquaintance of my Husband by the

Description you give of his Taste and elegant Conversation:[1] at least it would be strange should there be *two* such Men of any *English* Name. Scotch and Welsh Families are disposed in a different Manner: *We* have but so many Names, and all who bear those Names are related to each other. I find a great Resemblance between the two Nations in a hundred little Peculiarities, and the Erse sounded so like my own native Tongue that I wished for Erudition to prove the original Affinity between them.

The French Nation was never a favourite of mine—and I see little done to encourage one's Esteem of them—*as* a Nation. Their low people are very ignorant, their high ones very self-sufficient: You now read in every Paper the Effects of that Self sufficiency acting upon that Ignorance. Fermentation however will after much Turbulence at length produce a *clear* Spirit,[2] tho' probably 'twill be a *coarse* one; they will know in a Dozen years what they would have, and I fancy *that* will be once more an absolute Monarchy.[3]

Major Barry has been very good to write to me so.[4] We are here in the midst of Steward's Accounts &c.[5] or I would thank him as I ought; to tell him mean Time how highly Mr. Piozzi and I prize his Friendship——and tell dear Mrs. Byron how much I love her, and how sorry I am that my Letter should have vexed her: I only fretted for a Moment just because I *did* love her; if I had not loved her, what had I cared? The Stuff was of no Consequence, and the Publisher used *her* worse than he used *me:* He will play such Tricks no more though.

I am shocked for poor Mrs. Whalley;[6] the more so perhaps, if more is possible, because here are Mr. and Mrs. Parry whom you have seen at our house lying ill at a Place in this Neighbourhood—far from their own Home, with Contusions, Black Eyes &c. the Consequence of just such an Accident, only putting a Hedge for a Brook.[7]

I do not clearly comprehend the Account of Mrs. Siddons's project—but She is with Child it seems, and will hardly be able to act at all next Year.[8] Write often and direct hither till I say *Nay.* Mr. Piozzi has half a Mind to go further into Wales, and see *our* Highlands, but this is Head Quarters always—so direct here, and tell me the News of the Town. Tell me particularly that Mrs. Byron is pretty well, and very kind, and that She loves us still.

I have a good Opinion of a Woman esteemed by Major Barry, and *Trefusis* is a Name one respects.[9] Give your Family their proper Share of our Compliments and accept my Master's best Wishes with those of Cecilia and of Your ever Affectionate Servant / H: L: Piozzi.

I hear nothing from the Greatheeds. Where are they?

P.S. In a few days I intend go to see our Little estate, and chose the place for building a Little Cottage,[10] and a Little Room for our dear friend Miss Weston; accept my best Compliments and believe me for ever your Most Humble Servant / and good friend / G. P.

Text: Princeton University Library. With a postscript by GP. *Address:* Miss Weston / Queen Square / Westminster. *Postmark:* SE 5 89.

1. Thomas Knight (d. 1820), an independently wealthy actor and playwright with strong ties in Liverpool and, from 1787, with the Bath theater. In that year and city he married the actress Margaret Farren (d. 1804), sister of Elizabeth, later Countess Derby. In 1795 he was to move to London and the Covent Garden Theatre, in 1803 to Liverpool as one of the managers of the theater there.

2. Cf. Samuel Butler, "Miscellaneous Thoughts," lines 351–52:

> All love, at first, like gen'rous wine,
> Ferments and frets until 'tis fine.

3. HLP's timetable was close. From 1804, Napoleon as emperor worked steadily to make himself and the state omnipotent, suppressing not only political freedom but also private interests and civil rights. This had been accomplished by at least 1810.

4. The Barry letter is missing.

5. The steward, who managed the Bachygraig estates and additional property in Denbigh, was Edward Edwards of that town. See "Memorial against Cator" ([autumn 1792], Ry. 611).

6. Elizabeth Whalley in the spring of 1789 had been thrown from a carriage into a brook near Mendip Lodge, the Whalley summer residence. She never fully recovered from the accident and was to die in December 1801. See Anna Seward to TSW, 7 April 1789 (*Seward Letters* 2:301).

7. Caleb Hillier Parry (1755–1822) received his M.D. from the University of Edinburgh in 1778. In that year he married Sarah, née Rigby (1749–1831), of Warrington, Lancs. (Many years and several children later, the couple were to separate amicably.)

By 1779 the Parrys had moved to Bath, where he set up his surgery at 27 Royal Circus. His practice grew until it was one of the largest in the country. At the height of his career he earned as much as three thousand pounds annually. See his will (P.R.O., Prob. 11/1657/275), which clarifies the relationship with his wife.

8. SS refused engagements at Drury Lane during 1789–90 because of a quarrel with the manager, Richard Brinsley Sheridan (1751–1816), over money matters. In 1789, while visiting Bath and Birmingham, she began "modelling in clay [which] became her favourite amusement" (Campbell 2:163–67).

Her pregnancy ended in a miscarriage and lingering ill health. As she had written to her close friend Sir Charles Hotham-Thompson (1729–94) on 30 August: "The truth is that I have been in so miserable a State of health and Spirits for a long time, as not to have written a line to anyone except my Physician, dear good Dr Reynolds" (cited by Manvell, p. 174).

Except for seven performances in London (December 1790 to March 1791), she was absent from the stage from the autumn of 1789 until January 1792.

9. The friend of PSW and Major Barry, Elizabeth Trefusis (ca. 1763–1808) was a sister of Robert George William (1764–97), seventeenth baron Clinton (1791). She was the author of *Poems and Tales*, 2 vols. (London: S. Tipper, 1808). See *GM* 78, pt.2 (1808): 859.

10. The idea of Brynbella was conceived during this journey to North Wales. In her "Journey Book" HLP wrote: "my best Amusement here was planning a House with Windows every way. . . ."

TO SOPHIA BYRON

Denbigh Tuesday
1: September [1789]

My dear Mrs. Byron made the properest Answer in the World to Mr. Este: had he published a letter of yours to *me*——would you not have felt Resentment in the same Proportion? Would you not have blamed your Friend for putting the Letter in his *Power?* For after all, a Man *cannot* publish what he has *not:* at least I thought so; till your very kind Exculpation of yourself shewed me that he printed merely from Memory; a Thing capable I am sure to have much astonished even *yourself.*

I am now no longer angry for the best Reason, I have nothing to be angry about: you only read him a Passage, and he took advantages which he will never have again—Mr. Este cannot wonder if *you* express more Displeasure than I do, for you have Breach of Trust to complain of——I trusted him *not,*[1] but gave him such Prohibitions in my last Letter, that I have no Fears of his ever more publishing surreptitiously any thing of my writing——but here is too much about such Nonsense. Meantime do not say or suppose that I could think you guilty of any dishonourable Action: God forbid; I was jealous of *your* Kindness, and acted on that Impulse, as I am convinced *you* would have done in the same Case. I had no Claim upon Mr. Este but for the common Civilities of Society: now do dear sweet Friend be satisfied with yourself and with me, who have long loved you, and who will always love you, and who beg you to believe it.——

Now tell me you comical Lady some pretty Tittle Tattle, and take the *Matter* from the most *beautiful Subjects:* We have heard some imperfect Story of a Quarrel between the fair Duchess of Rutland and Mrs. Fitzherbert.[2] Make me understand the what, where, and why. Tell me too if Lady Haggerstone is not Sister to the last named of the Disputants—I think so.[3]

The Black Wax on your Letter frighted me less because you have so many Relations: I had forgotten Mr. Delme though.[4] Had we known that young Mrs. Strickland's Family and yours were intimate we should have had still more Chat. The amiable Woman you remember tall, active and elegant tho' never handsome——is now chained to her Chair by Infirmity: She has to comfort her however the attentions of her *second* Husband,[5] and the Dutyful Fondness of her Son by the *first;* besides two little Babies[6] whose Birth has been followed by their Mother's *Loss of Limbs.*

How variously does Heaven bestow its Blessings and Corrections! and how unreasonable are those who expect in this Life nothing but the first.

Poor Mrs. Lewis stays at Reading for the same Reason that Dear Mrs. Byron remains in London;[7] but her Daughter's health mends She says, so is the less concerned.[8]

Daniel was not the only Person at Liverpool who enquired much for you: the Kembles said every sweet and respectful Word in the Dictionary when you were mentioned.

Cecilia has too much reason to rejoyce that you remember *her;* She is very sensible of the Honour and so is Mr. Piozzi.[9] He wonders what ails the Hamiltons that they never answered a Letter I wrote from Scotland—and bids me ask *You*.

Adieu dearest Madam, and never cease to love / Your H: L: P.

Text: Ry. 546.22. *Address:* Hon: Mrs. Byron / Bolton Street / London. *Postmark:* SE 5 89.

1. HLP consistently distrusted Este's political and personal loyalties. See *Thraliana* 2:742; her letter to him, 26 June 1793.

2. As long before as 1787 in Brighton, each had hoped to be recognized as the reigning beauty. At the time, Mary Isabella Manners, née Somerset (1756–1831), duchess of Rutland, feeling morally superior to Mrs. Fitzherbert, "was by far the fairest of the fair." This praise was soon challenged on 9 August 1787 when the *Morning Post* remarked: "Mrs. Fitzherbert looks more elegant than ever. One could hardly help exclaiming with the Army of Mahomet II, when he showed them Irene: 'Such a woman is worth a kingdom.'" The rivalry over beauty and royal lovers persisted, especially after the recently widowed duchess appeared in the winter of 1788 as the favorite of the duke of York. See Nathaniel Wraxall, *Historical and Posthumous Memoirs* 5:36–37.

3. Frances Smythe (1762–1836) married Carnaby Haggerston (1756–1831), fifth baronet (1777), of Haggerston Castle (Northumberland).

Like Mrs. Fitzherbert, Lady Haggerston was the daughter of Walter Smythe (d. 1786), of Brambridge, Hants., and Mary, née Errington (d. 1807).

4. Peter Delmé (1748–89) of Titchfield, Hants.; Braywick, Berks.; and Erlestoke, Wilts. He was M.P. for Morpeth, Northumberland, from 1774 until his death on 15 August.

On 16 February 1769 he had married Lady Elizabeth Howard (1746–1813), daughter of Henry (1694–1758), seventh earl of Carlisle (1738), and his second wife, Isabella (1721–95), daughter of William (1669–1736), fourth baron Byron (1695).

5. Gerard (or Jarrard) Strickland. See HLT to Q, 3 July [1784], n. 1.

6. The second marriage produced three children: Charles, born 16 September 1779, died a few weeks later; George (1780–1843); Jarrard (or Gerard) Edward (1782–1844).

7. Sophia Maria, the youngest daughter of Mrs. Byron, was unmarried and apparently ailing at this time.

8. For Sarah Lewis's illness, see HLP's letter to Mrs. Byron, 13 [July 1788], n. 9.

9. Sophia Byron had informed HLP that she planned to add a codicil to her will in which she left "To Cecilia Thrale my little Gold and Ivory <   > Book . . . Instead of my Grand-daughter Augusta."

TO SOPHIA BYRON

Denbigh
11: September 1789.

Dearest Mrs. Byron

How tender, yet how dismal is your last Paragraph?[1] Oh pray send for that kind and skilful Friend Mr. Farquahar,[2] and make him tye that too active Soul tight in its thin Wire Cage, lest it should beat the house down with fluttering so.

I wish you safely and speedily at Bath and will hasten to meet you there;[3] tho' Steward's Accounts and Country Matters long neglected, are tedious Things to get through: my good-natured husband however, who sees my Anxiety, bids me assure you that he will make all possible dispatch, in order to bring forward the moment of our Meeting.

We are *here* till we are *there* My dear Friend; and Denbigh Direction will long be that my Heart most delights in——After all her Turnings and Windings and *Hunting* up and down, the Hare you know, loves to dye where She began first to live[4]——and so does another *Pussey* of your Acquaintance.

Well! I have heard *some* body say *some*thing of Colonel Balfour *some* Time or other:[5] but it was good, by what I can remember: an Irishman is often honest, and almost always brave, whatever Defects he may have;[6] but I find the *Nation* is angry at me for a Passage in Your favourite Travels——'tis too late to care about it, or I should be more sorry than glad.

Why will you be always doing Exploits of Valour in the Park? walking thro' it at Midnight one Time, and crossing it in a Storm at another: The Experiments might either of them have been fatal, yet I dread Lightning less for you than Leanness: and am very earnest for a Letter to tell me your Bones are covering.

Farewell and may God bless you; and keep your Spirits up till I can tell you personally at Bath how / Truly I am yours / H: L: Piozzi.

Cecilia sends Respects—her Health begins to *unsettle* you understand me, She grows too fast.

Text: Ry. 546.23.

1. Sophia Byron, whose letter is missing, was suffering the effects of pleurisy and rapid loss of weight.
2. Sophia Byron bequeathed to Farquhar a large black diamond-studded ring for his "friendship and attention . . . at all times and on all occasions."
3. The Piozzis were settled in Bath by mid-October, there to remain for about six weeks. They returned to Hanover Square by 27 December—after a journey of some thirteen hundred miles (*Thraliana* 2:749).
4. See *Oxford Proverbs*, p. 354: "The hare always returns to her form."
5. HLP had heard the false rumor that Colonel Nisbet Balfour (1743–1823) was to marry Q. He had been a distinguished officer under General Cornwallis in the American Revolution. At the war's end he was made a colonel and appointed aide-de-camp to the king. For his subsequent military and parliamentary career, see *DNB*.
6. Colonel Balfour was in fact born in Edinburgh, the son of a bookseller, and the last representative of the Balfours of Dunbog, Fifeshire.

TO SOPHIA BYRON

Denbigh
19: September 1789.

It was very kind of you to write so, I was beginning to be uneasy when the Letter came: my good-natured Husband bids me repeat his Assurances that we will come as soon as ever *we can*. God knows we have seen too little of our Estate here, and Mr. Piozzi will tell you how severely our Affairs have suffered by Neglect. *He* is excessively active and diligent to mend Matters however; is adored by the Tenants,[1] and delighted in by the Neighbouring Gentlemen; I am most happy in *Him* for every Reason.——But such Friends as there are in the World!! Let me preserve at least *one* who loves me, that is my dear Mrs. Byron: Bath will restore your Health, I am *sure* it will, it always *did:* and we shall meet at old Greenway's Cold Bath [2] I hope. Dear Mr. Hay is tender and gentle, and Dr. Harrington will be *so* attentive, and I will come Morning, Noon, and Night to see how your Sweet Spirits mend. Mr. Piozzi says *He* will have a Share in your Cure as soon as You can bear the Sound of his Forte Piano.

At present Farewell; These nasty Steward's Accounts crack my Brains, I know no more of Business *now* than Cæcilia does: and have [at] best just Sense enough to see that I am cheated, without knowing how to extricate myself.[3] Had not God given me always a large Fortune, I must have been in Prison Years ago.

Adieu my dearest Friend and believe me / Ever Yours / while H: L: P.

A fine Young Man here just come into a handsome Fortune has shocked us all sadly.

He had been with some Friends to Ireland on a party of Pleasure, and was safe returned to Holy Head—jumping on Shore however in a gay humour he struck his Head against some thing of the Ship, with such Violence that it stunned him; and falling into the Sea was taken up Stone Dead. What Accidents this World is full of! Mr. Piozzi and Cecilia join in all best and kindest Respects.

Text: Ry. 546.24. *Postmark:* SE < > 89.

1. The Bachygraig estates consisted of the following "tenements," which were sometimes further subdivided: Bachegraige, 273 acres; New Inn, 29 acres; Plâs-newydd, 72 acres; Cold Robin, 34 acres; Childaugoed, 62 acres; Rhewl, 20 acres; Cross fford, 6 acres; Fynno Beyno, 3 acres; Graige, 21 acres; Gwern-y-cŵm and Tyddyn-y-Doctor, 44 acres; Pant Glas, 37 acres (spellings as recorded in Ry. Ch. 1014).

In 1789 the Piozzis began to buy up meadow and wooded lands in Tremeirchion parish so that by 1790 the Bachygraig estates consisted of 832 acres, valued annually at £502 (N.L.W., 11103D and 11104C).

2. For Mrs. Greenaway [Greenway], see HLT to Q [27 June 1784], n. 7.

3. Edward Edwards, the Piozzis' steward, embezzled rents that were due the Piozzis from their tenants of the Bachygraig estates and of their property in Denbigh.

Within three days of this letter to Mrs. Byron, HLP asked John Perkins at Southwark what legal action could be taken. On 25 September Perkins replied (Ry. 600.8): "This days post brought me your favour of the 22d Instant. I am sorry you are likely to lose any Money by Edward Edwards. I always thought him a distressed man but I understood, that your affairs in Wales was long ago taken out of his hands for I think it's not many Months since I [saw] him in the paper a Bankrupt." For the amount of the Piozzi loss, see HLP to Charlotte Lewis, 20 September, n. 7.

TO HUGH GRIFFITH

Denbigh
19: September 1789.

Mr.and Mrs. Piozzi present their best Compliments to Mr. Griffith[1] with a Thousand Thanks for his very kind and friendly Invitation and Letter: the last they have been properly *attentive to;* and the first they hope for the pleasure of accepting another Season.

When Mr. Griffith remits his Money to London as usual,[2] he will be kind enough to send it no more to Mr. Cator,[3] but directed to Drummond's and Co. Bankers Charing Cross.

Text: N.L.W., Llanfair and Brynodol

1. Hugh Griffith (1724–95) was the third son of John (1697–1764) of Carnarvon and Margaret, née Rowlandson (1697–1784). About 1749 he married Mary Wynn (d. 1797), who bore his seven children: Jane (baptized 1751); John (1753–1830); William (1755–64); Hugh (baptized 1756); Wynne (baptized 1757); Richard (1761–64); Margaret (baptized 1763). For the Griffith family, see "Baptismal Registers," C.R.O., Gwynedd.

Griffith owned two Carnarvonshire estates: Brynodol in the parish of Tydweiliog and Plâs Llanfair in the parish of Llanfair.

2. Griffith had rented Salusbury land and buildings in Tydweiliog and Llangwadl at least as early as 1772. Almost immediately there was a misunderstanding between him and HLT's mother, Hester Maria Salusbury, née Cotton (1707–73). "He pays or proposes to pay the rent of *one* Year when *two Years* are due; this Mrs. Salusbury does not Approve and says the difference she expected to find between having a Gentleman for a Tenant instead of a Common Tythe Taker is the punctuality of paying every years Rent as it became due" (HLT's "Pocket Book" [1773], Ry. 616). Griffith agreed to the demand and continued to rent the same land, now owned by HLP, until he died.

3. When HLT was widowed, Griffith had sent his annual rent to John Cator as one of HT's executors. Ever since 1784 (but particularly after 1787), HLP thought Cator guilty of financial duplicity and wished no more of her monies to be placed in his care. See her "Memorial" [autumn 1792] against him.

TO CHARLOTTE LEWIS

Denbigh
20: September [17]89.

My dear Mrs. Lewis

You find yourself interrupted by Company—Yes indeed—while writing to your Friend——Thank God you have no worse Interruptions. Poor Mrs. Byron has had a Pleurisy, and Miss Weston writes me word that She is in a very dangerous Way: I am truly grieved for her, and there is Borghi[1] can't write at all, but employs old Tonioli[2] to tell us how bad he is. These are dismal Tales, but no better Proofs of the World's End I think,—tho' quite as good ones—as the

Madness which has seized on poor Loutherbourg.[3] How every body fancies their own little Circle the World! and how little the Circle is, even of the most expanded Fancier;—each passing Moment shews one.

A poor Peasant Fellow in these Parts about forty Years since was sent by my Mother to a still more distant County to buy or sell Barley—The Weather was unseasonable, and Things went badly enough. "Mistress says the Man at his return, I *thought* the World was coming to an End, and now *I'm sure* on't; for the Folks in Caernarvonshire know that Owen Lowgo[4] who was King of the Country 600 Years ago, is to rise again before the last Day; and I find he is got up now this Week as high as his Elbow.—"

Are the People in Berkshire much wiser yet in the Year 1789? With regard to French politics,[5] like Bottom's Plot for his Tragedy in the Midsummers Night's Dream; you shall see 'twill fall out *pat* as I told you.[6]

With regard to what detains us here in Wales, you are a naughty Lady not to remember that we have much serious Matter to mind—a Steward in Arrears,[7] a Mine in Hope,[8] and a new House in Idea.[9] When we have got Money from one however, and some Expectation from the other, we will leave the last for future Intentions; and drive towards Bath by the way of Shrewsbury, Hereford, Monmouth and Glocester. The Weather will have done its worst soon I trow, and the Roads will mend.

But not till the Bath Exploits are over, shall we see again our sweet Mrs. Lewis, to whom we may really be pretty well qualified to give a smart account of England, Scotland, and Wales by the Time we arrive at dear Reading, and bring little *Figaro* to keep Company with Mademoiselle *Robinette.*[10]

Mean Time our Health and Spirits are good, and Cecilia laughs when I am uneasy about *her,* and says She is stronger than myself. Do you hear that Miss Thrale marries Colonel Balfour? or is all that a Dream? She was five and twenty Years old last Thursday, and we illuminated our Windows and so did all Denbigh Town; *not upon her Account* but because young Mr. Lloyd of Pontriffeth came of Age that Day:[11] it was droll enough however.

Mr. Piozzi sees what Friends and Agents I had in my State of Widowhood, now he is come to look over old Accounts &c. His Diligence and Acuteness will I hope remedy many Evils, and prevent more of the same Nature——but there has been sad Work made indeed. I am weary of fretting over past Misfortunes, and would rather be thinking of Floretta[12]——but my Master gives me ne'er a Moment; he is however desirous I should send you his kindest Respects, and tell you with what Truth and Love I always [re]main Your most Affectionate / H: L: Piozzi.——

Love and sweet Words to your Household.

P.S. Dear Mrs. Lewis if you dont go to *Bath* to meet us, we must stay [one] months more absent of your charming and amiable Company; My presence in the Country [ ] was very necessary because I found the estate in Great disorder and principaly for the negligence of the Steward, and I [intend] to send him away. Well Last Night I made the agreement with the [ ] Manor for two years; the *Plan* of the Home Mr. Mead [he has done], if I can Save some money sure. I hope begining to build the House next year, but how ever may happen, I hope to see joy of Streatham. Adieu and / belive me [Your G.P.]

Text [with a postscript by Gabriel Piozzi]: Hyde Collection. *Address:* To / Mrs. Lewis / London Street / Reading / Berks. *Postmark:* SE 23 89.

1. See HLT to Q, [27 June 1784], n. 2.

2. Probably Girolamo Toniolo (fl. 1754–92), author of *Le Due Gemelle. A New comic opera . . . as performed at the King's Theatre* (Italian and English, 1784). Less likely is Vincenzo Tonioli, a composer of instrumental music best known for his six duets for two violins, a work published in London.

3. Philip James de Loutherbourgh (1740–1812), painter and book illustrator, was born in Germany of Polish extraction. Coming to England in 1771, he served Garrick as a scene painter at the Drury Lane from 1773 to 1776. He had first exhibited at the Royal Academy in 1772, was elected an associate in 1780 and an academician in 1781.

He became a disciple of the pseudoprophet Richard Brothers (1757–1824) and claimed for himself and his wife the gift of prophecy and faith healing. In 1789 there appeared under the imprint of Mary Pratt *A List of a few Cures performed by Mr. and Mrs. De Loutherbourg of Hammersmith Terrace without Medicine, by a Lover of the Lamb of God.*

4. Probably "Owain Lawgoch" or Owain ap Thomas ap Rhodri (ca. 1330–78). A soldier of fortune, once in the service of the king of France, he planned to invade Wales and claim kingship. The invasion (1372) failed, but the adventure, celebrated in poetry, song, and legend, elevated Owain as a folk hero. He was assassinated in France and buried in the church of Saint Leger.

5. For the events to which HLP alluded, see her letter to SL, 21 July [1789], n. 3. This period also saw the prudent self-exile of the comte d'Artois, the prince de Condé, the prince de Conti, the duc de Bourbon, marshal de Broglie, and others who were hostile to Jacques Necker (1732–1804), recently returned to power as *directeur général des finances.*

6. *A Midsummer's Night's Dream* 5.1.186–87.

7. Edwards, the "Steward in Arrears," was replaced by Thomas Lloyd (d. 6 May 1811), mercer at Denbigh, who immediately took up the Piozzi cause. He wrote on 15 October to summarize the situation: "Mr. Piozzi's demand against Edward Edwards . . . is 125£.16s.0d. and if that was scrutinized, I am afraid the Balance would appear more in Mr. Piozzi's favor." On 19 August 1790, Lloyd reported: "I am sorry to say I am afraid no prospect of Your recovering any of Your Cash from him, I have been requested to apply to him for the small sum of Four Pounds, his answer was he could not pay it." By 24 November 1791, Edwards had placed his assets "in an other person's Name, which," wrote Lloyd, "is rascally, and am afraid no prospect of Your ever being Paid." By 31 October 1793, Edwards paid Lloyd "on Mrs. Piozzi's amount the sum of Twenty Pounds, which is more than I thought he would have done, attaching which he hath sent a Note to say that he will annually pay the like sum, which is a kind of Security for the remainder and an acknowledgement." For this correspondence, see Ry. 603–4.

8. A shaft was sunk near Bachygraig and is still extant, but no evidence exists that the hoped-for lead was ever mined.

9. The future Brynbella was to be designed and built by Clement Mead. Only in 1793, however, did the site belong legally to the Piozzis. See HLP to PSP, 10 January 1793, n. 8.

10. Figaro and Robinette were Phillis's puppies.

11. The son of Bell Lloyd (1729–93) of Pontriffith, Edward Pryce had been born on 17 September 1768. An M.P. (1806–31), he was to succeed his great uncle as second baronet (1795) and to be raised to the peerage as Baron Mostyn (1831). He died on 3 April 1854.

12. HLP thought of "The Two Fountains" (Ry. 649) for a reason that she was later to explain to JSPS in "Harvard Piozziana" 3:1–2:

"I think I told you Dear Salusbury at the End—or toward the End of my last red Book,—

That having been so often solicited for Prologues, Epilogues, &c., my Heart began to pant for Dramatic Celebrity; and bring something—I knew not what—upon the *Stage*.

"Johnson's Fountains [with its character Floretta] would do well for a Masque—in the Manner of Milton's Comus I thought; where Sentiment and Show might supply the Place of Terror, Pity, or Merriment.

"Kemble and his Sister saw the Two first acts in 1789 as I remember, professed to like and bring it forward—— So I finished——and they *Shelfed* it."

For a slightly different version of the same situation, see "Harvard Piozziana" 2:215; cf. *Thraliana* 2:829, 836.

TO HENRY BARRY

Bath
19: October 1789.

Dear Sir

After so long a Silence I might make the Excuses and Apologies fill up a Side of Paper well enough——and plead Precedents innumerable for the proceeding—but 'tis better let your new Lapdog carry *such* sort of Compliments himself, while I have the honour to assure you that many people reckon him the handsomest Son of his Parents:[1] Mrs. Lewis has him with her at Reading just now, but earnestly wishes him safe in Town under his Master's Protection——Will you take the Trouble to send your Servant to one of the Coachmen who pass and repass perpetually, with a Charge that he may be taken Care of on the Road?

And now Dear Sir what think you of higher Matters? will my System of French Politicks come in Play within the Time I limited or no?[2] Yes, Yes, the prediction will prove as true about France as it proved about England I doubt not.[3] But why did I not foresee the Death of our amiable and partial Friend—our delightful Acquaintance and Companion Lord Huntingdon?[4] and why was I no less *surprized* some how than *grieved* at an Event every body ought to have expected, and I suppose the wise ones did expect.

We have made a long Journey this Summer, and seen nothing as agreable that's certain;[5] for People are better Things than Places as Terence told us long ago[6]——I have however seen and conversed with *Doctor Blair.*[7]

Wales did not look badly even after Scotland, and England looks lovely come from where one will. The Weather was favorable enough upon the whole, and the Highlands had not a Cloud upon them.

Excuse more Chat, Bath Chat is a poor thing heaven knows—a little solid London Talk would spread into many Plates of our thin Bread and Butter Conversations. Do send me some dear Sir, and I will make a Figure with it here whilst I stay. Mean Time accept Mr. Piozzi's best Compliments with those of your much Obliged Servant / H: L: Piozzi.

Text: Yale University Library, Tinker 2145. *Address:* Henry Barry Esq. / No. 10 St. James's Terrace / near Grosvenor Place / London. *Postmark:* BATH: OC 20 89

1. Figaro, the puppy.
2. See HLP to PSW, 1 September [1789].
3. Although HLP's analogy is casual, she here implies that Cromwell's regime began in a democratic frenzy with Pride's Purge in December 1648 and the execution of Charles I on 30 January 1649; that Cromwell and his eldest surviving son, Richard, ruled as absolute monarchs; that English despotism ended only with the return of Charles II to England in May 1660.
4. He died suddenly on 2 October while entertaining friends in the house of his nephew, Francis Rawdon (1754–1826), at Portman Square. Huntingdon's Saint James's Square residence was being repaired at the time. See the *Bath Journal*, 12 October; also HLP to Sophia Byron, 29 June 1788, n. 13, and 11 August [1788], n. 8; to PSP, 19 September 1793, n. 10.
5. In her "Journey Book," HLP wrote: "From Gloucester to Bath every Step is strewed with Beauty, and when one arrives there—'tis always fresh Admiration that fills the Mind. Every Day sees Population and Accommodation encrease——and *omne quod exit in* <*Ation*> I believe except Mortification, from which Bath affords best Refuge if Variety can allure one from thinking about Sorrow—or Friendships alleviate such Griefs as never can be forgotten."
6. For HLP's fuller statement on the Terentian assumption that all things material were subordinate in value to human beings, see her letter to JSPS, 28 January 1808, n. 1.
7. The Piozzis had met Hugh Blair in his native Edinburgh and admired him. For his part, in a letter dated 24 July [1789] to the Reverend George Husband Baird (1761–1840), he wrote: "Mr. Piozzi (who understands and speaks English very imperfectly) is an obliging and amiable man, and I am informed of very respectable character. Mrs. Piozzi (late Mrs Thrale) is exceedingly accomplished and agreable. She is not only mistress of all the modern Languages, but understands Latin perfectly, and is much conversant in all the parts of classical Literature. Her Conversation is lively and instructive; her information extensive; and her taste Excellent. I have seldom known any of the Learned Ladies with whom I have been so much pleased as with her" (Ry. 893.2).

TO PENELOPE SOPHIA WESTON

Bath
2: November 1789.

Dear Miss Weston

Not *one* Letter do I owe you, nor *three* nor four, but forty if they would make Compensation for your kind ones to Ludlow,[1] where Miss Powell's[2] Politeness made the Time pass very agreably indeed, spight of Rain which however provoking could not conceal the Beauty of its elegant Environs, even from an Eye made fastidious by the recent Sight of richer and more splendid Scenery.

Mrs. Byron read me the kind Words for which Mr. Piozzi and I owe you so many Thanks: She gains Strength daily, and will be quite restored if kept clear from Vexation and indulged in her favourite Exercises of Riding and the Cold Bath.

My Husband and She have many an amicable Spar about Bell's Oracle on Account of his Savage Treatment of Dear Siddons,[3] whose present State of Health demands Tenderness,[4] while her general Merit must enforce Respect. I wonder for my own Part what Rage possesses the people who wish to see or delight in seeing Virtue insulted[5]—Let us not learn to tear Characters in England as Persons are torne in France; and drink the *intellectual Life* of our Neighbours warm in our Lemonade.

Major Barry has written me a charming Letter,[6] do tell him that he shall find my Acknowledgements at Lichfield; I mean to write a Reference to Miss Seward about a Critical Dispute we had here at Bath some Evenings ago, concerning the two new Novels—which I find are set up in Opposition to each other, and People take Sides. You will easily imagine that Zeluco and Hayley's Young Widow are the Competitors.[7]

Give my kind Love to Miss Williams when you see her, and tell her that She is one of the persons I please myself with hoping to see a great deal of this winter.

We are all going to the Milkwoman's Tragedy tomorrow,[8] I fear with much Ill Will towards its Success—Her Ingratitude [to] Miss More deserves rough Censure,[9] but hissing her Play will not mend her Morals.[10]

Miss Wallis[11] is to play Belvidera next Saturday.[12] She is scarcely more of a Woman than Cecilia Thrale, and quite as young-looking; very Ladylike though, and a pretty-behaved Girl in a Room: I advised Dimond in Sport to act Douglas to her Lady Randolph as a still more suitable Part than Belvidera.[13]

Here's Nonsense enough for one Pacquet. 'Tis Time to say how much I am Dear Miss Westons / Affectionate Servant / H: L: P.

Text: Princeton University Library. *Address:* Miss Weston / Queen Square / Westminster. *Postmark:* NO 3 89.

1. On their journey from Denbigh to Bath, the Piozzis were forced to alter their anticipated route. Once they arrived at Shrewsbury, they found the city "was filled with Dancers all Night and Cattle all Day—it was Fair Time, and we went from there to Ludlow instead of Bridge North" ("Journey Book").

2. The Powell family originated in Worthen and Bank House between the counties of Salop and Montgomery. The family head, John Powell (1716–94), was born in Boston and had married Jane (Jannet) Grant (1735–74) of Newport, R.I. An ardent loyalist, he went to Halifax in 1776 and thence to England. His house and land in Massachusetts were confiscated and his wealth consequently reduced. He could, however, purchase property at Ludlow. He had two sons and three daughters: William Dummer (1755–1834), John, Anne (1760–92), Jane or "Jenny" (1766–1838), Margaret (fl. 1765–1835). For Jane, see the "Tolpuddle Burial Registers," C.R.O., Dorset; and for other details of the family, William Renwick Liddell, *The Life of William Dummer Powell, First Judge at Detroit and Fifth Judge of Upper Canada* (Lansing: Michigan Historical Commission, 1924).

The Miss Powell referred to here is either Jane or Margaret, both friends of PSW when she lived in Ludlow. See HLP to PSP, 19 September 1793, n. 3.

3. From the *Oracle. Bell's New World* (28 October 1789): " . . . Siddons, the prodigious, the miraculous Siddons (after vagabondizing through the *barns* in the *West,* to ease a gaping Peasantry of every superfluous shilling), is now alas! in a state of unpropitious inactivity—deaf to the supplications of Dullness, she is nestled in the *Crescent,* up to her ears in Clover—unapprehensive of those terrific sensations which occur in that *black interim,* when the Demons gladden—between calling for the bill, and discharging the sum total—*An Act of Benevolence is its own reward*—she was *houseless,* and Mr. Whalley took her in. 'Thus safe inborn heaviness to stray, / And lick up very Blockhead in the way.' Pope."

4. SS was recovering from a siege of depression. See Priscilla Kemble's letter to HLP, 23 November 1789, in Broadley, p. 149.

5. The *Oracle* attack was controversial. Even the loyal PSW expressed doubts to HLP

(12 December) about the actress's behavior. "My devotion," she wrote, "to the charming Siddons is nothing diminished, nor would [GP] suspect me of disaffection, could he witness the Battles I am Daily fighting in her Cause, or the *Paper War* I have had with that nasty Bell upon her Account:—yet I have always lamented the want of more *general* Conciliation in *her Manners* and must ever think that her Playing about the Country, particularly after these Theatres were open, very *bad Policy* and derogating much, from her own proper Dignity.—It is what no first rate Actor, or Actress has ever done—and I only deplored to Mrs. Byron that it gave to others . . . an opportunity of disseminating *such* and *such* Opinions and Impressions, as I was fearful would operate very materially and seriously to the mortifying and wounding of her Sensibilities, if not to the *actual* prejudice of her *Interests*.—" (Ry. 566.4).

6. The letter is missing.

7. On 21 December 1789 Anna Seward wrote to HLP, admitting that " 'Zeluco' is a work of considerable ability" that demanded—what she could not give it—a second reading. Moreover, she could not believe that the poet William Hayley (1745–1820) wrote a novel, *The Young Widow, or a History of Cornelia Sudley* (1789).

See *Seward Letters* 2:340–42.

8. On 2 November and for a few days thereafter, a verse tragedy by Ann Yearsley in five acts, called *Earl Goodwin*, was performed at Bath. By 9 November it was presented at Bristol, and it was published in 1791.

9. Ann Yearsley (1756–1806) was known as "Lactilla," or the "Bristol Milkwoman." Born in that city, she sold milk from door to door. A brother taught her to read and write. Her poverty and poetry brought her to the attention of Hannah More, who revised her poems and had them published by subscription. Over six hundred pounds was raised and the money invested under the trusteeship of Miss More and Elizabeth Montagu. Mrs. Yearsley was legally denied control of the money, and a subsequent quarrel with Miss More reached the press.

10. Numerous echoes, here, of familiar lines: Pope, "Imitations of Horace," Epistle 2.1.261–62; "To Mr. Lemuel Gulliver," lines 17–18; SJ, "Prologue to *A Word to the Wise*," line 18.

11. Tryphosa Jane Wallis (1774–1848), later Mrs. James Elijah Campbell, was born in Richmond, Yorks., and performed in Dublin as a child actress in the Smock Alley Theatre. Her first London engagement was on 10 January 1789 as Sigismunda in James Thomson's *Tancred and Sigismunda;* she appeared in Bath on 17 October as Rosalind in *As You Like It*. She continued to perform at Bath and at Bristol until 1794, when she returned to Covent Garden. In 1797 she married James Campbell of the Third Regiment of Guards and left the stage, except for a disappointing revival in 1813–14.

12. The female lead in Thomas Otway's *Venice Preserved* (1682).

13. An allusion to *Douglas*, a romantic tragedy by John Home (1722–1808), based on a Scottish ballad and first performed in 1756. HLP was amused by a casting incongruity in which a middle-aged Dimond might play Douglas, the son of a youthful Miss Wallis's Lady Randolph.

TO SAMUEL LYSONS

[Bath]
28: November 1789.

Dear Mr. Lysons

Your enquiry whether I had or had not received your Letter[1] was a very fair Reproach. It would not be much amiss to copy it, and send to *our Friend Mr. Cadell*.[2]

A propós, which Month's review contains the Criticisme on my Book?[3] for I cannot find it, and Mrs. Lewis protests it has been *wholly* forgotten only by the *aforesaid Mr. Cadell.*

Mrs. Lewis is here you will perceive, and so much improved in her Health that She walks out for her own Amusement; Mrs. Byron too, who came hither supported on Pillows—looks amazingly well again, even better than usual: General Burgoyne is quite alive[4]—and Mrs. Siddons has lost all Complaint by the use of these charming Waters.[5] Who would not love pretty Bath! I am sure we prove *our* Affection for it, by coming every Autumn so—but 'tis Time to get home after so long a Ramble, and on Tuesday 15 of December we set out.

You are kind in remembering Flo's wife and Son, he could live no longer without his Family; so we sent for them to give him the meeting here that the natural *Sweetness* of his Temper needed not be *ruffled by disappointment.* Yet see how falsely we accuse the Newspapers of mentioning every domestic Occurrence——when an Anecdote of this Importance has never been notified to the Public even in the most fashionable Gazettes.

But I will try to be serious. If you favour me with another Letter, do pray tell how poor dear Dr. Lort goes on, for my Heart is not happy about him; and let the kind charming Kembles hear of our Welfare and continued Regard for them. Mr. Piozzi has had no Gout this Year, he never looked so well since I knew him: People in this Town tell me much of Miss Thrale's intended Marriage——you are likely enough to know the particulars. Sir George and Lady Colebrooke[6] are often of our Coterie here, and some agreable Nesbitts[7]—are they of your Acquaintance?—I forget. Our Friends in Brunswic Place[8] are well, and happy in their growing Family. Every body sends you a Portion of Compliments and good Words how much more Your Faithful and Obliged Servant / H: L: Piozzi.

Text: Harvard Theatre Collection, Pusey Library. *Address:* To / Samuel Lysons Esq. / No. 17: / Cliffords Inn / London. *Postmark:* BATH; NO 30 89.

1. SL's letter is missing.
2. A critical barb at the silent Thomas Cadell as one of the publishers of the *Observations.* Apparently SL in his letter had alluded to the reception and successful sale of the book.
3. See HLP to SL, 13 August, n. 13.

HLP had been subjected to other, exceptionally hostile reviews of *Observations,* e.g., in the *Morning Post,* 15 June:

"The literary crudities of this lady afford a lamentable proof of what *Vanity* will do when it is associated with *Wealth.* This work, which would not be bought by the booksellers if produced by obscure life, exhibits no proof of capacity above the ordinary rate of women. It contains no reflection that can be supposed the result of philosophical mind, or of original observations.

"There is in it a strong and sometimes a very ridiculous affectation of extraordinary sensibility, vivid imagination, refined taste and poetical expression.

"These qualities are, however, assumed with such awkward or violent ostentation, that it is not possible to suppose the author possesses the realities, otherwise than in a moderate degree, or rather that they are perhaps only adopted for the sake of *Fashion,* like other casual modes.

"In private life Mrs. *Piozzi* displays a *superficial glitter* in her conversation, which supported by some anecdotes of her *former* literary connections, enables her to pass with tolerable credit; but if she properly estimated her powers, or regarded her intellectual character, she would never venture into *print*, for she really can give nothing new in the way of remark or description, and her language, rather distorted than strengthened by a tasteless selection from *Johnson*, and larded with an abundance of *Continental cants*, is destitute of force, elegance, and even ordinary correctness."

4. John Burgoyne (1723–92) was a British general during the American Revolution whose army was defeated at Saratoga in 1777, an event that led to a parliamentary investigation in 1779. Politically ambitious, he served as M.P. for Midhurst (1761–68) and Preston (1768–92). His last act in the Commons was as manager of the impeachment trial of Warren Hastings in 1787.

Not only was he active as a party writer, but he also wrote for the theater. His play *The Heiress* (1786) was a popular success that went through ten editions in a single year and was translated into several languages.

5. In a letter of 23 November Priscilla Kemble had written to HLP: "Mr. Kemble has had a letter from Mr. Siddons, who says Mrs. Siddons still continues mending" (Broadley, p. 149).

6. Sir George Colebrooke (1729–1809), second baronet (1761). Educated at Leyden, he was a fellow of the Society of Antiquaries. He was M.P. for Arundel (1754–74); deputy chairman (1768) and chairman (1769–73) of the court of directors of the East India Company. On 23 July 1754 he had married Mary, née Gaynor, or Gayner (1739–1818), of Antigua. A large landowner and banker (Dublin), he was nonetheless bankrupt in 1777. In a codicil to his will (written 10 September 1807), he stated: "I attribute my [financial] Misfortunes to my engaging in the East India Company to the Neglect of my Private Affairs" and, particularly, to the behavior of Warren Hastings, governor general of India. The cause of bankruptcy, however, was his speculation in raw materials (hemp, flax, wood).

The Colebrookes were the parents of George (1759–1809), James Edward (1761–1838), Henry Thomas (1765–1837), Mary (1757–post 1809), Harriet (1762–85), Louisa Sutherland (1764–95). They lived in the Marlbro Buildings, Saint James Square, Bath, from 1802 to 1809. See "Walcot Parish Poor Rates," Guildhall, Bath. For Sir George's obituary, see *GM* 79, pt. 2 (1809): 787–88; his will was proved at London, 14 September 1809 (P.R.O., Prob. 11/1503/679). For Lady Colebrooke, see *GM* 88, pt. 2 (1818): 282.

7. Walter Nisbet, or Nisbett, or Nesbitt, of Jamaica died in Bath in 1797. He was survived by his wife Anne (1752–1819), daughter of Robert Parry of Llanrhaiadr, and by six children. See his M.I. in Saint Swithin's Church, Walcot Parish, Bath.

8. The family of George and Frances James had resided at Brunswick Place, Bath, for several years. See HLT to FB [27 June 1784], n. 5.

TO THE REVEREND LEONARD CHAPPELOW

Bath Monday
7: December 1789.

Dear Mr. Chappelow

I should not have answered Your Letter so soon tho' it was a very kind one, because the Kindness had been too long o'coming: only that I had something to tell which I know will delight your feeling Heart exceedingly, and that I am impatient to write upon a Subject which engrosses the Attention of everybody here.[1]

Bridge Tower the African Negro[2] is that Subject, whose Son plays so enchantingly upon the Violin as to extort Applause from the first Professors[3]—while his

Father amazes me a hundred Times more by the showy Elegance of his Address—the polished Brilliancy of his Language, the Accumulation and Variety of his Knowledge, and the interesting Situation in which he stands towards an Absent Wife; who born a Polish Woman of high Rank in her own Country, has been forcibly separated from him, who seems to run round the Globe with an Arrow in his Heart, and this astonishing Son by his Side.[4] Was he sent hither by Providence to prove the Equality of Blacks to Whites I wonder, he would make a beautiful Figure at the Bar of the House of Commons; and charming Miss Williams will make such sweet Verses about him when they meet. Have you *stumbled* upon *her* as well as upon Miss Weston? I want her to see what a Man may come to, tho' born a Slave, and educated for no higher Purpose. When She hears him talk of his Wife, She will be really quite melted: The Ladies here wept when he presented his Son so gracefully in the Orchestra at a Benefit——for the Comforts and Profits of which he yesterday returned publick Thanks in our Abbey Church, and afterwards received the Sacrament——His Devotions at Home after the Sacred Ceremony made him so late he said, before he came to Dinner.

And now Dear Sir when you have said a pretty Word in Answer to this most unanswerable Letter, I will tell you that our Excursions for the Year 1789 are closing very fast—and that by the 26 of December we shall be comfortable at Hanover Square[5] and happy in your Company, at least I hope so. Mrs. Lewis's Hospitality and Friendship will delay us for a Day or two at Reading in Berkshire, She feels much relief from these Waters, and when Spring calls her to London, you will find her much improved: but we have lost poor dear Lord Huntingdon——and a dismal Loss that will be.

Meantime do not speak ill of Bath, it is a lovely Place, and our Master's Lungs were never in better Order; everybody said last Night that he sung beyond himself: and Mrs. Siddons has felt the Benefit of Bathing here, and how can one hate a Town that does such People good! We have the Cavalier Pindemonte too who is mentioned so honourably in your Florence Miscellany,[6] and a World of Foreigners beside, but the African carries off all the Applause——he is so very flashy a Talker, and has a Manner so distinguished for lofty Gayety, and universality of Conversation I can but think all Day how Dr. Johnson would have adored that Man![7]

Farewell, and believe us with the greatest Esteem your obliged and Faithful Servants and accept all our best Compliments from the Hand / of H: L: Piozzi.

Text: Ry. 559.11. *Address:* To / The Rev: Mr. Chappelow / Hill Street / Berkeley Square / London. *Postmark:* DE 8 89.

1. The subject concerned the Bridgetowers, whom HLP first met in Bath in 1789 and enthusiastically described in the "Journey Book." "At [Bath] some new Phænomena have this Autumn attracted attention—the Bridgetowers, Father and Son astonish and delight us. I will speak of the Boy first, as his Talents maintain them both: and such are his Powers upon the Violin as to have extorted Money and Applause from the professors themselves, who acknowledge the superior Merit of a Baby not yet ten Years old, with a Candour that does them Honour."

2. Little is known of the elder Bridgetower (fl. 1758–92). His full name never given, he

was referred to as "the Black Prince" or "the Abyssinian Prince." For HLP his "Accomplishments are various and amazing—Languages, Address and Elegance of Person he possesses to a Wonder: Was he less eager to display his Talents it were better, but he is a fine Fellow with all his Faults; and one is sorry to see that he might sink and extinguish like the Stick of a Sky Rocket, after entertaining us with a charming Blaze, and half alarming our Fears by the loud Noise made at his rising" ("Journey Book"). See also *Thraliana* 2:757.

3. George Augustus Polgreen Bridgetower (1778–1860). Of his European debut, the *World* (2 January 1789) reported: "He played at a public Concert on the 2d instant at Cleves, with very great applause, and promises to be one of the first players in Europe. His natural genius was first cultivated by . . . Haydn, and afterwards by the Sieur *Schick*."

HLP heard him at the New Assembly Room, Bath, on 5 December (see the *Bath Journal*, 7 December). From there he went on to a successful debut in London on 19 February 1790 and soon thereafter enjoyed the patronage of the Prince of Wales (*Bath Herald*, 10 March 1792). By 1803 he was on the Continent where Beethoven purportedly composed the "Kreutzer Sonata" for him and accompanied him on the pianoforte at its initial Viennese performances, 17 and 24 May 1803.

4. "This wonderful Child (young Bridgetower) is a Mulattoe, offspring of an African Negro by a Polish Dutchess: whose Marriage with her accomplished Moor being foolishly blazoned by the Father——a compelled Separation was the Consequence; and poor Bridgetower turned out to wander thro' the World with an Arrow in his heart, and this surprizing Son of theirs in his Hand. The Lady remained long at home locked up I trust till her relations thought her Passion past away, but She has escaped like Thisbe, and is run after her Husband as far as Ratisbon, whence he will bring her hither as he says, if in England any Establishment can be obtained" ("Journey Book"). HLP reports unauthenticated Bath gossip first circulated by the elder Bridgetower.

5. The final entry in the "Journey Book" is for the 27th, at Hanover Square.

6. See HLP to Q, 4 June 1785, nn. 10, 11.

7. HLP assumed that SJ would have reacted to Bridgetower as he had to another exotic foreigner, Omai, or perhaps to Francis Barber.

TO THE REVEREND THOMAS SEDGWICK WHALLEY

Monday
25: January 1790

Dear Mr. Whalley

In return for the best News here—that of our charming Siddons's gradual Recovery; let me beg some *Truths* from Bath, for the Tales poured into our Ears are such as one can say nothing about till 'tis known whether they are true or no.

Is Rauzzini going to marry an English Lady and his Scholar with a large Fortune?[1] and is Bridgetower in Prison for having had to do with Sharpers?[2] He was here last Week,—and calling on us asked Mr. Piozzi to lend him 30£ which was no Proof of his *Sharpness* I think, to suppose one should throw such Sums into the Lap of a Man one had not seen Six Times, and whose Son never played at our house. I gave him a Letter to you, did he ever deliver it?[3] We are curious to hear how the Story really stands. I am ashamed to send you a Letter of mere Enquiry so, but if I take the *Questions* you shall have the *Commands*——for nothing could make either my Husband or myself happier than knowing how to oblige Mrs. Whalley and you or Miss Sage[4] to both whom you must kindly present our best Compliments and believe me / Dear Sir / Your Obliged and faithful / humble servant / H: L: Piozzi.

Text: Berg Collection +.

1. Venanzio Rauzzini (1746–1810), an Italian operatic singer and composer, resided in England (1774–1810). In 1787, he left London and settled in Bath to teach voice and to conduct concerts. He was buried there in the Abbey Church. The gossip about his impending marriage was only that.

2. "Bath told somewhat a disgraceful Tale lately of his being connected wth Sharpers, but he is got thro' even *that* . . ." (*Thraliana* 2:757).

3. *Thraliana* 2:757 n. 2; HLP to LC, 7 December 1789, nn. 2 and 3.

4. See HLP to TSW, 5 January [1789], n. 2.

TO THE REVEREND THOMAS SEDGWICK WHALLEY

Hanover Square
Thursday, 3: June 1790.

My Dear Sir,—I have been a runner after remote interest[1] so long, that I am sure I pardon Mr. Nott[2] and Mr.Best[3] from my heart, and wish I could more effectually serve the friends of my dear Mr. Whalley; but how one of them should fancy I could promote the welfare of a language master, and how the other should dream of my influence in Exeter College, who can guess? Cizos[4] deserves everything, and has to me been the cause of so much pleasure in procuring me two such letters from Mr. Whalley and Miss Seward; but nothing can I do for him. Miss Weston is kind and partial to her friends, but her health is not what we all wish.

Sweet Siddons is my patient. Sir Lucas Pepys attends her at Streatham,[5] and she is there now keeping house with dear Mrs. Lewis, while we are come up for the Abbey music,[5] lest no places should be got when we arrive there. Adieu, and believe me most truly yours, H. L. Piozzi.

Text: Wickham 2:41–42. *Address:* Rev: Mr. Whalley / Crescent / Bath.

1. Cf. Edward Young, *Night Thoughts* 3.6–18; 5.164, 340; 7.47–48; 8.436, 798, 1353; and HLP to MF, 21 September 1820, n. 3.

2. John Nott (1751–1825) studied surgery in Birmingham with SJ's friend Edmund Hector; in London with Sir Caesar Hawkins; and in Paris. More interested in travel than in medicine, he probably did not take his degree until 1789. He was skilled in languages, particularly Italian and the classics. In need of employment, he sought the help of TSW and Dr. Richard Warren (1731–97), physician to George III. Upon the recommendation of Warren, Nott accompanied the duchess of Devonshire and her sister Lady Duncannon to the Continent (1790–93). After returning to England, he settled permanently at Bristol Hotwells.

3. Henry Digby Best (1768–1836), later Beste, matriculated at University College, Oxford, earned his B.A. (1788) and M.A. (1791) from Magdalen College. In September 1791, he was ordained deacon and in December was appointed to the curacy of Saint Martin's in

Lincoln. When in 1790 he sought a university fellowship, Exeter College became a possibility because its rector, Thomas Stinton (1748–97), had connections with literary people and SS. TSW assumed that HLP was either acquainted with Stinton or could approach him through the actress.

4. Cizo (fl. 1765–90) sang in Drury Lane oratorios in 1790. In February and March he performed in several Handel concerts. Thereafter he disappeared from the stage, fallen upon hard times. TSW on 10 May wrote fulsomely about this "young Man who cultivates the arts you love, and whose Talents are but the polishers of his virtues. Monsieur Cizo's, the unfortunate Frenchman for whom I sollicit your protection . . . [has] been struggling for years, and in various Places, with the Adversity which now holds him by the Throat, and threatens his quick and utter destruction. . . . *All* this amiable, clever, and unfortunate Being *asks*, is to be *recommended* as a French and Italian Master, for which, I believe, you will find him *well* qualified." TSW ended his letter: "At all events you [and Mr. Piozzi] may be able to procure him a few pupils, should you not think him worthy of further attention . . ." (Ry. 564.6).

Miss Seward's letter on behalf of Cizo is missing.

5. By 17 May, according to an entry in *Thraliana* (2:769), SS had "spent some Weeks with" the Piozzis. SS, however, recalled arriving 29 May, a date she associated with Charles II's Restoration and with the onset of her own restoration to health (2:771). In any event, Sir Lucas was treating her no later than 2 June, when she wrote to Bedina Wynn: "Doctors differ you know and it seems they are very much at odds about poor me, for Sir Lucas Pepys says my Complaint is *Nerves* and Nerves only . . ." (Harvard Theatre Collection).

For Bedina Wynn, see HLP to SL, 17 May 1792, n. 7.

6. In honor of the king's birthday, a concert attended by the royal family was held at Westminster Abbey on 1 June. It consisted "chiefly of chorusses, and with the strictest adherence to truth we may pronounce the performance magnificently grand . . ." (*The Times*, 2 June).

TO PENELOPE SOPHIA WESTON

27: June [1790].[1]

You are very considerate as well as very kind dear Miss Weston, and you deserve better of Streatham than to miss Mrs. Siddons[2]——but as the Footman at Bologna expressed himself—so run the *Combinations*. At Jacob's Intreaties my Master yields the Pleasure of fetching you; and I, knowing you will come the *earlier*, am the easier pacified.[3]

May you but come safe, and disposed to pardon the Liberty you so sweetly offer to your Affectionate Servant / H: L: Piozzi.

I am as Sorry to miss the Pleasure of Seeing you here my [dear] Miss Weston as I am glad to hear of your returning health.[4] God grant us all, reestablishment! But I fear my heart will fail *me* when *I* fail to recieve [*sic*] the company and consolation of our dear Mrs. P: There are many disposed to comfort me,[5] but no one knows so rationally or effectually how to do it as that unwearied Spirit of kindness. Adieu and believe me yours very Sincerely / S. *Siddons.*

Jacob is in great hurry, and I am disappointed for the plasure come to you next Tuesday; Pazienza! Our Charming Siddons, she goes away to morrow, indeed I am afflicted, because she is a great loss for us, but the Providence never fail, and we hope to see her again in little time; Pray come Tuesday very early, and stay with us great deal, then you did before, believe me, and I am your Sincer friend, / G. P[iozzi].

Text: Hyde Collection. With notes by SS and GP.

1. This follows two previous notes (22 and 26 June) arranging for PSW's visit to Streatham Park on the twenty-ninth.

2. Although delayed by illness, PSW was eager to meet SS. But as HLP wrote on the twenty-sixth: " . . . what Drawbacks there always are of one sort or another! Mrs. Siddons—which I little feared till now—leaves us o'Monday [28 June]" (Princeton University Library).

3. In the same letter to PSW, HLP noted, "You cannot think how busy we pretend to be here in the Country about our Hay, and how important Jacob thinks himself at this Time of Year: he shall however fetch you on Tuesday."

Jacob Weston (1742–1820) was the steward of Streatham Park. For his dates, see the "Walcot Parish Church Burial Register," C.R.O., Somerset.

4. HLP wrote on 22 June, "My dear Miss Weston's Physician now recommends Country Air, and I can assure the Possession of the Lilac Bed Chamber to her as long as she pleases" (Princeton University Library).

5. The most successful of SS's doctors was Sir Lucas Pepys (see HLP to FB, 30 June 1784), who had recognized SS's illness as recurrent depression. According to William Siddons (in a letter to Sir Charles Hotham, 21 June): "Mrs. Piozzi persuaded her she should try some other medical gentleman, as Dr. Osborne seemed at a standstill and had a fair and long tryal. Sir Lucas Pepys was fixed upon, and sent for, who gave her great hopes, and prescribed for her. To be as brief as possible, either from Sir Lucas, the air, or Mrs. Piozzi's attention and witty concorse [sic], she is amazingly better, and sleeps the whole night without waking—what she has not known for a year and a half past. She has got her flesh again, and I think looks as well as ever she did in her life." See A.M.W. Stirling, *The Hothams: Being the Chronicles of the Hothams of Scorborough and South Dalton from their hitherto Unpublished Family Papers*, 2 vols. (London: Herbert Jenkins, 1918 [1917]), 2:250.

[TO SAMUEL LYSONS]

Streatham Park
Saturday 14: July [1790].

My dear Sir

The Weather seems to mend, and Jacob says we must work hard at the Hay, that it may not be wholly ruined.[1] Should it keep on pouring as usual I desire no greater Pleasure than a Visit to you on Tuesday Morning, but my heart tells me it cannot be *then*. Accept us some other Day, and do you determine which. Meantime forget not our Anniversary the 25: of July:[2] and remind your Brother, or tell me how to direct him a separate Invitation.[3]

"A Friend or so, as old Capulet says—but we'll keep no great ado"——[4]

Adieu; and if you know anything of my Daughters *do* tell me; for I have some strange uneasy Impression on my Mind about their Health. Horrid Dreams &c. / Ever most sincerely yours / H: L: Piozzi.

How I hate this shining Paper!

Text: N.L.W.

1. "The Hay harvest this Year has been eminently prosperous round London; in many Places two Load to an Acre, a Proportion scarce ever known before" (July 1790, *Thraliana* 2:772).

2. In the spring of 1790 the Piozzis spent over two thousand pounds renovating Streatham Park and redecorating it with Italian vases, pictures, fabrics, etc. On 25 July an elaborate party celebrated the re-opening of the house and the sixth wedding anniversary (*Thraliana* 2:775).

"Mrs. Piozzi's Fete on Monday at Streatham was not confined to the dull insipidity of an Italian *conversazione.* Dinner, concert, dance, and supper, all contributed to set off the intellectual good things, and as the liberal hostess has long been of opinion that 'Every man should have his way,' why even the honest John Bulls and their ladies did not hop off without having their Hop in the Hall" (*The Times,* 31 July).

3. About this time DL had become curate of Putney and chaplain to Horace Walpole (1717–97), fourth earl of Orford (1791). The young clergyman was also gathering material for his principal work (dedicated to Walpole): *The Environs of London: being an Historical Account of Towns, Villages, and Hamlets, within twelve Miles of the Capital,* 4 vols. (London: Printed by A. Strahan, for T. Cadell, jun, and W. Davies, 1792–96).

4. *Romeo and Juliet* 3.4.23. "We'll keep no great ado—a friend or two."

TO THE REVEREND LEONARD CHAPPELOW

Streatham
21: September 1790.

Generous, comical, kind Mr. Chappelow! your Turkeys have brought Compliments upon their dusky Wings, and shall have every honour and Pleasure this Place will afford, in return for their obliging Intentions of stocking our little Colony. Don't you recollect in Don Quixote that the Duchess sends Sancho's Wife Money, Clothes &c. and only requires some Acorns for planting in return; which the Wench makes a Difficulty of getting for her.[1] I certainly am growing like poor Theresa Pança; for the more I watch your favourite African Oak, the fewer Acorns can I find upon it.

Here are some amiable Italians upon a Visit,[2] whose Talk about France, with the State of which they are well acquainted—refreshes my very Soul.[3] I am all Day wishing you to hear them; they are Men of Learning and Enquiry, and the Business very interesting: but above all their Conversation delights *me* who as a true Englishwoman rejoyce to know that rational and religious Liberty is best enjoyed in our Little Island, and that Imitation is but a poor thing at last.

The Dear Hamiltons! and how I love them: and how comfortable it is that we should think just alike so. Had it rained Money this Year instead of Expences, we would have made the Norfolk Tour, have heard a sweet Duet at Stanton,[4] and told Dear Mr. Chappelow at Diss[5] how sincerely / I have the Honour / to be Obliged and Obedient Servant / H: L: Piozzi.

Text: Ry. 559.12.

1 In *Don Quixote de la Mancha* the duchess sends Sancho Panza's wife a string of coral beads and a letter. The duchess in return asks only for a "couple of dozen acorns," but Teresa Panza says she will send her "a whole peck." See *The Second Part of the History of the Valorous and Witty Knight-Errant, Don Quixote of the Mancha* (London: Printed for Edward Blount, 1620), chap. 50, pp. 332–40.

2. HLP specifically mentions in her "Pocket Books and Journals" for 1790 (Ry. 616) Paolo Andreani (ca. 1763–1823), General Pasquale Paoli (1725–1807), and Pindemonte.

3. Ironically HLP implies the collapse of religious freedoms and institutions in revolutionary France. Religion was becoming more and more secularized, in fact as well as in spirit. The Civil Constitution of the Clergy (passed on 12 July) provided a framework for reshaping the ecclesiastical hierarchy within the mold of local government districts. Bishops and parish priests, for example, had to be validated like other public officials through elections. The papacy was stripped of influence in temporal matters. See Albert Soboul, *A Short History of the French Revolution, 1789–1799,* trans. Geoffrey Symcox (Berkeley, Los Angeles, London: University of California Press, 1977), pp. 69–71.

4. The Reverend Frederick Hamilton, his wife Rachel, and daughter Jane were apparently on a family visit. The duke of Hamilton owned at least two estates in Suffolk, one located near Stanton in west Suffolk.

5. Diss was relatively near Stanton. See HLP to LC, 9 October 1787, n. 5.

TO PENELOPE SOPHIA WESTON

Streatham
12: October 1790

I am watching the Moon's Increase with more attentive and more interested Care than ever I recollect to have watched it since your Project of coming hither with the Colonel[1] has depended on her getting fat.

I am glad he is much at Lord Sydney's,[2] and hope it bodes well for us all, and that he will soon have his Orders to fight these hateful French,[3] whose pretended Love of England and English Liberty—In good Time! ends at last in real Attachment to Spain, and to the Ratification of old Family Compacts.[4] I never expected better for my own part, and long for you to come and tell me all the harm of them You know.

My Master looks better, and gains Strength every day.

I can scarce be expected, or even desire to be more sincerely than I am / Dear Miss Weston's Affectionate / and faithful Servant / H: L: Piozzi.

Text: Hyde Collection. *Address:* Miss Weston / Queen Square / Westminister. *Postmark:* <   >. Franked by Pickett.[5]

1. Henry Barry was promoted to the rank of lieutenant colonel on 18 May.

HLP could not make up her mind about his social qualities. "That Colonel Barry," she later wrote (September 1794), "is just like a rainy Day—coming too often he wears one's Spirits quite down; but never coming at all, much Information—and *fructification* of the Mind is lost:—great *Refreshment* too may be found in his Conversation, when Life & its oft-repeated Tales grow arid, harsh & stale" (*Thraliana* 2:892).

2. Thomas Townshend (1732/3–1800), cr. Baron Sydney of Chislehurst (Kent) on 6 March 1783 and Viscount Sydney of Saint Leonards (Glos.) on 11 June 1789. He held various governmental positions: lord of the treasury, 1765–67; joint paymaster general of the forces, 1767–68; secretary at war, 1782; home secretary, 1782–83 and 1783–89; president of the board of control, 1784–90.

3. HLP anticipated the intensity of monarchical feeling in England that in a few years would culminate in war. Much of her current antigallicism was generated by accounts throughout 1790 of bloody engagements in which French monarchists struggled vainly to preserve the symbols of the Old Regime—in Nîmes, Montauban, and Lyons. She believed that English interest dictated support of French royalists.

4. Early in 1790 England's deepening quarrel with Spain over the area adjoining Nootka Sound on the western coast of North America (now Vancouver) made war seem inevitable. Spain called on France for help under "the Family Compact" (August 1761), and the response was positive. Montmorin, minister for foreign affairs, advised the president of the National Assembly that the scale of British war preparations necessitated the arming of fourteen ships of the line. See *GM* 60, pt.2 (1790): 656. The National Assembly, however, denied Louis the power to make war and cancelled the treaty with Spain. By October 1790 Spain had given way to England on all disputed issues, war was averted, and the Treaty of the Escurial was signed by both countries.

5. William Pickett (1736–96) was lord mayor of London at this time. He had been a successful goldsmith until his retirement *ca.* 1785. Among his public offices, he was alderman of Cornhill Ward (1782), sheriff (1784), lord mayor (1785, 1789–90). In 1790 and 1796 he failed to win parliamentary elections.

See Alfred Beaven, *The Aldermen of the City of London temp. Henry III.–1908 (–1912),* 2 vols. Published by the corporation of the city of London (London: E. Fisher, 1908, 1913); Arthur C. Grimwade, *London Goldsmiths, 1697–1837* (London: Faber, 1976).

TO JONATHAN STERNS[1]

Streatham Surrey
30: October 1790.

Sir

In Consequence of my worthy Friend Mr. Wetherhead's Recommendation[2] I take the Liberty of sending you a Power of Attorney to transact my Affairs in the Province of Nova Scotia, where John Salusbury Esq. styled in the Grants the Honourable John Salusbury possessed a good deal of Land;[3] from the Inheritance of which I, though his only Child and sole Heiress, have been hitherto kept out of Possession, though my first Husband Henry Thrale Esq. made such Enquiries as were then thought necessary; and though when a Widow I besought my Agent Mr. Cator to seek for these Grants that were at last put into my hands by the Kindness of Colonel Butler,[4] whose Sister is married to John Myddelton Esq. of Gwaynŷnog near Denbigh North Wales, my worthy old Acquaintance and Countryman.—

His Brother Captain Thomas Myddelton lately deceased,[5] was at Nova Scotia when my Father was; and knew of these Grants, and advised me to send a power of Attorney over to Halifax in the Year 1785. Being then at Leghorn with my present Husband Gabriel Piozzi Esq. we wrote to our Agent Mr. Cator, who sent the Letter of Attorney to Mr. Wylly;[6] but he was gone to another Part of the World, and it is scarce two Months since I received any Account of or from that Gentleman, in Answer to mine written five Years ago.

You see Sir how Fortune has hitherto treated my American Claims, of which my Father's personal Intimacy with Governor Cornwallis,[7] and particular Favor from his Friend Lord Halifax, then head of the Board of Trade—made him excessively fond.[8] You will therefore perhaps kindly take up a falling Cause; and partly from Justice, partly from Compassion, and partly from Friendship towards Mr. Wetherhead; be active in obtaining Possession of this Property for me, and likewise contriving so to ascertain its Value, that I may know in future what to trust to—and not consider all my Father promised me from that Quarter, as the mere Dream of his unshaken fidelity, and unrewarded Diligence. I *think*, but know not how I shall make *You* think; there is a little Island called by my Family Name, in Consequence of its being a Gift to my Father when the first Settlers arrived there, and of his having built himself a Hut or Cottage upon it—very near to the Spot he called *Dunk Cove*, and parted from the Main Land by an extremely small Space.

Do me at least the favour to enquire, and by your obliging Activity and Service on this Business[9]—bind Mr. Piozzi everlastingly your Debtor, with all possible Gratitude on the Part of Sir / Your most Obliged Servant / Hester Lynch Piozzi.

I have got our kind Friend Mr. Wetherhead to direct my Cover, and doubt not of his taking the Trouble to add some Solicitation on his own part, to press your Attention to my Affairs.

Text: Public Archives of Nova Scotia, MG1, vol. 144. *Address:* Jonathan Sterns Esquire / Attorney at Law / Hallifax / Nova Scotia.

1. Jonathan Sterns or Stearns (d. 1798) was a graduate of Harvard College in 1770. A loyalist evacuated from Boston to Halifax in 1776, he was appointed solicitor general of Nova Scotia in 1797. He was beaten to death by Richard John Uniacke (1753–1830), attorney general of Nova Scotia (1797–1830).

2. A relative of Charlotte Lewis, John Wetherhead (1735–1813), formerly of Nova Scotia, had settled in Richmond with his wife Rachel (1731–91) by 1788. Encouraging HLP to fight for her father's onetime property near Halifax, he wrote on 1 November 1790: "It is pretty Clear to Me that this same Island Mentioned to You by Mr Salusbury as occupied by Him by building a Hutt upon it, has not been granted to Him by a separate Patent, but is included within the Bounds running along the Beach att Dunks Cove, and Contained in the Second Patent *No. 144*—I should imagine however that this must appear by the Map or Plan annexed to the Grant itself, but also for the Plan of the 20 Acres described to be on the Peninsula of Halifax. . . . I have written on this, and indeed on Every other particular respecting your long Neglected Property in that Country" (Ry. 601.34). See "Richmond Land Tax Assessments," and the "Burial Register" of Saint Mary Magdalene, C. R. O., Surrey, Kingston upon Thames; HLP to SL, 21 September 1785, n. 4.

3. In a letter to the lieutenant governor of Nova Scotia, the secretary of the province, Richard Bulkeley (1717–1800), on 27 May 1791 described the Salusbury holdings: "In

answer to your Enquiries concerning certain Tracts of Land, which had been granted to John Salusbury Esqr., formerly of this Province; I have the honour of informing Your Excellency, that he had four Tracts.

"1st. One Consisting of 248 Acres, on the opposite side of this Harbour. This was forfeited 21 Years after it had been granted, for want of any kind of Improvement, conformable to the Condition of the Grant.

"2d. A Tract of 20 Acres about a Mile distant from this Town; forfeited 31 Years after granted, for want of Improvement.

"3d. A Small Tract of about 1/4 of an Acre in the North Suburbs of the Town, on this a Hutt had been erected, and had a slight fence round it, in course of time it became inhabited by people who committed Robbery and Murder, and became a Nuisance. After being 33 Years granted, it was Forfeited. . . .

"There yet remains a fourth Tract of about 70 Rods, at a Place called Dunks Cove. This is a Place for Fishing—the Condition of this Grant is, that the Grantee shall always occupy it for Catching and Curing Fish. As soon as he quits that Occupation, it becomes forfeited and the Place is given to another person" (Ry. 601.38).

Despite Wetherhead, Sterns, and the Piozzis' attorney Joseph Ward (fl. 1769–1827), of 21 Bedford Square, the Nova Scotia property could not be claimed by HLP, who by December 1791 abandoned the fight.

4. William Butler (1733–96), colonel in the Flintshire militia, was born posthumously, the son of William and Margaret Butler of Cornist. See "Flint Parish Registers—Baptisms" and "Flint Parish Registers—Burials," C.R.O., Clwyd.

5. Thomas Myddelton (1730–90) of Gwaynynog, Denbighshire, was in Nova Scotia ca. 1749 until the autumn of 1753.

John Salusbury, who departed from Plymouth in June 1749, sailed for England in August 1751. At home he found his family in want of money. On the advice of Lord Halifax, he returned to Nova Scotia in June 1752. But once again, in the summer of 1753, he returned to England penniless. See Clifford, p. 19; Ronald Rompkey, ed., *Expeditions of Honour: The Journal of John Salusbury in Halifax, Nova Scotia, 1749–53* (Newark: University of Delaware Press, 1982).

6. William Wylly (fl. 1748–1811), an attorney, had moved from Halifax to the Isle of New Providence, Bahama.

7. Edward Cornwallis (1712/13–76) served in the British army (ca. 1731–49, 1753–61), attaining the rank of lieutenant general. M.P. as well (1743–49, 1753–62), he was appointed governor and captain general of Nova Scotia in May 1749, arriving with twenty-five hundred settlers for the new town of Halifax. He returned to England in 1752, reassumed active military duties—in Minorca and Ireland—and spent 1762–76 as governor of Gibraltar, where he died.

8. George Montague, afterwards Montague-Dunk (1716–71), third earl of Halifax (1739).

On 2 July 1741, he married Anne, née Richards (1726–53), who brought him a fortune of £100,000 (inherited largely from the estate of Sir Thomas Dunk, whose surname he adopted). In the autumn, he assumed direction of the British board of trade and in that post did much to extend the commerce of Canada.

9. HLP's request was soon repeated by Joseph Ward. Sterns replied on 6 January 1791 from Halifax:

"I was favored with your Letter of the 2nd November last accompanying a Letter of Attorney from Mr. and Mrs. Piozzi, authorizing me to claim some real Estates in this Province to which Mrs. Piozzi is entitled as the representative of her Father John Salisbury Esquire deceased and have in consequence of that authority examined so far as the short time I have had would admit, the state of the Property, and on Enquiry find, that every Part of it which is valuable, has been on various pretences in consequence of inquests taken by the Escheator, resumed into the Kings Hands and regranted to others, in whose possession they now are. I am however pretty clear, that the Facts found by the Inquest of Office were in some instances untrue, and in others the proceedings were so informal that they will not stand in the way of a Recovery by the Representative of the late Mr.

Salisbury. No further authority will be necessary to enable me to prosecute the Business but the original Patents must be sent and it will also be necessary for Mrs. Piozzi to furnish me with proof of her being the Daughter and only legitimate Issue of Mr. Salisbury" (Ry. 601.37).

TO PENELOPE SOPHIA WESTON

Streatham
11: November 1790.

Dear Miss Weston

On Wednesday you shall if you please get the *Little Things* together, and come to Streatham.

Hanover Square is *deserted,* and we march for Bath at Xmas——I have lost two Friends whom I loved and valued,[1] and am in Mourning for a Relation of Mr. Thrale's[2] who neither loved *nor* valued / Your truly faithful / H: L: Piozzi

Text: Princeton University Library. *Address:* Miss Weston / Queen Square / Westminister.

1. Michael Lort and Sophia Byron both died on 5 November. She was buried in the Abbey Church at Bath on 12 November. For HLP's reactions to the deaths, see *Thraliana* 2:787.
2. Henry Smith "died in September [1789], only thirty-three years old. So ended the life of the young man in whom Thrale had placed his hopes" (Hyde, p. 257). See HLT to Q [27 June 1784], n. 12.

TO SAMUEL LYSONS

Monday 15: [November 1790].

It was very good natured of you to write so Dear Mr. Lysons, and very considerate. *My* Loss in poor Dr. Lort is irreparable, and pray tell his Widow how sensibly I feel for all that belonged to him.[1]

A fond and partial Friend was taken from me on the very Day too that *he* died——our amiable old Acquaintance Mrs. Byron: but Beauty and Learning have no Virtue in them to repel the general Devourer. We mean to go for a while to Bath soon after Christmas Holydays; that Water has more of Lethe in it than any other for my Constitution; and it will do Mr. Piozzi good too.

Here is fine Weather for Walking yet your Brother never calls—when you see him scold him for / Your Faithful / humble Servant / H: L: Piozzi.

There is an Italian Liturgy of the Church of England Service about the World,[2] small 8vo but 'tis out of Print——get it for me at your Leisure dear Mr. Lysons, I shall be much obliged to you.

Text: Huntington Library MSS 6592. *Address:* Samuel Lysons Esq. / Clifford's Inn / London.

1. Michael Lort had married in May 1783 Susannah, née Norfolk (1742–92). Shortly after her death on 5 February, she was buried in the same vault as her husband in the Church of Saint Matthew, Friday Street, Cheapside, and a commemorative white marble tablet was placed on its north wall.

2. *Il Libro delle Preghiere Publiche . . . secondo l'uso della Chiesa Anglicana; insieme col Saltero over i Salmi di David . . . e la forma e modo di fare, ordinare e consacrare Vescovi, Presbiteri e Diaconi,* trans. Giovanni Battista Cappello and Edward Brown (London: Appresso Moise Pitt, 1685). Or: *Il Libro delle Preghiere Publiche . . . Questa nuova impressione revista e corretta per Alessandro Gordon,* trans. W. Bedell (London: Alessandro Blackwell, 1733).

TO CHARLOTTE LEWIS

Streatham
8: December *1790*.

Dearest Mrs. Lewis

may Trust *me* that I should like of all things to spend a Week at Reading; and say to her about *half* of what I feel concerning Your *Seceders.*[1] My kind hearted Master was very angry indeed, when he heard that Sally had left you——and at such a Time too! He had a good Mind to go to Berkshire and fetch you home hither directly; but this eternal *House* in Hanover Square, *every body's Admiration, and nobody's Choice* as poor Mrs. Byron used to say of Sophia Streatfield.[2] It is a sad Plague sure enough; and when we are rid on't, doubt no doubtings that We shall come and tell you So.

Colonel Barry, Miss Weston, and Miss Williams have been our ten Days Guests, and we made it out very prettily with the help of agreable Mr. Jones,[3] whom you were all so in Love with last Summer.

Little Floretta and her Faery Train must lye by *till called for:*[4] I have seen Mr. Harris,[5] and a more hateful Gentleman did I never see, but no Manager can speak kindly of poor Dr. Delap, of whom to speak *un*kindly, is sure to offend *me.*[6]

Sweet Siddons made her triumphal Entry last Night—and the Acclamations, with the Distress of the Tragedy,[7] and all together, finished up my poor Titmouse strong as She is; and we had a *little Faint*. I think the Crowd was beyond all Credibility, such Clapping and Shouting too! it makes me laugh when I think how the Spiters told us that *Siddons had lost all her Popularity*——the Idea that She had lost her Senses was no Sillier. Kemble gave us a gay Supper, and She came in for a Moment, and kissed us all, but ran home to Bed almost immediately by Sir Lucas's orders, who sate in the Orchestra watching every Movement, and then followed with true Gallantry to her Dressing Room. So some Chivalry *is* left in the World notwithstanding Mr. Bur<ke>. His Book is the greatest Performance in Literature that has appeared for a long Time.[8] Helena Williams will please you however; I know of nothing else that is likely to do much for a Mind like yours harrassed with Thinking, does Miss Lewis at least write often, and write kindly?

I grieve She went not to Bath. Be as chearful as you can, and scold the new Maid. Miss Hull says She hopes Mrs. Siddons won't be ill again——for She do love Mrs. Siddons—She is so pretty——and so She is indeed.[9]

I have no more Chat just now, poor dear Mrs. Byron left me a Trinket by way of Remembrance,[10] and her fine Daughter in Law[11] sends me word that *'tis lost*.

Mr. Wetherhead will let us know when the Nova Scotia News comes over: meantime *You* have been the Cause if any good comes and to *you* I scarcely can be more than I have long been, a truly affectionate Friend and Servant / H: L: P.

Text: Collection of the late James Gilvarry. *Address:* Mrs. Lewis / London Street / Reading / Berks. *Postmark:* 9<DE>90.

1. Charlotte Lewis's daughter Sarah and son Patrick.
2. See HLP to Q, 25 November 1786. Sophia Streatfield had little patience with pretenders. As HLP wrote in "Harvard Piozziana" 1:108: "Where Sophy—like the Sun severe, / Soon dissipates each Flasher."
3. John Jones (1717–1806), of Cavendish Square, and Mitcham, Surrey, had married Lucy, née Fowler (b. 1731), a cousin of HLP's mother. "Good old Mr. Jones," as HLP habitually called him, "was no Hero . . . nor no Orator . . . but living rich, & living long are two great Distinctions" (*Thraliana* 2:999).
4. For HLP's dramatic aspirations, see her letter to Charlotte Lewis, 20 September [17]89, n. 12
5. Thomas Harris (d. 1820), proprietor and manager of the Covent Garden Theatre (1767–1820).
6. Delap had at least two undistinguished plays at the Drury Lane: *The Royal Suppliants*, which opened on 17 February 1781 for ten performances; and *The Captives*, whose first night was 9 March 1786. Even the acting of SS in the latter could not make the drama endure for more than three nights.
7. SS appeared on 7 December at the Drury Lane in Southerne's *Isabella or the Fatal Marriage*. Behind this performance was a history that began when she withdrew from the stage for the 1789–90 season. In poor health, she was also angry because Sheridan did not pay her either equitably or promptly, and because—according to Samuel Rogers—he made indiscreet advances (Manvell, pp. 172–73). Thereafter she appeared occasionally but did not fully return to the Drury Lane until January 1792.

SS performed in *Isabella* only after being assured of immediate compensation. Newspapers reported that the theater was packed to suffocation, that the shouting and applause after her performance lasted for more than five minutes. See the accounts in *St. James's Chronicle*, 7–9 December; *The Times*, 8 December.

8. The popularity of Burke's *Reflections on the Revolution* had been instantaneous upon its publication on 1 November.

HLP alludes to the eloquent lament that, following the downfall of Marie Antoinette, "the age of chivalry is gone.—That of sophisters, œconomists, and calculators has succeeded; and the glory of Europe is extinguished for ever. Never, never more, shall we behold that generous loyalty to rank and sex, that proud submission, that dignified obedience, that subordination of the heart, which kept alive, even in servitude itself, the spirit of an exalted freedom. . . ." See *Reflections on the Revolution in France, and on the Proceedings in Certain Societies in London Relative to that Event* (London: Printed for J. Dodsley, in Pall-Mall, 1790), p. 113.

9. HLP's housekeeper at Streatham, who helped to nurse SS when she was convalescing in the spring and early summer.
10. Sophia Byron bequeathed a "little Gold pencil to my much loved friend Mrs. Piozzi for with pen and pencil who can write so well."
11. For Henrietta Charlotte Byron, see HLP to Sophia Byron, 8 June 1788, n. 2.

TO PENELOPE SOPHIA WESTON

Tuesday
11: January 1791.

My dear Miss Weston did not use to be so silent, I hope it is not Illness or Ill humour keeps her from writing. Here have been more Storms—and very rough ones since you left us. Lady Deerhurst apprehends the End of the World, but I think her own Dissolution poor Dear is likelier to happen, for She is neither old nor tough like that; but very slight and feeble.[1]

We have fixed for going to Bath on Monday sennight; I have had some Pains in my Stomach, and Mr. Piozzi says (truly enough) that the Water will cure them: Change of Air too will carry away his little Nervous Complaints, so we set out on the 24: for dear Mrs. Lewis's at Reading.[2]

Send me some Commands, and believe / me ever equally and truly / Dear Miss Weston's Affectionate / Servant H: L: Piozzi.

Accept the united Compliments of the whole Coterie. We have lost our favourite Dog Loup.[3]

Text: Princeton University Library.

1. Margaret Pitches (1760–1840) had married in 1783 George William Coventry (1758–1831), Viscount Deerhurst, seventh earl of Coventry (1809). She was the daughter of Sir Abraham Pitches (d. April 1792), a brandy merchant and a Streatham resident. She now had four children and was about to produce her fifth: George William, born 16 October 1784 and baptized 10 November; Georgiana Catherina, born 10 September 1786 and baptized 16 October; Emily Elizabeth, born 27 November 1787 and baptized 18 December; John, born 3 June 1789 and baptized 26 July. On 16 February 1791 she gave birth to Thomas Henry, baptized 13 March (d. 2 October). Lady Deerhurst had four more children born after 1791: Thomas Henry, born 18 September 1792 and baptized 8 October; Jane Emily, born 3 July 1794 and baptized 10 August; William James, born 1 January 1797 and baptized 5 February; Barbara, born 15 July 1799 and baptized 15 August. See "Christenings 1756–1812," St. Leonard's Church, Streatham, at the Greater London Record Office.

2. The Piozzis did not leave for Reading on the 24th. In *Thraliana* 2:799, 27 January, HLP wrote: "Here's my Birthday returned; the first I have spent at Streatham for many Years, and quite the happiest I ever *did* spend there. Shortly thereafter she noted, "We are going to Bath for the Season, most of our great Debts paid, & our Hearts at ease" (2:800). See HLP to PSW, 11 February, n. 1.

3. The dog had wandered from Streatham Park but before 11 February had returned.

TO HUGH GRIFFITH[1]

Alfred Street Bath
Fryday 11: February 1791.

Dear Sir

I trouble your known Kindness with a Slight request: It is that you would obligingly procure me a Copy of the Register of my Birth, to be found in the Church of the Parish of Llanore County of Caernarvon, and Diocese of Bangor—as you know.[2]

That it was there in the Year 1774 I recollect, because my first Husband Mr. Thrale examined it—and I think took a Copy; which I cannot find. The Occasion for which I wish to be favoured with this Writing is solely the following.

My Father had Lands granted him in a Province of North America called Nova Scotia, which the present Possessors refuse to my Claim till I can *prove* myself Daughter, and *only* Child of my Parents.

Your friendly Assistance in this Business will be a real favour done to / Sir / Your Obliged / and faithful Servant / H: L: Piozzi.

My Husband and Daughter Cecilia Thrale send their Compliments.

Text: N. L. W., Llanfair and Brynodol.

1. See HLP to Griffith, 19 September 1789; *Thraliana* 2:691 n. 1.

2. In connection with the Nova Scotia property, the attorney Ward had written to GP from London, 9 February: "On the other side I send you a Copy of a Letter just received from Mr. Stern of Halifax for your perusal—

"This Letter does not go so far as I could have wished, because I fully expected he would therein have given some account of the nature of the property, and the probable value thereof, but it is some excuse to suppose that Mr. Stern wrote before he had time fully to investigate the subject.

"Mrs. Piozzi will be pleased to inform if there are any persons in this Town who can make proof of her being the only Child and Heir of . . . her late father, and I shall wait on them and explain the Business and draw a proper Affidavit to substantiate the Proof required by Mr. Stern.

"Who were present at her Marriage? as it seems to me necessary that a Certificate thereof should likewise be sent out at the time the other proof goes—.

"The Original Grants I have in my possession—and before I send them out, shall make regular attested Copies of them to guard against any accident.

"I hope, from the complexion of Mr. Stern's Letter, that the parts of the Estate resumed, will turn out to be of considerable value" (Ry. 601.37).

HLP also enlisted the help of John Wetherhead, who on 23 February wrote from Richmond that he intended meeting with Ward in London to discuss strategy: "If Mr. Sterns is convinced that the Proceedings of Government in Nova Scotia in the Escheat and reassumption of Your Estate, has been clearly illegal, the Risk of the Expence of 30 or, 40 Guineas at the utmost, would not deterr Prudence Himself from every Exertion for its Recovery—.

"I wish the Proofs and Testimonials you wrote to Wales for, may arrive in Time for next Wednesday's time—if Not, the Patents must be sent without Them" (Ry. 601.35).

Meanwhile an impatient HLP pressed her Welsh steward, Thomas Lloyd, for more action. Thereupon, he wrote from Denbigh on 26 March: "I am uneasy to know if Mr.

Griffith of Brynodol hath sent you proper Testimonials of your Birth, Parentage &c. &c. to your Satisfaction, in a Letter of His in answer to mine, upon the Subject, He informed me he would, if he hath not, pray write me a line, will make it my business to go my Self, or employ an acquaintance of mine in that neighbourhood" (Ry. 603.16). By 28 March, however, she acknowledged to Griffith the receipt of a copy of the birth register.

TO PENELOPE SOPHIA WESTON

Fryday
11: February 1791.

My dear Miss Weston must be among the very first to whom I give an Account of our safe arrival at a comfortable House Corner of Saville Row Alfred Street.[1] We left poor Mrs. Lewis as usual—happy in having spent her Money and Time to amuse us; and ran hither in one Day from Reading, but I found a strange Giddiness in my Head that was not allayed by the noisy Concourse of your Gamesters, Rakes &c. at York House[2] where we staid till this Lodging was empty: and here I have good Air and good Water and good Company—and at last—*good Nights:* so that I mean to be among the merriest immediately.

The Place is full, and the pretty Girls kind as my Master Says, so you must write pretty eloquent Letters, to hold his Heart fast.

Your Friend Mrs. Rundell has an exceeding handsome Daughter indeed;[3] and here is sweet Miss Hamilton who sings as well as ever She did—can I give her juster Praise?[4] and Mrs. Mullins no bigger round the Waist than usual, and no less able to bear her Part in the *Baronessa amabile*.[5] The dear kind Whalleys first with their Cards of Invitation, Mrs. Jackson[6] and Miss Lees in good humour—— and all asking after you.

Miss Hotham's Accounts[7] of our sweet Siddons are better than common, So when Things are at worst they mend you see. Mr. Kemble's illness, gained only by shining too brightly, and wasting the Oyl in the Lamp, while here at Bath; is recovered by now I hope, and his Spirits properly recruited.[8] All the World is to be at Dimond's Benefit on Tuesday 22.[9] He keeps his youthful Look and Step unimpaired still.

Did I tell you that *Loup* had Sense enough to find his own way home to Streatham, for which we rewarded him with a Bath Journey. The *indoor* Dogs send Duty.

Cecilia was fourteen Years old Three Days ago; and all the folks say how She is grown &c. Pray accept her's and Mr. Piozzi's kindest Thoughts with those of your Affectionate Servant / H: L: P.

11: February 1791. Fryday.

Text: Princeton University Library. *Address:* Miss Weston / Queen Square / *Westminster. Postmark:* FE 12 91.

1. The Piozzis had lodgings in Bath from early February through early April. According to the Bath directory for 1791, "The general price of Lodgings" in season (1 September to 31 May) "is 10s.6d. a week for the best rooms, and 5s.3d. for servants' rooms."

2. See HLP to Sophia Byron, 29 June 1788, n. 3.

3. Maria Eliza Rundell (1745–1828), only child of Abel Johnstone Ketelby, of Ludlow, and wife of the surgeon Thomas Rundell (d. 1800), who had served on the common council of Bath. In 1791, Mrs. Rundell had six children: Edmond Waller, Maria, Margaretta Catharine, Frances Amelia, Augusta Louisa, and Harriet Eliza. It is difficult to know whether HLP refers to Maria, the eldest daughter, who was soon to marry Thomas Briggs or to Margaretta Catharine, who in 1796 married George Booth Tyndale.

Mrs. Rundell was the author of two widely used books: *A New System of Domestic Cookery* (1808) and a *New Family Receipt Book* (1810).

4. That is, Jane Hamilton, through whom HLP in the spring of 1788 was invited to the amateur theatricals sponsored by the duke of Richmond at Richmond House. When Jane was rehearsing a role in Nathaniel Lee's *Theodosius,* she came to HLP for a special song. Finding a suitable Italian air, HLP had GP play the music several times and then dashed off a set of verses ("Vain the Breath of Adulation"). See "Harvard Piozziana" 2:102; HLP to Sophia Byron, 2 June [1788]; 11 July 1789; "Verses 1," p. 69.

5. Frances Elizabeth Sage became on 12 May 1790 the second wife of William Townshend Mullins (1761–1827), later second baron Ventry (1824). The marriage was dissolved by act of parliament in 1796.

6. The widowed Eliza E. Jackson (d. 1829 or 1830), "formerly of Clonmel, co. Tipperary; late of the Island of Ceylon," resided at 13 Portland Place, Bath, between 1789 and 1791. Early in 1792 she moved to London but returned intermittently to Bath and Bristol Hotwells. The mother of four children (three boys and a girl), she was a friend of TSW and of Anna Seward, who found her " 'a woman of first-rate abilities and virtues' " (Wickham 2:36–37). In 1806 Rivington published in London and Edinburgh her *Dialogues on the Doctrines and Duties of Christianity,* 2 vols. See "Prerogative Wills Index," P.R.O., Ireland.

7. One of the three nieces of Sir Charles Hotham-Thompson (d. 1794), eighth baronet. She was a daughter of Beaumont (1737–1814), second baron Hotham (1813), who in 1767 married Susannah (Norman), née Hankey (d. 1799). The possible identifications are: Frances (d. 1836), who in 1797 married Admiral Sir John Sutton; Amelia (d. 1812), who in 1798 married John Woodcock (1775–1813), secretary of bankrupts to the lord chancellor; Louisa (d. 1840), who married, firstly, Sir Charles Edmonstone (d. 1821) and, secondly, Charles Woodcock.

8. The autumn of the 1790–91 season vexed Kemble as one of Drury Lane's managers. The theaters had been closed by the marquis of Salisbury as lord chamberlain in memory of the duke of Cumberland, who had died on 18 September. During this hiatus, Kemble engaged in constant social activities and drank excessively, even at the Piozzis' two-day house party. When the theater reopened in the first week of November, its receipts averaged only £150 a night. He quarreled with Eliza Farren and Dorothy Jordan. He performed poorly as Charles Surface in *The School for Scandal.* He accompanied Thomas Linley to Bath, where more carousing occurred. His illness, the result of frustrations at the Drury Lane and dissipation, was temporary, and he was again active in the theater even before the spring social season. See Baker, pp. 167–72.

9. Two plays were performed for Dimond's benefit (22 February): Arthur Murphy's *The Way to Keep Him* and J. O. Keeffe's *The Farmer.*

TO THE REVEREND LEONARD CHAPPELOW

Alfred Street Bath
February 23: 1791.

Dear Mr. Chappelow

You are very kind always, and so are your Letters: we are well and merry I thank God; full of Engagements, and pretty near empty of Cares: if my Lord Dumfries[1] takes a fancy to the House, and will have it for our remaining Term, I shall be very happy indeed and comfortable.[2]

Bath is a mighty pretty Translation of London, and I like it better than the original——for the same Reason as I do Pope's Homer—because I *understand* It better; and because 'tis *easier.*[3] The dear Hamiltons say so too; many and kind are their Enquiries after you, so are Dear Mrs. Lewis's. Do you know that one of our little darling W's deserts next Summer? Fair Helena is the Person; and She is going to reside in France for two or three years.[4] I say She will come back a better Patriot than She goes away——a better or a more amiable *Woman* can She not be. Miss Weston is among you in London, but laments that She sees nobody. If you call on, or meet her; tell how I am engaged here in perpetual Nothingnesses, that keep me from writing——but *nothing* its very self shall longer hinder me from assuring You of my kind Husband and Daughters truest Regards with those of Dear Sir Your ever Obliged and faithful Servant / H: L: Piozzi.

I am glad you are amused by the new Opera.[5]

Text: Ry. 559.13.

1. Patrick Macdowall-Crichton (1726–1803), sixth earl of Dumfries (1768), an officer in the Third Foot Guards, 1762; grand master of Freemasons [Scotland], 1771–73; and representative peer [Scotland], 1790–1803. In 1771 he had married Margaret, née Crauford (d. 1799), of Edinburgh. They had one child, Elizabeth Penelope (d. 1797), who was to marry on 12 October John Stuart, Lord Mount Stuart (1767–94), son of the first marquess of Bute.

2. At the beginning of 1791 HLP had observed that the cost of maintaining Streatham Park warranted economy measures. "I am glad that Hanover Square house is let, or going to be Let to Lord Dumfries; our Establishment here [at Streatham Park] is too magnificent for the admission of other Expences" (*Thraliana* 2:797).

3. That is, translations of the *Iliad* (1715–20) and the *Odyssey* (1725–26).

4. Helen Williams planned to leave for France at the end of July.

5. The opera *Armida* was first performed at King's Theatre on 8 November 1774. The music initially was by Antonio Maria Gasparo Gioacchino Sacchini (1730–86). During the 1785–86 season, on 25 May, *Armida* was revived with music by Michele Mortellari (ca. 1750–1807) and a libretto by the Italian poet Giovanni de Gamèrra (1743–1803). Now, in the 1790–91 season, the opera was brought forth again at King's with Sacchini's music supplemented by the alterations and additions of Gaetano Andreozzi (1755–1826) and Joseph Mazzinghi (1765–1844).

The opera, performed on 17 February (and on four subsequent dates) at the recently refurbished Pantheon Theatre, was criticized for the poor quality of the facilities and production and for an excessively long performance.

TO HUGH GRIFFITH

Bath
28: March 1791.

Dear Mr. Griffith

I take Shame to myself that having lived in this World *so long,* as our Registers amply testify——I have not yet learned, as you will think, Good manners enough to answer so kind a Letter.[1] Accept my Thanks for it *now,* and spare my Excuses, which commonly but make bad worse in those Cases.

I hope the People in America will not be as dilatory, and then I perhaps need not despair of recovering some Property of which my Father has been cruelly wronged on *the other* Side the Globe; however Matters may have gone in *this Hemisphere.*

This Place is very chearful, and the Buildings much improved; but we are desirous to see home, and shall of Course return to Streatham the first Week of next Month.[2]

If you would then favour my husband or myself with any Commands at London, You should not find so dilatory a Friend, as you have found a Correspondent in / Sir / Your faithful Servant / and much Obliged / H: L: Piozzi.

Cecilia Thrale begs her Compliments may be added to ours—and pray tell us what Expence was incurred by your Inquiries.

Text: N. L. W., Llanfair and Brynodol.

1. Griffith had sent a copy of the register of HLP's birth, as she had requested.
2. HLP referred to the Bath buildings—those completed and those being constructed—by the architect John Eveleigh, among them Camden Crescent, Somerset Place, and Grosvenor Place.

By 9 April the Piozzis had returned to Streatham Park, "not sorry to come home" (*Thraliana* 2:801).

TO WILLIAM WILSHIRE[1]

Streatham Park
26: April [1791]

Sir

You have been very good, and it was very idle in me not to tell you so sooner; the Business must be settled and the Cash paid as before.[2] So end my Possessions in Hertfordshire it seems, the Place I earliest attached my silly Heart to.[3] That you Sir may long be happy there is the sincerest Wish of your Obliged humble servant / Hester Lynch Piozzi.

You will send the Account of the Interest.[4]

Text: Hitchin Museum, Paynes Park, Hitchin, Herts.

1. William Wilshire (1754–1824), a member of the law firm of Hawkins and Co., at Hitchin, Herts.

He was an important local figure—chairman of Bedfordshire Quarter Sessions, a partner in Whitbread's brewery, owner of a malthouse in Ware—all this in addition to an extensive law practice.

He and HLP shared political views. He so feared the French Revolution's effect on England that he built into his house in Hitchin "a secret chamber, with shelves for food, drink and valuables, air-tubes for ventilation, and a massive iron door." In 1803 he became lieutenant colonel of the Hitchin Volunteers, raised to meet Bonaparte's threatened invasion. See C.R.O., Hertfordshire; *[Hertfordshire] County Chronicle,* 7 September 1824.

HLP became acquainted with him in his capacity as legal adviser to Sir Thomas and Lady Salusbury.

2. During her adolescence, HLS had regarded Offley Park as a second home. Here she was educated by her mother, her aunt Anna Maria Salusbury, and Dr. Arthur Collier (1707–77). Here, also, she was the favorite of her uncle, Sir Thomas, and as his nearest blood relative was assumed to be his heir-at-law, a distinction that promised her a share of his large estate. But difficulties between HLS's father and her uncle were augmented by the second Lady Salusbury.

In 1773 HLT learned that she had been excluded from Sir Thomas's will. By late 1790, largely upon the advice of John Perkins, HLP discovered that she could claim title to some of the Hertfordshire copyholds once owned by her uncle. In a letter from Perkins, 2 November 1790 (Ry. 600.12), she was told the following:

"I am *convinced* Mr. Thrale *never received* any Money for Rents or Copyholds from the Estate of Sir Thomas—if I recollect the Case right, it was this—Sir Thomas forgot to mention the Copyholds in his Will. Therefore they came to you, and Mr. Robson went down to Offley to ascertain the Copyholds and have them layed out to him: I think (nay I know) he brought an Account of them or at least their Value which I think was £1500—therefore he can shew you that Account and tell you every thing you want to know, they are still yours. If their Value was not set off in the Account Lady Salusbury made out against you, but if they never were deducted from the demand she made of Mr. Thrale, why then you have a right to them and all the Rent from Sir Thomas's death. . . ."

But, as Perkins discovered, the resolution of the copyholds was both more complicated and less profitable than he assumed. In a letter of 12 November (Ry. 600.13), he informed HLP:

"This day I had a meeting with Mr. Norris and talked over the Copyholds, he tells me, that the Rents from 1773 to 83 was set off by the Master in Chancery when the Suit between you and Lady Salusbury was settled, and since that you have been paid the Rents up to 1789. . . .

"I find that the Rents don't exceed £40. a Year which at 20 Years purchase for Copyholds, makes their full Value £800—why they came to be Valued at more when Mr. Robson went to have them layd out, was that Sir Thomas had them all in *his own* possession; so that their value was *Nominal,* but *since* his death they have been let to Tenants, by which their value has become fixed, and their Worth more properly Ascertained. . . ."

3. Determined to sell her copyholds, HLP had made further inquiries of Ward, who answered on 3 March: "Mr. Wilshire informed me that you wished to know, what he meant by the Surrender which he wrote about; I understand by him that the Estates agreed to be sold, lay in four several manors, viz. King's Walden, Offley, Saint Ledgers, and Hitchin, and that before the Money for the purchase can be paid you must Surrender

the Estates to the use of the purchaser; such Surrender being the same as Executing a Conveyance of a Freehold or Leasehold Estate" (Ry. 605.4).

4. What HLP wanted, specifically, were the unpaid rents, with interest due her from 1789, and the earnings from the sale of the copyholds.

TO CHARLOTTE LEWIS

Monday
9: May 1791.

My Dear Mrs. Lewis knows Very well that No Concert is half as attractive to me as the Company of an old Friend: but I have no Chance of getting to London while the House keeps full with one Body or another; Mrs. Jackson comes today: She has been mortified by her Boy's running away from School, pawning his Watch for Money, and riding a hundred Miles an End upon the Strength on't.[1] But I find the Bath Tongues are all disserting upon Mrs. Light's Marriage with Captain Anstey, third Son of the Authour Anstey in Marlbro' Buildings.[2] She has written me a very affectionate Letter from onboard the Ship which carries her and her Husband to India, charging me with a Thousand Compliments to you and Miss Lewis—who I hope will continue well while She minds Sir Lucas Pepys's Directions. Mrs. Siddons seems to have prospered exceedingly under his Care, nobody can I think enjoy better Health than She.

Cecilia has a sore Throat, but will not let me send for him on her Account relying on old Buchan's Book[3] and little Kitchen the Apothecary;[4] with Rob of Elder, and Mrs. Piozzi for consulting Physician.

The Frost ruins all our Fruit, the Vegetables shrink and perish in the Ground, but the Gardeners Bills will not shrivel up. I suppose even with these Easterly Winds, which unless they bring marvellous Tydings indeed from America will not make me any Compensation for the Evil done at home.[5]

Fox our rough Terrier has had a vile Accident too, and nearly lost his Life by a Burn; so Things do not go quite right you find, and if my young Turkeys *do* come out while this Weather lasts—they must die.

So much for poor Streatham where dear Mrs. Lewis has many Friends but none more Affectionate than / H: L: P.

Mr. Piozzi and Cecilia send due Devoirs: our Friend Lysons is collecting Anecdotes of the Villiers Family and proving its Antiquity, Illustriousness &c. He seems much delighted with the Employment, and I fancy does it exceedingly well.[6]

Text: Hyde Collection.

1. Of Eliza Jackson's three sons, one remains unidentified; the other two were Henry and Thomas.

2. Emigrating in 1765 to Madras as a member of the East India Company, William Light

had become by 1776 a "Senior Merchant." He apparently died there about 1782. See Charles C. Prinsep, *Record of the Services of the Honourable East India Company's Civil Servants in the Madras Presidency. From 1741 to 1858* (London: Trübner, 1885).

Lucretia Luders (d. 1794), having married Light on 10 July 1776 ("Bath Abbey Registers, Marriages"), returned to Bath soon after his death.

As recorded in the "Walcot Parish Register, Marriages 1783–1793" (no. 507), "Robert Anstey, Esqr. of this Parish, a bachelor, and Lucretia Light of the Parish of Widcombe & Lyncombe, a Widow in this County, were married" 21 April (C.R.O., Somerset). See also the *Bath Journal,* 25 April 1791.

Robert Anstey (ca. 1760–1818) was a son of the Bath poet Christopher Anstey (1724–1805). Having prepared at Eton, Robert matriculated at Saint John's, Cambridge, in 1780. By 29 September 1781, however, he had become a cornet in the Twenty-third Dragoons (renumbered the Nineteenth Dragoons in 1786), a lieutenant on 2 March 1785, and captain lieutenant on 23 March 1791. A captain in the Seventy-sixth Foot by April 1792, he resigned his commission in 1793, returning from India to England.

Anstey was on 28 June 1796 to marry "Miss [Louisa] Cane, daughter and co-heiress of the late Colonel Hugh Cane, member of the Irish parliament for Imlagh, co. Waterford" (*Bath Herald,* 2 July 1796).

3. The Scottish-born William Buchan (1729–1805), M.D., was a skilled pediatrician. In 1769 he published in Edinburgh *Domestic Medicine; or The Family Physician,* the first British work of its kind. It was to go through nineteen large editions in Buchan's lifetime. In 1778 he came from Scotland to establish an extensive practice in London.

4. Matthew Kitchen (fl. 1769–93), an apothecary and surgeon, resided on the west side of the Streatham Common. He was appointed a guardian of the poor in 1790. See "Land Tax Assessments," C.R.O., Surrey, Kingston upon Thames.

5. HLP deplored the spread in England of French revolutionary principles and organizations allegedly propagating those principles. "Societies all over the country which had just been celebrating the centenary of the expulsion of James II remained in being to applaud the French. . . . The Society for Constitutional Information, suspended since 1784, was revived in 1791" (Watson, p. 324).

"Tydings from America" concerned the parcels of land, once owned by John Salusbury in Nova Scotia, that HLP now claimed (see her letter to Sterns, 30 October 1790).

6. HLP does not specify which branch of the Villiers family interested SL—whether it was that connected with the dukes of Buckingham, who claimed descent from a companion of William the Conqueror; with the earls of Clarendon and barons Hyde; with the viscounts Grandison and earls of Jersey.

SL, however, soon put this "Employment" aside. He was heavily committed to projects that finally emerged as *The Views and Antiquities in the County of Gloucester* (1791– [ca. 98]) and *Reliquiæ Britannico-Romanæ,* 2 vols. (1801, 1817); 3 vols. (1813–17).

TO CHARLOTTE LEWIS

Streatham Park
30: May 1791.

My dear Mrs. Lewis

I should have written sooner, but Cecilia has had some little Ailments, and kept my Spirits in Agitation. She is well now, and I have Leisure to be plagued for Letters to Italy in favour of a Mr. Gray who is going thither, and wishes for our Recommendation.[1]

Helena Williams begins her French Tour in August; the farewell Poem is mighty pretty, and will I hope bring her some *pretty Consequences:*[2] Mr. Merry is said to have actually lost Money by *Lorenzo,*[3] and I'm sorry for it, as the Play was very elegant: but Literary Anecdotes and Gossiping Stories alone can obtain Attention: Mr. Boswell's Book——full of your Name and mine, is said to sell excellently[4]——and so it must too, or the printing will not be paid for, it stands its Author they say in a thousand Pounds[5]——If I was to write any more these two or three Years——I would own nothing I wrote.

M[rs.] Lewis is right in following Sir Lucas implicitly; did *He* recommend the Sea? Some Neighbours of ours are going to reside in Topsham Parish—for Health: the Lady was Miss Fry, and kept the School here at Streatham where Cecilia was left by me on our going abroad; and whence Miss Thrale moved her, I never could guess why.[6] The Gentleman She married is a Mr. Sainsbury Alderman of London and very rich,[7] he has been in France and Italy a long Time, but finds Devonshire Air preferable to all other: it is indeed very famous——but you that hate Rain would be weary on't soon I think.

James your late Servant called to see us the other day and looked all alive. I have got Miss Owen with me,[8] but no Friend of ours ever tryed to lessen You in Mr. Piozzi's Esteem——that I know of——and certainly not in mine: I am very sorry you should suspect any such Thing.

Mrs. Siddons is gone to Oxfordshire handsomer and healthier than ever,[9] and so far happier as She has now the Company of her Daughter, whom of Course she admires no little.[10]

Your kind Cousin overrates my possessions terribly I doubt not, but we do not overrate his Civility and active Friendship:[11] Dr. Parker gave Mr. Piozzi an excellent Account of that Mr. Sterne he recommended to us as Agent for our Affairs in America.[12]

Farewell my dear Mrs. Lewis and God bless you and write often to / Your ever equally / Affectionate / H: L: Piozzi.

Text: Hyde Collection. *Address:* Mrs. Lewis / London Street / Reading / Berks. *Postmark:* JU 1 91.

1. The Reverend Robert Gray (1762–1834) was to become bishop of Bristol (1827). Having received the B.A. (1784) and M.A. (1787), RG would take his B.D. (1799) and D.D. (1802) from Oxford. His first published work was *A Key to the Old Testament and Apocrypha* (1790). At this time (i.e., 1791–92), when he was already vicar of Faringdon, Berks., he was planning a tour through Germany, Switzerland, and Italy.

2. See *A Farewell for Two Years to England. A Poem* (1791).

3. Merry's tragedy *Lorenzo* was performed at Covent Garden by Joseph George Holman (1764–1817), William Farren (1754–95), Ann, or Anne, Brunton (1769–1808), soon to become Merry's wife, and Elizabeth Pope, née Younge (ca. 1744–97).

Opening night was 5 April, receipts being £187 3*s*. *Lorenzo* was performed again on 7, 14, 27 April, and 7 May. The benefit for Merry on the last night earned £114 13*s*. 6*d*. Cadell published the play on 7 May.

4. On 16 May JB's *Life of Johnson* appeared, printed by Henry Baldwin (ca. 1734–1813) for Charles Dilly (1739–1807). It consisted of two large quarto volumes in blue-gray boards, with 516 pages in the first and 586 in the second. See Mary Hyde, *The Impossible Friendship* (Cambridge: Harvard University Press, 1972), pp. 148–61, for HLP's reactions to

what JB called his "*Magnum Opus.*" None of these, whether public or private, were as bland as the statement in this letter.

Despite its price of two guineas, eight hundred sets were sold in the first week or two. By August twelve hundred sets were purchased, and JB hoped that the whole of the first edition (1,750) would have been distributed before Christmas.

5. JB required one thousand pounds for a fifteen hundred pound mortgage applied to his purchase of Knockroon, once a part of the Auchinleck estates. The necessary funds would have been available had he sold the copyright to George Robinson (1737–1801). He was, however, unwilling to part with it or to sever a longtime association with Dilly. By 8 March he informed Malone that Dilly and Baldwin had each promised two hundred pounds advance credit on the biography and that he had been able to obtain another six hundred pounds credit on his rents in Scotland. Thus he was able to "get the £1000 [for Knockroon] paid in May" even while keeping "the property of [his] *Magnum Opus*" (Hyde, *The Impossible Friendship*, pp. 145–48).

HLP had apparently heard the sum of one thousand pounds discussed but misunderstood its purpose and was ignorant of the fact that the matter had already been resolved.

6. HLP had placed CMT in Russell House in 1784. Q, upon her own authority, removed her sister to the Miss Stevensons's school at Queen Square, Westminster. The change was made in the summer of 1786 allegedly because of the child's inadequate progress at Streatham. See HLP to William Parsons, 4 August 1786, n. 4, and to Q, 7 July 1787.

7. For Eliza Maria Fry and Alderman Thomas Sainsbury, see HLP to Q, 7 July 1787.

8. For HLP's relative Margaret Owen, see HLP to Q, 17 August [1784].

9. SS was at the Rectory House of Lord and Lady Harcourt at Nuneham Courtney, Oxon. HLP's optimism for the actress's health and appearance soon changed. See HLP to PSW [post-9 August–pre-15 August].

10. Sarah "Sally" Martha (1776–1803).

11. John Wetherhead, of Richmond.

12. Additionally the Reverend William Parker testified that HLP was her "Father's Daughter—this for the sake of reobtaining the Nova Scotia Property" (*Thraliana* 2:807). See HLT to FB, 20 May 1784, n. 2.

Sterns's enthusiasm for the Piozzis' legal cause began to abate, and on 25 August he recommended cautious waiting while a similar case was being adjudicated in Nova Scotia. By 3 December he warned Joseph Ward that the property was "in the Possession of lawless People, whom I shall find some difficulty to deal with." See Ry. 601.40, 41.

TO PENELOPE SOPHIA WESTON

Streatham Park
Thursday 28: July [1791]

My Dear Miss Weston

I was happy to find the Prescription—which after all I did not find, but made little Kitchen copy. Do not forget Streatham, nor remit of your Kindness towards me, or towards those I love——Dear Harriett in particular: I hope you will contrive to see her very often.

Marquis Trotti is sensible of your partiality,[1] and deserves all your Esteem: his Behaviour is such that were he my Son I should kiss him, were he my Brother I should be proud of him; and as he is only my good Friend, I pity and respect him.

There is much Tenderness joined with due Manliness in his Character——he is a very fine young Fellow.

Miss Jones has left us,[2] so has Mr. Jones now and we are desolate enough.[3] My Gentlemen are gone to Greenland's[4] at Carshalton this Morning in hope to drive Care away; they will find Care enough there; but 'tis a nice House for Foreigners——such good Italian is talked in it. Poor Emma[5] must wait long though I fear before that Language is of use to *her,* but as Hermia says in The Midsummer Night's Dream

> I never read in Tale or History
> That Course of true Love ever did run smooth;
> But either it was crossed in *Degree* &c. &c.[6]

Well! if 'tis of the right Sort Opposition will but encrease it, and as Marquis Trotti said to Buchetti[7] in my Company Yesterday—The Time is approaching when Aristocratic Notions about Marriage will fall to Ground, and then those who have sacrificed their Happiness to such Folly, will look but like Fools themselves.

Shew this Letter to our lovely and *much*-beloved Harriett; She is I think the Object of a very Honourable and a very tender Passion, and to a Mind like hers that ought to be a very great Comfort.

Adieu! and believe me / ever truly yours / H: L: P.

Write to me only in general, not *particular* Terms, write very soon tho', or I shall be gone to Mrs. Siddons's[8]

Text: Princeton University Library. *Address:* Miss Weston / at Mrs. Jackson's / Portland Place / Bath. *Postmark:* JY 28 91.

1. For Lorenzo Galeazzo Trotti, see HLP to SL, [5 April 1787], n. 7; *French Journals,* p. 202 and n. 1.

During the young man's visit to England in 1791, HLP and PSW played matchmakers, hoping to effect a union between him and Harriet Lee.

Under date of 16 July HLP wrote in *Thraliana* (2:812) of "serious Morning Readings with Marquiss de Trotti and Harriett Lee, who I once fancied had made impression on his Heart, so closely did his Lordship attend to the *Lecture:* but I believe he only wanted to gain the Language after all."

2. Lucy Eliza Jones (fl. 1772–1820), of Saint Marylebone, would on 12 May 1792 marry Alexander George (sometimes given as George Alexander) Mackay (fl. 1770–1815) at Saint George's Church, Hanover Square. Mackay, who owned a town house in Baker Street, shortly after the marriage rented Langham Hall near Bury, Suffolk. Of their six children, two died before adulthood: George, the eldest son, on 1 August 1808, aged eleven; Georgiana, the third daughter, on 23 December 1811, aged sixteen.

See J. H. Chapman [and G. J. Armytage], eds., *Register Book of Marriages belonging to the Parish of St. George, Hanover Square,* 4 vols. (London: Harleian Society, 1886–97), vol. 2 (1788–1809); and "Monumental Inscriptions at Bury St. Edmunds (in the Abbey Burying Ground)," in C.R.O., Suffolk.

3. For John Jones of Mitcham, see HLP to Charlotte Lewis, 8 December 1790, n. 3.

4. For Augustus Greenland, see HLT to Q [27 June 1784], n. 6.
5. The daughter of Augustus Greenland. See HLT to Q, 15 July [1784], n. 1.
6. A variation on Lysander's lines in *A Midsummer Night's Dream* 1.1.132–35.
7. For Lodovico Maria Buchetti, see HLP to SL, 7 December 1784, n. 13.
8. While GP accompanied Buchetti and Trotti on a tour of North Wales, HLP and CMT planned a visit to SS at Nuneham Courtney in August and part of September.

TO PENELOPE SOPHIA WESTON

Rectory house Nuneham
6: August [1791] Saturday.

I promised my dear Miss Weston a long Letter from sweet Siddons's fairy Habitation, but had not an Idea of finding as elegant a Thing as it is. England can boast no happier Situation; a Hill scattered over with fragrance makes the Stand for our lovely little Cottage, while Isis rolls at his foot, and Oxford terminates our View. Lord Harcourt's rich Wood covers a rising Ground that conceals the flat Country on the Left, and leaves no spot unoccupied by cultivated, and I may say peculiar Beauty.[1] How I should love to range these Walks with my own dear Streatham Coterie!—but now it is all broken up. The Marquis and my Master with Mr. Buchetti left us this Morning in search of Sublimer Scenes:[2] I have given them a Tour into Wales——Cecilia and my self sit and look here for their Return——*that is for my Husband's*—unless Miss Owen's summons, or Signal of distress lures me to Shrewsbury, where I could wait for *him* and be nearer.[3] They will reach Worcester tonight, and visit Hagley tomorrow I trow.

Never did mortal Nymph speed her *polished* Arrow more *surely* than has our Harriett done: never did stricken Deer struggle more ineffectually against the Shaft which has fixed itself firm in his heart, than does her noble Lover.[4] He has however no Mind I fancy to give up without an Effort——but no one better knows than I do the difficulty up to impossibility of such an Operation.

She too feels, and feels sincerely I'm sure; these are the true lasting Passions; where a Serpentine Walk leads they know *not whither:* for in Love as in Taste I see

He best succeeds, who pleasingly *confounds;*
Surprizes, varies, and conceals the *Bounds*.[5]

Console and Sooth her, *do* my charming Friend, She will find these five or six Weeks as many Years——but by then She will have her Admirer at the Hot Wells where he may drink the Water to Advantage. He is already much altered in Countenance but *so* interesting!

Give my kindest Compliments to Mrs. Jackson for whom I have very just Esteem. What a charming Company will you have at Bath now! and Miss Seward too—how charming! I warrant She has been at dear Mr. Whalley's Cottage all this while!—how is her precious health?[6]

There is nothing like living near a Nobleman's house for making a *Democrate* of one: here has been such a deal of Ceremony and Diddle Daddle, to get these

Letters franked as would make a plain Body mad——and I see not that you or Harriett will get them either quicker or Cheaper for all the Ado we have made at last. But now I am out of Parliament myself, I will beg no more Free post directions.[7]

Oh! would you believe the Gypsies have told Truth to Marquis Trotti? They said he would have a great Influx of Money soon—*Yellow* Boys you know they called them: and he said what Stuff that was, because his Fortune could not easily admit of Increase, as it was already an entailed Estate——and all his Expectations well known to himself.—But a few Days ago a Letter from Italy informed him of unclaimed Dividends found in the Bank of Genoa which might be his for asking. He *will not go over* to ask for them however; but sent his Father[8] word he was indifferent about the Matter—he had enough &c.—he is of Aspasia's Mind entirely—[9]

Love be our Wealth, and our Distinction Virtue; his Income can be in no Danger though, do what he will: at least a very considerable one of which I am glad: he is a deserving Character indeed, and will I hope lose very little by His Sentiments of Dignity and Sensitivity of Heart.

Let our Harriett read all this, I had no room for another Word in that I sent her. How beautiful a Bit of writing did She send me upon leaving Streatham! I wish when her Hand's *in*, some clever Verses would but drop from it: tell her I say so: this is Inspiration's favorite Hour.

How pleased it would make me if I were but addressed in them![10] Her Talents have really made a glorious Conquest and She ought to cherish them. I long for the sight of her dear pale Ink that I do: and do not you forget the Truth and Zeal with which I love my kind Miss Weston.

If you cannot bathe for Distance, and cannot drink——take my Pills——and half an hour before Dinner a Teaspoonful of Huxham's <fine> Tincture of Bark in a Glass of Pyrmont or Spa Water dropping in fifteen Drops of Elixir of Vitriol——the Dose may be gradually increased to twenty Drops without Danger.[11]

So Adieu! *I* hoped to bathe *Here*, but see things are not so easily obtained——and I scorn to go thro' Difficulties for such a Trifle. / Ever and Ever Yours / H: L: P.

Mrs. Siddons sends a thousand kind Words. She is very well as can be.

It appears so strange and so shocking to put up my Letter without speaking of Miss Seward that I can't bear it; nobody has such a notion of her Talents as I have, though all the World has talked so loudly about them——her Mental and indeed her Personal Charms when I last saw them, united the three grand Characteristics of Female Excellence to very great Perfection: I mean Majesty, Vivacity and Sweetness.[12] Well! you may speak as ill of Bath as you please, but I wish I was there, and never look at old White Horse Hill which one sees from the Terrace without sighing to pass it on the Road——but Fate calls to Shrewsbury——and thither I shall hie me on the 20 of this Month——and now remember Missey—that to kindle and keep up a Man's Love so as to make him want enough for the *overleaping* Objections, is the true duty of prudent Friendship;—not to make him *talk* of those *very Objections* which we know already, and which will only strengthen by talking of. So God bless you all and love / your / H: L: P.——

Text: Princeton University Library.

1. George Simon Harcourt (1736–1809), second earl Harcourt (1777). The estate at Nuneham Courtney was purchased by Simon Harcourt (1661–1727), first viscount Harcourt, in 1721. SS's "fairy Habitation," whose scenery had at first attracted HLP, soon took on the overtones of the actress's depression. See *Thraliana* 2:814–15.

2. HLP sent them "round by Oxford, Blenheim, Worcester, Hagley, Leasowes, & L[d] Stamford's fine Seat at Anville Park, thro' Colebroke Dale, Shrewsbury, Llangollen, Dynas Bran &c to Wrexham. whence they shaped their Course thro' Bala Dolgelly & Barmouth to Brynodol; visited Bodvel the Place of my Nativity, in good Time! & came round By Caernarvon Bangor & Conway to Anglesea . . . from these Places across the Ferry S[t] Asaph Holywell & Denbigh detained 'em a while with Llewenney's *Works,* & poor Bachygraig's Idleness" (*Thraliana* 2:814).

3. At some unspecified date Margaret Owen had invited HLP to Shrewsbury, "where She stood in serious need She said, of Advice and Consolation: I . . . set out to comfort one of my earliest, perhaps one of my most disinterested Friends" (*Thraliana* 2:816). HLP left about 20 September for Shrewsbury.

4. HLP's allusion to and adaptation of William Cowper's lines 108–11 in "The Garden" (*The Task,* bk. 3). Cf. *Julius Caesar* 3.1.209; *Hamlet* 3.2.271; "A Fit of the Spleen. In Imitation of Shakespeare." By Dr. Ibbot, in Dodsley 5:245.

5. See Alexander Pope, lines 55–56 of *Epistle IV. To Richard Boyle, Earl of Burlington* ("Of the Use of Riches").

6. Writing on 23 August from TSW's Langford Cottage, to an acquaintance, Anna Seward noted: "The week after I arrived here, Mr. W. was so good as to take me to Bath. We were the guests of his charming friend, Mrs. Jackson" (*Seward Letters* 3:104).

7. On 23 December 1765, HT had been returned as M.P. for Southwark, a seat that he held through several elections until 1780. See Clifford, pp. 59–60, 71–74, 189–90.

8. HLT had first met the marchese Lodovico Trotti (1729–1808) in Paris during her 1775 visit. Not only wealthy but influential, he had been named in 1767 *gentiluomo di camera dell'imperatore d'Austria.* The association continued with both generations of Trottis after the Piozzis arrived on the Continent in 1784.

9. In an exchange with Demetrius, Aspasia proclaims:

> Nor wealth, nor titles, make Aspasia's bliss.
> O'erwhelm'd and lost amidst the publick ruins
> Unmov'd I saw the glitt'ring trifles perish,
> And thought the petty dross beneath a sigh.
> Chearful I follow to the rural cell,
> Love be my wealth, and my distinction virtue.
> (SJ's *Irene* 4.1.106–11; *Poems,* pp. 176–77)

HLP looks to a Trotti-Lee alliance in which the virtuous love of both parties will transcend material concern.

10. Harriet Lee's "Bit of Writing" is missing, but she obliged HLP with "Verses . . . written 10: August 1791" (*Thraliana* 2:819–20).

11. John Huxham (1692–1768), M.D. His tincture is a compound of cinchona bark, bitter orange peel, serpentary root, saffron, and cochineal mixed in alcohol. It was used as a specific for fevers.

12. PSW must have shown HLP Anna Seward's letter (dated from Lichfield, 7 July 1791), which defends HLP from the suggestion of SJ's slights as reported in JB's biography. Indeed, the letter must have pleased HLP even more when the writer continued: "I both blame Mr Boswell, and wonder at him for the wanton, because unnecessary,

inroads which a number of those records must make upon the feelings of many. . . . [The book exhibits] spleen, envy, boundless haughtiness, and utter callousness to all the mental sensibilities of others" (*Seward Letters* 3:87).

TO PENELOPE SOPHIA WESTON

[post-9 August–pre-15 August 1791][1]

I know not my dear Girl whether the Great Dictionary is a good Incentive to Love or no, but if agreable Letters produce it—The Gypsie Prophecy[2] towards *you* will not surely be long in completing.[3] I never read any Book so interesting or entertaining, therefore recommend no novels, but write again, and that directly: for Peggy Owen has sent me word that I only can save her from Death or Distraction, so there will I be on the 20 without fail—and *there* as well as *here,* let me find a Letter from You.

Dear lovely sweet Siddons is better; and at last tolerably reconciled to parting with me for the Relief of those whose Anguish is of the Soul—while hers I thank God is confined wholly to the beautiful Clay that fits it so neatly with its truly well suited Inclosure.[4]

I sent Harriet word She has miscarried.—And now my beloved Friends do not think me wanting in my Duty about our Lorenzini; I never was remiss in bringing the Subject forward, never lost Sight on't but from thinking it prudent so to do: as Adriana says.

> It was the Copy of our Conference,
> Alone it was the Subject of our Theme,
> In Company I often glanc'd at it,
> Still did I place it in his constant View.[5]

The Verses I dispatched after them to Denbigh, which they cannot yet have reached, are a Proof I never shrunk one Instant from the Cause;[6] and as this Moment has brought me a *cold stiff* Letter from him dated Shrewsbury;—this Moment shall carry one back from me to tell him *I think it such.* Meantime you know I never said that it was likely he should marry in this manner unless from irresistible Impulse,——the Obstacles I *know* to be all *but,* if not *wholly* insurmountable; only my notion of his *Love* is stronger than yours can be who have seen so little of him; and proportionable Power will vanquish proportionable or rather *dis*proportionable Resistance——If Gunpowder *enough* is put under Mont Blance—*it must give way.* Such was my Reasoning always, and I still think it just: the last Evening he spent here, crying over Piozzi's Song, and applying every word on't as I could see, mentally to his own Situation; looking all the while like *very Death,* and never sleeping in the Night, but employing himself in penning his Journal forsooth, which consisted only of tender Saillies at Sight of the Bath road—at Thoughts of leaving Streatham &c., till his very Heart was breaking with Passion apparently increased instead of diminished by Absence;—vindicate my Hopes, and even *Belief* that he will relieve his Anguish when become totally insupportable, by a Union, which every *natural* Friend he has in the World will certainly disapprove.

As to the Letters which he brought down to the Library in his hand the Morning we left Streatham—they were Letters he had himself *written* not *received:* I suppose to say that he was resolved on remaining another Year in England. They had as he confest, cost him even *Tortures* to write them. Oh my sweet Sophy! I know most fatally from Experience every Pang that poor young Man is feeling——Yet I was an *Englishwoman!* of a Country where no such Aristocratic notions are acknowledged, as taint his hotter Soil; and yet three Years did I languish in Agony, Absence, and lingering Expectation.

If Fortune said he to me one Day (dancing to the Tune in his own head, for I had not mentioned Fortune) If Fortune were the only Obstacle, I hate it, I despise it, I have been offered Fortunes enough—the first in Lombardy I may say—but I abhor them all.[7] One may see was the Reply, you have no such mean Notions: "My Father pleased himself said he[8]—I made no Objections—if *People were generous!* but: but *what* my Lord? quoth I, He put his Handkerchief to his Eyes and changed the Conversation. Who would have pressed him further to tell that which I know already—and which no Person on Earth can dare—the Difference of Birth, Religion, and Country——If however he has but *Love enough*, all those three Things which would drown him if he swam across may be *leaped over;* and I who have taken the Jump before him, never cease to shew him how well I feel myself after it.[9] For the rest, he is now in bad Company for our Cause to be sure; but I shall have another Sight of him at Shrewsbury, before he gets to Bath; and will send thither all the Particulars.

When you write *thither* direct to me at Mr. Haycock's St. John's Hill Shrewsbury.[10] but let me have a long letter here first; immediately that is, and say this comes safe.

No room have I for Compliments. The good Wishes of the House and all its Inhabitants are innumerable towards Dear Sophia: I will write again soon. Mrs. Jackson has much of my heart, and *very* much of my Esteem: and I dote on Dr. and Mrs. Whalley—Adieu.

Text: Princeton University Library. *Address:* Miss Weston / at Mrs. Jackson's / Portland Place / Bath. *Postmark:*< >.

1. This undated letter was written between 9 and 15 August: On 9 August (Ry. 566.7) PSW in Bath alludes to matters discussed by HLP on 6 August (see n. 2). On 15 August (Ry. 566.8) PSW responds to the present mention of Trotti's "*cold stiff* Letter," his travels, and SS's miscarriage.

2. In the letter of 9 August PSW had written: "I was absolutely startled at the instance you mention of the Gypsies and 'the *Yellow Boys*'—'And can the Devil speak Truth'?—I do not much like trusting myself to think of these matters;—but certainly if *other* things turn out, as they certainly seem in a <train> to do, I shall begin to prepare in good earnest for my *two* Husbands and 5 *Children*." The gypsies, PSW wrote, had also "prophesied" a union between Trotti and Harriet Lee.

3. The coy exchange between PSW and HLP is the first intimation in the correspondence at hand that the former had active marriage prospects. Her future partner was

William Pennington (d. 1829), descendant of a Bristol merchant family. A onetime colonel in the British army, Pennington had served in Wilmington, North Carolina, as comptroller of the customs. On 21 February 1766, in the wake of colonial agitation over passage of the Stamp Act, Pennington, about to be forcibly removed from the house of Governor William Tryon (1725 or 1729–88), resigned his office lest he be compelled to betray it. Subsequently, the governor was instrumental in his reinstatement. Unequivocally loyal to the Crown, Pennington probably bore arms against the American forces. On 16 July 1781 he was taken prisoner in or near New York. Once released, he returned to England ca. 1783. The acquaintance that he struck up with PSW culminated in their marriage on 27 December 1792. Pennington, "admired for his wit and polished manners," became master of ceremonies at Clifton Hotwells in 1785 and remained in that office for the next twenty-eight years.

His will, P.R.O., Prob. 11/1756/310, was proved on 7 April 1829.

The Colonial Records of North Carolina, ed. William L. Saunders, 10 vols. (Raleigh, 1886–90), 7:172–73, 189; *The State Records of North Carolina*, ed. Walter Clark, 26 vols. (Raleigh, 1886–1907), 15:537; Lorenzo Sabine, *Biographical Sketches of Loyalists of the American Revolution* ([1864]; Port Washington, N.Y.: Kennikatt Press, 1966), 2:165; *GM* 62, pt.2 (1792): 1220; Knapp, pp. 57–58; *Thraliana* 2:851 n.1. For the Pennington marriage announcement, see the *Bristol Gazette and Public Advertiser,* 3 January 1793.

4. SS's miscarriage, the second in about three years, occurred probably in July.

5. Adriana, wife to Antipholus of Ephesus in Shakespeare's *Comedy of Errors* (5.1.62–67); as altered by HLP.

6. The "Verses to the Travellers written at the Rectory House Nuneham" consists of seven stanzas. They were intended for "Marquis Trotti and Mr. Buchetti [who] had a mind to see North Wales, and [for] my Husband [who] had a Mind to shew it them; so I wrote their Tour!" (*Thraliana* 2:814–16). See also "Verses 1, "pp. 51–53.

7. Despite his lofty rhetoric, Trotti never forgot that if he married below his station, he would forfeit half his inheritance. See HLP to PSW, 15 October.

8. Lodovico Trotti's second wife was the widow Teresa Fontana Belinzaghi (Beluschi), née Gaetano.

9. HLP's image may have been suggested to her by SJ's letter, 8 July 1784 (Chapman 3:177–78).

Despite HLP's hope, PSW on 15 August implied obstacles in the way of a Lee-Trotti marriage. "I have always found reason to put strong Faith in your Prophecies," she wrote to HLP, "and am well disposed to do so on this occasion—yet cannot bring my courage quite to the sticking Place.—However as you say, 'if the Love is strong enough,' it will do at last.—We have known weightier points atchieved by that Power."

10. John Hiram Haycock (1759–1830) designed the guildhall and shirehall (1783–85), and the county jail (1787–93) at Shrewsbury. He was responsible for the architectural alterations of Oakly Park, Salop (ca. 1784–90), the seat of the second lord Clive (afterwards first earl of Powis).

Haycock and his wife Elizabeth had a child, Edward (1790–1870), who was also to become an architect and the county surveyor for Salop in 1834.

TO PENELOPE SOPHIA WESTON

Nuneham Thursday
18: August 1791.

One more long Letter dearest Miss Weston, and then away to Shrewsbury,—whither direct your next. This last has been just as long reaching Oxford, whence I almost saw myself within five Hours of you; as a Letter yesterday received from Marquis Trotti at Wrexham a Place not less surely than 140 Miles off. They make a mighty slow Progress, which tires my Spirits to follow; and seem exceedingly well amused, a Thing I was not absolutely dying to hear. Meantime what he has written tho' cold, has pensive Passages in it which keep my Hopes alive—and 'tis not cold neither, but *guarded:* now I thought it my Duty to keep Harriet ignorant of nothing I knew, and as I have told her every good and desirable Symptom, so have I left in no doubt his present Disposition—for the first Letter I *copied* for her, and this last I *enclosed*.——

Was there ever such a Storm seen in England as this last dreadful one of the 15th?[1] Our December Lightning that frighted you so, was nothing to it. Where was my poor Husband *then* I wonder—perhaps on Snowdon incumbered with a Horse no less confounded than himself——We were all here much alarmed indeed, though Mrs. Siddons has mended ever since I think.

Miss Owen is in a sad Case sure enough. Her Brother is not *dead* but *worse* as you justly term it:[2] Her Prospects all seem shutting in so—not by a Morning Mist like our Harriet's which *must* dissipate and that very soon into a bright or a <coarse> Day——but by night's great black closing Curtain. Her Letter requiring my Company would have pitied the hardest Heart.—

Now for more public Concerns—of which your last Letter but one, gives me the best Information: it does really appear contrary to my Predictions that all Europe will joyn to reinstate a Descendant of that House of Bourbon which when represented by his Ancestor Louis *quatorze* all Europe united to humble: but this should be considered as Justice not Caprice: That last mentioned Prince sought openly to seize the Rights of others,[3] while his wretched Successor has been cruelly deprived of his own: and the World will not look on it seems, while the Crown of France is trampled on;[4] tho none stirred a Step even when the Sacred Head of an *English* Monarch was severed from his Body by the *Democrates* of that day.[5]

Helena Williams is a courageous Damsel, and I will I hope never be a distressed one in Consequence of that Conduct, which if anything happens but good to her will be condemned as rashness; and if She returns safe will be applauded as Curiosity after the great Objects in Life, while we are listening only to hear how go the small ones.[6]

I find that fierce Doings are expected, and I am much delighted with your *nine Thousand* Men: 'tis an admirable Anecdote of old Marshal Saxe,[7] and to me a new one, it will maybe divert you to hear that he married a Lady he did not much like, merely because her Name was *Victoria*[8] and that when He died—one of the Female French Wits said what a Pity it was, that no *De Profundis* should be said for him who had so often made all France sing *Te Deum*.[9]

He was a Lutheran you know.[10] You never sent me word you liked my Verses, and they were really ingenious ones too—did Harriett ever shew them to you? If much Applause ensues, I shall be tempted to copy over some Stanzas made for pretty Siddon's little Red Book where She keeps everything that has been ever said or sung in her Praise—*unprinted*.[11]

Talking of such Matters makes me add that Mr. Lysons comes tomorrow,[12] and my going was *necessary;* on your Principle of the nonelastic Houses.

I expect a Letter from my Travellers before I seal this: mean Time Heaven forefend that I should meet the Marquis at Shrewsbury——He will quit my Master at Denbigh *sure,* and go thro' S: W: to Bristol. Say every thing that expresses Esteem, Love, and Gratitude to Mr. and Mrs. Whalley, and tell Miss Seward how valuable her Health is even to *me* who see so little of her; if She neglects it She is doing public Injury, and is worse than a Democrate. Adieu. Give my best regards to Mrs. Jackson, and earnest Wishes for the Prosperity of her Boys;[13] who I really think send no particular Compliments to her. / Farewell and love / Your Affectionate / H: L: P.

No Letters come; I suppose they think me at Shrewsbury, or do not think about me at all.

Text: Princeton University Library. *Address:* Miss Weston / at Mrs. Jackson's / Portland Place / Bath. *Postmark:* OXFORD.

1. It was a sultry day with heavy rain, thunder, and violent flashes of lightning. See *GM* 61, pt. 2 (1791): 786.

2. John Owen (1741–1823) had been committed to Dr. Thomas Arnold's asylum at Leicester for "temporary Madness." When he escaped and returned to Shrewsbury, his sister refused to recommit him. According to HLP, Miss Owen "is next Heir, & fears lest Interest should mingle in the Motive—this is lovely, but in the mean Time her unfortunate Brother is left to inflame his Disorder by Intoxication, & destroy his Fortune by Freaks of Expence, while her own Life can scarcely be called safe, as his mistaken Fury often flies at her . . . for petty Offences which perhaps others have committed" (*Thraliana* 2:818).

3. Louis planned to become the foremost prince in Europe, aspiring even to usurp the role of Holy Roman Emperor for himself. He hoped to nullify Spanish power, to reduce the German and Italian princes and the English Charles II to the status of French dependents. The treaties of Nijmegen (1678–79) gave him new territory in the Spanish Netherlands and Franche-Comté. By 1680 he received the title of Louis le Grand. With the treaty of Regensburg (1684), he acquired Strasbourg, Luxembourg, and all the territories "reunited" with France before 1681. But various military coalitions finally brought on the War of the Spanish Succession (1701–14), after which French boundaries were reduced and England became the commercial arbiter of Europe.

4. On 20 June, Louis, accompanied by his family, attempted to flee to Metz and the army of Bouillé. The following day "the King and Queen of France were arrested . . . at Varennes, a small town on the road to Mons." See *GM* 61, pt. 1 (1791): 580. By the 24th the royal family were returned to Paris and by the 25th reentered the Tuileries under heavy guard.

5. Tried for treason on 20 January 1649 and found guilty on the 27th, Charles I was executed three days later in front of Whitehall. From the scaffold, he proclaimed himself "a martyr of the people."

6. A response to PSW's announcement of Helen Williams's recent departure for France: "Her Enthusiasm is nothing abated. She insists upon it that every thing is going on well in France—nay that all is perfectly *Quiet* and will remain so there, tho we know that the People are Murdering one another.—They are however lavishing Honors upon *her.*—Monsieur du Fossé [of the Société des Amis de la Constitution] has presented her Letters to the Assemblée at Rouen, and they have Voted her their Thanks and ordered the

Letters to be Printed and dispersed in Paris at their own Expence" (PSW to HLP, 24 July [Ry. 566.5]).

7. The comte de Saxe was a heroic figure in Europe. PSW and HLP may have read of his exploits, both military and amatory, in Louis Balthazard Néel, *Histoire de Maurice, comte de Saxe,* 2 vols. (1770); Antoine-Léonard Thomas, *Éloges de Maurice, comte de Saxe* (1756; 1773); his own work *Mes Rêveries,* 2 vols. (1757), translated into English in the same year; Baron d'Espagnac, *Histoire de Maurice, comte de Saxe* (1773). But what probably made the two ladies recall the comte de Saxe at this time was the *Manuscrit trouvé à la Bastille concernant deux Lettres-de-cachet lâchées contre Mademoiselle de Chantilly et M. Favart par le Maréchal de Saxe* (1789).

The anecdote was recounted by PSW in the letter of 9 August (Ry. 566.7): She referred to "old Marshall Saxe, who said whimsically, 'What will 9000 Troops, if he might *pick* them;—Why 3000 Scotch with their Purses empty; 3000 Irish with their skins full of Wine, and 3000 English with their Bellys full of Meat, he would conquer *the World.*' "

8. (Hermann) Maurice de Saxe (1696–1750), comte de Saxe (1711) was the natural son of Elector Frederick Augustus I of Saxony (later also king of Poland as Augustus II). In 1714 he married by paternal arrangement the heiress Johanna Victoria von Löban. The marriage was subsequently annulled. A brilliant military strategist, the comte de Saxe was by 1734 a lieutenant general in the French army, by 1744 a marshal of France, and by 1747 a marshal general. See Jon Manchip White, *Marshal of France, The Life and Times of Maurice, Comte de Saxe [1696–1750]* (London: Hamish Hamilton, 1962).

9. When news of Saxe's death reached Versailles, the queen of France remarked, "It is a pity that Catholic France cannot say a *De profundis* for the repose of the soul of one who has so often caused the nation to sing a Te Deum" (White, p. 255).

The "Wit" was Marie-(Catherine-Sophie-Félicité) Leszcinska (1703–68), daughter of Poland's King Stanislas and wife of Louis XV.

10. Born a Lutheran, he refused to become a Catholic even on his deathbed because for a man of little piety "it would be unbecoming to make a display of religion at the last" (White, p. 254).

11. SS copied poetic tributes to herself into red leather-bound books (now in the Bath Reference Library, Queen Square). For this volume HLP wrote three eight-line stanzas praising SS as the mistress of the rectory house at Nuneham Courtney and as an actress "Majestick in Charms too distressingly bright" (*Thraliana* 2:816–17. See also "Verses 1, pp. 63–64).

12. Probably SL.

13. PSW passed on HLP's good wishes and on 23 August wrote about Mrs. Jackson and one of her sons: "Tom Jackson charged me to thank you in his name and his Brothers for your kind remembrance of them. He is not a little proud of your *Prediction;* the fond and amiable Mother too happy in it, which she bade me acknowledge with her kindest Regards.—" (Ry. 566.11). Thomas Jackson was in October 1804 to be admitted to Jesus College, Cambridge, having attended schools in Bath (Mr. Morgan's) and Uppingham (Mr. Bull's).

TO PENELOPE SOPHIA WESTON

Shrewsbury, Monday
29: August [1791]

You are a noble Girl yourself dearest Miss Weston and a true Friend: if to be an elegant Letter Writer was Praise fit to mix with this—I think you the best in England. *Both* the sweet Epistles came safe, the *first* pleases me best tho', because most natural[1]——but if the Thing is credible—believe it, they have been come a little Bit and no Enquiries has he made, but treats me with a haughty reserve—in Consequence perhaps of my Verses,—[2] or I dream so; for when Buchetti praised them he said nothing.[3]

We are *none* of us going thro' S: Wales to Bath and Bristol—he has *Business in London* he says——and God knows we have *little Pleasure* here; so we all set out on Thursday Morning together.[4]

You will be sadly hurt at all this but tis true: no more does he follow me fondly about as at Streatham or the Rectory but I think apparently avoids me——bad Symptoms these; which poor Miss Owen polite by Habit and desirous of keeping her own Anguish down by hospitable Attentions in which the *Mind* has no share, though the kind Heart wishes it had—leaves me not an Instant to myself or to him.

Oh but I have caught my Spark at last—he begun talking to me of the Assizes—where said I Marquis Trotti shall be indicted on a new Statute for Heart-stealing, without Intentions of Payment—he coloured, laughed, and stared—Well he might—but asked my Proofs, and I produced *Your Letter.* We should have made a good Picture enough; and what says I is to be the End of all this? a Ride to Bath replyed he: I have begged Jacob to buy me a Horse and I will go—and *go alone* and I will see South Wales and all: As to the Letter Miss Weston is charming; but I hope has embellished a good deal——and who is going to Sea bathe?[several words obliterated] only her Sister in Law[5] answered I: Oh! that Seabathing frighted me——We were Interrupted; but I find by Mr. Piozzi that this matter has been discussed among them, and my Husband thinks *now* that there is *somewhat in it:* but he is always right, friendly and charming, and says just what he ought, but wishes our Harriet well too, and is reading your Letter *now.*

No Description can tell what I have suffered in another Friend's Cause since I came here, but my Death is not catched, and my Leg is not broken. So I'll say as little as possible on a Subject of more Horror than one can Express in words,[6]—tho Dear Miss Weston chose them.

The Dinner is waiting and so is the Post: Adieu then and direct to Streatham Park, whither I shall most willingly return after the sight of Sickness, the Terror of an unequalled Tempest, and my own Child in Fits[7]—at Nuneham; while worse,—ay *worse* my Maid Allen[8] says,—waited us here.

Love me my sweet Friend, for whom I have never either done nor suffered anything: and for ought I know you always will even < > than they to whom my Time and Trouble <have> all been given. God bless *you* from <such> Scenes and Farewell says your true / H: L: P.

Write directly to Streatham Park.

Text: Princeton University Library. *Address:* To / Miss Weston at the Rev. / Francis Randolph's / Corston near / Bath.[9]

1. PSW had written two letters, one a hurried scrawl on Thursday, 25 August (Ry. 566.12), and the other, the next day (Ry. 566.13).

HLP had schemed with PSW to intimate Harriet Lee's desire for a marriage proposal from Trotti. On 25 August PSW admitted that "Writing *purposely* to be seen is hard and up Hill Work to me. . . . I durst not *Date* it—you who can do every thing and imitate everyone's Hand—may do that according to your own Judgement. . . . You may depend upon me in all things—I will burn your Letter."

The details must remain speculative; HLP's initial letter was burned, and PSW's response has also disappeared. We must rely mainly on the latter's account, 26 August, that she has "endeavoured to manufacture a Letter, which containes the *Expressions* [HLP] wish[es] to bring forward, (in case [Trotti] desires to see it)."

2. In an occasional poem HLP muses: "From Pride and Prejudice as clear, / We read our Noble Traveller / Refining in his Course." The veiled hint becomes explicit in HLP's note identifying the "Noble Traveller" as Trotti, who "always says he means to marry an *English wife*" (*Thraliana* 2:815 and n. 1).

See also "Stanzas to the Travellers (Marquis Trotti and Mr. Piozzi) Written at Nuneham Rectory, 1791," in "Verses 1," pp. 51–53.

3. Trotti's companion is identified in the same poem as the author of "darling *Buchettiana*"——"a Collection of Epigrams" (*Thraliana* 2:815 and n. 3).

4. That is, on 1 September.

5. The wife of Gilbert Weston (fl. 1760–1800), PSW's brother.

6. John Owen's derangement.

7. HLP refers to SS's depression, to a storm "worthy of hotter Climates, which killed a Woman within our View, and fired ten Shocks of a neighboring Farmer's Corn under the very Windows. Our young Girls Cecilia and Miss Siddons fell into Fits, the Baby Boy George not 5 Years old was from home, gone o' merry-making with our Servants to some Village not far off—the Mother became a real Picture of Despair, supposing him killed by the Lightning" (*Thraliana* 2:814).

8. The sharp-tongued domestic, Elener Allen (fl. 1775–1810), who was to serve in the Piozzi household until 1806, when she married Robert Jones of Llŷs, a Denbigh apothecary. See HLP to JSPS, 2 December 1809.

9. Francis Randolph (1752–1831) is listed in the Bath directory for 1791 as rector of Corston and one of the proprietors of the Octagon Chapel. A Cantabrigian, he was vicar of Broadchalke, Wilts. (1786–88); rector of Chenies, Bucks. (1788), and of Aston (until 1804); prebendary of Bristol (1791–1831). Between 1800 and 1809 he was the proprietor and minister of Laura Chapel, Bath. Rector of Saint Paul's, Covent Garden, from 1817 to 1831, he died at Bristol and was buried in the cathedral churchyard.

TO PENELOPE SOPHIA WESTON

Monday 5: September [1791].

Kind! charming Miss Weston! Your Letter was a sweet Cordial after the Journey, for I did get home very tired and fatigued and latish on Saturday Evening—after suffering something sure enough in the Cause of Friendship: Miss Owen says like Harriett that *all* my Care was bestowed on *her*. Mr. Piozzi has not begun yet thank God, but a Fit of the Gout is not far off I fancy——The Marquis is making Jacob buy him a Horse to ride over *South Wales*,[1] and Mr. Davies[2] tells him that Bath and Bristol is the nearest way thither; sure he will never *ride* that way, however earnest to rid himself of his Companion's good Advice, which his Head probably applauds, while his heart resists it. There is a cold Reserve about the Man mixed with fine Qualities too: but he has only a half Confidence in me certainly—and seems odd enough to like teizing my Curiosity with Conjecture about his intentions towards Harriett which I have not yet penetrated. He waits in this Neighbourhood for his Servant from Paris whither he has sent him to fetch all his Goods away—so far looks well; and < > as he told me long ago, when he said I can at least give you *that* Satisfaction, that I do not leave England this Year. For my own Part he puzzles me completely, and *so* confounds my Conjectures that were I to hear within a Month that Harriet was Marchioness Trotti, or were I to hear he had informed her that such an Event was impossible I should in neither Case be surprized. He is gone to London this Morning under promise to return o'Thursday, and says his Servant will not be here before the End of the Week.—So much for Lorenzo.

My own Health has been shaken but will tye up again with Use of the Tub—and perhaps we may try the Sea too—but I feel so glad to get home that scarcely will Pleasure or Profit tempt me out again in a hurry.

Harriett talks of going to Weymouth or Southampton——if he should go and find Belvedere house[3] without his favourite Bird—how would he feel? Yet will I not tell him the Project lest he should make that an Excuse for not going: let him go, and hear, perhaps see that She is ill from those whom he will believe—better so—She may change her Mind too, and I hope She will; but I only give her Information always—not Advice, I have this Day acquainted her with all he says and does—tis She must act accordingly.

My dear Master is pleased to find me at Streatham Park once more in a whole Skin. The Danger will be better to talk than write about, and we shall meet again sometime I trust, and exchange Minds: Miss Owen is a good Woman indeed, and suffers only from Nicety of Honour and Scruples of Morality——What a World it is though after all, where nobody can be happy as the poor Marquis says—Yet Happiness spread for all too, and enough on't.

Dear charming Siddons is better,[4] we stopt at her *Village* not her *House* returning, and heard that Sheridan and Kemble were with her:[5] *on Business* no doubt, so we would not go in, but sent Compliments. <Thus> They may see I do not want any favours they have to bestow.

Adieu my charming Friend! Poor Harriett laments Your Loss most pathetically and I am very—very sorry for her: yet let us remember 'tis not now above six or seven Weeks suspense: I should from the first have thought it very fortunate if She had not to count by *Months* at least if not *Years*——Adieu! and love / Your H: L: P.——

My Master sends Love.

I cannot find Fanny Rundell,[6] her Mother has not put her to Mrs. Ray[7] as I hoped.

Text: Princeton University Library. *Address:* Miss Weston / at the Rev: / F: Randolph's / Corston / near / Bath. *Postmark:* SE 6 91.

1. Jacob Weston.
2. Reynold Davies (1752–1820) was educated at Jesus College, Oxford (B.A., 1773; M.A., 1816), becoming curate of Saint Leonard's, Streatham. Also a schoolmaster, RD was in time responsible for JSPS's early education. His primary school—dubbed "Streatham

University" by HLP—was built on land that she owned. He was buried on 20 August in Streatham. See "Register of Burials, 1813–1837" of Saint Leonard's Church, Streatham, in the Greater London Record Office.

3. For Belvidere School, see HLP to SL, 17 November 1787, n. 7.

4. SS had been ailing for about two years from what had been diagnosed as "Scorbutic Humours——[and was] dosed. . . with Mercurial Medcines, till they have torne the fine Vessells to pieces, & shattered all the nerves that her Profession had not ruined before" (*Thraliana* 2:769).

5. As patentee and manager respectively of the Drury Lane, Richard Brinsley Sheridan (1751–1816) and John Philip Kemble hoped SS was prepared to return for the 1791–92 season.

6. That is, Frances Amelia Rundell (fl. 1775–1828). HLP responds to a remark in PSW's undated letter (Ry. 566.10): "[Mrs. Maria Eliza Rundell] has lately placed one of her daughters, Fanny I think, at a school near Streatham. . . . The poor Child She took I understand is sick, of some sad undefinable Malady and her tender affectionate Heart is suffering much Maternal Agony on the Subject." Fanny was placed "not with Mrs. Ray, but a Miss Gregory on Clapham Common" (PSW to HLP, 17 September 1791 [Ry. 566.15]).

7. At Russell House, Streatham. See HLP to Q, 7 July 1787, n. 2.

GABRIEL PIOZZI TO JOHN CATOR[1]

[pre-13 September 1791]

Mr Cator
Sir

I am very earnest to have done trifling and very weary of our way of going on: for either you intend to pay me that 186£ odd money on account of which so many shuffling excuses, and I may add shameful ones—have already been made on your part—or you do not:[2] The last resource endeavoured at, namely the setting 100£ owing from me to you against the aforesaid Sum has been clearly shewn to be nugatory——for I owe you no Money, and you know that I owe you none, nor can you produce any Shadow of a Reason for supposing that I do. The Money therefore I must and will have; likewise the Account of My Wife's Affairs with regard to her Estates &c. while She was a Widow, and entrusted you as Manager for her:[3] these Accounts are necessary for me, to know by them what Balance was due for the Sale of her Trees in Wales &c. and I have a Right to claim the Account as her Husband, and I do claim it.[4]

Then good Sir let me this last Time be seriously listened to; nor force me upon a suit so scandalous to yourself—for if there is Justice in England, it will not be refused by the Courts thereof to your humble Servant / Gabriel Piozzi.

Text: Ry. 533.15; "Mr. Piozzi's Letter to Mr. Cator," a draft in HLP's hand.

1. For several years there had been omens of a deteriorating relationship with Cator, denounced as "a Hero of Rascality." As early as January 1788, e.g., GP suspected "that some latent Fraud might be lurking," although Crutchley assured HLP of Cator's honesty (*Thraliana* 2:707). On 10 November 1790 she complained to Perkins, "Mr. Piozzi cannot force from him any Book or Paper relative to my Affairs by any decent Methods, and so

what he received or paid . . . Heaven knows—not I" (Clifford, p. 354). By 1791 the acrimony virtually precluded a civilized exchange for the next several years.

2. Cator tacitly acknowledged his indebtedness when, under threat of legal action, he paid the entire sum by 13 September (*Thraliana* 2:812, 820). At issue was £136 6*d.* said to be rent paid by the Crowmarsh resident, Thomas Lovegrove. That is, Cator was charged with having remitted only £1,372 3*s.* of the £1,508 3*s.* 6*d.* collected between 1785 and 1788. An additional fifty pounds was owing from Hugh Griffith, a tenant in Carnarvonshire.

For further detailed allegations of financial mismanagement, see HLP's "Memorial against John Cator" (Ry. 611 [autumn 1792]) and HLP to Hugh Griffith, 20 October 1792.

Thomas Lovegrove (d. 1815), tithingman for the manor of Maidengrove (parish of Pishill, Oxon.), was the tenant at Preston Crowmarsh (parish of Benson) between 1781 (or earlier) and 1794. See "Land Tax Assessments," Vol. II / vii / 1; Vol. II / ix / 1 (C.R.O., Oxfordshire).

3. On 22 September Cator defended his management of HLP's business matters. "But in order to have no more trouble Mr. C. will give Mr. Piozzi all the Information in his power, which is only from Memory" (Ry. 602.10).

4. HLP was to recall (in the "Memorial") "that Mrs. Piozzi being obliged to cut Timber upon her Estates in Flint and Denbighshire for the Purpose of clearing the said Estates from a Mortgage—Mr. Cator did with her Consent order Timber to be cut" and sold to Peter Jackson, a Chester timber merchant. According to her indictment, Cator paid her only £2,164 4*s.* 6*d.* of £3,686 received.

In the Chester commercial directories between 1781 and 1797, Jackson is identified as a "ship-builder" located in Old Crane Street. The "City Assembly Minutes" for 1792 note his petition for a lease of Tower Field, to be used as a timber yard (C.R.O., Cheshire, AB/ 5, f. 29v.).

TO PENELOPE SOPHIA WESTON

Thursday
28: September [17]91.

Your Letters my lovely Friend are like the Places they describe; cultivated, rich and various: the prominent Feature Elegance, but always some Sublimity in Hope and Prospect. Make mine and my Husband's best Regards welcome to the Master and Lady of your sweet Mansion,[1] but never forget poor dear tranquil Streatham, in whatever fancy Regions you may dwell.

I have not seen London or would have looked at Queen Square—[2]all is well there however, or you would not write so calmly.

Our Italian Friends are still with us;[3] the Marquis talks seldomer than ever of his intended Tour thro' S: Wales to Bath, yet may mean it never the less; and I dare say he will go, and refresh his Passion.[4]

Make Harriet Lee tell you Cecilia's saucy Trick;[5] it will divert her to tell it, and I won't take the Tale out of her Hands: her Spirits mend I see, as to her Heart it scarce *can* receive Improvement; and the strong Sense She possesses, with such Variety of Resources too—will guard those Passes where Tenderness prevails over Prudent Apathy.

Your Friends Mr. and Mrs. and Miss Hamilton are with us,[6] so here is Musick and good Humour and Chearfulness,—but my Master went last Night to Town with good old Mr. Jones, to see what Sport the Transmigration of old Drury can afford.[7] We hear that all goes well, and that the Town accepts Kemble's new terms willingly and generously.[8]

I shall hope that Curiosity will prove to You an additional motive now for making haste home, though Harriett seems to think Mrs. Jackson has a wicked Design of stopping you on the Road.[9] What Weather here is! No foreign Climate sure ever exhibited so beautiful an Autumn: the Paintey Month as October is sometimes called, will now be in no Want of clear Light to shew its vanity of Colouring——but the want of Verdure is a Dismal Drawback.

Adieu! and distribute our kindest Compliments among your kindest Friends; never forgetting the Streatham Park Coterie, especially your / most Affectionate / H: L: P.

Text: Princeton University Library. *Address:* Miss Weston / at Langford Cottage / Rev: Mr. Whalley's near / Bristol / Somersetshire. *Postmark:* SE 29 91.

1. PSW was staying at TSW's Langford Cottage, near Bristol. In a letter of 17 September, she described her surroundings: "This darling Cottage is nestled into a sort of concave Recess in the Bosom of the Mendip Mountains. . . . The vale below is one of the richest and most beauteous in this fertile County. . . . Other Hills form an Amphitheatre to the North and East of the Horizon, while on the West, the Severn Sea stretches out its broad white Arm. . . . Nothing can be more elegant and commodious than our Dwelling.—a Rustic Hall, with Kitchen &c. below Stairs.—Above, an excellent Eating Room—a pretty withdrawing Ditto and a darling little Boudoir fitted up in the neatest style . . . and over these the Lodging Rooms—all so skillfully and artfully contrived that its wonderful to think, what abundant accommodation they have, within so small a space." PSW comments on the gardens around Langford Cottage and concludes, "At the Summit of this magic Circle, commanding the whole View, is an elegant, rustic Pavillion dedicated to dear Mrs. Siddons" (Ry. 566.15).

2. PSW and her mother lived at Queen Square, Westminster.

3. Trotti and Buchetti.

4. Of the women interested in promoting the Trotti-Lee nuptials, Harriet Lee was the least hopeful. She—according to PSW—suffered from sleeplessness, appetite loss, and "a constant, acute Head ach;—the effect of excessive, nervous agitation" (Ry. 566.10).

5. A reference to CMT's flirtation with James Drummond, "a Cadet of the great Banking house" (*Thraliana* 2:824).

6. For the Hamiltons, see HLP to Sophia Byron, 2 June [1788], n. 5.

7. On 27 September they saw Sheridan's *The School for Scandal* and the farce *No Song, No Supper.*

8. HLP alludes to a crisis faced by Kemble.

Having abandoned their old theater, the Drury Lane company moved to the Haymarket, where admission charges were raised. These the public accepted, but a riot occurred on 22 September—first night—because the doors were not opened on time. Once in the theater, about fifty patrons shouted for the manager and refused to allow the presentation of the prologue for *Poor Old Drury!!!*. Kemble appeared before the audience, and only after he promised reforms could the performance continue. See Baker, pp. 174–75.

9. Harriet Lee's surmise was correct. In a letter postmarked 10 October, PSW reported: "I shall therefore pass a few Weeks in Portland Place [after leaving Langford Cottage], and then take the first convenient opportunity of transporting myself to Queen Square, which I begin to feel some Yearnings after—" (Ry. 566.16). PSW remained with Eliza Jackson until mid–December.

HELEN MARIA WILLIAMS TO HESTER LYNCH PIOZZI

[Orléans]
October 12th, 1791

[The salutation is missing.]

I only yesterday received your charming letter, and I have heard this moment that an englishman who is just going to set off for London will put a letter for me in the post when he arrives—I therefore cannot resist scrawling a few hurried lines, which I shall send because they will cost you nothing, and will inform you of our safe arrival at Orleans—to which place we travelled by a crossroad, avoiding Paris, and shortening our journey more than fifty miles—but it was such a road as I believe few English ladies would have passed for all the national estates of France. Cecilia took the liberty of screaming pretty frequently,[1] but upon the whole we all behaved tolerably well, and often forgot the rough paths thro' which we were passing in contemplating the beautiful country about us—we saw to us new images of plenty, in a country covered with grasses, which crouds of people were employed in gathering, and then carrying home in great baskets, and in cart-loads—the whole scene was to us equally strange and delightful.

Orleans is a very pretty *french* Town, with a noble bridge across the Loire, and beautiful environs—of the society we can yet tell nothing, for we have not delivered our letters—we shall however, have the best the place affords, as Monsieur D'Orleans had at Madame <Sillery's> desire,[2] recommended us to the most considerable families here—he possessed immense domains round this Town before the Revolution which now belong to the nation— . . . The société des amis de la Constitution at Rouen sent me a very flattering letter of thanks for my french journal,[3] and ordered three Thousand copies of an answer I sent them, to be printed—these honors I find "play round the head but come not to the heart," nor do I feel any pleasure from the Democrats which at all compensates to my heart for this cruel separation from my friends at home—and you are unjust if you do not believe that among those friends there is none more tenderly regretted, or more truly beloved than yourself, by, my dear Madam, your most / obliged and faithful / Nell Williams.

Text: Ry. 570.3.

1. Cecilia (d. 1798) had first arrived in France in 1790, shortly before her younger sister Helen. During a brief visit to England, they persuaded their mother to return with them to France in July 1791. On 6 March 1794 Cecilia would marry Marie-Martin Athanase Coquerel, and she would die in childbirth a few years later.

See Lionel D. Woodward, *Une Anglaise Amie de la Révolution Française Hélène-Maria Williams et ses Amis* (Paris: Librairie Ancienne Honoré Champion, 1930).

2. Caroline-Stéphanie-Félicité Du Crest de Saint-Aubin (1746–1830) had married in 1763 Alexis Brûlart Sillery (1737–93), comte de Genlis and marquis de Sillery. For her role as tutor to the children of the duc d'Orléans, see "Letter 5," as in n. 3 below.

See also HLP to Q, 14 September 1784, n. 8.

3. *Lettres Écrites de France à une Amie en Angleterre, pendant l'Année 1790, contenant*

l'Histoire des Malheurs de M. du F[ossé], par Miss Williams. Traduit de l'Anglais, par M. . . . [le baron Pierre de La Montagne] (Paris: de Garnéry, 1791).

Translated from *Letters written in France, in the Summer of 1790, to a Friend in England; containing various Anecdotes relative to the French Revolution; and Memoirs of Mons. and Madame du F[ossé]* (London: T. Cadell, 1790).

TO PENELOPE SOPHIA WESTON

Streatham Park
Saturday 15: October [1791].

My Dear Miss Weston's Letter contained more agreeable Description of the Places I love, than of the People: I must hear better Accounts of our sweet Harriet before my Heart is easy,[1] yet I doubt not her Command over a Passion which no longer appears to disturb the Tranquillity of her once half-frantick Admirer; who told my Master in Confidence *no*—was his Expression to me—but in common Discourse: that if he married a Woman of inferior Birth, such were his *peculiar* Circumstances, that exactly one half of his Estate would be forfeited. He remains constantly with us, but the World seems a Blank to him; he takes no Pleasure as I can observe, and either feels no Pain, or pretends to feel none. If he ever does marry an Italian Lady he will be a very miserable Man however[2]—from being haunted by our Harriett's Form adorned with Talents, and radiant with Excellence[3]——Should he renew his Attachment to her, and sacrifice half his Fortune to his Love, every Child She brings will seemingly reproach him for lessening an Ancient Patrimony.——*Such is Life*.

Mrs. Siddons is at Harrowgate and we hope—mending;[4] Poor Sir Charles Hotham is going to change *the Scene* I hear; his State of Existence so far as relates to this World draws to an End, yet though the Physicians send him to Bath, he and Lady Dorothy[5] resolve it seems to see the *new* Drury Lane Hay Market, before their Curtain falls.[6]——Who says there is no ruling Passion? It appears to me that *any* Passion, or even Inclination nursed up carefully, will rule the rest, tho' naturally larger and stronger; as our little Flo lords it over the out-door Dogs, merely on the Strength of being his Mistress's *Favourite*.

Cavalier Pindemonte has written me a long Letter;[7] he sends particular Compliments to all our Friends and Coterie almost, and says a vast deal about dear Siddons. What cries Mr. Buchetti does he say of Helena Williams?—Oh not a Word replied I—Men never speak at all of the Woman whom they really like. A Painter would have enjoyed Marquis Trotti's Countenance at this Conversation. Meantime our little Democratic Friend is not doing a foolish Thing at last by leaving England I do believe: Such is the Advantage of exchange between London and Orleans,[8] that they say the very difference may make it worth her while; nor is that position a weak one, if it be true that a British Guinea is worth 32 French Shillings; and 'twas a Man just arrived who told it me for a Fact.

I'm glad Mr. Whalley has so much Comfort in his Mother, for whom he always seemed to have so great a Share of Regard:[9] Dear Mrs. Jackson's Fondness for her

Children is a commoner Sentiment; and I somehow was always willing to predict that She would be better rewarded for *Her* Maternal Affection than most Parents—The Boys I have seen of hers are to my Fancy very promising: How happy is it tho' to possess one's Faculties at such an advanced Age as the Lady at Longford Cottage.[10] I think we have one at Shrewsbury however that can match her, we will compare when we meet. Poor Miss Owen is still unhappy—and adds to her vexations and tormenting Misfortune, that of suffering it to corrode her Temper, and make her ready to quarrel with her truest Friends.

Della Crusca has married a Woman of elegant Person and Address, and who will bring him perhaps 500£: o'year with an unblemished Character, as People tell me: The husband meantime will congratulate himself charmingly on his *own Superiority*—no small Pleasure to some Minds;—and the World will always be on *his* Side in every Dispute, tho' he had neither Character *nor* Fortune when they met. His Family I hear are very angry.[11]

The Kembles get Money apace, Mr. Chappelow says he is sure that the Pit *alone* pays every Night's Expence, and People in general seem highly satisfied.[12]

Here's a long Letter from your Ever Affectionate / H: L: P.

No room for Compliments you must accept, and you must dispose.

Text: Princeton University Library. *Address:* Miss Weston / at Mrs. Jackson's / Portland Place / Bath. *Postmark:* OC 17 <91>.

1. Following a gloomy report from Anna Lee, PSW on 10 October informed HLP: "You will be sorry to hear that Harriet's Health and Spirits decline daily and I begin to think it necessary to her Peace, that a *certain* Subject should no more be mentioned to her——Indeed if you were to see how *very low* and Hysterical She is, and to observe how entirely She has lost her Rest and Appetite—you would be greatly alarmed, as I am" (Ry. 566.16). Harriet's decline was short. By 26 October PSW could find her "in excellent *good Looks* and *Spirits*" (Ry. 566.16, 17).

2. About 1795 Trotti married in Vienna the widow Antonietta Schaffgotsch, daughter of Antonio Gottardo, count of the Holy Roman Empire and free baron of Tochenberg, hereditary seigneur of Cravara, Wildshin, and Krautenwald.

3. HLP was convinced that Trotti's "Love" for Harriet Lee was "founded merely on her Virtue & Talents" (*Thraliana* 2:823).

4. Accompanied by her husband, SS visited Guy's Cliffe in late August and early September. There at dinner, wrote William Siddons, "we . . . met . . . a Lady Mordaunt, who had been for four or five years in the same miserable way [as SS], but had considered herself well for the last year and half, though still in the habit of taking three hundred drops of laudanum each day. She says . . . that Dr. Warren was the person who prescribed it, upon which we thought it right to come directly to town for his advice; but it was first necessary to consult Sir Lucas Pepys, who has so long attended her, and with so much care and attention, though with so little success. He has been here this morning, and says it is impossible that medicine can ever cure her . . . but he begged she would, in the meantime, so settle her affairs as to leave herself at liberty to go to Harrowgate. I imagine to that place we shall be obliged to go . . ." (Wickham 2:60). The Siddonses spent at least two months there, staying through Christmas and waiting futilely for her improvement.

5. Sir Charles Hotham-Thompson married on 21 October 1752 Dorothy Hobart (d. 1 June 1798), daughter of the first earl of Buckinghamshire. See HLP to PSW, 1 September 1789, n. 7.

6. The Drury Lane Theatre, in almost constant use since its reconstruction in 1674 (as

designed by Christopher Wren), had become shabby and outmoded. Once demolished in the summer of 1791, it was replaced by a new building that was opened on 12 March 1794 and made ready for dramatic productions on 21 April, when Kemble and SS acted in *Macbeth*.

In the first year of its exodus the Drury Lane company performed at the King's Theatre, Haymarket; in the 1792–93 season it alternated between the King's and the Haymarket; awaiting the opening of the new theater in the spring of 1794, the company was disbanded; many of its important actors sought engagements in other cities while others—like SS, Eliza Farren, and Dorothy Jordan—chose temporary retirement.

7. His letter is missing.

8. On 12 October Helen Williams had informed HLP that she and her sister had been introduced to the prominent families of Orléans by "M. [duc] d'Orléans." But because they found the city narrow intellectually and politically, they moved to Paris (Ry. 570.3).

9. TSW's mother Mary (1707–1803) was the only child of the Reverend Francis Squire (d. 1750), canon and chancellor of Wells; the wife of the Reverend John Whalley (d. 1748), master of Saint Peter's College, Cambridge (1733–48), regius professor of divinity (1742–48), and one of the king's chaplains in ordinary. Widowed at the age of forty-one, she reared seven children. Of her four sons, three took degrees at Cambridge. She made her home with her second, Francis Edward (b. 1743), at Winscombe Court. TSW admired her intelligence, her devotion to her offspring, her moral and physical fortitude.

10. PSW had written on 10 October: "At near 90 [Mary Whalley] is beautiful! well bred—clear in her Intellects . . . and animated and entertaining to a very uncommon degree in Conversation and Society, which She greatly enjoys.—She has still many resources of amusement within herself and tis quite delightful to see her sit down to the Piano forte and divert herself for an Hour together in as good Time and Task as most People.—Indeed She is *every* way a *Phenomenon*" (Ry. 566.16).

11. On 26 August Robert Merry had married Anne Brunton of the Covent Garden Theatre. Shortly thereafter they went to America. See *GM* 61, pt. 2 (1791): 872.

On 12 November, PSW responded: "I am not surprized that Della Cruscas Family are angry at the Connexion he has made,—because it is the way of the World, to take up everything by the wrong end.—The young Womans Friends have much more reason in reality to be dissatisfied, that she has bestowed her Personal Graces, fair Character and Competency upon a Man, who has neither (of the *latter* Goods at least) to give in exchange.—Yet his Friends may reasonably enough be hurt at his want of Spirit, in condescending to live upon the Talents of a Wife" (Ry. 566.18).

12. In September 1791, Kemble as one of the managers moved the Drury Lane company at great expense to the King's Theater, Haymarket. His difficulties with performers continued from the previous season. SS was reluctant to act, Eliza Farren remained petulant; and Dorothy Jordan squabbled about money.

The company opened its temporary theater on 22 September with two staples: *Poor Old Drury!!!* and *The Haunted Tower.* Opening night began with a riot, for "the workmen [could not] perfect what was intended so soon as was expected; nor could they be got out in time for opening the doors in the afternoon: this delay and the difficulty of finding the way to different parts of the house caused some disgust" (*Universal Magazine*, September 1791, p. 220). Because of the unfinished condition of the stage, *The School for Scandal*, scheduled for the 24th, had to be postponed.

But the season soon quieted down with an emphasis on revivals. The entrances and exits were clearly marked, and for this the audience was prepared to pay higher ticket prices. For almost a month nothing more significant was acted than *Poor Old Drury!!!*, but the house was making money. And when in November Kemble was to produce his annual offering of Shakespearean plays, the public accepted them with relish.

TO PENELOPE SOPHIA WESTON

[Streatham Park
8: November 1791]

My dearest Miss Weston would readily forgive my long Silence if She knew how heavily my hours are passing, and how happy a Moment I think even this—that I have stolen to write at last. Poor Mr. Piozzi has been, and *is* as ill with the Gout as I do believe a Man can possibly be. Knees, Hands, Feet—crippled in all; and unable even at this Hour to turn in the Bed—or perform *necessary Operations* without manual assistance:[1] this to a delicate Man and for Weeks together is dreadful; he took to his Room the Day I wrote last to our Harriet.

Marquis Trotti and Mr. Buchetti have both been excessively kind indeed, and I shall feel eternally obliged by their attentive Friendship. The Marquis has delayed his Journey till he sees our Master on his Legs again, and Mr. Buchetti keeps his Courage up—as nobody but a Country man *can* do, in a strange Land.

Colonel Barry has been here too for a Day, but is going back to his Regiment.[2] He loves you and yours, and is happy to find your Mother comfortable among her new Folk, who he says behave mighty sweetly, and he wishes you to stay at Bath till we fetch you to Streatham Park.[3]

Mr. Weston[4] called here the last day my poor Husband was *alive,* so never came in; because forsooth Piozzi was gone to London upon business—how it did provoke me! and as to getting up to Queen Square myself now for a long Time I despair on't: It shall be my first Visit tho', that it shall.

I rejoyce in our dear Harriett's recovery which *you* say proceeds from her Fate's being decided, a position I never believed, yet cannot contradict: for to me he never names her, notwithstanding I am confident he thinks of her still: not would I bet a large Wager he does not yet marry her——but it was not an Event ever likely to happen in three Months—and in three Years She may for Ought I see still be his, tho' I never more will tell her so.

Agitation of Spirits is the worst Illness, of which my present Situation is a Proof, and too much Love is good for nothing as I see except to make one wretched. Mr. Piozzi has had Gout upon his Throat, his Voice—all that could agitate and terrifie me: but now *Safe's* the Word, and I care little for his *Pain* poor Soul if we can but keep away Danger.

Tell our sweet Friend that I'll write the moment I'm able, to thank her for her last;[5] and to say if She wants telling, that I am truly her Affectionate as well / *Your* ever faithful / H: L: P.

Compliments to all Friends.

Text: Princeton University Library. *Address:* Miss Weston at / Mrs. Jackson's / Portland Place / Bath. *Postmark:* NO 9.

1. PSW reported to TSW on 18 November GP's suffering and HLP's reaction: "Poor Mr. Piozzi is laid up in a dreadful fit of the gout, and she has been excessively terrified! All danger, however, she says, is now over; but it has been upon his voice, in his throat, with

every symptom that could alarm" (Wickham 2:67). HLP was further worried that the gout was accompanied by "a Pain in the Side, darting thro' to his Back: which seems to gain Strength every Fit he has . . ." (*Thraliana* 2:828).

2. The Thirty-ninth Regiment, in which he served as a lieutenant colonel. See HLP to PSW, 11 June [1789]; 12 October 1790.

3. Colonel Barry presented HLP with a more optimistic view of the Weston household than circumstances justified. On 12 November PSW was to write: "Colonel Barry is I beleive a true Friend and a wise Man and I hope he speaks of the posture of affairs in Queen Square, from better knowledge than observation on the mere *Surface* of things:—but my Sister I find has very bad Health.—My Mother complains that the Evenings in general drag on very heavily, and seems impatient for my return.—However the Colonels *Prescription* pleaseth me well, and I should like to follow it *very much*" (Ry. 566.18).

The "Sister" is doubtless her sister-in-law, who earlier had been sea bathing for her health (HLP to PSW, 29 August, n. 5).

4. PSW's brother Gilbert, whom HLP found "good natured." See HLP to PSW, 6 July 1791 (Princeton University Library).

5. Eliza Jackson.

TO PENELOPE SOPHIA WESTON

Streatham Park, Saturday
20: November [1791]

My dear Miss Weston deserves twenty Letters, yet can I scarce write her *one* somehow.—That all have their Vexations is very true, and perhaps my Share has been hitherto not quite equal to my Neighbours—notwithstanding they would make no inconsiderable Figure if prettily dressed up——I mean *my own*.[1] Poor Piozzi gets on as the Crabs do he says—backward. Yesterday no Creature could bear to see his Agony, and tho' we all dined in the Library we wished ourselves back a'Bed.

So Mrs. Jackson is a Sufferer of bodily Pain too;[2] I am really very sorry: but your Return will be a nice Cordial, and I hope to take it soon. Long live the Causes of your coming back, both old and young;[3] and let us meet and tell Tales of Sorrow and of Joy.

I have had a Letter from sweet Helena this very Post, telling how She is got safe to Orleans; 'tis however written in a Strain less triumphant than tender I think, and if as She purposes—We may hope to see her next Summer, I shall have few Fears of her return to France.[4]

As to our Dear Harriett you know how much I love her but Old Barba Jove[5] and I have a vile Trick of laughing at Lover's Resolutions;[6] no matter: my Heart wishes her sincerely well, and I have too many Obligations to Marquis Trotti's Politeness and Attention while Mr. Piozzi was ill, not to wish and desire all Good for him, which he can desire for himself.

Adieu my dearest Miss Weston and accept this Apology for a Letter from Yours ever / H: L: P.

Dispose of my best Compliments.

Text: Princeton University Library.

1. This was a melancholy time for HLP: " . . . what a World it is . . . and what Wretches are we who inhabit it" (*Thraliana* 2:823). She worried about CMT—not yet fifteen—who was being wooed by James Drummond (b. ca. 1768); and about poor health. In the present letter, however, she acknowledges the "vexations" that also plagued her friends. That is, she responds to PSW's lament of 12 November: "Every Body has Gout, or Hands, or Heads, or Hearts, or Stomachs, or *something* to torment them!" PSW herself had suffered from a feverish "Bilious and Rheumatic Seizure" that left her languid and "most unusually depressed" (Ry. 566.18).

2. In this same letter of woe, PSW had reported that Eliza Jackson suffered "with a *Sprained Wrist*—got now 10 Weeks ago!—still suffering such misery, as will not allow her a Nights Rest!—and now they say there is an Inflammation upon the Tendon!"

3. As of 12 November, PSW planned to shorten her visit so that she could be in London before Christmas. "Mrs. Jackson's Children will all be at Home during the Holydays . . . *entre nous*—the uproar would then be *too wild* for any Nerves, but a fond Mothers to bear for 5, or 6 Weeks together."

4. See Helen Williams to HLP, 12 October (Ry. 570.3). PSW also had "a long Letter from our Democratic Helena, who writes me glowing accounts of the flourishing state of the New Constitution and of the Honors she has received, as one of its Champions." PSW, however, was also aware of Helen's nostalgia for "her English Friends—[HLP] and the dear Streatham Park Coterie in particular" (26 October, Ry. 566.17).

5. The characteristically bearded deity in contrast to the "beardless Jupiter" (see HLP to SL, 1 March 1786, n. 7). Jupiter is notorious in mythology for the varieties of his amorous disguises and stratagems.

6. According to PSW, 12 November: "Our poor, dear Harriets Heart begins to palpitate again with painful and Sickening Emotion, at the Idea of seeing [Trotti], whose Conduct and Sentiments has been so perplexing; and her Countenance betrays already the Effects of this encreased, and renewed agitation. . . . In the only Conversation I have had with her on the Subject, she declared to me;—were the Marquis at her Feet to Morrow and the Circumstances of his Fortune *such* as he once hinted to Mrs. P—the World should not tempt her to accept him;—neither himself, or his Posterity she said, should ever have to reproach *her*, with such a Sacrifice."

JOHN FIELD[1] TO HESTER LYNCH PIOZZI

Southwark
28 December 1791

Madam

Before Mr. Perkins[2] set out for Bath he desired me to recollect the circumstance how, and when I paid you the Balance of your Welch Estate, and delivered you the Papers concerning the same, and wished me to address you on the Subject—

I have now to inform you that it is perfectly in my recollection that you came to the Brewhouse, and called me into the inner Countinghouse, and said "I am come for the Balance of my Account," and at the same time, you said, "nay give me all the Accounts and Papers which you have as I will not trouble you any further with them," in consequence of which I took the Book and Balanced the Amount, and gave you the Money which you counted out before Mr. Barclay,[3] and said it was right. You did not give me any Receipt as there was no occasion for it, you taking the Cash Book where the Account was kept—I cannot remember the particular Sum but I think it was between Two and three hundred Pounds. You put the Money into a long Check Bag—and I delivered you all the Papers amongst which was a number of Letters &c. of Bridges and a quantity of Edwards with the Rentals &c.[4] They were all in a Box. I gave you the Key and you locked it, and I think you took the Box home with you in the Coach.

This is all I can recollect of the business, and which I hope will be sufficient to bring to your memory the transaction.

I am with the utmost respect / Madam, Your most Obedient humble Servant / John Field.

Inclosed is the Account of the Porter.

Text: Ry. 601.12.

1. The exchange with Field (also on 3 January 1792) was part of HLP's threatened litigation with John Cator. In this instance she sought £840 11*s*.6*d*. allegedly due her in rents "from the Estates of Flint and Denbighshire" for the period of 28 July 1783 to 30 July 1784 (Ry. 611). Apparently Cator professed ignorance, but HLP remembered having been told by John Perkins on 25 September 1789 that her steward Edward Edwards agreed "to remitt me every Quarter [these rents] as the Money came into his hands" (Ry. 600.8). If we believe John Field, HLP inflated the sum due her, and, further, she received something "between Two and three hundred Pounds" before 23 July 1784.

The exchange between HLP and Field reveals the former's financial naïveté, her distrust of the world's honesty, and her tenacious claims on what she considered hers. Despite the controversy with Field, nothing came of it, and HLP dropped the matter.

John Field (fl. 1755–1800), clerk in the Thrale brewery, was first in the employ of HT and then of his successors, Perkins and Barclay.

2. John Perkins (ca. 1730–1812), who had been HT's chief clerk, was also the able manager of the brewery during his employer's last years. Lacking confidence in HT's ability to make decisions after his paralytic stroke, he made his displeasure clear, even at the risk of his employment. Nevertheless, he was able to win over HT, who left him a bequest of one thousand pounds. On 31 May 1781, assisted by a loan from HLT, he became a one-fourth partner in the Thrale brewery. When he and his family moved into the Thrales' Southwark house, HLT left them all the furniture. See Elizabeth Montagu to Elizabeth Vesey, [25] July 1784, n. 3. With SJ's reluctant approval, HLT threw off a "Golden Millstone," as she informed Elizabeth Lambart on 3 June 1781 (Ry. 550.17). The transaction brought her about £135,000 over the next four years. On 1 April 1786, in Rome, the Piozzis assigned a power of attorney to HT's surviving executors for completion of the brewery sale: witnessed by William Coxe and Thomas Jenkins. Even so, the Piozzis faced prolonged dickering. See the notice of the newly surfaced legal document and a letter from Barclay and Perkins, 12 September 1797, Bernard Quaritch sale catalogue no. 1038 (ca. 1988), item 31; also *Thraliana* 1:491.

3. David Barclay (1728–1809), "the rich Quaker," was an active co-manager with Perkins. See *Thraliana* 1:494; Chapman 2:427–31.

4. The two stewards of HLP's property or of her parents' in the Vale of Clwyd.

Edward Bridge (d. 1792), of Bodfari and Aberwheeler, was the agent who untangled John Salusbury's property affairs during his absence in Nova Scotia and elsewhere. Late in 1772 he was briefly imprisoned for debt and declared a bankrupt. On 23 February 1773, his eldest daughter wrote to HLT: ". . . thank God my Father got home from Chester by 5 oclock on Sunday last . . . all his creditors are alarmed so that he confines himself to the house. What will be done we know not as yet, he writes to day to good Mrs. Salusbury. Our hopes are that he will be able to do her justice and every other Creditor" (Ry. 532.108). But according to HLT, "our worthy Steward" lined his pockets, "cheating us grossly all this while," as she determined during her Welsh visit in 1774. She quickly dismissed him despite her friendship with his family. For Edward Bridge's death, see "Bodfari Burial Register," C.R.O., Clwyd; also HLP to JSPS, 16 July 1810, n. 6.

Bridge was replaced by Edward Edwards of Denbigh. For the latter, see HLP to Sophia Byron, 19 September 1789, n. 3; and to Charlotte Lewis, 20 September [17]89, n. 7.

TO JOHN FIELD

Streatham Park
30: December 1791.

Mrs. Piozzi's Compliment[s]. She has received Mr. Field's Letter, and is more and more astonished at herself, and at her entire want of Memory concerning a Transaction so particular as he describes.

She is no less amazed that Mr. Field should pay her a Sum of two or three hundred Pounds, or even *say* that he paid it her without a Receipt or any Acknowledgment on her part. She has not (or cannot tell where to find) one Letter from Bridge; nor any Cash Book or Book of Accounts [and] earnestly begs him to say *what Day,* and what *Year* he *thinks* She fetched away this Box of Money and papers; where She lived at the Time, and where She ordered the Coach. He says she came in—to drive: if to the Adelphi or to her own house, or to the Bank of England in order to have the Box deposited.

It would really be but kind in Mr. Field to add these particulars, and might lead forward till some Light could be thrown round Mrs. Piozzi; who feels at present totally in Darkness with regard to what became of her Money *from Mr. Thrale's Death to her second Marriage* excepting only that she *confided in Mr. Cator* from whom She desired and received only *150£ per Month,* while he paid (or promised to pay) her Debts, *Mortgages* &c. with what remained of her Income, every Penny of which passed thro' his hands, and of which She can obtain no Account.[1]

Jacob who has been long her Coachman can recollect nothing of this matter (for she asked him). Strange that Mrs. Piozzi should go on this Errand when Perkins was from home! Stranger that she should forget so completely a Transaction so very striking! *Most Strange* that Mr. Field should not have her handwriting to shew for so considerable a Sum of Money!

Can Mr. Field recollect what Servants came with her to the Brewhouse.

Text: Ry. 533.10; a draft.

1. According to the "Memorial" against Cator, HLT in 1783 "went to Bath, leaving her whole Income to the Care of Mr. Cator," requesting that he send her £150 a month, and keeping "the rest for payment of Debts &c. relying on his Honour to make use of it for her best Advantage."

Appendix 1
Newspaper Accounts of Mrs. Siddons in 1784

Parker's General Advertiser, and Morning Intelligencer, Friday, 10 September:

> Mrs. *Siddons* returns to London, loaded with money, from Ireland and Scotland; but neither her theatric fame, nor her private character, have received a spark of lustre by the campaign. Poor Digges! he felt her *generosity* to a child of the stage in the hour of distress. A respectable body of gentlemen saw a respectable actor, by a stroke of the palsy, unable to earn his bread. They requested Mrs. Siddons to perform a part in tragedy, for the benefit of this once public favourite. She could not deny—because they were persons of consequence; but she was resolved to profit by the unhappy situation of poor Digges, who, she was sensible, must at all events have the benefit. She sent to him in the most *friendly* manner, and with a heart *sensibly alive* to the *softer* feelings of *Isabella*'s soul, she informed him that there were *two considerations* under which *only* she could perform. The nurse-keeper asked what they were. The *messenger* replied a payment of the sum of Fifty Guineas, and a solemn promise that Mr. Digges would never *mention* that such money *was paid or demanded.* Mrs. Siddons otherwise would be sick. . . . The bargain was struck—the money was paid; but the secret was not kept; for nurse told the tale to the baker's wife. . . . But this is not all; the person who brought over the news avers it to be a literal fact, and declares, if any of Mrs. Siddons's friends are bold enough to deny the assertion, he will step forward and prove it beyond the power of contradiction. So much for Digges. We have already mentioned how this heart-moving, woe-be-gone, tear-drawing, soul-melting *Jane Shore,* not *Lady Macbeth,* behaved to that very respectable gentleman, and excellent performer, Mr. Brereton. Now the only mode for Mrs. Siddons to get rid of those charges is, to prove them to be false. If she dares not to do so, John Bull may probably speak, *serpentinely* to her from the gallery. To be divested of humanity, though she were a very Garrick in her profession, will not do on a British stage. Who can join in Lady Randolph's tears for her son; or who will sympathize with Belvidera's woe, when it stands upon record that the actress's soul is callous as the stone that Sisyphus rolled?

General Advertiser, Saturday, 2 October:

Letter to Mr. Siddons

Sir,

I am heartily sorry that the document is lost, which would so amply have testified the falsity of the report of your wife not having either by herself, or by you, or by any other person, asked or received money for performing for the benefit of poor Digges. But, I dare say, *Mr. Digges* when he hears of the cruelty of the story, will, as a small return for the obligation he received, give the most ample and full contradiction to such malicious scandal.

Brereton being on the spot can have nothing more to say than to lament Mrs. Siddons being ill three times a week and sick three times a week, and that one of the latter days happened unfortunately on his night. God knows we are all subject to the visitation of Providence in this way; and there may be a Dramatic alternate ague among actors and actresses as well as among other people.

I wish to observe to you, that charity, benevolence, hospitality, and friendship, are public characters as well as private virtues, and that hinting a non-possession of them in her theatrical character, was no proof that Mrs. Siddons did not hold them near her heart in private. The recesses of family matters, I pry not into; not the conduct of Mrs. Siddons beyond the line of her profession on the stage. What I said of her, and what all the papers lately said of her, was in her character as an actress to perform for a benefit, and not as Mrs. Siddons in her own house, or in any house but the theatre.

The public now are in possession of the evidence on both sides, and let them give their verdict accordingly.

Dramaticus

The *Morning Herald and Daily Advertiser,* 4 October:

A brief list of the Enemies *of Mrs.* Siddon[s]

1. All the disgraced Partizans of the insulted Muse, *Melpomene.* Those who made pretences to her patronage, and called themselves her favorite servants, previous to the appearance of her real and genuine priestess, in the person of Mrs. Siddons, who feel the decline of their estimation, and execrate the object who has superseded them in the Muse's regions, and dismissed them to oblivion.

2d. Those who never had, but aspire only to the Muse's favors.

3d. Those who envy merit of any, and of every kind, and feel an enmity to all distinctions that remind them of their own inferiority.

4. All the people who have formerly played with her, in her probationary passage to excellence, who cannot be brought to understand why, and wherefore she who was in times past, little better than themselves, has now got beyond all reach of competition, and has attained a perfection, which they can see no good reason for their not having in their own persons arrived at.

5. Such (if any there be in her profession) who cannot conceive that the bond of conjugal union need be any impediment to the gratification of the pleasanter passions, or why a little *innocent* dissipation is not fair game, in spite of any obstruction arising from marriage duty. Insult is worse to bear than injury.

6. A select knot of angry critics of the *old school*, who revenge upon the actress the degradation sustained in their own judgment. *Rant* and *fury* for their money, and the simple nature which delights the intelligent spectator, excites no other emotion in their breasts, than disgust to the performance, and dislike of the performer.

7. A constant influx of *daily* enemies from Ireland. The scandalous aspersions which have been recently circulated from this land of liberty, are evidently *jobs* of the *alley*, and proceed from a Jew there, who, being reduced to the < >. . . . Let the Impartial Judge, if after such a refutation of the facts alledged against Mrs. Siddons, as has already appeared, there can be any other individual to express dis-approbation of her, but such only as come under some particular class of those descriptions that are above enumerated.

"Theatrical Intelligence" in the *Morning Herald*, 6 October:

Drury Lane

A very numerous and genteel audience, last night, honored this theatre, to give the return of their *favorite actress*, welcome. The galleries were so crowded, that a disturbance took place, for want of proper room. This confusion the *hireling* enemies of *Mrs. Siddons*, who were stationed to annoy her entrance, availed themselves of, and an uproar ensued, which suspended the performance for more than twenty minutes.—Mrs. Siddons, after making a few efforts to speak, was at length heard. Her address was to the following purport:—"That many *asperities* had been directed against her, upon the most idle pretences, and charges made without a shadow of authority; and that, as she shortly meant to submit to public decision, a relation of the transactions, which had been *perverted* to do her injury, she trusted, she should still be found deserving favor."—The Audience highly applauded her, and expressed the highest resentment against the *miscreants*, who were brought into the galleries to distress her.

The agitation this interruption occasioned, made her first scene the more interesting.—In her interview with Beverley, where she surrenders her jewels, she was astonishingly great.—Her scene with Stukeley was inimitably marked with fine touches of nature; and in the prison scene, when she exclaims to *Jervis*, "'Tis false, old man! They had no quarrel; there was no cause for quarrel!" Every feeling auditor was electrified by her manner. . . .

Mr. *Kemble*, in the soliloquy which begins the 2d act,—gave by his *whimpering* manner, a poor introduction to *Beverly:* if Mr. Kemble, thought he should thereby awaken the affections, he was mistaken; nothing is more contemptible than a driveller. . . . [See Edward Moore, *The Gamester.*]

Mr. *Brereton* was received with uncommon favour, for the zeal he had shewn, in rescuing the conduct of *Mrs. Siddons* from detraction.

The *Morning Herald*, Monday, 11 October:

The Tragedy of *Douglas* brought Mrs. *Siddons* forward in the part of Lady Randolph.—Whenever this distinguished actress appears, she diffuses an interest over the scene in which she is engaged. The performers catch fire from her vehemence; and the audiences feel no respite from the earnest attention, which is so necessary to their gratification.

The *Morning Herald*, Saturday, 23 October:

> "Sir,
> "I empower you to declare to the public, that I did not pay Mrs. Siddons for playing for my benefit. I thanked the lady by letter for her politeness, which I am informed she has mislaid. I think it is but justice to inform you of this." / "West Digges."

The *Morning Herald*, Saturday, 20 November:

> It has been observed, we believe with no very charitable intention, that no performer ever gained so great a reputation as Mrs. Siddons, by so few characters. But what is the just and obvious conclusion from this fact; for a fact it indisputably is? Certainly this, that no performer but Mrs. Siddons, ever had intrinsic merit sufficient to engage the attention of the public for the same space of time, without the additional charm of variety and novelty.

Appendix 2
Manuscript Draft of "Italian and German Journeys 1784–87"

These transcriptions are taken from Ry. 618.1,2, and include material not incorporated or the focus of which has been altered in *Observations and Reflections*.

Dover, Sunday, 5 September 1784:

Last Night I arrived at this Place in Company with my dear Husband and faithful Maid,—having left my Daughters reconciled to my Choice (all at least except the eldest who parted with me cooly, not unkindly:) and my Friends well pleased with my leaving London I fancy, where my stay perplexed 'em, and entangled their Duty with their Interest.

I am setting out for the Country which has produced so many People and Things of Consequence from the foundation of Rome to the present Moment, that my Heart swells with the Idea, and I long to leap across intermediate France. The Inn here is execrable, we came late last Night and put up at the wrong house. There never was a Coach and six at the Door till now I dare say—ours is a very elegant one, and Mr. Piozzi is on all Occasions kindly attentive to my being accommodated in every possible Respect (1: fol. 2).

Paris, 18 September:

This is Dr. Johnson's Birthday: may God give him many and happy returns of it; we used to spend these two Days [including Q's birthday on the 17th] in Mirth and Gayety at Streatham: but Pride and Prejudice hindered my longer Residence in a place which indeed had lost its charms for me—I am happier at this moment than I have been Two and Twenty Years (1: fol. 6v).

Paris, post-19 September:

I went to see my old Friends the Austin Nuns at the Fosseè one Morning; and found them all alive, and well, and not the least altered: I told them again how much happier they lived, than we who bustled in the World; and once more promised them to come to their Convent if my Husband used me ill.——I had told them so before, when married to Mr. Thrale: they laughed and said they saw no Sign of my disposition towards a *Nunnery* by my chusing to enter again into the married State, but acknowledged I had not been in haste (1: fol. 7v).

I shall let loose . . . in this Journey the Fondness for Painting which I was forced to suppress while Dr. Johnson lived with me, and ridiculed my Taste of an Art his own Imperfect Sight hindered him from enjoying (1: fol. 8).

Lyons, 30 September:

Letters from my Daughters . . . have contributed to make me see every Thing with good Humour, and tho' my Health is not all I could hope for, I have little coin on *that* Side to give me a just Cause of Complaint (1: fol. 10v).

Genoa, post–21 October:

I know not whether the peculiarly pathetic Manner of the Genoese Beggars has ever been mentioned—but they clasp their hands together, and conjure one to assist 'em by the sacred Wounds of our Lord Jesus Christ; and Oh pray, Dear Sir, help me, if ever you wish to enjoy the Glories of Heaven, or the Comforts of Paradise——I never saw such eloquent Misery; They break my heart, as well as ruin my Purse (1: fol. 16v).

Milan, 4 November:

The Sermons of Tillotson magnificently bound [in the collection of books at Brera] struck me exceedingly, but the Works of many Protestant Divines besides him have gained Admittance, and I saw with Horror Bolingbroke's Philosophy in admirable Preservation, and heard the Praises of Gibbon's Roman History from the Mouth of an Ex-Jesuit. Of Religion and Government it is however safest and best to say nothing—nothing therefore will I add upon the Subject (1: fol. 18v).

What I prize in the People is an utter absence of that Affectation which renders it so difficult to know whether an English-man or Woman have either good Parts or good Principles, the first is so overlaid with Literature and the last so perverted by Refinement: no need of a Miss Burney to develop the Passions or spy out the Interests of the People *here* however. They tell you their Minds too plainly for you to suspect their falsehood . . . (1: fols. 19–19v).

Milan, 10 February 1785:

I have had the Advantage of seeing a Play acted by Fryars—the Monks of St. Victor being permitted to amuse themselves this Carnival Time, wrote a little Play about the Events which happened in Milan 100 Years ago when the Torriani and Visconti disputed for Superiority: it surprized me to see how well they understood the Power of Parental Affection, and I came home astonished at the recollections that I had shed Tears at a Fryar's Play. Had they excelled in force or elegance of Language, I should have wondered little, for such Excellence is the result of mere Study: but I have no reason to think they *did* excel in *that*, it is however not right for a Foreigner to decide in matters of Language, even when he knows more of every Tongue than I do of the Italian. The Manners of the Ladies here are coarse, and their Voices loud, Comte de Shinigl says that when a Woman of Fashion says even kind Things to him here, he is afraid of her

Violence: there is *too* much Nature and too little Refinement in their Conversation certainly——Obscenity and Profaneness have not yet been banished even from the best Company——who sometimes laugh, sometimes return the Talk, and sometimes—but rarely—disclaimingly call out Porcheria! Porcheria! when they wish to have done with the Subject. Another Topick to which there is still less Temptation still keeps its Ground here; and Dean Swift would have been thought a *delicate* Writer and Sterne a chaste one, had they but been born in the Plains of Lombardy. Our Milanese indeed do not mince the Matter, and even those whose Faith is firm amongst 'em, do not forbear profane and gross allusions to the sacred Mysteries of holy Religion (1: fols. 19v–20).

Venice, post-10 April 1785:

I think . . . that the low People here seem somewhat less wicked than at Milan. In a word Vice is made agreable here, it disgusted me at the last named Place: but that may be the Effect of Habitually seeing it, and hearing of nothing else.

Vice is a monster of so frightful Mien
As to be hated need, but not to be seen;
But seen too oft, familiar with her face,
We first endure—then pity—next embrace.
[Pope, *An Essay on Man*, 2:217–20]

May God keep me and my Husband from becoming Examples of the Truth contained in these four elegant Lines: when I think of the Danger, it really takes off much of my Delight in the beautiful Objects daily offered to my Mind and Senses (1: fol. 32v).

Florence, 24 June:

Affectation indeed is not the Growth of Italy, what the People think in this Country that do they speak; when no End is to be served I mean by Change or by Suppression, for I am not talking now of *moral* but of *Civil* and *Social* Life: and this openness of Manners, this natural Carriage renders their company exquisitely refreshing to one who has been hacked thro' the Coteries of London—'Tis like going from the Parterres of France to walk in Ilam Gardens or the Leasowes; living in France, Venice, or Padua after the Conversations of Portman Square, Queen Ann Street or the Adelphi. No one is however good or bad, wise or foolish without a reason why. In our Country those who fairly profess Talking, must look over each Word and measure every Sentence in the Company tonight, or they will see themselves tomorrow hung up by some kind Newspaper to public Scorn perhaps, and lasting Abuse. If a pretty Woman puts on a new Hat for Ranelagh this Evening, the 1st Day of next Month shews her the Caricatura of herself exposed at every Window in the Town and Country Magazine, probably over against the Officer (or other Gentleman) who handed her to her Coach. Here no such Terrors restrain Conversation, no public Ridicule pursues fantastical Behaviour, and as it is always Fear which creates Falsehood, these People seek just such Carriage as becomes them, not such as they hope will ensure applause; and pronounce Sentiments for which they have a real value . . . (1: fols. 42–42v).

Lucca, post-24 June–pre-19 September:

. . . though it is Holyday Time just now, I do not perceive that they suffer their Agriculture to be neglected, either for the sake of attending to their Devotion or Diversion; which in these Countries are always mingled—whether that Connection is or is not a good and proper one, my little Book has nothing to do: Religion and Government are Subjects best avoided by Travellers, whose Duty to Society during their Pilgrimage is doubtless Conformity and Obedience to the Laws and Customs of every Xtian Land (1: fol. 45v).

. . . if I was to chuse a Place for Retirement, cheap living, free Government and genteel Company, in a very little snug Way——*I would live and die at Lucca:* where no Man has been murdered in the Memory of any of its Inhabitants—— where if any robs he is hanged with terrifying Circumstances of Penitence etc. and where every body being known to every body, and the Governed so few in proportion to the Governors——a great Boarding School in England is really rather a more licentious Place than the delicate Commonwealth of Lucca (1: fols. 46–46v).

Leghorn:

It is . . . a prodigious Blessing and Comfort to have such a Place as Leghorn to die, *and be buried in:* as for *living* there, I suppose no one not connected with Trade, or driven to seek Shelter from Distress would think on it: To those who are so circumstanced I believe no People can be kinder; the Purse of an English Merchant is open as his heart, and punctual as his Books. In this Town I got my Anecdotes of Dr. Johnson's last 20 Years, transcribed for the Press;—and sent it to Mr. Cadell by the Ship Piedmont, Joel Forster Captain. When that Affair was settled, my *worldly* Concerns at Leghorn were all done . . . (1: fols. 49v–50).

Rome, 24 October:

One must at least mention what has pleased me most in this Galaxy of the fine Arts, among which the two or three Statues well known in all Parts of the civilized World shine with distinguished Lustre. The Things however from which I received Pleasure unexpected, unaffected, and inextinguishable—was the Andromeda of Caracci, the Apollo and Daphne of Bernini—the old and young Woman of Guglielmo della Porta—the Christ carried to his Sepulchre by Raphael, a great Chalk Drawing of a Head by Michael Angelo, and the Marriage of Alexander and Roxana by Giulio Romano. St. Peter delivered from Prison in the Vatican has something of Trick in it—or I should have named it first. The figure of *Meekness* has no *Justice* done her by Mr. Strange: She is more divinely beautiful than I ever saw a female painted. Guido's St. Michael is an Angelic Performance, but I almost think it surpassed by his Baptist at Padua. In the Discovery of Calisto by Domenichino in Palazzo Farnese, one sees the Original of all other Painters Ideas on the Subject; and there is great Delight to me, in having suggested a Notion to the Connoisseurs that he whom they have so long called the fighting Gladiator, is no other than Isadas the Spartan Hero, who snatching up a Shield and Spear only, dashed naked into the Battle, and after having performed Prodigies of Valour, was punished for Breach of Discipline instead of being applauded for his Courage.

I am grown less fond of Bernini; his Expressions are over charged, except perhaps in the Groupe of Pluto and Proserpine which looks very well even in the same Room with Pætus and Arria the Work of an ancient Artist.

Guercino's Aurora struck me more than Guido's; and there is a plain Marble Bust, the head our blessed Saviour by Michael Angelo, that (excepting the famous Thing of all,) appears to be more alive than ever was any thing yet cut in Marble.

The Adam and Eve of Domenichino are excelled by Castiglione's Animals which surround 'em; the human Figures can hardly be called.

Two of far nobler Shape when one looks at this picture; and poor Eve is neither *Erect nor Tall*. In short the two Galleries at the Capitol have put me out of humour with all other Pictures: Guercino's Sibyl, Guido's Fortune, Tintoret's Magdalen, the two Sebastians by Master and Scholar; with the constant Bloom and Chearful Youth of the Girls painted by Romanelli——are all so adorable, one can hardly perswade oneself to quit the Rooms they hang in.

'Tis said by <Vopiscus> that the Statues and Pictures at Rome out number the People; and certain it is, that I like the dead Men's representations better than the living Personages: it is however unpleasant enough to see that all which remains of ancient Rome was built by the Emperors, who for the most part were such disgraces of human Nature that one would wish their Names expunged and their Deeds obliterated from the face of the Globe, and from the Memories of Mankind.

The two Columns of Trajan and Antoninus Pius must be forever excepted; and Marcus Aurelius's fine figure in Bronze which has perhaps no equal, any more than had the glorious Mortal which it represents. The Prison is however the Work of the *Kings*, and while others are doubtful about the Saints and Martyrs massacred in this blood thirsty City; I cannot help doubting the Possibility of Jugurtha being kept in that Dungeon for six Months during the Time when Rome was a polished State——that Xtians should be kept in a worse Place *still*, if a worse could have been found—is no wonder, when we reflect on the horrid Tortures inflicted on all professed Members of the primitive Church: but that any Nation could bear to look on while a Prince of Jugurtha, Consequence was so kept, appears impossible to People who live in less savage Days to conceive: Antiquarians assure us however that this was the very Place (1: fols. 56–58).

Having . . . observed the common people more than those of higher Rank, I had a Mind one Day to satisfie my Curiosity concerning their real Notions; and after wading through the Filth at the Entrance of the Palace Farnese to see the Toro; a young Wench who shewed it, appeared particularly attentive to what I said in Italian to Mr. Piozzi; so that I was tempted to take up a little broken Statue of Isis the Egyptian Deity very hideous; with many Breasts, and bound up like a

Mummy in their Country, or a Baby in this—and turning to the Girl——They worshipped these frightful Things said I once, before Jesus Christ came, but we are wiser now—*Che bel gusto!* added I contemptuously, to pray to this ugly Stone! was it not very foolish think you? *No,* (replies the Wench,) *I do not see that it was so very foolish* (1: fols. 59v–60).

Ancona:

The condemned Prisoners work on the Quay at Ancona, and as Italians know not the Words Honour and Shame, or the meaning of them: a Fellow accosts you with pray Sir give a Thief somewhat, I am a Horse Stealer please your Honour; another tells another Story with equal Insensibility of his Crimes, or of your Disgust——and begs you for love of the saints or of the Madonna to give him something for he only—a Woman in the Church. Comical enough! but when Mr. Piozzi mentioned it with Horror to the Waiter at the Inn, the Man laughed, and seemed to wonder that any one should annex Disgrace to wickedness, when Punishment was sufficient, for says he if they *do* steal they are *Castigato* (1: fol. 84v).

Bologna:

Our broken Coach has at last brought us safely to Bologna Thursday 27: April 1786. Two Englishmen we met on the Road gave us their kind Assistance or we should never have got hither I think: and now the Fatigue of driving late and early to get into the Towns, will be changed for the Fatigue of seeing the Sights they contain. The Traveller's Life is a continual Fever, and all his Relief is to turn from Side to Side. One of our English Friends said he should be glad to get home if it was only to be relieved from the Fatigue of seeing Sights. I had more pleasure however today Fryday 28. in looking over the Wonders of the Lampieri Palace than when we were here last (1: fol. 85v).

Ferrara, 2 May 1786

I looked ever so long for a *Beggar,* and could find none: A bad Account indeed for poor Ferrara; but it made me recollect how unreasonably my Daughters and I had laughed some few Years ago to read in an Extract from the foreign Gazettes that Talasi an Improvisatore who came to England about the Year 1770 had published an Account of his Visit to Mrs. Thrale eight miles from Westminster Bridge where he met all the Wits of London he said, and passed to her country Seat through the Village of Streatham—*luogo assai popolato ed ameno* which Expression we thought ridiculous but to a Ferrara Man the Idea was natural enough (1: fols. 86v–87).

Venice:

Lovely Venice! I have then been permitted by Providence to see my Husband's Country once again, May I but reach my own to Thank God in it for the Accounts I now daily receive of my Book's success, and my Favour with the generous Publick (1: fol. 88v).

Varese:

We came home to Varese, where on our Wedding Day 25: July, we received elegant Verses this Year from Mr. Piozzi's Italian Friends as last Year at Florence from Mr. Parsons, Mr. Greatheed, and Mr. Merry (1: fol. 103).

Vienna:

I saw the Danube first yesterday Morning, it is like Hercules who in his Cradle strangled two enormous Serpents:—this River scarce burst from the Spring is so rapid deep and strong, that tis difficult to build wooden Bridges that will resist it: and accordingly it did a few Months ago overwhelm many Cottages and Fields which we past. They call it Donau from its peculiar Swiftness, and it deserves beside any Name expressive of that singular purity which distinguishes the German torrents—(2: fol. 10v).

Men drawing Carts along the High Ways, in and near this Capital . . . ought to be looked on with Horror by every Nation, particularly ours—the lowest Subject of which would I trust rather submit to Death than to be levelled with the Beasts of the Field (2: fol. 11v).

I like Baron Borne exceedingly, have been happy in many charming Houses; and shall leave Vienna with very sincere Regret (2: fol. 17).

I would not chuse German Musick in preference to what we have been hearing in those Countries [Rome and Venice]; tho all ought to confess its intrinsic Merit, and complicated Excellence—whoever underrates what cannot be obtained without Labour and Study will be censured, and justly; for refusing the Reward due to deep Research, and prompt Execution in every Science:—Yet *de Gustibus non est disputandum* we know; and if a Man likes Cyprus Wine or Lachryma Christi—let him drink them, and content himself with *commending* the Old Hock (2: fol. 18–18v).

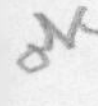

To day 22: of November 1786 we leave Vienna where every thing has appeared to me (in common Life I mean) a Caricatura of England—The Language like ours, but coarser; the Actors like ours but stupider, the Plays like ours, but their Plots worse contrived. Education of the Female Sex still more refined than in England—all the Girls speak three Languages at least, and are in haste to shew off their Improvements comically enough—while married Women are most attentive to shine in Conversation, praising our Country for its Literature, and condemning Italian Ignorance in terms that would gain at London the Censure due to Pedantry I fear, instead of those Applauses they who pronounce them expect (2: fols. 22v–23).

Dresden, post-17 December:

I saw an impudent Thing to-day among the Elector's Treasures, the Beast of the Apocalypse represented in Enamel on a very fine Dish—with the Woman on his Back—the Pope in his Tiara worshipping it. I said nothing because we were a mixed Company of Romanists and Protestants: Revelations the 17th Chapter was written under it however, so it could be no Mistake—but it shocked me (2: fol. 32).

Pre-1 January:

At Church to-day the sudden Stop of the Preacher when the Hour Glass had emptied all its Sand, put one in mind of our old Sermons in the early days of Reformation exceedingly; and would have made some moderns of more refined Notions laugh I believe: but there is little Jest at last in Things merely customary for either *all* Customs with out meaning are ridiculous or none are so (2: fol. 34–34v).

Brandenburg, post-13 January 1787:

From this Scene of Solitude without Retirement and of Age without Antiquity I was glad to be carried forwards. Peina tho poor and miserable, exhibits what ought to give every Christian comfort; the sight of Romanists and Lutherans living together in Harmony and brotherly Love, and agreeing neither to insult nor caress the wretched Jews who take Shelter under the charitable Bishop of Poderborn's Protection. Here I first saw the King of England's Livery on the King of England's Servants since I left home; 'twas comfortable somehow to feel ones self among one's fellow Subjects, but the Poverty of every Village, and apparent barrenness of the Soil thro' this Electorate, was such as excepting in Anglesea or Carnarvon (my *own* dear Country) I really never did see before . . . (2: fol. 42).

Peina, pre-24 January:

. . . The Windows and Looking Glasses which in France or Italy are encrusted with nastiness, are always kept clean in these Countries—but their sanded Floors, and stinking Privies are odious enough. The Streets are paved in this Town to imitate England, and the Lamps are round like ours, though not so frequent (2: fol. 43).

Molines:

Well! The Wind was so high no Bark big enough to hold our Coach could pass the Scheld, so we turned about, and came back to Bruxelles by that same delightful Road we had gone to Antwerp. Molines is a fine Place; I know not if 'tis the Town Sterne places his Maria near: but I caught myself looking for her, and listening to hear the Pipe as We approached it both Times (2: fol. 49).

Lille:

Lille I remember being at twelve Years ago, when I thought myself at the World's End almost—and now it feels as if one was in England: so much has every thing an Air of Approximation to the Old Place. If one was to go to Egypt I suppose, the sight of Naples would give just the same Sensations: and I remember the People who went round the World with Admiral Anson, considered Calcutta as home, and all their Toils as ended: whatever one acquires by Travelling (and 'tis too little to pay the pains to be sure:) the Mind does purify itself from little dirty Prejudices which haunt the wisest of those that stay within; but in return for such Advantages, one loses that fond Attachment to any thing, or any Person, or any Place which makes the delight of those very People; and when regard for one's own Country consists of mere dry Esteem, and well-weighed Preference the Return to it can give little Pleasure: for one loves nothing truly, tenderly and passionately without finding that alone capable to supply the want of every thing else (2: fols. 49–50).

Random epigraphs at the end of Ry. 618.2:

Sherlock says he who leaves Vienna unsatisfied is his own Satirist——I shall save my Enemies some Trouble.

False Friends are like the Lady in the Weatherhouse. True ones like the Gentleman.

Index

This index is limited to proper names.

Members of the British nobility are listed under family names with cross references from titles.

Members of the French, Italian, and other European nobility are listed under the names and titles by which they are usually known with cross references, if necessary, from other names and titles.

The title "Dr." is reserved for individuals who hold the degree of "M.D."

Names of major figures in the correspondence are designated by abbreviations (e.g., Samuel Johnson = SJ). For list of abbreviations, see pp. 39–40.